A GUIDE TO JEWISH PRACTICE

Volume 2

EVERYDAY LIVING

A GUIDE *to* JEWISH PRACTICE

Center for Jewish Ethics
Reconstructionist Rabbinical College
in cooperation with the
Reconstructionist Rabbinical Association

Reconstructionist Rabbinical College Press

1299 Church Road, Wyncote, PA 19095-1898
www.rrc.edu

EVERYDAY LIVING

Shabbat and Holidays

DAVID A. TEUTSCH, EDITOR

RICHARD HIRSH, ASSISTANT EDITOR

Reconstructionist Rabbinical College Press
Wyncote, Pennsylvania

Composition by G&H Soho, Inc.

ISBN 978-0-938945-02-4

Printed in the U.S.A.

Let all who are hungry come and eat.

Table of Contents

Commentators

Sylvia Boorstein (S.B.)
Lester B. Bronstein (L.B.)
Michael Fessler (M.F.)
Richard Hirsh (R.H.)
Margaret Holub (M.H.)
Leah Kamionkowski (L.K.)
Tamar Kamionkowski (T.K.)
Donna Kirshbaum (D.K.)
Jason Gary Klein (J.G.K.)
Myriam Klotz (M.K.)
Lori Hope Lefkovitz (L.H.L.)
Nina H. Mandel (N.H.M.)
Miriam Margles (M.M.)
Nathan C. Martin (N.C.M)
Vivian Mayer (V.M.)
Ela Merom (E.M.)
Jay Michaelson (J.M.)
Deborah Dash Moore (D.D.M.)
Barbara Penzner (B.P.)
Linda T. Potemken (L.T.P.)
Steven Carr Reuben (S.C.R.)
Yael Ridberg (Y.R.)
Jeremy A. Schwartz (J.A.S.)
Hugh Seid-Valencia (H.S.V.)
Jonathan P. Slater (J.P.S.)
Joshua M. Snyder (J.M.S.)
Toba Spitzer (T.S.)
Jacob J. Staub (J.J.S.)
Elsie R. Stern (E.R.S.)
Robert Tabak (R.T.)
Elliot M. Tepperman (E.M.T.)
David A. Teutsch (D.A.T.)
Deborah Waxman (D.W.)
Joshua Waxman (J.W.)
Elyse Wechterman (E.W.)
Sheila Peltz Weinberg (S.P.W.)

Advisory Committee

Rabbis Richard Hirsh and David A. Teutsch, *Co-chairs*
Rabbi Lester Bronstein
Deborah Dash Moore, Ph.D.
Chayim Herzig-Marx, Ph.D.
Leah Kamionkowski
Tamar Kamionkowski, Ph.D.
Rabbi Nina H. Mandel
Rabbi Yael Ridberg
Rabbi Jacob J. Staub

Preface

The introduction to Volume I of *A Guide to Jewish Practice* explains the purpose of Volume II as well, and the large section at the back of the first volume discusses these books' shared methodology, so the focus of this preface is on the many people who joined in the creation of this book.

Rabbi Richard Hirsh, co-chair of the editorial Advisory Committee for the *Guide*, helped with the assignment of chapters to authors and contributed early editing of several of the book's chapters. Also critical in producing the book were the sage guidance of the Advisory Committee; the thoughtful suggestions of commentators; the administrative work of Joan Hollenbach, Cheryl Plumly and Raela Forman; the copyediting and proofreading of Marilyn Silverstein; and the design and production expertise of printer Jim Harris and G&H Soho, Inc.

The support of the Levin-Lieber Program in Jewish Ethics of the Reconstructionist Rabbinical College and the commitment of the college's administration have been essential to the smooth development of this project. The enthusiasm of family and friends has buoyed my spirits as I pursue this work.

Any errors found in this book are the responsibility of the editor.

Sharing the rhythms of the Jewish calendar builds community and shared commitment. May this volume open the way for readers to experience deeper spirituality, greater insight, a broader connection to Jewish community, and an increased commitment to acting on Jewish values and improving the world.

David A. Teutsch
March 2013

EVERYDAY LIVING

Shabbat

Jacob J. Staub

> *More than Israel has kept the Sabbath, the Sabbath has kept Israel.*
>
> —Ahad Ha'am

Over the long and rich history of the Jewish people, the weekly observance of Shabbat has played a central role. The actual details of how Jews have observed Shabbat

As a cultural/spiritual Zionist, Ahad Ha'am wanted to shift the notion of what bound Jews to each other from an emphasis on nation state and territory to an emphasis on language and cultural practices. The Sabbath here is construed as a moral or spiritual Jewish practice, not necessarily as a religious one. Ahad Ha'am was concerned about saving Judaism, not Jews; hence, the emphasis on the Sabbath preserving Israel (Jews) rather than the reverse. Rabbi Mordecai Kaplan, of course, felt that one had to save Jews so that they could save Judaism. Thus Kaplan's commitment to reconstructing Judaism. —D.D.M.

have evolved over the centuries and varied according to where Jews have lived and which cultural traditions they have inherited. In all communities of which we are aware, however, Shabbat has been the primary axis upon which Jewish life has turned: preparing for Shabbat, lighting the candles before sunset on Friday, sanctifying the day over wine and hallah, eating, singing, praying and studying Torah. The day revolves around putting aside the cares of the week to create 25 hours devoted to holy, restful living until the moment on Saturday evening when the *Havdala* ceremony marks Shabbat's end. However the melodies, the foods and the customs have varied, Shabbat has sustained Jewish lives.

Many of us today find it challenging to receive this rich inheritance for a host of reasons—among them, because our lives are so busy; because the worlds in which we live do not stop on Friday evenings if they ever stop at all; because we were not raised in households where Shabbat was observed, and we are uncertain how to proceed;

The shift in our sense of mitzvah from obligation to opportunity implies the move that sociologist Peter Berger calls "a movement from fate to choice." Perhaps it is true that the world in which we live does not stop on Friday night—all the more important, then, that we see Shabbat as a choice, as a way of taking back some of the control that our 24/7, online and perpetually connected culture deprives us of. —R.H.

I learned in my meditation practice that it is when I don't want to meditate that I most need to meditate. Similarly, when I am "too busy for Shabbat," that's when I need Shabbat. —J.M.

because when we think of Shabbat observers, we think of the rigors of the practice of Orthodox Jews, and we do not find that appealing. This chapter introduces and explains a host of Shabbat practices and some of the underlying meanings associated with them so that readers may learn what they do not know or explore the significance of practices that may already be familiar. The chapter also celebrates the diversity of our backgrounds, spiritual interests and needs. Observing Shabbat offers joy and meaning to everyone who is interested, but the precise form of that celebration will necessarily differ since each of us is unique.

Kavanot *for Shabbat: Themes That Express How Shabbat Can Enrich Our Lives*

Revaluation

The list of *kavanot* (themes) that follows is a sampling of the ways in which Jews have looked at Shabbat over the centuries. In some cases, these interpretations contradict each other, reflecting the vast diversity of experiences and viewpoints of Jews throughout our history. Shabbat is so central to Jewish experience through the ages that every

For many Jews, it is the sense of Shabbat restriction, what they are "not allowed to do" that is off-putting. For many nonhalakhic Jews, mitzvot (especially the "shalt nots") feel like a direct threat to individualism and evoke a sense of being told what to do. So many Jews have had negative experiences of being exposed only to a Judaism defined by restriction and an external and judgmental authority without opportunities for spiritual nourishment, joyousness and cultivation of awareness. —M.M.

generation and every community has added its own interpretations, practices and understanding of Shabbat. This list of suggestions is designed as a tool to enrich the experience of Shabbat and as an impetus to generate new interpretations of the meaning of Shabbat.

Each of these *kavanot* is framed in traditional language and imagery. It is important to note at the outset that our employment of these mythic images does not necessarily suggest that we believe in them literally. They are presented here to illustrate how traditional biblical, midrashic and liturgical images can retain power for us even when we do *not* literally believe in them. You don't have to believe, for example, that God literally created the world in six days and rested on the seventh day in order to experience the transformative Sabbath rest that occurs when we leave our workweek behind at sunset on Fridays.

In *The Meaning of God in Modern Jewish Religion*, Rabbi Mordecai Kaplan applied the term "revaluation" to this method of interpreting rituals. We *consciously* look at the traditional poetic formulations of a ritual or prayer,

God is not something I believe in but rather something I experience in the everyday miracles of life. The power of Shabbat is not dependent upon belief in a supernatural being. That power lies in our opportunity, week after week, to create experiences that help add meaning and purpose to our lives. —S.C.R.

I love the idea of conscious reinterpretation. It is time to help people understand the great value of practice, indeed, Jewish transformational practice, without supernaturalism. That is why I, for one, am a follower of Mordecai Kaplan! —S.P.W.

Revaluation is not always about defining underlying values and expressing those values in a new idiom. Sometimes it involves keeping the ritual form and finding new significance for it—different values that can inhabit that ritual. —M.M.

determine the values underlying it, and then express those values in a contemporary idiom. To those of us who believe, with Kaplan, that Judaism is the evolving religious civilization of the Jewish people, it is clear that every generation of Jews has engaged in this process of reinterpretation. The difference is that prior generations did this largely *unconsciously*, believing that their new interpretations were what was originally intended.

In premodern societies that assumed the words of sacred text to be accurate records of revelations from God, innovation masquerades as interpretation. Otherwise, premodern interpreters would have experienced an intense cognitive dissonance between their fidelity to received tradition and their self-consciousness that they were changing that (presumably unchanging) tradition. But earlier generations do not speak with a single voice. Surely some interpreters labeled their innovations "original intent." But others used legitimations derived from other vocabulary, including "hidden meanings" and "symbolic story." —R.H.

One of the most exciting things about being a progressive Jew today is recognizing that the past is a gift given to us by our ancestors and that it is our privilege to embrace those rituals and ideas that continue to inspire us while at the same time adding our own ideas, rituals and new traditions to the ongoing evolution of Jewish civilization. —S.C.R.

One potential benefit, then, of revaluation (conscious reinterpretation) is that we remain connected to the sacred milieu of our ancestors, thereby allowing ourselves to be acculturated into and influenced by their values and perspectives—that is, we acknowledge that we do not know everything and that we have much to learn from the treasures of our traditions. In this way, we avoid distancing ourselves unnecessarily from the sacred experiences of prior generations.

The danger to revaluation is in simplifying the process so that it becomes reinterpretation to suit your own needs. This "anything goes" attitude is not the goal of revaluation; rather, we strive to engage deeply with the values that have motivated a ritual practice and to find ways to express those values in ways that are resonant with tradition, but contemporary in execution. —N.H.M.

Revaluation presumes that we want to stay connected somehow to our ancestors, that there is something of benefit to that connection spanning centuries, that our worldview and our values can and even should reflect more than our current moment. Yet revaluation also shatters a conservatism that insists that our ancestors' values are the only ones worth preserving. Revaluation creates space for the assertion that the best of our values and perspectives are worth entering into the chain of Jewish continuity. —D.W.

You can believe in God with your right brain and not believe in God with your left brain. —S.P.W.

Both the practices and words of our ancestors are worth preserving in our Jewish repertoire. While I don't say prayer words I find ethically or theologically offensive, I continue to say many words that I don't find particularly inspiring because of the countless times one of those previously uninspiring words has suddenly opened up deep meanings to me. New life circumstances or new understanding or just a new mood opens up these previously unrecognized gems. —J.A.S.

A Reminder of Creation
(Zekher L'ma'asey B'reyshit)

We usher in Shabbat on Friday evenings with candles, and we sanctify it with the Kiddush, a prayer that declares the day to be holy and recalls the story of the creation of the world as it is told in the first two chapters of the Book of Genesis. In that narrative, the Torah's writers imagined that God created the world in six days and then rested on the seventh. Traditionally, the celebration of Shabbat

Shabbat as rest was inferred from the prohibition against Shabbat work. The mitzvah of Shabbat is not to engage in activities that *halakha* labels as *m'lakha*—according to tradition, a series of 39 actions derived from the tasks needed to construct the portable sanctuary of the Exodus period. *M'lakha* thus does not easily translate as "work" in the sense of "effort." At the end of the story of Creation, the Torah says that God "ceased and drew a breath" (*shavat vayinafash*). Shabbat in our day may be more significant as a time for actively setting aside work and instead doing things that make the day special in ways we cannot on the other six days. Shabbat then becomes a day for catching our breath (literally as well as figuratively) rather than simply a day of rest. —R.H.

Each of us is a creature of Creation. It is a gift to be part of a world that we can use to our benefit during the week. On Shabbat, we open ourselves to the experience of not being creators (as we are during the workweek) but being creaturely, aware that we did not create our world or ourselves. We refrain from changing our environments but allow them to make an impression on us, to taste the wonder and awe of the natural world and of our own fragile, wondrous beings. —M.M.

A midrash suggests that the act of resting on the seventh day was not a cessation from creation but rather its culmination and completion. This teaches that our generative acts, like God's, are made whole through rest, not through further work. —D.W.

"*L'kha Dodi*" is a 16th-century poem by Shlomo Halevi Alkabetz used nearly universally in the Friday night Jewish liturgy. In "*L'kha Dodi,*" Shabbat is described as "*sof ma'aseh b'maḥashava t'ḥila*"—the last thing made when the world was created, but the first in mind. Lest we believe that the world was created for the sake of humanity, the poet reminds us that there was a seventh day of creation; the world was created for the sake of Shabbat. —J.G.K.

reminds us that there is a Creator of the world to whom we owe our lives and to whom we are responsible. Just as God rested on the seventh day, so should we rest in imitation of God.

Resting on Shabbat can thus be an important reminder

The traditional idea of imitating God can still inspire us to strive to incorporate our own highest ideals and values into our lives (to be more compassionate, more just, more loving, more caring, more patient, more kind) without having to believe in any particular theological image of God. —S.C.R.

It is an oft-repeated trope that we rest on the seventh day because God rested on the seventh day. But few pause to ask: Is God still resting? If not, does God continue to work and rest every seventh day? Implicit in the fact that these questions have no answer is an acknowledgment that Shabbat is ultimately a human creation, based on our meaningful cycles of work. The month and the year are respectively based on lunar and solar cycles. Not so the week, which is an arbitrary length of time. We rest every seventh day because we find it meaningful and necessary to do so. —J.M.S.

Just as Shabbat reminds us of Creation, and Shabbat practices encourage us not to create anything new, so we should be mindful not to destroy Creation on Shabbat. Shabbat can be a time to be with the created world just as it is. —B.P.

To my knowledge, the first chapters of the Book of Genesis contain the only ancient Creation myth that incorporates the notion that the Creator rested. This is a remarkable assertion! With the claim that God ended the creation process with Shabbat, the biblical authors imply that when we observe Shabbat, we are acting in accord with the fundamental structure of the universe. The idea of Shabbat rest, then, is clearly much more than mere rest and relaxation. To take a day each week when we honor Creation by ceasing from all creative (and destructive) acts helps attune us to the rhythms of Creation and the godliness that infuses it. —T.S.

Control is a primary spiritual issue, especially in our time. We delude ourselves into thinking we have more control than we have, and sometimes we even abandon the areas where we do have control, such as our practice and our priorities. If Shabbat were nothing more than a way to contemplate issues of control and self-understanding, it would still have infinite value. —S.P.W.

that we are not in control of our lives. Our time is not our own; we cannot determine the length of our lives. The work to which we are dedicated and the money that we are intent on earning are not ultimate values. No matter how urgent the work in which we are engaged on Friday afternoon seems to us, the weekly lesson is that it can wait.

Our time is not our own; neither is our world. In our six days of labor, we never fully finish the world—our work is endless. The traditional 39 categories of forbidden labor on Shabbat may be taken to hint at the limits of our mastery over the world. —J.A.S.

We imitate the divine. We come to know ourselves as creators, in the divine image, sharing that generative capacity with the source of all life. In connecting with the image that God rested on the seventh day, we experience rest as an essential part of the creative energy of the universe. Music has notes and silences. Creating needs periodic pauses for appreciating, gaining perspective, and experiencing humility and delight, and for imbuing our work with significance that connects small creations with a larger whole, that connects our creations to ultimate meaning (*ḳedusha*) and our deepest values. —M.M.

Indeed, our work should wait. Our priorities should dictate that ceasing from work on Shabbat is more important than engaging in work. —D.D.M.

By resting on Shabbat, I am also conscious that I am participating, in my own small way, in the healing of our planet by refraining from the consumption of some materials and energy that I would consume during a regular weekday. —N.C.M.

Religious practice connects us to ideas and values; it orients us. The religious experience our practice supports is embodied and internal, not primarily or initially cerebral, but our ideas and values shape our experience even as our religious experience reinforces our ideas and values. The weekly lesson is not only that the other work can wait but that other experiences and ways of being in the world are deeply valuable and are an important counterbalance to productivity. The nurturing experience of being comes into balance with doing. We connect with our essence as valuable not for what we achieve but simply for being amazingly alive. This balance enables us to cultivate ourselves as whole beings, richer beings, in abiding relationship with that which is larger than our individual beings and goals. —M.M.

Another mitzvah (commandment) that the Torah describes as a "Sabbath" is the commandment to observe the sabbatical year. In ancient Israel, land was to be cultivated for six years, but it was to lie fallow in the seventh year, called *sh'mita*. The seventh year is a Shabbat of God. We are to rest the land because it is not ours to exploit; it belongs to God. We use it on loan.

The weekly Shabbat works the same way. When we leave our busy lives behind for a day each week, it is not because we are incapable of continuing 24/7. To the contrary, we are supremely able to pursue our work without taking a break, and we often feel impelled to do so. We forget that whatever work we are pursuing, it ought to be God's work. Shabbat reminds us of this.

The biblical sabbatical concept underlies the premise of contemporary sabbaticals—time off for those of us who are lucky enough to work in fields (pun intended) that recognize the need to recoup our energy and insight by letting go of regular activities. —D.D.M.

Perhaps the original idea of *sh'mita* can remind us today to have reverence for the earth and to exercise our responsibilities to replenish and nurture our natural resources as a sacred act. —S.C.R.

There is a tension in our tradition between the responsibility that comes with ownership and the concept that nothing really belongs to us. Instead of reading, "This book belongs to..." Hebrew bookplates often read, "*Ladonay ha'aretz um'lo'a*"—"The earth is God's and all it contains." (Psalms 24:1) Once, I was sitting on an Israeli train typing on my laptop when an ultra-Orthodox child accompanied by his father pointed to the computer and asked me, "*Zeh shel'ḵha?*" "Is this yours?" I answered him in Hebrew with the line from Psalms, and said that aside from that, I supposed it was. —J.G.K.

Shabbat is like many of the spiritual practices of cultures (tea ceremonies, flower arranging, meditation retreats): The purpose of the focused activity is to enable us to bring that level of attention and mindfulness to the entirety of life. —R.H.

A Reminder of the Exodus from Egypt (Zekher Litzi'at Mitzrayim)

The Friday evening Kiddush (blessing over the wine) also indicates that Shabbat serves as a reminder of the Exodus from Egypt. In this central Jewish story, narrated most explicitly at the Passover Seder, we are each required to regard ourselves as if we personally were slaves liberated from Egypt. The Exodus narrative is not a historical account that reports events that happened long ago. Rather, it is a story in which we participate in our lived, felt experience. Individually and collectively, we are all restricted by our fears and passions, our family upbringing, our cultural context and society's economic and political constraints, as well as in many other ways. And just as God delivered Israel out of Egyptian bondage, so do we locate in God the power of liberation from personal limitations and political oppression in our own lives.

This theme resounds through the daily liturgy, morning and evening. Shabbat, however, is an extremely potent weekly opportunity to enact and experience our weekly

We locate God in the power of liberation. Every expansion from the limited, self-centered, habitual and self-serving "me" indicates the presence of a power greater than ourselves. Every such expansion is also an experience of connection, well-being and transformation. Every such expansion is also fundamentally a mystery, no matter how I prepare for its coming. —S.P.W.

liberation from bondage and to embody the belief that *avadim hayinu b'mitzrayim* ("We were slaves in Egypt"). We literally are freed from working—from the work of

Often, while studying Shabbat observance in a community, the issue of the *Shabbos goy* is raised. The *halakha*—Jewish law—allows for a variety of legal fictions that make actions permissible that appear to be forbidden. The *Shabbos goy* is a non-Jewish worker who performs acts that are traditionally understood as prohibited work. (Examples include feeding a fire [a vital winter activity before the invention of central heating], turning on an oven, performing maintenance on the synagogue and doing some cooking chores.) On the one hand, employing a *Shabbos goy* facilitates life in some Jewish communities and households on Shabbat. On the other, it calls into question the concept of allowing those who work for us to have a Shabbat, and, for many, it causes discomfort by creating a divide between Jew and non-Jew.
—N.H.M.

Shabbat is first introduced to the Israelites immediately after they escape Pharaoh's chariots at the Reed Sea. In chapter 16 of Exodus, Moses is informed that in response to the people's complaints about being hungry, God would send down "bread from the heavens," a special substance the Israelites call "manna." Each day, they were to collect enough for that day and not hoard any overnight because all manna that was left over would rot. On Friday, the people are informed that they should collect enough for two days, and lo and behold, it was still good the next day because, as Moses explained, "Today is a Shabbat of God, and you will not find it in the field." (Exodus 16:25) The manna comes not just as a miraculous daily meal, but also as a lesson in "enough"—in not grasping more than is needed and then, on Shabbat, having faith that what we have will suffice. Our two loaves of hallah on *erev Shabbat* hark back to this lesson, inviting us to accept as enough that which we have, without needing to acquire more for a period of one day. —T.S.

In premodern Europe, where Jews lived in close contact with other Jews, commerce shut down on Shabbat due to the weight of religious expectation. Thus, both rich and poor Jews rested on Shabbat. In an open and industrial society, commerce and industry churn on nonstop. Poor Jews who migrated to America in the late 19th and early 20th centuries were expected by their employers to work on Saturdays. For many, this was a painful and unprecedented conflict. —D.W.

our employment and any other activity in which we are constructing something or repairing it. Beyond that, the day offers us regularly scheduled rest, as well as an opportunity for good food, interpersonal connection, song, prayer, contemplation, study, self-reflection, pleasant recreation, and play—all of the things available to a person of leisure who is not burdened with the pressures of earning a living. It is truly a reminder of the liberation from slavery.

Yes, Shabbat involves liberation from earning a living, but also, so important in our current culture, liberation from the constant buzz and interaction of social media. For so many people, taking a day off from work is imaginable, but detaching from email, texting and the Internet seems impossible. And yet this is exactly where Shabbat can offer respite and reorientation—in relation to the seeming urgency of email and the types of information most of us feel we need to constantly take in. Shabbat offers an opportunity for very different input. —M.M.

In the words of *The New Haggadah* (the 1941 Reconstructionist Haggadah), the experience of the Pesach Seder involves liberation from all those things that warp the mind but leave the flesh alive. —D.D.M.

The idea of personal liberation is one of Judaism's greatest challenges. It is a constant reminder that each of us is enslaved in many ways in our own lives, both externally and internally, and that the challenge to free ourselves from our own enslavements is a lifelong task. —S.C.R.

Our generation knows unprecedented leisure through all kinds of laborsaving devices. I do not know how much energy it took my forebears to get the clothes really clean without the aid of any electric devices, or how long it took to harvest crops, process them into foodstuff, guard against spoilage and ultimately prepare three meals a day. Yet I know that the time freed up by technology is also consumed by it, and our lives are full of demands for our attention and the expectation of instant responsiveness. *Mitzrayim* can also mean "narrowness," and the liberation from Egypt led to a place of *merḥav Ya*, a wide-open, God-filled place. Observing Shabbat—setting limits so as to create expansiveness—seems extremely important in the digital era. —D.W.

Furthermore, the biblical command not to engage in work applies not only to the Israelites, but also to their servants. As we recall that we were once slaves, our commitment to human dignity is embodied in the extension of Shabbat rest to everyone in the community.

It is intriguing that keeping Shabbat is a commandment, and that the prohibition against working one day a week is included in the Ten Commandments. Why do people need to be commanded to rest? On the face of it, rest would seem to be a pleasurable thing to do, something we shouldn't need much encouragement for. The incessant urge to do, to produce, to make and take, must be a very primal human urge. If our ancestors were in need of this commandment in a world that moved at a much slower pace than our own, how much more so are we in need of it today!

—T.S.

The version of the Ten Commandments in Deuteronomy implies that the *purpose* of the Sabbath is to let servants rest "in order that your male and female servant rest as you do." Not only does Shabbat apply to us and our servants, it also extends to our animals, who are not to be required to work for us on Shabbat. Shelly Yachimovitch, a leader of the Israeli Labor Party, commented on the need for a weekly day of rest and sharply contrasted the depth of the Torah commandment with our overworked present: "What cattle received 3,000 years ago, even the high-tech guy doesn't get today."

—J.A.S.

This lesson can impact our lives outside of the specific realm of Shabbat, reminding us that no workers should be slaves.

—B.P.

The Terms of the Perpetual Covenant (Brit Olam)

The Exodus from Egyptian slavery was also the beginning of the covenantal relationship between God and the Jewish people. Shabbat is a sign of that perpetual covenant—*brit olam.* (Exodus 31:15) The terms of that relationship are particularly clear on Shabbat: Just as on Shabbat we commemorate our liberation from Egyptian slavery, so on

Normally, covenants are reciprocal, with both parties dependent on one another to some degree. Yet how can this be true of Shabbat, a covenant between finite human beings and an infinite God? I am reminded of the bumper sticker that says, "Where is God? Wherever you let God in." —J.M.

There is a difference between a *sign* of the covenant and the *terms* of the covenant. As with any durable relationship, the terms are continuously renegotiated as the parties change and grow. The way we might have observed Shabbat at one stage of life may not be the way we currently observe it. In this perspective, Shabbat is more a symbol of the covenant than a sign. As Rabbi Lawrence Hoffman teaches, symbols come before signs: Symbols speak to feelings, identity, familiarity and a sense of belonging. Signs are the explanations we create for the symbols we experience. —R.H.

For me, *brit* (covenant) first evokes mutual relationship. How do we feel that, enact that and make room for that sense of connection and relationship? That happens mostly through action/mitzvah, since the *brit* has terms for behavior, but I wouldn't want to lose the anchor of *brit* as connection—ways in which we make ourselves transparent to God and ways in which we open ourselves to mystery and awe. —M.M.

Through the way Jewish tradition tells the story of the Exodus from Egypt, it teaches us that our story is everyone's story and that all human beings have the divine right to freedom and liberation from their own enslavements. —S.C.R.

Shabbat we remember our commitment to work for the liberation of all who are enslaved, persecuted or oppressed today. The celebration of our own freedom on Shabbat comes with the reminder that it is not to be taken for granted.

A Foretaste of Paradise: The Joyous Appreciation of Life's Blessings (Oneg Shabbat)

During the Shabbat morning service, we sing, "*Yism'ḥu b'mal'khut'kha*": "Those who keep the Shabbat enjoy your realm; they call it delight. All members of a people who sanctify the seventh day are satisfied and delighted by your goodness."

Even as Shabbat reminds us that on the six days of creation we must work for justice, it also reminds us that adequate self-care is necessary in order to be effective in this work.
—D.W.

The first Passover in Egypt, before we were actually physically liberated, set up a system in which each Passover does not just celebrate a memory, but imagines a future time when all will be free. ("Next year in Jerusalem" articulates this metaphorically.) Shabbat is called *me'eyn olam haba*, a taste of the world to come. Each Shabbat is an opportunity to imagine a world without slavery, without injustice, in which all will be free to observe Shabbat or in which every day will be like Shabbat.
—J.G.K.

A similar *ḳavana*/theme can be found in another phrase from the Shabbat liturgy: "Let us be satisfied with your goodness (*sab'enu mituveḳha*)." This is a day when we practice being satisfied and not always wanting something else. Though things can be a wonderful blessing, our satisfaction comes not from things but from goodness.
—J.A.S.

Shabbat is a most enjoyable, blessed gift. As traditional Jewish imagery puts it, God loves us, so God gave us the seventh day to be happy, to be transported into another realm of living. The ideal for Shabbat is that we not worry about work or business or money, not use our free time to catch up on our errands, not travel or transport things from one place to another. In all of the prayers we recite on Shabbat, we do not even ask for anything; on Shabbat we simply praise, appreciate and give thanks, expressing the value of *hodaya* (gratitude). We act as if we have no

It is important not to let the difficulty in living the "ideal" version of Shabbat keep us from incorporating some elements of Shabbat into our lives. Sometimes it is enough to choose one new way of celebrating or acknowledging Shabbat at a time. —S.C.R.

For those of us immersed in consumer culture, praising, appreciating and giving thanks may not be so simple. We are habituated to evaluating and critiquing our experiences. While a pointed critique might roll off the tongue, a well-turned compliment often does not. The language of the Shabbat liturgy can encourage our capacities to accept, wonder and be grateful. —H.S.V.

It takes practice, weekly practice, to become skilled at setting aside workday concerns. As one gains skill, the anticipation of Shabbat lets one step back, take a deep breath and enjoy its rhythms, as well as the rhythm it gives to a week. —D.D.M.

Shabbat should be a day of pleasure and joy. That is part of the reason that sexual pleasure and intimacy are part of the delight of the day. They point to the connection between physical and spiritual delight. —M.M.

Keeping Shabbat as a practice implies that it is something we work at week by week. Cultivating an awareness of Shabbat as a state of mind can be something we work at moment by moment. The *mida* (quality) of *hodaya* (gratitude), for example, can be intentionally nurtured that way. Whenever we pause and let go of the grip of our busyness and grasping intentions, we can invite in a Shabbat of the mind in which we relax regarding the conditions of our lives in that moment. To pause, simply, for one breath, and to notice something for which we are grateful, however insignificant, is to invite in a moment of Shabbat for the mind. —M.K.

cares or concerns—and when we become skilled in this practice, we are actually able to put our preoccupations on hold, living more fully in the present moment, tasting food more acutely and noticing the blessedness of experiences that we otherwise take for granted. We might say that on Shabbat, we experience divine love. In many Jewish traditions, Shabbat represents a foretaste of paradise, where Jews have believed that figuratively speaking, one bathes in divine light for all eternity. The Shabbat experience that we seek to create should therefore reflect how we imagine heaven.

When we experience Shabbat by living fully in the present moment and make doing so a spiritual practice, we can then extend the experience into our everyday reality. We can bring Shabbat into every moment. —B.P.

My family had wide-ranging conversations over the dinner table. They were usually gregarious and energizing, but occasionally arguments would break out. Sometimes the arguments were about politics, sometimes merely sibling rivalry. When the temperature would creep upward on Friday nights, my Bubby would always say, "*Sha*, not on *Shabbos*." For her, heaven was a place with no one yelling at each other! —D.W.

It isn't heaven as a supernatural place that matters. It is the opportunity to imagine what a perfect vacation day, a perfect day of enjoying life in all its wonder might look like, and choosing to incorporate as many of those elements as you can into your own personal Shabbat. —S.C.R.

Shabbat oneg involves joy, delight and gratitude consciously enhanced by the day's experiences. That is the sense in which Shabbat is the embodiment of wholeness. For some Jews, the word "heaven" contains Christian associations. (Heaven is where the good dead people go.) By contrast, I connect *olam haba* (the world to come, Eden, paradise) to the embodiment of wholeness, that which is eternal and complete. —M.M.

Palpable Holiness (Shabbat Kodesh)

"*Z'khor et yom hashabbat l'kad'sho.*" "Remember the Sabbath day in a way that sanctifies it." (Exodus 20:8, recited as part of the traditional Ashkenazic Kiddush prayer on Saturday afternoon)

Sanctity (*kedusha*) is difficult to define. It is commonly associated with space. At a holy site, we might take off our shoes (Moses at the Burning Bush), wrap ourselves in a tallit (prayer shawl), cleanse ourselves (the Israelites at Mount Sinai), refrain from work-oriented speech, elevate our thoughts, and pray. When we leave the sacred space, we may carry some of the experience with us, but we know that we are no longer in that physical space. We can feel the difference between the mundane and the holy. In fact, the different, separate nature of the holy is what makes it sacred; the holy points us beyond the everyday to something greater, something that's not so easy to remember or express, something that transcends and/or underlies the apparent reality in which we live.

One ancient meaning of sanctity is "belonging to God." "*Shabbat kodesh*" would then mean something like "Sabbath that belongs to God" or "God-time Sabbath." What does "God-time" mean to you? —J.A.S.

One of the radical innovations of the talmudic rabbis was to transfer *kedusha* from a property of sacred spaces (Temple, altar, land) to one of sacred times (Shabbat, holidays, daily prayer times). This is still a great gift to those of us in the Diaspora, and all those seeking to avoid the potential idolatries of blood and soil. —J.M.

Do we see holiness in something that is different from everything else, or do we see holiness in things that we normally see, but now see in a different way? —R.H.

What makes time sacred? In his book *The Sabbath*, the great thinker Rabbi Abraham Joshua Heschel followed a line of Hasidic interpretations. These define Shabbat as the temporal equivalent of the Tabernacle (*Mishkan*), and Heschel called Shabbat "a palace in time." While he was a committed Zionist, he rejected the line of thought that bemoaned the Jewish loss of a homeland after the destruction of the Second Temple and before the establishment of the State of Israel. Heschel believed that it was fortuitous that for 2,000 years, Jews were not attached to the places where they lived. Instead, he maintained, the Jewish calendar became a palace in time, and Shabbat became our temporal palace. It went with us wherever we sojourned while we lived in the Diaspora.

The binary division between "space" and "time" as presented by Heschel is not neutral but hierarchical: Heschel implies that "time" trumps "space." Ironically, many English editions of Heschel's essay "The Sabbath" are bound together with his essay on the Land of Israel, "The Earth is the Lord's." One could make a plausible argument that Judaism is as much concerned with space as with time, and that it depends on what is under discussion as to where the emphasis falls. That said, Shabbat is certainly the primary prism through which Jewish tradition views the entire category of time.

—R.H.

Shabbat can be conceived of as an island in time. Shabbat is a day for itself, a time to be "in the moment" or "in the day." We avoid doing things in preparation for the days after Shabbat. This is the basis of the Shabbat practices policy at my congregation in Willimantic, Connecticut. (See *A Guide to Jewish Practice, Volume I*, pages 615–636).

—J.A.S.

One of our objectives for Shabbat, then, is to construct a temporal equivalent to a sacred pilgrimage site. As Friday sundown approaches, all of our preparations can be seen as the equivalent of entering a synagogue sanctuary or a holy shrine. Reality is altered with the lighting of the Shabbat candles. Because of the elaborate symbol and ritual system of Shabbat, time itself takes on a different quality, and crossing that boundary in time, we behave as if we have entered the sacred palace of the Blessed Holy One.

In the scheme of Jewish time, Shabbat is the primary fountain from which all sanctity springs; we look forward to the holiness of Shabbat all week long, and we yearn to keep Shabbat with us as long as we can, not rushing to end it at the earliest possible moment on Saturday evening.

Shabbat really does give meaning to every day of the week. It turns every week into a sacred pilgrimage. The week moves toward it and then is suffused with its light. —S.P.W.

Try the following as you walk down a street, or look into a shop window, or peer at a field as you drive by on a Friday evening as the sun sets, after you have set your intention to bring in Shabbat: Imagine that something magical has descended to make this ordinary place shine with an inner glow. Look closely and see how the place has colors, smells and sanctity that you didn't notice before. Now zoom out and see how everything has been imbued with that sanctity. Your intention to bring in Shabbat has changed the entire world as you perceive it. —J.M.S.

What can we do to shift our orientation to time from a cramped one in which we experience the press of minutes, hours and weeks to a more expansive orientation in which time is measured in epochs and eons? Can we reorient our sense of time from political to geological cycles? We can get out into the natural world. This, for me, is the role of a Shabbat hike. —H.S.V.

Shabbat ends slowly and on its own time. The liminal time of twilight following sunset invites us to gradually anticipate bidding Shabbat farewell. —J.G.K.

Living in Jewish Time (Hamavdil Beyn Kodesh L'ḥol)

Many Jews who are committed to living a rich and full Jewish life do not believe that Jewish laws and customs are literally commanded by God. They face a daily challenge: Given that the world in which we live is radically different from the world of our ancestors, how can we hope to relate to our inherited beliefs and practices? Are we just picking and choosing those aspects of the vast Jewish heritage with which we happen to agree? And if so, aren't we abandoning most of the opportunity to be shaped by the wisdom of our heritage? The Reconstructionist saying, "Tradition has a vote but not a veto," depends upon our ability to hear tradition's voices, an extremely tall order when so much of our heritage is expressed in idioms of an inherited culture whose terms and categories are difficult to understand, and whose values sometimes are unacceptable to us.

Because Judaism is a civilization, however, the wisdom of Jewish traditions is also available to us in ways that are not directly cognitive. Living a Jewish life entails far more than affirming certain principles of belief and observing Jewish rituals. It involves seeing reality through Jewish lenses. This happens gradually, for good and bad, as the result of experiences in a Jewish context. (You see an almond tree? Perhaps you think about *Tu Bishvat* [New Year of Trees] songs that mention almond trees. You hear a tune or inhale a scent that you can't quite place, but it takes you back to Jewish summer camp or to your grandmother's apartment.) We immerse ourselves in our heritage in order to become Jewishly acculturated, so that even while most aspects of our lives would be unintelligible to our ancestors, we can nevertheless integrate their voices into our consciousness.

The most powerful agent of Jewish acculturation is the Jewish calendar. It allows us to follow ancient rhythms that orient our lives in many subliminal ways, and thus to sense the resonance of countless generations who followed the same rhythms. To live in Jewish time means, for example, that the heat of summer (in the Northern Hemisphere) reminds us of the destruction of the First and Second Temples in Jerusalem (*Tisha B'Av*) and leads us to the self-examination that precedes the High Holy Days. The weeks preceding Pesach have us enslaved in preholiday preparation, and the seven weeks between Pesach and Shavuot have us moving toward the revelation of the Torah on Mount Sinai. Following the annual cycle of the reading of the Torah has us thinking about the matriarch Sarah in October and November, and Miriam, Moses' sister, in June. We inevitably bring new interpretations to the understanding of the holiday cycle and the re-reading of Torah, but in doing so, we are being acted upon by the sacred texts and practices that we encounter. We are becoming ever more Jewishly acculturated.

When we align ourselves with the rhythm of the sacred seasons of Judaism, we begin to see the world through Jewish eyes. We allow ourselves to bring to mind personal Jewish memories from our past to add color and emotional connections to our present, and we feel a greater sense of belonging, recognizing we are a small part of the ever-flowing, ancient stream of Jewish life. —S.C.R.

There is no more prominent and frequent occurrence in the Jewish calendar than the weekly arrival of Shabbat. Along with the remaining six days of the week, Shabbat provides the basic rhythm of Jewish time. Six days of work, one day of rest: mundane, holy. Hurry up, slow down. Get distracted, return to the Source of All. Worry about yourself and your loved ones, remember your blessings. In the *Havdala* blessing that marks the end of Shabbat, God is praised for distinguishing between holy and mundane (*hamavdil beyn kodesh l'ḥol*).

Traditionally, Jews bask in the light of the previous Shabbat through Tuesday, and on Wednesday they begin to prepare for the following Shabbat: cleaning, shopping, laundering, studying. A richly celebrated Shabbat colors all the days of the week. When we live from one Shabbat to the next, it becomes our primary temporal marker. Even as we look forward to next winter's vacation or to a family celebration, we are also thinking about where and with whom we will be eating in several days. And even as

Kadya Molodowsky's poem "Song of the Sabbath" imagines a week full of drudgery and destruction. "This is my whole week," she writes, "the dove's flight dying." On Shabbat, everything is restored to wholeness, even the damaged dove, and she enters into a world of peace and renewal. —D.W.

I have never liked the word "mundane," but I recognize Shabbat as the antithesis of the "everyday." The *Havdala* blessing is a reminder that time we set apart from the everyday becomes sacred by definition. That is one way we have the power to bring holiness into our lives. —S.C.R.

I studied an early Jewish mystical teaching that compares Shabbat to a fountain that waters the rest of the week. In this image, Shabbat is not the culmination of the week, but rather its center. What would it be like to have Shabbat be the center of our week rather than its culmination? —N.C.M.

we are calculating how we will find the hours to devote to a project we have that has a deadline in ten days, our calculations take account of Friday sundown to Saturday evening as time that we won't use for work. Shabbat affects the reality of weekdays as well.

Living in Jewish time inevitably affects our outlook, our priorities, our values and, often enough, our blood pressure. The rhythms of our observance shape us more completely than the words that we pray or the values that we espouse.

Returning to Our Ultimate Purposes (T'shuva)

The observance of Shabbat has often been associated with the purification or elevation of the soul, suggesting that immersing our consciousness in a different spiritual reality for 25 hours each week has a substantial effect on the quality of our spiritual lives. The proof text our rabbis

I am often struck by the contrast between Shabbat around the world, where Sunday is also a weekend day, and Shabbat in Israel, where Sunday is a weekday and Friday has both weekday and weekend qualities. In the Diaspora, one who works a weekday schedule often has a chance to rest on Sunday and recover from being overwhelmed with Shabbat guests, food, drink and conversation. In Israel, Friday daytime is a time to prepare both for Shabbat and for the week ahead. Shabbat is the single day to rest and recover from the week; there is a need for Shabbat itself to be the opportunity to rejuvenate. —J.G.K.

The rhythms of our lives are shaped by tradition and culture as well as by our unique biology and upbringing. Our lives are shaped by our responses to often-conflicting rhythms that provide frequent challenges. This *Guide* continually invites us to acknowledge these challenges and to make an effort toward more awareness in contemplating our choices. —S.P.W.

gave for this notion comes from the Book of Exodus. (35:1) Immediately following the account of the Israelites' worship of the golden calf at Mount Sinai and the consequent divine wrath, the commandment to observe the Sabbath is repeated. Why? Because, commentators have taught, observing Shabbat is the most effective means we have for *t'shuva* (return, repentance). More than any other mitzvah, it has the power to lift us up out of whatever we find ourselves mired in during the week. Whatever our very real and pressing concerns are in any given week—professional, financial, interpersonal, or medical—Shabbat arrives to remind us to look at them from a different perspective, from the vantage point of the ultimate meaning and purpose of our lives. That way we can keep our concerns from becoming idolatrous attachments—golden calves, if you will.

Cognitive neuroscience appears to confirm the efficacy of this function of Shabbat. Neural pathways and synap-

Shabbat and *t'shuva* are deeply intertwined. Creation recurs (mythically but truly) every Shabbat. We are (mythically but truly) reborn every Shabbat. New eyes make change possible. Nothing ever is the same except the perception that we have seen this before. But we really have not. Life, reality and the universe are always in flux; therefore, there is always the possibility of beginning again. This is the core of the spiritual message, the evolution of consciousness, and the hope for a better world. —S.P.W.

Books like Richard Davidson's *The Emotional Life of Your Brain* and Daniel Siegel's *The Mindful Brain* are new sacred texts for 21st-century contemplatives, because they show that spiritual practice has more in common with nutrition and exercise than with magic and superstition. Shabbat is the opposite of "working out." You might call it "not working in." Yet the transformative effects of spiritual practice are measurable even by Western scientific methods. —J.M.

tic connections are formed through mental activity. When we respond to stimuli the same way over and over again, these pathways do not grow; instead, they form the basis of habits and set ways of being. However, it is also possible to cultivate new habits, which correlate to the formation of new neural connections in the brain. Changing our response patterns—doing *t'shuva*—physically changes the brain and increases the capacity for calm, attention, mindfulness and gratitude. But this kind of *t'shuva* doesn't have to wait for Rosh Hashana or Yom Kippur. Indeed, to be effective, it must be more frequent than that. When our regular weekly Shabbat observance includes not only external behaviors but also an inner cultivation of peaceful, restful, states of mind, it has the power to transform our minds.

The discoveries of cognitive neuroscience suggest that repeated alternative behaviors can create new neural highways through the brain. This insight is related not only to the issue of *t'shuva*, but also to the entirety of Shabbat. Those who take on as a regular repeated routine the decelerated rhythms of Shabbat can, over time, create new habits whose effect can extend beyond that one day to the rest of one's life.
—R.H.

Shabbat as an instrument of *t'shuva* is amplified exponentially when Yom Kippur falls on a Shabbat.
—R.H.

Shabbat is fundamentally a state of mind. It is a weekly opportunity for us to choose not only to live differently on that one day from the way we live during the rest of the week, but also to think differently on that day as well.
—S.C.R.

Community (Am M'kad'shey Sh'vi'i)

Shabbat prayers refer to the Jewish people as "*am m'kad'shey sh'vi'i*"—"the people who sanctify the seventh day." That is, the prayers implicitly assert that Shabbat observance is one of the defining characteristics of a Jew. It certainly can be a primary factor in the building of a Jewish community (*kehila*). Those who mark Friday evening and/or Saturday join together. This occurs most publicly in the synagogue, where those who attend services come together for prayer and fellowship. Shabbat "regulars," who spend hours together in Shabbat services and at the *oneg Shabbat* (eating and social time) that follows, become well acquainted and develop bonds of connection that do not rest on prior friendship or even on common back-

The great poet Hayim Nahman Bialik introduced a religiously inspired version of the *oneg Shabbat* in prestate Israel. On Saturday afternoons, he would gather people together in Tel Aviv for communal singing, learning and meals. The topics were frequently on the Bible or religious themes, but the approach was cultural. Our use of the term "*oneg Shabbat*" to refer to the social time following services stems from the *oneg Shabbat* groups started by Hayim Nahman Bialik, the national poet of the early Zionist movement. These groups were intended to invent a new, cultural way of observing Shabbat based on Jewish learning, singing, shared food and sometimes drama. The term probably migrated to Friday night skits, socializing and Israeli dancing at Zionist summer camps and from there to synagogue life. I would love to see us reclaim the civilizational breadth and spirit of Bialik's *oneg Shabbat*. —D.W./J.A.S.

The *Mi Shebeyrakh* blessing, discussed below, can be a source of community building. In some congregations and *ḥavurot*, individuals going up for an aliyah receive personal blessings for milestone celebrations or in preparation for such major transitions as surgery or retirement. The individuals mark the milestones in community, and community members are informed about them and can offer congratulations or support. A similar dynamic can happen through the *Mi Shebeyrakh L'ḥolim*, the prayers for healing, when names of ailing individuals are recited aloud. —D.W.

ground or interests. A warm, welcoming group of people is the foundation of a thriving community. Some communities build on this by catering or hosting potluck meals on Friday evenings before or after services, or on Saturday afternoons after the Shabbat morning service.

Shabbat observance also builds community in other ways. Not everyone finds what they are looking for at worship services. People who celebrate a Shabbat dinner in their homes on Friday evenings gravitate to others who can join them or host them. Sometimes *ḥavurot* (small groups of individuals or households) form to meet for the Friday evening meal each month in one another's homes. Such groups sometimes become powerful extended families, and their deeply felt connections sustain subcommunities upon which the larger community depends. What makes a Shabbat meal different from other meals is that on Shabbat the participants are not rushing off to do anything else. There is plenty of time for talking and singing. There is a sense of *oneg*, of joy.

Similarly, if our observance of Shabbat means that we only engage in activities in the spirit of Shabbat, then we

While many members of our congregation, both Jewish and non-Jewish, celebrate Shabbat in a variety of ways over the course of the year, as a community we designate one Shabbat in the spring "Shabbat Unplugged," when we encourage one another to "unplug" in some way from email, from taking work home, from shopping, from doing the laundry during an entire Shabbat. In addition to individual "unplugging," we organize Friday night dinners in members' homes and encourage people to "plug in" to Shabbat morning services or to an afternoon walk in the woods, a bike ride or a Shabbat nap. The shared sense that we are enjoying Shabbat as a community, even if we are not all physically together, fosters a lovely sense of connection. —T.S.

are often looking for others to share the experience of a long walk or a trip to a park, museum or zoo. In the words of the liturgy, those who observe the Shabbat enjoy themselves together.

Linking the Chain of Generations (L'dor Vador)

"*L'dor vador nagid godlekha ul'netzaḥ n'tzaim k'dushat'kha nakdish.*" "From generation to generation we proclaim your greatness, and we will sanctify your holiness forever and ever."

We end the *Kedusha* part of the *Shabbat Amida* (standing, individually recited prayer) with this line, linking our observance of Shabbat with all preceding generations and generations yet unborn. Every ritual and prayer contains the power to transport us from the present moment into a sense of eternity at the moment when we remember that we are doing what we imagine our ancestors did and what we hope our descendants will do. We may use the candlesticks or Kiddush cup that we have inherited, or sing an uncle's melody or cook a grandmother's recipe. And when we have no intergenerational history—if we are Jews by choice or Jews by birth without memories of Shabbat

I have found that for Jews by choice, the ability to create their own new rituals and traditions for Shabbat is one of the most powerful gifts of becoming Jewish. Every ritual you create adds one more layer of sacred connection to the Jews throughout history who did exactly the same thing and passed down to us what we now call "tradition."
—S.C.R.

observance in our families—the observance of Shabbat provides a palpable path of entry into the bosom of the age-old community of Shabbat observers (*am m'kad'shey sh'vi'i*).

The opportunity that resides in this nostalgic power is that we are not only connecting to generations past and future. We are also connecting their most cherished experiences and values to our own. When we rejoice at the setting of the Friday sun and the sacred rest it signals, we imagine how they experienced this moment—how their images of paradise may enrich our own.

A Vision of Redemption (Sam'ḥeynu bishu'atekha)

Eviatar Zerubavel, a sociologist of time, argues that Shabbat may be the most important Jewish contribution to human civilization. He finds no evidence of the existence

Inevitably, connections across imagined generations may involve projecting values onto the past that weren't present then. Plenty of Jewish immigrants, for example, spent Friday night at the Yiddish theater, not in shul or around the Sabbath table. —D.D.M.

My favorite translation of the word "mitzvah" is "that which connects," from a Hasidic play on the Aramaic word "*tz̦'vat*" (Hebrew letters *tzadi-vav-vav-tav*), meaning to "join" or "attach." In this playful translation, a mitzvah is an act that connects us. The mitzvah of Shabbat connects us in so many ways: to our ancestors, to our communal past, to family and community in the present and to our children's future as we create Shabbat memories for them. —T.S.

The ancient Babylonians apparently had days of restricted activity on the seventh, 14th, 21st and 28th day of each lunar month, but these were also connected to the moon, leaving the "week" of the new month longer than the others, and maintaining cyclical time outside of human intention. —J.A.S.

of the week before its introduction in Israelite culture (*The Seven Day Circle: The History and Meaning of the Week*). The week does not correspond to anything in nature. The day follows sunrise and sunset, the (lunar) month corresponds to the cycle of the moon, and the solar year follows the rotation of the earth. But the week is arbitrary; seven days is an artificial period of time.

The biblical introduction of the week and its climactic Shabbat signals the introduction of linear time, which liberates us from the regularly repeating cycles of nature. The Jewish calendar looks forward to redemption, to the end of time, to a rupture in the order of reality when the world will be different, to a time when peace and justice will reign and the presence of God will be completely manifest. In rabbinic terms, this is the redemption that will occur in the future that is anticipated by the redemption from Egyptian bondage.

The Jewish tendency to look forward to a world that is repaired and healed and to work toward that world (*tikun olam*) stems from the development of the view of time as linear, as moving forward, rather than as being only cyclical, repeating itself. Shabbat is not only our attempt to create a reality every seventh day that feels as if we're in heaven; its very existence, punctuating the humanly crafted seven-day week, stands as a weekly affirmation that we are not completely subject to the elements of nature. We can jump off the carousel and move toward redemption. We know that we can do so because we do it every Friday at sundown. It is what we pray for in the *Shabbat Amida* when we say, "*Samḥeynu bishu'atekha*," "Cause us to rejoice in your salvation."

Rest and Renewal (Menuḥa)

"*Uvayom hash'vi'i shavat vayinafash.*" "On the seventh day, God rested and was replenished." (Exodus 31:17)

The *menuḥa* (rest) of Shabbat certainly includes napping and catching up on one's sleep, not an insignificant enterprise in an era when studies tell us that most of us are sleep-deprived. It thus also contributes to the value of *b'riyut*—health and wellness. But Shabbat *menuḥa* includes many other activities: praying, eating, leisurely conversation, singing, reading, studying, playing and

While Shabbat emphasizes living in a cycle of humanly constructed linear time, I find that it also connects me more deeply to the cycles of nature; when I slow down on Shabbat, I am better able to notice the natural processes happening in my environment and to remember how connected I am to natural cycles. —N.C.M.

Adolescents, with their sensitivity to perceived hypocrisy, often pull up short at the idea of mandated rest. They will argue that it takes added work (by which they mean effort) to observe Shabbat. With this in mind, it might be helpful to conceive of *menuḥa* not just as rest, but also as refraining from acts of creation and destruction. During Shabbat, we change our orientation to the created world. We work on being, not doing. —H.S.V.

other activities that renew the soul. The break from the weekday routine allows us to attend to, refresh and deepen our spirits.

What might the writers of Exodus 31:17 have meant in using the word "*vayinafash*" (replenished) to describe God on the seventh day? The Hebrew word has the literal meaning of being "re-souled," renewing one's energy, being revived. After a taxing work week, what does it take to make you feel whole and refreshed?

The halakhic literature recognizes that Shabbat is no different from any other day, except that we declare it so. The great medieval halakhic authority Maimonides, for example, addresses the challenge faced by a traveler who loses track of the days. His advice is that you should start counting from the day on which you realize that you have lost track, and then observe Shabbat on the seventh day of the new counting. It is not that it doesn't matter which day you choose to observe Shabbat. The point is that, even if you are observing Shabbat on a different day than everyone else, you can't give it up altogether because of your miscalculation. Counting to the seventh day is an essential act in the life of a Jew even when—or precisely because—it is arbitrary.

—J.J.S.

Maimonides's perspective that Shabbat occurs because we declare it so is in tension with the rabbis who understood that Shabbat happens with or without us, while holidays are sanctified by the Jewish people, who set the calendar. (See, for example, Talmud *Beytza* 17a.)

—J.G.K.

The Torah teaches us that human beings are created in the image of God. Just as the Torah describes God as having created Shabbat, we human beings have creative power to set one time apart from another and literally to create sacred time in our own lives.

—S.C.R.

In Exodus 23:12, "*vayinafash*" is applied to servants and strangers resting on Shabbat; elsewhere it is used to describe David and his weary fighters resting up. "*Nefesh*" can also mean "self," which was often its meaning in biblical Hebrew. Perhaps Shabbat is an opportunity to return to our true selves (*vayinafash*), to become ourselves again.

—J.G.K./J.A.S.

In his book *The Kuzari*, the medieval philosopher and poet Judah Halevi explains this as precisely the reason why Shabbat was given to us. He sees Shabbat as a gift of time that allows us to devote adequate attention to the care of our bodies and souls. For Halevi this involves contemplation of the divine presence through prayer and meditation. We each have our own methods of renewal. The *menuḥa* (rest) of Shabbat is an opportunity for renewal as well as rest.

Play (M'saḥeket B'tevel Artzo)

Sometimes it is difficult to play, to engage in enjoyable activities that have no purpose. Traditional Jewish values are very clear that "wasting time" (*bitul z'man*) is to be avoided because that time can and should be devoted to the study of Torah (*limud Torah*). In medieval Europe, ethical treatises cautioned fathers not to waste their time playing with their own children! In our own time, potentially playful activities lose their playfulness as we turn them into accomplishments by honing our skills to run the race faster or to lower the handicap.

Our work has no end. As *Pirkey Avot* teaches, "The day is short and the task is great. . . . It is not up to you to complete the task; neither are you free to neglect it." (2.15–16) Even when we finish a project, meet a deadline or fulfill an obligation, the next project may already have its grip on us. For those who fear the impact of "losing" one day a week, the value of *menuḥa* as renewal provides a useful rationale for taking time off. Unless our work involves saving lives, *pikuaḥ nefesh*, we might discover that we can indeed afford to give up one day for our own rest and renewal. —B.P.

The Book of Proverbs imagines Wisdom as a person. It says that Wisdom was created before all other things, (Proverbs 8:22) and it often portrays Wisdom as the blueprint for the created world. Proverbs quotes Wisdom as saying, "*M'saḥeket b'tevel artzo.*" "I played before [God] at every moment. I played with the inhabited world and delighted in humankind." (Proverbs 8:30–31) Similarly, the psalmist has no problem saying that God created the mythical beast Leviathan so that God could play with the sea creature. (Psalms 104:26) Clearly, biblical writers did not think it inappropriate or disrespectful to suggest that God plays.

Shabbat is the perfect time to play—to do things we enjoy without worrying about what we are accomplishing. And if we are to believe the writers of biblical wisdom literature, when we play, we manifest a divine quality as surely as when we love or act compassionately.

Some Jews who grew up in traditional homes have memories of Shabbat as primarily filled with rules about what not to do, with restrictions and "do not's." How much more joy will we create if we see Shabbat as a weekly opportunity to enjoy doing what we don't have time for during the week as we celebrate life, play and enjoy life's blessings with family and friends. —S.C.R.

One of the highlights of school *Shabbatonim* is the inevitable pick-up game of Ultimate Frisbee on Shabbat afternoon. Staff and students play together, no one keeps score, and we play until we are too tired to continue. —H.S.V.

Longing for the Blessed Holy One (Tzam'a Nafshi)

In the symbolic imagery of the Shabbat liturgy, we welcome the Shabbat Bride at sunset on Friday, and we escort the Shabbat Queen as she departs on Saturday evening. The assumption of these images is that the Jews who are praying are heterosexual men spiritually romancing a Shabbat who is their female consort. This is not the place to undertake a thorough deconstruction and reconstruction of this worldview. Suffice it to say that Jews of different genders may want to re-imagine Shabbat in a variety of gendered or nongendered ways.

If we can move beyond this obstacle, it may be meaningful to recall that the mystics' gendered Shabbat *also* is identified with the *Shekhina*, the feminine aspect of God that in their system was closest to, and most manifest in, our physical, created world. Thus, for them Shabbat is the manifest presence of God. Welcoming Shabbat is a way of discerning the divine presence, a presence that is always with us everywhere, but one that we can more easily notice and embrace when we enter into the temporal

Much like my feelings about Shabbat preparation rituals (hallah baking, candle lighting) that are traditionally associated with women's observance, I often find myself caught between feeling invisible as a gay man by the traditional Jewish norm of heterosexuality and feeling happy as a feminist that, even as early as the rabbinic period, important roles and images of women existed in Jewish practice and thought. —J.G.K.

sphere of Shabbat—literally embrace, as we sing "*L'kha Dodi*" ("Come, My Friend/Beloved") on Friday evening, welcoming the face of Shabbat as if she or he were a lover returning from a six-day journey.

In the terms of the Lurianic kabbalists of 16th-century Tzfat in northern Israel, the *Kadosh Barukh Hu* (the transcendent, awesome aspect of God) is united on Shabbat with the *Shekhina* (the accessible, beloved aspect of God). We might express this as the way that our practice of Shabbat helps us to embody a concrete version of holiness that is otherwise far too abstract to express in words. Sometimes the truth is best expressed in song and dance.

When singing "*L'ḵha Dodi*," the quintessential Jewish mystical vision of the heterosexual union of (male) God with (female) Shabbat, I like to imagine *Shabbat Hamalḵa,* the Shabbat Queen, entering the sanctuary as a glorious drag queen. —T.S.

Even though I am praying indoors when I sing "*L'ḵha Dodi*," I often seek to call up an image of what it feels like to be in a field at sunset experiencing the presence of the divine; this helps me to connect to the kabbalistic notion of *Sheḵhina*. —N.C.M.

Songwriter Benjamin Newman echoes the marriage metaphor in his song "*Shechinah*," in which God transcendent may feel less accessible to us but God's presence reunites with us each week: "The King is in His office, 'cause the work is never finished / But the Queen has gone to walk among the twisting streets below; / And the light that is Her Presence fills the houses of the people / Who remember, when She visits—about every week or so." —J.G.K.

While *Kabbalat Shabbat* literally means the "receiving of Shabbat," which requires a readiness to receive Shabbat, "*L'ḵha Dodi*" has us running out into the fields to greet the beloved, as if calling across the meadow, "Hey, Beloved! I'm coming to meet you!" It is not delicate or reserved, but full of longing and love. We lift ourselves out of sadness and wake up. We put on garments of light and dance with the divine

A Coat of Many Colors

Like all people, Jews span a range of different spiritual types. Some of us tend to manifest our spiritual journey in action, locating the divine presence in our acts of *g'milut ḥesed* (loving kindness), such as hosting guests for Shabbat, and *tikun olam* (repairing the world). Such people use the perpetual covenant of Shabbat as a reminder and spur to do the social justice work that is required of us. Some of us like to study and engage in intellectual activity, using the free time of Shabbat to engage in *talmud Torah* (Torah study). Others of us find meaning in an embodied spiritual practice, hiking or biking or cooking and eating

under the setting sun. It is sensuous, luscious and erotic. While it may be challenging to connect with images of God as the beloved, we can gather each and every experience of love that has kissed our lives as manifestations of God's love. We have become uncomfortable with erotic energy as part of our spiritual lives, or we are worried about the abuse of that energy, but the Tzfat mystics remind us how alive, intimate, transcendent and unitive spiritual experience can be. Eros is a fundamental quality of spiritual life. The prayers of "*Yedid Nefesh*" and "*L'kha Dodi*" enable us both to awaken and to direct that energy through prayer. —M.M.

For those whose spiritual lives are deeply connected to the work of social justice, Shabbat rest is a particular challenge and a gift. Full-time justice activists often suffer burnout, leaving little if any time for their own rest and renewal. Whether making a commitment to be home at a somewhat reasonable time on Friday to enjoy a Shabbat meal with a spouse or friends, or taking a few hours on Shabbat afternoon for meditation, yoga, or a walk in the woods, a Shabbat practice can be a vital part of creating a sustainable commitment to the work of peace and justice. —T.S.

Jewish tradition in general and Shabbat observance in particular raise the tension between the world as it is and the world as it could and should be. Shabbat provides an occasion to push the limits of our spiritual comfort zones. —J.G.K.

Shabbat meals that help us to taste our blessings, breathing in the beauty of the created world. And some of us are most comfortable expressing our spiritual needs emotionally, like those Lurianic kabbalists in Tzfat who dressed like bridegrooms and ecstatically danced Shabbat into town.

Of course, none of us is a pure spiritual type; we are each a mixture of all of the above types and many more. And, of course, none of us is static; each of us changes and grows, adopting new modes of experience while other modes in our repertoire diminish. Nevertheless, each of us may tend to believe (however secretly) that our way of experiencing the spirit of Shabbat is more compelling and elevated than others that we have not experienced personally. The miracle of Shabbat is that Jews of all types, in all the diversity of our approaches, are able to celebrate the seventh day together in our communities and contribute to the ideal of *klal Yisrael*—the unity and survival of the Jewish people.

We might believe that our way of experiencing Shabbat is less compelling, elevated, informed or authentic than that of others. The diversity of the Jewish people means that we can each learn, experiment and evolve in our own journey of Shabbat practice by observing others and ourselves without judgment. —J.G.K.

Shomer Shabbat: *Who Is a Shabbat Observer?*

Our definition of a *shomer/et Shabbat* (observer of Shabbat) is someone who sets Shabbat aside as a special day and who is in a perpetual, lifelong process of discovering how the *kedusha* (sanctity) and *menuḥa* (rest) of Shabbat can best be experienced.

The Halakhic Shabbat Observer

In the contemporary Orthodox world, a person is called *shomer/et Shabbat* (an "observer of Shabbat") if he or she observes all of the halakhic prohibitions for Shabbat—not lighting a fire or turning on electricity, walking rather than riding in any kind of transportation, not carrying anything in a public space, and not cooking or writing or building or repairing anything. The designation is very significant. In much of the Orthodox world, only someone who is *shomer/et Shabbat* is regarded as trustworthy

Liberated from the confines of a halakhic Shabbat and dwelling in a highly pluralistic world, we are all challenged to be more accepting of difference and to be clearer about what we need for our own fulfillment. This stance depends on high self-esteem. Individuals who are ashamed or confused cannot claim their particularity in an egalitarian system. This is Judaism for grownups, which can give it ultimate value when it is not undermined by the less mature parts of others and ourselves. —S.P.W.

Using fire and electricity—particularly electronics—strikes me as a clear example of the work in our regular lives, with fire ancient, and electronics contemporary. —J.G.K.

While most Orthodox legal authorities forbid the use of electricity, bicycles and baby carriages on Shabbat, several permit it. —J.G.K.

about all other aspects of *halakha*. In much of that world, someone may keep a kosher home, buying only kosher-certified food and separating milk and meat, but if he or she is not *shomer/et Shabbat*, then other observant Jews won't trust that she or he is sufficiently meticulous in observance for them to eat in his or her home.

Sh'mirat Shabbat (Shabbat observance) in the above sense is not technically about how our actions on Shabbat affect our state of mind. For example, you are not permitted to ride on an elevator unless the elevator is set on continuous motion before Shabbat, or unless a non-Jewish person happens to enter the elevator and push the button, so that you can ride it without turning on electricity. You can't carry in a public place, *unless* an *eruv* (a boundary that marks the circumference of a neighborhood) has been created by hanging a wire, thereby creating the legal

My personal Shabbat practice has varied over the years, but my *kashrut* practice has been more constant. I am strict about *kashrut* in my home—among other reasons, because I love food and I love the Jewish people, so I want to make the food I prepare as accessible as possible. Many Orthodox Jews are happy to eat in my home. —J.G.K.

The halakhic principle of the *eruv* is that carrying is permitted on your own property but not in public spaces such as a road. The *eruv* turns a public space into a mutually owned private space by symbolically fencing it off. This allows traditionally observant Jews to push a baby carriage or carry a bottle of wine to a friend's house. The *eruv* legal fiction would not ordinarily be used by a nonhalakhic Shabbat observer, but that person might ask questions such as, "Is this too heavy a burden to carry so far on Shabbat?" Or, "Should I bring over my contribution to the potluck on Friday afternoon so that I don't have to schlep this big pot on Shabbat?" —D.A.T.

fiction that it is actually a private and not a public place. And while one may argue that these two examples may enhance one's Shabbat spirit—by allowing you to visit friends who live in a high-rise building, or by making it easier to leave your home—it would be more difficult to make that argument about an electrical timer that would turn on the television at a preset time so that you could view programs or sporting events without violating the prohibition of turning on electricity.

Because of the well-known and widespread use of the term "*shomer Shabbat*" in the Orthodox world, non-Orthodox Jews sometimes say, "We observe Shabbat—we light candles, make Kiddush and have a meal as a family on Friday night, and we often go to synagogue, but we are not *shomer Shabbat*." In other words: "Shabbat occupies an important place in our week, but we do not observe Shabbat as Orthodox Jews do." When non-Orthodox Jews cede to the Orthodox the right to define

While we often judge ourselves and one another as overly enmeshed in technology, electronics, television and the Internet during our work weeks, for some this might be one of the few opportunities they have during the week to watch their favorite shows or play their favorite games and still feel in the spirit of the day. —J.G.K.

Even within Orthodoxy, there is a wide range of practice regarding Shabbat observance. Orthodox Jews maintain that while *halakha* is authoritative, it is also subject to interpretation, and they often choose to follow the teachings of a particular rabbi or community. The non-Orthodox approach presented here presumes that committed liberal Jewish practice is as authoritative—legitimate, empowered and filled with meaning—as Orthodox practice. —D.W.

the term "*shomer Shabbat,*" we inadvertently denigrate not only the value and importance of our own ritual practice, but also our overall approach to Jewish living.

A New Definition of Shomer Shabbat

In fact, it is entirely possible to cultivate a meaningful and transformative observance of Shabbat (some would say it is easier), even when one does not accept halakhic author-

It can be exceedingly difficult for non-Orthodox Jews to assert the validity of their approach to Jewish life in general, and specifically Shabbat, when living among Orthodox Jews. Often, the tolerance for non-Orthodox Jews involves their accommodation to an Orthodox common denominator. I am challenged daily in this regard in my home community of Pikesville and in my professional role in convening a pluralistic campus community. If we are to take ourselves seriously and invest in the long-term viability of a liberal approach to Judaism, the struggle against this standard must be undertaken. True pluralism emerges from mutual respect, not from Orthodox common-denominator Judaism. —J.M.S.

Promoting acceptance of diverse religious practice is an abiding interest of Reconstructionist Judaism. Mordecai Kaplan, the founding thinker of Reconstructionism, once declared that his efforts were dedicated to "making religious diversity safe for Judaism." He and his collaborators insisted that varying expressions of Jewish living were characteristic of the Jewish past and were absolutely vital to the Jewish present and future. In an age of multivocality and wide-ranging experience, no one can or should insist on a single, exclusively legitimate expression of Judaism. —D.W.

I agree that definitions for *shomer Shabbat* should not be narrow, but when liberal (non-Orthodox) Jews define certain actions as within the spirit of Shabbat and certain actions as outside the spirit of Shabbat, we run the risk of judging ourselves by another set of subjective standards, and of creating our own orthodoxy. —J.G.K.

I am uncertain about the advisability of using classical halakhic terms for things that do not conform to classical halakhic meanings. It is one thing to claim a pluralism of possibilities for Shabbat, and to encourage diversity and honor differences. It is

ities' decisions about what is permitted and what is prohibited on Shabbat. That is precisely the subject of this *Guide*. From our perspective, it is appropriate and important to think of ourselves and others who observe Shabbat in a variety of ways also as *shomrey Shabbat* (observers of Shabbat) since we believe that a wide range of approaches to Jewish ritual observance is legitimate and encouraged.

Several issues emerge as a nonhalakhic Jew develops a practice of Shabbat observance.

another thing to take a term that has a specific meaning and apply it to something else, something that is different in whole or in part in a way that makes common conversation among Jews problematic. I am not convinced we need to argue over "joint custody" of a halakhic term as much as we ought to be identifying an alternative paradigm. "*Shomer*" and "*shomeret*" derive from a Hebrew root meaning "to guard" or "to protect" and only derivatively mean "to observe" or "to celebrate." So much of Jewish practice is (or is perceived to be) *lo ta'aseh* ("you cannot do . . ."), and too much of Jewish identity is negatively defined. "*Shomer*" and "*shomeret*" to me fall at the same end of the perceptual spectrum, suggesting that Shabbat is something under siege and that our role is to defend it. A Reconstructionist approach to Shabbat might choose to revalue the terms "*shomer Shabbat*" and "*shomeret Shabbat*," but could as easily, and perhaps more invitingly, find an alternative concept. —R.H.

I believe it is helpful to use the term "*shomer Shabbat*" to refer to those who follow some version of the *halakha* regarding Shabbat observance. For that large group of Jews who take Shabbat observance seriously outside the framework of *halakha*, I prefer the term "*zokher Shabbat*." In the two versions of the Ten Commandments, one uses the term "*shamor*," ("observe the Sabbath"), while the other uses the term "*zakhor*," ("remember the Sabbath"). Using a different term indicates deep engagement with the tradition but reflects the necessarily different approach of someone making values-based decisions. —D.A.T.

Approaches to Shabbat Prohibitions

The original biblical commandment about Shabbat reads as follows:

> *Remember the Sabbath day and keep it holy. Six days you shall labor and do all your work, but the seventh day is a Sabbath of your God; you shall not do any work. . . . For in six days God made the heaven and earth and sea, and all that is in them, and God rested on the seventh day; therefore, God blessed the Sabbath day and hallowed it.* (Exodus 20:8–11)

The Book of Isaiah seems to understand the prohibition of work in this passage as a commandment to refrain from engaging in your own occupation. (Isaiah 58:13) In the authoritative interpretation of "work," however,

In the "fourth commandment" of the Decalogue, the mitzvah to observe Shabbat is stated alongside the requirement to work during the other six days. —J.G.K.

The prohibitions of Shabbat arise from the actions used to build the *Mishkan*, a process of human building and creating that shares many similarities in description to the Genesis account of God's creation of the world. The prohibitions of Shabbat are not only about not working (walking up stairs, for example, is more work than taking the elevator), but also about understanding *m'lakha* as involving actions that are world creating —M.M.

the rabbis defined work as any one of 39 activities in which the ancient Israelites engaged in constructing the *Mishkan* (according to the Torah narrative, the portable Tabernacle built in the wilderness, where worship occurred before the First Temple was built in Jerusalem). From these activities, which are specified in the Torah, they derived 39 foundational categories of "work" (*avot*

The sages of the Talmud understood these activities as prohibited by Torah law on Shabbat because the Torah's instruction on building the *Mishkan* immediately precedes another commandment to keep Shabbat (Exodus 31:12–17), creating an apparent contrast between the preceding acts of work and the necessity and covenant of Shabbat. —J.G.K.

The association of the definitions of work with the building of the *Mishkan* is a fascinating rabbinic midrash that probably doesn't really explain the origin of the traditional 39 categories. The arrangement of these 39 categories in Mishnah Shabbat 7:2 suggests that they involve all the activities involved in baking, sewing and writing a scroll, plus building, working with fire and transporting goods. In other words, they are the items that distinguish humans not intellectually or spiritually, but technologically—as transformers of our environment. —J.A.S.

One way to think about decisions around Shabbat practice is to consider how to understand the words here translated as "shall labor and do all your work." Other possibilities include "shall work/serve/slave away, do all your production and practice all your craft." How we understand labor and work influences how we understand rest. —J.A.S.

m'lakhot), from which all subsequent definitions of activities prohibited on Shabbat are derived.

The major categories of work prohibited on Shabbat include:

1. Carrying—This involves moving an object from one domain (*r'shut*) to another, most commonly, between private and public domains. We can carry things in our home, for example, but we may not carry them from our home into a public space. To circumvent this prohibition, communities can construct an *eruv*—a boundary that marks the circumference of a neighborhood—so that one can carry things or push a stroller or a wheelchair through the entire area as if it were a single domain.

Rather than "work," many Jews understand *m'lakha* as meaning "productive labor" or "actions that change the world." Obviously, it is less work to drive to shul than it is to walk, less work to push the "Up" button on the elevator than to trudge up seven flights of stairs. But if we understand *m'lakha* not as that which requires effort, but as that which changes the world, brings order out of chaos or yields a productive result, then these traditional prohibitions cohere more. —J.M.

It stands to reason that a functional, values-based approach to Shabbat practice is truer to the idea of Shabbat than a 2,000-year-old subjective list of prohibited categories of work (the 39 *m'lakhot*). —J.M.S.

I hold ever-shifting opinions about the legal fiction of the *eruv*. Some days, I think it is genius, an agreed-upon construction that enables a group of Jews to honor and preserve the law and yet function in a way that fosters ease and community-building. Other days, I think it is painfully artificial. Though I live in a community that has an *eruv*, it does not ordinarily shape my Shabbat practice, and it is not clear to me what causes the shift in my perspective. Such schizophrenia is, I suppose, what it means to be a postmodern Jew. —D.W.

2. Creating, Destroying and *Muktzeh* (Separated, set aside)—Making and destroying are forbidden on Shabbat, and we are not permitted to touch any object without an accepted use on Shabbat. Items that are set aside as *muktzeh* include money, writing implements and work tools.
3. *Sh'vut* (Resting)—Activities that are not in the spirit of Shabbat include discussing business matters or doing things that are not strictly directly forbidden on Shabbat but that involve preparations for Shabbat-prohibited activities we will do after Shabbat, such as packing a suitcase for travel or reading business correspondence or documents.

Many Orthodox people won't use an umbrella on Shabbat because opening an umbrella creates a shelter, and building on Shabbat is forbidden. Closing an umbrella eliminates the shelter, and destroying is also forbidden on Shabbat. —M.M.

The injunction to abstain from work on the Sabbath includes, for me, making sure my mind does not inadvertently pick up and spend time with angry feelings and hostile thoughts. Ruminating on negativity embitters the mind and disables its ability to celebrate or to bless. —S.B.

In earlier times, travel was work for the animal and the driver, who needed to make food along the way, jack up a cart that was stuck in a rut or deal with the wheel of a wagon if it came off. The driver would not have been allowed to fix the wheel on Shabbat, since that would be an act of creating. —M.M.

4. Traveling—The rabbis were concerned about the inadvertent damage one might cause to the environment in traveling with or on an animal. Such concerns are only magnified with contemporary modes of travel, such as the automobile.
5. Lighting a Fire—This prohibition has been interpreted to include turning on electricity. The original biblical injunction, "You shall not burn fire in all of your settlements," (Exodus 35:3) was interpreted by the rabbis as a prohibition against kindling a fire on Shabbat, thus permitting the use of fire that was kindled prior to Shabbat. Similarly, the use of electricity is permitted as long as it was switched on before Shabbat or if an automatic timer set before Shabbat turns it on without any human agency.
6. Preparing Food—Cooking is prohibited; keeping food heated that has been prepared before Shabbat is permitted, as long as the flame or burner is not ignited or adjusted on Shabbat.

Starting a car engine involves igniting a spark, and the power of the engine comes from creating fires in its cylinders many times a minute. The debate about electricity is more complex because it involves no obvious consumption of fuel. When turning on the lights, am I igniting a spark or only opening a valve? While after considerable debate, Orthodox *poskim* (halakhic decisors or deciders) ruled against flipping an electric switch on Shabbat, the halakhic authority of the Conservative movement, the Committee on Jewish Law and Standards, permits it. —M.M./J.A.S.

Another legal fiction is that the non-Jew in question is turning on the electricity of his or her own volition (that is, not at the request of a halakhic Jew). —D.W.

For some who were raised in halakhically observant households and who are therefore familiar with the wide range and great abundance of these Shabbat restrictions, the overall effect of halakhic Shabbat observance remains positive and rich. Food is prepared, businesses are closed, shopping is completed, and travel ends before sundown on Friday. The activities in which one engages during Shabbat are limited and relaxing: walking, praying, eating, conversing, singing, reading and napping. There is no engagement with one's occupation or profession. There is nothing to accomplish, and one's awareness of the outside world is temporarily suspended (without access to phones, television, radio or the Internet). Shabbat that is observed in this way is indeed a day of rest and an opportunity to be physically and spiritually refreshed.

Most Jews today, however, have not been raised in such an environment. Despite this lack of familiarity with halakhic Shabbat observance, some people find it powerfully attractive to contemplate absolutely shutting down

When my partner and I decided to turn off all of our electronic screens over Shabbat, we had to make an extra effort to engage our children in fun activities, since we couldn't fall back on letting them watch TV or play a computer game. Many Jews raised in homes with a long list of Shabbat prohibitions do not experience the day as joyful or meaningful, but as a stringent set of "don'ts" that feel constricting and, especially to a child, boring. The challenge for anyone who wishes to create a meaningful Shabbat observance is shaping not only the "don'ts" that help construct the palace in time, but also the positive "dos" that make the day special and meaningful.

—T.S.

the workweek and entering into an uninterrupted, sanctified period of time. Abstaining from regular, habitual activities can be an effective way of freeing oneself from unwanted distractions, elevating one's perspective, and focusing contemplatively on what is truly important. The challenge one then confronts, of course, is that unless you are in an environment in which many are observing Shabbat in similar ways—a summer camp; a Jewish retreat center; some Israeli neighborhoods; *kibbutzim* and *moshavim*; and some sections of North American cities, such as New York City and Montreal—it is extremely dif-

Many of us live Jewish lives that are neither completely isolated nor completely immersed in a community that observes Shabbat traditionally, so one approach to Shabbat observance could be that the more immersed we are in a Shabbat community, the more we might aspire toward traditional observance, while the more isolated we are, the farther we may step away from traditional observance to experience the pleasure of Shabbat. —J.G.K.

There are other reasons *not* to observe Shabbat in the traditional/Orthodox way. Our historical understanding lets us know that the Torah itself actually records multiple understandings of the meaning and import of Shabbat, not all of which have been encoded in rabbinic Shabbat practice. Our practice should reflect our encounter with tradition in all its variety, and also our own understanding of the nature of Shabbat. —J.A.S.

ficult to observe all of the traditional Shabbat prohibitions and simultaneously to experience the joy and pleasure of Shabbat celebration.

For those outside of such Shabbat-friendly environments, Shabbat observance requires an ongoing series of decisions concerning which activities promote a positive sense of rest and renewal and which do not. Individuals will reach different conclusions, and they may find that their decisions vary over time and in different contexts. Sometimes, these decisions may lead someone to consider

The criteria by which a progressive Jew or a progressive Jewish community will define their Shabbat observance are always subject to reconsideration. Promoting a positive sense of rest and renewal and fostering the spirit of Shabbat are two good, broad criteria, but they are not the only ones, and they may not be sufficient by themselves. Here are some other possible criteria: What will promote connection to sacred community, Jewish tradition, Jewish learning and/or Jewish time? What will engage me/us in spiritual practice/connection with God? Spiritual practice can be quite rigorous and disciplined, not necessarily "restful" per se. What is it about traditional observance—its spirit, values and forms, and what it potentially cultivates inwardly, interpersonally, communally and outwardly/socially/culturally—that can be revalued? —M.M.

When our children were younger, we introduced them to the concept of the Shabbat exception. On occasion we would do things on a specific Shabbat that as a rule we would not do on Shabbat. Sometimes that would mean driving several hours on Shabbat afternoon to get to a vacation destination rather than waiting until early Sunday morning so as to have an extra day away together. Sometimes it would mean watching something on television on Friday night, a time when we normally would not turn on the set. Or it could mean delaying Friday night candle lighting, Kiddush and dinner until our son got home from one of his theater performances at 11 P.M. In naming such things "Shabbat exceptions," we were, paradoxically, reinforcing the sanctity of Shabbat and affirming the norms of our usual family Shabbat rhythm. —R.H.

traditionally prohibited activities as permissible, while considering traditionally permitted activities as prohibited. Should we restrict the use of the phone to topics appropriate to Shabbat, while not making or taking calls related to work, or should we give up phone use altogether? Should we not watch television at all, even if it has been set by a timer, because its programming is disruptive to the spirit of Shabbat? Should we watch a movie, carefully selected for its Shabbat spirit, on a DVD player? Does a family trip to the zoo or the museum on Shabbat afternoon preserve the spirit of Shabbat (but only if we are members, so that we don't have to pay for admission, and only if we bring snacks rather than buy them? Or can we be selective about when we do and don't handle money or

My own idiosyncratic practice, which perhaps makes sense only in New England, is that I don't watch TV on Shabbat, with the exception of Red Sox games (with the "mute" turned on during the commercials). —T.S.

It takes attention and intention to be *shomeret Shabbat* outside of halakhic structures. I find looking at art deeply nourishing, and since I have little free time, I may choose to pay for admission to the art museum on Shabbat afternoon. However, once I have my wallet out and I am in an environment with others who are simply having a lovely Saturday, not a holy Shabbat, I need to remind myself not to enter the gift shop or purchase a museum membership. I relish the challenge, but it is a challenge nonetheless. —D.W.

I view money as part of the world of instrumental "I-It" relationships, not appropriate to the "I-Thou" covenantal relationships of Shabbat. We should also consider that when use money, someone else is being required to work for us on the weekend, perhaps out of economic necessity and not fully out of free will. —J.A.S.

For much of the last century, it has been downright patriotic to shop. America has become a nation of citizen-consumers. Refraining from shopping is radically countercultural. —D.W.

credit cards—perhaps not using money for weekday concerns (such as shopping), but using it for activities that we deem in keeping with the spirit of Shabbat (such as recreation)?

In all of these many decisions, the positive objective of the *shomer/et Shabbat* is to live with a sense of sanctified time, in which we experience the rest and renewal of Shabbat that comes with moving more slowly, putting our cares aside, and devoting ourselves to a spiritual practice and awareness that may be neglected during the workweek. In pursuit of creating that positive sense of holiness, many people who do not choose to abide by halakhic Shabbat prohibitions nevertheless find it meaningful to abstain from activities that have work-like connotations for them. Here are just a few examples to consider:

A suggestion I often make to people whose jobs require them the work on Shabbat (especially healthcare professionals) is to incorporate a Shabbat-like practice into their workday. Light candles when you get home; pack a special lunch that you have only on Shabbat; or keep a beautiful plate or glassware on the job that you use only on Shabbat. This way, you can create small openings of *oneg Shabbat* in your otherwise work-focused day. —N.H.M.

Our congregation's ritual committee compared the usefulness of adopting local communal rules of Shabbat practice to the usefulness of rules in games or the rules of writing a haiku. These are structures that promote communal activity, challenge us to excel, and help create meaning. —J.A.S.

As we spend more and more of our time wired, wireless and otherwise tethered to the online world, Shabbat is a time to unplug. At the very least, it's a great excuse to temporarily withdraw from the insane notion that one must immediately reply to all texts, emails and phone calls. More than that, however, logging off for a day returns the virtual to its proper place and offers us a powerful reiteration of the real. —J.M.

1. Reading, Listening to, or Viewing the News—If you find the prospect of missing 25 hours of the perpetual news cycle startling or even unimaginable, you may want to give it a try. What would it be like to cut yourself off from your globalized interconnections and to devote yourself to mindful attention to your inner life and to the people with whom you are personally connected?
2. Planning for the Future—This may involve ruminating about a career change or a potential investment, rehearsing a conversation you want to have with a family member or work associate, or planning an outing or get-together with friends or family after Shabbat. Perhaps, if the only way to let go of a train of thought is to jot down a brief note—and you write on Shabbat—you might try writing it down so that you can return to awareness of the present.

Many Jews who choose to avoid accessing the news, current events, politics and related issues on Shabbat often find the peace and tranquility they try to create disrupted by sermons, *divrey Torah* and synagogue dialogues that address exactly (and often stridently as well as polemically) the issues of daily life that they have tried to avoid on Shabbat. —R.H.

As a Jewish communal professional, I sometimes find little time during my work week to pay attention to the world around me, and I think that Shabbat might be the best time for me to reconnect with the rest of humanity. —J.G.K.

Be careful not to let jotting down a few notes explode into having Shabbat be the time to work on your to-do lists! —J.A.S.

3. Engaging in Self-Criticism—Imagine living one day each week satisfied with what you have done over the previous six days as good enough, in imitation of the God of Genesis who is said to have "rested and been renewed" (*shavat vayinafash*) on the seventh day after creating a world that is good. We can resume our efforts to improve ourselves and the world after dark on Saturday evening. The created world from which God stepped back was and is certainly not perfect.
4. Hurrying and Multitasking—This may be the most difficult challenge of all. Paradoxically, we often find ourselves rushing on Shabbat—preparing for and serving guests and cleaning up after them, getting family members ready to go to synagogue, and so on. The day of rest is best lived with a restful, focused consciousness.

On this day, we ask God to take pleasure in our rest—to accept us the way we are, not because we are doing anything, but just because of our being us in a state of rest. We can also practice that same self-compassion. —J.A.S.

Perhaps the greatest gift of Shabbat is the opportunity to accept ourselves for who we are. As God looked at what God had created and said, "This is very good," we should look in our own mirrors each week and, with all our imperfections and weaknesses, say of ourselves, "This is very good" as well. Self-acceptance can be a sacred act that aligns us with the very same Torah idea that we are created in the divine image and sacred just as we are. —S.C.R.

Commitment to the principle of not rushing on Shabbat might also include not undertaking long-distance travel on Shabbat. The hustle and bustle of waiting for trains, planes or buses, accompanied by the exhaustion we can feel during long trips, can diminish the sense of calm that these 25 hours afford us. —B.P.

5. Shopping—This may include refraining not only from buying things in stores or online, but also from window shopping, visiting websites to see what's available, and discussing best brands or best buys—anything that coaxes us into the role of consumer.

These five categories are intended to be suggestive sparks to encourage you to consider activities from which you may want to abstain so that your Shabbat can be more mindful and holy.

Consistency of Practice

One of the obstacles that many people confront in thinking of themselves as Shabbat observers is the notion that Shabbat observance must be consistent. You may catch

In shaping one's own Shabbat practice, it is important not merely to choose activities that we already deem relaxing or enjoyable. Shabbat observance is a spiritual practice, and any practice involves some element of challenge and discipline. There is an element of discernment in figuring out what is true "rest," in a Shabbat sense, and what is merely a form of entertainment that we use to distract ourselves during the course of a regular day. Surfing the Web might be relaxing to some, but I would argue that it is not a Shabbat practice; neither is going to the mall or playing video games. There is something profoundly countercultural in the ways in which Shabbat invites us to slow down the pace of our lives, which are now geared to the speed of computers counted in nanoseconds, and to simplify our day, over against the constant onslaught of input from cyberspace and the incessant calls to consume from the surrounding culture. —T.S.

I encourage people to ask questions: Is there something I want to make sure to do once a week? Is there something I wish I didn't have to do for at least one day each week?" The answers to these questions are often, though not always, things to do and not do on Shabbat. —J.A.S.

yourself thinking: "If I decide that I will not cook on Shabbat, what will happen when a week arrives in which I am simply not able to have everything prepared before Friday sundown?" Or: "I can commit to eating cold cereal on Shabbat mornings, but I'm not willing to refuse to cook eggs or oatmeal for my partner or children, so I guess that I'm not prepared to be a *shomer/et Shabbat.*"

In the context of the Orthodox community, the term "*shomer Shabbat*" entails consistency, as explained above. If you are consistent and reliable in your observance of Shabbat, then you are assumed to be reliable in all other matters of halakhic practice. In that universe, intentionally violating a Shabbat prohibition creates a serious ethical dilemma because hiding the violation misleads others into assuming that you are trustworthy in all matters of halakhic practice—that they can trust, for example, the kashrut of your kitchen.

In Orthodox practice, the halakhic observance of Shabbat is understood as God's will, so it is not perceived to be the place of human beings to choose some practices and not others. Consistency entails bringing one's will into consistent alignment with God's will. There may be some element at work of how it looks to others, but the primary factor is to accept mitzvot as a total system. No individual mitzvah has more value or meaning than another. —M.M.

Some *ḥaredi* (strict Orthodox) authorities differentiate between ramifications of private violations of Jewish laws and public, willful violations of them for the purpose of making such decisions as whom to trust in matters of *kashrut*, for instance. —J.G.K.

Consistency of practice is an issue of a lifetime, not only of the moment. While some Jews take on a certain pattern of Shabbat observance and maintain it for decades or even a lifetime, others find that as they change and grow, the ways in which they approach and engage Shabbat change and grow as well. I once knew a rabbi who did not travel by car on Shabbat. Upon retirement from his congregation, he moved to a home that was too far from any synagogue to walk and changed his practice. —R.H.

In the rest of the Jewish world, however, there is no absolute virtue in consistency of practice. To be sure, consistency in ritual and spiritual practice, like any other kind of practice, has many benefits. Sanctity accrues to a given behavior as our cumulative associations reappear each week. The more we observe or recite them, the more rituals and prayers serve a mnemonic function, sparking in us reminders of the values, insights and experiences that we associate with them. There are certainly advantages to regularizing our Shabbat observance rather than deciding over and over again how to observe Shabbat each week.

There are many reasons, however, why you may choose to perform a particular Shabbat practice—or to refrain from doing a particular activity on Shabbat—on some occasions but not on others. Here is a sampling of such reasons:

One of the benefits of consistency of practice is that it encourages us to move beyond self-focus to a focus on the other. It reminds us that our lives are not lived only for our own convenience; we are obligated/commanded by the presence of the Other/other.

—J.A.S.

My most consistent Shabbat practice over the past 20 years has been to refrain from shaving. Here, traditional definitions and my personal sense of labor coincide.

—J.G.K.

I prefer an approach to Shabbat practice that grows out of a basic principle/value understanding of the day. A standard-seeking understanding of Shabbat leads to a practice close to the traditional rabbinic practice. An in-the-moment understanding leads to my community's practice. A social-justice understanding probably emphasizes an avoidance of commerce and maybe even forbids hiring a rabbi on Shabbat!

—J.A.S.

- You may be experimenting with unfamiliar observances. You may decide to walk to synagogue for a few weeks and then find that walking there in the rain or in subfreezing weather diminishes rather than enhances your Shabbat practice, so you decide to ride to synagogue when the weather is uninviting.
- Relative to any given mitzvah, you may be in a state of what the German philosopher Franz Rosenzweig called "not yet." You remain open to practices that have never been yours until now, but you are not yet prepared to undertake them. Remaining open, you try them but experience discomfort. So it takes a while before you are moved to try again.
- You may find that different contexts require different approaches to Shabbat observance. In your home, you observe Shabbat in one way; perhaps you don't listen to the radio, for example. But when you are visiting your family or friends who do listen to the radio, it may be impractical and/or unappealing to ask them to change their behavior to accommodate you. You may not want your ritual observance to cause you to distance yourself from them.

Families that choose to send children to Jewish day school through middle school often find themselves renegotiating Shabbat observance once these children enter public high school. Open discussion as to how to preserve a spirit of Shabbat while not isolating students from their peers and peer activities is an important part of helping emerging adults to take on the process of decision making about Shabbat.
—R.H.

Or, you may be committed to participating in a political demonstration that occurs on Shabbat, though participation will require that you do things that you don't usually do on Shabbat.

- You may be committed, on principle, to inconsistency. You may love the value of ritual observance in your life, but not want to elevate it above all other things in a way that could become idolatrous. You don't want to forget that you are choosing to perform a given mitzvah, that it was not commanded by God at Mount Sinai for all time. You may not want to be enslaved to ritual practice in a way that keeps you from acting according to your values when they conflict with a given ritual proscription. So perhaps you decide, for example, that any Shabbat ritual practice that you observe will be kept for a maximum of 51 times each year, or that your Shabbat practice can and ought to be modified if it has negative consequences in a given circumstance—for example, if it would cause another person pain or embarrassment.

Consistency also enables us to experience impact over time. Shabbat observances are so markedly countercultural that it takes time to get used to various restrictions and limitations so that they become normative. We can then cultivate within us the awareness, orientation, and states of mind and heart they have the potential to generate. I think there is value to exploring what it is like to place personal will and desire second to larger shared norms, to experiencing surrender in a way that doesn't constantly put my own likes and dislikes at the center of what I do. This is a challenging perspective to discuss in the context of progressive Jewish practice, but I think it addresses one of the weaknesses of a "choose-your-own-Judaism" approach. This leads me to ask when I should decide to set aside choice and what might arise from that.

—M.M.

For any of these reasons and many others, we can take on observances of Shabbat without being sure if we are ready to commit to doing them forever. And there is no reason to be self-critical about the lack of such commitment to consistency. You are not necessarily a better or a worse Jew or human being because you are not thoroughly consistent. To the contrary, by this *Guide*'s definition, a *shomer/et Shabbat* is "someone who sets Shabbat aside as a special day and is in the perpetual, lifelong process of discovering how the *kedusha* (sanctity) and *menuḥa* (rest) of Shabbat can best be experienced." The observance of Shabbat entails change, growth and flexibility. It is a perpetual, lifelong process.

Experimentation can be an important element to a dynamic and rich Jewish life. Give yourself permission to be creative with your Shabbat practice and then reflect on how that difference enhances or detracts from your Shabbat experience. —J.M.S.

Becoming comfortable with being inconsistent is a necessary developmental step for liberal Jews. As Walt Whitman says in "Song of Myself," "Do I contradict myself? / Very well then I contradict myself, / (I am large, I contain multitudes.)" —H.S.V.

In our family, the choices of Shabbat observance are an evolving practice. We currently refrain from watching TV and movies, but we do play music (in the car) that honors the spirit of Shabbat. It's hard to know at this moment what our practice will look like ten years from now. —N.C.M.

Many progressive Jews are uncomfortable with imposing a greater degree of traditional observance on another Jew by, for example, asking someone to turn off music. It is easier to make demands if you believe that you are following the one right way to do things, but progressive Jews can be just as committed in their practice, and they are just as deserving of accommodation. Progressive Jewish communities struggle with commitment to being consistent, and I think their members are very ready to make exceptions in order to avoid conflict or to avoid standing out. The greater challenge is in trying to stick with patterns of observance that no one else is going to hold you to but yourself. —M.M.

Having said all that, it is important also to note the advantages and benefits of consistency. We all know what it is like to ask the questions, "What shall I do on Sunday?" or "What shall I do on my day off?" Faced with "free time," we choose among a myriad of options: catching up on sleep, running errands, watching a ball game, visiting with family or friends, reading a novel, playing golf and so on. Days off are wonderful, but they are not Shabbat.

What distinguishes Shabbat from days off is the sanctity we invest in it. Sanctity accrues to regular rituals and activities that one associates with values and feelings, which then trigger the rich, complex and multivalent experience of Shabbat. The lighting of Shabbat candles on Friday evening may be the most widely practiced of such moments. To the extent that one has many such regular ways of observing Shabbat—reciting Kiddush over wine, eating leisurely meals, singing, attending Shabbat services at synagogue and celebrating *Havdala*—one is able to enter the alternate Shabbat reality more seamlessly, without having to generate it each week. One can do this even if one's Shabbat observance practice varies occasionally or week to week.

Living in a Multicultural World

Many of us live in heterogeneous communities. Many members of our nuclear families, our families of origin, our close friends and our social and business acquaintances do not observe Shabbat the way we do, if they observe it at all. In fact, many of them are not Jewish.

Halakhic Shabbat observance can have the effect of separating Jews from non-Jews, and observant Jews from non-observant Jews. A great deal happens in the larger society on Friday evenings and Saturdays in which a halakhic Shabbat observer does not participate. Many of us today may not want our Jewish lives to separate us from others. We may not want to prevent our children from playing in Little League games, for example, or from participating in recitals that are scheduled on Shabbat. We

When we lived and studied in Israel, my wife and I would occasionally designate an upcoming Shabbat as a "*Shabbat ḥiloni*," a secular Shabbat. By this, we meant that we would experience Shabbat in the way that *ḥiloni* Israelis do: with picnics in the park or trips to the beach. When we returned to the United States, we continued this practice. —H.S.V.

While halakhic observance of Shabbat may have the effect of separating Jews from non-Jews, that is certainly not among its major purposes. —J.A.S.

Being different is one of the things that marks a Jew in a non-Jewish society and often allows the person to resist other demands of the society. I still remember one of my sons saying to me, as a teenager, that he didn't smoke, didn't drink, and kept kosher—what more could I want? "Do your homework," I replied. But his point was well taken: One form of difference supports other forms of difference. —D.D.M.

may welcome non-Jews and nonpracticing Jews to our homes for Shabbat and holidays, not because we aspire to convince them to be like us, but because we enjoy their company. This enhances our experience of Shabbat, and we may find it necessary to modify our practices in order to make our guests feel comfortable. When they celebrate events (including *b'ney mitzvah* services and celebrations) in their lives on Shabbat, we may not want to miss celebrating with them just because it would involve activities we normally abstain from on Shabbat.

We perpetually balance conflicting values. The importance of regular Shabbat practice does not always supersede all other considerations. Being a *shomer/et Shabbat* requires ongoing decision making of some complexity.

My parents and I often spent Shabbat afternoons during my childhood visiting the home of my father's lifelong friend, Ira, and his family. We parked our car several blocks from their apartment in order to respect the religious sentiments of Ira's Orthodox neighborhood. We sat, parents and children, in the living room, talking and laughing, and waited until the room was quite dark and, in winter, quite cool, before Ira said *Havdala*. Then we had light and heat and hot tea. Notwithstanding any challenge I might have experienced, I was always content and happy there. I think it was the love that my father and Ira had for each other, a love that I knew transcended their diverging beliefs and practices, that warmed the room and made it feel holy. —S.B.

Not engaging in observances that cause pain or embarrassment to someone else or that keep you from acting on your values may mean that you cannot always observe in exactly the same way. That is an ethical calculation regarding conflicting commitments. Wanting not to make observance idolatrous does not seem like a significant issue for non-halakhic Jews. More relevant perhaps is ensuring that observance holds both *ḳeva* (structure) and *ḳavana* (intentionality), holding a fruitful tension among regularity, consistency, discipline, commitment and meaningful aliveness. When *ḳavana* flags, it may be time to alter observance, at least temporarily. —M.M.

Pluralism

Because the full observance of Shabbat assumes interacting with other people and participating in community for meals and services, Shabbat is one of the primary ritual locations (along with kashrut observance) in which we confront the ways that our practice differs from the practice of friends and neighbors. Given these issues, it is important to consider observance alongside the value of *klal Yisrael,* the unity and diversity of the Jewish people. What can we do to avoid or transcend tensions and insults that may be sparked inadvertently when people who have diverse practices encounter one another?

First, in a pluralistic community, we don't assume homogeneous practice, and we are not offended by its absence. Your child's best friend may be permitted to go on a class trip that occurs on Saturday, and your child may wonder why she is not allowed to participate as well.

Just the notion that our Shabbat choices involve practices and not mythic imperatives is crucial. A practice is something undertaken for its effects. With *kavana*, the mind is inclined toward whatever subtle transformations may transpire. Choices about these various behaviors are pragmatic, and they will be at least slightly different for each of us. This is not some wishy-washy compromise; it's an affirmation of our integrity and authenticity as human beings. —J.M.

A Hillel setting is often the first place where people encounter very different Shabbat experiences. This encounter can be jarring, alienating and frustrating, or eye-opening, cathartic and growthful, depending on one's background and approach. The main key to having a positive experience is to respect one another's humanity and Judaism. —J.M.S.

The pluralistic answer is not necessarily that you are Shabbat observers and the other family is not. They may observe Shabbat in a different way. Or they may be Jews who are secular and not observant of religious rituals. Or they may not be Jewish. Such situations are opportunities to affirm your household's commitment to Shabbat while acknowledging and affirming that different people have varying beliefs and practices. Conversely, if your dinner guest does not participate in candle lighting before you sit down to dinner because he has already lit candles at home before sunset, the pluralistic response is to respect his variant practice without taking offense. The operating expectation is that we are all different, and that this is a good thing.

Second, being clear with others about one's own needs and practice is always helpful. "I know that you don't ride on Shabbat. Is it okay with you if I drive to and from your house for Shabbat dinner? Is it okay if I bring dessert when I drive over, even though it will already be dark?" "It is not our practice to turn on lights on Shabbat, so

For a novice, the idea of sharing Shabbat can sound very complicated. It does not need to be. Most Jews who care about Shabbat would be very happy to receive an invitation to share Shabbat with others. Members of liberal communities, including rabbis, are highly unlikely to be offended by the host's Shabbat practice. —J.A.S.

Asking some Orthodox people whether it is okay to drive over for Shabbat dinner could be a little tricky since they believe that the *halakha* requires them to say no because you asked. If you don't ask and simply arrive, then it is totally your decision and responsibility. If they are asked, they share the responsibility for your violation of *halakha*. —M.M.

please try to remember not to switch them off." The more we know about one another's practices, the more we can be mutually respectful.

Third, we often make the implicit assumption that more ritual observance is better. "There is so much to learn," we say effusively, "so many opportunities to enrich our lives by increasing our observance of Shabbat!" This assumption elevates one person's level of practice over another. It may be, for example, that you only recite the blessing over the wine before the meal on Friday evening and do not recite the full Kiddush prayer because that's what your grandfather did, and you honor his memory by following his practice. It would not necessarily be an "upgrade" of your Jewish life to chant the full Kiddush. More is not always better.

Fourth, there is a halakhic category called "a fence around the Torah" (*siyag latorah*) that prohibits activities on Shabbat not because they are forbidden in themselves, but because engaging in them might lead us inadvertently to do something else that is prohibited. Halakhically, we are not permitted to play the guitar, for example, because a string might break, and we might then forget that it is Shabbat and try to replace it. Playing would be permitted, hypothetically, but since repairing is prohibited, playing is prohibited as well because of where it might lead.

Since playing guitar is one of my greatest joys, I engage in it almost every Shabbat whether a string might break or not, since the joy of playing (and writing music as well) is its own reward. My personal observance includes replacing strings if they break so that the joy of playing can continue. —S.C.R.

There is something in the halakhic practice of creating a fence around the Torah that the nonhalakhic *shomer/et Shabbat* may find helpful. Which recreational activities are and are not likely to allow you to maintain your sense of Shabbat? Cycling in the park may help to bring you to a desirable relaxed or contemplative state; you ride, you return home, and you don't encounter another world. You may choose to refrain from embarking on a challenging climb up an unfamiliar mountain trail, not because hiking is less conducive to creating a Shabbat state of mind than cycling, but because it may lead to stress, or to the need to problem-solve. You may conclude that playing basketball with one group of people is a Shabbat activity, while playing with another group is not, perhaps because of the aggressiveness of the game, or because one group generally goes out for a beer afterward, and it would be difficult for you not to join them.

The point is that decision making for a nonhalakhic *shomer/et Shabbat* can be subtle and complicated—far more so than for someone with a halakhic practice who follows the rulings of halakhic *poskim* (experts). Achieving a balance between Shabbat observance and participation in the greater world requires ongoing thought, and sometimes creating a behavioral fence around us may be essential.

Fifth, the halakhic principle of *pikuaḥ nefesh* (saving a life) always applies on Shabbat. Any prohibited activity

Disconnecting from our electronic devices can be seen as a "fence" for non-halakhic Jews. While the Internet can be a source of pleasure, it has the potential to lead us back into the weekday modes of multitasking, engaging in business or generally taking us away from the uniqueness of sacred time. —B.P.

becomes permitted if it is in the service of saving a life or getting needed treatment to a person who is ill. The non-halakhic *shomer/et Shabbat* may find an expanded version of this principle helpful in formulating his or her own practice. Is your observance of Shabbat undermining your physical and/or emotional health? Is your practice doing damage to others? If the answer to either of these questions is "yes," you may conclude that you ought to modify your behavior on Shabbat.

Preparing for Shabbat

Ideally, it would be wonderful to experience automatically a radical transformation of consciousness at sunset on Friday: from multitasking to letting go, from mundane to holy, from narrower objects of focus to an awareness of

Many liberal Jewish households mark the start of Shabbat at 6 P.M. or at dinnertime on Friday evening since many people are still working when sundown occurs in the winter and families often cannot wait for Shabbat dinner until sundown in the summer. —J.A.S.

Even though Jewish days begin at sunset, there is a progression from traditional candle lighting times (before sunset) to sunset itself, to the twilight after sunset, to nightfall. While there may be a single moment when the cosmos tells us that it is Shabbat, this nightly cycle of nature also suggests that our experience of fully embracing Shabbat on Friday evening can happen in phases. —J.G.K.

It is remarkable how often people who would not think of taking a vacation, attending the theater, arranging a dinner party or planning a birthday celebration without adequate preparation expect to have a significant religious experience with no similar degree of planning—and then cite the emptiness of the experience as an explanation for why they "find nothing in religion." —R.H.

the greater scheme of things. Alas, while the sun does set at regular and predictable moments, we are not often able to redirect our focus abruptly. It requires planning and practice.

Preparing Ourselves Internally in Advance

A midrash relates that as the sun sets on Friday, the ministering angels peek through our windows. If they see a home that has been cleaned for Shabbat, with a table set with a clean tablecloth and candlesticks, then they enter and contribute to our spiritual uplifting on Shabbat. If not, we're on our own, perhaps without the "additional soul" that doubles our spiritual capacity on Shabbat. Without preparing for Shabbat, it is much more difficult to experience the *oneg*, the pleasure, of Shabbat.

The insight on which this midrash is based is that the physical acts of cleaning and preparing your home for Shabbat enhance your ability to take in the Shabbat spir-

After years of Shabbat practice, I find that even when I'm running until the last minute to get things done, lighting the Shabbat candles is a sufficiently powerful signal that it usually snaps me into a different mode. —J.A.S.

Significant preparation for Shabbat provides us with an opportunity to strongly feel the contrast between work and rest. —J.G.K.

it. You may also want to expand this insight into other areas: In what ways might you want to cleanse yourself emotionally and spiritually? Has the week involved conflicts at work or with friends or loved ones? Are you harboring feelings of pain or anger? Are you mourning any losses? Are you feeling isolated, or cut off from the Source of life? Conversely, perhaps it has been a week of successes and accomplishments, of progress made toward your larger goals, and you are bursting with pride and energy, eager to work on the next stage. Or perhaps you are excited but also a bit agitated about a new relationship that has an uncertain future.

Imagine those angels peeking into the windows of our souls. In order to make room for them, to be receptive to the energy and ambience of Shabbat, you probably need to set the figurative table of your psyche, clearing away the clutter—whether pleasant or unpleasant—so that you are more present, breathing at a more relaxed pace and appreciating the scent of all of the flowers that may have gone unnoticed for six days. The "clutter" of the week is noisy and ever changing. When Shabbat comes as a reminder of what is ever-present, unchanging, and ultimately important, we can leave the bustle behind and take comfort beneath its wings.

Before beginning services on campus each week, I ask the students to think about what they are leaving behind at the threshold of Shabbat, and what they are bringing along. A brief reflection like this is often all you need to create a cathedral in time. —J.M.S.

At the start of the *Kabbalat Shabbat* (Welcoming the Sabbath) service, Rabbi Levi Weiman-Kelman of Congregation Kol Haneshama in Jerusalem leads a guided meditation that has been widely adopted in North American congregations. Sitting at dusk on Friday, he invites participants to recollect something that happened on the preceding Sunday and then to let go of it, leaving it behind as they enter Shabbat. He then repeats the instruction for each succeeding day of the week. The practice can be very effective in helping us to demarcate the transition from mundane time to sacred time and consciousness. It is also helpful in shifting our gaze from the future (What do I need to accomplish next week?) to the past (Look at everything that I have done this week!), so that we can remain in the present, in gratitude for our blessings. This meditation is available to us when we are alone, as well as when we are in community. It is also effective on Fridays before dusk, or whenever we are about to turn our attention to preparing for Shabbat.

You may also find it helpful to begin your inner preparation for Shabbat before Friday. Traditionally it is on Wednesday, midway through the week, that we have been encouraged to begin anticipating the upcoming Shabbat.

At the table of one of my friends, each family member and guest augments Kiddush by sharing one thing from the week for which they would like to offer up a blessing. —D.W.

Sometimes when I have had a particularly hard week, I perform *n'tilat yadayim*, the ritual rinsing of my hands, before I light Shabbat candles. —J.G.K.

So on Wednesday or Thursday, you may want to begin your preparation, perhaps by reflecting on such questions as: What burdens are you carrying that you would like to relinquish when Shabbat arrives? Whose company on Shabbat is likely to enhance your sense of peace and rest? How might you spend your time on Shabbat in ways that will increase your sense of freedom and ease? While you want to avoid over-planning the details in a way that might make your Shabbat "schedule" feel like any other day of the week, the quality of your Shabbat experience can be enhanced with some intentional forethought.

For the bakers among us, there are few ritual pleasures more gratifying than baking our own hallah for Shabbat. It is an embodied activity that is literally and concretely preparation for Shabbat. It is thus an ideal way to trigger our anticipation of the coming Shabbat; while we are kneading the dough, we may find ourselves shifting our consciousness and addressing some of the questions mentioned above. And because the process takes a substantial amount of time, many people bake the hallot in advance, on Thursday evening. The scent of hallah thus generated also serves to whet the appetite of the entire household for Shabbat.

I love the way hallah is described here. I am struck by the contrast with Rav Joseph Soloveitchik (a leading 20th-century American Orthodox rabbi), for whom material times and objects gained significance only from their status within the halakhic system. Here, it's the feel, the smell and the taste that matter. Fresh baked bread is its own sacrament, regardless of whether it is designated as such by religion. —J.M.

In Hasidic and other traditional communities, it is the custom to go to the mikvah (ritual bath) on Friday afternoons in order to undergo a spiritual cleansing for Shabbat, washing away the dust of the week's journey. If you have access to a mikvah that you find pleasant and welcoming, or to a lake or stream where you have privacy, you may want to try it. Many find it extremely powerful. You submerge yourself unclothed three times, allowing the waters to touch every pore of your body, emerging with a renewed awareness of the precious nature of each moment, recalibrating your sense of what is important.

Taking a shower or a bath right before Shabbat is another way to let go of the workweek and enter a more relaxed and restful consciousness. Further, the traditional practice of putting on fresh clothes for Shabbat is an effective external manifestation of the internal transition that one hopes to achieve.

Other practices that are often used to get in the Shabbat spirit include: chanting a word, phrase, or verse (for example, "Shabbat shalom" or "Shalom"); reciting a set of prayer-phrases that are preset and regularly used (for example: "May I feel safe, may I feel peaceful, may I feel strong"); taking a walk; reading from a book or a set of

Some dress in white on Shabbat as an external manifestation of purity and a connection to the metaphor to which the Shabbat song "*L'ḳha Dodi*" refers—that Shabbat greets us like a partner at the *ḥupa* each week. —J.G.K.

poems that sets the right mood; journaling to reflect on the week gone by and the approach of Shabbat; studying a text with a study partner (Traditionally the focus was on the laws of Shabbat, but that can be extended to any text that engages you in the themes and customs of Shabbat.); calling family or friends to wish them "Shabbat shalom"; swimming or jogging; using an aerobic workout to clear your mind; or practicing yoga. Obviously the choices are innumerable. We can experiment until we hit upon a practice that works to trigger "Shabbat consciousness" in ourselves. After only a few repetitions, this practice can become your pre-Shabbat ritual, enabling you to be at rest as you usher in the evening.

Of course, we don't always have the time to prepare ourselves before Friday evening. Sometimes we have to tear ourselves away from our work, fully immersed until the very last moment. That is why it can be helpful to begin the preparations on Thursday or even Wednesday. But when we find ourselves in a state of weekday agitation and preoccupation on Shabbat, it is helpful to remember that all of the pre-Shabbat practices described above work on Shabbat itself as well.

My brother, who identifies as a committed Reform Jew, writes a weekly email to my sisters and me on Friday afternoons to catch us up on his family and to wish us all "Shabbat shalom." —B.P.

Preparing the External Environment

Equally as important as attending to our spirit are the practical preparations. Without such planning, we might grab a bite to eat after work on the way to a late Friday evening synagogue service, for example, and nevertheless have a meaningful, elevating experience, but planning increases our odds of having that kind of experience.

Company

It is certainly possible to celebrate Shabbat alone. Some call it a Shabbat retreat and relish such Shabbatot as opportunities for deep renewal. We don't need a minyan or anyone else to light candles, chant the Kiddush, eat a delicious meal, sing Shabbat *z'mirot* (songs) and recite the *Birkat Hamazon* (prayers after the meal). Even when we attend synagogue services on Friday evening and/or Shabbat morning, we may choose to return home alone for a contemplative, quiet experience, spending the time in ways that bring us rest and peace.

When I was growing up, the only dinner rule in my house was that every Friday night at 6 P.M., my three sisters and I knew we had to be sitting at our Shabbat table without arguing with each other (at least for the duration of the meal). The consistency of this Shabbat practice was one of the most powerful Jewish influences of my childhood. —S.C.R.

My father worked as a traveling salesman and slept away from home three or four nights a week. However, he always came home for Friday nights, and dinner on *erev Shabbat* was the one meal of the week when my entire nuclear family was together. Even as my siblings and I became teenagers and made plans to see our friends on Friday evenings, we always scheduled those plans after dinner rather than during it. Shabbat and the importance of family were inextricably intertwined in our household. —D.W.

When you prefer company for Shabbat, it is best to plan in advance. Do you need to confirm with the members of your household that they will be present for the meal(s)? In many households, there is an understanding that everyone is present on Friday night for the Shabbat meal; if anyone is going out, that happens after the meal. Especially for families that do not often share meals, this can be a grounding and cherished practice. It also works to balance among the different Shabbat practices of household members—that is, we may not all choose to observe Shabbat in identical ways, but for the duration of Shabbat dinner, we sit and celebrate together.

If you want to host a meal with guests, you may want to invite them days or weeks in advance, given our busy schedules. If you would rather eat in another home and you feel sufficiently comfortable with particular friends or family, you may want to ask in advance whether you would be welcome at a particular meal. Often communities have a standing hospitality committee that matches those who are hosting on a given week with those who need an invitation. Sometimes *ḥavurot* meet biweekly or

I often find Shabbat meals fun to orchestrate. They are a great way to develop community because they provide a built-in structure for hosting community members and creating a way to deepen our connection to one another. —N.C.M.

I have found it moving to be a stranger at certain Shabbat services (oftentimes in traditional communities) and to be approached and offered a place to go for a Shabbat meal. This is a practice that I think should be adopted in all Jewish communities. —N.C.M.

monthly for a potluck Shabbat meal, rotating among homes. Or if eating in a restaurant with friends feels more Shabbat-like than cooking a meal, we may want to arrange to go out with friends, perhaps before or after services that we attend together.

Because it can be challenging to have a festive Shabbat meal when you are eating alone, the mitzvah of *hakhnasat orḥim* (welcoming guests) is especially encouraged for Shabbat. In the premodern Jewish world of Europe, the community regarded it as a primary responsibility to distribute bread to those who needed it on *erev Shabbat*. Elsewhere, the most important challenge was caring for travelers or for people who were unable to afford to prepare a Shabbat meal, and people would not leave the synagogue service until everyone in attendance was headed to a house for the Shabbat meal. In our society, that function has been assumed by rabbis (who are often aware of people's needs), by hospitality committees that match guests and hosts, and by community listservs that put people in direct touch with one another. Beyond the admirable mitzvah of caring for those acutely in need of a meal or of company, however, Shabbat can be a time to focus on close friends or people whom we may not have seen or connected with in a long time and to invite them over.

In the liberal Jewish world, the standard meal for hosting is often Shabbat dinner, when Shabbat lunch would better serve the purpose of a leisurely, shared meal. A communal Kiddush is nice, but it doesn't provide the same intimate social experience. How often do we really get to sit and enjoy one another's company in the middle of the day during the busy workweek? Shabbat provides that counterbalancing opportunity. —J.M.S.

Eating and davening are not the only ways to enjoy one another's company. You may want to invite people over for tea or a drink, to go for a walk or a hike, to meet in the park or at a playground, or to go to the zoo or a museum. If you drive on Shabbat or are comfortable using public transportation, the list of destinations expands exponentially, as long as everyone on the outing agrees about whether a given activity promotes the spirit of Shabbat for them. The key point is that when you live in a community in which many people are observing Shabbat, there are many opportunities to get together with others whose day, like yours, is far less encumbered with weekday time commitments.

Frequently enough, today's Shabbat observers share homes with people who do not share their interest in observing Shabbat in the same way. If you have roommates or housemates whom you have not chosen because of their interest in Shabbat observance, this is likely. It is also often the case that your child or parent or life partner may not be interested in Shabbat or may have very different approaches to Shabbat observance. Addressing these challenges is one of the many issues that need to be negotiated in a healthy relationship.

One of the keys to making different modes of observance work is for the more observant person to find ways of sharing the points of overlap. I do not drive on Shabbat, for example, but I take pleasure in inviting guests who I know will arrive by car and who will often bring with them food to be shared at dinner. —D.A.T.

To address Shabbat-related challenges, clear communication is essential. We all need to express personal values and concerns clearly and to feel as if we are being heard respectfully and nonjudgmentally. If a long-term relationship is involved, the parties can expect of one another that there will be a lot of stretching, accommodation and compromise. It is not helpful to harbor the assumption that greater observance of traditional Shabbat practices is superior. The challenge, however, is not to be minimized. For someone who wants to live in a home where the atmosphere transforms substantially on Shabbat and who values Shabbat meals, it is very challenging to do so individually in the presence of others who are not participating.

I spend a lot of joyful time with my family, but I dread some of the negotiations about Shabbat practices since I am the person in my family who organizes her life to be most aligned to Jewish time. I love the American holiday of Thanksgiving because, aside from my food practices, that Thursday is virtually the only holiday I celebrate in the identically same way as my family. —D.W.

As posthalakhic Jews, how do we say that any act is forbidden or required on Shabbat? Given the range of personal practice, the one thing I was willing to tell the congregants and their children at the Reconstructionist congregation I used to serve was, "No homework." I would like to think that forbidding schoolwork on Shabbat is also a way to raise our children with a particular love of Shabbat. Of course, we still want to imbue them with a love of learning, but perhaps that is another matter. —J.G.K.

A useful distinction in communicating about differences in Shabbat observance might be to distinguish between things that impose a non-Shabbat atmosphere on others and things that can be done without others being significantly affected. —J.A.S.

Renegotiating Shabbat practices with other household members can be particularly challenging if one's Shabbat practice changes significantly during a relationship or gains or loses a degree of consistency. —J.G.K.

Cleaning

The image from the midrash of angels peering through the windows to check on our Shabbat preparations is an interesting metaphor for the correlation between our inner state of consciousness and the external environment. Minimally, work-related materials should be cleared away or shut off so that we are not inadvertently drawn into a work-planning or problem-solving mindset. Beyond that, we each have our own sensibility about what a Shabbat-ready home looks like. Before Shabbat—and before Friday, for those who are not able to get to it on Friday—is the time to straighten up and clean our homes so that they are a sanctuary for the Shabbat spirit.

I struggle with physical clutter. It is hard for me to let go of papers or memorabilia, and much too easy for me to rush into the next seemingly urgent task without cleaning up. When I prepare for Shabbat by clearing away the clutter, I feel a sense of gratitude and expansiveness that is not ordinarily present in my day-to-day life. —D.W.

In 15th-century Spain, Christian descendants of Jews who had converted 90 years before were accused of being secret Jews and arrested by the Office of the Inquisition. Frequently, a piece of evidence used in such cases was that the household changed the linens on Fridays. The rhythms of the week, including the patterns of housecleaning, were so imprinted upon their psyches that, even several generations later, they adhered to them. —J.J.S.

Rabbi Danielle Leshaw has suggested that we eat better on Shabbat because we are not just feeding our ordinary selves; we are each feeding our *neshama yetera*, the additional soul tradition tells us we have on Shabbat. —J.G.K.

Food

Except for bread and wine or grape juice, there are no mandated foods for Shabbat. There are, however, many traditional foods that vary from community to community. They derive from the following considerations:

- Delicacies—It has long been traditional for Jews who live without luxuries to serve meat or poultry meals on Shabbat even if they cannot afford these dishes during the rest of the week. This is one explanation for the ubiquity of chicken soup, which allows a little bit of meat to go a long way. (In some parts of the Hasidic world today, it is permissible to be a vegetarian six days of the week, but on Shabbat, one is required to eat meat in honor of Shabbat!) The essential principle here—for those who eat meat and those who don't—is that we should eat *well* on Shabbat, whatever that means for you. For some, that may mean rich desserts, while for others, eating fresh, organic fruit is the way to eat well in honor of Creation.

Anthropologists have observed that the diet of indigenous cultures is usually simple and even sparse, interspersed with abundant feast days. In Jewish culture, Shabbat is our most regular feast, with meat and egg-enriched bread and even dessert. —D.W.

- Stews—Because cooking is work, the food that we eat on Shabbat is traditionally prepared in advance. It can traditionally be kept warm only if it is cooked and warm before Shabbat and then heated in an oven or on a stove that is lit before Shabbat and then remains heated throughout the night and the following day. This is the origin of Ashkenazic *cholent* and Sephardic *ḥamin*, slow-cooked stews that do not require preparation on Shabbat itself.

Slow-cooked, hot Shabbat meals have been traditional since talmudic times as an embodied affirmation of rabbinic tradition. Conversely, Karaites (who did not accept the authority of the Talmud) sat in the dark on Shabbat and would not take advantage of heat to keep food warm. By preparing *ḥamin* or *cholent* before Shabbat and letting it cook slowly overnight, we join ourselves to the legacy of a tradition in which the written word of Torah is always paired hand-in-hand with an oral, interpretive tradition. Ingredients for such Shabbat stews vary among Jewish communities around the world—Moroccans include chickpeas and rice, Ashkenazim onions and potatoes—but the concept of a Shabbat stew is ubiquitous, and it can be adapted for omnivorous and vegetarian palates alike. —J.G.K.

Informal Jewish environments like Jewish summer camp lend themselves to people's being involved in Shabbat food preparation by preparing *cholent*, and maybe even having a *cholent*-making contest among families or bunks of campers. —J.G.K.

We also respond to visual signals. Dishes and utensils passed down through the generations help to lend special meaning to the Shabbat meal when they are set aside for Shabbat. —M.K.

Some families make Shabbat special for children by restricting the eating of sugar cereals to Shabbat mornings. —J.M.S.

The power of association is strong. There are stories of new college students who do not understand how their campus Hillel foundations can host *Havdala* on Saturday nights if there is no lake, since every time they participated in a *Havdala* service before (at Jewish summer camp), there were wine, spices, a candle and a lake. —J.G.K.

- Sensory Triggers—If there is a dish that your grandmother or father prepared every week for Shabbat, then that may become central to your traditional Shabbat celebration, even if nobody else has ever heard of that custom. If your first regular celebration of Shabbat occurred on a kibbutz or at summer camp or at a *bayit* (communal Jewish house) at college, there may be tastes and scents that trigger for you a sense of the arrival of the Shabbat Queen. So much about the *menuḥa* (rest) of Shabbat is sensory that it is important to be mindful about what we each think constitutes a Shabbat meal.

I once asked my mother whether it was okay for my wife and me to serve a West African peanut stew for Shabbat dinner. What made me ask this question, I can no longer imagine. I was astounded when my mother, who was not a very traditionally observant person, said, "No." For a long time, I alternated between thinking that she was wrong because anything special is good for Shabbat, and that she was right because Shabbat is a time for connecting to Jewish civilization, including our food culture. Then I thought that maybe the perfect Shabbat food for an American Jew was Jewish-American fusion food since our food has historically been fusion: for example, noodle kugel with cranberries or maple-glazed chicken. Now Rabbi Staub suggests an intriguing new possibility: West African peanut stew will be especially appropriate if we serve it often enough that it becomes a Shabbat "trigger." —J.A.S.

Clothing

Jewish people once had specially designated clothes that were worn only on Shabbat and that were nicer, dressier, cleaner and fancier. Dressing up to greet the arrival of the Shabbat Bride and to acknowledge the presence for 25 hours of the *Shekhina* (God's presence) and the palpable difference in the quality of Shabbat time was and remains an effective way to mark the distinctiveness of Shabbat. In our era, however, the distinctiveness of Shabbat is not necessarily most effectively invoked with our most formal clothing. If you spend your workweek in executive garb, for example, you may find that a switch to more casual clothing works better. And even when we are dressing up for Shabbat, that means different things to different people. The key principle is that before the arrival of Shabbat it is customary to change into clothing that represents the distinctiveness of Shabbat in our minds.

The request that teens and children change into special clothes for Shabbat can be challenging for them. For many of us, the culture of dressing up for synagogue is something that turned us off in the past. In our synagogue we request that "message T-shirts" not be worn on Shabbat and, in an effort to stress the power of wearing Shabbat clothes, children are encouraged to set aside favorite shoes or articles of clothing or jewelry that can be worn with other, more familiar items. —N.H.M.

I vary what I choose to wear on Shabbat (sometimes casual, sometimes a button-down shirt with a tie), but when standing in front of the clothes closet, I often ask myself what outfit will allow me to honor Shabbat most deeply and also to feel most personally authentic at this particular moment. —N.C.M.

Friday Evening at Home

When Candles Are Lit

This is the moment that traditionally marks the beginning of Shabbat. The traditional time of *likht bentshn* (Yiddish), or *hadlakat nerot* (Hebrew) (lighting and saying the *b'rakha* [blessing] over the candles), is 18 minutes before sunset, so that we are not still lighting them after Shabbat has begun. Candle lighting occurs as early as around 4 P.M. in December and as late as around 8:30 P.M. in June in North America. The time varies with your exact location as well, since the sun sets at different times in different places in a given time zone, and locations closer to the equator do not vary as much between summer and winter. The exact time each week is provided on standard Jewish

The practice in most traditional communities in the Diaspora is to light candles on Friday afternoon 18 minutes before the sun sets, not waiting until the last possible moment to welcome Shabbat. There are several opinions about the origin of the custom, and the *minhag* itself is not consistent—some communities light a few minutes earlier, some a few minutes later. The mountainous terrain around the cities of Tzfat and Jerusalem raises questions about defining when sunset takes place there. Many Jews in Jerusalem welcome Shabbat a full 40 minutes before the sun sets. Curiously, the Jews of Petach Tikva, built as a new settlement by Jerusalemites, use Jerusalem candle-lighting times each week to this day. —J.G.K.

How we prepare for, come into, make space for and welcome Shabbat has a very different set of dynamics and determinants in the late fall and winter than in the late spring and summer. While there is something to be said for adjusting one's Friday afternoon to make it home by 3 P.M. on a Friday in December, for many people such adjustments are impractical. Similarly, keeping sleepy toddlers (and adults!) awake until 8:30 P.M. or 9 P.M. on a summer Friday night to begin Shabbat and then start dinner can be a challenge. When to start Shabbat is a meteorological and mathematical question for which there is a ready answer: 18 minutes before sunset. But for

calendars and on many Jewish websites. Traditionally it is permitted to light the candles and say the Kiddush earlier out of eagerness to usher in Shabbat and extend its stay. Nevertheless, a powerful magic is generated by aligning candle lighting with the setting sun—and thus with the arrival of Shabbat. For many, however, this is not possible when the winter sun sets earlier than they are able to return home. It may thus be preferable for you to light the candles when you are ready to usher in Shabbat, either when you are sitting down for the Friday evening meal or

many contemporary Jews, it is really a question that needs to be answered individually or in the context of a family or household negotiation, a question that has more to do with calling up the light of Shabbat from within than determining how dark it is outside. When deferring candle lighting and the welcoming of Shabbat on a fall Friday, we can begin to make a transition in the way we manage activities between sunset and when we arrive home and are ready for Shabbat. If we commute by public transit, we can bring a Jewish text to read on the way home on Friday. If we commute by car, we can bring music or a podcast that has Jewish content for the ride home. If we work at home, we can listen to Jewish music in the background, or light a single, non-Shabbat candle in our workspace, or light some incense, or take a five- or ten-minute break every hour between sunset and when we start Shabbat—something that calls our attention to the shift into Shabbat. —R.H.

Rabbi Elyse Goldstein and her husband Baruch Sienna start Shabbat at the same time each Friday (6 P.M., if I recall correctly) and end it 25 hours later. They like the "mitzvah/commandment" aspect of having the beginning of Shabbat imposed by a rule outside their convenience, and they like the 25-hour Shabbat, but they find that the traditional 4 P.M. winter start time and 9:30 P.M. summer end-time conflicts with other important values in their family. —J.A.S.

In our home, Shabbat starts on Friday evening when we light the candles, not according to the position of the sun or the clock on the wall. Some weeks, the transition is breathtakingly dramatic, and we suddenly and gratefully find ourselves in holy time. —D.W.

as you are departing for synagogue services. Some people, however, prefer to light the candles at the traditional moment before sundown, even if they have not completed all of their preparations. Cooking after the candles are lit, for example, can be transformed by the spirit of Shabbat, so that it can be done in a more relaxed and mindful way.

Why Candle Lighting?

Rabbinic sources mention that we light Shabbat candles in honor of Shabbat (*likhvod Shabbat*), as we might turn on the lights as guests arrive. They also mention *sh'lom bayit* (the peace of the household) as another intention of candle lighting.

Since the practice of lighting candles predated by centuries the use of human-made electric power, the practice of lighting candles on Friday night had the practical purpose of providing illumination when no lamp could be kindled after nightfall. The onset of Shabbat meant dinner by candlelight. Unlike Hanuka candles, which we light to gaze upon and enjoy but not to use, Shabbat candles are utilitarian, and warm lighting over a delicious meal on a set table can be very useful for peace in the home. —J.A.S./J.G.K.

I sometimes think about the light of the Shabbat candles as bringing forth a piece of *or haganuz*, the mysterious hidden light of the divine stored away after the first days of Creation. It is as if, for a moment, I can slip into the timelessness of Shabbat. —N.C.M.

The siddur of the communities of Rome and Milan places Psalms 36:10, among other verses about light, in a mystical candle-lighting *kavana* (meditation) in which we ask for light that is hidden to be revealed. —J.G.K.

That is, we light to express our hope that the members of the household are well and in harmonious relations. Even when that is not the case during the week, the lit candles are intended to remind us that at least on Shabbat there should be amity among us. Those more mystically inclined see the light of the candles as symbolizing the arrival of the extra Shabbat soul, or the increased spiritual capacity that each of us is said to receive on Shabbat. "By your light, we see light." (Psalms 36:10) Others also speak of the connection they feel at this moment with recent and distant ancestors who lit candles just as we do, as if their spirits, too, arrive at this moment to embrace and surround us for the coming day. Traditionally one does not leave a lit room on Friday evening to sit in a dark room. The list of *kavanot* (explanations) for candle lighting that has developed over the generations is long. Each of us should feel invited to generate our own associations and meanings with this and other ritual practices of Shabbat.

People tell me over and over that one of the most powerful aspects of lighting candles is their sense of belonging and connection to Jews all over the world who are doing the exact same thing, perhaps at the exact same moment, by lighting their own candles and ushering in Shabbat. The simple act of lighting a candle can transform our individual lives with a profound sense of belonging to a sacred community. —S.C.R.

It is spiritually informative that the blessing of Shabbat candles originated in a rabbinic polemic against the Karaites. The rabbis cited Isaiah's instruction to "call the Shabbat a delight" as part of their argument for not sitting in the dark on Shabbat, as the Karaites did. Thus, the candles themselves are a symbol of delight and our affirmation of pleasure and delight. —J.A.S.

Who Lights Candles?

Traditionally candle lighting has often been a silent, private event performed by the woman of the house, with the blessing whispered inaudibly and without the expectation that anyone else would be present. Indeed, it usually occurred after the men had left for the synagogue. It was one of only a few time-specific mitzvot that the rabbis believed were incumbent upon women. When more than one woman was sharing a house on a given Shabbat, each of them would light her own candles. Only in the absence of a woman would a man light the Shabbat candles. Since we support egalitarianism and no longer assume rigid gender roles, women are as likely as men to go to the synagogue, and men are as likely as women to be involved with cleaning and cooking. Thus, the reasons for a gender-specific association with candle lighting have long faded. Today, both men and women light candles. In fact, it is quite common for all willing adults (and sometimes children, too) to light their own pairs of candles, or to say or sing the blessing together over shared candles.

How Candles Are Lit

At least two candles are used, corresponding to the two different words used in the Bible concerning Shabbat. In Exodus 20:8, we are commanded to remember (*zakhor*) the Sabbath and keep it holy; in Deuteronomy 5:12, we are commanded to observe (*shamor*) the Sabbath and keep it holy. Both are accounts of the content of the Ten Commandments at Mount Sinai. Several midrashim imagine God to have said "remember" and "observe" simultaneously. When we light the two candles, we are recalling this two-faceted commandment. Some families follow the custom of lighting an additional candle for each of their children.

There are no particular requirements for Shabbat candlesticks. In fact, there are travelers' candlesticks that are anything but elaborate. They serve the purpose, which is to hold the candles securely and safely. Shabbat candlesticks, however, are not customarily used for any other occasions; they ascend in sanctity by virtue of their function on Shabbat, and thus they should not be used for more mundane purposes. Shabbat candlesticks are often also heirlooms, handed down from generation to generation, or bought, for example, by grandparents for their grandchildren at birth or for *b'ney mitzvah* or weddings.

Are Shabbat candlesticks considered sacred? I would not ascribe sanctity to candlesticks. They are special, yes, for sacred use, yes, since we mark time as sacred by using the candlesticks for candle lighting and making a *b'rakha*. —M.M.

When my mother gave my partner the candlesticks that she had used throughout my childhood, I knew that he had become a member of the family, and that the home we were building together had become as sacred as the one in which I grew up. —J.M.

Boxes of standard white Shabbat candles are widely available for purchase, though long tapers of any kind may be used. The candles should burn for several hours, from the time of candle lighting through the evening meal. They should not, however, be so large that you will need to extinguish them at the end of the evening; traditionally, fire is not extinguished on Shabbat.

The practice for reciting the *b'rakha* (blessing) over lighting the Shabbat candles departs from the usual sequence. The standard practice for saying a blessing (over a food, for example) is to say the blessing and then to perform the act (such as taking a bite). In the case of Shabbat

Some have adopted a custom of "spreading" the light of the candles to each person present before lighting them, and sending the light as well to beloveds who are not physically present. The hands scoop the light from the candles and spread it toward the person or people, from head to toe. The intention is to help each other open up to the new moment of "extra light" and soulfulness that is about to begin as the blessing over the lights is said. This practice provides another moment in which to pause, soften and prepare oneself to receive Shabbat in fullness and presence. —M.K.

While the custom of saying the blessing after lighting Shabbat candles rather than before is nearly ubiquitous in the Jewish world, contemporary modern Orthodox Rabbi Alan Yuter points out that the notion that Shabbat begins with a blessing was invented by Abraham Gombiner in 17th-century Poland, likely as a codification of a folk tradition of preceding the blessing with candle lighting even though every other time a Jew says a blessing over a mitzvah, the blessing precedes the mitzvah. This is one example of the many practices called "Orthodox" that are actually examples of reforms or reconstructions—departures from Jewish law as presented in the Talmud and codes. —J.G.K.

In our family, we have taken on the practice of shaking out our hands—symbolically shaking out all that no longer serves us from the week—before drawing in the light of the candles. —H.S.V.

Even after the most hectic of weeks, keeping my eyes closed for a few breaths as I welcome Shabbat at candle lighting allows me to be more centered for the evening to come. —N.C.M.

candle lighting, by contrast, we first light the candles and then recite the blessing. This is because once we recite the blessing, it is Shabbat, and we do not traditionally light candles once Shabbat has begun. Therefore we light them first. This anomaly gave rise to the practice of covering one's eyes while reciting the blessing, acting as if the candles have not yet been lit. Some people wave their hands three times from the lit candles to their eyes before covering their eyes with their hands, as if they are drawing in the candles' special energy. Then, after the blessing, they open their eyes and "see" the Shabbat lights for the first time.

The words of the blessing are "*Barukh ata Adonay Eloheynu melekh ha'olam asher kid'shanu bemitzvotav vetzivanu l'hadlik ner shel Shabbat,*" "Blessed are You who commanded us to light the light of Shabbat." (*Kol*

Historians believe that the blessing over the Shabbat candles, which states that God commanded us to light the candles, was first instituted as a mandated practice only in the tenth century. The blessing would have been a response to the challenge of the movement of Karaite Jews, who questioned the authority of rabbis and the rabbinic interpretation of the Torah. The Karaites took literally the biblical prohibition against burning fire in our homes on Shabbat (Exodus 35:3), and thus celebrated Shabbat in darkness. Rabbinic Judaism taught that you could use lights lit before Shabbat that continued to burn. By instituting the blessing over kindling the lights, the rabbis took the argument further; not only are we permitted to light fires that continue to burn on Shabbat, but we are also *commanded* to do so. (Maimonides, for example, asserts that even if you have no food for Shabbat, you must first beg for oil for the Shabbat light before you ask for food! See *Mishneh Torah, Hilkhot Shabbat* 5.1.) All of us who find the candle-lighting blessing central to our Jewish lives have the Karaites to thank for the development of this practice. —J.J.S.

Many American Jews use a melody that was first sung when lighting candles on Hanuka, leading sometimes to confusion about which words to say at the end. Others use one of several melodies designed expressly for Shabbat. —D.W.

Haneshamah: Nashir Unevareḥ, page 79). Whether the candles are lit by one or many, it is most often the case that the *b'rakha* (blessing) is chanted out loud, either solo or in unison, so that others can hear the blessing and respond by saying, "Amen." Nevertheless, many people prefer to whisper the blessing privately and then to take some time in silence for their own personal contemplation, gathering themselves after all the tumult of last-minute preparations to enter the psychic space of Shabbat. Then, if people are gathered together, this is a moment for greetings of "Shabbat shalom" or "*Gut Shabbos,*" accompanied by hugs and/or kisses.

While I was growing up, my family had a tradition of adding the *Sheheḥeyanu* blessing after candle lighting when one of the children came home after a long absence. The Shabbat table was the place where we felt like a family and, thus most keenly felt the absence of family members. —B.P.

One of the practices in my home is to greet every Shabbat guest with a kiss, something we would never think of doing at an ordinary dinner gathering. This is one of the ways we know it is Shabbat. —D.W.

Some parents choose to place their hands on their children's heads or shoulders as they recite the blessing. Others gather in a familial embrace or hold hands. Our young children prefer a tickle blessing! The connection of touch gives a palpable sense of our hopes and love made manifest in the words of the priestly blessing. —J.M.S.

Blessing One Another

Parents traditionally bless their children at the beginning of Shabbat with the *Birkat Kohanim*, the Priestly Blessing.

When each of our children left home for college, we continued the practice of saying the blessings for them despite their not being present. Giving a blessing can sometimes be as much for the one who gives as for the one who receives. —R.H.

Long before we were regularly using mobile phones or emailing electronic photographs to one another, when my friend Shira Schnitzer left home for university, her father, who had placed his hands on her head and said this blessing to her since the time she was very little, sent her a photocopy of his hands and left her a voicemail blessing, both of which arrived in time for Shabbat. —J.G.K.

I use the egalitarian practice that blesses both boys and girls with the same blessing—"May God make you like Sarah, Rebecca, Rachel and Leah, Ephraim and Menasheh." Both boys and girls deserve to be blessed with the distinctive qualities of each and all of these spiritual/cultural ancestors. —M.M.

There is a well-known tale of Rebbe Zusya, who told his disciples that when he got to heaven, he wouldn't be asked, "Why weren't you Abraham?" or "Why weren't you Moses?" He was concerned that they would ask, "Why weren't you Zusya?" Based on this tale, Rabbi Elyse Wechterman innovated a blessing of children that says, "May God make you like (fill in child's name). This innovation can also be combined with the traditional blessing: "May God make you like Ephraim and Menasheh, and (add child's name)"—acknowledging the desire to have our children become their own unique selves in addition to having them emulate our ancestors. We follow the traditional blessing with additional hopes and blessings that we have for that child's Shabbat and week. —N.C.M./J.A.S.

At Havurah Shalom, Portland, Oregon's Reconstructionist Community, each family receives a laminated handout with all these blessings, augmented with an additional one drawn from Marcia Falk's *The Book of Blessings*: "Be who you are, and may you be blessed in all that you are." —D.W.

In our home each Friday night, my wife and I would individually place our hands on our daughter's head and give her our own personal blessing for Shabbat that reflected something that had happened in her life during the previous week, either acknowledging a quality we admired in her or encouraging her to find that quality we knew would be part of her character in the week ahead. This weekly ritual was so powerful for her that even in times of adolescent rebellion she would insist (sometimes through gritted teeth) on her Shabbat blessing each week. —S.C.R.

(Numbers 6:24–26) Often this happens immediately after candle lighting if the candles are lit in the presence of the whole family. When blessing a daughter, the blessing is preceded by the line, "May God make you like Sarah, Rebecca, Rachel and Leah." When blessing a son, this is preceded by the line, "May God make you like Ephraim and Menasheh." (*Kol Haneshamah: Nashir Unevareḥ,* page 80) These words may be supplemented or replaced with other words of blessing. Many find that the weekly repetition of this standard text takes on the power to contain innumerable wishes that are often difficult to express spontaneously. When children and parents no longer live under the same roof, many find it extremely meaningful to call their children each Friday afternoon to continue to recite this blessing and to wish them a "Shabbat shalom." In some families, the children bless the parents as well. Others recite all together, "May the Merciful One bless all of us together with the blessing of peace." (*Kol Haneshamah: Nashir Unevareḥ,* page 81)

This is also a time when many people find it meaningful to take a moment to reflect on the week that has ended. This can take many forms. Each person may share one blessing that occurred during the week, one difficult moment that they are happy to leave behind and/or one wish for the Shabbat that has just begun. Or people might take a minute to reflect privately about these questions.

"Shalom Aleykhem"

This first Shabbat song, which dates from the 17th-century kabbalists in the town of Tzfat in northern Israel, welcomes in the ministering angels, who are said to accompany us home from synagogue on Friday evening. Whether

My children love the practice of walking around the prepared table while we sing "*Shalom Aleykhem*." For me, this is a way of physically demarcating the table as set apart. —H.S.V.

The four verses of "*Shalom Aleykhem* depict the hope that the angels will come in, bless us and leave us in peace and wholeness. This movement of the angels can also be understood as the movement of the breath within the body. Inviting the angels of *nishmat ḥayim,* the breath of life (Genesis 2:7), to enter our bodies, fill them with blessing, and then depart echoes the connection between the Hebrew words "*neshama,*" "soul," and "*neshima,*" "breath." An intention for chanting this first Shabbat song can be to open up to the *neshima yeteyra,* the extra soul breath, that can fill and "inspire" consciousness during this day if one's intention is that it should do so. —M.K.

When songwriter Debbie Friedman wrote music to "*Shalom Aleykhem*" just before her death, she altered the last verse slightly. Instead of saying "*tzet'khem l'shalom*" ("leave in peace"), she amended the verb to "*shuv'khem*" ("return"), meaning we are reluctant to send the angels away. Rather, we encourage them to leave and return. This might also serve as a *kavana* (intention) when we bid farewell to our real-life Sabbath guests. —B.P.

you believe in the presence of angels, feel the presence of the souls of ancestors, experience the inspiration that comes from connecting to the spirit of Shabbat or simply delight in the palpable atmosphere of rest and reflection that accompanies candle lighting, "*Shalom Aleykhem*" (*Kol Haneshamah: Nashir Unevareḥ,* page 38) offers a moment when we can sing out our gratitude.

Blessings of Life Partners

On Friday evenings in generations past, many husbands would sing the poem, "*Eshet Ḥayil*"—"A Woman of Valor" (Proverbs 31:10–31), extolling their wives' virtues in the hyperbolic language of the Bible. While some still include the poem because it connects them to the practice of parents and grandparents, this custom is rarely continued in contemporary egalitarian households. When it is, the wife usually sings something in response to her husband, often a selection from the Song of Songs. More

The example of "*Eshet Ḥayil*" provides an opportunity for romantic creativity. I wrote a personalized Hebrew alphabetic acrostic poem patterned on "*Eshet Ḥayil*" that I recite privately to my wife each Saturday night before we go to sleep. In this way, it serves as a weekly reminder of our love, which sustains us as Shabbat departs. —J.M.S.

Another lovely ritual is to thank each other for something in the past week. —J.A.S.

Rabbis Arthur Waskow and Phyllis Berman resanctify their commitment to each other each Shabbat after hand washing by reciting the Jewish marriage vow to each other: "Behold, you are sanctified to me . . ." This is another way of elevating partner love and connection on Shabbat. —N.C.M.

often, couples of all genders find other ways to bless each other in their own words or with passages from the Song of Songs, the Book of Psalms or more contemporary poetry. Shabbat is the moment each week when the Shabbat Bride is married to the Creator or to the people Israel. It is an ideal time for the renewal of vows in one form or another.

Kiddush

The Kiddush (*Kol Haneshamah: Nashir Unevareḥ,* pages 82–85) is chanted over a full cup of wine or grape juice. The Kiddush cup itself is elevated in holiness because of its function in sanctifying the Shabbat, and so it is customary not to use it for ordinary, weekday purposes. A wonderful array of beautiful Kiddush cups made by talented artists from all over the world is available in a wide variety of designs, colors and materials. In line with the value of *hidur mitzvah*, beautifying Jewish observance, using a

When I was growing up, each of us had a specific Shabbat role in our family. Mine was to chant the Kiddush. I always saw it as a great privilege and responsibility, and each week it was a personal self-esteem booster. —S.C.R.

People often stand for Kiddush as a posture of bearing witness, as the Kiddush speaks of the Creation of the world and the liberation from Egypt, to which we bear witness. —M.M.

Kiddush cup that is a work of art can enhance the sanctity of the day.

The Kiddush is chanted while standing, according to one custom, and while sitting, according to another. Yet another custom is to chant the first section while standing and then to sit down at the conclusion of the first blessing. The cup is customarily filled to overflowing, signifying our hearts bursting with gratitude or overflowing with joy. According to some customs, the cup is held with the right hand while resting in the left hand (for those who are right-handed, and the opposite for those who are left-handed).

The first paragraph of the Friday-evening Kiddush is the Genesis account of the seventh day of Creation, when God rested after the creative work of the first six days. (Genesis 2:1–3) We who are created in the divine image (*b'tzelem*

Sometimes we associate the words of the 23rd Psalm with hard times, but through this Shabbat joy, "my cup runneth over." —J.G.K.

I have learned that the cup should rest in the palm of an open hand to remind us to open ourselves to fully embrace Shabbat, which we join with the divine in sanctifying through the Kiddush prayer. Perhaps right over left has its origin in kabbala, since the mystics teach that, on Shabbat, the *s'fira* (mystical emanation) of *ḥesed* (loving kindness), symbolized by the right hand, triumphs over the *s'fira* of *g'vura* (judgment). Holding the cup in the right hand is physically embodying God's *ḥesed*, God's loving kindness, and seeking to have it infuse the experience of sanctifying Shabbat time. —J.G.K./N.C.M.

It is traditional to precede Genesis 2:1-3 with the last words of Chapter 1, ". . . the sixth day—*yom hashishi.*" In this way, our first four words in Hebrew, *yom hashishi vay'ḳhulu hashamayim,* form an acrostic of the divine name "YHVH." Divinity is found both in creation and in rest, and in the cycle of creation and rest. —J.A.S.

The *Vay'ḳhulu* is also traditionally repeated out loud following the *Amida* shortly before the rest of Kiddush said in synagogue. That is why *Vay'ḳhulu*, the first paragraph of the Friday evening Kiddush said at home, is not part of the Kiddush in the synagogue. —J.G.K.

Elohim) are reminded that when we cease working on the seventh day, we are acting in imitation of God. We are also affirming that the need to rest is embedded in the cosmic rhythms of the universe. (*Kol Haneshamah: Nashir Unevareḥ,* page 83) This paragraph is omitted in the Kiddush that is recited as part of the synagogue evening service because it has already been recited in the *Amida*. Many households also omit it for the sake of brevity.

At this point, the person chanting the Kiddush lifts the cup and says, "With your permission (*savrey*)," and everyone else responds "*L'ḥayim!* (For life!)" The first *b'rakha* (blessing), "*borey p'ri hagafen*" over the wine, then follows—"Blessed are You . . . the creator of the fruit of the vine."

The second paragraph of the Kiddush (*Kol Haneshamah: Nashir Unevareḥ,* pages 84–85) praises God for making us holy by giving us the mitzvot (commandments), specifically by lovingly bestowing on us the mitzvah of Shabbat as a remembrance of Creation and of the

Many people chant Kiddush in unison. In that case, "*savrey*" would be skipped, since one person is not seeking the permission/attention of the others. In this case, "*l'ḥayim*" would traditionally be said at the very beginning, in order to avoid interrupting between the blessing and the drinking. But our family, like many, says it at the end, with much clinking of glasses before we drink. —J.A.S.

Most of us probably learn to pronounce this blessing in its Ashkenazic formula, "*borey p'ri hagafen*." Although the Hebrew word for "vine" is "*gefen*," lengthening the first vowel to make "*gafen*" makes the form pausal, which means that the punctuation mark at the end of the blessing is contained within the word *hagafen* itself. The Sephardic formula is "*borey p'ri hagefen*"; the pausal form is not added. A Moroccan friend once taught me that the "*amen*" said by the listener after this blessing is what completes the blessing. It is no longer about one person drinking wine or grape juice, but about a community's interactive expression of thanks. May we always have the blessing of others surrounding us to echo our blessings as we drink the fruit of the vine. —J.G.K.

Exodus from Egypt. It ends by blessing God for sanctifying Shabbat *(m'kadesh Hashabbat)*.

The traditional Ashkenazic version of the second paragraph includes the line, "*ki vanu vaḥarta v'otanu kidashta mikol ha'amim*"—"for you have chosen us from among all peoples and sanctified us." The Reconstruc-

I am a card-carrying religious naturalist who finds the rejection of the idea of the chosen people to be one of Reconstructionism's most important contributions to Jewish modernity. Nonetheless, we chant the traditional Friday night Kiddush at our Shabbat table for a number of reasons. Among them is this: One of the few Jewish memories I have of growing up was the dramatic moment at Friday night services when the cantor lifted the silver Kiddush cup and we all sang the Kiddush together. Each Friday night, I have a chance to reconnect with that memory. Most Jews who make their way to our table know the traditional version, and so we can share a sense of belonging without having to digress into a discussion of ideology about believing. When our children were attending Jewish day school, this was the version they learned and knew. —R.H.

If your custom is to recite the Reconstructionist version of Kiddush, you may find yourself leading the Kiddush outside of your own home in a situation where others only know the traditional version and you have not prepared them for the difference in wording. In that situation, you may want to chant, "*ḳi vanu vaḥarta v'otanu ḳidashta* im *ḳol ha'amim*"—"for you have chosen us *with* all peoples and sanctified us." While this may be a bit awkward grammatically, it does capture the Reconstructionist belief that each people has its own path, and that just as our reconstruction of Jewish traditions is a vehicle for Jews to move ever closer to lives of holiness and virtue, so the traditions of other religions and cultures are opportunities for members of those groups to move ever closer to lives of holiness and virtue. The change of one syllable preserves your integrity and avoids the confusion that occurs when people sing different words simultaneously. Note that even with this modification, non-Jews may not be comfortable joining in. —J.J.S.

Some recite "*asher baḥar banu im ḳol ba'aley ḥayim*"—for you have chosen us together with all species. Thus we sanctify Shabbat by allowing our worldview to expand beyond the supposed centrality of humanity. —J.M.S.

For decades, Isaac Imber used the formula "*asher baḥar banu la'avodato*"—"who chose us for divine service." —Y.R.

tionist liturgy has altered that to "*ki eleynu karata v'otanu kidashta la'avodatekha*"—"for you have called to us and made us holy for your service." The change was made out of the conviction that God has not singled out and elevated the Jewish people above all others. Rather, all peoples are called to divine service in their own cultural idiom, and it is incumbent on all peoples, including the Jewish people, to work within their own traditions toward ever more elevated and ethical levels of belief and practice. Saying "for you have called to us and made us holy for your service" also makes it more comfortable for non-Jews to join in, since it applies to everyone.

"Kiddush" means sanctification. In Jewish practice, we transform reality with a combination of words and concrete action; in this case, we first declare the sanctity of Shabbat verbally, and then we do it concretely by drinking

In groups where there are people who will be singing both the Reconstructionist and non-Reconstructionist liturgy of the Kiddush together, rather than hearing dissonance (some singing "*ki vanu vaḥarta*" and some singing "*ki eleynu karata*"), I seek to appreciate the mixture as an opportunity to truly appreciate Jewish diversity. But I admit that this can be challenging. —N.C.M.

Like many Reconstructionist Jews, I don't recite the traditional liturgy of "*ki vanu vaḥarta mikol ha'amim*"—"for you have chosen us from all nations." But when I'm in a pluralistic space where that is the recited form, I think of this aspect of Shabbat: that it is indeed particular to the Jewish people, and a gift we have offered to the world. —J.M.

The prevalent Sephardic version of Kiddush does not include the problematic words at all. (See *Kol Haneshamah: Shirim Uvraḥot,* page 12.) —J.G.K.

In the central blessing of the *Shabbat Amida* and in the concluding blessing of the Shabbat haftarah, we sanctify Shabbat through words; at Shabbat meals, we sanctify Shabbat with our other senses with the help of wine and food. —J.G.K.

the wine (after the second blessing). That is the action that sanctifies Shabbat.

Hand Washing

After Kiddush, it is customary to wash your hands ritually before eating the hallah. The hand-washing cup (*natlan*) is another opportunity for *hidur mitzvah* (beautifying Jewish observance); many beautifully crafted cups are available to be acquired or given as presents. Ideally, the cup should have two handles, so that it can be passed easily back and forth from hand to hand. Lifting the filled cup with your right hand, you pour the water over the left hand. You then take the cup in your left hand and pour the water over the right hand, alternating until each hand has been doused three times. Another custom is to pour

Traditionally, the act of eating any kind of bread, not just the hallah we eat on Shabbat, is preceded by hand washing and recitation of the *motzi*. This is based on an early rabbinic/pharisaic innovation of nonpriests taking on priestly rituals formerly done only in the Jerusalem Temple. Some of us might embrace this daily practice, with its democratizing roots and spiritually uplifting message of the holiness of food. Others might reject it as too connected to troublesome notions of purity and to Temple practices we don't want to reclaim. —J.A.S.

Many people remove their rings to ensure that the water touches every part of their hands. My partner and I follow a practice we have seen among other Reconstructionists. Before hand washing we take off our wedding rings (sometimes this requires a little soap for swollen fingers!), and afterward we place the appropriate ring on the other's finger. As we look into each other's eyes and kiss, we are reminded of our wedding day and of all that we mean to each other. In our family, this takes the place of spoken words of blessing between us. It is quick and private, but deeply meaningful to both of us. —B.P./D.W.

Some Jews carefully follow the *halakha* that one should precede the act of rinsing one's hands by reciting the blessing for hand washing. —J.G.K.

the water three consecutive times over the left hand and then three times over the right hand. Refilling the cup for the next person's use, you then dry your hands, reciting the blessing "*al n'tilat yadayim*"—"Blessed are You . . . who has commanded us to wash our hands."

It is customary not to speak between reciting the hand-washing blessing and eating the hallah. While people wait for others to rejoin them at the table, many people join in singing a *nigun*, a wordless melody. Any wordless melody will do the job of bringing everyone together in a unified focus on the moment—for example, the tune to a song that many people know, such as "*Bim Bam Shabbat Shalom*." There are also many exquisite and elaborate *nigunim* that are worth learning if you want an elevating experience of being transported to another, more Shabbat-like realm.

Hallah

The type of hallah that has come down to us from Europe is a braided loaf, but that form is not required. The requirement is to have two whole, uncut breads. These could be two pieces of matza, or two rolls, or one of each. Nor does

How rare it is to spend time with friends and family without chatter! Rather than fill these few moments with a tune or with awkward gestures, I relish these few seconds of silence before the conversations resume. I continue this quiet moment throughout the eating of the hallah, which I like to perform mindfully as an eating meditation. —J.M.

Many contemporary recordings of *nigunim* are available. Hasidim have been at the forefront of creating new *nigunim* since the movement began in the 18th century, and many recordings of these are available as well. —J.J.S.

the grain need to be wheat. Nevertheless, many people find great meaning in the taste, scent and braided shape of the European-style hallah because of childhood memories or grandmothers' recipes or the sweet and yeasty taste.

The hallah plate is yet another opportunity for *hidur mitzvah*. There is no requirement to have a special plate on which the hallahs rest, but inasmuch as the hallah is a successor to sacred offerings in the ancient Temple in Jerusalem and serves as one of the portals to Shabbat, it is natural to give it a place of honor and beauty on the table. In addition, whether it is one's practice to slice the hallah or to tear it with one's hands, it is easier to do so when it is on a plate of some kind. Exquisite wood, ceramic and glass pieces are available, as well as simple Israeli olive wood platters.

The hallah cover, by contrast, is traditionally mandated. While a simple napkin can serve this function, we beautify the mitzvah by using crafted hallah covers of every imaginable design and fabric.

Folk midrash has it that the hallah would be upset to witness the precedence over it that is accorded to the wine and Kiddush each week. To save it that embarrassment, the hallah is left hidden, uncovered only when it is time to recite the blessing and eat it. —J.J.S.

I have never liked the midrash about the embarrassed hallah. It makes no sense to anthropomorphize the dough we are about to chew in order to explain why we cover the hallah. Each *b'rakha* is separate. Each serves its own function, so we focus on each one in turn. —M.M.

The hallah cover can serve another, more practical purpose—concealing the treat from an enthusiastic child. —J.G.K.

The two Shabbat loaves are also a reminder of the double portion of manna in the desert, from which the Temple practice developed. —M.M.

The Motzi

It is customary to have two loaves on the Shabbat table, both on Friday evening and Saturday afternoon, in memory of the two cereal loaves offered on Shabbat when the Temple stood in Jerusalem. One of the most valuable contributions of the rabbis to the transformation of Judaism after the destruction of the Second Temple in the first century was the way they regarded the tables on which we eat as the successors to the Temple's altars. When we recite the blessing over the bread (*motzi*) on the Shabbat table and eat a morsel, we are reenacting the animal and vegetable sacrifices that our ancestors offered two millennia ago as worship of God. When we join together to recite

Hallah is named after the piece of bread that is traditionally separated by the baker before the dough is set to rise before baking. Separating this bit of hallah from the rest of a large quantity of dough comes with its own blessing, *l'hafrish ḥala*. The removed piece can be burned or otherwise disposed of. While the origin of the tradition may be providing food for the priests in Temple times, for me taking hallah when we bake bread is a concrete reminder to give *tzedaḳa* before Shabbat, when we focus on abundance. —J.G.K.

When traveling in Poland some years ago, I struggled to find food that met my *ḳashrut* requirements. One morning I smiled, pleased to find braided bread called "*ḥalḳi*" in Polish, which I ate for breakfast, hoping that the ingredients matched the name and the form. —J.G.K.

There is a Sephardic custom of reciting several lines from Psalm 145 before reciting the *motzi*. The verses read, "All hopeful gazes turn toward you, as you give sustenance in its appointed time. Your opened hand satisfies desire in all life." These words serve as a hopeful *ḳavana* that the satisfaction we enjoy through our eating is truly meant to be enjoyed by all, especially those who suffer from hunger throughout the world. —Y.R.

motzi, having prepared ourselves to enter the sacred rhythm of Shabbat, the divine presence is palpable.

According to one custom, you uncover the hallahs before the blessing, sprinkle salt on the loaves—the practice with the meal offerings in the Temple, which also

Just as two hallot can evoke for us the image of our ancestors gathering a double portion of manna in the desert before Shabbat, the plate below and cover above the hallah can remind us of the two layers of dew that protected that manna for our ancestors each morning. —J.G.K.

For some, Shabbat meals may be the only time in a busy week when they pause to bless food before eating. There are many *ḳavanot,* intentions, available for helping one to focus and cultivate one's awareness of the gift of nourishment before saying this blessing. One *ḳavana* is to pause and think of the endless elements and efforts that contribute to creating this bread, and how interconnected all elements truly are at root: Sun shining on the fields enabled the wheat to grow and be gathered and crushed and further transformed so that those who labored could produce the bread on that Shabbat table. —M.K.

Many Sephardic Jews lift the hallah and add the verse, "*Pote'aḥ et yadeḳha umasbia l'ḥol ḥai ratzon*"—"You open up your hand and satisfy the needs of every living being" (Psalm 145:16) before saying *motzi*. This focuses attention on appreciation of the source of nourishment that flows through all of life. This practice aids us to become more fully present to the moment of blessing the gift of the Shabbat meal. —M.K./J.G.K.

Some salt the bread three times while reciting, "*Adonay meleḳh, adonay malaḳh, adonay yimloḳh l'olam va'ed*"—"The Eternal reigns, the Eternal reigned, the Eternal will reign forever," an apparent play on similar sounds of "*meleḳh*," the word for "king," and "*melaḳh*," the word for "salt." The *gematria* (the numerical value of the Hebrew word) for salt is three times the numerical value of God's four-letter name. —J.G.K.

While breaking bread together is a universal symbol of amity, it is prudent to inquire in advance if guests have gluten allergies or keep a vegan, no-egg diet. In many places, it is possible to buy vegan hallah and in some places, even gluten-free hallah. In any event, hosts ought to ensure that this occasion of sharing includes a sufficient variety of breads so that all can partake. —R.H.

makes it more likely that we will mindfully taste the bread—and lift up the two loaves together. You then recite the *b'rakha* (blessing) over the hallah, which is identical to the blessing recited over bread on any other occasion: "*hamotzi leḥem min ha'aretz*," "who brings forth bread from the earth." (*Kol Haneshamah: Nashir Unevareḥ,* pages 86–87) You then slice or tear off pieces and distribute them. According to another custom, you recite the *b'rakha,* slice or break the hallah into pieces, and then salt the pieces before you distribute them. According to yet another custom, salt is poured, and then the hallah is dipped in it. After everyone eats a bit of bread, the meal is served.

Tear or slice? Many of us rarely have the pleasure of eating unsliced, freshly baked bread. Taking a knife to the hallah is reminiscent of the biblical prohibition against using metal to hew the stones for the altar in the Tabernacle. (Exodus 20:22; this is also cited in I Chronicles 28:3, in the admonition to King David not to build the Temple because he was a man of war.) If we welcome Shabbat as a time of peace, then we may choose to avoid putting a knife to the hallah. —B.P.

When I was a kid, our rabbi loved to toss people pieces of hallah at the synagogue Kiddush luncheon. I later learned that receiving the hallah from the air also evokes the image of manna from heaven. —J.G.K.

In our family, we break the hallah and throw the pieces to one another. This is both fun and a way of reminding ourselves that our bread does not only come from our own hands. —H.S.V.

Some choose to substitute honey for salt to symbolize the hope for a sweet week. Children love this practice. —J.M.S.

Salt was an extremely valuable commodity in ancient times. I like to think that by salting the bread we are adding the food equivalent of jewels to the meal. —N.C.M.

The Meal

Aside from the Kiddush wine and hallah, there are no mandated dishes for the Shabbat meal. As explained above in the section "Preparing for Shabbat: Food," the culinary customs of Jewish communities through the centuries have varied widely. What all of these customs share in common is that Jews saved their delicacies for the Shabbat table. Many impoverished Jews in Eastern Europe and elsewhere, including many new immigrants to the United States, ate meat only on Shabbat, and sometimes that meat was a bone in a stew or a watered-down chicken soup. In many other places and eras, wealthier Jews prepared sumptuous multicourse feasts.

Thus, it is up to you to define what a special meal is for you and your guests. Dishes and ingredients that were regarded not so long ago as *de rigueur* now seem to some to be hazardous to our health and/or environmentally

Eating gefilte fish may have its origin in the Shabbat prohibition against *borer*, separating the nondesirable parts out from the desirable parts. A deboned (and reconstituted!) fish solves this problem since it has no bones to pick out. Another explanation is that by making gefilte fish, our impoverished forebears could turn the least expensive fish into a delicious Shabbat morsel. —J.G.K./D.A.T.

One important Shabbat meal custom is sharing words of Torah, speaking about the weekly *parasha* or sharing other teachings from Jewish texts. These words can spark interesting conversation (not connected to work or other weekly concerns), enabling everyone around the table to learn, to reflect personally on a section of Torah and to get to know each other through a wonderful lens. You don't have to be a scholar to share a *vort* (a word of Torah) and there are countless websites that can be helpful in offering direction or inspiration. —M.M.

counterproductive. While some might argue that chicken fat and noodle kugel (pudding) are essential to a Shabbat meal, you need not be persuaded.

More important than the items on the menu is the pace with which they are served. A Shabbat meal is a leisurely one, with multiple courses served with plenty of time between them. It's a time to talk in an unhurried way and to savor every morsel because we are not hurrying to get anywhere. We have the freedom to rest in the moment.

Singing

One traditional way that this leisurely pace is manifested is through group table singing, traditionally the singing of Shabbat *z'mirot* (songs). *Kol Haneshamah: Nashir Unevareḥ* offers a wide variety of songs (pages 37–77), and *Kol Haneshamah: Shirim Uvraḥot* provides musical notation for them. These traditional Shabbat songs are intricate and gorgeous in their Hebrew poetry, and there are endless numbers of melodies to which they are set. The point of singing them is to envelop us in the spirit of Shab-

It can be difficult to have a relaxing and lengthy Shabbat dinner when small children demand constant attention and tire quickly of sitting still. Some deal with this by reciting opening blessings together and serving a first course, then taking a break to put the children to bed before resuming the meal. —J.M.S.

Song is nourishment for the soul as food is nourishment for the body. The practice of including *z'mirot* at a Shabbat meal creates space for the spiritual dimensions of one's life to move toward the foreground of awareness as one's physical needs, such as hunger and thirst, have been sated. In this embodied practice of *z'mirot*, we utilize the physicality of our vocal chords, diaphragms, lungs and more in an act of spiritual expression. —M.K.

bat. That objective, however, can be achieved equally as well by singing wordless *nigunim* or singing songs in English that feel restful and sacred, especially if the intricate Hebrew is an obstacle to wholehearted participation.

Shabbat table singing can be an interesting and transformative experience. Most of us do not sing together very often. We sing with small children, with musical recordings or at concerts. Perhaps we have fond memories of singing with friends accompanied by a guitar—something we still get together to do occasionally. But all too often, it becomes something we leave behind, something from summer camp or undergraduate days. Singing can bring us together in ways that speech does not; many people cite the group singing that happens in a synagogue service as one of the most moving, prayerful moments they experience there. But even in synagogue, we are being led by a *hazzan* (cantor) or another *sh'li'aḥ tzibur* (communal prayer leader).

Sitting around a table with friends and family and taking turns selecting songs that everyone sings together is a different experience. Without a professional, designated leader and without an expectation that participants have fine singing voices, table singing is not an artistic performance. It is something we can do together, lowering our guard, each of us raising our voices. Repeating the same *z'mirot* week after week makes the tunes emotional prompts that transport us into a sacred realm, sometimes

The sound of Shabbat songs sung by a group rarely fails to amaze and transform me.
—J.G.K.

triggering fond associations and memories. Learning yet another tune to the same, familiar words can be fun and exciting. And occasionally, something mysterious clicks, and we somehow feel transformed and moved in unaccountable ways.

Birkat Hamazon

It is traditional practice to recite *Birkat Hamazon* (The Grace after Meals) at the end of every meal at which we have eaten bread and recited the *motzi* blessing (See *Kol Haneshamah: Nashir Unevareḥ*, pages 3–33, for several different versions). On Shabbat, the *Birkat Hamazon* is preceded by the singing of *Shir Hama'alot* (Psalm 126). Many people only make time for *Birkat Hamazon* on Shabbat and holidays. Some others recite a short version during the week and sing the full *Birkat Hamazon* on Shabbat. Gathering together for the Shabbat meal provides a particularly good opportunity to express our gratitude for the blessings of our table. Ideally, we are always mindful that the food we eat is a blessing to be savored and appreciated. If in the relaxed pace of Shabbat we remember to be more mindful and thankful, this is yet another piece of Shabbat practice that we can carry with us into the week.

Before Retiring

If the Friday evening service follows the meal, the challenge afterward is to preserve the spirit of Shabbat once we leave the synagogue. In more traditional practice, you return home, perhaps read a book or study some Torah, and quickly go to bed. If you do not feel restricted by Shabbat prohibitions, you may nevertheless want to take care not to slide right back into weekday consciousness. Perhaps you will avoid listening to or watching the late evening news, checking your messages, or accessing the Internet, so that you can remain under the spell of Shabbat.

One very traditional practice on Friday evenings is to make love with your partner. The halakhic obligation of a husband is to "satisfy" his wife at least once each week. Since many Jewish men worked away from home and returned for Shabbat, Friday night became the time for fulfilling one's minimal obligations. With the expansion in kabbalistic circles of images of the marriage between the Shabbat Bride or the *Shekhina* with the Blessed Holy One, sexual intimacy on Shabbat acquired an additional importance: Our unions reinforce and are reinforced by the heavenly union that occurs on Shabbat. This is yet anoth-

In my family, we often play board games while reclining and sipping after-dinner drinks to draw out our enjoyment of *oneg Shabbat*. —J.M.S.

Having sex is a "double mitzvah" on Shabbat—traditionally because the sexual act fulfills two discrete commandments, procreation and the enjoyment of Shabbat. This act fulfills many other purposes as well: connecting with one's partner, triumphing over loneliness, celebrating the pleasures of life (*hakarat hatov*) and so on. —J.M.

er example of how the observance of Shabbat in Jewish traditions is much more than a disembodied transformation of consciousness. We experience a foretaste of the world to come with all of our senses by sanctifying them through Shabbat observance and celebration.

Those of us whose observance of Shabbat takes a less regimented shape may choose to observe in some of the many ways outlined below in the section "Nontraditional Observance." If you are a *shomer Shabbat* (Sabbath observer) who may observe by eating out in a restaurant, attending a concert or film, or meeting friends for drinks in a bar, the ever-present question may be: How do you distinguish engaging in such activities on Shabbat from engaging in them on any other day? Do the topics of your conversation differ? Do you treat people differently? Do you choose to keep your *kipa* on even though you are doing something that is not traditionally done on Shabbat because you are observing Shabbat in your own way and wearing a *kipa* reminds you of this?

Friday Evening Synagogue Service

The underlying themes of Shabbat can be identified as creation, revelation and redemption. At the start of Shabbat on Friday night, the liturgy and songs emphasize the creation of the world, as we celebrate the wondrous blessings of this created world, blessings that we are better able to discern and appreciate with our Shabbat eyes wide open. On Shabbat morning, the service climaxes at the reading of the Torah, when we reenact the mythic revelation of the Torah at Mount Sinai. Constituted as a sacred community joining together in song and prayer, we are renewed and invigorated—prepared to receive and take on the divine mandates mythically revealed at Sinai. On Shabbat afternoon, at *minḥa* (the afternoon service) and during the *se'uda sh'lishit* (the third meal, traditionally eaten between *minḥa* and *ma'ariv* (the evening service, which marks the close of Shabbat), the emphasis is on redemption. Having experienced a foretaste of paradise on Shabbat, we cling to the sweet moments that remain and longingly await the messianic age that we hope will be a time that is "all Shabbat" (*kulo Shabbat*). The three themes of creation, revelation and redemption are reflected in the liturgical words of each service.

In kabbalistic practice, the quality of God's presence is thought to change throughout the day of Shabbat. In the evening, we feel the warm immanence of God's feminine presence, the *Shekhina*. On Shabbat morning, the formal prayer service and morning light offer a more transcendent, masculine presence. In the afternoon at the time of *minḥa*, God's feminine and masculine aspects are for a moment unified, giving us a glimpse into a world beyond our inherited gender boundaries. This is reflected in the pronoun referring to Shabbat in the final paragraph of the central *Amida* blessing for each service of Shabbat, which changes gender and person for each service—from *ba* (upon her) to *bo* (upon him) to *bam* (upon them)—according to some liturgies. —J.M.S.

Most non-Orthodox communities have fixed times for Friday night Shabbat services. I think this is a mistake. Yes, it makes it easier to plan. But what is lost is the natural connection between Shabbat and the rhythms of the sun. I like the fact that Shabbat feels different in December than it does in June, and I like the subordination of my electronic calendar to the rhythms of the heavens. —J.M.

Some communities that begin the *Kabbalat Shabbat* service early precede it with the *minḥa* (afternoon) service. —J.J.S.

The late service is an accommodation to the demands of the industrial and postindustrial workweek, which doesn't wind down at the setting of the sun. —D.W.

Some communities hold *Kabbalat Shabbat* services late, at 8 P.M. or 8:30 P.M., presuming that Shabbat dinner will be eaten first. Others hold an early service, between 6 P.M. and 7 P.M., before dinner. Some move the starting time of *Kabbalat Shabbat* services during the year, holding it close to sunset. Therefore, though this discussion of the service follows the description of the Friday evening home ritual, it does not presume a particular sequence. The service remains the same regardless of whether it precedes or follows dinner.

The first section of the Friday evening Shabbat service is called *Kabbalat Shabbat*. It is a relatively new section of the liturgy, having been added in the 16th century by the kabbalists (Jewish mystics) in Tzfat. Their practice was to begin Shabbat by going to the town gates to welcome the Sabbath Bride and dance her in. A remnant of this practice occurs when we rise and turn to

The originality and playfulness of this relatively new service are reminders that Jews have always created new Jewish expressions. —D.W.

Formal mourning does not take place on Shabbat, so instead of holding a shiva minyan at home, mourners return to the synagogue on Friday evening. It is customary for mourners who are in the middle of the week of sitting shiva after a funeral, or who are attending a communal service in the synagogue for the first time since getting up from shiva, to remain outside the sanctuary until the end of "*L'kha Dodi*." The whole congregation, still standing and facing the entrance as it welcomes in the Shabbat, also welcomes them with ritualized words of comfort as they make the transition from the isolation of mourning to re-entry into the community. It is a moving and effective way to acknowledge the significant passage experienced by mourners without resorting to words that are often awkward at such moments. This also spares the mourners from pressure to sing during *Kabbalat Shabbat*. —J.J.S.

face the sanctuary entrance as we sing the last stanza of the prayer "*L'kha Dodi*," bowing twice as we sing "*Bo'i, kala*" ("Enter, bride!").

In line with the Friday evening theme of Creation, the *Kabbalat Shabbat* service is composed of six psalms (95–99, 29), that represent the six days of Creation, followed by "*L'kha Dodi*" the central prayer of the *Kabbalat Shabbat* service that introduces the seventh psalm (92), the psalm for the Sabbath day. Those first six psalms emphasize the created world, its majesty and wondrousness, and God as its sovereign, ruling over mountains and thunderstorms, the regularity of nature and its marvelous exceptions.

There are countless melodies to which the different psalms are chanted and sung. The mood and tempo are joyous; the service is meant to invoke a weekly coronation of the ruler of the universe, a celebration that we reenact on Shabbat after having gone our separate ways during the week. "*L'kha Dodi*" then celebrates the arrival of Shabbat, the Bride/Queen/*Shekhina*, the divine presence as it is most manifest in the created world—especially on

Sephardic Jews recite Psalm 100 as the sixth Psalm of *Kabbalat Shabbat*, following the series with Psalm 29. —J.G.K.

The descriptive natural imagery in the psalms helps me to feel linked to the psalmist because we both experience the power of the divine within the natural world. —N.C.M.

For regular synagogue attendees, the joy of singing these psalms contrasts with the tradition of omitting some or all of them when Shabbat occurs after a holiday has begun. The liturgical change suggests that the joy of the holiday has already made space to usher in Shabbat. —J.G.K.

Shabbat. Some of its melodies are energetic; others are much softer, evoking the slow march of a wedding procession as we escort the Shabbat Bride in, finally rising at the final stanza of "*L'kha Dodi*" and turning to the entrance as one does for a wedding procession—or as a partner standing in front of the *ḥupa* (wedding canopy), waiting expectantly for the other partner to proceed down the aisle after the two have been separated for six days. The arrival of Shabbat can set our hearts aflutter.

The *Kabbalat Shabbat* service is often preceded by the communal lighting of the Shabbat candles (*Kol Haneshamah: Shabbat Veḥagim*, page 5) and by songs intended to set the Shabbat mood. "*Shalom Aleykhem*" (*Kol Haneshamah: Shabbat Veḥagim*, page 13), described in greater detail above in the Friday Home Ritual section, is one such song. Another, "*Yedid Nefesh*" (*Kol Haneshamah: Shabbat Veḥagim*, page 7), also deriving from 16th-century Tzfat, expresses the longing of our souls to be aligned and at one with the Merciful One, as well as the yearning to be healed and made whole on this Shabbat. Passages from the Song of Songs are also sometimes read to set the mood, including the song "*Dodi Li*" ("My Beloved Is Mine"), because of the traditional interpretation of the love poetry in that biblical book as expressing the love of the Jewish people for God. Sometimes, just prior to "*L'kha Dodi*," the song "*Ana B'kho'aḥ*" is added. It is another song of love and yearning for holiness. All of

Some traditional communities recite the biblical Song of Songs every Friday evening in synagogue. —J.G.K.

these additions aim to center us and elevate us into a sacred, restful mode of consciousness.

In some communities—especially those that meet for *Kabbalat Shabbat* before dinner, when it is less likely that there will be an extended sermon—there is a custom of studying a little bit of Torah at the conclusion of *Kabbalat Shabbat*, before continuing with *ma'ariv* (the evening service). We are each "spiritual" in our own unique way. Some are transformed by prayer, some by song, some by study, and all of us by a mixture of different approaches. Services should offer several spiritual modes.

The *ma'ariv* service is structured much like the evening service during the week. The special Shabbat evening *nusaḥ* (chanting melody mode), however, creates a soft and celebratory mood, quite different from the more prosaic *nusaḥ* of the weekdays.

Before the *Shabbat Amida*, the congregation rises for the singing of "*V'sham'ru*" (Exodus 31:16–17), the biblical passage that identifies Shabbat as an everlasting sign of the covenant between God and the Jewish people, marking the completion of Creation at the end of the sixth day.

The Talmud (*Shabbat* 119b) says that that one who recites "*V'shamru*" is as if he or she were a partner with God in Creation. German Jewish scholar Ismar Elbogen cited a Persian *nusaḥ* in which the entire seven-day Creation story, from the first verse of the Torah, is read on Friday night. Those with whom the imagery or assurances of good resonate at week's end may wish to adopt this practice. —J.G.K.

While the version of Shabbat found in Exodus emphasizes the events of Creation, Deuteronomy sees Shabbat as a weekly release of servants commemorating the exodus from Egypt, creating a link between Shabbat and a historical event. —J.A.S.

Unlike most of the holidays in the Jewish calendar cycle, Shabbat does not primarily commemorate a historical event. It celebrates the natural world. Similarly, the Shabbat *Amida* does not include all of the petitionary prayers that are contained in the weekday *Amida*. The liturgy gently urges us to rest and be refreshed (like God on the seventh day) in the moment. With our figurative additional soul, we set aside our weekday concerns and aspirations, as if we are complete, as the world is complete. The central blessing of the *Amida* for Friday evening features the Genesis account of God's resting on the seventh day. It concludes by praising God for sanctifying Shabbat. The Mishna (*Avot* 5:8) charmingly asserts that at dusk on the sixth day, ten things were created miracu-

On Friday evening we speak intimately and passionately to God in the *Amida*, joyfully and silently proclaiming, "*Ata ḳidashta et yom hashvi'i lishmeḳha*"—"You sanctified the seventh day for your name!" For those who did not light candles, this phrase halakhically begins Shabbat. What we are really doing is giving cosmic resonance to our personal sanctification of Shabbat. —J.M.S.

The rabbis' enumeration of the ten things created on the eve of Shabbat also serves to explain, and sometimes reassure us—from the mouth of Bilaam's donkey, which spoke to the ram that Abraham sacrificed in place of Isaac, preordaining that God would not make Abraham go through with it. My favorite on this list is the possibility of "tongs, which are made with tongs." After all, how did the blacksmith take the first pair out of the fire? I came to appreciate this rabbinic sense of practicality—and humor, as well—a few years ago on a visit to Belfast, where the enormous cranes that built the RMS Titanic still stood. My tour guide explained that a developer had investigated how he could take them down. The engineers responded that he would need to build new cranes, larger than the ones there, in order to do that. Chuckling, I told my tour guide about this passage from the Mishna. —J.G.K.

lously, so that nothing else was needed once night fell on Shabbat.

There is no repetition of the *Amida* for *ma'ariv*, but on Friday evening there is a pseudo-repetition, an abridged summary. It is preceded by *Vay'khulu* (Genesis 2:1–3) and then continues with *Magen Avot*.

The Kiddush, the sanctification of Shabbat over a cup of wine, was intended primarily to be recited at the home table. It was incorporated into the synagogue service after the *Amida* so that any traveler or wayfarer with nowhere else to go would hear the Kiddush with a group rather than have to recite it while all alone.

Following the late Friday evening service, there is usually a spread of food and beverages that has come to be called the *oneg Shabbat*, or *oneg*, for short. The word "*oneg*" means "pleasure" or "delight," and the phrase *oneg Shabbat* has traditionally referred to much more than food. The *oneg Shabbat* includes the pleasure of

Many explanations have been offered for the addition of *Magen Avot* to the Friday evening service. It may be helpful to recall that before the invention of the printing press in the 16th century, most worshippers did not have a text in front of them. They relied on the leader to chant the words of the prayers to which they could then say, "Amen!—We affirm what you say!" Since there is no repetition of the *Amida* on Friday evening, the congregation hears *Magen Avot* instead, and we express our wishes for the Shabbat that has just begun: May we be satisfied with divine goodness. May we be made joyous through divine deliverance. May our hearts and minds be purified to serve God in truth. —J.J.S.

Some wayfarers were lodged overnight in synagogues, so they might have continued their meals in the same place where they heard Kiddush. —J.G.K.

It is common in American Jewish communities to call the Friday night snacks "*oneg*" and the Shabbat morning snacks "Kiddush." —J.G.K.

studying Torah or singing during a relaxed meal without responsibilities and time constraints, of whiling away the hours of the day with nothing to do but engage in delightful Shabbat activities. *Am m'dushney oneg*, a liturgical phrase referring to the Jewish people, means "a people full of the joy of Shabbat."

Accordingly, the *oneg Shabbat* that follows the Friday evening or Shabbat morning service is about much more than eating and drinking. It is a time and place to welcome newcomers and become acquainted in ways that can lead to further connection and relationship building, to catch up with old friends and maintain a connection with people with whom you are not otherwise friends but whom you value as part of your community. It is also an opportunity to relax with people with whom you may have a more businesslike relationship through serving together on synagogue committees. Ideally, on Shabbat all members of the Jewish community shed their weekday roles and become simply human beings celebrating Shabbat, so

The increased challenge of creating welcoming environments is a direct consequence of the breakdown of traditional Jewish communities in the modern world. In smaller, more homogeneous towns and villages, for better or worse, the locals knew almost everyone in the congregation, and a stranger was easy to pick out in the crowd. Even in North American areas of first and second settlement in the early-to-mid-20th century, neighborhoods were pretty stable. That is no longer the case. Given the frequency with which people move, the fact that Jews no longer live in Jewish neighborhoods or suburbs, and the much greater diversity in the lifestyles of Jews, synagogues no longer automatically feel like home. Often in smaller communities, individuals take it upon themselves to approach and engage people with whom they are not acquainted and who are standing alone. In larger congregations, it is often helpful to have a rotation of "greeters"—people who assume this role in a given week. —J.J.S.

that political tension, hierarchy and other interpersonal barriers are diminished significantly.

While communities should generally create welcoming environments in which strangers and newcomers feel comfortable and enthusiastically embraced (*hakhnasat orḥim*), that value is even more important at events such as the *oneg Shabbat*. It is difficult to enter a synagogue building and service if you don't know anyone there, and that difficulty is magnified exponentially at a social hour.

In keeping with the value that a community places on promoting health and wellness (*b'riyut*), those responsible for ordering and providing food for the *oneg Shabbat* do well to offer sugarless desserts and nonalcoholic alternatives to wine. For a significant number of people, attending the *oneg* can be a stressful experience of resisting the temptation to eat food or drink that can damage their

People often report that they join synagogue communities because they feel welcome, but that they remain in synagogue communities because of the people they have met there with whom they have become close. This dynamic reveals that welcoming is not automatic; it takes the conscious efforts of individuals and communities. —J.G.K.

We should also create a culture in which people feel as comfortable as possible about sharing their struggles to receive support. The myth that there are "no Jewish alcoholics" is alive and well in some quarters, and not talking about addiction, recovery and sobriety risks making people feel alone or invisible. —J.G.K.

Many communities serve nondairy baked goods at their Friday night *oneg* so as to avoid a *ḳashrut* conflict for those who have eaten a meat dinner. As our nutritional knowledge of the destructive role of trans-fatty acids increases, we should also be thoughtful about the ingredients in pareve (nondairy, nonmeat) desserts from the local kosher bakery—often margarine or shortening—that contain problematic partially hydrogenated oils. —J.G.K.

health and well-being. The food alternatives provided by the community signal its support of their efforts to transcend compulsive behavior. Providing alternatives follows the biblical instruction that "you should not place a stumbling block before the blind." (Leviticus 19:14)

Shabbat Morning at Home

Shabbat morning is a particularly good time to awaken with the words that Jews traditionally recite every morning: "*Modeh/Modah ani lefanekha*"—"I am thankful and acknowledge you . . . for compassionately restoring my soul to me; great is your faithfulness." It is a morning when we are not compelled to rush to work, when we have some leisure to appreciate our lives and everything that is good in them.

It is up to each of us to determine how best to extend the sense of sanctity and blessedness that was generated on Friday evening, but it is important to do something

Writing in 1934, at a time when most American Jews had to work on Saturday, Mordecai Kaplan suggested that people try to arrange their work and other schedules to allow them to keep Shabbat morning free to attend synagogue, even if they then had to report for work in the afternoon. This early foray into avoiding the "all-or-nothing" approach to observance became a foundation of future Reconstructionist discussions about Shabbat, including the one you are holding in your hands right now. —R.H.

that keeps Shabbat time sacred, lest we inadvertently reinforce the larger society's prejudice that moments of holiness happen exclusively in the synagogue or in formal prayer. You may devote some time to meditation or chanting, perhaps to some journaling or a leisurely walk or a vigorous jog—something that you would love to do every morning, if you just had the time. On Shabbat we have the time.

Breakfast

Traditionally Jews do not eat a full breakfast before going to synagogue and davening *shaḥarit* (the morning prayer service). This is an unremarkable practice on weekdays,

There's a Hasidic story about a *tzadiḳ* who didn't come out of his bedroom one morning. His worried students came knocking at the door, only to find their *rebbe* stuck in the throes of one line of prayer. The *rebbe* had recited each word with such *ḳavana* that when he began the phrase, "Grateful am I before You," he felt the divine presence right in front of him and thus couldn't finish the word "*lefaneḳha*." (Conveniently, this meant he didn't get far enough to assign a gender to the divine, either.) —J.M.

When I was growing up, I ate a bowl of cereal first thing each morning, and when I went to Jewish summer camp for the first time, it was challenging to me that breakfast came after *shaḥarit* on weekday mornings. As an adult who loves food, I have become more tolerant of not eating right away. —J.G.K.

When I was a kid at Jewish summer camp, we said Kiddush and ate cake and hard-boiled eggs before the Torah reading on Shabbat morning, a model I have also seen at a minyan in Jerusalem that is known for its lengthy services. The tradition at Camp JRF is to make breakfast on Shabbat the one optional meal of the week. Campers can eat at a leisurely pace, sleep late or split the difference. Shabbat morning services and lunch follow. —J.G.K.

when the service occurs early and ends quickly. On Shabbat morning, however, neither of these conditions apply, so traditionally observant people usually have some coffee and cake (something less than a full meal).

For many of us, this custom does not work. Shabbat services often begin midmorning and extend past noon; nothing less than a full, satisfying meal can sustain many of us through these hours. Whether you cook on Shabbat or not, this is an opportunity to enhance the celebration of Shabbat by serving a festive Shabbat breakfast or brunch for everyone in the household.

Competing Activities

North American Jews live in two civilizations. Along with all of the blessings and benefits of residing in an open society in which we are fully integrated, there are inevitable and persistent challenges as the greater culture competes for our time. As adults, we can choose to schedule activities so that they do not compete with synagogue attendance or do not occur on Shabbat at all.

If we are parents, however, the challenge increases as we decide whether or not to permit our children to participate in recreational programs that occur on Shabbat. Few

In my household, we consider it a mitzvah to have cake for breakfast on Shabbat if there is some left over from Friday night—not because it's less than a formal meal, but because it's a delight! —J.A.S.

A seemingly mundane but actually meaningful interfaith initiative on which Jewish and Christian leaders could collaborate would be requesting—perhaps demanding—that games not begin until weekend afternoons. —J.G.K.

of us live in neighborhoods or towns where there are sufficient numbers of Jews to warrant that Little League games, for example, not be scheduled on Saturday mornings. Parents inclined to keep their children with them in synagogue and at home on Shabbat risk facing their children's resentment at being deprived; success requires that we ensure that our Shabbat observance have meaning, power, joy and commitment that can be conveyed intergenerationally. Shabbat is indeed a treasure worth bestowing as an inheritance, but that is no small task.

As discussed above, the difference between contemporary Jews and previous generations is that we have a choice about whether and how to observe Shabbat. When we don't have a choice—such as when the synagogue requires pre-*b'ney mitzvah* students to attend services on Shabbat morning as a requirement for becoming *b'ney mitzvah*—we comply. In most other cases, we do have a choice, and we exercise it. On any given Shabbat, most

Because I am a parent of young children, my current Shabbat morning synagogue practice focuses on experiencing Shabbat through the eyes and play of my children. My *ḳavana* (intention) is to appreciate the moment as holy time (whether we are at "tot Shabbat" or the on playground) and not as a forfeiting of my own davening experience. —N.C.M.

Orthodox communities tend to be far more welcoming than liberal ones (especially to men). Visitors are welcomed warmly, offered honors and invited for Shabbat meals. Formal surveys and anecdotal reports agree that many individuals who visit synagogues feel tentative or even frightened, and they are turned off by the inaccessibility of services and of the community of regulars attending them. Most congregants don't realize we are perpetuating a culture of exclusiveness. To better translate our intentions into reality, we need to willingly assume the mitzvah of *haḳhnasat orḥim* and get better at adopting patterns of behavior that concretely demonstrate we welcome guests. —D.W.

Jews do not attend synagogue services. This is not primarily because prayer services have become less meaningful; vibrant communities and inspiring services increase attendance, but even with them, most people do not attend.

If Shabbat observance is attractive and important to you and you do not warm to the idea of spending Friday evening and/or Shabbat morning in a synagogue, then it is up to you to craft a Shabbat practice that speaks to you. In the section "Nontraditional Practice" below, there are suggestions for ways to approach that challenge.

Shabbat Morning Services

Jews who attend a synagogue service on Shabbat morning are there for many different reasons. They may find it meaningful to spend time with members of their community. They may find meaning in personal prayer. They may have a nostalgic attachment to the words and melodies of the prayers. They may be honoring their grandparents or parents, with whom they attended services when they were younger. They may find the *d'var Torah* or sermon stimulating, and they may enjoy the interactions during the congregational discussion. They may be uplifted and inspired when they join together with others in song. They may be committed to showing up because they want the community to survive. They may find deep connection to their Jewish heritage by developing liturgical skills such as chanting from the Torah. They may feel a loyal attachment to the rabbi for pastoral services that s/he has rendered, and/or to the community for having been helpful during a difficult period. They may be there to attend a bar or bat mitzvah ceremony, or to recite Kaddish.

All of these motivations—and many more—are honorable and significant. Belonging to the Jewish people as a whole or to a particular Jewish community is the basis upon which all Jewish beliefs, practices and values rest. It is remarkable nevertheless that so many people who attend synagogue worship services are less than completely comfortable with praying. Large numbers of non-Orthodox North American Jews are uncomfortable with the idea of communicating with God in prayer. Many are uncertain about the existence of God, and if they do believe, their image of God often does not resemble the images that they find in the words of the siddur (prayer book). They may think of God as a force, the Source of Life, the Ground of Being, or the Mystery of Existence. Most of them rarely think of God as a being who listens to and responds to petitions. In a pinch, they may ask God to heal or comfort a loved one. However, on an ordinary day when they have no pressing needs, addressing God may be embarrassing.

Many non-Orthodox North American Jews do not have the same level of literacy with Jewish practice and the prayer book that their Orthodox counterparts have, and many feel challenged or embarrassed by this as well. —J.G.K.

Any list of God's names is usually made up of all nouns, encouraging us to think of God as Being/Entity. We might also think of God as verb: Becoming, Liberating (not the Liberating One, but Liberating itself). Or we might think of God as an imperative: Love! —J.A.S.

Another reason to pray is that it provides an opportunity for reflection and for *musar*—reflecting on our values, on what ways we are living in accordance with our

What might it mean to pray if we are not asking for something? Here are a few suggestions that you may want to explore in the interest of cultivating a prayer life:

- Cultivating gratitude (*hodaya*). Since we are alive, we have a lot to be thankful for. It is easy to take our blessings for granted. The way to become a more grateful person is to practice noticing things for which we are grateful.
- Cultivating equanimity *(hashva'a*). Left to our own nonprayerful devices, we tend to focus on how to manipulate reality to correspond to our desires. Through prayer we develop the capacity to be grateful for reality as it is, with all of its positive and negative aspects. We are then better able to remain in the present moment and appreciate it.
- Blessing practice (*b'rakha*). If we do nothing during the service other than send blessings and good wishes to others and to ourselves, chances are that we will emerge more openhearted.
- Discerning holiness (*kedusha*). Try to scan the last day or week, asking at every point: Where is the holiness/mystery/divine opportunity in this situation? You will emerge with a heightened appreciation for the sanctity of every moment.

values and in what ways we want to sharpen and refine our actions and awareness to be more thoroughly in line with our deepest values and ideals. —M.M.

As the Habad Hasidim say, better to eat in order to pray, than to pray in order to eat. —J.M.

Each of these is a prayer practice. There are countless others. Most forms of prayer are not requests. Prayer is primarily a discipline that shapes the way we think, feel and experience the universe. If you so wish, any of these practices can develop in you a sense of ongoing awareness that there is more to reality than can be measured in a laboratory.

The siddur is an anthology of prayers composed over the centuries that seek to lead us into a prayerful state. Traditionally, a Jewish man would recite the same words over and over again, so that the words became embedded in multiple layers of his consciousness. At any given worship service, one or another of the phrases of the familiar liturgy may have sparkled unexpectedly with meaning. Even when that did not happen, the repetition of the words was an ample reminder of the reality of God and of one's relationship with God.

The siddur, which accumulated Jewish prayers through centuries and millennia, is a history of the Jewish heart. —J.G.K.

I believe that the siddur, the Torah and all holy texts were written by individuals grasping for language to describe their own apprehension of the divine. They are not always successful in capturing such experiences in words. Much of our sacred text is written in poetry and metaphor intended to convey an impression rather than to describe God literally. If we can approach these words with curiosity and openness to the mystery that they conceal, holy texts can open doorways to our own experience of the holy. Each generation writes its own texts and commentaries in an effort to reframe the experience of the divine in contemporary language. —B.P.

The siddur is not a haphazard anthology, but an intentional and carefully structured one, leading us step by step along a spiritual journey. —J.A.S.

Prayer serves the dual purpose of reminding us of our responsibilities and internal truths and demonstrating our constant need for God's goodness. The overlap of these lenses produces an emotional and spiritual yearning for God's presence. —J.M.S.

Because so many of us no longer have the experience and expertise to employ the traditional liturgy as it was intended, we modify worship techniques in order to achieve a similar objective. Those of us who attend services may want to adopt one of the suggestions above, engaging in our own private personal practice while sitting in synagogue.

Shaḥarit—*The Morning Service*

The Shabbat morning service consists of the following components:

- Preliminary prayers—the morning blessings (*Birkhot Hashaḥar*)
- *P'sukey D'zimra*—a collection of psalms and other songs of praise
- The *shaḥarit* (morning) service—the Shema and its surrounding *b'rakhot* (blessings), and the *Amida* (standing, individually recited prayer)
- The service for taking out and returning the Torah scroll, and the Torah reading
- The *d'var Torah* (homily) and its discussion
- The *musaf* (additional) service (usually omitted in liberal worship)
- Closing prayers—including the *Aleynu* and the Mourners' Kaddish

Preliminary Prayers

Atifat tallit (donning the prayer shawl). The *b'rakha "lehitatef batzitzit"* (*Kol Haneshamah: Shabbat Veḥagim*, page 143) is a blessing for the mitzvah of wrapping oneself in a tallit, often a daily practice for Jewish adults. Those who have a daily prayer practice sometimes own a weekday tallit and a more elaborate or decorative tallit for Shabbat, but that is not required. Many synagogues provide tallitot near the entrance to the sanctuary for those who do not bring their own.

The tallit is an aid for concentration and focus. It brings a sense of being *taḥat kanfey Hashekhina*, protected beneath the sheltering divine presence, and intimately connected with God. On Shabbat the sense of being enveloped in the presence of God is often particularly

In many progressive congregations, women as well as men now wear tallitot, though this practice was unimaginable 50 years ago. —D.W.

Donning the tallit as one enters into the service, whether at the beginning or when the service is already underway, is an opportune time for centering oneself. With the tallit gently cascading over one's head and face, one can add an intention for the morning's prayer, or a personal prayer, or even a request that one's heart be opened in prayer. Beneath the folds of the tallit, one can feel both separate from all of the surrounding commotion of life and connected to the Source of All and to one's inner life. —B.P.

When I am reciting the blessing while covered by my tallit, I sometimes imagine being inside the *Mishkan*, the holy tent of God, breathing in the divine presence. —N.C.M.

Some choose to linger a moment under the canopy of the tallit and read a series of verses from Psalm 36, beginning, "How dear is your loving kindness, O God, for humans take shelter in the shadow of your wings." The image of a crane or stork shielding its young with its wings is such a tender way to enter prayer with a palpable feeling of being surrounded by God's love. —J.M.S.

intense because of all the other Shabbat practices that lead us in this direction.

Before reciting the *b'rakha* (blessing), you hold the tallit up in front of you, with the *atara* (neckband) facing you. You recite the words, kiss the *atara*, and then drape the tallit over your shoulders, so that the *atara* is at the top, resting against the back of your neck and facing outward.

Preliminary Blessings (*Birkhot Hashahar*)

(*Kol Haneshamah: Shabbat Vehagim*, pages 152–161). These 15 *b'rakhot* were originally intended to be recited in the home upon awakening and were only later added to the synagogue service. For this reason, they are expressions of gratitude for an assortment of blessings that one might appreciate upon first arising, but, in truth, most of the sentiments expressed here are relevant at any time of day. Their recitation starts the day on a note of apprecia-

A *kavana* for tallit builds on the teaching that being wrapped in a tallit is like being enfolded in the wings of the *Shekhina*—the loving presence of the divine: As you drape the tallit around your head or shoulders and recite the blessing, invoke memories of a time or person with whom you have felt wrapped in protective love. Allow that memory to fill the space between you and the tallit so that you can enhance the feeling and carry it with you into your prayers. —N.H.M.

These morning blessings can be read literally or figuratively as opportunities to count our blessings. As we begin the day, we take an accounting of our lives and express gratitude for what we have: the parts of our bodies that are working, the steady earth beneath our feet, the clothes and food and other gifts that fill our needs, and the fact that we are alive. The blessings express appreciation for nonmaterial gifts as well: freedom, strength to face the day and the spiritual awareness that lifts us above the challenges we will certainly face. —B.P.

tion. If you arrive after they are recited, you may want to recite them individually.

Also included in this preliminary section are *Ma Tovu* (*Kol Haneshamah: Shabbat Veḥagim*, page 141), a meditation on being in a house of worship, *Asher Yatzar* (page 163), an appreciation of the wondrous workings of the human body, and *Elohay Neshama* (pages 164–167), recognition for the gift of a pure soul and of the fragility of life. Other poems and prayers are often added as a way to set the tone for the themes of the service.

P'sukey D'zimra

In rabbinic literature, "pious ones" are lauded for praying for an hour before they begin praying. A prayerful state is not something that one can jump into without some preparation. This value has been concretized in the Jewish liturgy with the introduction and expansion of *P'sukey D'zimra* (*Kol Haneshamah: Shabbat Veḥagim*, pages 176–241), a collection of psalms and prayers that

Maimonides explains that *Elohay Neshama* is actually the conclusion of blessings we might say before we go to sleep at night. Perhaps our entire night of sleep, together with our subconscious anxieties, hopes and dreams, is all part of one great nightly prayer. —J.G.K.

When I shared with congregants that my friend has a personal practice of saying all 150 psalms every morning at the Western Wall, some of the synagogue members suggested that we try it. One Shabbat morning, a small group of us gathered early. By the time services began, we were about 80 percent through reciting the psalms. The framers of most siddurim place Psalm 150, the final one in the Book of Psalms, at the very end of *P'sukey D'zimra*. Thus, we have an opportunity to complete the Psalter every morning, regardless of whether or not we begin it! —J.G.K.

function to enhance our awareness of the blessedness, majesty and mystery of this world, for which we are grateful.

Traditional Ashkenazic liturgical practice has historically accomplished this objective by having each worshipper whisper the words of this section of the service individually, as if in private conversation with the addressee. The *sh'li'aḥ tzibur* (service leader) reads openings and closings aloud in order to keep everyone roughly in the same place. While this mode may seem exotic and off-putting to those accustomed to a North American (Protestant-influenced) worship style, it can be very effective as a way of deepening one's state of prayerfulness.

One obstacle is that this presumes that the worshipper is familiar with the words of the liturgy and able to read rapidly. If you are not familiar with the prayer and you find yourself attracted to this mode of prayer, you may want to read as quickly as you can, without being concerned about the amount of ground you are able to cover. With repetitive practice, you will move more and more quickly. And since the whole of *P'sukey D'zimra* is there as a preparatory prayer practice, you needn't worry about the content of what you are omitting.

Other traditional Jewish communities have historically proceeded through *P'sukey D'zimra* with the hazzan leading the congregation in chanting each line out loud, or in alternating lines responsively. The individual worshippers recite the words of the psalms in singsong fashion, but when one has been chanting fixed texts for one's whole life and knows the liturgy inside and out, there is considerable room for individual internal reflection even as everyone chants the same words together. The words can function as an extended mantra.

In 21st-century North American communities, most worshippers do not possess an intimate familiarity with the Hebrew liturgy. *P'sukey D'zimra* is therefore shortened to a few selections from the traditional texts and/or a few contemporary readings in English. In many groups it is a time for spirited singing from the Book of Psalms, through which people who are otherwise largely unfamiliar with the experience of prayer have their hearts touched profoundly, losing themselves in song. Often, participants say that this is the highlight of the service for them.

Sometimes one or two lines are chanted over and over again, either in contemplative melodies or in ecstatic modes. People whose sparse knowledge of Hebrew keeps them from comprehending long passages are able to learn the approximate meaning of a single line or phrase that they chant for substantial periods of time. At a certain point, the chanters no longer pay attention to the words they are chanting, and the prayer transcends a cognitive, linear experience, becoming more embodied and uniting. In the silence after the chant ends, important prayers arise from somewhere other than the conscious mind.

Alternative ways of davening *P'sukey D'zimra* are not necessarily accommodations to ignorance! People with substantial Hebrew literacy may also find repetitive chanting or abbreviated singing to be more useful prayer tools than the traditional full recitation of these psalms. —J.A.S.

I love being in communities that have multiple Shabbat morning options, ranging from meditation to Torah study to yoga to davening. It signals for me a vibrancy and appreciation of pluralism and Jewish diversity. —N.C.M.

In some communities, Jewish meditation services precede or run parallel to the regular *shaḥarit* service. Those who are so inclined thus have a period of time to devote to contemplative practice, and that becomes the functional equivalent of the *P'sukey D'zimra*. Following the medieval philosopher Maimonides, these people often cite the line from Psalms, "To You, silence is praise." (Psalms 65:2) There is a long and distinguished tradition of Jews who have believed that God is beyond verbal description and that contemplative silence is the best way to worship.

In some communities, a Torah study session precedes the worship service. After an hour of reading and discussing the weekly Torah portion, participants, with their minds ignited and their hearts inspired, are better prepared for worship. *Talmud Torah*, the study of Torah, is frequently characterized in rabbinic texts in terms of heat, light and fire. Sacred Torah study is itself a form of prayer.

Sḥaharit

The main part of the morning service on Shabbat morning begins with *Shoḥen Ad Marom* (*Kol Haneshamah: Shabbat Veḥagim*, page 241), a section that pictures God dwelling on high, being praised and thanked by the righteous and by myriads of worshippers. The scene, which extends through *Yishtabaḥ* (page 243) and paints an image of the mightiest of rulers in an unimaginably vast palace

I have heard Rabbi Shawn Zevit insert the completion of the verse (Isaiah 57:25) from which *Shoḥen Ad Marom* is drawn: God dwells on high, but is with the downtrodden and lowly of spirit to bring life [to them]. —J.A.S.

filled by masses of grateful subjects, may be off-putting to contemporary worshippers who are not comfortable with the implicit hierarchy and obsequiousness. There are many ways to relate to this image. Here are a few:

- Given that God is a mystery beyond conceptualization and accurate description, every image is by definition inaccurate. Liturgical images do not aspire to describe God; rather, they employ metaphors from our experience to evoke desired responses in us. In this instance, they seek to evoke awe at the unfathomable and wondrous vastness of Creation.
- Many of us find ourselves caught in the lure of the illusion of self-reliance, as if we could control our destiny if we but acted optimally. Imagery that reminds us of our vulnerability and inability to control our fortunes is a great and ever needed gift. Attributing omnipotence to God, however accurate or inaccurate that is, serves to reassure us that we are not solely responsible for everything.
- Expressing praise and gratitude is never gratuitous because of their beneficial effect on our own souls. If there is a God who is aware of what we utter in prayer, that God is not enhanced by our praise and gratitude. We, on the other hand, can transform our own lives by appreciating this morning's sunrise or

this glass of water. Taking things for granted reduces the scope and significance of our lives.

Bar'khu (page 247)—Having worked thus far to achieve a sense of praise and appreciation, we rise to bless the Holy One of Blessing.

Shema and Its Surrounding Blessings (Sh'ma Uvirkhoteha) (pages 246–291)—Two blessings precede the Shema. The first gives thanks for the natural world, and the second gives thanks for the gift of Torah. On

The *Bar'ḳhu* is often described as the call to prayer. In many liberal congregations, this is the first time in the service that we check to be sure we have a minyan, a quorum of ten adult Jews. When we respond as a minyan to the leader's call, we acknowledge that we have come together as a holy community, all of us contributing in our own unique voices, to create a whole that is larger than the sum of its parts. We also acknowledge our interdependence, with the *Bar'ḳhu* inviting us to explore the many ways, known and unknown, that we are connected to all the other people who are worshipping with us. —B.P.

In the call to worship, we bless the transcendent God, the source of life, the creator of the universe, and we bless the immanent God, who dwells within the community that is gathered, and who shines in the faces of our family and our friends. Sometimes I invite members of the congregation to acknowledge God's immanence by introducing themselves or saying hello to someone sitting nearby. —D.W.

The cycle of creation-revelation-redemption is acted out through the cycle of the three blessings that surround the Shema: *yotzer, ahava rabba,* and *ga'al Yisrael.* —J.M.S.

The core focus of the first blessing before the Shema is on the heavenly lights, which are mentioned in its concluding blessing. While this *b'raḳha* can be broadly understood to be about nature, its broad focus can also be understood to be morning or creation or physics or, attitudinally, awe (as opposed to the focus on love in the second *b'raḳha*). —J.A.S.

Shabbat, the poem *El Adon* (pages 252–255) is sung as part of the nature blessing. It pictures God reigning in splendor over the celestial world. Also part of the text of the nature blessing is a passage that describes the heavenly hosts as engaged perpetually in a single activity—attesting to the holiness of God, repeating "*kadosh, kadosh, kadosh*" ("holy, holy, holy") for all eternity. This image is intended to prompt us to inch closer to a state of being in which everything we do at every moment attests to the blessed existence of the Source of All. We recite "*kadosh, kadosh, kadosh*" in the *Kedusha*. What if the entirety of our lives reflected the fact that we are created in the divine image?

The second blessing, for the gift of Torah, begins on Shabbat with the words "*Ahava raba ahavtanu*" ("You have loved us with a great love") and ends "*ohev amo* Yis*rael*" ("who loves the people Israel"). In this rabbinic liturgical formulation, God's love for us is manifest primarily in the gift of the Torah and the commandments—

Franz Rosenzweig, the German Jewish existentialist philosopher, suggested that this prayer arc is a model for learning about love—as we are loved and experience love, we then must go out and, inspired by divine love, give love to others. —N.H.M.

In non-Reconstructionist siddurim, the ending of the second *brakha* before the Shema is "*haboḥer b'amo Yisrael b'ahava*"—"who chooses his people Israel with love." —J.A.S.

Another connection between love and Torah is that loving relationship implies thoughtfulness and obligation. Torah and mitzvah are ways of living thoughtfully and recognizing the obligations that arise from our relationship with others, with our heritage and with God. In this sense, Torah is not so much a gift motivated by love as it is the implication of the love itself. —J.A.S.

that is, the Jewish heritage. We are the recipients of divine love collectively as a people. Since most of the liturgy is phrased in the collective, the individual must address God personally in her or his own voice beneath the collective formulations. Focusing on or chanting "*Ahava raba ahavtanu*" is an opportune place in the liturgy to cultivate a sense of being loved individually.

The Shema is the central prayer of the Jewish liturgy, traditionally recited daily in the morning and evening services, as well as before retiring for the night. It is also the declaration made by a Jew before death. Its opening line is a declaration of God's unity. Three paragraphs, each with its own themes, follow: first, the commandment to love God, to be perpetually mindful of the commandments, and to transmit them to the next generation; second, the promise of blessings if and only if we obey the commandments; and third, the commandment to wear fringes (*tzitzit*) as focal objects that remind us to follow the commandments.

The Shema is the boundary prayer. It is said at the boundary of day and night, night and day, and life and death. It is placed physically in the mezuzah at the boundary of inside and outside. It proclaims the unity of God on both sides of all these boundaries. —J.A.S.

In his book *Seek My Face: A Jewish Mystical Theology*, Rabbi Arthur Green describes the first line of the Shema as connecting to the unity we experience between our souls and the divine, and the second line of the Shema, "*Barukh shem k'vod*," connecting us to the sparks of divinity that exist within the diversity of all Creation. —N.C.M.

The practice of gathering the *tzitzit* is supported by the command, "*uritem otam*"—"and you should look at them"—in the third paragraph of the Shema. —J.G.K.

In some communities, it is customary to gather the fringes of the tallit together in one's hand before the start of the Shema. Then you cover your eyes as you say or chant the first line. In other communities, the congregation rises to sing the first line of the Shema, treating it as a public declaration of faith. It is customary in some communities to kiss the fringes when you reach each of the three occurrences of the word "*tzitzit*" in the third paragraph, as well as when you utter the final word, "*emet.*" In other communities, one simply looks at the fringes without kissing them.

The blessing following the Shema (pages 286–291) has the theme of redemption (*g'ula*). It recalls our redemption from Egyptian bondage in the past and anticipates the redemption that will occur in the messianic age, implicitly a consequence if we follow the commandments. It is a moment to cultivate an awareness of the injustices and imperfections in our world and to rededicate ourselves to realizing our vision of an age that we would call "messianic."

Recalling the redemption from Egypt and the joyous celebration of the Israelites after miraculously crossing the Red Sea provides an opportunity to reflect on our own oppression and liberation. The Exodus as an archetype for struggle and deliverance gives us hope as we face our own challenges—personal, communal and universal. —B.P.

The themes of creation, revelation and redemption all contribute to the Shabbat morning service. The opening blessings and psalms remind us of Creation. The passages surrounding the Shema and referring to the light of Torah point to revelation. And the *mi ḳhamoḳha* and ensuing blessings that link to the *Amida* bring us to redemption. In this way, we experience the unfolding themes of Shabbat all within one service. —B.P.

The *Amida* (standing individually recited prayer) for Shabbat (pages 294–323) shares the first three and last three *b'rakhot* (blessings) with the weekday *Amida*. However, the 13 middle weekday *b'rakhot,* each of which asks for something, are replaced by a single blessing for Shabbat. This is because on Shabbat, we don't engage in petitionary prayer. It is a day to appreciate our blessings rather than focus on things we don't have.

Communities take different approaches to the *Amida*. On the most traditional end of the spectrum, some communities stand toward the end of the *g'ula* blessing, and each individual davens the entire *Amida* individually. When everyone has finished, the *sh'li'aḥ tzibur* (prayer leader) chants the *Amida* from the beginning, with everyone rising for the *Kedusha*, after which the leader continues to chant the remainder of the *Amida*, through the blessing for peace (page 321).

Some communities begin by chanting the first three *b'rakhot* together, including the *Kedusha*. After the *Kedusha*, each individual remains standing and completes the *Amida* individually. This method is called *Heykha Kedusha*. In other places, after the *Kedusha*, everyone sits down, and selections from the rest of the *Amida* are sung communally.

The *Amida* contains the space in the service that is dedicated for individual, private prayer. The words of the liturgy are intended as aids, prompting us to enter into a variety of different prayerful states. *Kol Haneshamah* offers a thematic heading at the beginning of each blessing, so that the worshipper can be prompted thematically without having to read the liturgical text, in case doing so would be an obstacle to prayerful experience. *Kol Haneshamah* also offers several "Alternative *Amidot*" (pages 725–730). In addition, a *Shiviti* (traditional art for contemplation) precedes each *Amida* (pages 89, 293, 595) for the worshipper who prefers a visual prompt to a verbal one. Finally, we are always invited during the individual time of the *Amida* to set aside all of these aids and to pray in our own words or to stand or sit contemplatively and wordlessly.

There was a time in the middle of the 20th century when many liberal synagogues restricted individual, quiet, prayer time to a few moments or eliminated it altogether. This reflected the discomfort of the Jews of that time with the practice of prayer; they did not know "how" to pray, sometimes confusing their ignorance of the traditional liturgy with their inability to pray. This practice has become less common. Increasingly, people have come to cherish the opportunity to pray individually alongside fellow worshippers in a synagogue setting. Individual prayer and communal prayer nourish each other.

The Torah Service

As discussed above, while the theme of Creation is predominant on Friday evening, on Shabbat morning the theme of revelation is most prominent. The reading from the scroll of the Torah is a weekly reenactment of the mythic moment of the revelation of the Torah on Mount Sinai to Moses and the Israelites and a reaffirmation of the *brit* (covenant) between God and the Jewish people upon which our communities are founded. Rabbinic midrash affirms that the divine voice that spoke to Moses and the Israelites continues to speak at every moment, so that each of us can hear the voice if we prepare ourselves to listen.

The Torah scroll has a central place in the universe of Jewish meaning. In the simplest sense, the Five Books of Moses are written on parchment by a scribe (*sofer*), whose work conforms to an elaborate set of specifications—number of columns, number of lines on a column, and specially designated words. Some rabbinic traditions claimed that the entire five books were dictated by God to Moses on Mount Sinai. Other traditions limited the reve-

I see the marriage metaphor of Mount Sinai and *Kabbalat Shabbat* repeated in the way we approach the Torah scroll with a special level of care and reverence, similarly to the way in which we treat an intimate partner. —J.G.K.

Every time we hear, read and interpret Torah, it is as if we are experiencing revelation anew. We may bring new life experiences to our reading of Torah. We may hear a new interpretation from someone else. Each generation adds a new understanding to what has been spoken in the past. When we take out the Torah scroll, the verses of the liturgy invite us to imagine that we are standing at Sinai, as if for the first time. —B.P.

lation at Sinai to the two tablets that contained the Ten Commandments (*Aseret Hadibrot*).

In a broader sense, the Torah scroll represents the entirety of Jewish tradition. For the early rabbis, the oral Torah (*Torah sheb'al peh*) was revealed at Sinai to Moses with the written Torah (*Torah shebikhtav*) and was transmitted intact through the generations, so that the entirety of Jewish law (*halakha*) and lore (*agada*) literally derives directly from the words on the scroll. For those of us who

In the 1940s, Rabbi Ira Eisenstein and Judith Kaplan Eisenstein collaborated on a very popular cantata—a combination of spoken word and sung performance—called "What is Torah?" In a 20-minute piece, choirs ranging from as small as 12 singers to as many as 400 sang and spoke their way through nine expositions about the breadth of Torah:

> Torah is the Creation of the world . . .
> Torah is the Sabbath . . .
> Torah is the pastoral life . . .
> Torah is the epic of Egyptian slavery and emancipation . . .
> Torah is ethical idealism . . .
> Torah is a parchment scroll . . .
> Torah is a study room, a lullaby, a prayer . . .
> Torah is a land . . .
> Torah is a light unto the nations . . .

—D.W.

Extending the mythic truth of the oral Torah opens for us the possibility that the very conversation we are having about Torah at this very moment was given at Mount Sinai. Sometimes I think that for Reconstructionists, the idea that oral Torah in the broadest sense of the term is revealed by God makes more sense than the idea that the written Torah was divinely given; Judaism does not exist without the Jewish people. —J.G.K.

In his book *Sacred Fragments: Recovering Theology for the Modern Jew*, Rabbi Neil Gillman talks about the plasticity of Jewish myth as embodied in the concept of written and oral Torah. Our ongoing interpretation needs to be flexible enough to accommodate the needs of changing times (oral Torah) while still grounding ourselves in a fixed, firm and unchanging text of (written) Torah. —N.C.M.

do not believe that this is literally the case and instead understand Judaism to be a religious civilization that has evolved through the centuries and continues to evolve today, the mythic truth of this claim nevertheless remains powerful. That is, as we ourselves continue to adapt our inherited traditions in our own day, we do so by interpreting and reinterpreting the words of the Torah—the same words in this scroll that prior generations of Jews have interpreted. The scroll stands as the clearest and most moving link that we have to the ongoing chain of tradition.

Aron Hakodesh—Torah scrolls are kept in the *Aron Hakodesh* (Holy Ark), most often located on the eastern wall of the sanctuary (in the Western Hemisphere), so that the Holy Ark is in front of the congregation, which faces it. When the ark is not on the Eastern wall, many congre-

The Holy Ark is usually placed on the wall closest to Jerusalem so that the congregation will face in that direction; which wall that is depends on where in the world you are. An exception occurs when the building served another function before it became a synagogue, and it is not architecturally practical to place the ark on the traditional wall. —D.A.T.

There is no halakhic requirement that the *aron hakodesh* or the *bima* be raised, though it often is. In our recent project to rebuild our synagogue, we chose to keep the *aron* and the *bima* on the same level as the pews. This reflects our desire to have a completely accessible Torah for everyone. While ramps and handrails are important accommodations, we wanted to equalize the experience. —N.H.M.

In facing toward Jerusalem, we form a great circle whose mythic center on the Temple Mount is and was physically empty space. And on the other side of the circle are the faces of other worshippers. The Talmud (*Berakhot* 30a) teaches: "In the east, turn your face to the west; in the west, turn your face to the east; in the south, turn your face to the north; in the north, turn your face to the south. So you find all Israel to be directing their hearts to one place." And Martin Buber teaches in *I and Thou*, "The extended lines of relation meet in the eternal Thou." —J.A.S.

gations face it for the service and turn to face east for the *Amida*. Thus, regard for the Torah scroll supersedes even regard for Zion and Jerusalem.

Taking the Scroll Out of the Ark (pages 382–393)—As the ark is opened, all those who are able to rise do so. The liturgical melodies are up-tempo, almost martial, as we praise God's sovereignty and majesty and pledge our loyalty and trust, hoping that all of our wishes will be fulfilled for the good. The scroll is then removed from the ark, and the leader sings out the first line of the Shema in a call-and-response pattern. The Torah scroll is then carried around the sanctuary. As it passes, people often touch its cover with their *tzitzit* (fringes) or siddur and then kiss

Children may come up to open the ark. For the congregation, this has the effect of juxtaposing the greatest symbol of our tradition (Torah) with the inheritors of its future. For the children, they are vouchsafed a personal experience of the mystery and awe engendered by the Torah. —J.M.S.

Some communities add special prayers at this moment when the congregation is standing before the open ark. Congregants in a Moroccan synagogue I used to attend in Israel would say a blessing for the well-being of soldiers of the Israel Defense Forces at this time. —J.G.K.

In addition to standing when the ark is opened or a Torah is being held during a service, we show our respect for the Torah in other ways. It is customary not to turn one's back on a Torah scroll. For this reason, the ark is normally closed while the Torah is carried in procession. Although it may seem rude to turn around when the Torah passes by and to look at the people behind you in the congregation, this is perfectly acceptable! All of these customs demonstrate our reverence for learning, in the same way that some people stand when a sage or an elder enters the room. —B.P.

The Torah procession can be a confusing ritual to see, experience or even explain. Where does the line get drawn between revering the Torah and idolatry? One way to look at the practice is that by reaching out to touch the scroll as it processes, we are each claiming it as our own inheritance. —N.H.M.

the *tzitzit* or prayer book. In some places it is customary not to touch or kiss the scroll directly because of the sanctity attributed to it.

Reading of the Torah—As the Torah procession concludes, the service leader places the scroll on a table at the front of the sanctuary. Its coverings and adornments are removed, and the scroll is then lightly re-covered, so that it does not remain bare when not in use. At this point, there are generally three people at the table: the person who will *leyn* (chant from the scroll); the *gabay rishon*, who supervises and runs the Torah reading service; and the *gabay sheni*, who follows the reading closely, assists the reader as needed, and corrects any significant errors in pronunciation. Chanting or even reading from a Torah scroll requires much skill and preparation since the scroll's

"*Leyn*" is Yiddish for "read." In Hebrew, the person who reads from the Torah scroll is called the *ba'al(at) ķ'ri'a* or, in a popular, if grammatically incorrect, folk Hebrew, "*ba'al(at) ķorey.*" —J.A.S.

Different communities have different standards for chanting Torah. In some communities, precision is the most important priority. In these communities, reading is limited to a few highly skilled individuals and occasionally, only to professionals (the rabbi, the cantor, the ritual director or a paid Torah reader). In other communities, participation by the greatest possible number of Torah readers is a priority. Inclusion is usually accompanied by a tolerance for less precise readings. —D.W.

The second *gabay* must find a delicate balance. In some settings, the accurate reading of all of the words and sentence structure is of vital importance. Thus, the *gabay* should correct any mistakes that render a change in meaning. But given that extensive Hebrew knowledge is required to do this well and not overcorrect, how should we proceed? A skilled *gabay* is able to be generally consistent with corrections but tailors his/her approach to the reader's confidence and expertise. Above all, the *gabay* should strive to serve as a guide on the side rather than upstaging the reader. —J.M.S.

text is neither punctuated nor vocalized, nor are the markings for the *trop* (cantillation) found on the scroll. The *leyner* prepares in advance by memorizing the words, the sentences and the melody. Hence, the second *gabay* is needed to assist when the *leyner* needs help. Sometimes one individual chants the entire week's *parasha*. Sometimes a different person chants each aliyah. Before the reading itself, there is often an introduction to the weekly portion that is about to be read.

The *Parashiyot* (weekly Torah portions)—The rabbis divided the Torah into weekly portions so that in ancient Palestine, the Torah was read over three years. In Babylonia and eventually throughout the Jewish world, the entire Torah was read each year on Shabbat, beginning and ending on Simchat Torah. While Orthodox communities and some others chant the entire *parasha* each Shabbat, many now choose to follow what is called the triennial cycle, covering the whole Torah over three years, chanting the first third of the *parasha* in the first year of the cycle, the second third in the second year, and the third in the third. *Kol Haneshamah: Shabbat Veḥagim* includes a chart sug-

The reader doesn't exactly "memorize the words," since it is traditionally required that they be read from the scroll, not recited from memory. The reader memorizes the proper vowels for the words. A reader with sufficient aptitude in biblical Hebrew simply reads the words, having made sure in advance about the pronunciation of any difficult or confusing words. —J.A.S.

Because the Jewish calendar is based on the lunar cycle and an extra lunar month is added seven times in a 19-year cycle in order to keep the lunar year aligned with the solar cycle, and because special holiday portions are read when Shabbat coincides with a holiday, on a few Shabbatot each year a double portion is read. —J.J.S.

gesting how to break each *parasha* in thirds (pages 710–722). Some communities read less than one-third of the *parasha*. There is a balance to be struck among competing priorities: the amounts of time allotted respectively to prayer, to the reading of the Torah and to the study and discussion of the text.

Aliyot—Traditionally, the *parasha* is divided into seven aliyot (literally: ascensions) on Shabbat. In some communities, this number has been reduced to three aliyot, so that each one of them is of greater length. This saves time by reducing the number of persons who are called up to the Torah for an aliyah and recite the *b'rakhot*. Traditionally, the first aliyah was given to a *kohen*, a descendant of the priests who worked in the Second Temple in Jerusalem before it was destroyed in 70 CE, and the second aliyah was given to a *levi*, a descendant of the Levites who worked in the Temple assisting the priests. The other five of the seven aliyot were then given to any other Jew—*Yisrael*. Reconstructionist and many other liberal communities do not reserve aliyot for the *kohen* and the *levi*, in part on egalitarian grounds and in part because if one does not

The performance of interlinear translations—reading or chanting a line in Hebrew, immediately followed by an English translation—can be especially powerful. It preserves the sanctity of the Torah service and at the same time boosts understanding and highlights the Torah's ancient history as an oral text. —D.W.

Although we avoid the *kohen/levi/Yisrael* hierarchy in assigning aliyot in Reconstructionist synagogues, individuals who consider themselves descendants of the *kohanim* and *levi'im* often take great pride in noting their ancestry. This is often a way to pay homage to parents and grandparents and to feel connected to the ancient roots of our tradition. —B.P.

look forward to the messianic rebuilding of a third Temple in Jerusalem and a restoration of its cultic worship, there is no good reason to preserve the special status of descendents of former Temple officiants.

The *gabay rishon* calls up each person honored with an aliyah by name, usually by his or her Jewish name and two parents' Jewish names. If you are being honored and are not already wearing a tallit, one will usually be offered to you for the aliyah. You stand in front of the scroll, generally to the right of the reader, who will open the scroll and point to the place with a *yad* (a ceremonial pointer used so as not to touch the scroll with one's finger). You take the fringes of the tallit and touch the place on the scroll with

It is customary to take the fastest route to the *bima* for an aliyah, as this avoids a delay in the service and demonstrates the person's desire to approach the Torah. It is also customary to take one's time on the way back to one's seat, so as to further treasure one's time at the Torah. —J.G.K.

As structures of families become more diverse, the way people are called up to the Torah may change as well. Jews may choose to be publicly recognized by more—or less—than one patronymic or matronymic. —J.G.K.

In earlier times, the person who came up for an aliyah also read from the Torah scroll itself. By separating the role of Torah reader from that of the one who recites the blessings, we make it possible for many more people to be close to Torah. When you touch the scroll with the *tzitzit* and bring the fringes to your lips, it is as if you yourself were chanting the words of Torah. —B.P.

Many people kiss the *tzitzit* after touching it to the word in the Torah where the *leyner* will begin chanting. —M.M.

"Kissing" the scroll by touching one's *tzitzit* to the blank column nearest the word that begins the aliyah is the most practical choice for extending the longevity of the written script. —J.G.K.

When I hold the *atzey ḥayim*, I have a sense of being connected to the Tree of Life itself, grounding me in the vital force of our heritage. For those who are more com-

them. (If you do not want to don a tallit, you may want to use the fringes of the tallit of the reader, or you may want to use the wimple (the belt that ties up the scroll). You then hold the two wooden handles (*atzey ḥayim*, literally: trees of life) and recite the first Torah blessing. In most settings, the words of the blessing, in Hebrew and transliterated in English, are written in large print on a card next to the scroll for you to read. The reader (along with everyone else) responds to your blessing with "*Amen*" and then chants the aliyah from the scroll. At the conclusion of the passage, the reader points to the endpoint. You touch your fringes to that spot, kiss the fringes, take the scroll handles and recite the second Torah blessing.

The experience of ascending to the Torah for an aliyah, kissing the scroll with your fringes, reciting the blessings

fortable with the blessings, taking hold of the rollers can be a powerful experience. Many people are so nervous about saying the blessings properly that they are distracted by the need to hold a book or page with the blessings. For those who are nervous, taking a breath and grasping the *atzey ḥayim* can create calm and turn the experience into a true honor. —B.P.

When individuals are nervous, they sometimes read the first word of the blessing as the very familiar *barukh* (blessed) rather than the less familiar *Bar'khu* (bless in the imperative). The words are very similar, but their meanings are different. —D.W.

Customs of what or how we touch the Torah vary. I have seen many Jews touch the Torah cover with their hands or even kiss the cover directly. Others avoid touching the Torah cover altogether because they believe such gestures are idolatrous. —J.G.K.

As a congregational rabbi, I have often seen the powerful connection to Jewish tradition reflected in the conscious decision by *b'ney mitzvah* parents to choose a Torah portion for their son or daughter that is the exact same portion that one of them chanted at his or her bar or bat mitzvah many years before. This becomes a literal and spiritual embodiment of *l'dor vador*, passing Jewish tradition from one generation to the next. —S.C.R.

and receiving the blessings of a *Mi Shebeyrakh* prayer is a significant communal honor. You are representing the community as revelation is reenacted and the text of the Torah is symbolically revealed once again. For everyone, but especially for those who are rarely in close proximity to a Torah scroll, it can be a powerful and elevating moment.

Traditionally, an individual adult (actually, a man) was called up for each aliyah. In many communities, it is now also a practice to call up women, couples, or whole family units, reflecting the commitment to egalitarianism. In some communities, aliyot are sometimes defined by category (for example, everyone who is home on break from college) or by experience (for example, everyone who has been troubled by a certain event in the news in the previous week). Aliyot are restricted to adult Jews, but in some communities, non-Jews accompany Jewish members of their households to the Torah.

I want to offer a dissent from the increasingly prevalent custom of making all aliyot into group aliyot. Like the near-ubiquitous custom in liberal synagogues of a congregational recitation of the Mourner's Kaddish, group aliyot submerge individuality and suggest a sameness that on closer inspection is often artificial. My experience of group aliyot, especially those that fall into the category of what I call "liturgical profiling" (for example, "all those who are feeling particularly challenged in some way in their lives this week") is that the people reciting the blessings become the focus and the Torah becomes a prop—especially when those called up are asked, for example, to tell the whole congregation about their specific challenges. —R.H.

The Reconstructionist version of the first blessing differs from the traditional text. Instead of the words, "*asher baḥar banu mikol ha'amim*" ("who has chosen us from among all peoples"), the Reconstructionist text substitutes "*asher kervanu la'avodato*" ("who has brought us close to divine service") (*Kol Haneshamah: Shabbat Veḥagim*, pages 396–399). Traditionally, Jews believed that we were chosen by God to receive the Torah and its commandments and to observe the commandments. For those who do not believe that the Torah was supernaturally revealed by God and who do not believe that all of its commandments continue to be binding, the affirmation of chosenness turns into a claim that the Jewish people are superior to other people, which was not the original intention of the belief in chosenness. To dissociate ourselves from this chauvinistic interpretation at the very moment when we reenact the receiving of the Torah, we alter this phrase in order to affirm that all peoples are equally capa-

Like many liberal synagogues, Reconstructionist communities often find that Shabbat morning attendance is dominated by the family and friends attending the bat or bar mitzvah celebration. Most of those guests, if familiar with the Torah blessings at all, will know the traditional version, but not the Reconstructionist variant. The mitzvah of *hakhnasat orḥim* (hospitality) suggests to me that those invited to recite the blessings for an aliyah ought to be offered the option of which version to use rather than requiring people to stumble over an unfamiliar set of words. If a grandparent says, "*asher baḥar banu mikol ha'amim*"—"who has chosen us from all peoples"—little will change in the balance of the universe. If that same grandparent experiences a moment of awkwardness, embarrassment or discomfort because of unfamiliar words, then something of consequence has happened. That could have been avoided simply by giving priority to comfort and choice over ideological conformity. —R.H.

ble of service to God when they choose to live godly lives. Just as Jewish people have a moral imperative to continue to reconstruct our heritage to reflect our most elevated values, so do all people have a moral imperative to improve their own cultures.

Using the Reconstructionist version of the first *b'rakha* is not required in Reconstructionist communities. It is common to find both versions used for aliyot, even among members of the community. Not everyone finds the above rationale compelling. In fact, you may hear other variations of the wording in a Reconstructionist community—different names for God, different genders for God, modifications of the word "*melekh*" ("king") by people who have difficulty relating to monarchic images for the divine. Some of these variants can be found in *Kol Haneshamah: Shabbat Veḥagim*, page 5.

Gomel Benschen—When a person has recovered from an illness or an accident, has completed a journey, or has

The most powerful moment in the *gomel* blessing occurs when the congregation responds to the one who has said the blessing: "Amen. May God, who has bestowed every goodness on you, continue to bestow every goodness on you *sela*." This exchange signals the recognition of life's ongoing fragility, and our reliance on God's presence to be our aid. —J.M.S.

In caring communities, the sight of someone bensching *gomel* is an opportunity to offer support. When individuals approach me to say they want to *bensch gomel*, I encourage them to think about what they want to share with the community about the occasion so that they are not put on the spot. This allows people to get the support they need without feeling overwhelmed. —D.W.

Many women *bensch gomel* after childbirth. —J.G.K.

otherwise experienced some kind of personal relief from a potentially difficult circumstance, it is customary to recite publicly *Birkat Hagomel* (The Blessing for Deliverance and Good Fortune). (*Kol Haneshamah: Shabbat Veḥagim*, pages 400–401) This *b'rakha* is often recited just after a person has completed an aliyah. It does not have to be connected to receiving an aliyah, however. One can come up to the Torah between aliyot to *bensch gomel.*

Mi Shebeyrakh Prayers—A "*Mi Shebeyrakh*" is a prayer form known by its initial two words, "May the One who blessed." The opening line is "May the One who blessed the Patriarchs and Matriarchs bless ___." It is customarily recited while the Torah scroll is outside of the ark and undressed, because the sense of the proximity and power of the divine presence is most palpable when the scroll is among us.

A range of different *Mi Shebeyrakh* prayers can be found in *Kol Haneshamah: Shabbat Veḥagim* on pages

The traditional list of ancestors of our people—Abraham, Isaac, and Jacob, Sarah, Rebecca, Rachel and Leah—are named one by one. Both here and in the *Amida*, some add Bilha and Zilpa, handmaidens who birthed some of Jacob's children, as a way of redeeming them from the invisibility caused by their social status. Some add additional biblical names for special blessings, such as the names of biblical warriors Joshua and Yael in a blessing for soldiers, or of biblical same-sex intimate friends David and Jonathan or Ruth and Naomi at an *aufruf* for a gay or lesbian couple. —J.G.K.

684–693. In some communities, the *gabay rishon* offers a *Mi Shebeyrakh* at the end of each aliyah for the person who took the aliyah. If the aliyah was taken for a special reason—such as a birthday or a personal event that one wants to celebrate or for which one wants communal support—the specifics are incorporated into the prayer. In some communities, a single *Mi Shebeyrakh* is offered at the end of the Torah reading for all the people who have taken aliyot on that day.

Healing Prayers—In many communities, the *gabay rishon* or the rabbi offers a *Mi Shebeyrakh* at some point in the Torah service for those in need of physical or spiritual healing. This prayer may take a traditional form (*Kol Haneshamah: Shabbat Veḥagim*, page 685), or it may take the form of a chant recited repeatedly by everyone in the congregation. Alternatives include the words of Moses' prayer for the healing of his sister Miriam, "*El na r'fa na la*" ("God, please heal her." [Numbers 12:13]) or the interpretive "*Mi Shebeyrakh*" song composed by Debbie Friedman. Sometimes the leader reads aloud a list of names that have been submitted in advance. Sometimes the leader invites members of the congregation to stand up and call out the names of those to whom they are sending healing prayers. Of course, we may pray for people whom we know to be in need of healing without calling out their names. Healing prayers support and comfort the ones praying as well as the recipients who know that people are holding them in prayer. Some believe that such prayers have an impact on individuals who are ill even if they are unaware that the prayers are being offered because the energetic interconnections between human beings are active even if they do not operate on a conscious level.

The *Maftir* and Haftarah—A passage from the biblical prophetic books called the haftarah is traditionally chanted following the Torah reading. The person who chants the haftarah is called the *maftir*. Prior to chanting the haftarah, the *maftir* is traditionally called to the Torah for the *maftir* aliyah, which is a repetition of the last few lines of the Torah portion on Shabbat or a reading from the second Torah scroll on holidays. Blessings precede and follow the chanting of the haftarah. Not all communities include the haftarah every week. (*Kol Haneshamah: Shabbat Veḥagim*, pages 408–411)

Hagba and *G'lila*—At the conclusion of the reading of the Torah, the scroll is lifted by the *magbia* (the lifter) and

There is a popular legend that the recitation of the haftarah originated in a period of oppression, when a wicked ruler forbade the public reading of Torah. Scholars of Jewish liturgical history agree that that is almost certainly not the true origin. After all, why would the wicked ruler allow the recitation of one part of the *Tanakh* and not another? More likely, the haftarah started as a jumping-off place for an exploration of the text's meaning in a *d'var Torah*. Comparing and contrasting thematic and verbal links between the two passages provided a tool for discovering deeper meanings. —J.A.S.

This is the moment of honor for the bar or bat mitzvah. He or she takes the *maftir aliyah* and is called up with a special, celebratory chant. Depending on the practices of the community and the child's abilities, she or he may read from the Torah and chant the haftarah, and will probably give some kind of interpretation of the text in a *d'var Torah*. —D.W.

In Ashkenazic communities, the *magbia/magbiha* shows the writing in the open Torah scroll to the congregation before the scroll is closed and tied. Many Sephardic communities show the scroll before the reading rather than after it. —J.G.K.

wrapped by the *golel/et* (the one who rolls). As the scroll is lifted, the community rises and recites a phrase that begins, "*V'zot Hatorah*"—"This is the Torah that Moses delivered to the Israelites . . ." or "This is the Torah that is a tree of life to those who embrace it." (*Kol Haneshamah: Shabbat Veḥagim*, pages 406–407) The community remains standing until the scroll is completed dressed and placed back on the table or on a stand; while this occurs, many communities join in song.

Returning the Scroll to the Ark (pages 432–441)—The scroll is carried in a procession that often parallels the procession when the scroll is taken out of the ark, described above. It is customary to sing Psalm 29, which actually appears to be a description of God's manifestation in an overpowering thunderstorm, something of which few people singing are aware. As the revelation of the Torah at Mount Sinai is described in Exodus 19 as occurring amid thunder and lightning, Psalm 29 is sung at this moment to suggest the momentous (and celebratory) nature of the reading from the Torah scroll that has just occurred. With the conclusion of the procession, the scroll is placed back into the Holy Ark. Just before the ark is closed, we sing "*Etz Ḥayim Hi*," "It is a Tree of Life to those that hold fast to it. . . . Renew our days, as you have done of old."

Sermon or D'var Torah

In some communities, words of Torah (used in this sense to mean "teaching") are shared after the Torah scroll is wrapped and before it is returned to the ark. In other communities, this occurs after the scroll is returned to the ark. In some communities, it is always the rabbi who teaches. In others, this role is shared with lay members of the congregation. Until the 19th century, the community's rabbi gave a full sermon only twice each year, on the Shabbat before Yom Kippur (*Shabbat Shuva*), in order to review the rules for fasting and to encourage community members in their work of *t'shuva*, and on the Shabbat preceding Passover (*Shabbat Hagadol*), to review the laws of ridding one's house of *ḥametz* (leaven) and rendering it kosher for the holiday.

The weekly sermon was introduced in the modern era as a result of the influence of Protestant church practice, in which the homily is central to the service, and in response to the unprecedented circumstance after political emancipation in which attendance at synagogue services on Shabbat became optional. Thus, when communal prayer was not sufficiently compelling to induce attendance, rab-

When I am writing a *d'var Torah*, I will often first read through the section I want to focus on without referring to any commentary and ask myself, "What in this section of Torah particularly stands out for me at this moment?" —N.C.M.

Weekly sermons entered into Jewish services in emulation of Christian practice. Sermons were once a mesmerizing form of moral instruction, especially in the days before television. Today there is increasing questioning in most faith communities about the pedagogic and spiritual effectiveness of sermons. —D.W.

bis thought that sermons addressing topics of interest might do the trick. Sermons are not necessarily related to the weekly Torah *parasha*. They may not even be obviously related to "religious" Jewish concerns. Sometimes they address compelling social or political issues, based on the premise that Jews ought to act in these areas on the basis of Jewish values. For some community members, the sermon may be the highlight of the service. For others, it may be regarded as a break from the more important activity of prayer.

Beginning in the 1960s, Reconstructionist communities sought to alter the format of the sermon, which some perceive as turning the congregation into passive receivers of sermonic wisdom. Thus, the sermon dialogue has been common in Reconstructionist congregations for many decades; it reshapes the sermon into an initial presentation followed by responses from members of the community. When the numbers attending grow very large, often the responses may occur within small groups or in conversational pairs. In addition to helping community members become active listeners, the sermon dialogue also opens the discussion to a wider variety of viewpoints.

The *d'var Torah* form (sometimes referred to as a *drash* or "interpretation") stays much closer to the weekly Torah portion. The speaker derives his or her points out of a close reading of the biblical text, combined with a reading of a variety of postbiblical commentaries on the text, including contemporary interpretations. Again, most commonly, the initial *drash* is followed by a wider discussion by those in attendance.

The underlying assumption is that the Torah has been a living document for millennia, expanded and reinterpreted as each set of readers has engaged in transgenerational conversation and debate with its predecessors. Thus, each new *d'var Torah* joins that conversation, augmenting it with our points of view and experiences. Sometimes the text of the Torah may be inspiring; at other times, it may be upsetting. As long as we retain the structural format of the *d'var Torah*, however, beginning with the biblical text and continuing with interpretations, we remain connected to prior viewpoints and open to reexamining our own preconceptions. What is difficult for one generation may be inspiring to the next.

For people interested in delivering a *d'var Torah* who have not studied the Torah or its commentaries extensively, translations of rabbinic *midrash*, medieval and Hasidic commentaries, as well as contemporary interpretations, are available in print and electronically.

The demise of the classic sermon and the rise of the congregational Torah discussion may be an appropriate response to changing needs and alternative approaches, but many communities fail to require or provide the sort of training necessary to guide an effective Torah dialogue. Equally important, open dialogues can often leave participants vulnerable when others use their opportunity to speak to attack another comment, or to advocate a position as a statement of opposition rather than as an alternative, or to speak insensitively even if inadvertently. —R.H.

Musaf (The Additional Service)

Traditionally, an additional *Amida* is added after the Torah service. It corresponds to the additional *korbanot* (animal sacrifices) that were offered on Shabbat when the Jerusalem Temple stood. The traditional *musaf Amida* consists of a recitation of the specifics of ancient Shabbat cultic worship and the yearning for the rebuilding of the Temple and the restoration of the sacrificial cult. Reconstructionist and Reform communities generally have eliminated the *musaf* service because they do not look forward to that rebuilding and restoration. Some communities have a service segment called "an alternative *musaf*," at which time the service leader offers an additional poem, reading, teaching or song; during this time, in some congregations, members of the community who wish to *daven* a version of the traditional *musaf Amida* are invited to do so.

Communities that daven a *musaf* (additional) service or do a little something extra in memory of the additional Shabbat and holiday offering in the ancient Temple might consider that in this classification, *musaf* is the bridge from creation and revelation to redemption. Just as the traditional *musaf* service associates the path to redemption with a restored Temple service of sacrifices, we might reconstruct *musaf* to reflect themes of *tzedaka* and *tikun olam*, pathways to a redeemed world. —J.G.K.

Some of the most beautiful Jewish music has its origin in *musaf*, the additional synagogue service added after the Torah service on Shabbat and holidays in traditional congregations. People strolling into synagogue at a leisurely pace on Shabbat morning and service leaders not rushing through davening are not contemporary innovations, so Shabbat is linked with a long history of musical creativity designed to inspire and engage—particularly nearer the end of services, when synagogues were as full as possible. —J.G.K.

Concluding Prayers and Songs

The conclusion of the Shabbat morning service consists of one or several songs, including traditional ones, such as "*Eyn Keyloheynu*" (pages 442–3), "*Shir Hakavod*" (pages 452–457), "*Adon Olam*" (pages 458–459), "*Yigdal*" (pages 460–463), and contemporary songs with which the community may be familiar. These songs precede or follow the *Aleynu* (pages 444–449), in which the community affirms its responsibility to live in ways that make the divine reign manifest and to work to repair suffering and injustice in the world.

Mourner's Kaddish

There are several forms of the Kaddish, which is an Aramaic declaration of the greatness of God and an expression of hope for peace in all worlds. The Kaddish functions as a capstone for each section of the service, as well as for the conclusion of study. It is often recited by mourners, (pages 450–1) particularly at the end of worship. Its literal meaning notwithstanding, the Kaddish functions poignantly and effectively to allow mourners to give voice to whatever they are feeling and to enable the community to respond

Closing songs also provide a particular opportunity to bring in themes of the life cycle of congregants (Is someone celebrating a wedding this week?) or secular calendar (Is there a national holiday on Monday?) through selecting unusual tunes or substituting Jewish or secular songs. —J.G.K.

to them in ritually prescribed ways. In some communities, the Kaddish is recited only in the first eleven months after the death of a loved one and, subsequently, on the Yahrzeit (anniversary of the death). In some communities, the entire congregation rises in solidarity to join the mourners midway through the Kaddish. In other communities, everyone rises and recites the entire Kaddish in unison. And in most communities, there is a mix of these variant customs, reflective of the diversity of the members.

Kiddush

The *oneg Shabbat* following the morning service functions symbolically as the traditional second meal of Shabbat and is thus preceded by a Kiddush (pages 464–465) recited over wine or grape juice and often a *motzi* recited over hallah. In some places, this occurs in the location where the *oneg* food is waiting. In other places, this occurs in the sanctuary immediately after the end of the service, so that people do not have to wait in the *oneg* location before beginning to eat.

The Shabbat morning Kiddush functions similarly to the Friday evening Kiddush, but the text chanted before the blessing over the wine is different. It is the "*V'sham'ru*" (Exodus 31:16–17), which portrays Shabbat as a sign of the covenant. It is generally sung communally

Another custom is to recite the entire 23rd Psalm as a prelude to Shabbat morning Kiddush.
—J.G.K.

to one of an assortment of melodies. The leader then holds up the *kos* (wine cup) and calls out "*Savrey*" ("With your permission"), to which everyone responds "*L'ḥayim!*" ("To life!"), and everyone joins in chanting the blessing over the wine. This Kiddush has only one blessing, not two, as the observance of Shabbat, the focus of the second blessing on Friday evening, is well under way. Traditional Jews add another paragraph, the fourth of the Ten Commandments (Exodus 20:8-11), which focuses on giving everyone a day off for Shabbat.

Shabbat Lunch

Many communities have adopted the custom of providing a substantial Shabbat lunch after the service, either weekly or monthly, so that people can sit and mingle together, catching up and enjoying the leisure of Shabbat afternoon, when there is nowhere else one is required to be. These lunches often include the singing of Shabbat *z'mirot* (songs) and the *Birkat Hamazon* (Grace after Meals).

Shabbat Afternoon and the End of Shabbat

Hosting others or being hosted for Shabbat lunch is a traditional and pleasurable way to spend Shabbat afternoon. Because cooking is not a traditional activity on Shabbat, the meal generally consists of cold fare, such as salads, cold meats or cheeses, pita and hummus or other dips. Also traditional, especially in cold weather, are hot dishes cooked in slow cookers, such as Ashkenazic *cholent* or Sephardic *ḥamin*. The food, while it is essential, is not the main attraction. Leisurely time spent with friends and family is the epitome of the experience of Shabbat. As on Friday evening, Shabbat singing and the chanting of the *Birkat Hamazon* are also spiritually uplifting. For that purpose it is helpful to have *benschers* or *birkonim*, booklets containing table songs and prayers, close at hand.

Traditional Shabbat activities after lunch have long included napping, taking walks, visiting with friends, studying Torah, playing games and reading anything that is not related to one's work. For the nonhalakhic *shomer/et Shabbat* (Shabbat observer), the options are much more numerous. As discussed above in the section "A New Definition of *Shomer Shabbat*" and below in the

In some communities and for some people, Shabbat observance winds down after Saturday morning services. There is a sweetness to Shabbat afternoons if we allow time and space for it to emerge. —D.W.

A particular sport may serve as your return to Shabbat. As far back as I can remember, Shabbat meant football with friends; more recently, it's Ultimate Frisbee. The ritual of a game you enjoy with people you enjoy can be a great source of *oneg Shabbat*. —J.M.S.

In previous times, chess was particularly favored as a Shabbat game, and in some of the stricter communities, one of the few games sanctioned at all. It was valued as a game that sharpened the mind as opposed to games that emphasize chance, which were viewed as frivolous—a waste of time. If a preference for games that sharpen the mind is an important value for you, there are now many more games that suit that Shabbat value. —J.A.S.

Shabbat afternoon practices and liturgy are the least familiar to the liberal Jew. This is a loss, since this time is often the most accessible for families, for sharing with friends or for individual contemplation. When a community shares an entire Shabbat together, through a *Shabbaton* or retreat or at summer camp, the flavor of Shabbat deepens through the course of the day. It gives us the opportunity to savor the full cycle of the day and to experience fully the joy of pausing from our everyday routine and daily concerns. —B.P.

section "Nontraditional Shabbat Practice," the personal choices made by liberal Jews who are attentive to Shabbat flow from our judgments about what contributes to maintaining the spirit of Shabbat and what does not. Indeed, nonhalakhic Shabbat observers often find that their observance of Shabbat closely resembles halakhic observance, perhaps modified to accommodate specific, varying circumstances and the people with whom we are celebrating Shabbat.

Shabbat Minḥa

The afternoon (*minḥa*) service on Shabbat afternoon has the overall theme of redemption (*g'ula*). The *nusaḥ* (melodic mode) of the prayers is wistful and yearning. The day of rest and peacefulness is nearing its end, and we are sad to see it go. Having experienced a foretaste of the mythic world to come, we look forward with heightened intensity to the coming of the messianic age, when every day will be Shabbat-like.

On Shabbat, the *minḥa* service includes a short Torah reading, the beginning of the following week's *parasha* (weekly portion). This is another indication that this Shabbat is nearly done, and we are already looking forward to the next one.

Se'uda Sh'lishit (The Third Meal)

In communities that reassemble for *minḥa* and *ma'ariv* (the evening service), *minḥa* is scheduled shortly before sundown, and there is a third, light Shabbat meal (*se'uda sh'lishit* in Hebrew, *shaleshudes* in Yiddish) that occurs between the two services. In addition to eating, it is a time for leisurely singing of *z'mirot* (traditional Shabbat songs) that tend to have a slower, more relaxed tempo and lyrics that celebrate the gift and blessings of Shabbat. Traditionally, the *se'uda sh'lishit* lasts until the first stars can be seen in the night sky, at which point the community davens *ma'ariv*.

In some communities, *se'uda sh'lishit* is organized without *minḥa* and *ma'ariv* and is followed directly by *Havdala*. It is also a time for a *vort* (bit of teaching) by an individual or the collective study of texts. For example, between Pesach and Shavuot, a different chapter of the tractate *Pirkey Avot* (Ethics of the Fathers) is traditionally studied each week. In the month of Elul preceding the Days of Awe, texts on *t'shuva* may be studied.

Whether there is song and study or one of these, the *se'uda sh'lishit* feels like the last remnant of Shabbat, a period in which we are not rushing to go anywhere or get anything done. Time is out of our control. In summer in places far away from the equator, Shabbat seems to go on and on, and we linger, waiting for the darkness. In winter, evening falls quickly. From week to week the rhythms change in ways we cannot control.

Havdala (Separation)

Rabbinic Judaism is famous for the way it makes distinctions—between holy and profane, ritually pure and impure, kosher and nonkosher, female and male, Jew and non-Jew, and among food categories that determine which *b'rakha* to recite. Distinctions create meaning and significance; they are human cultural constructions that sort and define our perceptions and experiences.

Havdala, the ceremony that divides and distinguishes Shabbat from the week, is a preeminent example of this phenomenon. It is the way we declare the end of Shabbat and make a very clear distinction between Shabbat and non-Shabbat (*ḥol*/weekdays). It has a significant function—Shabbat actually can continue well into the night (technically, through Tuesday!) if we delay *Havdala*. It provides a moment that often turns celebratory; when a community spends the whole of Shabbat together, one of the transformations that occurs is in their relationships to one another, and *Havdala* is a moment to rejoice in that sacred bonding process. Or, if members of a household have spent Shabbat afternoon apart, *Havdala* may be a time of reunion.

The rituals of *Havdala*, with their concrete use of the senses (taste, smell, seeing, hearing and touch), are particularly appealing to young children. *Havdala* can be introduced as a simple, brief family ritual at an early age. Likewise, the symbolic power of these objects, accompanied by community or family singing, speaks to all ages. —B.P.

Havdala in a house of mourning is also a time to return to shiva observance; the transition reinforces the reality of the still recent shock of separation. —J.G.K.

The ceremony is often conducted with the lights dimmed and with participants in a circle, holding hands, or arm in arm. It begins with the lighting of the *Havdala* candle, which is actually composed of multiple candles braided together, symbolizing this unique moment in which holy Shabbat and ordinary weekday are joined together fleetingly. Some people recite an introductory series of biblical verses that laud God as the source of our strength, song, light and joy, and that express the hope that we will receive all of these blessings.

Four *b'rakhot* (blessings) then follow:

- Over a cup of wine, which the leader holds up to the light. According to most customs the wine is not drunk at this moment, however.

The lighting of the *Havdala* candle, the rekindling of the flame of creation, is the first act of creativity in the new week. —M.M.

If the weather is nice, I always choose to conduct *Havdala* outside. I use the requirement to check for three stars in the sky before beginning the ceremony as an opportunity to linger in stargazing with friends and family. To my eyes, the light of the braided candle takes on additional beauty under the night sky. —H.S.V.

Another explanation of the braided *Havdala* candle: At the beginning of Shabbat, the distinct people and things of our world, like the distinct lights, seemed separate. The practice of Shabbat has reminded us that they are truly one, combined in one intertwining braid. —J.A.S.

The verse "The Jews had light, happiness, joy and dearness," recited jointly in the opening paragraph of *Havdala,* is from the book of Esther (8:16) and may be understood as a reassurance that just as every new week comes with its new anxieties, so we should also bring some Purim into every week—we should be careful not to always take ourselves too seriously. —J.G.K.

- Over spices, such as cinnamon and nutmeg. Though it is not required to keep the spices in a special vessel, the *Havdala* spice box is another piece of ritual art, dating back to medieval silver workers who constructed spice boxes in the form of castles. Contemporary spice boxes come in all shapes and materials. The blessing expresses gratitude for the creation of spices. Each person takes a turn inhaling the spices. One interpretation is that they serve as smelling salts, reviving us as we become faint from witnessing the departure of the beloved Shabbat. Another is that the spices help us carry the sweetness of Shabbat into the week.
- Over the candle's flame. After the blessing is recited, some people follow a custom of looking at their fingernails to see the flame's reflection, and then

I find that smelling fresh herbs or spices enhances the celebration, and it gives us the opportunity to say special *b'rakhot*. At the *Havdala* ceremony during the rehearsal dinner preceding a friend's wedding, the chef supplied us with the same herbs and spices that were used during the meal for *Havdala*, which created a more unified experience for our senses of smell and taste. —J.G.K.

Looking at your fingernails curved over your hand gives you the visual experience of *Havdala*—the distinction between the light reflected on your fingernails and the darkness of shadow on you palm. It is moving to me to look at the reflection of the *Havdala* candle's light in the eyes of the people around the circle, to see the last glimmer of Shabbat's light mixed with the first spark of the week's creativity shining in people's eyes. —M.M.

I understand that examining our fingernails in the light of the fire gives us an opportunity to put the fire to good use, the first transition to the new workweek. Making shadow puppets with one's fingers on the walls or ceiling is another way to put the fire to use, and it is particularly fun for children, and perhaps for our inner child. —J.G.K.

holding up their fingers and looking at the flame that is framed between them. A folk tradition suggests that the second, additional soul that we receive at the start of Shabbat departs at this moment through our fingernails. However we conceive of the nature of our souls or spiritual selves, something palpable does occur at this ceremony. If we have been living in a spiritually elevated Shabbat zone, we find ourselves facing outward into the world once the *Havdala* ceremony ends, as if our inner selves are somehow altered or diminished.

- For the creation of distinctions. We bless God for distinguishing between holy and profane, between light and darkness, between Shabbat and the six days of the week. The traditional text includes the distinction between Israel and all the other peoples, but this is omitted from the Reconstructionist text to avoid triumphalism and claims of exceptionalism.

A Hasidic teaching states that when Adam and Eve were first created, they wore garments like scales that radiated light ("*or*," spelled with the letter *aleph*). After they ate the forbidden fruit, God covered them with garments of skins ("*or*," spelled with the letter *ayin*). According to the teaching, our fingernails are the last remnants of those radiant scales that shine by the light of the *Havdala* candle. —M.M.

The distinction we have just seen between the light and darkness on two sides of our hands concretizes this *b'rakha* of distinction. —J.G.K.

Following the final *b'rakha*, the leader drinks from the wine cup, and then the candle is doused in the remaining wine. The song "*Shavu'a Tov*" ("A Good Week") is often then sung, followed by "*Eliyahu Hanavi*"/"*Miriam Hanevi'a*" (Elijah and Miriam, the Prophets). Elijah is traditionally believed to be the herald who will announce the onset of the messianic age. Since our hope is that each Shabbat will be the last one before the time when it will be perpetually Shabbat, we sing with the wish that Elijah is arriving with the good news.

When I'm feeling more like a Hasid (stereotypically mystically inclined), I like dipping the candle in the wine. When I'm feeling more like a *Litvak* (stereotypically Lithuanian-rationalist), I am more than happy to blow out the candle. Often, the choice I make at this moment is a choice of contrast; the more Hasidic a Shabbat I just experienced, the more I want to begin the week on a Litvish note to provide some balance, and vice versa. My less rationalist side enjoys taking drops of *Havdala* wine and placing them on my eyelids (expressing a hope for seeing good in the coming week) and pockets (expressing a hope for prosperity) to symbolically link the blessings of Shabbat with the new week. —J.G.K.

When our children were small, at the end of *Havdala* we would sing, "Bye-bye Shabbat, bye-bye Shabbat" (to the melody of *Shavu'a Tov*). Saying goodbye to Shabbat is akin to bidding farewell to a houseguest. We welcome guests into our home with enthusiasm and graciousness; we also send them away with good wishes and a sense of sadness (or, perhaps, relief). In any case, it is fitting to add a ritual to end Shabbat that mirrors our welcome to Shabbat. No matter how we have spent the day, we express appreciation for the sacred time we have had. —B.P.

Why is Miriam the counterpart to Elijah? One Jewish folk custom was "to draw water (from a well) on Saturday night because Miriam's Well supplies all the wells each Saturday night, and one who does so and drinks will be cured of illness." (*Kol Bo*, *Oraḥ Ḥayim*, 299:10) As Elijah represents redemption and the hope that we might witness the day when it is always Shabbat, Miriam represents the healing and repair that we need now, while we wait for that messianic day to arrive. —B.P.

Melaveh Malka
(Accompanying the Shabbat Queen)

Communities sometimes gather festively on Saturday evening to usher out the Shabbat Queen (*Shabbat Hamalka*). The celebrations may include music, dancing, viewing films and playing games. A *melaveh malka* is again a way of building on the beauty of the Shabbat experiences and prolonging Shabbat and all of its blessings.

Issues in Synagogue Shabbat Practice

Synagogue communities inevitably consist of individuals whose Shabbat practices vary widely from one another. Some members may walk to synagogue and avoid the use of electricity, while the entirety of others' observance of Shabbat may consist of attendance at synagogue services. And there may be members who strongly believe that activities that are traditionally prohibited on Shabbat should not be permitted within the synagogue building, even though they themselves do not observe these prohibitions in their own personal lives.

Melaveh malḳa is also called "*se'uda revi'it*," the fourth meal, since—even though Shabbat is technically over—it is as if we are extending Shabbat into one more celebratory feast. The meal might begin with the flames of *Havdala* itself or by lighting a new candle from the *Havdala* candle before it is extinguished. Even in the absence of another formal meal, some households leave a candle burning Saturday night to accompany Shabbat on her way out. —J.G.K.

How do synagogue communities decide about communal practice in such situations? It is recommended that each community involve as many members as are interested in studying texts and considering the competing values involved in each case, reaching a decision that includes the views and sensibilities of as many people as possible. (See the "Decision Making" section in Volume I of this *Guide.*)

Shofar

Sounding the shofar is traditionally prohibited on Shabbat. Thus, when the two days of Rosh Hashana fall on Saturday and Sunday, traditional congregations sound the shofar only on Sunday.

The digital revolution presents many challenges to Shabbat practice in the synagogue. Even as we may want to refrain from the use of personal electronics on Shabbat, we can imagine ways in which they may bolster our experience in synagogue—not just through the amplification of the sound system, but also through projecting teaching texts or new sheet music or loading multiple translations for Torah study onto tablets. This presents a whole new set of challenges to sort through, urging each of us to consider what we want to embrace and what we want to set aside. —D.W.

Our congregation recently began live audio streaming of Shabbat services. Our amplification system is linked to a computer program that allows homebound members the opportunity to "connect" with the community, even if it is only a virtual connection. The decision to do this involved a working through of congregational values in which we chose to underscore accessibility. —N.H.M.

The halakhic origins of the prohibition against blowing the shofar, like the prohibitions involving *lulav*, are to avoid transporting these things to the synagogue. The mystical echoes of this practice suggest that sounding the shofar—to arouse God's *ḥesed* (loving kindness)—is redundant on Shabbat since on every Shabbat, God's *ḥesed* eclipses God's *g'vura* (judgment). —J.G.K.

Some of the issues and values to be considered: On the one hand, people with traditional sensibilities may find it jarring to hear the shofar sounded on Shabbat. Those who observe Shabbat in a traditional way will regard blowing the shofar on Shabbat as offensive. Not sounding the shofar is an opportunity to teach about the sanctity of Shabbat. On the other hand, people who attend Rosh Hashana services with the expectation of hearing the shofar blasts may find it strange and off-putting not to hear them. The sounds of the shofar contribute to the feeling of a Rosh Hashana service. If the practice of most members of the community is to listen to the radio or to music on Shabbat, then abstaining from hearing the shofar may not make sense. How many members attend services on both days of Rosh Hashana? Those who only attend on the first day will not hear the sounds of the shofar at all if the first day falls on Shabbat that year and the shofar is not blown.

Rabbi Ira Eisenstein, the first president of the Reconstructionist Rabbinical College, once explained why he accepted the sounding of the shofar on Shabbat. Most people who come to synagogue only occasionally very much look forward to hearing the shofar sounded. When they are told that because of the sanctity of Shabbat (a Shabbat they most likely do not celebrate by conforming to customary Shabbat restrictions), there will be no sounding of the shofar, they are not only disappointed; they are also confirmed in a sense that "Judaism is always about what you can't do." —R.H.

When Shabbat and Rosh Hashana coincide, one option is to leave out the shofar sounding after the haftarah as a nod toward Shabbat but to leave in the shofar sounding in *musaf* as a nod toward contemporary Jewish realities. If *musaf* is not recited, the same idea can apply to wherever the *musaf* additions with shofar are placed. —R.H.

Lulav

Similarly, the four species (*etrog* and *lulav*) are traditionally not used on the day of Sukkot that falls on Shabbat in order to avoid carrying them to the synagogue. In many communities, most people attend services only on Shabbat, and many of them do not own a *lulav* and *etrog*, so they would not have an opportunity to bless and shake the *lulav* if the *lulav* and *etrog* were not used on Shabbat. The prohibition makes sense if many people come to the synagogue on the other days of Sukkot and some members are traditionally observant of Shabbat.

Musical Instruments

While musical instruments were used on Shabbat in the ancient Temple in Jerusalem, the rabbis later prohibited the use of them on Shabbat. They were placing "a fence around the law" because of the danger that an instrument might break and the person playing it might forget that it was Shabbat and repair it. It is the repairing, not the playing, that is the primary Shabbat prohibition. There is also

The restrictions against the use of *lulav* and shofar on Shabbat come from a time and place long past, when Jews could and did come to synagogue both days of Rosh Hashana and every day of Sukkot, and so there were always "the other days" to do what you couldn't do on Shabbat. The prohibitions that deny access to powerful Jewish symbols for the presumed sake of avoiding the transgression of carrying in a public place on Shabbat are long overdue to be archived and ignored. —R.H.

a prohibition against carrying an instrument outdoors on Shabbat, but this issue is irrelevant to the use of a piano or an organ. In regard to other instruments, communities ought to decide together whether the danger of making a repair outweighs the potential enhancement of the service by the use of musical instruments.

Microphones

Traditionally, microphones are not used on Shabbat because doing so involves the use of electricity and the potential need to adjust the sound system when it is in use. In most systems, speaking into the microphone alters the amount of electricity used. The advantage of the use of a sound system is that it enables congregants to hear what is being said and sung, enhancing their experience of Shabbat and prayer. The vast majority of liberal Jews do not consider electricity to be a prohibited form of fire, in which case there is no reason to avoid using a microphone, though the spirit of Shabbat should be considered when deciding on the volume and the material broadcast.

A study by the Hartford Seminary on vital congregations across faith denominations found that one factor shared by all vital congregations is the inclusion of musical instruments, especially drums, in religious services. —D.W.

A Hebrew proverb reads, "*Al ta'am v'al re'aḥ, eyn l'hitvake'aḥ*"—"There is no sense in arguing about matters of taste." While communities can use values-based decision making to articulate their public Shabbat standards, let us take care in judging what is or is not in the spirit of Shabbat. —J.G.K.

Videography

Often, families of *b'ney mitzvah* want to visually record the service or parts of it. In communities in which the custom is to use microphones, the issue is not about electricity. Rather, it concerns potential disruptions to the mood and solemnity of the service. The service should not take on the feel of a performance. Sometimes communities compromise by permitting fixed cameras stationed at a distance from the *bima* that do not require special lighting or obstruct anyone's view. Some congregations build a fixed video camera with a suitable lens into the back wall of the sanctuary and link it to a microphone on the *bima* so that the proceedings can be filmed in a way that does not detract from the service in any way.

My community decided that videography and photography conflicted with our definition of Shabbat as a day unto itself on which we do not create for the future. We therefore prohibited the use of these things in the synagogue, although we had gone into our study of Shabbat assuming we would end up permitting them. There were other things, such as the use of computers and writing on chalkboards, that we surprised ourselves by permitting, again based on a principle of Shabbat observance that grew out of tradition and that we found we could agree on. —J.A.S.

Given the distances that often separate family members, as well as the issue of aging relatives who cannot travel, prohibiting the videography of a bar or bat mitzvah ceremony or an *aufruf* or another *simḥa* on Shabbat seems pointless and even punitive as long as the videography can be done in a way that is not intrusive or distracting. Our two children celebrated their *b'ney mitzvah* ceremonies in different congregations. From the first one, we have a video that we were able to share with distant relatives and friends back then, and that we can take out at any time now to relive a wonderful day. From the second, we have no video of the service (prohibited by the synagogue) but lots of video of the Shabbat lunch (permitted by the synagogue). We still regret and resent that we do not have the opportunity to enjoy viewing the second service because of an antiquated sense of what is prohibited on Shabbat. —R.H.

Electronic Music

For congregations that permit microphones and musical instruments, the use of electronic music, whether live or recorded, is a question of *ruaḥ Shabbat*, the spirit of Shabbat. Loud, harsh music violates that spirit, so a congregation may want to put limits on electronic music or bar it altogether so that *ruaḥ Shabbat* is preserved. On the other hand, many families may insist on such music at bar/bat mitzvah celebrations. Some make a distinction between congregational activities and private, invitational activities that take place within the building.

Nontraditional Shabbat Practice

Not everyone finds that attending synagogue services is always the best way to usher in and celebrate Shabbat. For those who prefer to celebrate at home alone or with family and/or friends, or to go to others' homes, a previous section describes Shabbat home observance on Friday evening. Others, however, may not find the practice of prayer and communal worship to be meaningful, and they may not be able to create meaningful observance of Shabbat at home. Yet they may be very interested in maintaining an observance of Shabbat. Those who fit this description face the challenge of being a *shomer/et Shabbat* (Sabbath observer) without clear guidance from inherited Jewish traditions.

Some of the general issues raised by this challenge are addressed above in the section, "A New Definition of

Shomer Shabbat." The current section is more specific, naming some of the possibilities in order to accord them weight and respect. They are not inferior to the choice of attending synagogue services on Shabbat and spending the better part of the evening and afternoon singing around a Shabbat table. Judaism is a civilization, not only a religion; Shabbat can be a significant practice in your life even if you do not think of yourself as particularly religious or spiritual. Each of us answers the questions of practice in our own way. What are some of the possibilities for a serious, meaningful, nontraditional Shabbat observance?

First, it should be noted that there may be pieces of traditional practice that resonate for some people, evoking treasured experiences and associations and bringing thoughts and memories of loved ones to life. Lighting Shabbat candles is one example. Even if you do not engage in any other traditional Shabbat activity on a given Shabbat, you may find that lighting the candles is the concrete marker that brings you into a different realm of consciousness. Or that marker could involve eating hallah, or calling your grandmother, or timing your arrival at synagogue so that you miss the service but participate in the social time of the *oneg*.

Second, many people find that engaging in an activity on Shabbat that they also engage in on weekdays can be a substantially different experience, just because they do it in the spirit of Shabbat—breathing more deeply and eating more slowly and mindfully. You might luxuriate in reading the newspaper because you enjoy it, rather than skimming through it for information before hurrying off to work or school. You might enjoy the company of family and friends, without having to accomplish anything. It may be helpful to think of Shabbat observance as much more than doing specific, Shabbat-related things such as reciting the Kiddush over wine or attending synagogue services. Even if you don't engage in any traditional practices, you can still designate Shabbat as a day when you relate to the world in a totally different way, with an awareness of your ultimate values.

It is useful to determine the goals that you seek to achieve in your observance of Shabbat. Here are some suggestions:

- *No Work*—If the way you want to align with the sabbatical rhythm of the seven-day week is to do absolutely nothing related to your profession or

How should you decide whether a traditionally prohibited creative activity, such as gardening, painting or knitting, might contribute to your contemporary, liberal Shabbat? One useful consideration is whether you are engaging in the activity for the sake of the process or for a product. One view of Shabbat is that it is a day for enjoying the process of living, not for production. —J.A.S.

There is a difference between needing rest and needing recharging. While we often have the need to rest physically, we also may feel depleted emotionally, intellectually, sexually or spiritually. So while going away for a retreat-style Shabbat weekend might charge us up spiritually and intellectually, the drive home afterward might also leave us physically exhausted. Awareness of each of the five realms of our energy provides not only a key to avoiding fatigue during the week, but may create the possibility of a deeper level of replenishment on Shabbat. —J.G.K.

Choosing an activity in which we specifically do not engage on Shabbat also echoes another piece of tradition, even if the activity we choose is not one of the 39 traditional categories of work prohibited on Shabbat. —J.G.K.

business, then your practice may consist of not taking calls or checking electronic messages or reading the business section of the news. The measure of your success may be whether you avoid planning on Shabbat for what you need to do once Shabbat is over. If you feel as if your life is consumed by your work, a Shabbat practice offers the opportunity to reconnect each week for an extended period (25 hours!) with the rest of your values, interests and priorities.

- *Focus on Nature*—For some people, Shabbat, the celebration of the creation of the world, is the time to connect with the natural world by hiking in the woods or gardening. If your life is structured in such a way that you find yourself generally unaware of or unable to appreciate the natural beauty that surrounds you, this may be a path that works for you. The traditional Shabbat prohibitions of planting and weeding, for example, were first established when most of our ancestors lived agrarian lives. These were prohibitions of engaging in what you did for work. Unless you are a farmer, these prohibitions may function to undermine your Shabbat rest.

When we observe a full-length Shabbat from before sunset Friday until Saturday's nightfall, we remind ourselves that something is bigger than us, and that we do not and cannot control everything. —J.G.K.

- *Family*—For parents who spend too little time with their children during the week or partners who find it helpful to have a designated period of time to spend together, Shabbat offers a regular designated time to focus on these priorities. It is not always easy to do, but establishing Shabbat dinner on Friday night as a time when you are reliably at the table for candle lighting can be transformative in a family's or relationship's dynamics. Similarly, going regularly to synagogue services together, whether or not the services themselves always speak to you, can have this effect, as can other regularly designated shared times on Shabbat morning and afternoon. Or Shabbat may be the day when you travel to see grandparents or grandchildren, older and less mobile aunts or uncles, or siblings or cousins whom you miss. You may find that when such visits come to be associated subliminally with Shabbat, they acquire an additional sense of sanctity and purpose.

I learned from beloved friends the nontraditional practice of bringing a phone to the Shabbat table. They would call an elderly parent who lived far away and was otherwise isolated on Shabbat, so that they could share in the moments of making Kiddush and blessing the hallah and exchange Shabbat greetings and blessings between the generations. That parent has passed on now. However, the memories of those precious moments linger and inspire the act at my own Shabbat table until this day.

—M.K.

Ideally, it may be better to travel long distances before Shabbat, but if it is not logistically possible to do this, you may decide that the unpleasantness of traveling on Shabbat is outweighed by the value of the visit and the Shabbat spirit that it generates.

- *Friends*—Most of us are not able to spend as much time with friends as we would prefer because of work demands, family responsibilities and the hectic nature of our lives. For many people, time spent with people we choose to see is a lived experience of the divine. In fact, the Jewish philosopher Martin Buber asserted that it is precisely in a dialogical relationship between two people that God's presence is most manifest. On Shabbat we can seek out people with whom we are at ease. These may be people with whom we have fun, feel safe and let our guard down, people who perhaps share long histories with us or who may be new to our lives, offering the excitement that accompanies the building of a new relationship. Shabbat is ideally the time when we receive a second soul; God's presence, the *Shekhina*, is often identified with the Shabbat Bride. Some may indeed find time spent with good friends to be the best way to celebrate Shabbat.

- *Leaving the Web Behind*—In traditional settings, Shabbat-observant Jews go beyond not walking into a store to make a purchase; they do their best to avoid a business district in which others are engaged in weekday commerce. Some find that switching off access to the Internet serves an equivalent function. Far more than the shops and people on Main Street,

How to practice leaving behind the Web when smartphones enable us to carry the Web in our pockets and tallit bags? If you deem it necessary to carry a phone and keep it on in case of emergency, you might decide to turn off the Web/email part of the phone. The act of disabling part of the phone sets the distinction between Shabbat and the rest of the week and can help allow the mind to relax and break out of patterned actions of habitually grabbing for the phone to text, email, check the calendar, surf the Web, and also receive and make calls. —M.K.

The discussion of prohibited and permitted activities on Shabbat inevitably draws us into the ancient debate about the letter of the law vs. the spirit of the law. While this can be helpful by way of organizing conversations, we should understand that the argument about letter vs. spirit is not simply about opposing positions. They are actually two ends of a continuum along which we move when making decisions about Jewish behaviors. Consider the use of technology on Shabbat. Jews who choose to be governed by *halakha* will not use liturgy apps on a smartphone or a tablet reader. The reasons given for avoidance vary, some being based on the prohibition against manipulating electricity ("fire") on Shabbat, others on prohibitions against inscribing/writing/copying on Shabbat since every keystroke is entered somewhere. These reasons follow the letter of the law. Still others suggest that in light of the siege of connectivity under which we increasingly labor, we need a Shabbat from technology simply to re-engage in unmediated human-to-human contact. This is a spirit-of-the-law position. Increasingly sophisticated and ubiquitous versions of Jewish liturgy (as well as text, commentary and story) are available online, and increasing numbers of Jews, certainly those under a certain age, see those resources as things that could enrich their Shabbat experience by using the devices they have come to rely on for daily access to information. For these Jews, bringing a device to Shabbat services that allows them to follow on an e-reader the same siddur being held by their neighbor is a preferred way of engaging the text. The determination of what is prohibited and permitted on Shabbat is likely to be a much more personal determination in the future. —R.H.

the Web draws us in. It is virtually impossible to do anything on the Web without links and pop-ups that take us elsewhere. It is a virtual world that never sleeps; it is always not Shabbat somewhere.

- *Acts of* Tikun Olam (*Improving the World*)—One of the central and repeating Shabbat themes is that it commemorates the Exodus from Egyptian slavery (*zekher litzi'at Mitzrayim*). The ability to refrain from engaging in our everyday occupations is a consequence of our having been liberated from slavery; we don't have to work all of the time. Thus, some people find that engaging in activities that help others fulfill their needs, such as attending a demonstration or lobbying government officials, is an ideal way to concretize and embody a commemoration of the Exodus from Egypt in the spirit of Shabbat.
- *Acts of* G'milut Ḥesed (*Deeds of Loving Kindness*)—Some find that helping out less fortunate people—visiting sick people (*bikur ḥolim*) or shut-ins, serving as a big brother or big sister, serving as a reading or math tutor—is a way of being part of

I view Shabbat as a day to rest from building and repairing, a day for appreciating the world as it is. Even liberal rabbinic authorities have tended to discourage work-like *tikun olam* on Shabbat, such as building a house with Habitat for Humanity or conducting a soup kitchen fundraiser, which might be done on a day other than Shabbat. Of course, the principle of *pikuaḥ nefesh* – that saving a life overrides the prohibitions of Shabbat – might sometimes justify *tikun olam* efforts if there is a reason they need to take place on Shabbat. We all look forward to a time when our weekday work activities are all acts of *tikun olam* and Shabbat takes place in a world that is already *m'tukan* – already repaired. —J.A.S.

am m'kad'shey sh'vi'i, a people that makes the seventh day holy. If the rest of your week does not include such service work, doing it on Shabbat may create a clear distinction for you between the sacred and the everyday.

- *Working Out*—Swimming, jogging, hiking, playing in a weekly basketball game, practicing yoga, lifting weights: For some of us, such activities are a contemplative practice, a spiritual experience in which our consciousness slows down and expands, a way to get out of our minds and to be fully present in our bodies. Physical activities are one of the ways that we "pray." As such, they can be central to the celebration of Shabbat.
- *Play*—This is a broad category. Play is not explicitly in the traditional repertoire of Shabbat activities, in part because of rabbinic Judaism's historic aversion

More and more Jewish communities have begun to offer Jewish yoga sessions on Shabbat morning in synagogues. A common occurrence is to practice yoga in the early part of the morning at shul, and then to join the community during the larger service afterward. In such cases, yoga is offered as an embodied Jewish spiritual practice, a way of praying with our bodies in the context of Jewishly themed yoga sessions. This practice offers nourishment and stretch for body and soul, creating a communal expression of integrated prayer experience in the company of a nontraditional kind of minyan. Yoga practice can help some people find deep rest, and by practicing yoga on Shabbat, they find their experience of the day of rest greatly enhanced and deepened. —M.K.

The physical and the spiritual can be one and the same. This is reflected by the prayer book citing Psalms 35:10: "*Kol atzmotay tomarna Adonay mi ḳhamoḳha*"—"Let all my bones say, 'God, who is like you?'" —J.G.K.

to wasting time and its focus on devoting oneself to God at every moment. But many of us live pressure-filled lives that are largely oriented to accomplishing specific goals, both professionally and personally. As we noted at the outset, Shabbat is the perfect time to play, to do things we enjoy without worrying about what we are accomplishing. For some of us, it may be the best way to get off life's treadmill and experience the *menuḥa* of Shabbat.

- *Reading*—Those of us for whom reading is a pleasure know what nourishes our souls—fiction, poetry, history, memoirs, contemplative practice, Jewish or other religious teachings or page-turning murder mysteries. It is important to define your goals for Shabbat reading—the acquisition of new knowledge or insight, reading authors or genres for which you have no time in the remainder of your week, escaping into a fictional world—so that your choices reflect those goals and you do not find yourself reading work-related material that you are unable to squeeze into your hectic schedule.
- *Expressing Ourselves Creatively*—Writing (if you are not a writer by profession), drawing, painting, composing, choreographing, sculpting and landscaping are all traditionally prohibited on Shabbat

Perhaps through play, we can return to some degree to being children. Thus, the seventh day as a reminder of Creation can return us to the creation of ourselves. —J.G.K.

because they involve (among other prohibitions) creating something new, when the goal of Shabbat is to rest and appreciate what is already created. Many of us find, however, that creative activities such as those listed here can be an experience of opening up to the greater cosmos and aligning with forces that we don't ordinarily access. In this sense, it is indeed a prayerful yielding that is in the spirit of Shabbat; it is as close to that spirit as many of us will come.

- *Cultural Events*—Of course, a museum exhibit, a gallery show or an artistic performance of any kind has the capacity to elevate one's spirit, increasing our awareness of the intricate majesty of Creation.
- *Physical Rest*—If it is physical rest (*menuḥat Shabbat*) that you seek, then you may want to establish a regular routine of retiring early, sleeping late or taking afternoon naps. Depending on your level of exhaustion on Friday afternoon, or on whether you find services or visiting with people relaxing or exhausting, your goals for Shabbat rest may sometimes indeed be best accomplished by spending a part of the day catching up on sleep.

Jewish cultural or civilizational pursuits are especially appropriate ways of celebrating Shabbat. These include such activities as singing Jewish songs, playing in a klezmer band, studying the work of philosopher Baruch Spinoza and listening to Israeli music. The Jewish institutional world would do well to provide more opportunities for this sort of Shabbat celebration. —J.A.S.

In each of these instances and in countless other possibilities, the challenge is finding a way to enter into the spirit of Shabbat. If you are so inclined, consider saying a traditional *b'rakha* (blessing) such as *m'kadesh Hashabbat* (giving thanks for the gift of Sabbath holiness). Or you may want to compose your own blessing, through which you can declare (and remind yourself of) your intention to engage in this activity in the spirit of Shabbat, whatever that means to you. Part of the potential power of Shabbat is that it provides a regular, weekly opportunity for us to switch into the realm of *menuḥa*/rest, both in what we do and in our mode of consciousness.

A Full Day?

Shabbat observed for a full 25 hours remains the ideal. Carving out one-seventh of our week and living in a Shabbat consciousness in which we are able to dial down the busyness of our lives and focus on things that have ultimate meaning offers the promise of transformation. This is true whether or not we set foot in a synagogue. Including many alternatives to traditional Shabbat observance here illustrates that each of us can find a distinct path into Shabbat experience, determined by our upbringing, experiences and spiritual proclivities.

Can you find friends or other people with similar interests to share these activities *as Shabbat activities?* For many people, that would deepen the power of the Shabbat experience. —J.A.S.

Perhaps most daunting is the challenge of observing Shabbat for a full day. That is the ideal. However, it is not an all-or-nothing choice, as so many people know who regularly light candles, make Kiddush, and have a Shabbat meal on Friday evenings without continuing Shabbat practice on Saturdays. Obviously, a piece of Shabbat is far better than none, and two or three pieces—for example, a leisurely Saturday afternoon stroll, a *Havdala* ceremony on Saturday evening—are better than one. You might also choose to make a resolution to concentrate on one or more of the Shabbat-spirit values that you find most powerful—to focus on family, for example, or to remain in a mindful, contemplative mode. With practice—as with any spiritual practice—you may find that pockets of Shabbat consciousness expand and eventually join to make a full day.

"More than Israel has kept the Sabbath," the great Hebrew essayist Ahad Ha'am wrote, "the Sabbath has kept Israel." Shabbat is a gift, available for our enjoyment and the deepening of our lives.

Yamim Nora'im: *Days of Awe*

YAEL RIDBERG

Approaching the serious spiritual challenges of the High Holy Day season can be a daunting task. The Hebrew name given to the holidays of Rosh Hashana and Yom

More than anything else, the melodies, or *nusaḥ* of the *Yamim Nora'im* service distinguish these days from the rest of the year for those who attend services regularly. They are alternately complex and simple, majestic and humble, allowing us to get lost in the awesome and then to come back to the familiar. The *ma'ariv* (evening) service, usually minor with a hint of the darkness of the night, is transformed into a warm and golden tune sung in major melodies. The *shaḥarit* (morning) service, usually resolute and confident, is transformed into an ethereal and mysterious journey. Most haunting are the muted strains of the *n'ila* service on Yom Kippur, pleading and otherworldly. The melodies of the *Yamim Nora'im* throw us off balance musically and cause us to reframe our relationship to the words of the liturgy, which, despite their embellishments, follow the same patterns as those of the rest of the year.
—J.M.S.

Kippur is *Yamim Nora'im,* the Days of Awe. The celebration and commemoration of these days invokes a mixture of anticipation and anxiety, self-evaluation and enjoyment. Contemporary Jews experience all of these emotions and more because these days are devoted to the most fundamental questions about what it means to be human, about the meaning of life, and about the tension between intentions and actions. These days also provide meaningful opportunities to gather with family and friends and to celebrate in community.

Rosh Hashana and Yom Kippur are for many the most solemn and significant days on the Jewish calendar, the days when many more Jews gather for prayer than at any other time of the year. However, many of us are unprepared when we come to synagogue on these days. Uncertain about what to expect and what is expected of us, we

The word "*nora'im*" carries with it both a sense of awe and a sense of fear. It reminds us that in these awe-filled days, the difficult work of seeking forgiveness carries with it the anxiety of not being spiritually prepared for Yom Kippur. —N.H.M.

Awe is sometimes unhelpfully understood as a synonym for fear. Awe is evoked by an experiential awareness of the vastness of the galaxies in the cosmos, for example, or by the majesty of the flight of an eagle. Awe is connected to a sense of wonder, and a corresponding sense of my individual minuteness in the greater scheme of things. I go through my days as if my concerns are central and of the greatest importance, but then, in a state of awe, I realize what is really important. —J.J.S.

The *Yamim Nora'im* can be especially challenging for people who come to synagogue rarely if ever during the rest of the year. The themes of the High Holy Days are intense, but the key metaphors of the liturgy are extremely problematic for anyone who has difficulty with traditional God concepts. From Rosh Hashanah through Yom Kippur, the image of God as king is central. It can be very helpful to remember that this is a metaphor. God is not a king or a ruler or even a supreme being. The function of a metaphor is to describe something that cannot actually be described

are unprepared to confront the personal, spiritual and religious challenges of these days. We are unprepared because these days deal with the difficult, fundamental questions of human nature. We are confronted in the liturgy with the ideas of sin and repentance, justice and mercy, life and death, as well as with our relationships with other people,

directly; a good metaphor opens up our thinking in new ways. The question to ask ourselves, as we encounter potentially difficult images of God in the liturgy, is not "Do I believe this?" but rather, "Where is this image trying to take me?" The metaphor of God-as-king can help to give me a sense of my relative smallness in the cosmos and the truth of the ephemeral nature of my own life. It can also give me the sense that I am obligated to something far greater than myself. Whether I name that power "God" or "reality" or "the source of life," I am invited to contemplate my place in the universe and the ways in which I am called into service to something beyond myself. —T.S.

Part of the challenge of the High Holy Day season is that Rosh Hashana and Yom Kippur make the most sense in the context of ongoing observance. Then the cumulative themes offer a counterpoint. When they are the only elements of Jewish observance, it can feel like jumping into very deep, very cold water—shocking and uninviting. Prayer leaders and participants together can find ways to make the experience meaningful and welcoming. —D.W.

We are also unprepared for this season because, while High Holy Day prayers are designed to prompt us to face these central questions, many of us find that they are phrased in idioms that are no longer resonant. Sometimes the prayers are an obstruction to prayer and transformative experience. —J.J.S.

Many additional challenges make these days daunting: the notions of guilt and sin that pervade the *Yamim Nora'im* are problematic or offensive to many. The dominant metaphors of God as king or ruler or judge likewise raise issues for many, especially for Reconstructionists. Yael Ridberg and the commentators address these challenges throughout this chapter. —J.A.S.

Those who come to worship on the High Holy Days are confronted not only with difficult issues but also with liturgy that may be unfamiliar since it takes this form only during this one season of the year. However, for Jews who join for communal prayer primarily during this season, it may be the only liturgy with which they are at all familiar. —J.G.K.

our understanding of God and, most profoundly, our sense of self. Facing oneself and the need to change one's life can feel like an overwhelming challenge. As with most intense and important experiences in our lives, we need to prepare for these holiest days in order to understand them and find meaning in their observance. Before one prayer is said, one sermon heard, one apple dipped in honey or one greeting of "*Shana tova*" ("a good new year") expressed, there is much work to be done.

At the heart of our preparations for the Days of Awe is the concept of change and transformation. Jewish tradition understands that human beings are not perfect. We make mistakes that affect others as well as ourselves, but these errors of judgment, omission and commission need not

Entering into the longest and most emotionally demanding services of the year without preparation is like deciding to run a long distance race without any training. We can appreciate the depths and distances of the Days of Awe so much more fully when we are sufficiently spiritually prepared. The regular weekday and Shabbat prayers, the daily awareness of careful and kind speech, regular Torah study—all help to prepare us to run the full distance that the *Yamim Nora'im* are designed to take us. Through regular, thoughtful practice, we may become more primed for working with the difficult fundamental questions of this season. —V.M.

Preparation for the Days of Awe is the work of the entire year. Imagine a year that held that awareness every day! —S.P.W.

While human beings are not perfect, the traditional notions that each person has a pure soul and is made in the divine image are affirmations that change is possible and that there is no limit to the potential growth of our capacity for goodness and love. —J.A.S.

Acknowledging and responding to human imperfection is at the heart of most religious and philosophical traditions. The Jewish approach to *t'shuva*—understanding that we make mistakes and that we can atone for them—can be deeply redemptive. —D.W.

remain with us forever. On Rosh Hashana, we celebrate life and the possibility of new beginnings. We affirm the freedom and responsibility we have to conduct our lives with decency and morality. On Yom Kippur, we focus on the mistakes we make when we fail to exercise our freedom with responsibility. We seek atonement and forgiveness for our mistakes, and we experience the fragility of life. We realize that we want to make a meaningful difference by the way we live our lives while we still can.

The Days of Awe are a communal reenactment of ancient rites, and at the same time they serve as an individual confrontation with our current reality. What are we called to do at this time of year? Are these days just a burdensome obligation? How can they be as meaningful as possible? An essential message of the *Yamim Nora'im*

Rebbe Nachman of Bratslav taught: "If you believe that you are able to ruin things, then believe that you are able to fix them." (*The Chambers of the Palace: Teachings of Rabbi Nachman of Bratslav,* ed. Y. David Shulman) —T.S.

On Rosh Hashana we also begin to acknowledge our fragility and lack of ability to control our future, a theme that is further emphasized on Yom Kippur. —N.M.

The rituals of the *Yamim Nora'im* allow us to re-encounter the mythic truths of our existence as human beings, particularly our fragility and our desire to do better. —N.M.

The *Yamim Nora'im* unabashedly address big and challenging themes. There are many practices—meditation, prayer, journaling and more—that can help us to carry the insights gained during this season through the rest of the year. —D.W.

What feelings arise as we mark the passage of another year? There any many possibilities: I'm a year older, and I'm sad. I really haven't succeeded in doing the *t'shuva* I had planned on doing a year ago, and I'm discouraged. Or, life is so precious, and my longevity and health are not to be taken for granted, and I'm so grateful for all of my blessings. On Rosh Hashana we get to choose: who will be sad, who will be discouraged, and who will be grateful. —J.J.S.

is about the miracle of having lived another year, and the renewal of our awareness that life is a gift. The *Yamim Nora'im* are an opportunity for solemn rejoicing, for awareness of the ability to seek and grant forgiveness and, above all, for recognizing the human capacity for change.

T'shuva, repentance or returning to one's true self, is the core concept of the *Yamim Nora'im*. But the related categories of sin, atonement, forgiveness and pardon are also central, and each has its own nuances.

Sin

Jewish tradition does not understand human imperfections as being the result of an "original sin" by Adam and

The most profound human characteristic is the capacity to change consciously, but it is not easy to tap into that capacity. The changes we make pay our debt to the future. —S.P.W.

T'shuva involves realignment. The work of this time is to seek realignment with our inner nature and its optimal outward expression. —M.K.

Original sin is a fundamental principle of Christianity. In our Christian-dominated society, we tend to define sin through this lens rather than the lens of Judaism. Unless we first provide a Jewish definition of sin, this can cause the discussion of sin in a Jewish context to sound awkward and uncomfortable. We all "miss the mark" from time to time, but that is very different from the idea of original sin. —N.H.M.

It may be unavoidable that we sin, but Jewish tradition never calls us sinners. The *Tanya*, the seminal work of the founder of Habad Hasidism, begins with an analysis of the idea that all Jews should see themselves as *benonim*—people in an intermediate status, neither fully sinners nor fully righteous. The Kol Nidre service begins with a self-granted permission to pray with sinners. The statement establishes that, while sinners are allowed in the service on principle, all of us who are praying see

Eve in the Garden of Eden. Sin is the result of our negative human tendencies or inclinations, known in Hebrew as the *yetzer hara* (the inclination toward evil), which must be channeled in ways that affirm life by the influence of the *yetzer hatov* (the inclination to goodness). The word in Hebrew for sin (*ḥet*) literally means something that goes astray, like an arrow that misses the mark. When an

ourselves as something other than complete sinners. Identity is key. If we walk into synagogue with the identity of sinners, we will not be able to move beyond that identity to make the changes in our actions and in ourselves that are necessary. —J.M.S.

According to one Jewish understanding, sinning is the act of becoming distant from God. That alienation in itself cuts us off from goodness. When we regret our actions, we return to God or to godliness. As Mordecai Kaplan puts it, "If we identify God with that aspect of reality which confers meaning and value on life and elicits from us those ideals that determine the course of human progress, then the failure to live up to the best that is in us means that our souls are not attuned to the divine, that we have betrayed God." (*The Meaning of God in Modern Jewish Religion*, page 165) —B.P.

The *yetzer hara* has been much explained and much misunderstood. This "necessary enemy" is sometimes described in terms very similar to the definition of the Freudian id: our raw, urgent desires—"I want, I want, I want." Similarly, the *yetzer hara* has been understood as our drive to preserve our separate, physical selves without understanding our connections to others and the world around us. Desire and self-preservation are important and useful, but they do sometimes lead to harm, even to evil. —J.A.S.

One understanding of the word "Torah" is that it is related to the Hebrew word "*yara*," "to shoot." The Torah guides our actions so that our efforts come closer to their target. —J.J.S.

archer misses the target, it is not a permanent failure. Rather, an archer can keep trying to get arrows closer to the target and ultimately to its center. There is no guarantee of immediate success, nor does success ensure that the goal will be reached in all subsequent attempts.

The story of Noah and the flood teaches that human beings are imperfect, even permanently flawed. The Torah

"Sin" is a difficult word for many Jews, who know it primarily through its Christian connotations. Rabbi Adin Steinsaltz has written about traditional Jewish understandings of sin: "Sin is viewed as a correlate of mitzvah; it is treated not as a separate, independent entity but rather as a shadow-essence or even, at times, a reverse image of mitzvah." (*Contemporary Jewish Religious Thought*, eds. Arthur A. Cohen and Paul Mendes-Flohr) A useful Reconstructionist understanding of "mitzvah" can be developed from a Hasidic play on words that derives the word "mitzvah" not from the Hebrew "*l'tzavot*," "to command," but from the Aramaic root "*tzavta*," "to bind together, to connect." Thus, a mitzvah is that which connects us—to the ultimate, to our past, to our family and our community, to the earth, to our own deepest values and to others in need. Sin, then, is an action that leads to a disruption of these connections. —T.S.

In contrast to *ḥet*, the Hebrew words for "teaching" ("Torah") and "teacher" ("*moreh*" or "*mora*") evoke similar imagery since they are derived from the Hebrew root "*yud-resh-hey,*" which means "to shoot" or "to aim for the target." Sacred texts and teachers are meant to aim us onto the right path. —J.G.K.

Remembering the flood and the possibility of forgiveness is a significant part of the Rosh Hashana liturgy. It appears in the *zikhronot* (remembrances) section of the *musaf* service (*Kol Haneshamah: Maḥzor Leyamim Nora'im*, pages 638–9): "And so, with love, did you remember Noah, and appoint him for a fate of mercy and redemption, even as you brought the Flood upon the world … as it is written in your Torah: 'God remembered Noah and every living thing, and all the beasts with him upon the Ark, and God caused a breeze to pass throughout the earth, and all the floodwaters withdrew.'" (Genesis 8:1) —V.M.

imagines that upon reflection, God realizes that to destroy the world every time there is corruption and lawlessness would be an endless exercise. Human beings are flawed from the time of our youth, from our encounters with the world, and from the challenges we face as our lives unfold. Jewish tradition does not expect us to be perfect, although we are always responsible for our actions. Jewish practices provide ways of transforming our lives for the good. We understand the imperfections of our biblical ancestors as powerful reminders that, despite our flaws, we can be good people, even if we sometimes act in ways that conflict with kindness and justice. Our characters are shaped by how we respond to our failures more than by our failures themselves.

Forgiveness

The Torah portrays the first collective sin of the Jewish people as the making of a molten calf (Exodus 32) and

An early midrash suggests that even before the flood, God had learned that the world could not survive if it was held to a standard of strict justice and perfection. For the world to remain viable, God blended compassion into it during its creation. (*B'reyshit Raba* 12.15) —N.M.

Some practices aid us in transforming our relationships with ourselves; some assist in changing our relationships with the wider world or with members of our communities; and some help us to achieve a deeper relationship with the divine. —D.W.

Rashi, a medieval Bible commentator, wrote that the instructions for building the *Mishkan* were given before the sin of the golden calf because God does not supply the disease without first supplying the antidote. —J.G.K.

presents a model of forgiveness in the people's healing from that sin. We first learn of the concept of *s'liḥa* (forgiveness) in this story when the Israelites ask God, "Pardon our iniquity and our sin." (Exodus 34:9) This story and several others in the Bible establish the God of Israel as a forgiving, compassionate and even merciful God, in addition to being a God of justice and law. These two themes—justice and mercy—are at the center of the *Yamim Nora'im*.

The Bible expanded the concept of repentance and atonement with the institution of the ancient Temple's sacrificial system, which held that atonement could be achieved through expiation rites. While one biblical

The Jewish Publication Society's five-volume *Tanakh* contains an amazing diagram by scholar Jacob R. Marcus. It is a graphic mountain constructed of verses in the Hexateuch, the five books of the Torah plus the Book of Joshua, beginning at either end and converging toward the center of these six books. The center is the 13 *midot*, the revelation of God as the God of compassion and forgiveness. This is the center of our holiest text, the center of our faith, the center of our holiest festivals. —S.P.W.

In the process of asking for forgiveness, we sometimes overlook the fact that the divine balance between justice and mercy also applies to us. Many of us who are well practiced in being judgmental of ourselves are less practiced in the enterprise of self-compassion. It is difficult to forgive ourselves for mistakes that we have made. When we ask God for mercy and forgiveness, we can also ask for divine support in helping us to have compassion for ourselves. —J.J.S.

On a certain level, the sacrificial system reflects the idea that each individual and communal sin disperses God's essence and protective presence. Offering sacrifices was the way to restore that presence in its fullest concentration. Doing *t'shuva* each year is a way of refocusing on God's presence, on restoring our focus on leading a godly life. —N.H.M.

understanding of reward and punishment holds that there are consequences for sinful actions, the goal of expiation rites was not just avoiding punishment, but a redirection of one's life toward godly behavior. The choice of which way to go belongs to each person. In Deuteronomy, the Torah imagines God saying, "I put before you the blessing and the curse, life and death; therefore, choose life, that you may live." (Deuteronomy 30:19) Humanity is God's partner in the betterment of the world, a process that must begin with each individual.

Kapara and *m'ḥila* (atonement and pardon) are introduced in the priestly and prophetic texts of the Bible, which speak of the atonement of the people Israel, their return to God, and God's acceptance of them anew. Rab-

In the Torah's sacrificial system, an additional consequence of sinful action is the loss of God from the community; our personal transgressions are linked to the health of the group as a whole. —N.M.

In early biblical traditions, "*ḳapara*" connoted "wiping off." Our ancestors understood sinful behavior as impacting the body as well as the mind/spirit. As an embodied experience, atonement required the sinner to cleanse his or her body, in essence wiping off the effect of wrongdoing. —T.K.

binic sages believed that *t'shuva* was created even before the actual creation of the world. In the Babylonian Talmud (*Yoma* 86a–b) the rabbis describe *t'shuva* as bringing redemption and healing to the world that reaches up into the heavens. *T'shuva* is possible for all who are able to acknowledge wrongdoing, express regret and ultimately change their conduct.

Although "*t'shuva*" literally means "returning" or "going back," the process of *t'shuva* really involves a break with the past to create something new. Going back actually requires doing something creative to move oneself past old pains and behaviors. In nature, that act of making something new is evident in the Big Bang and in evolution. In this sense, such renewal is present in Creation, if not before Creation, but the nature of renewal reaches a new, deep level with the evolution of conscious beings who have free will. —J.A.S.

The Talmud (*Pesaḥim* 54a; *N'darim* 39b) lists seven things that were created before the world: The Torah, *t'shuva* (repentance), *Gan Eden* (the Garden of Eden or paradise), Gehenna (purgatory), the throne of glory, the Temple and the name of the Messiah. Why did the rabbis say that *t'shuva* preexisted the world as we know it? Mistakes are a part of the very fabric of our lives, as they were meant to be. When we see our capacity for reassessment, regret and transformation as part of our original design, rather than beating ourselves up for our mistakes, we can rejoice in our flexibility and in the gift of second chances. —V.M.

What might they have meant when they said that *t'shuva* was created before the creation of the world? Perhaps this means that part of the perfection of the universe is that it is imperfect in all of its components, and that each imperfect creature (you and I) is born with an innate predisposition to fail and then to improve—that it is never too late, and that second chances are the warp and woof of creation. —J.J.S.

Certainly *t'shuva* is integral to creation. It is a principle of possibility, creativity and love, and all healing depends upon it. An integral part of Creation, *t'shuva* sustains our temporary and fragile lives. A principle that underlies the possibility of a life of meaning, it is what makes freedom so cherished. —S.P.W.

T'shuva opens us to change in our relationships to others and in our sense of ourselves. On the *Yamim Nora'im*, we have an opportunity to recognize the blessings, remember the challenges, and acknowledge the failures of the year gone by. We pray for the strength, courage and wisdom to enter the New Year and face the future without knowing what is to come. Through our quest for meaning, wholeness and holiness we can confront what weighs us down, makes us cynical and separates us from others. When we engage in this process of *t'shuva* on an individual level, in our families, in our local communities, in the Jewish community as a whole and in the global community, we can accept the imperfections in our past and become better able to face whatever lies ahead.

The rabbis teach that the work of *t'shuva* is two-fold. During the month of Elul, which precedes the *Yamim Nora'im*, we engage in *t'shuva beyn adam laḥavero* (reconciliation between human beings), and when we come together on Yom Kippur, we are seeking *t'shuva beyn*

Sometimes we need to bridge the walls of separation between others and ourselves. At other times, we need to establish boundaries, so that we can become less enmeshed in relationships that are unhealthy and hurtful. —J.J.S.

True repentance is not sustainable if it is practiced only once a year. Franz Kafka commented, "Only our concept of time makes it possible to speak of the Day of Judgment by that name; in reality it is a summary court in perpetual session." The work of *t'shuva* must be a year-round process for us to truly transform our lives. —B.P.

The Mishna clearly expresses the need to seek forgiveness from others: "Those transgressions that are between human and the divine, Yom Kippur does atone; those transgressions that are between human and human, Yom Kippur does not atone until one has appeased the other." (*Yoma* 8.3) —V.M.

adam lamakom (reconciliation between human beings and God). The first kind of work is more readily understood. We make mistakes; we treat others badly; we are selfish and self-absorbed. We apologize; we repair the damage we have done; we seek forgiveness and forgive others. The medieval commentator Maimonides teaches in his code, the *Mishneh Torah*, that *t'shuva* is a three-stage process. First we must regret our actions, confront the reality of what we have done, apologize and make rec-

Some psychologists teach that practicing best behaviors even when they do not feel right may lead us to practice those behaviors more naturally. Perhaps there are times when Rambam's three-stage sequence goes in reverse: Right behavior in the present can inspire regret for wrong behavior in the past. —J.G.K.

Some of the most meaningful moments of the *Yamim Nora'im* are the moments when I ask others forgiveness for hurt that I have caused; by acknowledging my imperfection, being forgiven, and strengthening bonds with those I love, I can more fully experience being human. —N.M.

There is a custom of saying, "If I have inadvertently hurt you in any way over the last year, please forgive me." I personally dread such encounters. I have no choice but to say, "Yes, I forgive you," whether or not that is accurate. If *t'shuva* requires acknowledgement of and regret for what we have done, then it would be much more transformative to ask, "Have I done anything to you for which I ought to ask forgiveness?" It would be good to ask that long enough before Yom Kippur to be able to find time to have a serious conversation. I really am not able to forgive you unless I have some assurance that we share a perspective on what happened, so that I have some assurance that it is less likely to happen again. —J.J.S.

Jewish teachings on *t'shuva* insist that true repentance is possible. However, even if an individual repents and is granted forgiveness by those whom she or he has wronged, this does not necessarily mean that things will go back to "the way they used to be." Repentance does not mean erasure or reset, but rather a new beginning. —D.W.

ompense. Then we must reject that flawed conduct for ourselves. Finally, we must resolve to live differently in the future, and if confronted with the opportunity to sin again, we must behave differently, for that is when we know we have really repented.

Confronting our "sins against God" is a different matter, and the liturgy of Yom Kippur takes us beyond the actions that are between people to our actions that affect our interior, personal world. As mentioned earlier, the rituals regarding sin and atonement in the Torah were to be carried out through expiation and sacrificial rites, first in the portable sanctuary of the Exodus period, and later in the Jerusalem Temples. Only after the Second Temple was destroyed in 70 CE did these rites fully evolve into prayers and individual actions of repentance, forgiveness and atonement.

Of course, biblical and rabbinic understandings of God made the approaches to sin and atonement visceral and all encompassing. In our time, many Jews do not believe in a God who possesses personality, feelings, vulnerability and a will to act, punish and then forgive. How do we express our more global, human failures? How are our confessions "heard," and how do we experience "forgiveness"? It is possible to conceive of God as the power in the uni-

One way to experience forgiveness viscerally, even if I don't believe in a God who is aware of my thoughts and actions, is modeled by the Slonimer Rebbe in his book *Netivot Shalom* (*Pathways of Peace*). In his eyes, divine love, compassion and forgiveness flow constantly and perpetually from God to each human being. *T'shuva* is the process of acknowledging my lack of control, my limitations and errors, and my yearning to be loved and held. At that point—the point of heartbreak—I let divine love in, unobstructed by my ego defenses. I am changed, even though God has not done anything other than what God always does. My *t'shuva* is the variable. —J.J.S.

verse that makes for unity and creativity and helps us to experience life as worthwhile. When we encounter the liturgy of Yom Kippur that deals with *t'shuva beyn adam*

Mordecai Kaplan, in his discussion of Yom Kippur and the Jewish notion of sin, suggests that the thread that runs from the Bible to our own time is the idea that sin involves "a disturbance in the relation between humanity and God." (*The Meaning of God in Modern Jewish Religion*, page 165) If, according to Kaplan, God is understood as "that aspect of reality which confers meaning and value on life," then "sinning" means the failure to be attuned to the godliness that functions within and through us. The relationship we disrupt here is not between ourselves and some supernatural being. It is rather a disruption of our relationship to a fundamental aspect of reality that we can call "divine": the potential for good and wholeness that manifest both in individuals and within human society. *T'shuva*, then, entails intentions and actions that repair that disruption and disconnection. *T'shuva* fosters wholeness both within ourselves and in the world around us. —T.S.

"*Makom*" is a name of God that literally means "place." Perhaps we can understand the rabbis' choice of this name for God as suggesting that our deepest inner work involves realigning with the place of godliness within us, a "place" in our inner landscape that is sacred and divine in essence. As human beings, we must work if we are to return to this place. —M.K.

In Hebrew, "*Adam*" is spelled "*alef-daled-mem*." A human being is both the "*aleph*," understood in the Jewish mystical tradition to be the ineffable spirit from which all existence is derived, and the "*daled-mem*"—"*dam*," literally, the "blood." A human being thus comprises both spirit and flesh and blood, or physicality. The work of *t'shuva beyn adam lamakom* can be understood as working to remove the impediments that cause a rupture between the "letters" or parts of one's humanness in order to sit in right alignment with the "place" of one's true existence, at once both fully human and fully godly in nature. —M.K.

lamakom, we must grapple with actions that are "ungodly"—actions that have the potential to affect us on the deepest level. Judaism teaches that we are called to God's service. The *t'shuva* that we seek goes beyond how we treat one another and into the very essence of who we are, into the realm of the soul.

On Rosh Hashana and Yom Kippur, we have the opportunity to make amends, wipe the slate clean and begin again with our loved ones, our friends and the larger community. We can change how we act in the world.

Grappling with our inner need for *t'shuva* requires that we pay attention deeply and fully so that we notice these innermost realms in which the reverberations of our actions are felt and absorbed. In Hebrew, "*sim lev*" means "pay attention." This term literally means "to put one's heart," or "to attend with the heart." The Yom Kippur liturgy asks us to pay attention from the depths of our hearts. The *t'shuva*, the turning of our lives that we seek on this day, is a turning that begins from the depths of the heart, not from the periphery of the body or from a mind disconnected from the more interior layers of consciousness and conscience. —M.K.

In addition to crucial soul work, another type of *t'shuva* may be included in the category *beyn adam lamakom* (between human beings and God). Traditionally, this category included what many would describe as ritual mitzvot. Jewish rituals may not directly affect our relations with others. But in more naturalist terms, we may ask whether the relationship we are forging to Jewish civilization, including its rituals, is able to help shape our lives in godly ways. —J.A.S.

Do we wipe the slate clean? That may be our intention, but it may be an overly ambitious goal that leads to frustration and disappointment. I may pray to begin anew, but I am also the product of every interaction that has created this reality. I would rather wipe a passageway for forgiveness and *t'shuva* across the slate than expect to wipe it clean. —S.P.W.

I do not find the phrase "wiping the slate clean" to be helpful or realistic. When I forgive or I am forgiven, the past is not erased. Rather, we have the opportunity to be healed and to proceed in a new way together. We may even be able to let go completely of injured feelings. But it's not as if nothing happened. Sometimes the relationship becomes deeper and closer as the result of a conflict and its resolution. —J.J.S.

The "script" for these days is largely the same—many prayers that appear in the machzor, the prayer book designated for the Days of Awe, are standard prayers of the siddur, but there are insertions and *piyyutim* (liturgical poems) that are exclusive to these days. "Machzor" literally means "cycle," and it reflects the very nature of the Days of Awe—how we cycle through the year, bring it to a close, and begin again, identifying the aspects of ourselves and our lives that are in need of evaluation and renewal. The prayers may be familiar, but very often our circumstances have changed, as each year brings its own unique story of our lives and our world.

There is a Hasidic story about a cantor who was studying the prayers before the holidays. He came in a rush to the rabbi in his community and asked to be dismissed from additional duties. The rabbi asked him why he was hurrying, and the cantor replied that he had to look at the machzor and get his prayers in order. The rabbi replied that the prayers were the same as last year, and it would be better if the cantor would look into his own deeds and put himself in order.

For those who do not regularly attend synagogue, the High Holy Day liturgy with its *piyyutim* can be challenging, unfamiliar and hard to access. I appreciate it when service leaders give me and others permission not to stay "on the page." —N.M.

The predominant imagery of the High Holy Day additions to the liturgy about God—sovereign, judge and parent—can sometimes obscure other conceptions of God that may speak to contemporary Jews, such as God as the source of life or God as an ever-renewing process. As we teach about the High Holy Days, drawing on other metaphors may prove helpful. —D.W.

Preparations During the Month of Elul

Jewish tradition understands that the *Yamim Nora'im* can be difficult and all-consuming. To get the most out of our prayers, celebrations and rituals, we must prepare ourselves. It is easy to let the summer months come to an end, return to work or school and the yearly routine, and then be unprepared when Rosh Hashana comes. We often describe the holidays as coming "early" or "late," when really they come exactly on time, and it is we who need to be ready. The month of Elul, which immediately precedes the *Yamim Nora'im,* is a time of preparation. The general mood of the month of Elul is one of introspection and renewal. As the month begins, we begin the process of *ḥesh-*

I am always keenly aware of the moon during the month of Elul. The August sky of the Northeastern United States where I live is frequently clear, and as the moon moves through its phases, I count off the days of spiritual preparation for the onset of the *Yamim Nora'im*. As the moon wanes, I feel an increasing sense of urgency: The Day of Judgment approaches! —D.W.

The holidays do come early or late compared to those of the other civilization in which we live and the other calendar we use to orient our time. This is not insignificant. —S.P.W.

Rabbinic teachings remind us that even as the mood of Elul is a sober one of introspection and inner stocktaking, it is also a joyful time, for it is one when we can become aroused spiritually and stir ourselves to inner awakening. We can imagine God as our beloved who yearns for us to return to her. The letters of "Elul"—*aleph, lamed, vav, lamed*—are said to be an acronym of "*Ani l'dodi v'dodi li*" ("I am my beloved's, and my beloved is mine") from the Song of Songs 6:3. (*Mishnah Berurah, Arukh Hashulḥan*) We reclaim our deeply loving relationship to God, to our own inner beloved. This mystical imagery also has a profound psychological impact: As we do the work of facing all that we have done wrong, neglected and failed at, we might enter into despair and depression. The acronym suggests that we are lovable and desired, claimed and embraced, even in the midst of our human shortcomings. Only with this abiding sense of ultimate well-being and acceptance can we dare to undertake the work of repentance that Elul beckons us to do. —M.K.

bon hanefesh (literally, accounting of the soul; taking stock of oneself). This process is a personal one in which we are asked to look back on the year that is coming to a close, to look carefully at our lives, to re-evaluate and reexamine who and where we are, and to look forward to the ways in which the year that will soon begin can be different. It is also a time to seek to heal relationships, to offer overdue apologies and to repair the damage we have caused to others.

The journey of Elul is heralded by the sounding of the shofar (ram's horn), which is sounded daily (except on Shabbat) throughout Elul in synagogues that have a daily morning service. The shofar can also be sounded at home. The shofar serves as a literal wake-up call to the work of *t'shuva*. The commandment is to hear the sound of the shofar, thereby underscoring the need to listen. Much like human relationships, in which hearing is simple but truly listening to what another person is saying requires great

While we have a sense of urgency about doing *t'shuva* in the month of Elul because of the upcoming Days of Awe, *t'shuva* is actually a practice to be undertaken throughout the year. Self-examination need not wait until August. If I feel there is reconciliation work that needs to be done, for example, it is better for everyone if I do not put it off. —J.J.S.

I often wonder how to deal with the Elul agenda of self-examination in a culture of intense, yearlong introspection. Many of us who are engaged in spiritual practices or psychotherapy are always dealing with these issues. How, then, is Rosh Hashana different? Is it that the introspection is now couched in Jewish language? That the spiritual journey is now a Jewish communal excursion? —S.P.W.

Some of those who sound the shofar each morning during Elul take a break from sounding the shofar on the morning before Rosh Hashana. —J.G.K.

attention and intention, the mitzvah of hearing the sounding of the shofar means something deeper than just being able to hear the sound. During the High Holy Days, there are so many words spoken. Hearing and listening to the sounding of the shofar provides a primal connection beyond words. During traditional Rosh Hashana services, 100 blasts of the shofar are heard. They call us to remember both our personal and our communal past, and to rebuild our relationships and renew our lives.

There are 40 days from the beginning of Elul until Yom Kippur. According to a rabbinic midrash (interpretation), these days correspond to the 40 days that Moses remained on Mount Sinai after the incident with the golden calf. When he descended from Mount Sinai the first time, he saw that the people had created a molten calf to worship. Out of anger and frustration, Moses broke the first set of tablets, which had been inscribed by God. They were the symbol of the covenant between the Jewish people and God. The calf was then burned and the ashes strewn into water for the people to drink as a punishment. When Moses told the people they were guilty of a great sin, he also told them that he would attempt to make atonement on their behalf. Moses entreated God on behalf of the people to spare them from collective punishment, but the Torah describes God as bringing a plague upon those who sinned. According to the text, a second set of tablets was later written by Moses himself, and as the cloud of God descended, the divine voice is said to have uttered the 13 descriptive attributes of God: "compassionate and gracious, slow to anger, abounding in kindness and faithfulness, extending kindness to the thousandth generation, and forgiving iniquity, transgression and sin." (Exodus 34:6–7) It still took Moses quite some time to recover from his first response and return from Mount Sinai to the people, once again holding the tablets, the symbol of the covenant, in his hands.

The midrash implies that the first set of tablets represents that which has been broken—promises, hopes, dreams and covenants. The 40 days can be understood as a metaphor of longing, of a deep desire to return to things as they were before they were broken. At the close of Yom Kippur, having done all that we can to repair what has been broken, we embrace the New Year, grateful for the opportunity to begin anew, to strengthen relationships and start new projects.

The 13 attributes reappear regularly in the liturgy at this season, as well as when the Torah is taken from the ark on festivals. The overwhelming image that these attributes convey is of a forgiving, patient and loving God. By repeating this phrase, the prayer book encourages us not to be afraid of divine judgment. Rather, we should aim to be honest with ourselves and to become vulnerable in order to avail ourselves of God's love and to feel divine forgiveness. —B.P.

We can never return to things as they were before they were broken. That is not possible. And that is not what healing is. We are returning to something that can never truly be broken after it has appeared to be broken. We return with a new tenderness, a new depth of wisdom, kindness and confidence. —S.P.W.

The broken tablets from Sinai remained broken. An ancient teaching tells us that both the fragments of the broken first tablets and the whole second tablets were placed in the Holy Ark. We need not pretend that brokenness does not exist. But we can respond to the brokenness by creating something whole and new. Both the broken and the new remain part of us. —J.G.K./J.A.S.

Another tradition of the month of Elul is the daily recitation of Psalm 27. The theme of this psalm is trust in God—trust that the power that makes for judgment can become further manifest in the world by the presence of justice and mercy in all inhabitants of the world. The psalm opens with these lines: "God is my light and my life; whom shall I fear? God is the foundation of my life; whom shall I dread?" The psalmist expresses fear and doubts about the unknown, but ultimately ends the psalm with a message of hope: "One thing I ask of God; one thing do I seek: to dwell in the house of God forever. . . . Look to God for hope, be strong and of good courage. Look to God for faith." In this way, the text mirrors the work we are called to do at this time of the year. We are called to reflect upon the challenges of our lives and to resolve to seek the godly attributes of love, hope, repair and belief in the future.

Hasidim recite Psalm 27 morning and afternoon, while the custom of other Ashkenazic Jews is to recite it in the morning and evening. —J.G.K.

The Psalmist says, "One thing I seek ... to sit in God's house all the days of my life, to gaze on God's pleasantness." This can be an instruction for practice during the days of Elul. It can be a good thing to sit for a few minutes each day with a sense of being "in YHVH's house"—to experience the godliness of our physical "house," our own bodies. This requires little more than finding ten minutes of quiet, settling into the body, and becoming aware of the sensations of sitting and breathing. In addition to exploring the ways in which we have gone astray in the year past, Psalm 27 invites us to bring a sense of that which is pleasant and good in our lives into our contemplation. Strengthening our capacity for compassion toward ourselves and fostering an ability to sit calmly with our thoughts or sensations helps us to build a foundation for the work of *t'shuva*. —T.S.

The month of Elul is full of opportunities for deep introspection. Jewish tradition invites us to work from the broken parts of ourselves toward wholeness so that when we come together on Rosh Hashana, we are aware of our triumphs and our failures, and we are more humble and sensitive to the random nature of life, which can bring suffering, tragedy and sorrow. We begin with ourselves, even as we also focus on the complicated and often confusing world in which we live, where suffering, hatred and violence are so commonplace, and we set new goals to work for justice and peace. The month of Elul is understood by the Hasidic masters as an *et ratzon*—a time of willingness—that ends with transformation or rebirth at Yom Kippur. Each of us can seek out others and have the difficult conversations about our relationships that we need to have with family, friends and community members. We

Rabbis spend a great deal of time during Elul reading, thinking and writing. These practices can be helpful to anyone who wishes to enter the *Yamim Nora'im* prepared with the tools of *t'shuva* and *s'liḥa* (forgiveness). Keeping a journal during Elul can help us to focus on areas we seek to change or to notice the triggers that send us onto an undesirable path. —B.P.

The Hebrew letters that spell "Elul" are an acronym for "*Ani l'dodi v'dodi li*"—"I am my beloved's and my beloved is mine." In rabbinic understanding, this verse speaks to the relationship between God and the people Israel. Elul, then, is a time of intimacy between the source of compassion and us, a time when we turn toward God and God turns toward us. I like to think of this as meaning that as we engage in the hard work of *t'shuva*, of examining our deeds and making amends, the universe is on our side, supporting us as we turn onto a path of wholeness and peace. —T.S.

I often learn best what my Elul work will require each year by sitting and listening to my heart. —N.M.

can prepare to change our lives for the good in the coming year.

During the month of Elul, seeking out those one has unintentionally hurt or with whom one has had a difficult encounter or a breakdown in relationship can begin the process of seeking *m'ḥila* (forgiveness). A story is told about Rabbi Levi Yitzhak of Berdichev, a Hasidic rebbe of the late 18th century. Before going to bed each day, he would make a list of all that he had done wrong. He would recite the list over and over until regret and grief overcame him. The flow of his tears would be so great that the paper would be wiped clean of his transgressions. The teaching here is not that we need to attain perfection, but rather that we need to acknowledge our very real human imperfections and fragility before we can successfully move into the New Year.

Self-reflection is critical as one prepares for the *Yamim Nora'im,* but there are also Hasidic teachings that caution against being so hard on oneself that one becomes filled with depression and despair, guilt and shame. In such an extreme, one is mired in *yir'a,* fear in the sense of fear of punishment, perhaps fear of one's own being and the bad things one is capable of doing. Such self-alienation is counterproductive. An important counterpoint to the accounting of the soul is to remember one's *n'ḳuda tova,* the good inner point at the center of one's being. Rebbe Nachman of Bratslav offers a practice in which we actively seek out our good points and draw them forth in order to counter the inner voices of self-condemnation that may keep us mistrustful of ourselves and isolated from others. Those voices may also keep us from engaging the form of *yir'a* that the Hasidic masters understood as the more elevated form: awe—awe at the majesty of creation and at our ultimate place in the larger scheme of universal truths that embrace the mysteries of birth, life, joy, suffering, death and rebirth. Both of these practices—focusing on the suffering one has caused oneself or others, and focusing on the inner goodness of one's being and actions—help us to hold ourselves more lightly and fluidly, understanding that it is our human nature to shift and change, and that we can both prune and fertilize the godly aspects of our characters throughout our lives. —M.K.

Some people seek forgiveness face to face, others by phone or letter. Seeking and granting forgiveness are not easy. When approached by a friend or a colleague to forgive her or him, we can see that forgiveness is not casual or even accidental. It is a conscious act that requires us to recognize our own errors and acknowledge our own

How does one seek forgiveness from people or grant forgiveness to them when they are out of reach—those who have passed on, those who refuse to engage, or those to whom we choose not to speak in order to protect ourselves from further harm? What does it mean to forgive someone who does not ask for it? What does it mean to ask for forgiveness when we have no way of knowing if we have been forgiven? One important outcome of seeking or granting forgiveness is the loosening of the rigid places within our own hearts. When we decide to forgive someone who will never know of our forgiveness, we become capable of lifting the burden of anger and the pain of bearing grudges. The same is true of asking for the forgiveness of those who cannot hear our plea. When we truly regret what we have done and resolve to do and be better, we can relieve ourselves of debilitating shame and turn our lives toward goodness. —B.P.

I am deeply moved when an individual approaches me to seek forgiveness, and I learn more in each encounter, no matter how personally challenging, about how to gain the courage to do my own *t'shuva* work. Conversely, I am left cold when acquaintances publicly announce to a group of which I am a part that they apologize for any harm they have done, and urge all listeners to follow up with them if they feel they have been wronged. The onus for seeking forgiveness rests on the person who has transgressed, not on the ones she or he has wronged. The work of atonement is difficult, sometimes mortifying, and there are no shortcuts. —D.W.

faults. In light of our own failings, we are better able to forgive others' mistakes and recognize their humanity. There is no simple formula for granting forgiveness. Many people live their entire lives never forgiving someone who has profoundly wronged them. Elul can be an opportunity to transform our grudges into gratitude and our hardened hearts into healing ones.

Just as there is a deep intersection between the judgment of others and self-judgment, there is an equally deep interconnection between compassion for oneself and compassion for others. God—however we may understand God—may judge. We humans are well served by concentrating our efforts on deepening our compassion. —D.W.

An ongoing part of my process of *ḥeshbon hanefesh* (soul searching) is working on the reality that at times I am far more interested in being right than in seeing something broken become transformed through forgiveness. Sometimes I invest great energy nurturing a garden of bitterness and resentment. What might grow if I were to direct that energy toward forgiveness? —D.W.

The daily bedtime Shema ritual includes a passage in which we individually grant forgiveness to anyone who has harmed us. The formula, "Hereby I forgive," sounds like a completed action, but it may be hard to say it and mean it. The Hebrew can be understood as being in the present-progressive tense: "I am hereby forgiving." We acknowledge the value in the process we are in, even if the process of forgiving is incomplete. —J.G.K.

Are there some acts for which it is impossible to grant forgiveness? Heinous crimes of violence or abuse might qualify. Forgiveness does not mean forgetting that an offense occurred, nor does it require that a relationship be restored. It can sometimes be a letting go of the pain or anger so that the victim of abuse can move forward. —N.H.M.

Another custom during the month of Elul is to visit family graves. This practice may be tied into the theme of *zikaron*, memory—one of the names for Rosh Hashana is *Yom Hazikaron*, Day of Remembrance. We remember our loved ones, their expectations of us, and the values they imparted to us. This custom also underscores the confrontation with the uncertainty and fragility of life that lies at the core of much of the *Yamim Nora'im*. By remembering the dead we are better able to appreciate the sweetness of the gift of life that we renew a few days later at the start of Rosh Hashana.

Finally, it is customary to give *tzedaka* (righteous action to those in need; also, charitable contributions) during this time. The giving of *tzedaka* should not be seen as a penalty for wrongdoing, nor should it be used as a justification for bad behavior. It can be an act that encourages an open heart and a sacred expression of hope for a better world. Just as we conduct *ḥeshbon hanefesh* (soul searching), so may we conduct an accounting of how our resources have been spent and how our values are reflected in our expenditures and our giving.

There is a *minhag* (a Jewish custom) of asking forgiveness from the deceased while visiting the grave. —Y.R.

Sometimes the person from whom we need to seek forgiveness is inaccessible or has even died. In those cases, the culmination of *ḥeshbon hanefesh* may be to offer *tzedaka* in that person's memory or as a personal recognition of atonement. —N.H.M.

Most Jewish organizations use this season to remind us to support their causes. Choosing which organizations to support and determining how much to give can be an Elul practice all on its own. How we give reflects our deepest values. By carefully reviewing the appeals, we can recommit ourselves to our most cherished principles as we enter the new year. This can be an especially powerful lesson for our children when the family discusses such decisions together. In my family, we emptied our *tzedaka* boxes at the holidays and determined together where those funds would go. —B.P.

S'liḥot

One of the traditional practices of the month of Elul is the recitation of special penitential prayers known as *s'liḥot* (forgiveness). Customarily recited late at night or early in the morning, the prayers of *s'liḥot* are recited as a formalized liturgical expression of supplication for seeking forgiveness. Sephardic communities (those with roots in the Mediterranean area) recite these prayers for the full 40 days between the beginning of Elul and Yom Kippur.

The practice among Ashkenazic communities (those from Germany, Russia and Eastern Europe) is to wait until the Saturday night before Rosh Hashana to begin the *s'liḥot* prayers. That Saturday evening service is known as *S'liḥot*. If there are fewer than four days between the closest Saturday night and Rosh Hashana, then *S'liḥot* is held the previous Saturday night to allow for enough days of preparation before the holiday.

We enter into the liturgy and music of the Days of Awe with a special late-night service, traditionally begun at midnight, although many contemporary communities

S'liḥot is one of only two communal rituals that takes place near midnight. The other is *tiḳun leyl Shavuot*, the night of study on the first night of Shavuot, when many attend study sessions that last throughout the night until the earliest time for prayer around dawn. These rituals share a common goal of transformation through substituting prayer or study for sleep. With *S'liḥot*, the goal is for the prayer to be a catalyst for one's own transformational process that continues through the end of the ten days of repentance. —J.M.S.

begin earlier. Many congregations precede the service with study or stories on the themes of repentance and forgiveness, or with a program of High Holy Day music. The *S'lihot* service helps to open the gates to the spiritual and liturgical journey through Rosh Hashana and Yom Kippur. The prayers are pleas for compassion, mercy and forgiveness. The melodies and High Holy Day *nusah* (musical modes) are like a musical overture to Rosh Hashana and Yom Kippur. They are often haunting and full of longing, stirring people's connections with their past.

Even if families or individuals do not attend a *S'lihot* service at a synagogue, the evening can be an opportunity

Before the *S'lihot* service at the congregation I used to serve, congregants individually did a writing exercise about their successes and shortcomings in the previous year. The results were incorporated into the congregation's Yom Kippur liturgy as part of a communal *Al Het* or *Ahavnu* (a contemporary positive counterpoint to the *Vidui*).
—J.G.K.

During *S'lihot*, Kehillat Lev Shalem, the Woodstock Jewish Congregation, does a ritual undressing and redressing of the Torah scrolls in the white mantles of the High Holy Days. The changeover parallels our breaking down our own barriers to do the work of *heshbon hanefesh* (soul searching). —J.G.K.

The *S'lihot* service can be a time to concretize the work of reviewing the past year and preparing for the New Year to come. One practice our community has observed is to have individuals create a visual "intention" for the coming year through making crafts or writing. Participants choose a quality, set a goal, and articulate a desire to bring into the New Year. Having a physical reminder during the year can be powerful; at the end of the year, we will have a visible way of charting our progress. —B.P.

My father died when I was 21 years old. I cannot clearly recall his speaking voice, but I have no problem hearing the sound of his tenor voice as he led the *musaf* services for Rosh Hashana and Yom Kippur (and Shabbat). It is how I am best able to remain close to him. —J.J.S.

for reflection and introspection at home. The short service of *Havdala* that marks the transition from Shabbat to the rest of the week can be a natural place for a home *S'liḥot* observance. Marking the transition between the year coming to a close and the new one about to begin can resonate even for young children. What are they hoping to do better in the coming year? What are they most looking forward to? What are they sorry about? The family members might sound a shofar, sing some of their favorite melodies from the *Yamim Nora'im*, apologize to each other, share situations over the past year when they hurt someone or were hurt by someone, and consider how those situations can be resolved. Some families may even write their own version of the *Al Ḥet* ("For all these sins . . .") prayer and share it on that night together.

There are many explanations for why the *S'liḥot* service begins so late, but most have to do with the mysteries of the night. At night, we might be more relaxed and attentive, and, according to the Hasidic tradition, the mind is more composed since the body is less active. It is also traditionally "the hour of divine good will," when

A parallel exists between the late-night *S'lihot* service and the tradition of a *tikun leyl Shavuot*, studying Torah late into the night (some say all night) on Shavuot, the festival of receiving the Torah. On Shavuot, we open ourselves up to revelation from God. During *S'liḥot*, the Holy One is open to our revelations as we delve more deeply into our souls. —J.G.K.

According to some, God sits on the throne of judgment during the day but not by night, so God's attribute of loving kindness may be more available to us by night. —J.G.K.

prayers are thought to be more powerful since metaphorically speaking, God is understood to be more attentive and receptive, perhaps because we are more open and vulnerable. In a more modern interpretation of this idea, the stillness of the night encourages innerness, and gathering together as a community at a time when people are usually asleep can help to create a different kind of experience.

The ritual of *S'liḥot* is first mentioned in a ninth-century text, *Tana d'vey Eliyahu Zuta*. There, King David is described as being troubled by the lack of prospects for atonement in Israel's future, given the destruction of the Temple, which he knew would occur through prophetic insight. The author imagines God telling David that when troubles come upon Israel, "They should stand before me together as a single unit, make confession before me, and say the *S'liḥot* services before me, and they will be forgiven."

In this midrash, the description of Israel's future confession relates not only to the essential nature of what we

In another scene of seeking divine forgiveness, the Talmud (*Rosh Hashana* 17b) describes Moshe up on Mount Sinai receiving the second set of tablets while receiving forgiveness for the sin of the golden calf. In the rabbinic imagination, God, wrapped in a tallit, demonstrates to Moshe how, in the event of future transgressions, Jews can urge forth divine forgiveness by wrapping themselves in their tallitot, a symbol of God's love, and calling out the divine name of the 13 attributes (Exodus 33:19). As with the *Kedusha* and the Kaddish, Jewish tradition requires a minyan for calling out the 13 attributes of the divine name. —V.M.

do on these holiest of days, but also to the evening service of *S'liḥot* in particular. The community comes together, recites the *Vidui* (*Ashamnu*, the confessional prayer) and prays for a better year to come. While the traditional idea of God answering prayers the way one would answer a letter is challenging for Reconstructionists, we can interpret this process as one in which we humans have a role to play in bringing about the answers to our prayers and our most fervent hopes and dreams.

According to the midrash, God even showed Moses the order of these prayers and indicated that the recitation of the "13 attributes of God" from the book of Exodus (34:6–7) should be included. This passage emphasizes the compassionate and forgiving nature of God. Over the centuries, the liturgy added to the *S'liḥot* service has underscored this idea. While traditions differ as to which prayers are to be included in the service, the basic elements have remained the same.

The traditional *piyyutim* included in the *s'liḥot* were composed between the eighth and 16th centuries CE. The poems focus on the supreme power of the forgiving God, invoking the merciful way God dealt with our ancestors and offering hopeful pleas for the same attention and remembrance for ourselves. Many contemporary communities omit most of the classical *piyyutim* from the service because they are so difficult linguistically, theologically and intellectually. In many Reconstructionist communities, the *S'liḥot* service has been reframed by introducing the familiar melodies and liturgy of Rosh Hashana and Yom Kippur. In addition, many communities include contemporary readings about repentance, forgiveness and renewal. Some of the more popular prayers in the service include *Sh'ma Kolenu* ("Hear our Voice"), the liturgical poem *Ki Anu Amekha* ("For We Are Your People"), the *Vidui* ("Confessional") and *Avinu Malkeynu* ("Our Parent, our Sovereign").

S'liḥot is the opening night for coming together and for furthering our transition into a period of reflecting upon our actions and confessing our mistakes. Its use of the resources of an ancient service of transformation and forgiveness reminds us of the mysteries of life and death, and of the renewal that is possible. When the *S'liḥot* service ends, the community heads off into the night with an awareness of the work that still needs to be done: the introspection, self-evaluation, renewal, and seeking and granting of forgiveness that are at the core of the approaching Days of Awe.

Rosh Hashana

The biblical origins of Rosh Hashana explain very little about the current nature of the holiday and the way we observe it. There are three places in the Torah where the

The words of the *S'liḥot* prayers are more like Yom Kippur prayers than Rosh Hashana prayers. Rosh Hashana is an island of celebration with a different tone from the *s'liḥot* (penitential prayers) that precede and follow it. I am accustomed to *S'liḥot* services that conclude with a blast of the shofar, another parallel to Yom Kippur. —J.G.K.

festival cycle is laid out (Leviticus 23:1–44, Numbers 28:9–29:39 and Deuteronomy 16:1–17). Despite certain differences between them, the references in Leviticus and Numbers refer to the first day of the seventh month of the year (counting from Nisan, the month in which Pesach falls) as a *shabbaton zikhron t'ru'a mikra kodesh* (a complete rest, a sacred occasion commemorated by loud blasts) and *yom t'rua* (a day when the horn is sounded). The sacred number seven seems important to the dating of this commemoration. The seventh day of the week and the completion of a seven-year cycle are considered holy; so too is the seventh month. Rosh Hashana has antecedents in pre-Israelite, Middle Eastern annual rituals for the re-enthronement of the king.

The rabbis of the Mishnah (200 CE) designated the month of Tishri as the beginning of the year. The Talmud explains its function in this way: "On Rosh Hashana, all human beings pass before God as troops, as it is said, 'God looks down from heaven; God sees all of humanity. From God's dwelling place, God gazes on all of the inhabitants of the earth—God who fashions the hearts of all, who discerns all their doings.'" (Psalms 33:13–15; Babylonian Talmud, *Rosh Hashana* 1) The development of the Days of Awe has continued since then. Rosh Hashana, which began as an agricultural observance, was eventually transformed so that it focuses on God's judgment and ultimately on a new beginning for humanity: *hayom harat olam*—the day the world is born anew.

Like all Jewish holidays, Rosh Hashana begins in the evening. Lighting the festival candles at home, creating a festive meal, and enjoying the beginning of the holiday with family and friends ushers in the New Year in a meaningful way. Communities differ as to the starting time of services, thereby determining whether one eats the festive meal before the service or after. Special foods are prepared. The hallah, the sweet braided bread that we eat each Shabbat, is made in round loaves during the *Yamim Nora'im* to remind us of the continuous and never-ending

"*Harat olam*" ("*the birth of the world*") implies the world's conception. Perhaps whatever happens "today" (Rosh Hashana) is a prerequisite for the world to be born, or born anew. Maybe this is why the midrash (found in *Kol Haneshamah: Maḥzor Leyamim Nora'im*, page 185) teaches, "Great is *t'shuva*, for it existed in the world before Creation. …" —J.G.K.

The day the world is born anew is likened to the day a child is born. We experience each as having unlimited possibility. We celebrate to recall our unlimited nature. —S.P.W.

From leeks to carrots, fish heads to dates, several foods are associated with good luck in the new year because either their form ("may our merits multiply like the seeds of a pomegranate") or their name includes a wordplay in a language that Jews have spoken—Hebrew, Aramaic, Yiddish, Russian, Arabic or others. (The pun "May our enemies beat it" works in Hebrew as well as we eat beets on Rosh Hashana.) Inventing blessings in English for common contemporary foods can be a fun exercise for the whole family. These are among my favorites for sweet treats: for sandwich cookies, "May you be surrounded by love"; for cotton candy, "May you always take time to look at the clouds." —J.G.K.

cycle of life. We dip hallah and apples into honey to signify the hope for a sweet New Year. It is customary to wear new clothes on Rosh Hashana. On the second day, it is customary to eat a fruit we may not be accustomed to eating. These rituals give us additional reasons to recite the *Sheheḥeyanu* prayer—the thanksgiving blessing recited on special occasions.

The evening service for Rosh Hashana is brief, and it does not differ significantly from other festival *ma'ariv* (evening) services, but it has its own *nusaḥ* (melodic line). It contains a few specific references to Rosh Hashana, but traditionally the service is short so as to allow for a timely return home in order to share the festival meal. The Reconstructionist machzor includes a special section called *Kabbalat Hashanah (Kol Haneshamah Maḥzor Leyamim Nora'im*, pages 30–54) that can serve as introductory songs, readings and additional prayers that can expand the evening service if it is being held after people have already eaten dinner.

Agave nectar and maple syrup are among vegan alternatives to honey. —J.G.K.

As our awareness of sweatshops and slave labor increases, buying new clothes for Rosh Hashana can be an opportunity to begin the year on the right foot by increasing our commitment to purchasing only fair trade clothing. —J.G.K.

The first addition to the service comes just before the *Amida*: "*Tik'u vaḥodesh shofar* ..."—"Sound the shofar at the new moon, at the appointed time for our festival day." (Psalm 81:4) No matter how much I have prepared for Rosh Hashana, this moment makes me tingle, as if the declaration of the day connects me with preceding generations who have made the same declaration. —J.J.S.

The additions to the service that refer to Rosh Hashana appear in the *Amida* prayer and focus on the themes of remembrance and our hope to be in the Book of Life: *Zokhreynu l'ḥayim*—Remember us for life; *zokher yetzurav l'ḥayim b'raḥamim*—remember your creatures for life in mercy; *u'khtov l'ḥayim tovim kol b'ney v'ritekha*—write down for a good life all the people of your covenant; and *b'sefer ḥayim b'rakha v'shalom*—in the Book of Life, with blessing, peace, and proper sustenance may we be remembered and inscribed.

Thus, the evening service introduces the major themes of Rosh Hashana: the creation of the world, the sovereignty of God, divine judgment and remembrance. These themes present an opportunity to identify the creativity that persists every day—the sovereignty of God as

The plea to be written for life continues from the beginning of Rosh Hashana throughout the ten days of repentance. At the *n'ila* service at the close of Yom Kippur, the metaphor culminates in our asking to be sealed, rather than written, for life. —J.G.K.

Even though we might not relate to the traditional image of God deciding whether or not to inscribe us in the Book of Life, Rosh Hashana and Yom Kippur help us to acknowledge our mortality. We may look away from that abyss for the other 50 weeks of the year, but on the High Holy Days, the words of our prayers encourage us to reflect on the fact that there are no guarantees regarding events in the year ahead. Awareness of mortality moves us toward an appreciation of our blessings while we are alive. —J.J.S.

the power or energy in the universe that makes for a renewal of humanity, of the world and of community. It becomes the responsibility of humanity to make manifest "God's Kingdom" on earth through acting upon our moral principles and values in order to bring about justice, peace and beauty for all people.

The prayers imagine God as judge and king scrolling through the Book of Life, which is said to contain all of our actions of the past year, written in our own handwriting. God is said to weigh all the good that we have done against the bad that we have done, and to set our fate for the year ahead. This is a hard concept to embrace literally. Without the traditional belief that it is God who

Part of making God's presence manifest in the world is discerning that we already live in God's kingdom. The practice of saying blessings (*b'rakhot*) is designed to keep us perpetually aware of the divine presence in all of our experiences. Through the practice of discernment in Jewish spiritual direction, we endeavor to see the holiness and mystery in all things. "*Shiviti Adonay l'negdi tamid*," the psalmist says, "I place God before me perpetually." First we acknowledge the divinely inhabited world in which we live. Then we can work to make it more just, loving and peaceful. —J.J.S.

For individuals who are suffering and who feel that their suffering is unjust or unwarranted, the concept of reward and punishment can be especially challenging. What could we have done to deserve such harsh punishment—cancer, bankruptcy, fire and violence? Many of us who have health, financial solvency and the good luck to avoid calamity do not always have a sense of gratitude that would lead us to ask what we have done to deserve such bounty. All of us can cultivate an attitude of equanimity in response to all of the vagaries of life—positive as well as negative—and try to deepen our relationships with ourselves and with others, as well as with the source of life. —D.W.

judges humanity, we can still embrace the need to review our own deeds, weigh the good with the bad ourselves, and set a new course for the future.

First and Second Days

Like the pilgrimage festivals of Pesach, Shavuot, and Sukkot, Rosh Hashana is traditionally celebrated in Diaspora communities with an additional day of the holiday. For the pilgrimage festivals, most Reform and Reconstructionist congregations and some Conservative congregations have shifted to a one-day, full holiday celebration in keeping with the Israeli calendar. But, unlike the pilgrimage festivals, Rosh Hashana is celebrated for two days in Israel. Therefore the vast majority of Diaspora congregations observe Rosh Hashana for two days, though some congregations in the Diaspora observe the holiday for only a single day.

I find the image of the "Book of Life" evocative as an allegory for our self-contemplation. It is we who are the authors of our lives, and our actions are imprinted on the world just as type is printed on paper. We do not need to believe in a judge on high to help us make a new beginning on Rosh Hashana. We can instead investigate the stories we tell ourselves, and see if they are helpful or if they have become an obstacle to our process of *t'shuva*. Perhaps it is time to let go of some of those stories if they bind us to habits that are counterproductive or to attitudes that get in the way of believing that we can indeed make change. —T.S.

We might ask how our deeds measure up against the standard of the divine in the universe. What ripple will we leave in eternity? I suggest we consider God not as a ruler (king), but as the ruler (yardstick) against which we measure our deeds. That measurement fills me with as much *yir'a* (awe or dread) as the traditional image. —J.A.S.

Rosh Hashana is the only major Jewish holiday to begin on *Rosh Ḥodesh* (the new moon). As a result, the rabbis declared that Rosh Hashana would last two days. In contemporary times, liberal congregations often focus on the traditional liturgy on the first day and use the second day for more innovative and alternative services and programs.

In ancient times, witnesses heralded the arrival of a new month. Their task was to watch for the sliver of a new moon and quickly tell the high court in Jerusalem. Although the moon would reappear after a 29½-day cycle, the witnesses did not always see the moon in time to report to the court on the 30th day and, accordingly, the new month would be proclaimed on the following day. Some months on the Hebrew calendar are 29 days and some are 30 days because the lunar month lasts for 29½ days. The last day of each 30-day month is considered the first day of a two-day *Rosh Ḥodesh*; 29-day months have only one day of *Rosh Ḥodesh*. Because of 30-day months, Rosh Hashana, which is the *Rosh Ḥodesh* of Tishri, would sometimes last for two days. To establish a uniform observance, the rabbis decreed that Rosh Hashana would be observed on two days of the new month that were to be treated as one long day. —Y.R.

The tradition of the extra festival day could have been based on uncertainty about the exact day of the new moon. In ancient times, that exact date (which was determined in Jerusalem) could be reliably reported to all of *Eretz Yisrael* in time for the midmonth festivals, but Rosh Hashana's occurrence on the new moon left no time for informing even the people of *Eretz Yisrael*. —J.A.S.

Even before the calendar was set, Rosh Hashana was observed for two days in the Land of Israel because it fell at the new moon and no one knew for sure on which of the days the moon would be sighted. —J.G.K.

It is ironic that in most congregations, the more innovative day is the second day of Rosh Hashana. The congregants who return for the second day are usually those who self-identify as more traditional. Perhaps we should toy with inverting this custom. —J.G.K.

Both days of Rosh Hashana emphasize the sovereignty of God, the celebration of creation and its renewal, judgment of the past in order to strengthen the future, and remembrance of our individual and collective past. These themes are woven throughout the Rosh Hashana liturgy, rituals and Torah and haftarah readings. The prayer book for Rosh Hashana and Yom Kippur, the machzor, comes from the Hebrew word for "cycle." This reflects an essential aspect of Rosh Hashana—a process that returns annually to encourage personal renewal and to support efforts to reconnect with self and community.

Sovereignty

The *shaḥarit* (morning) service is full of poetry and majesty. Its *piyyutim* (liturgical poems) deal almost exclusively with the theme of God's sovereignty. The service shifts early on with the cantor's elaborate rendition

The prayer books for the five major festivals used to be called "machzorim," books for the annual cycle of festivals. It would be useful for us to regain a consciousness of Rosh Hashana and Yom Kippur not as uniquely holy, but as part of a cycle of festivals that includes includes Pesach, Shavuot and Sukkot. Indeed, in ancient times, it was Sukkot that was called "*Heḥag*"—"The Festival." Rosh Hashana and Yom Kippur were occasions for spiritual cleansing in preparation for Sukkot. —J.A.S.

Holidays are an intersection between linear and circular time. Rosh Hashana celebrates the birthday of the world more than 5,000 years after it was created, according to the Jewish way of counting. At the same time, it reminds us that we are here at the start of the year again. We are the same, and yet we are changed. The spiral continues onward. —D.W.

of this phrase: "*Hamelekh yoshev al kisey ram v'nisa,*" "The sovereign sits upon the high and lofty throne." The service focuses on the coronation of God, and this prayer is the announcement heralding God's presence. Though

The metaphor of God on a throne is related to the theme of *din* and *raḥamim*, justice and compassion. An early rabbinic midrash explains that on Rosh Hashana, God sits upon a throne of *din*, strict judgment, intending to judge the world according to a harsh accounting. But when we blow the shofar, God gets up from the seat of judgment and moves to the seat of compassion. We are made in the image of God, and thus we, too, encompass *midat hadin*, the attribute of strict judgment, and *midat haraḥamim*, the attribute of compassion. We certainly need to hold ourselves accountable, to sit with the truth of our lives and not to distort that truth through denial or an overwhelming sense of shame. But true discernment must be accompanied by the quality of compassion. Sitting on the throne of love and compassion, I am invited not to judge myself harshly, but simply to see the truth of this moment and to resolve to do better next time. I am invited to let go of the negative voices that discourage any attempt at change, and to believe instead that I am capable of becoming who I want to be. I am invited to forgive myself and those around me, and to focus not on past wrongs, but on future possibilities. —T.S.

The kabbalists teach that "*melekh*" is an acronym for "*moaḥ*" ("brain"), "*lev*" ("heart") and "*k'layot*" ("kidneys"). In the biblical and rabbinic world, kidneys were said to be the seat of conscience. Thus, the divine king is understood to be the divine brain, heart and kidneys of the universe. This rendering of "*melekh*" suggests that God is not a distant ruler, but rather the powerful consciousness, life force and conscience of the universe itself. How would we behave differently toward ourselves and each other if we really believed that we were created *b'tzelem Elohim,* in the image of God? The invocation of *Hamelekh* is a call to our own beings to sit in the seat of our dignity and capacity to be our best selves from moment to moment. How would we act toward ourselves and each other if we believed we could perceive, feel and discern ourselves and others as God does—and if we believed that God flows through our veins? —M.K.

Dr. Israel Knohl asserts that the Israelite designation of God as *melekh* (king) was originally meant not as a metaphor but as the "real thing." According to Knohl, the pre-monarchal Israelites would not have said that they did not have a king. They would instead have said that they did not have a *human* king, that God alone is their king. In this light, our annual coronation of God on Rosh Hashana reasserts our ancient ancestral perspective, dismissing human sovereignty as a weak and distant imitation of the ultimate power that is truly in charge of everything. —V.M.

the metaphor of God as king is powerful, for many contemporary Jews it is a challenge to understand it in a way that makes sense to them.

For many, the royal metaphor seems outdated, and to some, it even seems offensive. For some, belief in a personal, supernatural divine presence seems wrongheaded; for some, it is meaningless. A Reconstructionist understanding of God is not that of a king on a throne, but rather that of the power that makes for fulfillment, the power that impels human beings to be fully human, the power that elicits our best from us and strengthens us against the difficult moments life deals to humankind—the power inherent in nature's order. It is a power beyond us and bigger than us, and yet we can strive to be aware of its presence and to live in harmony with it. This understanding of God carries a moral message and challenges us to enthrone the divine presence in our lives.

During Rosh Hashana and Yom Kippur in particular, we are striving to connect with that power. We face parts of ourselves and parts of the world that need healing and

I experience the metaphor of God the king as a visceral reminder of my limitations—a reminder that goes hand-in-hand with the process of *t'shuva*. No matter what I do, I am mortal; I experience aging; I experience unforeseeable loss and unearned blessing. I am not the ruler of my universe. Metaphorically speaking, I do not have knowledge of or control over what the Judge writes in for my destiny in the year to come. My *t'shuva* does not guarantee my health or my material status; doing a mitzvah is its own reward. —J.J.S.

How to enthrone the divine presence in our lives is our great religious challenge. That challenge is why we gather to celebrate this festival! —S.P.W.

wholeness. Seeing ourselves as approaching a ruler or a judge has an impact on that confrontation with our humanity. At the heart of these prayers about sovereignty is an emphasis on our ability to hold ourselves accountable and to surrender ourselves. We are called to acknowledge that the control we think and perhaps wish we had over the totality of our lives is illusory—that our lives are often shaped by events we cannot control.

The liturgy provokes us to surrender the capacity to withhold forgiveness that we have held over our families, friends and colleagues, and to surrender our egos enough to acknowledge our failings, apologize to those we have hurt, and rededicate ourselves through *t'shuva*. This is not easy to embrace. Surrender can be understood as an abdication of our dignity, our security and our freedom,

There is a special blessing for being in the presence of a ruler who has power over life and death. Imagining God as a king or queen allows us to ask ourselves to whom and to what we are accountable, even for whom and for what we would be willing to die. —J.G.K.

The God of the *Yamim Nora'im* is imagined to weigh human life on the scales of *din*, judgment, and *raḥamim*, mercy. We humans frequently resonate with the quality of judgment, but we are most transformed through the practice and process of surrendering our egos and allowing mercy and loving kindness to enter. —D.W.

The great balance we need to maintain in life is to hold ourselves accountable for what is ours to control and to surrender what is not ours to control. The trick, of course, is to know the difference—or, as the famous Serenity Prayer puts it, the wisdom to know the difference. —S.P.W.

Praying to surrender the capacity to withhold forgiveness is a splendid intention. It is a prayer of willingness, a prayer of melting resistance to change, and a prayer for releasing one's identification with being a victim. —S.P.W.

but without that surrender, we lose access to the opportunity for renewal offered by Rosh Hashana. The surrender we are encouraged to experience on Rosh Hashana is one that deepens our connections to the world around us and to our loved ones, and that deepens our relationship to the divine as well.

Other additions to the service that underscore this theme include *Avinu Malkeynu* (a penitential prayer that originated in talmudic times as a plea for rain on specially declared fast days); the inclusion of the 13 attributes of God (Exodus 34:6–7) mentioned earlier; and the *musaf* (additional) service that includes many biblical texts on the theme of God's sovereignty. In *Avinu Malkeynu* we experience the tension of imagining a God that is both

"*Avinu Malkeynu*" literally means "Our Father, our King." In addition to these names, *Kol Haneshamah* provides alternative names for God here: "*Mekoreynu*," "*Eloheynu*"—"our Source," "our God." —J.G.K.

A practice: Meditate on each of the 13 attributes of God, sometimes referred to as *midot* or attributes of mercy. Pause and spend time with each attribute. Do I experience this quality in my life? Do I feel I embody this quality with myself, with others, with God? How can I cultivate it inside myself, and how can I manifest it in my actions? What helps me to experience this quality? What hinders me? How will cultivating these attributes within me help me to do the work of the *Yamim Nora'im* this year? —M.K.

Urban legend has it that the jam band Phish inadvertently scheduled a concert on Yom Kippur one year, to the chagrin of their Jewish bass player. The band members pride themselves on not letting down their passionate fans, so rescheduling the concert was not an option for them, but they acknowledged the holiday by including an extended session of "*Avinu Malkeynu*" in that performance. The crowd responded powerfully, and it is now a regular part of their set list. —D.W.

near and far: near, like the presence of a parent, and far, like the transcendent, awe-inspiring and ethical presence of a sovereign. The sequence of the prayer is significant. God as parent comes before God as sovereign as if to recognize the intimacy and reverence needed to approach and understand God's presence in the world. The familiar words and melody, as well as the memories that the prayer evokes, help contemporary Jews to grapple with its meaning and theology. Whether sung in Hebrew, read in English, or read as an interpretive payer (using, for example, feminine God language or alternative imagery), the fervent pleas for grace, responsiveness, righteousness, love and redemption are powerful and unmistakable.

God's sovereignty can be understood as being present when people assert personal power in order to make positive change in the world; when individuals assert communal power in order to effect the transformation, the *tikun*, of our world; and when individuals and entire communities empower humanity to live fully. When Jews engage in

In the prayer-poem *Hayom Harat Olam,* recited after the sounding of the shofar, the dual role of child and servant found in *Avinu Malkeynu* is developed: "Today the world was conceived. Today all the world's creatures will stand trial, whether as children or as servants. If as children, have compassion upon us as parents have compassion upon their children. But if as servants, we set our eyes upon you until you graciously behold us and bring to light our final ruling, awesome and holy one."
—V.M.

It is vital to keep connecting our inner work with the outer world. Ultimately, they are one.
—S.P.W.

the process of *t'shuva*, we can acknowledge the holiness of striving toward a path that is uniquely our own, but one that has the potential to have a positive impact on the larger world. We can catch a glimpse of the royal robe when we engage in *g'milut ḥasadim*, acts of loving kindness, and even when we are buffeted by chaos and happenstance. We can be awestruck at the divine within ourselves that we experience as conscience when we acknowledge that we have the power to hurt people unintentionally. And we can be sheltered by the royal shadow when we accept the lessons in our present reality—no matter how difficult or painful—and let them be our guide and teacher regarding what we should do next.

From the eighth century on, poets composed *piyyutim* for the *Yamim Nora'im*. Many were used solely in the community where they were composed, but others became more broadly used, despite their often-intricate structures and difficult rhyme schemes and diction. The printed traditional machzorim contain large numbers of these *piyyutim*, though there is considerable variation regarding which are included. Liberal machzorim leave out the more difficult *piyyutim* and include modern poetry and readings in their stead.

God's sovereignty *(malkhut)* can be understood in many ways. It can be a statement of the awe-inspiring majesty of the universe. It can signify a negation of human claims to any individual's right to power or rule over another. It can signify the source of our commandedness or obligation, whether one considers that source to be natural law or the fact of our being faced by the Other, by the Eternal Thou.
—J.A.S.

Torah and Haftarah Readings

The Torah and haftarah readings for Rosh Hashana are complex, multilayered, rich tales of birth, renewal, family, obligation and commitment. They deal with relationships and conflicts—between husband and wife, between women, between parents and children, and between people and God. Reading these stories in the synagogue on these days offers community members an opportunity for heightening their spiritual and psychological experience. Rather than presenting us with reassuring bromides, these biblical narratives contain stories of conflict and of tense, messy human lives that serve as another important reminder that humanity has never been perfect.

At the same time, these biblical stories represent some of the most difficult tales of our sacred texts. On the first day of Rosh Hashana, we read about the relationships between Sarah and Hagar and between Isaac and Ishmael, and their multiple triangulated relationships. (Genesis 21) The story of *akedat Yitzḥak*, the binding of Isaac (Genesis 22) is read on the second day. Some congregations focus

Some people argue that the High Holy Days are not the time to raise difficult topics, but the assigned Torah readings for these days almost dare us not to talk about such things as domestic violence or child abuse. —N.H.M.

This is a good time of year to be challenged by the most difficult relationships in our lives. —S.P.W.

The "birth" day of the world is a good time to remember the women among our ancestors. —S.P.W.

on the theme of creation by reading from the first chapter of Genesis on the first day, instead of reading from all of the traditional texts. This is one alternative suggested in the *Kol Haneshamah* machzor as well as in the Reform movement machzor. The traditional readings from the second scroll on these days recount the sacrifices offered on each day in the ancient Jerusalem Temple. A reading from the beginning of Genesis is often substituted for the reading from the second scroll in liberal congregations that do not make this the primary reading on the first day.

One common explanation for the choice of the main readings has to do with another major theme of these days—that of *zikaron*, remembrance. On the first day, the Torah and haftarah readings depict God remembering Sarah and Hannah in their dreams of having children. Sarah gives birth to Isaac, and Hannah to Samuel. Although the circumstances surrounding these two women are quite different, they each are "remembered by God" in their difficulty. This can serve as a metaphor for our understanding of God's presence in the world, and our desire to have the hopes expressed in our prayers fulfilled, even if we do not expect supernatural intervention.

Another theme that comes out of the two Rosh Hashana readings is birth itself—Isaac is born when Sarah least expects it, and according to some midrashim, he comes back to life after death at Abraham's hand on Mount Moriah. The liturgy for this time of year reminds us over and over again that through *t'shuva* we, too, may be born anew.
—J.G.K.

The stories of the Torah do not generally focus on the lives of women so directly, and therefore these tales open up unusually expansive opportunities for hearing women's voices through the text, despite the focus on the importance of the sons they bear. The complicated nature of the relationship between Sarah and Hagar underscores not just the particular details of the conflict between two women. The stories of the births of Isaac and Ishmael, both sons of Abraham, who are claimed as fathers of the Jewish and Arab peoples, respectively, have historic, religious and political meanings to be gleaned as well.

Seeing is at the heart of the Rosh Hashana Torah portions. In the first day's reading, the joyful moment of Isaac's birth, a moment of laughter, quickly descends into jealousy. Later, Sarah sees Ishmael laughing and desires to expel him. Sometimes we cannot enjoy our blessings when we see others who are happy, too. Their joy causes us pain, and we cease to see the joy and laughter in our own lives that once lifted us above petty rivalries. Hagar's situation is the opposite. She is cast out, rejected, helpless. She descends into darkness, where she can see only the imminent death of her son. Sometimes we give up hope, unable to see the blessings and the goodness that keep us alive. Sarah does not see Hagar as a human being worthy of compassion; she can see only the rivalry between their sons. Hagar cannot see the well in front of her; she can see only despair. In the haftarah, Hannah's problems are exacerbated when, like Hagar, she is not seen. As she prays at the holy shrine, the priest Eli can see only that she is talking to herself. Even a holy man like Eli can forget that things are not always what they seem. Eli judges Hannah, assuming that her actions are those of a drunkard. He then takes the next step and condemns her verbally (1 Samuel 1:14). In each of these instances, we are reminded of the gift of vision: not only our physical sight, but our insight, our ability to look beyond the obstacles immediately before us and to see the deep wells of sustenance, love and life that surround us at all times.

—B.P.

Hannah's prayer may be the earliest biblical text of an individual's prayer. It is interesting and significant that it is attributed to a woman. —J.J.S.

The *Akeda* (binding of Isaac), the reading for the second day of Rosh Hashana, is equally challenging and in some ways more difficult to understand. Genesis 22 opens with God's command to Abraham to take his son Isaac up a mountain as an offering to God. This narrative is traditionally understood as the consummate trial of Abraham's faith and devotion to God, but many contemporary Jews have a hard time equating a commitment to faith and covenant with the sacrifice of our children. The story has multiple layers of difficulty: God's shocking request,

The moment that I find most arresting in the narrative of the near sacrifice of Isaac is the midpoint: The son is bound, and the father raises the knife. The text gives little indication that anything will occur other than the unimaginable act of sacrifice. In this instance, we the readers know the end of the story. We have heard it year after year, so we can listen to this tale with a sense of anxiety or incredulity while safe in the knowledge that ultimately there is a surprise resolution that lets us breathe more easily. We know from our own lives that most stories do eventually unfold so that we can be shape them into a coherent and manageable narrative. We also know from our own lives about those middle moments, the times when everything is uncertain at best, and sometimes truly and legitimately terrifying. I find some comfort from this tale at moments in my own life when I am suspended without yet knowing the ending. —D.W.

We are hardly the first generation to be so disturbed by the story of the *Akeda*. In *Pirkey Avot*, the rabbis imagined that the ram (which would be sacrificed by Abraham in place of Isaac) was created right before sunset on the first Friday of creation. Our sages thus suggested that the end of the story had been ordained 20 generations before it even began. —J.G.K.

Sarah's absence from the *Akeda* narrative is, in my view, the most important aspect of this story. These events would never have happened if Sarah had been present. —S.P.W.

Abraham's ready response, Sarah's absence, Abraham's silence, Isaac's silence save for a single question ("Where is the lamb for the sacrifice?") in the entire 13 verses of text. The haunting conclusion is that because Abraham did not object to God's request, Abraham will be blessed forever. Congregations read this story year after year. Why is it read on Rosh Hashana? Perhaps because on this day of remembrance and renewal, we are meant to identify with Abraham and the "test." On Rosh Hashana, we

The test for Abraham is whether he can be present, whether he can say "*Hineni*" ("Here I am"), even at the most difficult moments. Three times God calls to Abraham, once directly, once through Isaac, and, at the most intense moment at the altar, repeatedly through an angel. Perhaps Abraham passes the test because he is able to be present in a moment when even God (an angel stands in for God) could not be. —J.G.K.

Seeing is a recurring theme in the story of the *Akeda*. What does Abraham see when he looks at his son and when he "sees the place from afar?" It is only when his focus is drawn away from the knife and from his son bound before him that he is able to see the ram in the thicket. The name of the place, Mount Moriah, the mountain of seeing, emphasizes that opening our eyes is essential to doing what is right. In that way, "seeing" leads us to an experience of holiness. —B.P.

God's silence, too, is striking. The last time the text tells us that God ever speaks to Abraham is when God asks him to bring his son to Mount Moriah. —J.G.K.

Another possible reason for reading the story of *Akedat Yitzhak* is for us to experience what Isaac experienced: an encounter with our own death. This is the blow to the gut that the *Yamim Nora'im* deliver. We are limited beings with a limited time on earth, and each year we should remember that and revisit our values. —J.M.S.

A number of biblical commentators through the centuries (such as Radak in the 13th century and Ralbag in the 14th) contend that Abraham's achievement, for which he and we are rewarded, is that he realized that he had been mistaken in his understanding of God's command—that God had never wanted him to kill Isaac. Read this way, the story teaches us not to act zealously without deliberation. —J.J.S.

examine our lives—the trials and tribulations—and pray that they will lead us to understand ourselves better and to see how we can be more present to our loved ones and the world around us. Few of us escape this life without experiencing our own personal version of an *akeda*—an experience that shakes us to our core and perhaps makes us question the very essence of life, so that we are fundamentally changed as we move forward in our lives.

The haftarah for the second day of Rosh Hashana comes from Chapter 31 of the Book of Jeremiah. This text emphasizes the promise of a renewed future and a restored land. Israel is depicted as a maiden rejoicing over this renewal and rebuilding. God promises that *t'shuva* will lead to reconciliation after the exile and destruction of

Jeremiah portrays God as recalling wistfully how Israel was so loyal in its youth when it followed God in the wilderness before entering the Promised Land. We moderns are obviously not unique in the way that we compare ourselves negatively to the authenticity of past generations. But the past is never as uncomplicated as it appears in retrospect. —J.J.S.

the people. The text reads, "*hashiveyni v'ashuva,*"—"bring me back, let me return," and underscores the possibility of redemption even in the face of devastation. Again, the text echoes the themes of the liturgy and of the day itself. Our desire for unification — of self, of community, of Israel—is a timeless theme of Rosh Hashana.

There are many ways to make these stories come alive in services. Many congregations highlight one of the salient themes or stories in dramatic or personal ways. Several actions can draw people into the power of these texts for greater meaning and understanding—a *d'var Torah* from the perspective of one of the characters, a sharing of poetry about the *Akeda*, a facilitated bibliodrama between the protagonists of either Torah reading, or a dramatization of the stories.

The haftarah for the first day of Rosh Hashana describes a personal redemption, Hannah's giving birth to a son. Among the miracles we have experienced in our own lives, conceiving and bringing a child to term, under any circumstances, is one worthy of awe and joy. The haftarah for the second day describes an even greater redemption, the return of the Jewish people to their home following destruction and exile. A hint of that communal redemption touched our lives in the past century, as we witnessed the ingathering of the Jewish people from all corners of the earth after the unthinkable evil and devastation of the Shoah. On Rosh Hashana, we come seeking redemption: redemption from the barrenness of pain, loss, isolation and loneliness. We also come to renew our hope in humanity, and to be reminded of the promise of God's holy community. Jeremiah lived through such suffering—the destruction of so many souls when the Temple was destroyed. His words carry even more weight as he urges us to seek out God's love and not to lose hope. Rosh Hashana is our time to rekindle the awe and joy that make life not only livable, but also worthy of blessing and celebration. —B.P.

Our community comes up to the Torah for group aliyot during the *Yamim Nora'im*. The theme of each aliyah is suggested by the text, which helps members of the *ḥavura* to map their own lives onto Torah. —D.W.

Shofar Service

The most familiar and central ritual of Rosh Hashana is the sounding of the shofar. Traditionally, the sounding of the ram's horn is heard 100 times during services on each day of Rosh Hashana, except for when Rosh Hashana falls on Shabbat.

Since the central biblical mitzvah of Rosh Hashana is the sounding of the shofar, it seems strange that Jewish law forbids this on Shabbat. This is not, as some might think, because it is work to sound the shofar. The Talmud teaches (*Rosh Hashana* 16a) that according to the written law, it is allowed, and it is the rabbis who prohibited it as a precaution; as stated by Raba, "All are under obligation to blow the shofar but not all are skilled in the blowing of the shofar. Therefore, there is a danger that perhaps someone will take it in his hand [on Shabbat] and go to an expert to learn how to blow it, and carry it four cubits in the public domain."

How are the 100 blasts of the shofar counted? For the first shofar blowing, *t'ḳiya sh'varim-tru'a t'ḳiya*, counted as four sounds, is repeated three times. That's twelve. *T'ḳiya sh'varim t'ḳiya* (three) and *t'ḳiya t'rua t'ḳiya* (three) are each repeated three times, for another 18. That's a total of 30. Another 30 are blown during the public recitation of the *musaf Amida*. That's 60. Some traditional congregations blow another 30 during the private recitation of the *musaf Amida* and ten during *Kaddish Titḳabal*, while others blow 30 during *Kaddish Titḳabal* and ten after the Mourner's Kaddish. —J.A.S.

If we recite Psalm 27 twice daily beginning on the first of Elul and continuing through *Hoshana Raba*, the seventh day of Sukkot, our 100 recitations parallel the number of shofar blasts. There are many ways to cry out to God. —J.G.K.

Indeed, we sound the shofar at the end of Yom Kippur, even when the High Holy Day falls on Shabbat. —J.G.K.

This is a challenging tradition for many more liberal Jews since we can easily leave the shofar in the synagogue before the holiday so as not to carry it in a public space. Also, for many of us carrying the shofar on Shabbat would not violate our personal practice. So what might this prohibition teach us? The sounding of the shofar has been likened to an externally produced wake-up call to the work of *t'shuva* and a sign that we need to change our ways. In a similar way, Shabbat has been likened to an externally created sign of the covenant between the Jewish people and God.

Not blowing shofar on Shabbat can be a vivid reminder of the traditional priority of Shabbat over Rosh Hashana. Although the practice stems from Shabbat rules that most of us don't observe, it nonetheless reminds us that Rosh Hashana has the most meaning when celebrated in the context of a rich Jewish life, which includes the practice of Shabbat. —J.A.S.

When Rosh Hashana falls on Shabbat, our congregation recites the liturgy of the shofar service, but instead of listening to the shofar blast, we listen to the silence. This reminds us that many cries for attention and action go unanswered. In that silent space, we can reflect on when we have failed to act. —N.H.M.

The halakhic particularities against sounding the shofar on Shabbat seem less important than the underlying message that the observance of Shabbat trumps this central mitzvah of Rosh Hashana. For that reason, it does make sense for Reconstructionist communities to observe this prohibition, as it helps highlight the importance and uniqueness of Shabbat. At our congregation, we don't do a shofar service when Rosh Hashana falls on Shabbat, and during the *malkhuyot-zikhronot-shofarot* section, I chant the call for the shofar and then invite congregants to listen for the *zikhron t'rua*, the "memory of the blast," in their imaginations. These moments of silence, when we sit with our memories of hearing the shofar's call, are quite powerful. —T.S.

When Shabbat and Rosh Hashana coincide, sounding the shofar may seem superfluous to the experience of divine majesty evoked in the liturgy and the holiday itself. Some congregations sound the shofar on the Sabbath despite the prohibition so as not to miss out on this unique ritual experience, especially if they celebrate only one day of Rosh Hashana.

The commandment to sound the shofar is found several times in the Torah. "In the seventh month, on the first day of the month, you shall observe complete rest, a sacred occasion commemorated with loud blasts." (Leviti-

Musical instruments and shofarot were permitted in the Jerusalem Temple because they were an integral part of the prescribed Temple sacrificial service. After the Temple was destroyed, the rabbis were concerned that the tuning and repairing of instruments would occur if the use of instruments were to be allowed on Shabbat. The rabbis also recognized that there was a danger of carrying musical instruments outdoors on Shabbat (another forbidden activity), and they wanted to differentiate synagogues from the Temple that had been destroyed. Therefore, the rabbis forbade the use of musical instruments on Shabbat. Now that the use of musical instruments in contemporary synagogues has become common, it can easily be argued that the blowing of the shofar should be permitted as well. —D.A.T.

There are so many words spoken and sung on Rosh Hashana. When Shabbat and the holiday converge, the shofar service without the shofar blasts can serve as an opportunity to notice the stillness and the quiet evoked by the same themes of sovereignty and remembrance, and by the call to repair our deeds and transform the world in holiness. Sometimes it is when we are quiet that we are the most awake. —Y.R.

Jewish mysticism suggests that when Shabbat and Rosh Hashana coincide, this *Yom Hadin* (Day of Judgment) is already eclipsed by God's great *ḥesed* (loving kindness), which is associated with Shabbat. —J.G.K.

When Shabbat coincides with the first day of Rosh Hashana, some communities compromise by sounding the shofar less than they otherwise would. —J.G.K.

cus 23:24) "You shall observe it as a day when the horn is sounded." (Numbers 29:1) The sounding of the shofar is the only biblical commandment that has been uniquely associated with Rosh Hashana across the generations. The Torah does not indicate when or how these horns are to be sounded, only that the ritual is to be a part of the holiday.

Over the course of time, layers of meaning and interpretation developed around the shofar blasts. In one rabbinic midrash, a connection is made between the blowing of the ram's horn and the horn of the ram that was caught in the thicket in the story of *akedat Yitzḥak* (the binding of Isaac). According to the midrash, God instructed Abraham that whenever the children of Israel were in danger of being punished because of sin, they were to blow the shofar. The sound of the ram's horn would "remind God" of the merits of the people "earned" by the binding of Isaac, and therefore the Jews would be forgiven. (B. Talmud, *Rosh Hashana* 16a) Another interpretation connected to the *Akeda* is that the sound of the shofar is the weeping of Sarah over her son Isaac being bound upon the altar.

Abraham does not argue with God before the *Akeda* the way he did on the eve of the destruction of Sodom. In the midrash, Abraham negotiates with God on behalf of his descendants. Because he went through this harrowing process, he asks that the telling of the story and the sounding of the ram's horn will summon God on Rosh Hashana to forgive us. —J.G.K.

A midrash in the Talmud (*Rosh Hashana* 38b) connects the shofar's sound to the cry of Sisera's mother waiting for her son to return from battle. Because Sisera was an enemy of the tribes of Israel who was defeated in war by the prophet Deborah, this association is stunning. On the holiest of days, we feel empathy for the mother of our enemy! —B.P.

Later rabbinic interpretations extrapolated from the earlier teachings, and pointed more toward the sounding of the shofar as a literal wake-up call for humanity, not for God. The sound of the shofar should awaken all who hear it to turn from their ways, consider their actions and make amends. The sound of the shofar is a visceral, stirring sound like no other that for some of us can penetrate more deeply than the thousands of words of the liturgy. It is a great honor to sound the shofar in a community. That role is traditionally given to particularly pious members of the congregation. It can also be given as a special honor on

Waking up is a universal metaphor for the transformation of consciousness. It is about moving from ego to soul—from a small, petty frame of mind to a compassionate connection to all of life. —S.P.W.

If the shofar is a wake-up call to rouse us from spiritual slumber, the implication is that it is not just enough to wake up. Once we awaken from sleep, we must engage in *t'shuva*, in acts of repentance that turn us toward a life of wakefulness and awareness. Our community augments the shofar with two other sounds: drumming and silence. As a framing intention, I ask members of the congregation to think about the almost unconscious behaviors from which they need to be awakened, the broken places to which they need to give attention, the relationships in need of repair. A drummer beats a drum, another ancient technology designed to warn, awaken and call to battle. After the drum beats, we stand in silence, while members of the community think about *t'shuva*, how they want the shofar to affect them, how they want to be transformed through this practice. After 30 seconds, we begin to call out the commands for the shofar blasts. —D.W.

Once, the Baal Shem Tov's disciple was to call the order of the shofar blasts for the Baal Shem Tov to blow on Rosh Hashana. The Baal Shem Tov taught his disciple the deep mystical meanings of the shofar sounds in preparation. The disciple wrote the meanings on a piece of paper and put it in his pocket, but the paper soon fell out of his pocket. On Rosh Hashana morning, the disciple discovered that the paper was missing and tried to remember, but he could not. He began to weep and, with tears in his eyes, he announced the calls simply, with no mystical intentions at all. Later, the Baal Shem Tov told him, "There are many halls in the King's palace, and intri-

these days. In many contemporary communities, all who are able to sound the shofar are invited to blow the horns in unison.

Rabbi Arthur Green's interpretation of the three blasts of the shofar—*t'kiya*, *sh'varim*, *t'rua*—is that they contain the whole message of the *Yamim Nora'im*. Each series of shofar blasts begins with *t'kiya*, a long, whole sound. It is followed by *sh'varim*, a three-part broken sound whose very name means "breakings." The blasts conclude with *t'rua*, a staccato series of nine blasts, followed once again by the long sound of *t'kiya*, as if to say, "I was whole. I became broken. I was entirely smashed to pieces, but I shall become whole again."

There are two places in the service when the shofar is traditionally sounded. The first occurs after the reading of the haftarah. Traditionally we begin by reciting Psalm 47,

cate keys to open the doors, but the axe is stronger than all of them... What are all the mystical intentions compared to heartfelt grief?" (This is based on "The Axe" in Martin Buber's *Tales of the Hasidim: The Early Masters.*) —J.A.S.

The congregation I serve has the nontraditional practice of asking a high school student to blow the shofar when such a student with the requisite skill is available. There is a sweet intensity in a young person's taking on this big, wordless mitzvah. It feels fitting and affirming. And it relieves me and the ritual committee from having to judge anyone's piety! —J.A.S.

Including everyone who can blow a shofar is a particularly lovely custom for *t'kiya g'dola*, the final long blast, or shofar blowers can take turns sounding the final ten blasts in *Kaddish Titkabal* near the conclusion of services. —J.G.K.

In our congregation, we station different people in the front, back and sides of the room, each sounding the shofar in unison. The stereo effect is dramatic. —B.P.

which contains several verses about the sounding of the shofar as a way to herald God's presence and power. The community then recites two blessings—"to hear the sound of the shofar" and the *Sheheḥeyanu* prayer. After three sets of blasts, the final *t'kiya* is prolonged (called "*t'kiya g'dola*"—the great blast), and the section concludes with the recitation of Psalm 145, *Ashrey* (named after the first word of the text, "Happy are they who dwell in your house"). The second time the shofar is sounded is during the *musaf* or additional service, which will be discussed below. Congregations that omit the *musaf* often include its themes with the first set of shofar blasts.

Musaf

The *musaf* or additional service on Rosh Hashana is complex and lengthy, and it contains powerful liturgy and rituals. The service mainly consists of an additional *Amida* with *piyyutim* (poems) and prayers, but the *Amida* is expanded considerably to focus on the themes of *malkhuyot* (sovereignty), *zikhronot* (remembrance), and *shofarot*

Often, the sounding of *t'ḳiya g'dola* becomes a moment of competition for the longest sound and the reddest face. Afterward, congregants giggle and sigh and chat about the fortitude of the *ba'al t'ḳiya* (the shofar player). Not only is this practice potentially hazardous to the *ba'al t'ḳiya,* but it also diverts attention away from the ancient sound itself. In our congregation we follow a practice (one that I learned from Rabbi Richard Hirsh) of remaining silent after the blasts, in order to pay attention and absorb the shofar's call within each of us. —B.P.

(redemption). The weekday *Amida* has 19 blessings. The middle 13 are omitted on Shabbat and holidays because they are petitionary. They are replaced by a blessing for the holiday, making for a total of seven blessings in a Shabbat or holiday *Amida*. The Rosh Hashana *musaf Amida* is unique because it has nine blessings—the standard three at the beginning and three at the end, with the three special blessings in the middle. Traditionally a series of shofar blasts is included with each of the three special blessings.

Between each of the three sections there is a passage that evokes the theme of Rosh Hashana as the birthday of the world. "*Hayom harat olam*"—"Today the world is born"—invites the understanding that Rosh Hashana is the day on which all creatures, all life is recreated. Such pure potential rests in our hands as we begin a new year.

One way to understand these themes is to see them as representing present (*malkuyot*), past (*zikhronot*) and future (*shofarot*). Another is through their parallels to the names of Rosh Hashana: sovereignty speaks to *Yom Hadin* (the Day of Judgment), remembrance to *Yom Hazikaron* (the Day of Remembrance) and *shofarot* to *Yom T'rua* (the Day of the Shofar Blasts). —J.G.K.

The *Amida* for Rosh Hashana and Yom Kippur is very long. It is also unfamiliar. Whether it is read in Hebrew or in English, many find it to be an obstruction to a state of prayerfulness. Some prefer to stand or sit in silent contemplation or to speak (silently) their own words of prayer that arise at that moment. —J.J.S.

"*Hayom harat olam*" is usually translated, "Today, the world is born." But in fact, "*harat*" refers not to birth but to pregnancy: "Today is the world's pregnancy." Today is full of potential. What sort of world will we bring forth tomorrow? —J.A.S.

It is curious that after God's first creative actions in Genesis, the text says, "It was evening and morning, *yom eḥad*—one day." Creation and therefore recreation happen afresh day by day, not as part of a linked sequence stretching across the weeks. Each day can be filled with glorious, creative energy, not to be squandered or underestimated in its potential. On Rosh Hashana, we can tap into that same energy to begin anew. —Y.R.

The Rosh Hashana *musaf Amida* is traditionally introduced by a prayer of unknown authorship called the "*Hin'ni*" ("Here I stand"), expressing the prayer leader's humility in approaching God on these Days of Awe. In many congregations, the cantor begins the recitation of this moving poem from the back of the sanctuary, slowly walking forward as he or she sings. By walking through the community, the *sh'li'aḥ tzibur* (prayer leader) emphasizes his/her membership in the congregation and displays humility as the community's representative before God: "Here I am, poor in deeds, trembling and apprehensive. I have come to stand before you and plead for your people, who have delegated me though I am not fit or worthy." Some communities have eliminated this prayer because of its formality and its dominant theme of the unworthiness of the prayer leader.

In some communities, the idea that the service leader is a member of the community is obscured by the highly dramatic entrance in conjunction with *Hin'ni*, a prayer about humility. —J.G.K.

The *Hin'ni* prayer provides a wonderful opportunity for leaders to acknowledge that this is truly not about them. Too often, services revolve around how well the rabbi or the cantor did. This prayer reminds the community that this is about each person in the pew and not about what happens on the *bima*. The leaders have their own work to do. —S.P.W.

Though the public *Hin'ni* prayer may be grandiose and out of place in some congregations, reciting a private, personal *Hin'ni* can be a powerful vehicle for preparing to lead a service. Sometimes we leaders need to remind ourselves of the grandeur of the task and to pray that we enter into it with humility. —B.P.

I have attended a service where the leader began *Hin'ni*, after which the whole community read the translation about all of us seeking to pray with our whole hearts. —N.M.

The unique High Holy Day themes in the *musaf Amida* become evident soon after the opening three benedictions of the prayer. The themes of *malkhuyot, zikhronot*, and *shofarot* are emphasized by including ten biblical verses for each blessing. They reflect each theme in turn. The verses are preceded by an introduction affirming a quality of God and concluding with an epilogue and final blessing. The traditional understanding of the inclusion of these themes suggests that first we accept God as our ruler (*malkhuyot*), then we ask to be remembered by God (*zikhronot*), and only then do we declare our desire and need for redemption (*shofarot*). We can understand these ideas more generally as aspects of divinity that we, as beings created in the image of God, seek to embody and understand. How much control do we have over our lives

For previous generations, the piling up of biblical verses probably had a sort of drumming, crescendo effect that is hard for us to perceive. Sometimes, I accompany the reading of the verses with a literal crescendo of rhythmic drumming that helps to regain some of that intensity. —J.A.S.

Some communities ask members to share personal reflections on the three *musaf* themes as part of the service. —D.W.

Malkhuyot comes as a powerful reminder of our place in the larger scheme of things, our relative smallness on the cosmic scale. It is a call to a certain kind of humility, to knowing that we are not the center of Creation. *Zikhronot* then tells us that despite our relative insignificance, we are "remembered"—the universe needs us, notices us, calls to us. *Shofarot* wakes us up to the potential we each hold to make a difference. Taken together, these three themes teach us that there is a moral structure to the universe that both holds us accountable and grounds us in compassion. We are invited to hear a call to justice that affirms our power and value as individuals and as a community. —T.S.

and the lives of others? How do historical recollections, the memories of our past experiences and our families' stories influence and affect our present circumstances and the way we see the future? How can we communicate and act with clarity, passion and justice? These themes teach us how we can realize aspects of the divine in our own lives and actualize godliness in the world.

The power of the *malkhuyot* section comes right at its beginning, with the chanting of the Great *Aleynu*. The *Aleynu* prayer, well known as a closing prayer during most Jewish services, was originally composed for the Rosh Hashana service as a statement of God's sovereignty. When it is recited in the daily liturgy, it is customary to bend one's knees at the phrase "and so we bend the knee and bow." On Rosh Hashana, this phrase is often accompanied by one's complete prostration on the floor. Today, sometimes only service leaders act out this physical demonstration of surrender, but traditionally adults in the

Customs of choreography for the Great *Aleynu* vary. Some kneel, while others prostrate themselves completely. —J.G.K.

For ten years I led High Holy Day services for a *ḥavura* in a lovely Episcopal church. While the Christian iconography was sparse, a wooden cross hung directly above my head. As the rabbi, I usually had my back to the cross, though members of the *ḥavura* had it in their line of vision throughout the service as they looked at me on the *bima*. I was extremely aware of that as I reflected on how to lead the Great *Aleynu*. While I personally find the full prostration very moving, I did not want any member of the *ḥavura*—or any members of the church who happened to stop by—to misinterpret my action in any way as a prostration before the cross. Because of the setting, I eliminated this dramatic gesture from our services. —D.W.

congregation prostrate themselves as well. This practice has become more common in recent years. The *zikhronot* and *shofarot* sections have less drama but share several things with the *malkhuyot* section. In all three sections, the shofar is sounded after the recitation of the biblical verses, and a common refrain is sung to conclude each section. (Congregations that do not have a separate *musaf* service can place these themes in the *shaḥarit Amida* or weave them into the shofar service.)

Un'taneh Tokef

Of all the *piyyutim* traditionally included in the Rosh Hashana service, only one always appears on both days of Rosh Hashana as well as on Yom Kippur. Inserted just before the *Kedusha* of the *Amida* (the third blessing of the

In the congregation I grew up in, it was not just the adults who prostrated themselves. The intensity of this rare ritual deepened my sense of spirituality as an early adolescent. —J.G.K.

A silent *musaf Amida* of Rosh Hashana can provide an opportunity to do something we are not used to—punctuate the silence by shofar blasts three times throughout the prayer. The blasts are not named out loud; rather, they are sounded by the *ba'al(at) t'ḳiya* from his or her place in the community at three points in the silent *Amida*. The interplay between silence and shofar and called and uncalled blasts is striking. —J.G.K.

Amida) is the haunting and deeply stirring prayer *Un'taneh Tokef* ("Let us ascribe holiness/weight to this day").

The prayer is a plain and clear reflection of the uncertainty of life, asking the most painful of questions: Who will live and who will die? This prayer emerged in a far different world from the one we live in today. It was a world where people associated natural disasters with punishment from God. Plagues, wars, illness and death could happen suddenly, changing life forever. Although times have changed in many ways, the feeling that life's tragedies are largely externally imposed and beyond our control is one we know all too well. There is so much about our lives that we simply cannot control. That is perhaps the most powerful paradox of these holy days. We swing precariously

The exact origins of *Un'taneh Tokef* are not known, but there is a popular though historically inaccurate legend of its origin. According to the legend, Rabbi Amnon of Mayence, a wealthy eleventh-century scholar, was asked by the town bishop to convert to Christianity. In order to stall for time, Amnon said he needed three days to think it over, but as soon as he left, he regretted asking for extra time. After the appointed three days, Amnon was arrested and forced to plead guilty for not converting to Christianity. In his profound regret for his lack of faith, he asked to have his tongue cut out, but the bishop had his hands and feet severed instead. As Amnon lay dying of his wounds, he crawled to the synagogue for Rosh Hashana. When the cantor was reciting the *Kedusha* of *musaf,* Rabbi Amnon asked the cantor to pause, and he spoke the *Un'taneh Tokef* just before dying. Three days later, it is said, Rabbi Amnon appeared in a dream to Rabbi Kalonymous ben Meshulam and taught him the prayer. Kalonymous then wrote it down as a memorial prayer to be recited on Rosh Hashana and Yom Kippur. —Y.R.

Sometimes disasters still change our lives forever without advance notice. —J.G.K.

between a sense of fragility and a sense of stability, between the quest for security and trust and an awareness at the edge of our consciousness that wakens us in the middle of the night—an awareness telling us that at any moment everything we take for granted might change or end or disappear. We live most days feeling secure, but our vulnerability can show itself at any moment.

Un'taneh tokef kedushat hayom ki hu nora v'ayom, "Let us declare the holiness of this day, which is the most awesome and solemn of days." The litany of terrible circumstances that the prayer invokes is not beyond the pale of possibility. The text teaches us that, indeed, these are

The very first word of *Un'taneh Tokef*, "*uv'khen*," ("and so") appears only twice in the Bible. In both instances where it is used, the fate that befalls people is random, not a consequence of their merit or lack thereof. (Ecclesiastes 8:10, Esther 4:16) The medieval poet's deliberate choice of the word "*uv'khen*" as the initial word of this *piyyut* acknowledges life's randomness and unfairness. It suggests that righteousness is not a protection against the outer circumstances of our lives. We are not in control of our ultimate fates. But we do have agency in how we respond to the situations in which we find ourselves. Within the parameters of these situations lies our power to choose responses that are redemptive and integrative, and that mitigate the harshness of the suffering we experience. —M.K.

Individuals living with serious illness or with other forms of clear danger live an *Un'taneh Tokef* experience every day. The illusion that most of us usually carry is that one day will be like the next and that the days will stretch on pleasantly one after another toward a hazy and far-off horizon. That illusion is stripped away for individuals who have an intense awareness of their own mortality. This can be harrowing, but also, in many instances, deeply clarifying. —D.W.

Although the *Un'taneh Tokef* describes God as a judge, implying that all the listed disasters might be punishments, the prayer also introduces an image of randomness: God is described as a shepherd letting the flock pass under his staff. This was the ancient procedure for tithing; The shepherd let the sheep pass in a line under the staff and each tenth one was destined as a gift for the Temple priests. The poem is acknowledging that sometimes our "outcomes" have nothing to do with our deeds; our number just comes up, like that of a tithed sheep. —J.A.S.

the things we *can* count on seeing in this world. We just do not know when they will occur, or to whom.

> On Rosh Hashana it is written and on Yom Kippur it is sealed: who will live and who will die, who in a timely manner and who not, who by fire and who shall be drowned, who by the sword and who by the beast. . . .

This moment in the service is a profound opportunity to acknowledge the fragility of existence and the ever-encroaching reality that the longer we live, the more likely that we and those we love will be touched by pain, grief and sadness.

And yet the prayer does not leave us without hope. The conclusion of the prayer says, "*T'shuva, t'fila,* and *tzedaka ma'avirin et ro'a hag'zera*"—"The acts of repentance/return, prayer and charity avert the severity of the decree." It is

The challenging reality of our fragility is one reason why religion remains relevant in the postmodern era. We must build up resources that help us to respond to loss and enable us to embrace life in spite of it. —D.W.

Some Hasidic interpreters read the phrase as "ameliorate the evil of the decree." That is, my *t'shuva,* prayer, and righteousness do not render me immune from worldly misfortune. They are efficacious, however, in "sweetening" my experience of misfortune. Once I open my heart in prayer, I have relinquished my pretension to autonomy and isolation, and I become connected—to God, to my community, to humankind. —J.J.S.

important to note that the text does not say that these things *cancel* the decree altogether, as we cannot prevent every bad thing that might happen. But these three actions can fill our lives with meaning and make it easier to bear the challenges that life deals to humankind. Perhaps this is why, despite its supernatural imagery, the poem remains resonant on many levels. We need to face our fragility and mortality. We can learn that living lives directed to making meaning, reflecting on our contributions and needs, and connecting to the world around us can give us perspective on our individual difficulties and remind us that we are not alone.

The *Yamim Nora'im*, and especially Yom Kippur, are intended to strip us naked, to tear away our fancy clothes and any other protections we might wrap around ourselves, and to force us to face our intentions, our actions and, ultimately, our deaths. The *Un'taneh Tokef* liturgy tries to evoke that reality, as does the requirement of fasting and the traditional dress of Yom Kippur, which is the white *kittel* that is part of the death shroud. The idea is that at the end of the day, we should rise up from our minideaths reborn, with a fresh opportunity to try to align our intentions and our actions, and to fill each day with meaning and holiness before our ultimate death. We may not be able to "avert the severe decree" entirely, to forestall death, but the tradition teaches that, until then, we can fill our days with life through cultivating our connection with the divine, through self-work and through just action on behalf of our community. —D.W.

How can acts of *t'shuva, t'fila* and *tzedaka* help ease the bitterness of the decree? Through each of these actions, we choose to open ourselves to the powers that are larger than our individual selves, powers that carry us collectively through life and death. As we stand in our vulnerability and choose to mend our ways, to open our hearts in prayer and to give to others, we affirm that we stand in the present moment and yet lean into eternity. In this leaning, we can find strength and sweetening, even though some of us will encounter great suffering and loss in the year to come. Reciting *Un'taneh Tokef* offers provisions for the road, provisions that we affirm together in our shared fragility. —M.K.

The end of the *musaf Amida* on Rosh Hashana and Yom Kippur can be a good opportunity for the high-energy singing of such prayers as *Sim Shalom, Hayom Harat Olam* and *Kaddish Titkabal.* —J.G.K.

Tashlikh

On the afternoon of the first day of Rosh Hashana, (but if the first day coincides with Shabbat, then on the second day) Jews perform a ritual called *tashlikh,* which is designed to rid us symbolically of our sins, mistakes and missed opportunities of the past year. The word *tashlikh* ("to cast off") comes from the prophet Micah's description of casting forth sins into the sea. (Micah 7:18–20) It is a ceremony conducted by a body of water—a stream, river, lake, ocean or even a well—and it commonly includes the reading of passages from Psalms and the Prophets. Leftover crumbs and pieces of hallah or other bread are cast into the water as if we were literally ridding ourselves of our sins. One can do this ceremony alone,

While the *tashlikh* ritual evokes the symbolic cleansing value of praying near a body of water and the symbolic expiation of throwing bread crumbs—our sins—into the water, the practice of *tashlikh* raised concerns about idolatry—the fear that the community might appear to be propitiating water deities or underground deities. However, folk tradition was strong enough to withstand that critique, and most liberal Jewish communities continue to practice the ritual of *tashlikh*. —J.G.K.

Another *tashlikh* tradition prefers pocket lint to bread crumbs. Our sins are not necessarily as obvious and consciously chosen as bread crumbs. We may need to carefully examine ourselves to find them. —J.A.S.

Not wanting us to upset the ecological balance of streambeds by littering them with bread crumbs, Rabbi Arthur Waskow has proposed casting stones instead of bread crumbs during *tashlikh*. —N.M.

with family or in a group, and it can be an opportunity for an innovative ritual on Rosh Hashana.

Why would a Reconstructionist community participate in this ritual, given its supernatural overtones? Unlike all of the prayers spoken during these days, the ritual of *tashlikh* is a tangible expression of what we hope to accomplish. We want to enter into the New Year unencumbered by our failings. We want to cast off our mistakes but

Tashlikh persists not for theological reasons, but because it is concrete and physical and it takes us outdoors. Our bodies crave activity and fresh air after a full morning of sitting and speaking words. *Tashlikh* is the physical embodiment of the *t'shuva* we seek throughout these holy days. —B.P.

The *tashlikh* ritual gives both adults and children an opportunity to viscerally experience the release of those obstacles that stand in the way of our *t'shuva*, our turning/returning to the path we want to walk in the New Year. *Tashlikh* can be a wonderful opportunity for families to discuss together those things that they want to let go of—perhaps impatience, unkind speech, anger, disrespect, or selfishness—and then to name each negative trait or quality as a piece of bread or a bean is thrown into the water. —T.S.

retain the lessons learned from them. *Tashlikh* is a physical metaphor for the emotional and psychological process of *t'shuva*.

Why do we toss bread into water on Rosh Hashana? On Rosh Hashana we use water to carry away the bread that embodies our sins and failures. Water is the element of fluidity, birthing and flow. Our bodies are comprised of at least 50 percent water. Our very cells contain water. It is also an essential component of the earth's body. The *tashlikh* ritual thus expresses the intention that we can let go of our individual holdings, grudges and failures, and that they will be carried along and absorbed in the greater life-giving flow of streams to rivers to oceans to vapors and then again to rain. The waters in which we are held in utero, the waters that are within our cells during our lifetime, and the waters of the *tahara* (cleansing ritual) to prepare a body for burial are invoked on the sacred days of Rosh Hashana. Water carries away impurities and also makes possible the life of the body and the cleansing of the soul. On this day of new beginnings, we let go of the old as we are born into the new. —M.K.

A more playful approach to *tashlikh* is a communal recitation of sins that are organized, like medieval *piyyutim*, in alphabetical order and called out by members of the congregation. "We cast off avarice, aggression, anger. … We cast off blasphemy, bigotry, bias. …" (Hint: For "y," try casting off "yellow journalism.") This can be followed by alphabetical affirmations. "We embrace caring, compassion, courage. …" —D.W.

Both complexity and simplicity can be useful spiritual tools. Generations of rabbis opposed the practice of *tashlikh*, partly because the ritual made it seem too simple a way to do *t'shuva*. No soul-searching—just toss a few crumbs in the water. But I find a useful teaching in the simplicity as well: I tell myself, "I don't need these sins any more (if I ever did!); I can just toss them away!" —J.A.S.

Aseret Y'mey T'shuva— Ten Days of Repentance

The work of *t'shuva* continues during the days that fall between Rosh Hashana and Yom Kippur. During this time, we take the meaning of the *Un'taneh Tokef* prayer to heart ("Repentance, prayer and acts of charity avert the severity of the decree.") and think about how the mitzvot of repentance, prayer and acts of loving kindness may be deepened in the coming year. Between the two islands of prayer and communal ritual that are Rosh Hashana and Yom Kippur, we have the opportunity to focus on day-to-day life and open ourselves to the unfolding future. Since the rabbinic period, these *aseret y'mey t'shuva*—ten days of repentance—have been designated as a special unit of time. In a passage from the Talmud (*Rosh Hashana* 16b), Rabbi Yoḥanan describes the function of these days by referring to the Book of Life that is understood to be open on Rosh Hashana. He explains that three books are open on Rosh Hashana: one for the completely righteous, one for the completely wicked, and one for those in between.

Each year on Rosh Hashana, I invite members of the *ḥavura* to reflect on their sins. I encourage them to list their sins on a card, to seal the card in an envelope, and to drop the envelope in a basket at the Kol Nidre service. In the *shaḥarit* service of Yom Kippur, I augment the traditional *Al Ḥet* list with the sins that members of the community have listed. The lists are arresting—honest, brave and full of spiritual struggle.

—D.W.

According to Rabbi Yoḥanan, the completely righteous are sealed immediately in the Book of Life, those who are entirely wicked are inscribed in the Book of Death, and the fate of those in between is suspended until Yom Kippur.

The rabbis understood that few people live at the extremes of righteousness or wickedness. Most of us try to be good people, and we all make mistakes. In the imagery of these days, it is as if each one of us is on trial—we are the defendants; God is the judge; and life is at stake. While Reconstructionist Judaism does not take this imagery literally, we should take it seriously. We can use these days leading up to Yom Kippur as an opportunity to think about how in the coming year we will truly live and not merely exist. If we really want to make our lives more meaningful, how can we do it? What changes would we have to make in order to live life more fully aware of our own existence, but even more, to be deeply connected to

During the *aseret y'mey t'shuva*, we encounter our own mortality, and it seems during that period that the veil separating the living and the dead is more transparent. Thus, it is a custom to visit the graves of one's relatives who have died, to remember them, and even to ask them to intercede on our behalf. While we may not believe our forebears to be literally capable of accomplishing this, we look to the example of their lives to learn about how to live ours rightly. —J.M.S.

Entering into the imagery of the *Un'taneh Tokef* is similar to entering into a dream (or, in our day perhaps, experiencing a film). After visiting the dreamscape of the heavenly throne and the heavenly court, we, the dreamers, have a visceral and emotional understanding of the awe and trembling that might not have been quite as accessible before our visit. This is the fine art of tapping into the religious imagination. —V.M.

T'shuva work is not only for the ten days. Having a structured time on the Jewish calendar to do our *t'shuva* work can help us to develop this as a practice that we carry into the rest of our year. —N.M.

others and to the world around us? The days between Rosh Hashana and Yom Kippur afford us one more opportunity to approach those whom we have hurt, apologize, repair the relationship and enter the gates of Yom Kippur having done all we can to better the landscape of our personal relationships.

Several changes in the daily liturgy during *aseret y'mey t'shuva* highlight the themes of remembrance, judgment and inscription in the Book of Life. Most of these occur during the central prayer section of the *Amida*. *Avinu Malkeynu* is inserted immediately after the *Amida*. The High Holy Day themes also emerge in the liturgy for the Shabbat that falls between Rosh Hashana and Yom Kippur, known as *Shabbat Shuva*, the Sabbath of Return. The name for this special Shabbat is derived from the same root as "*t'shuva*," which literally means, "to return." *Shabbat Shuva* focuses on the prophetic reading from Hosea 14:2–10 that replaces a haftarah for the weekly

I do not relate to the image of returning to God from our sinfulness. I do warm to the image in the early morning prayer, "My God, the soul that you have given me is pure." No matter what I do, no matter how badly I have acted, my soul remains pure; there is an "original" innocence that remains if I excavate deeply enough: "*Hashiveyni v'ashuva*"—"Help me to return, and I will return"—to my center, to my internal wellsprings that I have ignored over the course of the year. —J.J.S.

Most years, the Torah reading that falls on *Shabbat Shuva* is *Nitzavim-Vayelekh* (although in some years, it is the next portion, *Ha'azinu*). In this portion, repentance, *t'shuva*, rises to prominence, as the root "*shuv*" appears seven times (Deuteronomy 30). This coincidence enhances the theme of this Shabbat, as it is woven into both the Torah and haftarah readings. —B.P.

Torah portion. The haftarah begins with these words: "Return (*Shuva*) Israel, to your God, for you have fallen because of your sin. Take words with you and return to God. Say to God, 'Forgive all guilt and accept what is good; instead of sacrifices, we will pay with the offering of our lips.'" The rabbis appended two additional sections from the writings of other prophets to complete the message of the text. The first, from the prophet Micah, emphasizes God's forgiving nature. The second is from the prophet Joel. It anticipates a ceremony with the blast of a horn and the conclusion of a fast—very much like what happens at the conclusion of Yom Kippur. The message of *Shabbat Shuva* is traditionally understood to be that God is a forgiving God. Our task is to repent and prepare for the fast of Yom Kippur. In rabbinic and medieval times, *Shabbat Shuva* was an opportunity for rabbis to

The second line of the haftarah for *Shabbat Shuva* sums up the work we do in these ten days: "Take words with you, and return to godliness." (Hosea 14:3) Most of the work of *t'shuva*, like most of the sins we commit, is done via words. We have little else beyond words to offer: "I'm sorry" and "I forgive you." This passage in Hebrew (*ḵ'ḥu imaḵhem d'varim, shuvu v'shuvu el Adonay*) has been set to music and can be a regular refrain throughout the ten days. It reminds us of the power of our words. Just as our words can harm, they also have the power to heal. —B.P.

Prior to the publication of the Hertz *Pentateuch and Haftorahs* in 1936, some communities read Hosea and Micah, and some read Hosea and Joel, depending on whether *Shabbat Shuva* fell on *Parashat Vayeleḵh* or *Parashat Ha'azinu*. Current custom throughout North America, however, is to read all three. —J.A.S.

give lengthy and weighty sermons explaining the laws of Yom Kippur and urging people to repent and change their lives. Today, greater emphasis is placed on the sermons that rabbis deliver on Rosh Hashana and Yom Kippur, so *Shuva* can be an opportunity for a member or members of the congregation to share reflections on the impact and import of these days.

Yom Kippur

Making mistakes is part of what makes us human. Our ability to learn and grow from those mistakes makes our lives meaningful and helps us to discover more of who we are as human beings. When we come to the synagogue on Yom Kippur, we should be prepared to strip away all of our pretenses and our resistance to vulnerability. We are being called to account for our actions, and we must take responsibility for the change that needs to happen.

We attempt to do all of this in the context of the most sacred day on the Jewish calendar. Of course, throughout the year we must work to repair relationships that are broken, make amends with people we have hurt, and try to be better people. Those efforts should increase during the month of Elul and reach a peak in the days leading to Yom Kippur, but Yom Kippur itself provides this one day of intense self-scrutiny and self-affliction within which to undertake looking inward with the primary goals of atonement, forgiveness, and spiritual cleansing and renewal.

Yom Kippur in the Torah

While the spiritual themes of Rosh Hashana primarily developed during the rabbinic period, the core meaning of Yom Kippur is already evident in the Torah's description of the day, even though we no longer offer sacrifices. The Torah discusses Yom Kippur not just once, but in three separate passages. The biblical rites involved a cleansing and purging of ritual impurities in the sanctuary through the priest's atonement for himself, his family and the larger community. Two of these three passages are included in the Yom Kippur Torah readings. The first of these, Leviticus 16:1–34, is read during the morning service of Yom Kippur. This section recounts the service of the high priest and concludes with the following declaration:

> And it shall be for you an everlasting statute: In the seventh month, upon the tenth day of the month, you shall afflict your souls. No work shall you perform, both home born and the stranger in your midst, for on this day atonement shall be made for you, to make you clean from all of your wrongdoing. Before God you shall be clean. (Leviticus 16:29–30)

The second passage comes from chapter 29 in the Book of Numbers, which details the special sacrificial offerings for each festival. The verses regarding Yom Kippur state:

> And on the tenth day of the seventh month, you will have a holy convocation, and you will afflict your souls (*v'initem et nafshoteykhem*). No work will you perform. And you will offer a burnt offering . . . (Numbers 29:7–11)

This passage is read as the special *maftir* (concluding) reading from a second Torah scroll on the morning of Yom Kippur.

The third passage, not included in the liturgy, is also from the Book of Leviticus. It states:

> Mark the tenth day of the seventh month as the Day of Atonement. It shall be a sacred occasion for you; you shall practice self-denial. You shall bring an offering by fire to God, and you shall do no work throughout the day, for it is a day of atonement on which expiation is to be made on your behalf to God. Do no work whatever; it is a law for all time, throughout the generations in all your settlements. It shall be a Sabbath of complete rest for you, and you shall practice self-denial; on the ninth day of the month at evening, from evening to evening, you shall observe this as your Sabbath. (Leviticus 23:27–32)

The Israelites understood the somewhat obscure concept of soul affliction (*inui nefesh*) as referring to fasting

Although this passage seems to be a logical choice to include in the Torah readings, perhaps on the afternoon of Yom Kippur in the *minḥa* service, it is not included. Presumably, this is because in order for a reading to be used for the three aliyot (persons being called to the Torah), the reading must have a minimum of nine verses (by tradition, at least ten verses), and this one only has seven. More likely, it was not used because that would have meant rolling the Torah a considerable distance before the afternoon reading, which is not the case with the reading selected. —Y.R.

The root for "*inui nefesh*" ("self-affliction") is *ayin-nun-hey*, the same as for the Hebrew verb meaning "to answer." We need to strip away distractions and pretense so that we can answer the primary question of Yom Kippur: "Have we moved toward being more loving and compassionate human beings?" —N.M.

and self-denial. Outside of the mention of afflicting one's soul or practicing self-denial in the Torah, there is nothing to indicate that this day was nearly as important in biblical times as it would later become. It has been suggested that Yom Kippur was originally just a preliminary to the rituals and observances of the holiday of Sukkot that follows four days later. Sukkot was a holiday of great rejoicing over the abundance of the harvest. Making the sacrifices of atonement beforehand added to the rejoicing.

In biblical times, Yom Kippur was considered a priestly ritual and institution. Since atonement was to be achieved through sacrifices, the high priest was responsible for enacting the ritual, and the presence of the community was not required. The priest did all of the rituals out of the sight of the people in and around the sanctuary.

The Book of Leviticus offers us a mechanism for forgiveness in the form of animal sacrifice. Leviticus never suggests that repentance alone can bring forgiveness for

The Torah calls Sukkot "*Heḥag*," (The Holiday), indicating that Sukkot was the greatest holiday of Temple times. Re-emphasizing Sukkot's prominence can take the edge off the anxiety that many feel going into Yom Kippur. —J.G.K.

The concluding verses of the Torah reading (Leviticus 16) may be one of the first commentaries on Yom Kippur itself. Many scholars believe that these concluding verses were added onto the chapter in order to emphasize that this ritual was incumbent not just upon the priests, but upon all of Israel. —T.K.

The great Biblicist Jacob Milgrom suggested that animal sacrifices were simply a means of accessing blood that was needed to purify God's sancta. He referred to blood as "ritual detergent," a life-force cleaner to counter the negative energies of impure activities. —T.K.

violations of the laws or that one can successfully appeal individually to God's mercy, grace or kindness for atonement. Words that later rabbinic literature uses in conjunction with Yom Kippur—for example, repentance (*t'shuva*), mercy (*raḥamim*), grace (*ḥen*), and kindness (*ḥesed*) are not used regarding Yom Kippur in Leviticus. Later biblical texts, such as the books of Joshua and Ezekiel, have references to the role that human beings must play in the process of repentance, which is likened to an internal "returning" to one's essence. The verb "*shuv*" occurs frequently in the Bible, sometimes connoting turning away from something, and sometimes connoting turning toward something. The motion of turning implies following a direct path and having the potential to find the right way in life. The word "*shuv*" shaped the rabbinic understanding of *t'shuva*.

Leviticus 16 outlines the rituals of atonement and instructs Moses' brother Aaron, the high priest, to follow the ritual in order to make the people ritually pure: "Before God shall you be clean." (Leviticus 16:30) Sin and repentance were understood to be very much a part of life, with cleansing from sin and making a sacrificial form of atonement serving as the communal methods of expiation and forgiveness. Leviticus does not explain different categories of sins and their reparative sacrifices, only that the *asham* (guilt offering), and the *ḥatat* (sin offering) were categories of *korbanot* (sacrifices) offered in the *Mishkan*.

Leviticus does not outline a separate process of atonement for sins committed by human beings against each other. The Bible tells us only that certain crimes and actions carry consequences, including payment for damages, death and *lex talionis*, the law of retaliation ("an eye for an eye"). But none of these effect atonement or forgiveness between the transgressor and God.

The atonement rituals performed in the Temple in Jerusalem conformed to the instructions in the Torah. The high priest would lay his hands on a bull, confessing his sins and that of his household. Later, he offered a second confession for the *kohanim* (priests), and then one goat was sacrificed and one was sent off to *azazel*, the wilderness, carrying the symbolic load of the sins of all the Israelites. The high priest then went into the Holy of Holies to pray for forgiveness. In the afternoon, young women in white would seek husbands in the fields. This ritual is outlined in Leviticus 16 and included in the Torah reading in the Yom Kippur morning service.

Most Bible scholars understand *lex talionis* as setting limits on vengeful instincts, not harming the criminal in the same way the crime victim was harmed. —J.G.K.

In our modern-day context, we miss something profound about Yom Kippur that was present in Temple times. The primary concern in those times was that the sins of Israel somehow adhered to the Temple itself. Thus, the ritual to cleanse the Temple of its sins meant that all of Israel's sins were wiped clean, and the Temple could again serve as a fully functioning conduit to God. When the high priest emerged whole and uninjured, the people felt certain that their sins were actually forgiven, and they rejoiced. The description of the priestly service serves as a guided meditation to recapture the sense of relief and joy that accompanied the successful completion of the ritual. A traditional *piyyut*, *Mar'eh Kohen*, captures the power of the appearance of the high priest as he emerged and the joy that followed. —J.M.S.

The meaning of "*azazel*" remains obscure. Some believe that *azazel* was a demon of the wilderness upon whom all the sins of Israel would be thrown. Others suggest that *azazel* is the wilderness itself, the site of chaos and danger. —T.K.

The Talmudic Understanding of Yom Kippur

The beginning of larger discussions on atonement and repentance occurs later in rabbinic literature. The Mishna (*Yoma* 8.9) teaches that Yom Kippur allows us to atone for transgressions against God, but does not allow us to atone for transgressions against our fellow human beings unless we have first made peace with one another. The Jewish textual tradition evolved to emphasize the idea that by repairing ourselves and our relationships with others, we are doing our part to repair the larger world.

The Talmud records additional rituals performed by the high priest. These include preparing himself by immersing in a mikvah (ritual bath) (*Yoma* 19b), saying a prayer on behalf of the people, and tying a thread of crimson wool to the door of the sanctuary—a thread that would turn white when the goat reached *azazel*, a sign that Israel had been forgiven. (*Yoma* 68b) Not much more is known about the rituals of Yom Kippur during the Sec-

The high priest immersed himself in the mikvah twice. Both the intensity of entering the Holy of Holies and the intensity of returning from the holiest of places were disruptive of the priest's state of purity, and the ritual of immersion helped him to return to a middle ground between the extremes of the sacred and the profane. —J.G.K.

Pirkey Avot enumerates ten miracles of the Holy Temple, including the surprising statement that even though the people in the courtyard stood shoulder to shoulder, there was still room for them all to prostrate themselves when the high priest pronounced God's name. What an incredible sight! —J.G.K.

ond Temple period, except for further confirmation that the day was to be spent immersed in prayer from morning until night.

Once the Second Temple was destroyed in 70 CE, the sacrificial system was no longer the means by which Jews could achieve atonement. The rabbis needed to devise a new atonement process for when a Jew committed an *avera* (transgression or wrongdoing). "*Avera*" stems from the verb "*avar*," "to cross over." *Averot* are considered to be rejections of God's will, whether by commission or omission. They are believed to stem from the *yetzer hara*, our negative inclination, which drives us to mistakes. However, the rabbis also understood the *yetzer hara* to be the source of our passion and some say, of our creativity.

Several categories of wrongdoing emerged in later rabbinic texts. The word "*ḥet*" means "an inadvertent sin." As in archery, missing the mark or aiming off course constitutes a particular category of sin. This concept of sin refers to straying from the ways of godly living that Jewish tradition lays forth. An *avon* is a sin committed out of desire when we know the action is wrong but we can't stop ourselves. Finally, a *pesha* is a sin involving intentional rebellion against God, a parent or another person.

In the Talmud (*Shabbat* 153a), Rabbi Eliezer says, "Repent one day before your death." Not surprisingly, his students ask him how they can possibly know when they will die. Eliezer replies that is why it is important to rec-

When we seek to gratify only our own drives and ambitions, we are more likely to let our arrogance direct our lives and potentially hurt other people. —Y.R.

ognize your sins and mistakes right away and repent immediately, just in case your tomorrow never comes. Yom Kippur is built upon the stark realization that death is very much a part of life. When we embrace that mystery, we can transcend ourselves and our wrongdoings and engage more fully with life.

On this day, traditional clothing mirrors burial shrouds, and we do not eat or drink, have sexual relations or even bathe. Yom Kippur provides an opportunity for us to act as if we were physically dead and simultaneously to feel spiritually so alive! At the end of the day, we are resurrected to a balanced life in the New Year. —J.G.K.

Later in the evolution of Jewish life, Hasidic masters taught that Yom Kippur is a most joyful day. On this day, we turn to our innermost nature, our souls, and we can experience attunement with the source of our lives. Atonement becomes an opportunity to know a deep sense of at-one-ment with ourselves and with the power that is life and death itself. We participate in an act similar to that of biblical sacrifice. Sacrifice, *ḳorban* in Hebrew, has the same root as the word "*ḳarov*," close. The act of making a sacrifice is an act of drawing close. As we make sacrificial offerings through our prayers and our full attention, we draw very close to the mysterious power at the heart of existence. In the view of Hasidic teachings, this intimacy is a cause for great joy. —M.K.

Religious systems aim to generate a set of coherent answers to such questions as: "Why are we here?" "What is our purpose?" Ideally, the answers guide our day-to-day actions and behaviors. Much of liberal religious thought answers these questions through the rubrics of love and connection. We are on this earth to be in relationship—with God perhaps, but certainly and undeniably with other human beings. We are here to love. But with love comes loss. Joy and pain are inseparable twins. What can we do? To protect ourselves by not loving is lonely and soul-stunting. It goes against our human nature, our reason for living. Yom Kippur's extended meditation on mortality and fragility helps us to cultivate a deepened awareness of life and our engagement with it. At the end of the holiday, with the sounding of the shofar, we are considered reborn. When we return to our daily routines, we have an opportunity to apply what we have learned over the long fast. We can fine-tune our lives and make adjustments to the ways in which we have been acting. We can emerge from the holy day with an increased capacity for openheartedness, for love and connection. —D.W.

Preparations For Yom Kippur

There are several traditional preparatory rituals especially for *erev* Yom Kippur. These preparatory acts are *kaparot* (an atonement ritual), *t'vila* (immersion in a mikvah, a ritual bath), and *tzedaka* (righteous giving). While two of these rituals are rarely observed by liberal Jews, there is something to be gained from understanding each of them.

The ancient ritual of *kaparot* is a visceral approach to atonement, underscoring that on Yom Kippur our very lives are at stake. The original form of the ritual calls for a chicken to be waved in a circular motion over the head of the person repenting. The chicken is then slaughtered, and either the bird or its cash equivalent is given to the poor. For the past few centuries, most communities have abandoned this practice, and some have actively opposed it as cruel to animals. Instead, some people place coins in a handkerchief, swing that over their head, and then give

By the time I was born in the 1950s, my family had progressed to swinging coins above our heads—coins that were then given to *tzedaka*. But my older sisters and cousins have memories of chickens, of accompanying our grandmother on the bus to the slaughterhouse with the chicken in a basket, of chickens running around the slaughterhouse after their head had been chopped off. The chicken was then cooked for the *se'uda mafseket*—the meal consumed just before the fast. As a child, I regretted having been born too late, thus missing all the mystery. —J.J.S.

Jews from some Arab countries stuff the slaughtered chicken with pomegranate seeds and other symbolic foods. Then they roast it and serve it to the individual who has used the bird to atone. —D.W.

The ritual of *kaparot* is medieval in origin, and the opinions of Jewish scholars of the middle and later medieval period differed about whether to permit it. —J.G.K.

the coins as *tzedaka*. Whatever the ritual, today it is clear that atonement can be achieved through means other than sacrifice.

The ritual of *t'vila*, immersion in a mikvah, is now practiced across the Jewish denominational spectrum. The traditional reasons to immerse oneself in a ritual pool are for purification from any ritual impurity and preparation for *t'shuva*. Today, immersion in a mikvah is also used to mark the transition from one spiritual state to another. As one prepares to atone and turn back to one's true self, the mikvah can move us to repair our hearts, our souls and ultimately the world.

These rituals are important because we often need visceral and tangible acts in order to evoke spiritual change. Though we may be modern, this is still very true of humans in the 21st century. If these rituals seem archaic, we need to create new ways to tangibly mark our process of *t'shuva*. —J.M.S.

I went to a mikvah and immersed myself for the first time several years ago before my wedding. Until then, I had no idea how powerful and transforming an experience it can be. I had accompanied many others in my role as rabbi, and I had seen the impact of the experience on them, but I really didn't know. I have not ever engaged in *t'vila* (immersion) before Yom Kippur, but I'm sure that it would be a wonderful psychic portal to the day. —J.J.S.

At the Mayyim Hayyim Living Waters Community Mikveh in Newton, Massachusetts, immersing oneself at this time of year has become a popular practice for men and women across the denominational spectrum. Clergy are given precedence for preholiday immersions. The mikvah has created a special set of *kavanot* (meditations) for this season of repentance for one to read and contemplate prior to immersion. The ritual of immersion helps to purify our inner being, which we will then outwardly portray by wearing white for the service. —B.P.

Rabbi Alan Yuter describes Jewish ritual as choreographed values. Mikvah on the eve of Yom Kippur is a beautiful dance back toward our purest selves. —J.G.K.

Yom Kippur Observance

Yom Kippur is called *Shabbat Shabbaton*—the Sabbath of Sabbaths, a Sabbath of complete rest. All labors that are forbidden on Shabbat are also forbidden on Yom Kippur. (By the same token, as on Shabbat, the saving of a life takes precedence over the holiday observance.) What constitutes work in the modern world is different from that in the world of the rabbis of old. Many Jews refrain from going to their places of business on Yom Kippur and instead, spend the day in synagogue with family and community. In some places, public schools are not open on Yom Kippur to respect the observance of the Jewish students and faculty.

All of the rites of self-denial are meant to deepen the meaning of the holiday. The Mishna (*Yoma* 8.1) teaches that on Yom Kippur we are forbidden to eat or drink, to

Only oppressive employers will have a problem with their employees taking Rosh Hashana and Yom Kippur off. And Jews should not internalize the values of oppressive employers. —J.A.S.

I have never found that fasting enhances my *t'shuva* work. I get headaches, and I feel faint, and my physical discomfort distracts me from introspective and prayerful states. —J.J.S.

A key aspect of *t'shuva* is regaining our ability to choose with free will how to respond to our own desires. Fasting is an exercise in free will. —J.A.S.

One way of understanding these acts of self-denial is that on Yom Kippur, we are rehearsing for our own deaths. Another way of thinking of these prohibitions is that on Yom Kippur, we reach a spiritual peak. For one day, we have pure souls, and we have no need of our bodies. —B.P.

wash, to anoint ourselves, to put on leather shoes, and to have sexual intercourse. One rabbinic interpretation of these five rituals of affliction is that they are meant to correspond to the five books of the Torah. The rabbis also imagine that the second giving of the Ten Commandments was completed on Yom Kippur. Another interpretation offers the notion that the afflictions correspond to the five senses with which we either keep the commandments or commit transgressions. The medieval Jewish philosopher Maimonides, in *The Guide for the Perplexed,* offers the instruction that every person should engage in self-denial on Yom Kippur so as to limit material and physical pleasures while in the process of *t'shuva.*

Physical self-denial reminds us that the time will come when we will no longer have any physical pleasures, reinforcing the day's theme of confronting our own mortality. —J.A.S.

Every spiritual practice is based on self-denial, asking for some renunciation or redirection of intention, energy and action. This trains us to control our unskillful reactivity and our habitual tendencies to harm ourselves and others; it also trains us to manifest the eternal and universal values that lead to peace, justice and happiness. By developing the capacity for renunciation, we develop an inner freedom to see cause and consequence and to choose what is wholesome and life affirming. —S.P.W.

Our tradition notes parallels between Purim and Yom Kippur. Yom Kippur's formal name is *Yom Haḳippurim*, which we might translate as "the day that is like Purim." On Purim, we limit the spiritual and exaggerate the physical; on Yom Kippur we do the reverse. Each day is a day of extremes, and in this way they are like one another because during all the rest of the year we balance between the spiritual and the physical. Another connection between the two holidays is that Purim is a day of costumes and masquerade, and on Yom Kippur we act as if we were pious!
—J.G.K./D.A.T.

The fast is traditionally 25 hours long, one hour longer than a day. The verse in Leviticus regarding the fast says, "You shall practice denial on the ninth day of the month at evening . . ." (23:22) This verse puzzled the rabbis since the holiday begins on the tenth day of the month. The rabbis interpreted this to mean that there should be a *tosefet*—an additional segment—taken from the previous afternoon/evening during which Jews should refrain from food and drink. No set amount of time was traditionally added to the fast, only that it should begin before dusk in order to "add from the non-sacred to the sacred." (*Oraḥ Ḥayim* 608:1) Thus Yom Kippur, known as *Shabbat Shabbaton,* is traditionally observed for the same length of time as Shabbat.

If one is sick, pregnant, nursing or on certain medications, one should not undertake a full fast. Children under the age of 8 should not fast for a full day. Fasting is

Many individuals, especially elders, experience the fast as such an integral part of the holiday that they refrain from eating even if that is bad for their health. From the pulpit, I expressly urge those individuals not to fast, and I recite for them a blessing of *pikuaḥ nefesh*, saving a life. Fasting is a means, not an end; fasting is designed to heighten our awareness, not to put us at risk physically. The goal of fasting is to facilitate repentance. We cannot do this crucial spiritual work if we are compromising our health. —D.W.

I loved Yom Kippur as a child. My mother would pack me a bag of seedless grapes and marble cake to hold me over until she would walk me home for lunch at around 2 P.M. After my lunch, we would walk to my bubbe's *shtibl*, a tiny Satmar shul. She would also have brought treats for me. By the time I was 10, we would bargain about how long I would be allowed to fast, and at 12½ , I managed to make it through the whole day, ready to become a bar mitzvah. —J.J.S.

encouraged but not required for children under bar/bat mitzvah age. One who must refrain from fasting may undertake a different kind of fast by abstaining from favorite foods or warm foods, or by eating less than normal quantities. Many members of congregations collect canned food before Kol Nidre as a way for the fast to have meaning beyond their own individual atonement by benefitting people in need. It is customary to wish people a "*tzom kal*"—"an easy fast," and a "*g'mar ḥatima tova*," "to be sealed [in the Book of Life] for good."

Abstention from food and drink is considered mandatory in the Torah. The Talmud discusses at length what measure of food or drink would render a person in violation of the fast, and other forms of self-denial are derivative of this. (*Yoma* 74a) One of the reasons Yom Kippur never begins on a Thursday night or a Saturday night is that, respectively, there would not be sufficient time to prepare food before Shabbat or before the fast. Eating and rejoicing are associated with Shabbat, and while Yom Kippur may fall on Shabbat itself, the calendar demonstrates the clear importance of preparing sufficiently for Shabbat and Yom Kippur.

Fasting is traditionally understood as a kind of self-denial. In encountering a physical experience that is outside the norm for most American Jews, we are invited to really sit with the pleasant and unpleasant sensations that arise from fasting and to notice our reactions. Can we be compassionate with our bodily weakness, with the changes we experience? Freed from the ability to mask emotional needs with the open refrigerator door, can we more deeply enter into ourselves? The act of fasting radically disrupts our normal day. Whether or not we spend Yom Kippur in synagogue (although that can certainly help us to get through it!), fasting provides a foundation for a transformative experience. —T.S.

In addition to fasting and refraining from work, traditionally we do not wear leather, which was—and in many places still is—a sign of luxury inappropriate to the mood of the day. Dressing less elegantly and more simply is also a way to prepare ourselves to confront our mortality. The custom of removing one's shoes in a house of mourning parallels the prohibition against wearing leather shoes on Yom Kippur, again invoking our physical fragility and the need to see past material things. Even in biblical times, leather shoes or sandals were considered a luxury, and they certainly were removed in a holy place. The Mishna (*Berakhot* 9.5) teaches that a person may not enter the Temple Mount carrying a staff, wearing sandals or bearing a wallet.

In addition, it is customary on Yom Kippur to wear white, which is the color of purity. A white robe called a *kittel* is traditionally worn during Yom Kippur. A garment customarily worn by men at life transitions, the *kittel* is often worn by the groom at a wedding and then later serves as a burial shroud for its owner. On Yom Kippur, the *kittel* underscores our confrontation with our mortality and the need to make atonement while there is time to

Another reason for not wearing leather shoes and other leather clothing items is to avoid benefitting from the harm that has been done to animals in conjunction with a day on which we seek compassion for ourselves. —T.S.

When putting on my *kittel*, I find it particularly powerful to contemplate that I am dressing up in the same clothes that I will wear at my death. It helps me to get in touch with the essence of the day. —N.M.

live differently. Today many women and men choose to wear *kittels* as a way to set apart this day from other festivals and holy days on the calendar. Other Jews wear white or off-white clothing. The Torah scrolls and the cover for the reading table are also adorned in white and traditionally rabbis and cantors wear white robes and tallitot.

Yom Kippur is also a time to refrain from bathing and showering, as well as from sexual intimacy. These regulations are meant to heighten our experience on Yom Kippur since by abstaining from such activities, we are closer to the experience of what it means to no longer enjoy the earthly pleasures of the world. On a deeper level, when we are satiated, we can avoid the problem of the hungry; when we are well heeled, we need not be reminded of the poor; and when we are wrapped in the embrace of a partner/spouse, we can easily forget the lonely. None of those in need chose their difficult situation, but by choosing this abstinence ourselves, we can underscore the fragility of the world and our awareness of the suffering in it.

Jews of all denominations and affiliations observe Yom Kippur in some fashion. Regardless of how traditional one's observance is, engaging in some form of self-denial connects the individual with the communal endeavor of atonement and forgiveness. Those who do not choose to participate in communal worship might fast, gather for

Near the turn of the 20th century, radical Jews held banquets and balls to mock traditional religious practices and to shock members of the bourgeoisie. Liberal Jews presume that Jewish religion can be strengthened by the critiques offered by such "freethinkers." —D.W.

family discussions, engage in social justice work, meditate and reflect, or design a Yom Kippur observance that includes a number of these activities.

In the late afternoon before Yom Kippur begins, families gather for the meal known as *se'uda mafseket*—the last meal before the fast. The meal includes neither special rituals nor blessings such as Kiddush (the blessing over the wine), since this meal must be completed before the fast day. The meal should be substantial since it is the last one we will have for the next 25 hours.

Before lighting the holiday candles, a *Yizkor* candle is lit in memory of loved ones who have died, but no special blessing is recited. The *Kol Haneshamah* machzor (page 688) offers a meditation for the lighting of the *Yizkor* candle. Yom Kippur is not only a confrontation with the reality of the individual's life and eventual death, but an opportunity to remember those who have died and left us a legacy that can help shape our lives.

Before sundown and before leaving for services, holiday candles are lit, with the blessing: "*l'hadlik ner shel Yom Hakippurim*" ("to kindle the lights of Yom Kippur"). (*Kol Haneshamah Maḥzor Leyamim Nora'im*, p. 688) This is followed by the *Sheheḥeyanu* blessing,

The *se'uda mafseket* should be substantial, yes, but be careful not to overeat. Indigestion does not enhance the *t'shuva* process. —J.J.S.

Perhaps the most important preparatory ritual before Yom Kippur is eating. The day before Yom Kippur is considered a small holiday, so after the *se'uda mafseket*, the prefast meal, it is customary to recite the celebratory Psalm 126 before reciting *Birkat Hamazon*. —J.G.K.

"who has kept us in life." Some communities also light candles at the beginning of the Kol Nidre service.

Kol Nidre

The evening service of Kol Nidre traditionally begins just before sundown, while it is still light outside. This reinforces the idea that a trial or court proceeding that must be conducted during the day is taking place. Yom Kippur is known also by the name *Yom Hadin,* the Day of Judgment. The setting is imagined as the earthly court of humanity, with the *bet din* (court of three judges) symbolized by the prayer leader and at least two people holding

In some communities, past and current board leaders or presidents stand at the *bima* holding the Torah scrolls (if the congregation has more than one) during the recitation of Kol Nidre. In some congregations, the scrolls are carried in a procession from the back of the sanctuary to the front at the beginning of the service. —N.H.M.

In many congregations, the Holy Ark is emptied and leaders are honored with holding the Torah scrolls while Kol Nidre is recited. Sometimes leaders are rotated for each repetition of Kol Nidre. This is the only time in the year when the Torah scrolls are removed from the ark without the intention of reading from them. Here, the Torah scrolls stand as witnesses to the awesome ceremony of Kol Nidre. —J.M.S.

The image of a heavenly court begs to be reconstructed! Perhaps in place of a supernatural judge and the sense of ourselves as defendants, we can think of this moment as one in which we stand together in the process of discernment, with the intention of bringing clarity and honesty to an appraisal of our individual and communal lives. We are the "judges" of ourselves, and we pray for the strength and wisdom to fulfill that function in a helpful, compassionate way. We stand with respect and a measure of awe before this challenge and display the Torah scrolls as symbols of the wisdom of our Jewish tradition, which is here to aid us in the task before us. —T.S.

Torah scrolls (or one scroll, when only one is available), and the heavenly court where God alone sits in judgment. Even if we take this as a metaphoric legal proceeding, on this day we—and our actions—are the defendants, God is the judge, and our spiritual lives are at stake.

The words "*kol nidre*" ("all vows") refer to the opening declaration, but the entire service is commonly known by that name. The Kol Nidre service is experienced by many Jews as the most important of all the High Holy Day services. Synagogues and meeting places are often filled to capacity, with people arriving on time to hear the opening strains of the melody, which is better known than the words themselves. The melody is from the Middle Ages, and its haunting tones evoke memories and deep connections to Jewish tradition, even among more secular Jews.

Kol Nidre is the only evening service in which the tallit (prayer shawl) is worn. The biblical verse concerning the *tzizit* speaks of seeing the fringes (Numbers 15:39), and thus *tzizit* are required to be worn only during the day. Since the Kol Nidre service begins before the sun has set, and the cancellation of vows must happen before nightfall prior to the beginning of Yom Kippur, the leader of the service customarily wears a tallit. Gradually, it became

One of the associations of Kol Nidre is with the Conversos—the secret Jews who were forced to convert to Christianity during the Inquisition. Many Conversos continued to secretly identify as Jews. The image is of Conversos hiding in cellars chanting this melody as they forswear their forced conversions. —J.J.S.

customary for all those in the congregation who wear a tallit to do so for Kol Nidre as well. That they continue to wear tallitot into the evening portion of the service serves to further differentiate Kol Nidre as a time more sacred than other holy days. Yom Kippur is considered "one long day," so no blessing is recited the next morning upon donning the tallit, as if the prior service had lasted through the night.

The Kol Nidre service precedes and opens the evening service of Yom Kippur. It begins with the ark open, with all the Torah scrolls usually held by individuals in the community, and with the prayer leader delivering a most powerful declaration:

> By the authority of all who congregate above and all who congregate on earth, and with the permission of the omnipresent One, and by consent of this assembly, we accept into our midst whoever seeks to pray.

Some machzorim include blessings for putting on a tallit in the morning. I believe that since Kol Nidre evening services conclude with *Aleynu* and the Mourner's Kaddish, this makes sense. It may still be the tenth day of Tishri, but we wake up in the morning to a new day of life, just as we do every other day. The daytime services, however, generally omit the usual closing prayers between them. —J.G.K.

This opening declaration of Kol Nidre permitted the presence of people who had been excommunicated and could not otherwise enter the synagogue. The legal formula in Kol Nidre mirrors the one imposed by a *bet din* on an individual placed in *ḥerem*, that is, excommunication. A simple translation of the third line of the Kol Nidre declaration is, "We grant permission to pray with those who have sinned." This proclamation lifts the ban, if only for the duration of Yom Kippur. Even those cast out of the community may rejoin it, at least temporarily, at this holy moment. —J.G.K./DW./J.J.S.

> Whether righteous or unrighteous, all shall pray as one community.

The Kol Nidre prayer is introduced with this meditation as a way to bring to mind the essential work of this season. The idea of praying with sinners brings together an entire community—those within and those on the fringes.

The second part of the service is made up of the words of "Kol Nidre," a legalistic formula. The opening meditation reminds us that we stand alone with our own experiences, yet we are amid community—our actions within that community matter; and we stand before God—our actions and who we are in body and soul matter, as well. A kind of unity of purpose is effected through the interconnectedness of God and humanity. Each of us is righteous and unrighteous; we have all been wronged by someone at some time in our lives, and each person has wronged or will wrong someone else. Kol Nidre is the beginning of a time to come together with other, complex souls, directing prayer and action inward as well as outward.

The Kol Nidre prayer is in Aramaic. Its formula is designed to nullify unfulfilled personal vows, and to help us leave the *Yamim Nora'im* with a *tabula rasa*—a clean slate. The traditional text, composed in the ninth century, imagines the annulment of vows from the past year to the present. The text begins:

> All solemn vows—all promises of abstinence and formulas of prohibition and declarations of austerity and oaths that bear the name of God and pledges to our-

selves assumed on penalty . . . from the last Day of Atonement to this Day of Atonement (may the day come upon us for the good!)—from all of them, we now request release.

Rabbenu Tam changed the text in the 12th century because it was thought impossible to annul vows after they have been made. In order to truly impact any vows made, one would have to declare them null and void before one made them. As a result, the Kol Nidre text found in most traditional machzorim today imagines that the vows we make from this Yom Kippur until the next will be annulled. The Reconstructionist machzor returns to the original ninth-century text, and declares our past vows to be annulled. The assumption in annulling past vows is that only those vows that were impossible to ful-

The Rabbenu Tam version of Kol Nidre reminds me not to hold myself to a series of "shoulds" in the coming year that might keep me off my true path. The work of discernment is to become aware of what is asked of me in this moment, in this situation. If I am laboring under a set of expectations of what I should be doing, based less on the reality of this moment and more on my past baggage, I will be unable to respond as wholeheartedly and with as clear a mind as may be required. To release myself from future "vows" is to say, "I am setting an intention to be as present as possible to whatever arises in the coming year, with no preconceptions or false assumptions." —T.S.

Rabbinic leaders in the Middle Ages tried to eliminate Kol Nidre because it provided Christians with evidence that Jews could not be trusted, and it also had the potential to encourage people to take oaths more casually. But the leaders were unable to prevail over the will of the people, for whom Kol Nidre struck a powerful chord. —J.J.S.

fill, or that could be fulfilled only by causing significant harm, or that are not remembered should be annulled. The text is not intended to annul legitimate business agreements or personal commitments.

We humans are imperfect, and we know very well that despite our best efforts, we have made promises and vows that have gone unfulfilled. On Kol Nidre, we imagine that as we stand before the heavenly court, all of our mistakes and unfulfilled promises of the past year are rendered void before God. This, too, is part of our process of atonement laid out in the rituals of Yom Kippur.

Rabbi Mordecai Kaplan first articulated his statement, "The Thirteen Wants," at the dedication of the new building of the first Reconstructionist synagogue, the Society for the Advancement of Judaism, in 1926, and he later printed them in the first Jewish Reconstructionist prayer book. He may have been responding to the accusation that Kol Nidre's undoing of vows meant that Jews were not trustworthy: "We want the Jew so to be trusted that his yea will be taken as yea, and his nay as nay." —J.G.K.

A rabbinic story (*Vayikra Raba* 33.1) tells how Rabbi Shimon ben Gamaliel once told his servant Tevi to buy the best food in the market. The servant bought tongue. The rabbi then instructed Tevi to buy the worst food in the market. Tevi bought tongue again. Rabbi Shimon said to him, "What is this? When I asked you to get the best food, you bought me tongue. When I asked you to buy me the worst food, you bought me tongue again!" Tevi replied, "Both good and bad come through the tongue. When the tongue is good, there is nothing better. When it is bad, there is nothing worse." —M.K.

Scholars agree that each Jewish generation has given Kol Nidre a different meaning and significance. While the words themselves have remained constant, each generation has perceived them through the lens of its own cultural constructs. At some times, the lens was one of the magical thwarting of demonic forces, and at others one of precise legal formulas. What has remained constant is the sense that our words and our vows have great power and that we are to be held accountable for the forces we set in motion through them. —M.K.

Kol Nidre is chanted three times, which, according to the laws of the absolution of vows (see the *Shulḥan Arukh, Yoreh De'a* 228:3), must be recited in this fashion. Some cantors or service leaders will chant each repetition a little louder, thereby encouraging the community to sing along. This custom also parallels the custom of the high priest in the *avoda* service of Yom Kippur. The priest is imagined to make atonement first for himself, then on behalf of his family, and then for the community of Israel.

A more contemporary understanding is that the threefold recitation of Kol Nidre enables latecomers to the service to hear it at least once. Some communities may have one of the repetitions played on cello, violin or another instrument, as a way for the melody to fully evoke the depth of our feelings. The text of Kol Nidre does not warm the heart to the essential work of forgiveness. The melody, however, evokes a depth of prayer that is resonant for many Jews.

It is a musical custom to raise the key by a half step on each recitation of Kol Nidre. —J.G.K.

When Rabbi Mordecai Kaplan was serving the Society for the Advancement of Judaism in New York City, he sought to solve the ethical problem of dissolving vows as well as the disconnect between text and melody by substituting Psalm 130 for the traditional legal language, while keeping the melody. His congregants reacted very negatively because no matter how foreign the text may have been to them, they were moved by the emotional attachment of the words and melody together. —Y.R.

Following the Kol Nidre prayer is the recitation of several biblical verses. These verses underscore the forgiveness granted to the Israelites following God's decree against them when they refused to enter the Promised Land because of the frightening report by the scouts who had been sent in to investigate the Land of Israel. (Numbers 13) The verses from the Book of Numbers highlight God's compassion and the people's need for forgiveness.

The Kol Nidre section of the service ends with the *Sheheḥeyanu* blessing, which acknowledges how much we have to be thankful for in this season. It is the most important recitation of the *Sheheḥeyanu* of the year. More than

The story of the scouts can be read as a metaphor for how we approach our unknown future lives. Will we see the future as a land of promise, knowing that we will encounter difficulties along the way? Or will we see the future as a promised land, and be unwilling to embrace challenges because we think we should have a trouble-free future? —Y.R.

"*Salaḥti ḳid'vareḳha*," "I have forgiven according to your word." (Numbers 14:20) God spoke these words to reassure the Israelites after they had supported the despairing message of the twelve spies. In synagogues all over the world for many generations, reciting those words has reassured Jews that although they have sinned, forgiveness has and will be given. The inclusion of this verse in immediate response to the recitation of Kol Nidre has the power to ease the fear of punishment and the remorse over failures, so that an individual can move forward and continue the work of atonement that this day affords. The psychological dimension of this ritualized form of atonement, forgiveness and renewal is potent: Redemption is possible; forgiveness occurs. I can do this work. —M.K.

I like it when the congregation chants the *Sheheḥeyanu* following Kol Nidre with an upbeat melody. We might look toward the next 24 hours with trepidation, but we look toward both a joyous fast and a happy year. —J.G.K.

anything, we gather together to acknowledge our gratitude for having lived through another year, with all of the challenges and blessings it brought, and with a profound sense of humility about the fact that we never really know what will happen from one year to the next.

After the *Sheheḥeyanu* blessing, the Torah scrolls are returned to the ark. The structure of the rest of the service includes all the elements of the daily evening service, consisting of two major sections—the Shema and its blessings, and the *Amida*, followed by *Aleynu*. This service also contains several substantial additions that make the Kol Nidre service special, creating the longest evening service of the year.

The recitation of the Shema on Kol Nidre contains one significant difference in practice. When we recite the Shema on weekdays, Shabbat and festivals, the line that immediately follows is customarily said in a whisper. On

Many congregations find a time on Yom Kippur evening for their leaders to make a public appeal for community support. Someone once pointed out to me that the weight of Yom Kippur might strengthen our sense of commitment to the Jewish community in a world where so many things are competing for our attention. —J.G.K.

An apocryphal explanation for not reciting the second line of the Shema aloud suggests that an emperor forbade it after the Jews had been exiled from the Land of Israel. The emperor, the story goes, thought it was subversive for his subjects to be celebrating any king other than himself—even if it was an invisible monarch in heaven. So the Jews acquiesced in murmuring it all year, except on Yom Kippur. On this holiest of days, they defied the emperor's order and recited the second line of the Shema in full voice. The Reform movement returned to saying it aloud all year long, reasoning that in a free society Jews do not have to continue to act like victims. —D.W.

Yom Kippur, the words, "*Barukh shem k'vod malkhuto l'olam va'ed*" ("Blessed is the name and glory of God's realm, forever!") are recited in full voice. This line is understood to have been recited by the angels, thereby signifying their special connection to God, a closeness that humanity has not yet achieved. On Yom Kippur, as we stand before God stripped of pretense and ego, wearing white, not eating or drinking, we are more like angels than human beings usually are, and therefore on this day we merit the full response to the Shema.

The evening *Amida* contains special references about Yom Kippur as a day of forgiveness. For the first time, the two sections of *S'liḥot* (forgiveness) and *Vidui* (confession) are included in the *Amida*. They are repeated in each of the subsequent services throughout Yom Kippur. Atonement, as the rabbis understood it, could not be achieved without one's confession of wrongdoing. By the

Another explanation for reciting "*Barukh̤ Shem*" out loud: This phrase is traditionally said when one recites a blessing mistakenly, such as if one accidentally says the blessing for wine over bread. It proclaims that although one just spoke of God in a "false" statement, God's name is still blessed. When we say the Shema, we are usually not quite aware of the distance between our understanding of God's unity and the full truth of that unity. On Yom Kippur, we are at a high enough spiritual level to at least understand how much we don't understand! And so we proclaim out loud: "Nonetheless, God's name is blessed!" —J.A.S.

same token, without the assurance of forgiveness, what is the point of confession? The entire Yom Kippur liturgy is suspended between the divine attributes of *din* (justice) and *raḥamim* (mercy). The prayers imagine that God's abundant mercy and forgiveness come about through humanity's confession.

The *Vidui*—prayers of confession—include the personal and communal acknowledgment of offenses. They are traditionally repeated ten times during Yom Kippur: twice each during the evening service (Kol Nidre), the morning service (*shaḥarit*), the *musaf* service, the afternoon service of Yom Kippur day and the concluding *n'ila* service; once at the end of the silent *Amida*; and once during the repetition of the *Amida*, if the repetition is included in the service. These repetitions reflect the fact that confession is not primarily an intellectual exercise. They create oppor-

Din can be understood as the rule of law with its built-in punishments. Nature follows a different kind of law by which some actions cause harm, but not everything in the universe behaves like billiard balls in a physics problem. *Raḥamim* can be understood as the open, forgiving part of our world—the possibility of creation and renewal through free will, love and *t'shuva*. Our sages taught that the world is able to exist because of a careful balance between these two principles. —J.A.S.

Mercy is not without justice. We can understand *raḥamim* (mercy) as the balance of *ḥesed* (loving kindness) and *din* (judgment). —J.G.K.

In an early midrash, there is a discussion of the proper way for a person to confess his or her wrongs and to ask for forgiveness on the eve of Yom Kippur. Rabbi Isaac says, "It is like a person fitting together two boards and joining them together." (Leviticus Raba 3.3) William Tyndale captured this sense of "joining together" in his 1530 translation of the Hebrew Bible, in which he coined the English phrase "Day of At-one-ment," in translation of the Hebrew "*Yom Haḳippurim*" in the Torah. In his translation, Tyndale affirmed that the response to the defiling power of sin is the restorative power of connection between the individual and God. —T.S.

tunities to gradually increase our emotional and spiritual openness to confession.

The Talmud offers the first Jewish reference to a specific formula for individual confession. In the Talmud (*Yoma* 87b), several rabbis engage in a dialogue about what would be appropriate to include in a confession. The texts offered are prayers already well known at the time, until a teacher named Mar Zutra concludes that all of the suggestions are fine if one has not said, "Truly we have sinned." If one says, "Truly we have sinned," nothing more is required.

The simplicity of this teaching is powerful. All the flowery language of prayer cannot replace the direct confession of wrongdoing. We are not so arrogant as to think we have nothing to confess, and so we stand, reciting *Ashamnu*, a short alphabetical listing of offenses. The language is in the plural—*we* have acted wrongly, *we* have been untrue—once again acknowledging individual

The recitation of the alphabetical lists of sins in the machzor is not a sufficient confession by itself. Over the course of the day, we should speak of our own particular failures. —J.A.S.

A member of our congregation refers to the tapping of the chest as "spiritual CPR." We should not beat ourselves out of guilt; rather, the intention of tapping the chest is to open our hearts. —B.P.

There is a teaching that all our prayers are made more powerful when we pray for our needs in the context of praying for the needs of others. By the same logic, my confession and my pursuit of forgiveness are made more powerful in the context of our confession and our pursuit of forgiveness for all of us. —J.A.S.

wrongdoing in the context of community. It is customary to tap or beat our chests as we recite each transgression, adding a physical action that amplifies the depth of what we have done, as well as our heartfelt desire to repent. The categories are general but comprehensive in what could constitute wrongdoing in each asserted sin.

It is often easy to think that we have not sinned or that whatever we have done is not so bad. It is too easy to look over the *Vidui* and declare that we have done nothing on that list. Such arrogance alone deserves a rap on the chest, since none of us is perfect. By the same token, sometimes we can be overwhelmed by the list of wrongdoings we *have* committed, thereby not recognizing the goodness that resides inside, sometimes covered over by the harshness of life. The alphabetical nature of the list enables us to focus on a finite list and to set our personal course for atonement. The liturgy affirms that ultimately there is no hiding from our true essence, the divine power within our-

Sometimes the heavy-seeming language of "sin" and the broad categories in the prayer book blind us to the everyday hurts we impose without considering them sins. Have you endangered others by speeding or tailgating? Do you engage in water-cooler gossip or other hurtful speech? These and similar deeds need to be atoned for on Yom Kippur. —J.A.S.

I appreciate the acrostic lists of transgressions as a reminder that helps me to recall various aspects of my own behavior. How have I been this year in my speech, in my economic transactions, in my intimate relationships? The long lists give me permission to acknowledge that somewhere in there is something I have done not quite as well as I would have liked. —T.S.

selves that propels us to acknowledge the secrets we harbor if we will heed it.

The longer confession, the *Al Ḥet*, expands on the sins committed and invites the entire community standing together to speak as a collective: We have done these things, and we are accountable. The Talmud teaches that one who has the ability to protest against the wrongs of his or her household, city, or the entire world but does not, is held accountable for all wrongs committed (*Shabbat* 54b). In some communities, in addition to the versions included in the machzor, alternative *Al Ḥet* prayers are offered with a contemporary global focus or a very personal one.

Following the *Amida*, the *S'liḥot* prayers and poems offer a window into the soul's journey toward forgiveness and atonement on Yom Kippur. *Piyyutim* are expressions

Some tunes to the *Al Ḥet* are plaintive; others are upbeat because we celebrate the fact that we are being forgiven and starting anew. —J.G.K.

Jules Harlow's *Maḥzor for Rosh Hashanah and Yom Kippur* framed the *Al Ḥet* of the *musaf* service around sinning not only against God, but also against those who were martyred in the Shoah. —J.G.K.

Some communities provide index cards and pencils prior to the beginning of Kol Nidre. Congregants anonymously write on them the sins for which they wish to atone. In addition to the words of the traditional liturgy, some of these cards are read each time the *Al Ḥet* prayers are offered. We atone not with words from someone else's community and about sins committed somewhere else, but in this community about wrongs we have committed in our real lives. —M.K.

The opening word of each line of this *piyyut*, "*ya'aleh*," "*v'yavo*" and "*v'yera'eh,*" are drawn from the opening words of a prayer that is inserted in the *Amida* on every holiday, known as "*Ya'aleh V'yavo*." This insertion asks that our prayers be heard and accepted, and it includes a plea for "goodness and grace, love and care, life, well-being and peace." On Yom Kippur, this *piyyut* augments the traditional prayer dramatically, as befits this awesome day, when we most seek to be heard. —B.P.

of the mystery of existence, and they add depth and meaning to the traditional liturgy. Beginning with "*Ya'aleh*" (*Kol Haneshamah Maḥzor Leyamim Nora'im,* page 782), an anonymous poem written as a reverse acrostic, these *piyyutim* voice a plea for the supplications to rise up in the evening, the forgiveness to arrive by the dawn, and the transformation by dusk—thereby mirroring the time spent at services from Kol Nidre to the concluding service of *n'ila.* As time passes during Kol Nidre and Yom Kippur, one's experience may change. As we move through the process of introspection and examination throughout the day, and as the light changes from sunset to sunrise to another sunset, our perceptions of self may change as well.

Other poems add to the deepening experience of the evening service. Just before the recitation of the 13 attributes of God (Exodus 34:6), we sing the phrase, "*Haneshama lakh, v'haguf po-olakh, ḥusa al amalakh*" ("The soul is yours, the body your creation; have compassion on your handiwork.") (*Kol Haneshamah Maḥzor Leyamim Nora'im*, page 786) These words are part of a collection of biblical verses about mercy. They address God as the power that makes for creativity and development, and asks for compassion as we make our way through the work of atonement. The *piyyutim* that follow—"*Ḥatanu L'fanekha*" ("We Have Done Wrong Before You"), "*Ki Hiney Khaḥomer*" ("Like a Lump of Clay"),

"*Sh'ma Kolenu*" ("Hear Our Voice"), and "*Ki Anu Amekha*" ("We Are Your People")—underscore how our destiny is shaped and determined not by our own efforts alone, but by a source of support and attention that molds us, connects us and ultimately calls forth compassion and mercy. We may feel fragile and unstable when confronted with the challenges that life deals to humankind, but forgiveness is godly, and that is what we seek as we begin the holiest day of the Jewish year.

Toward the conclusion of the evening service, the ark is opened for *Avinu Malkeynu.* (If Yom Kippur begins on Friday evening, the prayer is traditionally omitted because of its petitionary nature.) As challenging as the traditional God language is, the prayer calls us into relationship with a divine presence that can feel at once like a parent—close, nurturing and loving—and at the same time like a

The *piyyutim* of Yom Kippur are rich in metaphoric imagery of the divine. Here, we find poetic descriptions of God as creative power, as source of compassion, as beloved, shepherd, farmer and potter. These images remind us not to take any of them literally, but rather to add our own imagery and metaphors. For some people, it feels more fitting to describe God as a verb, not as a noun—becoming, enlivening, creating. Finding a name for the divine that works for each of us is an important part of making the High Holy Day liturgy into an aid, rather than an obstacle, to introspection and prayer. —T.S.

When Yom Kippur coincides with Shabbat, the prevailing Ashkenazic custom is to omit *Avinu Malkeynu* from Kol Nidre evening through Yom Kippur afternoon and to recite it only at *n'ila*. Italian and Sephardic customs vary; some recite *Avinu Malkeynu* throughout the ten days of repentance—even on Shabbat—while others omit particular verses for Shabbat. —J.G.K.

When Yom Kippur falls on Shabbat, *Avinu Malkeynu* eventually appears, at the very end of *n'ila*, the closing service of the day. At that point, singing the plaintive melody sounds more like an assurance of divine forgiveness, rather than a petition. —B.P.

sovereign—more distant, demanding and powerful. On Yom Kippur we dwell in various states of surrender that *Avinu Malkeynu* potently reflects, and we will chant the refrain of the prayer at least twice more before the end of the holiday. We surrender our souls through repentance and atonement; we surrender our bodies by fasting, and we surrender our pretense of control in a ritual of confrontation with our mortality. In our times of greatest need and deepest vulnerability, we pray for grace—the divine response to our prayers—and in our humility, we ask to be dealt with out of righteousness, love and redemption.

Yom Kippur Morning

Yom Kippur is one of the few occasions during which Jews stay in the synagogue for most of the day. Throughout the four services of *shaḥarit* (morning service), *musaf* (additional service), *minḥa* (afternoon service), and *n'ila* (closing service), there are special additions to the liturgy,

As we sing the last line of *Avinu Malḳeynu* together, the phrase that always chokes me up is "*aseh imanu*"—"do with us." I get the feeling that we, individually and as a group, are asking to be acted upon, that our best efforts are not good enough, that we need help and that we are asking for it. —J.J.S.

Rabbi Sharon Kleinbaum has suggested that in the spirit of making all five Yom Kippur services into one contiguous service and keeping our prayer space sacred, we should push ourselves to recite the forgiveness ritual found in the prayer book at the bedtime Shema at the conclusion of services on Kol Nidre night ("... I hereby forgive anyone who has wronged me" ... "Let no one be punished on my account" ...), and then exit the sanctuary in silence. —J.G.K.

and in particular to the *Amida*. The additional sections of *Yizkor* (memorial service), the martyrology service, and the *avoda* service add depth to the journey. They create the opportunity for each of us to walk out of these prayer services not the same person as when we began, thereby making the experience truly heartfelt and worthwhile.

The *shaḥarit* service of Yom Kippur follows the same basic structure as Shabbat, weekday and other festival services. For those who attend services regularly during the year, the morning blessings, *P'sukey D'zimra* (Verses of Song), the Shema and its blessings as well as the *Amida* all provide comfort through the familiarity of liturgy and practice. It is during the *Amida* and its subsequent repetition (in some communities) that the additional liturgical

In our synagogue, as in many others, congregants are invited to stay for the entire day, and there are opportunities for engagement beyond the traditional services, including yoga, tai chi, text study and walks in the woods. —T.S.

Yom Kippur is a day on which to prepare for our dying. We allow part of the selves we have been to die in order to more fully live into our expansive potential of holiness. To do this work, we turn to prayers and rituals that impel us to let go of our attachments to our external roles and to go directly to our inner souls. In order to facilitate the loosening of our identification with the personality level of the self, some communities use their bodies to help actualize this transformative process in an innovative way. In some places, the Yom Kippur *shaḥarit Amida* is prayed not standing up, as are all other *Amida* prayers during the year, but rather lying down, face up. Drawing on the physical practice of asana or yoga postures, this asana is called the corpse pose. As community members lie down, they are guided to connect with the gift of breath and life within them, to recall that their bodies will eventually return to the earth they lie upon, and to release the ego's hold—not by force, but by letting go. In this way, the *shaḥarit Amida* is offered with a physical expression appropriate to the unique way in which we confront our impermanence and the eternality of the power that sustains us. —M.K.

poems and themes of Yom Kippur are found. Once again, we recite the *Vidui* and the *Al Ḥet*. This time, perhaps, we can more easily identify mistakes we made by accident, or those we made by succumbing to our primal inclination, or maybe we can even recognize something that is a reflection of our weaknesses and insecurities.

Torah Service

The Torah reading for Yom Kippur morning is from Leviticus 16:1–34. The chapter begins by recalling the

The *Vidui* most comes alive for me in the waning hours of Yom Kippur, when my resistance is lessened and I can feel the communal transgressions and shortcomings as I recite them. —N.M.

Even the Torah reading on Yom Kippur reminds us of our mortality. The passage opens with the death of Aaron's two sons and the admonishment by Moses of his brother Aaron not to enter the holy place "at will," lest he die. Then the reading launches into a description of the sacrificial rites for Yom Kippur. Rather than dwell on grief and loss, the portion moves directly into Aaron's responsibilities. Likewise, the tone of Yom Kippur is neither morbid nor mournful. It is as if on this day we are called, like Aaron, to honestly face our own deaths. From that encounter, we regain the will to re-emerge whole in body and spirit at the end of the day. The promise is not death, but life with renewed vigor and dedication to the holiness of human existence. —B.P.

The deaths of Nadav and Avihu took place in the desert sanctuary in the course of its dedication. By placing the Yom Kippur ritual in this context, the Torah is telling us that Yom Kippur addresses the terrible tension between the awesome holiness and beauty of the divine presence in our world and the fact that no place in our world, even the most holy, is free of death and sin. On Yom Kippur, we and God overcome all that mars life in order to strengthen the presence of holiness and love. —J.A.S.

The Torah reading from Leviticus is perhaps the best exemplar of Judaism as an evolving religious civilization: It makes quite obvious how radically different our own observance of Yom Kippur is from that of our biblical ancestors! And yet there is a thread that connects us somehow, running from those archaic rituals right into our own sanctuaries, from the hearts and minds of the ancient Israelites right into our own. —T.S.

untimely death of Aaron's sons, Nadav and Avihu. (See Leviticus 10). The portion describes the rituals of the service of atonement performed by the high priest in the *Mishkan*, the tabernacle/sanctuary. Unlike the Torah readings on Rosh Hashana, which contain the narratives of the matriarchs and patriarchs, the focus on Yom Kippur is on the ritual and ethical rites of our people. The rituals of expiation, as outlined in the portion read on Yom Kippur, have two main parts. One concerns the cleansing of the sanctuary, and the second is about cleansing the people of sin. Aaron makes a selection by lottery to determine which of two goats is to be sent out to *Azazel* (the wilderness) carrying the burden of the sins of the people as a scapegoat, and which goat is to be sacrificed. Through the scapegoat, Israel can be returned to a state of purity, free of sin.

As elaborate as this ancient rite may seem, we can recognize in ourselves the same desire to rid ourselves of our wrongdoings and the feelings and memories that cloud our judgment and our capacity to do the right thing. In our cleansing rituals, we too must "afflict ourselves" by fasting and denying ourselves the pleasures of luxury and intimacy. The *maftir* section read from the Book of Numbers (Chapter 29) outlines the sacrifices offered on that day, and the portion regarding Yom Kippur is prefaced with the same instruction to practice self-denial.

Kol Haneshamah presents *parashat Nitzavim* as an alternative *maftir* reading. Just as our ancestors about to cross the Jordan into the Land of Israel were on the verge of a new beginning, so are we poised to enter the New Year. —J.G.K.

The haftarah portion for Yom Kippur morning comes from the Book of Isaiah (57:14–58:14). Isaiah excoriates the people for fasting without taking seriously the real meaning and intention into the ritual. The fast is of no avail if it does not inspire a just and merciful relationship with other people and righteous action in the face of injustice:

> This is the fast that I desire:
> The unlocking of the chains of wickedness,
> The loosening of exploitation,
> The freeing of all those oppressed,
> The breaking of the yoke of servitude. (58:5–6)

It is a powerful message for us on Yom Kippur. Just as we are beginning to feel the effects of our own fasting, the prophet reminds us that fasting is not godly in and of itself. Justice is godly, and if our fasting leads to a more just and peaceful world, then it is of value; ritual action of this nature must lead to moral action if it is to be meaningful.

Instead of chanting the haftarah from Isaiah one year, a group of congregants created a dramatic reading that wove Isaiah's words together with words describing contemporary social ills that the prophet might call to our awareness today—statistics about hunger, poverty, failures of our educational system, global warming. Stationed around the sanctuary, their voices calling our attention to the "chains of wickedness" that bind us today, they seemed to bring Isaiah into our midst that morning. —T.S.

Isaiah asked what Yom Kippur was really about for his time. In our congregation, the Yom Kippur morning *d'var Torah* (sermon), given by the president of the congregation, addresses the question of what Yom Kippur is really about for our congregation this year. —J.A.S.

After the Torah and haftarah readings, many congregations begin the *Yizkor* service while the Torah scrolls are still out of the ark. *Yizkor* was originally recited only on Yom Kippur, and its observance later spread to the three pilgrimage festivals. The service ties together the themes of loss and memory and underscores our awareness of the absence of our loved ones at holiday times. In some communities the *Yizkor* service is what brings people back to the synagogue later in the day after a short afternoon break, and before or after the *minḥa* service. Though *Yizkor* is recited on other festival days, the themes and somber ambience of Yom Kippur can make this *Yizkor* service feel especially meaningful. During the *Yamim Nora'im,* we may feel a deeper longing for those in our lives whom we have loved and lost, as well as a sense of our own impermanence.

Some hold the custom that those blessed with two living parents should not remain in the room for the recitation of *Yizkor*. This tradition, which is based on the superstition that sitting through the memorial service could tempt the "evil eye," often results in many people leaving before the *Yizkor* service begins. In many communities

Three sections of the Yom Kippur service evoke memory: *Yizkor*, *Eleh Ezk'ra*, and *avoda*. With these sections, we fill our sanctuary with reinforcements from the past—our own loved ones, our people's martyrs and the ancient high priest. They add strength to our Yom Kippur efforts. —J.A.S.

In order to deepen people's engagement with the *Yizkor* service, I set up an empty glass vase and put a bowl of small stones next to it. I then invite people to come to the vase and place a stone in it in memory of a loved one; in some congregations, members place the stone directly on a table. These actions invoke the practice of placing a stone on a grave as a sign of remembrance, and they give people the opportunity to add physicality to their prayer experience. —N.H.M.

today, rabbis and service leaders encourage everyone to remain in the sanctuary both to support community members who have experienced loss and to stand in memory of the untold number of Jews throughout history for whom there is no one left to say Kaddish. *Yizkor* becomes an opportunity to remember family, friends, fellow congregants, victims of the Shoah (Holocaust), martyrs of the Jewish people and members of the Israel Defense Forces.

Musaf

The *musaf* service on Yom Kippur is an extended *Amida*. The Yom Kippur *musaf Amida* includes additional selections to amplify the themes of the day. Once again, the *Vidui* and *Al Ḥet* confessionals are recited. In some communities, the cantor/service leader repeats the *Hin'ni* prayer that is chanted on Rosh Hashana. (For an explanation, see the discussion of *Hin'ni* in the Rosh Hashana section above.) In addition, the *Un'taneh Tokef* is included, underscoring the sacred power of the day. We remind ourselves once again of the fragility of life and the stability that can come through *t'shuva, t'fila,* and *tzedaka*—repentance, prayer and righteous action.

The community of Kibbutz Beit Hashita in the Eastern Galilee has been a longtime archival center for secular Israeli ritual, largely linked to the agricultural cycle, but kibbutz members were befuddled by the question of how to connect with Yom Kippur. After the Yom Kippur War of 1973, when eleven kibbutz members were killed, the kibbutz members began to regard the day with greater intensity, as a time of memory and anticipation. Israeli songwriter Yair Rosenbloom composed a setting of *Un'taneh Tokef* for the kibbutz's 60th anniversary that has become the most popular version of the *piyyut* in contemporary Israeli society. —J.G.K.

Some communities include two major additions to the *musaf Amida—seder ha'avoda* and the martyrology service. Other communities include these additions in the *minḥa* service, and some may exclude them altogether. *Kol Haneshamah Maḥzor Leyamim Nora'im* intersperses the *avoda* service with the rest of the *musaf* service, thereby placing the individual worshipper in the role of the high priest and leading each person through a deeper process of atonement and forgiveness of self, family and community. In *Kol Haneshamah,* the martyrology section appears in the second confession for the Jewish people, and it is a discrete liturgical unit that, like the *Yizkor* service, could be moved elsewhere according to the customs of the community.

Seder Ha'avoda

Seder ha'avoda contains a description of the service in the Temple, and it is meant to serve as a reenactment of that service. Although the Temple has not existed for 2,000 years and liberal Jewish communities today do not hope for a third Temple to be built, evoking the service through words and song can have a powerful effect.

The idea that the contemporary worshipper is connected to the high priest is also reflected in the Shlomo Anski poem that appears in *Kol Haneshamah: Maḥzor Leyamim Nora'im* (pages 845-847). —J.G.K.

While the idea of building sacred spaces is a beautiful one, plans for the construction of a temple on Mount Moriah are particularly problematic, given that the Temple Mount is a holy site for our Muslim brothers and sisters as well; two great buildings frame this large pilgrimage and prayer space. —J.G.K.

The rituals of the high priest on Yom Kippur were mysterious, and they were believed to be quite dangerous for the high priest himself. He would prepare himself completely and with great care over seven days for the moment when he would enter the Holy of Holies to atone for himself, his family and the community of Israel. His personal expiation was critical to the process because in order to confess on behalf of others, he had to be free of sin himself.

After the destruction of the Second Temple in 70 CE, the Jewish community needed a substitute for the power of the Temple's ritual sacrifice. Without the Temple, there could be no centralized sacrificial system. In the early midrashic work *Avot Derabi Natan* (11a), Rabbi Yehoshua and Rabbi Yohanan ben Zakai are described as walking past the Temple, which was then in ruins. Rabbi Yehoshua cried, "What will we do now without the place that atoned for the sins of Israel?" Rabbi Yohanan ben Zakai responded, "We can still atone, just as we did through sacrifices, but now we will do so with deeds of loving kindness."

The rabbis replaced sacrifices with study, prayer and acts of loving kindness. The reenactment of the *seder ha'avoda* gives us an opportunity to recall the detail and

Two aspects of some *avoda* services particularly move me: being guided through a visualization of oneself as the high priest undergoing the meticulous rituals of purification, and receiving the invitation to completely prostrate oneself (as did the high priest). These connect me to our ancient past in an embodied way. —N.M.

care we Jews once took in order to encounter the supreme power, blessing and glory of God. We thereby remind ourselves that we can channel that same attention to detail into our contemporary process of atonement. Each of us begins by asking forgiveness of ourselves, then of our families, and then of our communities, our people, our nation and the world. Confession begins with oneself.

Eleh Ezk'ra ("These I Remember"), the service of martyrology, began as a poem based on various rabbinic midrashim concerning ten rabbinic sages who chose death over the abandonment of Torah and Jewish tradition. It is sometimes referred to as an *Akeda* poem because it references the *Akeda*—the story in Genesis of the binding of Isaac that is read on the second day of Rosh Hashana. Different versions of the poem include different stories of martyrdom, which points to the lack of historicity of the poem. This has never seemed to matter much to the generations of Jews who have included the martyrology in their Yom Kippur observance because the commemoration highlights the persecution Jews have faced throughout history and martyrdom serves as a symbol against tyranny. While this understanding may not resonate for some modern Jews, reading the traditional martyrology

The martyrology is closely connected to the *avoda* service. The *avoda* recalls for us the loss of the Temple; the martyrology recalls the loss of one of the greatest generations of rabbinic minds, primarily as a result of the Hadrianic persecution (132–136 CE). The two are juxtaposed purposely, as we are meant to see that Judaism's heart now resides in the rabbis rather than in the Temple. The loss of ten of them is equal to the loss of the Temple. —J.M.S.

passages can afford us an opportunity to remember what making such a choice meant at the time.

The echoing refrain, "*Eleh ezk'ra v'nafshi alay eshp'kha*" —"These I remember and pour out my soul"—transitions the worshipper from the texts about Rabbi Akiba's martyrdom to the stories of other rabbis in Rome who chose *kidush hashem*—the sanctification of God's name—rather than turn themselves over to their enemies. Modern machzorim have added passages about Jews who suffered in the Crusades, in the expulsion from Spain and, of course, during the devastating years of the Shoah. *Kol Haneshamah* offers the understanding that although the

When we read the martyrology on Yom Kippur, we recall times when choosing to be a Jew and to behave Jewishly was dangerous. Many who chose to risk their lives maintained their faith that God was with them. On Yom Kippur, when we are feeling most vulnerable and afraid, we can draw strength from their stories. When we feel most helpless, friendless and hopeless, God is with us. When we read of the persecutions, the exile, the destruction and the pain of each individual Jew who lived and died in a realm of extreme hatred, we feel sorrow for them and for our people. But we must also hear the strains of faith in the face of destruction, hope in the face of fear, and pride in the face of hatred. Their courage enabled our people to endure and ensured that our heritage would continue for generations. As we enter the latter part of Yom Kippur, we pray that we, too, may have the faith, hope and pride of our ancestors, even as we live in a broken world. And with that faith, hope and pride, we will heal the world. —B.P.

Rabbi Arthur Waskow encourages us to remember an additional sort of Jewish martyr—not only those who were killed because they were Jews, but those whose Judaism inspired them to put themselves in harm's way for the sake of others. Thus, we might remember Andrew Goodman and Michael Schwerner, along with their African-American colleague James Chaney, who were killed while taking part in Freedom Summer, working for civil rights for southern African-Americans. And we might remember the late Israeli Prime Minister Yitzhak Rabin, who was killed in the pursuit of peace. —J.A.S.

placement of this service after *seder ha'avoda* was originally meant to assert that the stories of these Jewish martyrs take the place of animal sacrifices, we can choose a different interpretation. We remember stories of instances in which Jews were forced to make the ultimate choice because they were Jews, for their own sake—not because such a choice could stand in place of their sins. No matter how meritorious such Jews were, we are still responsible for our own wrongdoings. And no matter how pious we are, we can still find inspiration in their lives and thoughts.

Minḥa

As the sun begins to head toward the horizon, the *minḥa* (afternoon) service signals a move toward the end of day. The least complex of all the Yom Kippur services, *minḥa* contains only a brief Torah service with three aliyot, the

Yom Kippur's rituals and prayers serve in many ways to make us feel vulnerable and to knock down the barriers that we create. The martyrology service, which we say about three-quarters of the way through the day, can crack our hearts wide open if nothing else has yet done so. —J.G.K.

I have found that Jews from many backgrounds and affiliations have a lot to say about the break between services on Yom Kippur. Some prefer to daven quickly and then to nap for hours in the midst of the fast day. Others do not choose to sleep and prefer a shorter break before services resume. Sometimes the break is a good time for text study, meditation or discussions that allow people to stay engaged at the synagogue for the entire day. —J.G.K.

A community that has a Torah study session or discussion between services might choose *minḥa* as a time to omit the Torah reading entirely and to delve more deeply into the Book of Jonah. —J.G.K.

chanting of the Book of Jonah as the haftarah, and an *Amida*. Unlike the other readings from the Torah on Rosh Hashana and Yom Kippur that are chanted with a special cantillation (*trop*) used only on the High Holy Days, the *minḥa* reading is done to the regular year-round *trop*.

The traditional Torah reading for *minḥa* is from Leviticus 18, a portion that outlines categories of forbidden sexual relationships in the quest for holiness. The 1948 Reconstructionist machzor substituted a section of Leviticus (19:1–14), known as the Holiness Code, to focus more on the holiness of mind and general societal conduct. Modern machzorim, including *Kol Haneshamah,* the Reform movement's *The Gates of Repentance,* and the Conservative movement's *Maḥzor Lev Shalem* all contain this alternative reading, and the Reform and Reconstructionist prayer books also contain another alternative from

While the Yom Kippur afternoon Torah reading is thematically connected to Yom Kippur, we read Torah on Yom Kippur afternoon only because it is a fast day. As on every other fast day afternoon, we read with ordinary Torah cantillation. —J.G.K.

Rabbinic tradition associates Yom Kippur and the 15th day of Av with matchmaking, so reading about sexual prohibitions may have provided limits on the community's desire for eligible people to connect. —J.G.K.

Contemporary communities committed to full inclusion for LGBT (lesbian, gay, bisexual and transgender) people may find that reading the biblical prohibitions on some sexual acts between men once a year (in the springtime, during the regular Torah reading cycle) is enough, and that to read them again on a day when there is so much liturgy—and less time to delve into the verses' context and to deliver explicit messages of LGBT pride and celebration—is reason enough for an alternative reading. Yet for some LGBT people, confronting these verses, particularly on Yom Kippur, can feel empowering. Some years ago, an openly gay friend of mine was called up for *hagba* (to raise the Torah) at *minḥa* on Yom Kippur. The rabbi apologized to him for what had just been read, and he was taken aback not by the reading but by the apology. —J.G.K.

Deuteronomy 30, whose focus is on the renewal of the covenant between God and Israel.

Leviticus 19:1–14 contains some of the most central ethical teachings of Judaism, echoing the Ten Commandments as it commands us to act in ways that imitate the holiness of God. The text also exhorts us not to curse the deaf or place a stumbling block before the blind, not to stand idly by the blood of our neighbor, and to "love your neighbor as yourself." In these last hours before the gates are closing on our day of self-examination, these verses give us another opportunity to assess the state of our commitments to our loved ones and relationships with them as well our connection to the community at large. They come under the heading that the great sage Hillel called the greatest law of the Torah: "What is hateful to you, do not do to another."

At first glance, the inclusion of the Book of Jonah in the *minḥa* service is a curious one. The Talmud (*Megila* 31a) gives no explanation for its choice of Jonah as the haftarah for Yom Kippur *minḥa*. We can see several obvious reasons. The Book of Jonah concerns a community ravaged by corruption and sin. At its center is Jonah, a man who flees from God to avoid being the one to call for the communal atonement of a foreign people, a man who is

Curiously, the old *Union Prayer Book* of the Reform movement omitted the first two paragraphs of Jonah in the haftarah for Yom Kippur afternoon. God told Jonah to go to Nineveh—and he went! —J.G.K.

enraged by God's forgiving nature toward the people of Nineveh. The story is about sin and forgiveness, and it is thereby completely appropriate for the day. Jonah is not a

As we read the story of Jonah, we see ourselves all too clearly. Jonah is a prophet, meaning that he has demonstrated his commitment to justice in the past. Yet a time comes when he just doesn't feel like it. He would rather run away; he would rather sleep; he would rather do anything else, even die, than fulfill his responsibility. Yet in the belly of the great fish, Jonah faces his own truth. He expresses gratitude to God for saving his life and realizes that his life does have a purpose after all. But Jonah is not completely transformed. After he goes to Nineveh to fulfill his duty, he still struggles with his high expectations and his severe need for justice. We hear the words of the Book of Jonah from the depths as well—the depths of Yom Kippur afternoon. We have worked hard all day. We have tried to rethink our lives and repair our relationships. We would all like to be wiser than Jonah. We want to believe that we are more compassionate in dealing with others. We hope that we can be more honest with ourselves. Perhaps our changes will be modest, but the story of Jonah helps us to accept our own human limitations and yet continue to strive to be better in the coming year. —B.P.

If Jonah, a dubious and dysfunctional character, could save an entire city, surely we, too, can do *tikun olam* effectively! —J.A.S.

There is literary and psychological wisdom in the reading of Jonah at this moment in the Yom Kippur experience. This wisdom is a counterpoint to the sustained liturgical points of male priestly service that mark the day. Jonah's confrontation with God and with himself takes place not in the Temple, not with formalized ritual, but rather in the oceanic depths and in the belly of an untamed, vastly powerful animal. Water often represents the unconscious or the womb in literary works. In reading Jonah, we find ourselves entering the underwater depths of our own psyches to explore where within us there still remains an unwillingness to come toward the work of *t'shuva*. Through this text we can connect to a metaphoric process of preparing to be reborn into the daylight, on dry land, where we are freshly inspired to listen to the depths of our consciences, to repent where needed, and to act in service to the greater good. —M.K.

The plant that grows over Jonah's head is a *kikayon*, perhaps a plant similar to ipecac or a similar plant, since its Hebrew root is the same as that of the verb "to vomit"—as in what the fish did in order to spew Jonah onto the land. Perhaps, in spite of the weaknesses of Jonah's character, we can look to him as an example of choosing a new path, even when we feel chewed up and spit out. —J.G.K.

historical figure, but the story is conceived as a fable with important messages about atonement and forgiveness, God's mercy and kindness, and our responsibility to the larger community and to ourselves, despite our fears and perceived weaknesses.

Minḥa concludes with the *Amida*. Once again, we have the opportunity to confess our wrongdoings in the *Vidui* and *Al Ḥet,* to pray for compassion and righteousness in *Avinu Malkeynu,* and to look forward to the end to our journey of Yom Kippur. What other work do we have left to do in the remaining time we have? This is the question of the *minḥa Amida,* but it is also the question we pose to ourselves about our lives.

N'ila

The sun has begun to set on this day of return and renewal. The word "*n'ila*" means "closing," and it originally referred to the closing of the gates of the Temple. Later, the phrase "*n'ilat she'arim*" ("closing of the gates") came to refer to the gates of heaven. This deeper spiritual mean-

During most of Yom Kippur, we work at opening our hearts to God, asking for help and support. With Jonah, the emphasis shifts. The *brit*, covenant, includes more than our capacity to ask for help, forgiveness and mercy. We also have an obligation to show up when God asks—when we are asked to step up in courage, in service and in love. —S.P.W.

We are also standing in front of our own gates; *n'ila* is the time to explore them. Have we allowed our gates to be open to discovery, to possibility, to light, to new beginnings, to action, to change? Are we letting the gates close without exploring all that could be before us? Will we stand up to the challenge? —L.K.

ing underscores the urgency, determination and edge of anticipated joy that accompanies this culmination of the day. Unlike *ma'ariv*, *shaḥarit*, *musaf* and *minḥa*, which are recited on festivals and Shabbat during the rest of the year, *n'ila* is unique to Yom Kippur. The tone of the service is at once joyful and confident, even as it expresses urgent pleas for a little more time before the gates close.

Many congregations begin *n'ila* with the Sephardic *piyyut* "*El Nora Alila*" by Moses Ibn Ezra or with *Ashrey* (a compilation of verses from Psalms 84, 144, and 145) before beginning the silent *Amida* for *n'ila*. The liturgical poem "*El Nora Alila*" repeats the refrain, "At the closing of the gates," which is a fitting opening to this last service of the day. The third stanza of the poem reads:

> *They pour their souls in prayer to you,*
> *To blot out their wrongs, their lives renew;*
> *Grant pardon to all who pray to you,*
> *In the hour of the closing gates.*

Rabbi Zalman Schachter-Shalomi notes in *Kol Haneshamah* that when one is awake, it is possible to awaken even more to the world around us. He teaches that "*ar*," the bilateral root of the word "*sha'ar*" ("gate"), means "to be awake." As we look toward the conclusion of Yom Kippur, we are encouraged to awaken even more. —Y.R.

Even congregations that choose to do the *Amida* silently and then aloud for *shaḥarit*, *musaf* and *minḥa* often choose to recite just the first three blessings together, to continue silently and then to join together for *s'liḥot* prayers, as the day wanes and the hour for *n'ila* approaches. —J.G.K.

The Israeli singer Meir Banai sings a beautiful *El Nora Alila*. Though the setting might be difficult to reproduce in synagogue, listening to the recording at other times has been inspiring for me over the years. As Betsy Teutsch's *Shiviti* drawing on page 738 of *Kol Haneshamah* reminds us, the gates of heaven are always open. —J.G.K.

The ark remains open during the final *Amida* that makes up almost the entirety of *n'ila*, and we are encouraged to stand for as much of it as is physically possible. The open ark is symbolic of the gates of heaven that are said to remain open to us as we pray for forgiveness. In some communities, the rabbi/service leader will encourage congregants to come up to the *bima* (prayer platform) to stand before the open ark and offer whatever silent, personal prayers they still feel the need to say.

The *Amida* by now is a familiar text, yet there are two differences in the last version we say. We no longer ask, "*Kotvenu l'ḥayim,*" "Inscribe us for life"; at *n'ila,* we ask, "*Ḥotmenu l'ḥayim,*" "Seal us for life." We pray that all of the hard work of the day will yield renewal and forgiveness. As with every other Yom Kippur service, forgiveness and confession are very much a part of *n'ila*. But unlike all the other Yom Kippur *Amida* recitations that include both the *Vidui* and the longer confessional of the *Al Ḥet,* the *n'ila Amida* contains only the *Vidui.* The mood has changed since the evening before, and as the day has waned, the detailed confessing shifts to an awareness that our Yom Kippur work is nearly done. Still, we should ask, "*Ma anu?*" "What are we?" Yom Kippur is an oasis of time within which we can immerse in the deepest questions of who we are yet to be.

Following the custom of saying 100 blessings every day is more challenging when one is not eating. One Yom Kippur custom is to smell herbs or spices and then to recite the appropriate blessings. When we do this late in the day, the aromas may smell fuller than they do at other times of year. —J.G.K.

The opening lines of the *piyyut* "*P'taḥ Lanu Sha'ar*" ("Keep the Gates Open for Us") are stirring as they plead: "Open for us the gates, in the hour of the closing gates, for the day is passing away." We chant the 13 attributes (Exodus 34:6–7), which speak of God's love, and we repeat the medieval poem "*Ki Anu Amekha*" ("For We Are Your People") that completes the *S'liḥot* section and transitions us to the last *Vidui.* Perhaps in the last repetition of the *Vidui* we no longer need to beat our chests, but rather hold our hands over our hearts as we treat ourselves with some compassion, having nearly reached the end of Yom Kippur.

How does one close such a dramatic and profound day? The conclusion of the service includes one final *Avinu Malkeynu.* Even if Yom Kippur has fallen on Shabbat, this *Avinu Malkeynu* is sung, even though *Havdala* has not yet been performed, for by now it is dark outside. It is a moment replete with layers of meaning. We have acknowledged our wrongdoing and asked for mercy and compassion, and now we pray to be sealed for a life of goodness, merit, sustenance and forgiveness.

Some time ago, Congregation Bet Mishpachah in Washington, D.C., created a prayer called "*Ahavnu*" ("We have loved") as a counterpoint to the repetitions of self-criticism in the *Vidui*. Taking a true account of ourselves means that we must balance facing our failures by embracing the ways in which we have done well and by appreciating that part of ourselves. —J.G.K.

With the final shofar blast, there is always a joyous sense of "We made it!" in our sanctuary. The fast day ends with a sense of completion and hope, and a readiness to move into the New Year. —T.S.

With exhaustion and exhilaration, we stand ready to complete the service with *Kaddish Titkabal*, the Kaddish for the completion of prayer, followed by the verses of the Shema, *Barukh Shem* (Blessed Is the Name), and *Adonay hu ha'elohim* (The Eternal One is God). There are two customs for the order of the section. One holds that the verses should be recited first and then the Kaddish; the other, that the Kaddish comes first followed by the verses. The Shema is chanted a single time; *Barukh Shem* is chanted three times, and *Adonay hu Ha'elohim* is chanted seven times. Finally, the sound of the shofar is heard, this time only as a *t'kiya g'dola*—the long, unbroken cry that reaches us deep inside as well as to the highest heights.

This shofar blast echoes the ancient practice of blowing the shofar to proclaim the beginning of the 50th year—the Jubilee—the time of freedom. (Leviticus 25:9–10) We no longer know the exact year of the Jubilee, so upon hearing the shofar blast each year, we should recall that the promise of freedom can and should be attainable for all people. —Y.R.

In our community, anyone who has a shofar and the ability to sound it is encouraged to bring a shofar to the *n'ila* service. At the end, we hear a very big *t'ḳia g'dola* from all corners, creating a sense of a strong and joyful community, ready to enter the New Year together. —B.P.

As at the Pesach Seder, the final words spoken on Yom Kippur are "*L'shana haba'a birushalayim*"—"Next year in Jerusalem." It is our prayer that after all we have been through—all the praying, fasting, learning, singing, weeping and dancing—we might enjoy redemption and freedom in the year to come. *Yerushalayim*—Jerusalem—evokes the phrase "*ir shalem*," "city of wholeness." Ultimately, what we are seeking each year is greater wholeness of being, of community and of the world.

The *Shabbat Shabbaton* (the Sabbath of complete rest) that is Yom Kippur concludes with *Havdala,* the ceremony that ends Shabbat and begins a new week. The braided candle and the wine revive our senses, which have been muted by our fast. (If Yom Kippur is on Shabbat, spices are included as well.) We recite the blessings and celebrate this most profound shift of the year from the holy, profound intensity of Yom Kippur to the ordinary awareness of a new day dawning for us all.

Breaking the Fast

After the conclusion of Yom Kippur, we are instructed to eat, drink and rejoice. The midrash teaches, "A heavenly voice declares on this night: Go and eat your bread joyfully and drink your wine in good spirit, for God has accepted your efforts." (*Kohelet Raba* 9.7) Many congregations will share in the breaking of the fast by having a communal meal immediately following the service, or they will hand out apple juice, honey cake, hallah dipped in honey,

Rabbi Simcha Bunim of Przysucha responded to a student whose practice of fasting had not yielded the expected spiritual rewards. Simcha Bunim then told a story of the Baal Shem Tov, whose horses magically flew past one inn after another one night. After passing the first inn, the horses believed that they had become people since they did not need to stop to eat. After passing the second inn, they believed that they were actually angels because they had gone for so long without food. Yet when the journey suddenly ended and the horses were stabled, they thrust their heads into their feedbags and stuffed themselves, just like horses. The message is: "It's not how you fast; it's how you break your fast." (*The Quest for Authenticity*, pages 220–221) We should be just as attentive to what we do after Yom Kippur has ended as we have been for the previous 25 hours. —B.P.

For me, the contrast between *n'ila* and the break-fast after Yom Kippur is one of the most dramatic moments of the year. I find myself craving a special greeting for this particular hour of the night; I have noticed that people sometimes have gone from "*shana tova*" to "*g'mar tov*" and back to "*shana tova*" again. Perhaps "*l'shana haba'a birushalayim*" is the most appropriate greeting. But because I have such a strong desire to say the perfect thing and I am feeling so joyous and overwhelmed, I do not know what to say. That, in itself, is one of the things that makes this post-Yom Kippur time so special. —J.G.K.

On one local college campus, the Roman Catholic community graciously offers to cleans up the room after Yom Kippur services so that the Jewish community can go straight to its break-fast; the Jewish community reciprocates the gesture later in the school year. —J.G.K.

or other simple foods that sweetly revive the spirit. Some carry on the tradition of beginning to build the *sukkah* upon returning home that very night as a way of committing with alacrity to disciplined action in the coming year. The meal with which we break the fast brings us from our confrontation with mortality and our examination of life in the face of death back to life and joy. We are newly motivated to live life more intensely, with more awareness and more gratitude as the New Year opens before us.

Sukkot Theology

Richard Hirsh

Sukkot: Spiritual Perspectives

Sukkot is one of three festivals (along with Pesach and Shavuot) linked by narrative as well as by the customary Hebrew word *ḥag* ("[pilgrimage] festival," like the Arabic cognate *haj*). A *ḥag* is one of the festivals of the biblical calendar when Israelites were expected to make a pilgrimage to Jerusalem.

Sukkot, Pesach and Shavuot orbit around the Jewish master story of the Exodus as told in the Hebrew Bible and expanded upon by later rabbinic tradition in lore, law and liturgy. Pesach inaugurates the story with the narrative of the liberation of the Israelites from Egyptian servitude. Shavuot emerges in the later Jewish tradition as the festival commemorating the revelation of the Torah at

Sinai. (In the Hebrew Bible, this association is absent, and Shavuot is noted only as an agricultural festival celebrating first fruits.) *Sukkot* were originally the booths used to house the agricultural worker force during the fall harvest season in order to maximize their work time by having them domiciled in the fields where they would be working. Our festival of Sukkot thus has its origins in a harvest festival tied to the agricultural cycle. Sukkot became linked to the story of the Exodus when the booths were interpreted as symbols of the 40 years of desert wandering between the Exodus and the arrival in the Promised Land. The *sukkot* are then said to represent the transient shelters one might imagine being used during such a trek. The themes of Sukkot derive from this context.

Traveling

Much of spiritual discourse centers on the motif of "a journey" with its implications of movement, just as is recorded in the opening chapters of the fourth book of the Torah, *B'midbar*: "The Israelites journeyed from (place) to (the next place) and then to (the next place). . . ."

"Being on a journey" is a significantly different way of framing a spiritual or religious idea from "believing in God." Believing implies an act of faith or of will, or perhaps both, in which a decision must be made about affirmation, doubt or denial. Believing "in" something further implies that there is "something" (or "Someone") in which (or in whom) one believes.

The language of Jewish liturgy often embraces this sort

of relational assumption: "Praised are You, God . . ." Notable 20th-century Jewish thinkers such as Martin Buber, Abraham Joshua Heschel, Emil Fackenheim and many others all take for granted that when speaking of God, Judaism is speaking of a presence that is in some way "personal," however that is understood.

Reconstructionist Judaism as first formulated by Rabbi Mordecai Kaplan anticipated much of contemporary Jewish spiritual discussion, which more often takes for granted that "belief in God" is not only a problematic proposition, but perhaps not even a particularly helpful way of framing the question of religious meaning. Kaplan spoke of God in many ways—as a power, as a process, as a dimension of existence, as that which is more than "just natural" but less than "supernatural." But in whatever ways Kaplan (and his disciples and conceptual descendents) understood God, it was not "as a person(ality)" with whom one could enter into relationship.

So Kaplan took an important first step away from a conception of God as a supernatural Being in whom one could (or could not) "believe" and toward different conceptions of God that could evoke a religious sensitivity without compromising intellectual integrity. But Kaplan retained the framework of rabbinic Jewish discourse, especially as embodied in the language of the siddur (Jewish prayer book), and was often insistent that the conceptions of God he was formulating were also susceptible to "belief."

In our postmodern era, one of the challenges for Jewish religious life is to reframe and, consequently, to reformulate the ways in which spiritual discourse occurs. The imagery of "journey" helps to turn such discourse from debates about the nature of God to explorations of human spiritual growth, discernment and discovery. Our questions become less like "What are the Jewish ideas of God in which I can believe?" and more like "How can the resources of Judaism help me to cultivate spiritual sensitivity and an awareness of the sanctity inherent in everyday experience?"

Or, to link a Kaplanian concern to a reframed conversation: "How can I use the resources of Judaism to continue on the journey of growing into a more aware and responsible human being?" "How can Judaism help me to become more fully human?" "How can Judaism and being part of the Jewish people support and sustain me on the journey?" And more specifically in terms of Sukkot, "What resources can sustain and shelter me in the wilderness?"

Wilderness

It may seem odd to imagine a holiday as communally oriented as Sukkot as a time for reflecting on the meaning of solitude. The days and nights of Sukkot are often filled with people sharing meals, and the tradition of inviting imaginary guests (traditionally biblical heroes and heroines, but not necessarily limited to them) expands the sense of community. But insofar as Sukkot is linked to the 40 years of wanderings, the festival also offers an opportunity to consider the spiritual implications inherent in the imagery of the wilderness.

One way of looking at the spiritual meaning of the wilderness is to distinguish between whether one goes there voluntarily, or is sent there by someone else, usually as a consequence of something negative. The first suggests that "the wilderness" may be any place of solitude to which one goes for reflection, purification, communion or transformation. The second suggests that "the wilderness" can represent those places where we experience a sense of isolation and/or banishment not of our choosing.

While the wilderness in biblical thinking is clearly a geographic as well as a typological external location, for many contemporary spiritual seekers the wilderness can be a metaphor for an internal experience of solitude freely chosen, even amid the often frenetic demands of daily life. Periods of silence, a practice of meditation, keeping a journal or brief moments of deep and focused breathing, for example, can be "wilderness moments." The wilderness, in other words, can be a gateway from the interpersonal to the intrapersonal—a place of disengagement with others and engagement with oneself.

There is also the solitude that results from isolation when we yearn for connection, or from banishment when we seek reconciliation. Such solitude is a spiritual, religious and psychological reality each person encounters at one time or another. It is a "wilderness" from which we yearn to return. In invoking the 40 years of wanderings, Sukkot can sustain us with the ironic awareness that we are not alone in our isolation. Each person will at some point have to endure a period of wandering, when direction and destination may be equally elusive. The Israelites were challenged to find sources and resources that could sustain them in the wilderness, and no less than our ancestors, we must also seek the things that will support us in our moments of isolation and uncertainty. How will we find the faith that the things we need will be provided? Where will we find what we need? Who will help us in our seeking?

Story

While not all of the mythic 40 years of wandering took place in the wilderness—there were often stations of rest in settled areas—the imagery has become iconic. In the imaginations of the biblical writers, the dominant sense is that the wilderness period reflects poorly on the Israelites, who are frequently depicted as faithless, quarrelsome, complaining, doubting and opposed to the leadership of Moses, Aaron and Miriam. The Torah itself is divided, however, as to whether the 40 years are a punishment as well as a purging of the generation that left Egypt (Deuteronomy 1:34–40) or whether the 40 years are a preparation and a purification in anticipation of entering the Promised Land and creating a covenantal society. (Deuteronomy 8:2–6)

What is often lost in the inherited assumption of the wilderness trek as a time of turmoil is that among some of the biblical prophets, there seems to be a quite different interpretation. Jeremiah (about 625–580 BCE), for example, says: "Thus says God: I accounted to your favor the devotion of your youth, your love as a bride—how you followed after Me in the wilderness in a land not sown . . ."

(Jeremiah 2:2) In this reading, the wilderness represents the effusive outpouring of emotional attachment between God and Israel at a time when the newly covenanted partners were fully devoted to each other.

One central spiritual insight of Sukkot is that memory can be multidimensional. One person may remember the same event very differently from another who was present at the same time. Our own perception of events may change as we ourselves change. The one who is telling the story determines what the story means by way of what gets left out and what gets mentioned, what is marginalized and what is at the center, what is exaggerated and what is abridged.

Sukkot suggests that the nature of a story is that it is both continuous and constantly re-imagined. Insofar as the "self" each of us imagines ourselves to be is in fact "the story we tell about ourselves," it too is continuous and constantly re-imagined. We always have a choice about the self-story we offer to others, how much to disclose, what to share sooner and what later, what we do and do not want to have known.

The divided imagery of the wilderness that the Bible presents suggests that we also have a choice about the self-story we offer to ourselves. Over time, the way in which we come to see ourselves can become rigid and redundant. We can forget that the opportunity of innovation is always available, and that patterns we have come to perform as if scripted can be revised and rewritten. We can become so accustomed to a dominant way of thinking ("wilderness" equals "rebellion") that we forget there are other choices we can make ("wilderness" equals "betrothal"). Sukkot helps us to remember that who we are becoming is an ongoing achievement, not a playing-out of a predetermined destiny.

Transience

Among the key spiritual themes embedded in Sukkot are those of transience and impermanence. The requirements of Jewish law are explicit as to what can appropriately be understood as a sukkah in order to fulfill the mitzvah of "dwelling." A sukkah must be stable enough to convey a sense of stability and of being sheltered, yet fragile enough that it not be construed as "permanent."

This balance between fragility and stability has its spiritual correlation in the awareness that life takes place between the boundaries of birth and death, and is by definition transient. Whatever we seek to make of life, whatever contributions we create, however we try to ensure that our efforts are durable, to one degree or another each person remains aware that she or he is constantly in process and moving through time.

The awareness of impermanence can lead in different spiritual directions. It can become a motivation for tenacity and devotion, inspiring efforts at personal as well as professional accomplishment that almost defy the boundaries of life. It can help to mitigate disappointments as well as the inevitable distresses of life—not by diminishing them, but by helping to keep them in perspective.

In spiritual philosophies derived from Eastern traditions, impermanence is often linked to the term "grasping," by which is meant the tendency to ignore or avoid the implications of transience. Grasping or holding is a reaction to what happens to us that can subvert us. For example, when we lose our patience with a partner or a child or a parent and we say something hurtful, we may (we should!) experience remorse. But when that remorse leads us to dwell on "being a bad person" rather than on accepting that "we have done a bad thing," grasping or holding onto the remorse becomes a source of suffering. In some strands of the Hasidic tradition, a similar attitude is evident in the teachings that center around a belief that all things are "from God," and thus even the bad things that happen, or those that we cause or create, have within them a lingering if hidden spark of transformative holiness.

Rabbi Milton Steinberg suffered a serious heart attack some years before his untimely death at the age of 45. His experience of stepping outside into the daylight after his hospitalization yielded a moving sermon titled, "To Hold with Open Arms." Steinberg's illness had made him vividly aware of how brief our time in this world is, and that therefore what we embrace—a loving partner, a meaningful career, an appreciation of the arts, an awareness of the beauty of nature, all of these—are only "on loan" to us, and each can only truly be "held" with "open arms," with an awareness that all we have been given will one day have to be relinquished.

This awareness of impermanence is reflected in the closing lines of Psalm 90: "May the work of our hands endure . . ." where the psalmist evokes our hope that even within the boundaries of life and death, what we achieve will survive, will make a difference, will be remembered, will endure. Jewish tradition is emphatic about the responsibility for remembering. In the memories of those who keep our names and stories alive, we are granted a fragile shelter of stability, and are entered into an unshakable engagement with eternity.

The Many and the One

In addition to the *sukkah*, the other primary symbol of Sukkot is the cluster of palm, myrtle and willow branches commonly called by name of the dominant palm branch, "the *lulav*," used alongside the *etrog* (citron) and known together as the four species. This cluster is used during the festival in fulfillment of the mitzvah of "waving the *lulav*" both as an independent act and as an accompaniment to the recitation of festival liturgy.

It does not take an advanced degree in anthropology to recognize the fertility imagery that underlies this symbol and the ways in which it is used. In the agricultural cycle of the Land of Israel, the season just beyond the cycle of Rosh Hashana/Yom Kippur/Sukkot/Shemini Atzeret/Simchat Torah is "the rainy season." While most traditional explanations for waving the *lulav* in six directions (north/south/east/west/up/down) suggest it is ". . . to show that God is everywhere," the underlying urgency of furthering fertility by symbolically seeding the sky and the earth and then gathering a circle of protection from all directions of the compass is transparent.

Midrashic explanations of the *lulav* cluster suggest that

fragrance and taste stand in for deeds and learning. Each of the four species is different: The *etrog* has both taste and smell, the willow has neither, myrtle has only smell, and the palm has only taste (in its fruit). The analogy suggests four types of Jews who similarly display knowledge (smell) and deeds (fruit) across a symbolic spectrum. In gathering the four species together, it is often suggested, we are demonstrating that despite our differences, there is a unity that exists among Jews.

Whether we reference God or humans, the common concept is that what we divide by category, by time, by space or by definition remains one and not many at its core one. This can be understood through one Hasidic reading of the declaration *Sh'ma Yisrael Adonay Eloheynu Adonay Eḥad* that many learned as "Hear O Israel, the Lord our God, the Lord is One." This Hasidic interpretation understands the Shema as "Understand, people of Israel, there is nothing else but God."

Contemporary spiritual seekers often frame this issue as "dualism and non-dualism," which refers to the profound question of the nature of reality itself. Are the binary ways in which we most often experience life—dark and light, hard and soft, gentle and harsh, old and young, female and male, sacred and secular—an accurate reflection of reality? Is God/world dualism an appropriate reflection of our spiritual experience and seeking? Or are all of these experienced dualisms just that—the ways in which we humans most often experience reality, but not the way in which existence itself is actually constituted? Non-dualism affirms a fundamental unity underlying our human perceptions, within which God and world simultaneously exist, and to which we are consequently connected in some profound, poetic and perhaps only partially perceived way. Is this framing of our thinking about God a helpful support for our spiritual seeking?

Put differently, if we manage to experience the occasional flash of insight or intuitive experience or emotional tremor or timeless moment in which differences disappear and even, if but for a moment, an experience of unity and connectedness is felt, how shall we weigh such moments? Such moments, which are inevitably the exception and not the rule, may yet be determinative in grounding our religious experience and shaping our souls. In gathering the four species into one cluster, in waving that cluster in all directions so that in effect there are no distinct directions, we can perhaps begin to explore the unending question of "the many and the One."

Sukkot

Nina H. Mandel

Introduction

The final shofar blast on Yom Kippur is the exhilarating culmination of a two-week period during which Jewish communal spiritual life has reached its peak. The intensive services of Rosh Hashana and Yom Kippur, plus Shabbat in the intervening days, have brought many Jews into prayer communities and synagogues more frequently than

The echo of Rosh Hashana and Yom Kippur reverberates throughout Sukkot in part because one rabbinic teaching holds that the gates of repentance remain open until *Hoshana Raba*, which is the last day of the festival. A subtler but perhaps equally significant connection can be found in the High Holy Day prayer *Un'taneh Tokef*, with its familiar theme of "... who will live and who will die. . . ." The uncertainty and anxiety captured in this liturgical poem parallel our awareness of the impermanence and fragility represented by the *sukkah*. In many ways, the *sukkah* is an embodied version of *Un'taneh Tokef*. —R.H.

at other times during the year. Although the High Holy Days are over, the holiday season is not. Five days after the end of Yom Kippur, the festival of Sukkot begins.

Sukkot is a weeklong holiday dedicated to bringing worship outside, literally, and it can be understood as our opportunity to face the world anew after the powerful experience of introspection and *t'shuva* (commitment to change) of the preceding days. A time for appreciating our blessings, Sukkot reminds us to pause and acknowledge the abundance of our tangible and symbolic harvests.

It is clear that in biblical times Rosh Hashana and Yom Kippur were the opening acts for the truly major festival of Sukkot. How might you experience the *Yamim Nora'im* differently if you understood them as spiritual preparation for accepting the abundance of Sukkot or practicing the gratitude central to Sukkot? How might Sukkot be different if you began your preparations in June, when many High Holy Day committees start their work? —E.M.T.

Sukkot blurs the binary distinction between inside and outside. We step outside in order to go inside, moving from a residence that is permanent to one that is temporary. —R.H.

Taking trips and hikes in the outdoors is a very widespread Israeli Sukkot tradition, especially during *ḥol hamo'ed*. During Sukkot, most institutions do not follow their regular work schedules, and schools schedule vacation. This means that families can spend time together enjoying nature. After the long, hot Middle Eastern summer, the weather is milder at last, and trails are full of families hiking together. In Israel Sukkot provides a natural connection between joy (*z'man simḥatenu*) and the outdoors. —E.M.

In addition to being a time of gratitude for our symbolic harvests, Sukkot is an opportunity for practicing gratitude for the physical bounty we experience in the world—the fall harvest, the world's natural beauty, and the homes and buildings that shelter us. We can also practice gratitude for our ability to create community in our homes and synagogues. —N.C.M.

Because Sukkot follows Yom Kippur so closely, preparations for the holiday can be a transitional time from the somberness of the Day of Atonement to Sukkot's joyfulness. The midrashic work *Pesikta Rabati* describes the preparations for Sukkot as the natural next step after Yom Kippur:

> When the Holy One sees Israel resolved upon complete penitence, God forgives all sins and writes off Israel's debt, as it is written, "For on this day, atonement shall be made for you to cleanse you of all your sins." (Leviticus 16:30) When Israel sees that the Holy One has made atonement for them and written off their debt, what do they do? During the four days between the Day of Atonement and the Feast of Tabernacles, they go and fetch myrtle and willows and palm branches and build booths and sing praises to the Holy One. The Holy One says to them: Let bygones be bygones. From this moment on commences a new reckoning. Today is to be the first day in the new reckoning of iniquities. (*Pesikta Rabati* 51:8)

While ancient authorities might have experienced the proximity on the calendar between the end of Yom Kippur and the beginning of Sukkot to be naturally joyful, most years I feel fatigued and harried as one holiday concludes and the next rushes toward me. It is an act of spiritual discipline to immerse myself in Sukkot preparations. Most fortunately, the rewards of this discipline—a beautiful *sukkah*, engaging guests and delicious food—are always and immediately delivered. —D.W.

Sukkot is also a reminder that no matter how thorough and sincere we are in the work of *t'shuva*, there are no guarantees. The joyfulness of Sukkot comes from delight in our current blessings that is heightened by our emergence from the security and protection of our comfortable homes and our entrance into temporary huts that remind us of our own fragility. —J.J.S.

Whereas preparations for many holy days involve a process of internal spiritual readiness, the preparations for Sukkot are primarily physical: the gathering and construction of the ritual objects needed for the celebration—the *sukkah*, the *lulav* and the *etrog*. The physical work of gathering the materials, planning the structure, and going outside to build brings us from what the kabbalists might describe as the world of *atzilut* (spiritual ethereality) on Yom Kippur to the world of *assiya* (physicality) on Sukkot.

What Is Sukkot?

God spoke to Moses, saying: Say to the Israelites: On the fifteenth day of this seventh month, there shall be God's Feast of Sukkot (booths) that will last seven

Occurring six months apart at the full moon, Sukkot and Pesach are both physically demanding. One involves the construction of a *sukkah*, and the other, cleaning and changing dishes in the kitchen. These activities are, perhaps, an early anticipation of the contemporary concern captured in the term "embodiment." —R.H.

In many households, it is also a time to "harvest" the year's blessings—to give thought to things for which we are grateful, to post lists of those blessings on the walls of the *sukkah,* and to read those lists on each evening of the festival. —J.J.S.

How perfect! Our deep inner work on the High Holy Days is intended to prepare us for a new relationship with our bodies, our homes, our communities and our earth. On Sukkot we get to embody a new clarity, a new perspective, a new level of energy. —S.P.W.

Reconstructionist Jews often speak of "experiencing God" rather than "believing in God." The very physicality of Sukkot is ideally suited as a celebration of how we can experience the godliness of creation in the everyday miracles of the food we eat and the shelter in which we live. —S.C.R.

> days. The first day shall be a sacred event: You shall do no work; for seven days you shall bring offerings by fire to God. . . . On the first day you shall take the product of goodly trees, branches of palm trees, boughs of leafy trees, and willows of the brook, and you shall rejoice before your God for seven days. You shall observe it in the seventh month as an eternal law, throughout your generations. You shall live in booths for seven days; all citizens in Israel shall live in booths, in order that future generations may know that I made the Israelites live in booths when I brought them out of the land of Egypt, I your God. So Moses declared God's festivals to the Israelites. (Leviticus 23:33–36; 40–43)

The Torah prescribes three pilgrimage festivals in the Jewish year, Pesach (Passover), Shavuot (Festival of Weeks), and Sukkot—the Festival of Booths. Known in rabbinic texts as the *sh'losh r'galim*—the three pilgrimage festivals—they are linked to the harvest cycle and the injunction to bring seasonal sacrifices that were offered in the Temple by the biblical-era priests. As a harvest festival, Sukkot is sometimes called *Ḥag Ha'asif*, the Festival of Ingathering. This recalls the holiday's roots in an agri-

Getting out sleeping bags and camping in the *sukkah* with my father at the age of 5 had a powerful impact on me. I may not have fully understood the holiday or what we were doing, but it created a strong sensory memory. Sukkot lends itself easily to creating powerful, memorable experiences for young and old alike. We don't have to understand every aspect of a holiday for its rituals and practices to begin to touch our souls. —E.M.T.

cultural society where people lived in huts in the fields during the rush of the final harvest.

Scholars suggest that the pilgrimage festivals are linked to the Near Eastern practice of bringing offerings to the monarch at harvest season. Emergent Israelite and Jewish traditions understood the king to be God and understood the practices as a God-given opportunity to offer sacrifices, as explained in Leviticus 23:37–38:

> Those are God's set times that you shall celebrate as sacred events, bringing offerings by fire to God—burnt offerings, meal offerings, sacrifices, and libations, each according to the day. These are separate from the Sabbath sacrifices, and apart from your gifts and all the votive offerings and freewill offerings that you give to God.

With the destruction of the Second Temple, the rabbis necessarily transformed the pilgrimage components of the harvest holidays. Rabbi Lawrence Hoffman points to a way to recover the spiritual elements of pilgrimage by drawing on Martin Buber's theology. Hoffman suggests that a pilgrim is an individual who cultivates an "I-Thou" relationship with place. A pilgrim is distinct from a traveler, a visitor or a tourist because a pilgrim is open to being transformed through an encounter with a place, with the divine and with others encountered on his or her journey. —D.W.

Sukkot is an opportunity not only to recall our ancestors' temporary harvest huts, but also to sensitize ourselves to the plight of the unseen and disempowered migrant agricultural laborers who harvest much of our food, and to commit some *tzedaka* (a modern offering) to support the rights of this population. —N.C.M.

The *sukkah* is a kind of *mikdash m'at* (small sanctuary) where we have the opportunity to offer our food and hospitality with the same sacred intention with which our ancestors offered their Sukkot sacrifices in the Temple in Jerusalem. —N.C.M.

In addition to the harvest aspect of the festivals, each holiday is linked to a pivotal moment in the mythic history of the Israelites as found in the book of Exodus. Pesach recalls the liberation from Egypt, Shavuot the revelation at Sinai, and as the passage from Leviticus above indicates, Sukkot is linked to the narrative of the Exodus by recalling the time when recently freed Israelites built fragile lives and homes in the wilderness.

The Talmud (*Sukkah* 11b) relates that Rabbi Akiba considered the *sukkot* in which God housed Israel as actual, physical booths (*sukkot mamash*), while Rabbi Eliezer understood them to be the clouds of glory, our divine escort through the wilderness. —V.M.

The trilogy of pilgrimage holidays echoes the mythic substructure that Franz Rosenzweig (a 20th-century German Jewish existentialist) identified in Judaism: God's redemption (Pesach), God's revelation (Shavuot) and God's creation (Sukkot)—the moment when we acknowledge the generative forces in our world that bring forth natural creativity and food from the earth. —N.C.M.

According to our mythic history, it was on Yom Kippur that Moses descended from Mount Sinai with the second set of tablets. The sin of the golden calf was forgiven. The divine presence returned into the midst of Israel. In direct response to that restoration, we began the construction of the *Mishkan*, the tabernacle. (See Exodus 34–35.) The *Mishkan* is a structure of beauty. It is built as a result of an outpouring of generosity. It becomes the resting point for the clouds of glory that represent God's presence. Its construction began in a joyous response to atonement. In short—in building a *sukkah,* we call forth all the images of the *Mishkan* itself. —V.M.

In much of Jewish tradition, the wilderness is understood as a wild and uninhabited place where it is much easier to encounter the divine than one can amid the noise, distraction and corruption of cities and towns. Dwelling in the *sukkah* invokes a simpler time when contemporary Jews imagine, it was easier to hear the divine voice. —D.A.T.

In *The Meaning of God in Modern Jewish Religion*, Mordecai Kaplan notes, "[By] utilizing the nature festivals to recall historical experiences, the Jews directed the human mind to the consciousness of history as an ethical and spiritual influence in human life." (page 188) As is the case with many Jewish holiday celebrations, marking Sukkot requires us to step back in time not only to recall historical experiences, but also to reenact the essence of them. For seven days we bring the experience of the wilderness to our own private and communal backyards

In practical terms, our ability to replicate the experience of the wilderness in the urban and suburban areas where Jews often reside is limited. Perhaps our *kavana* (intention) for Sukkot should be less imagining the wilderness and more living in the awareness of the contrast between wilderness and settlement. —R.H.

At times when economic pressures rise in society, unemployment rises as well, and many who once felt secure suddenly find themselves living increasingly on the economic edge. At such times the sense of fragility that the temporary *sukkah* evokes becomes all the more poignant and relevant in our communal life. —S.C.R.

Sukkot doesn't only recall a time when we lived with a closer connection to our environment; it compels us to be outside and to connect more with the natural environment. When Sukkot falls in October in the Northeast United States, the air is just starting to chill. After the warm summer it is tempting to head to indoor comforts. One of the pleasures of this holiday is its gentle nudge encouraging us to be outside even when the weather is no longer "perfect." This push allows us to rediscover the spiritual dimension of being outside during all kinds of weather. —E.M.T.

On Sukkot it is easy to include children and make the holiday meaningful and memorable for them because it is fundamentally a tactile, physical celebration. Children can make decorations, shake the *lulav*, sing songs, help to make and serve food, and invite guests of their own. —S.C.R.

by building temporary *sukkot* (huts; singular: *sukkah*) and, according to tradition, living in them as we would in our own homes. We gather branches and fruit in the form of the *lulav* (a bundle of willow, myrtle and palm greens) and *etrog* (citron) and each day shake them toward the corners of the universe to invoke the Source of Abundance around us. These practices evoke a time when awareness of and connection to nature were essential for survival and rituals often involved tangible physical action beyond prayer and study.

Shaking the *lulav* in six directions continues to work well as a spiritual practice that connects us to the sanctity of the entire universe and reminds us how interconnected all things are, beyond our ability to see or even to conceive of it. —J.J.S.

Each of the *r'galim* (pilgrimage festivals) has an appellation for recitation in the Kiddush and the Amida for the holiday. Pesach is "*z'man ḥerutenu*," "the season of our liberation." Shavuot is "*z'man matan toratenu*," "the season of the giving of our Torah." "*Z'man simḥatenu*," "the season of our rejoicing," the appellation for Sukkot, strikes me as a curiously nonspecific generic invocation. Isn't each festival a season of our rejoicing? I would have expected something like "the season of our journeys" or perhaps "the season of our settling." —R.H.

Sukkot is also referred to as *z'man simḥatenu*, the "season of our rejoicing." It is a festive holiday during which we bring joy into our lives through hospitality, celebration and gratitude.

On Sukkot we cultivate gratitude by moving away—if only temporarily—from our material gifts. By stepping outside of our homes, whether humble or grand, we realize that we can be thankful for the people surrounding us, and for the ways we make meaning in our lives.

The origins of Sukkot probably date back well before those of Rosh Hashana and Yom Kippur, the Jewish holidays we now consider the most important. The early rabbis called Sukkot *Heḥag*, simply "The Festival." The joy and gratitude that emerged after the harvest provided an opportunity for one last celebration before the onset of winter, which is the rainy season in Israel. In our day we can also celebrate the transition of the holiday season toward the arrival of winter. —B.P.

During Sukkot in Israel, countless festivals, concerts and art exhibitions take place. Some examples are the colorful Jewish-Arab theater festival in the old city of Akko; the Haifa International Film Festival, with its many musical and art events; and the Tamar (Date) Festival happening all around the Dead Sea. The latter combines musical concerts by major Israeli performers with an opportunity to see the magic of the Judean desert. Some of the festivals have been happening for decades now, and they are an inseparable part of Sukkot as experienced by Israelis and visitors. —E.M.

Letting go or renunciation is at the heart of many spiritual practices. On Yom Kippur there is the practice of letting go of food, drink, sexual relations, leather shoes and work—a reminder to let go of unwholesome patterns in our lives. On Sukkot we let go of the security and comfort symbolized by the roof over our heads. All of this letting go is in service of being more conscious of the divine voice within. —S.P.W.

The many hours that I spend in community worship throughout Rosh Hashana and Yom Kippur rarely evoke for me the power of warm, nurturing, sacred relationships that I experience while sitting around a *sukkah* table with a dozen people. In the *sukkah*, somehow individuals palpably represent to me the communal embrace in ways that sitting with hundreds does not. —J.J.S.

The hospitality of Sukkot brings into focus our connections not only to family and friends but also to the broader community. The open design of our *sukkot* encourages us to share our holiday meals with friends, neighbors and even strangers, and to follow the kabbalistic tradition of inviting the biblical matriarchs and patriarchs to our festivities.

Despite the fact that living in *sukkot* is meant to take us out of the comfort of our ordinary lives, the tradition has always encouraged *hidur mitzvah*, bringing beauty and splendor to our preparations. The lulav and etrog used should be in optimum condition, and they are often kept protected in elaborate holders and boxes. The *sukkot*

In the Torah we find a commandment that is to be fulfilled every seventh year on Sukkot. At that time the Israelites are "to bring together" (*hak'hel*) the whole nation—men, women, children and strangers (non-Jews who are in the community)—and read the Torah. (Deuteronomy 31:10–13) Inspired by this text, PANIM for Jewish Renaissance convenes a creative and inspirational festival every Sukkot in Israel. Called the Hakhel Festival of Jewish Learning, it celebrates Sukkot, religious pluralism and love of Torah by convening a myriad of teachers from all religious streams to teach and speak on panels. Jewish music and theater are performed in the many *sukkot* built in the festival area. —E.M.

The *sukkah* should awaken all of our senses: sight, sound, taste, touch and smell. Fragrant pine needles add to the sensual experience. They also have the advantage of remaining whole and intact for the full week, unlike cornstalks or the leaves of deciduous trees. —B.P.

themselves are made inviting by decorating them with pillows, tapestries, pictures, harvest fruits and vegetables, and even lights. This focus on beauty and splendor enhances the rejoicing of the holiday. The rabbinic sages expanded the practices described in the Torah into the *halakha* of Sukkot, and as Jewish civilization has continued to evolve, so have the interpretations and lessons of the holiday.

The Sukkah

The name Festival of Booths comes from the verse in Leviticus 23 and the commandment that each year the "citizens of Israel," now and in the future, should dwell in booths, or *sukkot*, as a reminder of the Israelites who lived in *sukkot* in the wilderness. The rabbinic sages sought to define what was required to fulfill the commandment of "dwelling," including how the *sukkah* should be constructed, how much time an individual must spend in the *sukkah* to fulfill the commandment, and what rituals and daily activities should be performed in the *sukkah*. This section discusses basic teachings about the sukkah and explores contemporary options.

The guidelines for building a *sukkah* may seem counterintuitive. We are instructed to erect this structure annually as the central symbol of the holiday, and it needs to be suitable for habitation for a week. It would seem reasonable to invest effort and energy in building something that would be ready when you needed it and that would stand for years. But as a symbol that invokes living in huts during the harvest season and the fragility of our material lives, the *sukkah* is an impermanent structure by definition. It is erected each year for the express purpose of dwelling in it to observe Sukkot.

When putting up a *sukkah*, we experience the simple joy that comes with building something we know will not last forever—just as when we build a sandcastle. We are building simply for the joy of creating. Getting it perfect or making it last is not the point. The message of the *sukkah*—to loosen our ties to what is material and permanent—is hammered home with each temporary nail or tie used to construct this short-lived celebration space. —E.M.T.

Rabbi Yehudah Aryeh Leib Alter (the second Gerer Rebbe, 1847–1905) suggests that the *sukkah* is meant to remind us that we are sojourners, *ushipizin* (guests), if you will, in this world. (*S'fat Emet, Parashat Vayishlakh*). While we mostly live in an illusion of permanence, our physical bodies are like *sukkot*—impermanent structures that will wither away. This truth should encourage us to search for what is beyond the regular structures of the world to which we cling most of the time. —E.M.

The minimum halakhic requirement for a *sukkah* is two-and-a-half walls, which is barely enough to make a structure. The halakhic requirements for the covering spread over the top specify that you must be able to see through to the open sky, preventing full protection from the weather. When you are in the *sukkah*, whether you are outside or inside is ambiguous. —R.H.

In addition to being impermanent, the *sukkah* should be an open and welcoming structure. According to *halakha*, a *sukkah* should have at least two complete walls plus a partial one. The roof of the *sukkah* is flat but never solid. Its frame is covered with leaves and branches that allow for more shade than sunlight, but also provide a view of the stars at night. The Hebrew word for these roofing materials is *s'khakh*, which shares a common root with the words "to entangle" and also "to be enlightened."

The laws in the Mishna about the construction of the *sukkah* include practical considerations for building a liv-

A Hasidic teaching from the book *Bil'vavi Mishkan Evneh* (written by Itamar Schwartz, a contemporary Israeli rabbi) suggests that the form of the *sukkah* embodies the spiritual transformation taking place among the Jewish people at this time of year. From the focus on *ḥet*/sin during the High Holy Days, we shift to Sukkot, represented by the fragile, open *sukkah* that can be built with two-and-a-half sides like the Hebrew letter *hey*, one of the ways that God's name is written in Hebrew. The indwelling presence of the divine is with us as we live in the *sukkah*. —N.C.M.

It is easy to build the roof for a *sukkah* using bamboo poles and bamboo mats. Some suppliers weave the poles into the mats for you, making them easy to put on. —D.A.T.

According to some, the *sukkah* gets its name from its upper covering, *s'khakh,* which means "thatch," but which also means "that which covers or conceals." Because the *s'khakh* must not be so thick that it prevents one from seeing stars through it at night, it can remind us that everything we see has meaning beyond the surface level we grasp immediately. All existence is a parable, an analogy, a *mashal*, always pointing beyond itself to its own deeper meaning: God is hidden everywhere, waiting to be found and seen, known and loved. Peering through the *s'khakh* at night and glimpsing a glittering star, if only for a moment, is a reminder to us to look beyond the surface to find the truth hidden inside. —J.P.S.

able, if temporary, dwelling. The *sukkah* walls need not touch the ground or reach the roof of the *sukkah*. The walls can be made of wood, burlap, plastic, canvas or decorative fabric.

The size of the *sukkah* will depend on its anticipated use. It should be big enough for a person to stand upright in it, and it should accommodate more than one person. A communal *sukkah* can be designed to hold a crowd, but a home *sukkah* should not be bigger than your permanent dwelling. Typically the *sukkah* is made large enough to accommodate guests around a table for a meal.

After I had built my first *sukkah*, someone complained that its walls were too flexible to comply with the *halakha*. My reaction has been to celebrate all creative interpretations of the *sukkah*, seeing the creativity of design and construction as reflective of the Jewish diversity that we see in conjunction with holiday observances, especially during the Passover Seder. —N.C.M.

The mitzvah is literally *leyshev*, to dwell in the *sukkah*, but some commentators reinterpret the Hebrew as if it meant "*lashuv*," "to return," and understand that the promises of Yom Kippur repentance (*t'shuva*) can first be enacted through opening our hearts (and homes) on Sukkot to those from whom we have been estranged. —S.C.R.

Every Shabbat morning, my father would kiss my mother and me goodbye as we headed off to synagogue. Sitting in services for several hours was not his idea of personal renewal. However, every year when the synagogue put out the call for volunteers to help put up the *sukkah*, my father was the first to put his name on the list. Building, helping to educate the children, aiding in celebration: This was his kind of Judaism! —D.W.

Building the *sukkah* usually begins any time after Yom Kippur ends, and the structure should be complete before the festival begins. Some people prefer to erect the frame of the *sukkah* during the time between Rosh Hashana and Yom Kippur, putting the finishing touches on after Yom Kippur. Still others will begin erecting the *sukkah* the evening Yom Kippur ends so that it is among the first things they do after breaking their fast. Community-based *sukkot* are often built to coordinate with school and work schedules, and in some neighborhoods people go from house to house helping with the work of erecting *sukkah* frames.

The one and only year that my family managed to complete the construction of our *sukkah* a day in advance, I was pleased that the job would not have the usual last-minute pressure. Alas, that was the year in which a tornado kissed lightly down in our neighborhood on *erev* Sukkot and twisted the *sukkah* frame like a pretzel. It was a perfect Sukkot lesson about impermanence. —J.J.S.

In this busy season of the Jewish year, even the thought of constructing a *sukkah* can be daunting. As with a barn raising, building a *sukkah*—whether it is located at home or at a communal building—calls us to reach out to our friends and community to work together on a fun and sacred project. This is a great opportunity to lighten the task of *sukkah* building and to reinforce our interconnectedness. —N.C.M.

The act of building up and tearing down the *sukkah* year after year serves as a reminder of our power to rebuild what is broken in both our physical and our spiritual lives. —S.C.R.

Building plans for a *sukkah* can be found online and in resource books such as *The First Jewish Catalog: A Do-It-Yourself Kit*, by Richard Siegel, Michael Strassfeld and Sharon Strassfeld. *Sukkah* kits can also be purchased online and in some Judaica stores. The kits include plans as well as all the necessary hardware. All you need to provide is the wood or other framing materials.

Sukkah walls can be made of any material. Wall choices are generally made based on the local climate and the extent to which the *sukkah* will be used. Burlap will not be as sturdy in a windy, rainy climate as heavy canvas or wood plank. Those hoping to sleep in their *sukkot* may choose walls that provide more coverage and privacy, including a door or door flap, so that all four walls can be enclosed. If the *sukkah* is to be used solely for meals and periodic programs, a more open plan may be appropriate.

I have learned the hard way that simplicity can also be a value. Making the construction of the *sukkah* simpler by using prefabricated frames (or ones that require less assembly) can leave more time for decorating the *sukkah* and preparing meals. —N.C.M.

If you are planning to sit in the *sukkah* for leisurely meals, think about cutting out windows or using latticework that will keep things bright and airy. —J.J.S.

In our town, right about the time when we are taking out the family *sukkah* decorations, buying pumpkins and gourds and joining together to decorate, our neighbors are putting up Halloween decorations. We crave rituals that mark the passing of the seasons. There is something fulfilling in gathering the local produce for our *sukkah*, and in building and decorating it. Unlike other autumn holidays, Sukkot has the added benefit of teaching the values of gratitude and hospitality. —B.P.

The walls are just the beginning of the decorations in the *sukkah*. The idea is to make your *sukkah* beautiful and inviting, so even ornate carpets or tapestries might be used. Bundles of corn stalks make attractive additions to walls, as do sunflower stalks. Lights can be hung if you have access to an electrical source, and candles and lanterns can be used (but with care; these should never be left unattended because of the fire hazard). Decorating the *sukkah* is often (but not exclusively) the realm of the children in the community or household, and any number of paper chains, mobiles made out of gourds, pictures or murals can be hung from walls and ceilings. The ground in the *sukkah* can be covered with carpets. Bamboo, rattan and sea grass are particularly weather-friendly materials, as are rugs specifically designed for outdoor use. A table and chairs are a must for eating your meals in the *sukkah*, and people living in drier climates might add large

Twinkly strands of LED lights can light a *sukkah* beautifully. —D.A.T.

Decorating the *sukkah* is a fabulous opportunity to bring families together through planning, creating and hanging decorations as a family project. This provides an excellent occasion to teach the concept of *hidur mitzvah* (making the observance of mitzvot beautiful) to young children. —N.C.M./S.C.R.

Gourds are not just decorative. They emphasize the principle of *bal tash'ḥit* (not wasting). Rather than hanging food that will spoil, which is wasteful, we use gourds, baby pumpkins and Indian corn in our New England *sukkah*. —B.P.

One of my fondest memories of living in Israel is of walking through Jerusalem during the week of Sukkot and gazing in awe at the hundreds of *sukkot* that adorn nearly every balcony and every yard in the city. —S.C.R.

pillows for lounging. In decorating your *sukkah*, you are limited only by your imagination. Consider planning a tour of the *sukkot* in your neighborhood to see what other people have done.

A little advance planning can greatly enhance your *sukkah* experience. In some areas, decorations of fruit, gourds and dried corncobs will make your *sukkah* an attractive snacking ground for birds and animals. This may or may not enhance your experience, so plan accordingly. Bees and wasps are attracted to many of the materials used to decorate *sukkot* and can be a nuisance, but many hardware stores sell deterrent hives that can be hung around the *sukkah* to keep them away.

In the Sukkah

Like most Jewish holidays, Sukkot begins with candlelighting on the eve of the holiday. This is something that can be done in the *sukkah*. The standard candlelighting blessing for "kindling the festival lights" (*l'hadlik ner shel yom tov*) is recited. This is followed by the *Sheheḥeyanu* blessing, which is traditionally said upon performing an act (or encountering a new experience) for the first time or

Some congregations schedule a *sukkah* walk, arranging for food to be available at each stop. This can be a kind of progressive lunch, with one course in each *sukkah*. A *sukkah* walk can be a delightful communal event. —D.A.T.

The contrast between the simple, almost rudimentary nature of the *sukkah* and the plenty of a full meal is yet another reminder of the abundance in our lives. —E.M.T.

after a long hiatus. If there is a danger that the wind will extinguish the candles, they can be moved inside after being lit. When you are ready to eat on that evening, the festival *Kiddush* is recited over wine or grape juice, followed by the blessing "commanding us to dwell in the *sukkah*" (*vetzivanu leyshev basukkah*), and followed again by the *Sheheḥeyanu* blessing. The blessing for dwelling in the *sukkah* is repeated each time you eat in any *sukkah*, but is not recited when you visit without eating, or when you return to the same *sukkah* on the same day.

Spending time in the *sukkah* is an essential and unique feature of the holiday. Gathering in the *sukkah* for meals, prayer, learning and leisure is strongly encouraged. (See the section on Community Practice below for more ideas on programming in the *sukkah*.) We are encouraged to at least to eat the festival meal in the *sukkah*, though it is preferable to move a meal indoors if inclement weather

Dwelling in the *sukkah* is a mitzvah that is available to anyone, whether learned in Jewish tradition or not. The nature of this experience reinforces the universality of the human condition: In the end, our material possessions are meaningless. Both rich and poor are ultimately judged by the quality of our character, not the size of our estates. —S.C.R.

When rain falls during Sukkot, it is easy to feel disappointment. Decorations may become sodden, and the evening meal may be uncomfortably damp or may even need to be moved inside. This is one of the central teachings behind raising the *sukkah*: All structures we humans build for ourselves are fragile. This insight can bring gratitude for how much shelter most of us have most days of our lives. —D.W.

Since the joy of Sukkot should not be turned into suffering, during rainy or frigid weather you can limit your time in the *sukkah* to the time it takes to recite *Kiddush*. —D.A.T.

interferes with comfortable dining. People who do not have their own *sukkah* can share *sukkot* at synagogues, community centers and Jewish schools, often with scheduled public programs.

The *Zohar*, the primary kabbalistic text, teaches, "Those who sit in the *sukkah* see themselves in the shade of *emuna* (faith)." (*Emor* 103a) Mordecai Kaplan envisioned the *sukkah*'s contemporary meaning as a "protest against developing material civilization." (*The Meaning of God in Modern Jewish Religion*, page 207) Whether as a symbol of faith or a protest against the materialism that pervades most lives, the *sukkah* is a focal point for hospitality and community.

Ushpizin

One of the primary roles of the *sukkah* is to foster hospitality, and we are encouraged to celebrate the holiday by

It is all too easy to get caught up in a materialistic approach to Sukkot: There are ever more products to buy to decorate the *sukkah*. It is important to find a balance between *hidur mitzvah* and excessive consumerism. One way to decorate the *sukkah* is to laminate brightly colored Rosh Hashana cards from friends and colleagues and hang them on the walls. —D.W.

Unlike Noah's construction of the ark as a structure that protected him from the force of God's wrath, the *sukkah*'s construction places us on the side of God's compassion. Even when we can't stay in the *sukkah* very long because of inclement weather, we can still appreciate that all the structures we have built are more porous than we like to think, and recognize that we are not really so separate from the natural world around us. —N.C.M.

inviting guests to join us in our *sukkot*. Jewish tradition often connects the welcoming of *sukkah* guests to the biblical story in which Abraham and Sarah invite visitors into their tent, becoming paragons of hospitality. Spiritual guests to the *sukkah* are called by a special name: *ushpizin* (an Aramaic word meaning "guests"). A kabbalistic tradition teaches that the first guests we welcome into the *sukkah* should be the biblical ancestors. Starting with Abraham, a different forefather is formally invited to sit in the *sukkah* each night. Though practices vary, a common order is: Abraham, Isaac, Jacob, Joseph, Moses, Aaron and David. In our egalitarian communities, we also invite such biblical women as Sarah, Rachel, Rebecca, Leah, Hannah, Miriam, Abigail and Esther. These guests are welcomed with an Aramaic formula that translates as: "Enter, exalted sacred guests; enter, exalted sacred ancestors; be seated, exalted guests; be seated, faithful guests." (See *Kol Haneshamah: Shirim Uvraḥot*, pages 76–79.)

It is increasingly common to invite people who are not Jewish to share a meal in the *sukkah*. Explaining the custom of *ushpizin* in advance allows them to give some thought to names they may want to share, including spiritual figures from their own faith tradition. —R.H.

In addition to reciting the traditional blessings, our family custom is to ask every person in the *sukkah* each night to share at least one thing (other than sustenance) for which they are grateful that day, that season or that year. —S.C.R.

The term "*sukkat shalom*" (a tabernacle of peace) is found in Jewish prayer. Some Israeli progressive congregations combine the tradition of welcoming guests with the idea of *sukkat shalom* by making Sukkot a time to invite people of other faiths, particularly Arabs, to special events in the *sukkah*. Having gone through an internal process of forgiveness on Yom Kippur, we can take the next step on Sukkot by inviting people with whom we have been in conflict into the midst of our *sukkat shalom*, moving from forgiveness toward peace. —E.M.

Ushpizin need not be limited to biblical ancestors. On the first night of Sukkot, while lighting the candles, you can have tea lights available (most safely in votive cups) and invite everyone present to invite in their own ancestors by lighting one of these candles. Other practices also invoke the spirit of hospitality and generate conversation and remembrances—hanging pictures of friends and relatives in the *sukkah*; hanging gourds with people's names written on them; and discussing pertinent topics, such as which historical figure you would like to invite into the *sukkah*.

Of course, the physical guests we invite should receive invitations well in advance. They may include family and friends, but when considering whom to invite to our *sukkot*, special attention should be paid to reaching out to newcomers and to people without access to transportation or to those who are homebound. If rides to a *sukkah* cannot be arranged, a representative group can go to people's homes with *lulav* and *etrog* and a holiday meal.

During the *ushpizin* ritual, some people invoke the presence of relatives who have passed away. This can be a poignant and touching moment at the start of the *sukkah* meal. —N.C.M.

Inviting ancestors to join us in the *sukkah* sanctifies the moment and the space. We feel the presence of countless generations before us who have sat in the *sukkah* and recited the same blessings. We might remember a great aunt or grandfather whom we hold dear in our hearts. Sitting in the *sukkah* not only brings us outdoors, it also helps us to get in touch with the wider canvas and meaning of our lives. —J.J.S.

Sukkot themselves are generally accessible to those with disabilities in that they don't involve stairs or narrow doorways, though care may need to be taken to provide flat and stable ground leading into the *sukkah* and adequate room to accommodate wheelchairs or other mobility aids.

The Lulav *and* Etrog

In addition to dwelling in a *sukkah*, waving the cluster of the *lulav* and *etrog* is the primary observance of Sukkot. In halakhic literature, these ritual objects are also referred to

Many communities use the time of Sukkot to engage in communal-mitzvah building projects (like those of Habitat for Humanity) so that personal gratitude and appreciation for the material blessings of our lives translate into material blessings for others. —S.C.R.

The *S'fat Emet* (literally, *Language of Truth*, a book written in the nineteenth century by Rabbi Yehuda Aryeh Leib Alter) conveys a teaching from the Zohar that the *sukkah* corresponds to Aaron, who is like a bride, while the *lulav* corresponds to Moses, who is like the bridegroom. In this image (both gender-conformant and non-conformant!), we see the *sukkah* as the containing space into which we enter, while the *lulav* is the shaft that we thrust in all directions. Aaron is the high priest associated with the *Mishkan*'s spatial splendor. Moses is the prophet associated with divine communication. Inside the *sukkah* we sit enclosed, basking in the blessing of the past year. Shaking the *lulav,* we reach out, actively pleading for continued blessing for the future. —V.M.

The halakhic prohibition against carrying objects when outdoors on Shabbat leads to the tradition of not using the *lulav* on the Shabbat of Sukkot out of concern that the *lulav* would be carried to the synagogue. But many Jews may get to Sukkot services only on Shabbat. Using the *lulav* in synagogue on the Shabbat of Sukkot is an adaptation that ought to be encouraged. —R.H.

as the *arba minim* or four species—myrtle, palm, willow and *etrog*. The term "*lulav*" refers both to the specific palm branch and the bundle of greens for which it forms the spine. The bundle is formed by one *lulav* or palm branch flanked by three twigs of *hadas* (myrtle) and two branches of *arava* (willow). They are held together in a bunch by a braided palm-frond holder, and often lashed together at the bottom by a palm leaf. An *etrog* is a large citrus fruit also known as a citron.

Each component of the *lulav* should be fresh and in good condition. The palm should be long enough to be waved, it must not be wilted or torn at the ends, and its leaves should be bunched together. The myrtle branches should have more leaves than berries on them and, like the willow, should not be withered. Some people store the *lulav* in the refrigerator during Sukkot in order to keep it fresh. Wrapping the ends of the branches in a damp paper towel and then encasing the ends in a plastic bag will help keep the plants fresh.

Finding an exceptional *etrog* can be like finding a perfect gem. Its qualifications are exacting, and some people invest considerable time and money to obtain just the

I dissent from the quest for an exquisite *etrog*. The obsessiveness of the search for the perfect *etrog* in anecdote, legend and fact seems to me contrary to the values of modesty that we encourage in almost every other area of Jewish life. It is, after all, only a piece of fruit. —R.H.

If you are in Jerusalem on the days prior to Sukkot, the *etrog* market on *Reḥov Meah She'arim* is not to be missed. See the film "Ushpizin." —J.J.S.

right one. An *etrog* generally looks and smells like a large lemon (though a lemon is not a substitute for an *etrog*). It should not be scabby or withered, and it should have a minimal amount of green on its skin. Like most tree fruits, the *etrog* has a stem end and a flower end. The best *etrog* will be nicely shaped, and it will have smooth skin and a pleasant fragrance. In order for an *etrog* to be considered kosher (fit for ritual use), the stub of the withered flower, called the *pitam* (often pronounced "*pitom*" by Ashkenazic Jews, but derived from *pitma*, nipple, and therefore correctly "*pitam*"), must be intact. The *etrog* should be neither smaller than the palm of your hand, nor too large to hold with one hand.

Though they are made of materials found in nature, the *lulav* and *etrog* are rarely gathered together from scratch. Individual components or *lulav* and *etrog* sets are most often purchased from sellers who gather appropriate branches and fruits from sources in Israel and other places where they grow indigenously. The *etrog* is packed separately, wrapped carefully to prevent damage; traditional practice requires that the *pitam* be intact when the blessing is said. The palm, myrtle and willow are usually packaged separately along with a braided palm-frond with three holders for assembling the *lulav* on arrival. As it faces you, the palm goes in the middle; the willow is

Some Israeli farmers now grow *etrogim* in which the *pitam*, the stub of the withered flower, does not extend beyond the fruit, making it almost impossible to break and render the *etrog* ritually unfit. —S.C.R.

placed in the holder on your left, and the myrtle in the holder on your right.

In areas with larger Jewish populations, it may be possible to find the individual components in a market and pick them out yourself. It is also easy to purchase sets at a Judaica store or online for arrival before the beginning of the festival. Some synagogues, day schools and Jewish community centers place orders for members. Prepackaged sets vary in price, and they are often graded according to the quality of the component pieces. Regardless of the price, you can expect that all of them fit the halakhic guidelines, and they should have a warranty in case they arrive damaged or are otherwise unacceptable. Once purchased, the *lulav* and *etrog* should be carefully stored. Special ornate bags and boxes are available for both; they not only protect the items but make them easier to carry to the synagogue or *sukkah*.

The ritual for *lulav* and *etrog* celebrates the worship of God with the hands by asking us to gather the *arba minim* daily during Sukkot (except on Shabbat)—not just to hold but also to bless, uplift and shake. This is typically performed communally as part of the morning service, just before *Hallel* (see below), or it can be done at home or in your *sukkah*. If you are participating in a communal ser-

When sharing a *lulav* and *etrog*, keep in mind the principle that one must actually "own" the four species. Instead of loaning them to someone, give them away! Your intention to offer them as a gift adds a dimension of *ḥesed*, loving kindness, to the ritual of the *lulav*. Then the one who has received the gift can also offer it as a gift back to you. —B.P.

vice, it is customary to bring your *lulav* and *etrog* and share them with members of the congregation who do not have their own.

The procedure for saying the blessing of the *lulav* and *etrog* takes into account the halakhic requirement to say a blessing immediately before performing the coordinate act. That is why we hold the *pitam* end of the *etrog* facing downward at the start of the blessing and turn it upright at the end. To begin, hold the *lulav* in your right hand, with the spine of the palm frond facing you. Hold the *etrog* in your left hand with the *pitam* facing down. Holding your two hands together, recite the blessing, ending with *al n'tilat lulav* (taking and waving the *lulav*). On the first day, this should be followed by the *Sheheḥeyanu*

The act of shaking the *lulav* in all directions is commonly explained as affirming the presence of God everywhere and in everything. Shaking the *lulav* outside, where we can see the earth, sky and perhaps the horizon, increases our sense of God as expansive. Shaking the *lulav* in public, where we might be seen by others, turns this ritual into an act of witness. Just as our ancestors affirmed the oneness of God in the fields during the autumn harvest, we in the cities, suburbs or wherever we might live, publicly declare, "All is God." —E.M.T.

blessing. The *etrog* is then turned with the *pitam* facing up, and the ritual of shaking the *arba minim* begins. (See *Kol Haneshamah: Shabbat Veḥagim*, pages 354–355.)

Begin by facing east and shaking the *lulav* and *etrog* in front of you three times. Continue three times to your right, three times over your shoulder behind you, three times to your left, three times up above your head, and then three times down toward the earth. In this way, the divine presence is invoked all around us, with the number of shakes being the symbolic 18—indicating life (the numerical value of the Hebrew word for life, *ḥay*).

There are few occasions when we can feel that our entire bodies are celebrating the gift of life and expressing gratitude for the blessings we share. Engaging in the ritual shaking of the *lulav* and *etrog* is a spiritual act that allows for just such total physical involvement. —S.C.R.

I sometimes experience the shaking of the *lulav* as a meditation on connecting the life force within me to God's presence around me in all directions; it is the quintessential ritual of creating sacred space. —N.C.M

Shaking a *lulav* in six directions is a Jewish shamanistic rite. It casts a sacred circle and invokes the energy of each of the directions. Indigenous cultures are intuitively connected to the earth and the forces of nature. They seek the protection of alignment with those forces. This is a good intention for these times of a troubled relationship between our planet and the human species. —S.P.W.

It seems to me almost impossible to shake a *lulav* "the wrong way." Once you are holding the four species and shaking them, there is a kind of self-conscious awareness that seems to arise regardless of how many times you shake the *lulav* or what direction you are shaking it in. The very act of bringing together this combination of frond, twigs, leaves and fruit propels us into a state of mind more closely tied to the natural world and to our more agrarian ancestors. —E.M.T.

A midrashic tradition teaches: "All my bones shall say: 'God, who is like You?' (Psalms 35:10) This was said in allusion to the *lulav*. The rib of the *lulav* resembles the human spine; the myrtle resembles the eye; the willow resembles the mouth, and the *etrog* resembles the heart. King David said, 'There are none among all the limbs greater than these, for they outweigh in importance the whole body.'" (*Vayikra Raba* 30:14)

As the quotation from *Vayikra Raba* above suggests, the *lulav* and *etrog* are rich with symbolism, including that of nature mirroring the way that humans are created in the divine image. In addition to equating the *lulav* and *etrog* to eyes and limbs, some descriptions equate them to male and female genitalia. This particular comparison has enhanced the connection between the *lulav* and *etrog* and fertility rituals, which rites and folklore reinforce. Often egg or oval-shaped, the *etrog* is a symbol of fertility. One folk custom says that at the end of Sukkot, women should bite off the *pitam* for fertility; another says that you can sleep with an *etrog* under their pillows in order to dream of future spouses.

Another midrash compares the four species to the Jewish people. The *etrog*, which is edible and has a pleasant

The midrash comparing the four species to the Jewish people is an ancient illustration of the importance of our diversity and pluralism. Just as each part of the four species is holy, we are all counted equally in the holiness of the Jewish people. As God loves each individual, so do we. Without judging the merits of someone's learning or deeds, each one of us makes a valuable contribution. —B.P.

fragrance, is like people with knowledge of Torah who do good deeds. The palm tree, with edible fruit but no fragrance, is like Jews with knowledge of Torah who do not do good deeds. The myrtle has fragrance but not fruit, like Jews who perform good deeds but have no knowledge of Torah. The willow has neither fruit nor fragrance, resembling Jews with neither knowledge of Torah nor good deeds.

Observing the Holiday

The sacred timespan of Sukkot is divided into the "full" festival days and the intermediary days (*ḥol hamo'ed*). Traditional Jewish communities outside the Land of Israel add a day to the festival days of observance in accordance with a practice of reckoning time in relation to Jerusalem. (See Appendix One for an explanation of this practice.) In this model, Sukkot has two festival days at the beginning of the holiday and five intermediary days, the last of which is called *Hoshana Raba* (for the special ritual performed that day). Reconstructionist, Reform and some Conservative communities generally follow the practice in *Eretz Yisrael*, celebrating the first day of the festival as a "full" holiday day and *Hoshana Raba* on the seventh day. Including *Hoshana Raba*, there are six *ḥol hamo'ed* days.

The first day of Sukkot, as a "full" festival day, traditionally has many of the same restrictions as Shabbat. It is a day dedicated to worship and observance of the holiday:

Regular activities are curtailed, no work is done, and communal worship is planned. The most significant distinction from traditional Shabbat observance lies in the freedom to cook food in order to celebrate the holiday. Cooking and most actions related to preparing the festival meal are permitted, while many of these actions are not traditionally permitted on Shabbat.

Communal worship is marked by liturgical additions and, of course, the rituals involving the *lulav* and *etrog*. As with any festival or holiday, special Torah and haftarah readings are prescribed. On the first day of Sukkot, in many communities that celebrate the first day as the only full festival day, we read from Deuteronomy 8:1–18 and 10:12–22, in five divisions or aliyot (seven, if the first day falls on Shabbat). Orthodox congregations read Leviticus 22:26–23. The final line of the liberal communities' first Torah reading, Deuteronomy 8:18, invokes the Sukkot theme of remembering our mythic ancestors' journey in the wilderness, and it contains a humbling reminder of the source of wealth: "Remember that it is God who gives you the power to obtain wealth, in fulfillment of the ongoing covenant that God made by oath with your ancestors."

We can bring the beauty of the harvest into our synagogues as well. Large pumpkins and gourds, Indian corn and squash add autumn's colors to our congregation's Sukkot celebration. At the end of Sukkot, we hold a raucous auction of all the *bima* decorations on Simchat Torah. Families take home large pumpkins to place on their front porches as well as Indian corn you can pop in the microwave right on the cob.
—B.P.

The *maftir* (additional) reading from Leviticus 23:39–44 contains the prescription to observe Sukkot as part of the cycle of yearly festivals.

The haftarah reading, Zechariah 14:1–21, includes a passage suggesting that in the future messianic age, all nations will celebrate Sukkot: "All survivors who are left of the nations that came against Jerusalem shall make an annual pilgrimage to worship the Monarch, the God of hosts, and to keep the Feast of Tabernacles." (Zechariah 14:16) Those who fail to do so will be punished by drought, famine and plague. Many contemporary worshipers no longer believe in supernatural reward and punishment based on our ritual observance. However, Zechariah's message underscores the centrality of Sukkot in the biblical writer's mind and offers a model in which all nations come together under one *sukkah* in order to rejoice in peace.

Historical and contemporary accounts of Islam's haj can serve as a springboard to imagining what it must have been like when tens of thousands of Israelites streamed from all corners of the Diaspora to crowd the provinces of the Temple. What planning, what effort, what excitement for those ancient pilgrims. Some remnants of these major undertakings are preserved for us in the pilgrimage psalms sung by the Levites and possibly even ordinary Israelites as they ascended toward the Temple to fulfill the commandment "to appear before your God in the place that God will choose." —D.W.

The passage we read from the prophet Zechariah is stunning and visionary. At the end of time, when this world will realize the messianic, divine ideal, *all* peoples will make the pilgrimage peacefully together, worshipping the one deity, celebrating together in temporary huts. More than two millennia old, this is a vision worth pursuing today. (Of course, the sacred pilgrimage sites would include Jerusalem, as well as others.) —J.J.S.

During the weekdays of *ḥol hamo'ed,* tradition assigns a daily Torah reading from Numbers 29:17–34. This passage details the number and types of sacrifices that were to be brought to the Temple on each day of Sukkot. As the five days of *ḥol hamo'ed* proceed, subsequent passages are read corresponding to the appropriate day of the holiday, beginning with the second day of the sacrificial service. For example, on the first day of *ḥol hamo'ed*, which is the second day of Sukkot, the sacrifices listed for the second day are read; on the second day, the sacrifices for the third day are read, and so on.

On *Shabbat ḥol hamo'ed,* the Torah reading is Exodus 33:12–34:26, which ends with the commandment to observe the three pilgrimage festivals—Sukkot, Pesach and Shavuot. The *maftir* portion from the second Torah scroll is Deuteronomy 16:13–17, which refers specifically to *Ḥag Hasukkot*, the Feast of Booths, as a joyous harvest festival. It ends with a repetition of the injunction to observe all three festivals. The haftarah reading is Ezekiel 38:18–39:16.

In addition, the Book of *Kohelet* (Ecclesiastes) is customarily read on this Shabbat. *Kohelet*, named after its narrator, (The name "*Kohelet*" translates loosely as "the

Kohelet is a canonical curiosity. The message conveyed by the author is antithetical in almost every respect to the messages found in the rest of the Hebrew Bible. *Kohelet* bluntly acknowledges that there is no obvious connection between personal moral behavior and health, wealth and prosperity. While some may find this insight to be spiritually challenging, others may be equally pleased to see that the Hebrew Bible, at least in this one book, sees the world in the same way that they do. —R.H.

community expositor.") is often thought of as the ultimate nihilist. He writes as an old man looking back at the trajectory of his long and powerful life, and he realizes that much of what he pursued was in fact an exercise in futility. His message seemingly contradicts the spirit of rejoicing in the festival. However, if we link these teachings to the passage from Deuteronomy quoted above, we can also understand it as part of the teaching of humility that goes along with Sukkot.

Although the literary style of Ecclesiastes is of a later era, traditionally the author of *Kohelet* is identified as King Solomon in his old age. The words of *Kohelet* are like the falling leaves; some words drop with sadness and cynicism. *Shir Hashirim* (Song of Songs), which is attributed to King Solomon in his youth, is read on Passover. By evoking the lifespan of one man from the vernal to the autumnal equinox, we bridge Passover and Sukkot, the first and last of the pilgrimage festivals. Spring fever and the freshness of love are juxtaposed with the hopelessness and cynicism that sometimes occur in old age. —B.P./V.M.

The reading of *Kohelet* fits well with Sukkot's theme of vulnerability. Rather than nihilism, this is an autumn awareness of the incontrovertible reality of impermanence. When we recognize the impermanence of all of the things to which we are attached, we can enjoy our blessings as we are graced by them, and we can let go of our fears and worries about losing what we have. This is conducive to joy—joy in the aliveness of this very moment, the face of this friend, the savory taste of the Sukkot soup, the feel of the cool fall air on our cheeks, the next complete breath. There need be no conflict between living joyously and recognizing that we are mortal creatures who are not in control of many of the most important things in our lives. —J.J.S./S.P.W.

The *Hallel* of Sukkot, recited with the shaking of the *lulav* and *etrog*, is an intense sensory experience. The songs, the fragrant air and the movement of the body all enliven the senses, creating a multidimensional opportunity to experience physical and spiritual joy. —E.M.T.

Another distinction of the Sukkot liturgy is the addition of the blessing for waving the *lulav* and the *Hallel* service, which are recited after the morning *Amida*. During specific verses of *Hallel*, additional shaking of the *lulav* and *etrog* provides punctuation and a chance for group participation. The *lulav* and *etrog* are shaken during the *Hallel* recitation beginning with the words *Hodu ladonay ki tov* (Give thanks to *Adonay*, who is good), again at *yomar na Yisrael ki l'olam ḥasdo* (Let Israel declare: God's lovingkindess endures forever), and finally at *Ana Adonay hoshi'a na* (We implore you, *Adonay*, save us).

The *lulav* and *etrog* are also featured at the beginning of the Torah service during the *Hoshanot*—the recitation of specific verses with the repetition of the words "*hosha na*"—"save us." After the opening *Hoshana* prayer, a

Spending time in the impermanent *sukkah* reminds us of the limitations of bricks and mortar and the dangers of becoming overly attached to physical structures. The *Hoshanot* remind us that our spiritual intentions amid those physical structures can nonetheless be transformative. The act of circling a synagogue sanctuary reminds us that our actions and prayers can impact the physical world that we live in, that our prayers and spiritual practices really do affect the world outside ourselves. —E.M.T.

The invocation "Save us!" leaves open the question, "From what?" In its biblical setting, *hosha-na* (the Hebrew root means "redeem") likely meant something like "send us salvation" in the person of an earthly king-messiah. In rabbinic Judaism, *hosha-na* might have meant "bring on the end of days and the redemption of history" and/or "confer eternal life on me." None of these allusions is likely to excite the imagination of contemporary Jews. One potential adaptation is to invite people to offer their own conclusion to the invocation "*Hosha-na*, save us from. . . ." —R.H.

The *Hoshanot* service can be very moving. Our ancestors lived in a semiarid climate and appealed to God to save them by sending the rain after a six-month dry season. As we parade around chanting "Save us, save us," we have the opportunity to acknowledge that in spite of technological advances, or perhaps because of them, we really don't know how the human species is going to survive the meteorological and environmental storms that we are facing. Recognizing our vulnerability can move us to action. —J.J.S.

procession is formed behind the person carrying the Torah, with participants carrying their *lulavim* and *etrogim* and making one circuit around the synagogue or prayer space. (See *Kol Haneshamah: Shabbat Veḥagim*, page 646, for a complete description.) Plush (or stuffed) *lulav* and *etrog* sets can be purchased or made for younger children to carry.

While these liturgical changes remain the same throughout Sukkot, on Shabbat the *lulav* and *etrog* are not generally carried or shaken. *Hallel* is said without being preceded by the *lulav* blessing, and the *Hoshanot* are recited without the *lulav* and *etrog* as well. The challenge of these prohibitions is that in many contemporary communities, the only time people gather for a Sukkot service is on Shabbat. These communities need to weigh the impact of not having a chance to wave the *lulav* and *etrog* at all against including the *lulav* and *etrog* even though

When I chant the *Hoshanot*—either as the leader of the service or in response as a member of the community—my mind is busy in an effort to engage my heart. I imagine my ancestors pleading with God and praying for direct intervention. I seek to emulate their intensity, even as I have no expectation of succeeding. I try to discern what I am asking for, and how I might act to bring this deeply held desire into fruition. —D.W.

The *Hoshanot* ritual can seem strange, foreign or even humorous. Why are we all circumambulating the synagogue chanting "Save us!" as we hold our four species? Despite its strangeness, this is a moving ritual for me because of the opportunity to acknowledge our frailty and dependence on the world around us. Circling the sanctuary also connects me to my Muslim brothers and sisters, who have sacred circling rituals around the Kaaba during haj. —N.C.M.

they are proscribed on Shabbat by talmudic law. Similar discussions may also occur around the question of whether or not to blow the shofar when Rosh Hashana falls on Shabbat.

On the last day of Sukkot, *Hoshana Raba*, (The Great *Hoshana*), the Torah reading is again taken from Numbers 29:26–34, but is divided into four aliyot. During the *hoshana* ritual, multiple Torah scrolls may be removed from the ark even though the reading is done from a single Torah scroll, and the procession is expanded to include seven circuits of the synagogue or prayer space. At the end of the last circuit, willow branches (either from the *lulav* or ones especially set aside for this ritual) are beaten five times against the floor or the back of pews or chairs. This

Because *Hoshana Raba* usually falls on a workday, this service typically starts very early in the morning. As a consequence, this intimate service is one of the often-missed gems of our tradition. It is the perfect seal to the Days of Awe, with its focus on both the lingering *t'shuva* that may be arising in our hearts and the earthy practices of Sukkot, including one last explosion of *Hoshanot* circles, *lulav* shaking and willow beating. It seems almost to protest the fact that the Torah stops short of bringing us into the Land of Israel by repeatedly invoking our connection to the land. *Hoshana Raba* is one last outward-focused and highly physical moment before we return to the cerebral project of beginning the cycle of reading Torah again.
—E.M.T.

The penitential period actually ends on *Hoshana Raba*. The time from Yom Kippur until *Hoshana Raba* gives us an additional short period to work on repairing the damaged relationships in our lives. The more intense communal energy of Sukkot can fortify us to do this challenging work. —N.C.M.

practice echoes a ritual performed since Temple times and is sometimes thought of as the beating out of any last remaining sins from the High Holy Day period. The ritual also invokes a time when sympathetic magic—in the form of beating the willows to simulate rainfall—was thought to bring about the necessary rain for abundant crops in the year ahead.

The plea for rain continues on the next day as part of the Shemini Atzeret service when a prayer for rain, *T'filat Geshem* (*Kol Haneshamah: Shabbat Vehagim*, page 330) is added during the *Amida*. From that time until Pesach, a line invoking God as the bringer of rain—*mashiv haruah umorid hagashem*—is part of the *Amida* prayer.

Community Practice

Though Sukkot is traditionally prescribed as both a home holiday and a communal one, many of us celebrate primarily in community. Many traditions have evolved

To Diaspora Jews, the timing of the start of the prayer for rain may seem random. To residents of Israel, it is natural in its close ties to shifts in the weather and to agricultural cycles. —D.W.

After the establishment of the Jewish community in the Americas, many rituals that Jews previously celebrated exclusively in the home—Yahrzeit observances, Passover Seders, eating in *sukkot*—also came to be observed in synagogue settings. —D.W.

around utilizing communal rather than individual *sukkot*, and applying the themes of Sukkot to contemporary issues.

Creating Communal Sukkot Experiences

Communal *sukkot*, erected in synagogues, community centers, schools and apartment complexes, are the perfect places for an *oneg* and/or *Kiddush* after services.

A progressive meal can be scheduled in neighborhoods where several *sukkot* are close by, with each course being served in a different *sukkah*.

During *ḥol hamo'ed,* it can be a challenge to spend time in the *sukkah*, especially if you do not have one at your

The *sukkah* is also a great place to pray. Being outside in the *sukkah* for *Kabbalat Shabbat*, *shaḥarit* or a meditation circle on a cool autumn day is a fine expression of the festival spirit. Remind everyone to dress warmly if necessary and then enjoy the pleasures of outdoor prayer. —E.M.T.

On some college campuses, both Jewish and non-Jewish students are invited to build and decorate a *sukkah* at the center of campus and then to spend several days focusing on different aspects of homelessness. —N.C.M.

One year our congregation's Green Committee used the occasion of Sukkot to begin our policy of banning plastic water bottles from the synagogue and introducing environmentally friendly water bottles with the name of the congregation on them to encourage greater consciousness of water and plastic usage within the congregation and community. —S.C.R.

Year-round, our liturgy refers to *sukkat shalom*, God's shelter of peace. Make your *sukkah* a shelter of peace, a place for bringing people together in reconciliation or for sharing a vision of justice. The vulnerability of the *sukkah* reminds us that it is essential to guard the structures of peace and justice with care and devotion. When we leave the safety of our houses to dwell in the *sukkah*, we lift up a prayer for security in troubled times. —B.P.

home. However, individuals and communities can create opportunities through programming. A midweek "pizza in the hut" potluck meal, lunchtime workshops or discussions, or a music performance are some examples. The *sukkah* can also be used as a backdrop for a social justice or *tzedaka* project focused on the environment, and the *sukkah* can be decorated with unusual recycled materials or hung with informational posters. The *sukkah* can also be used as the drop-off point for donations. These can go well beyond money or canned goods to include warm blankets, winter outerwear, and heating and insulation materials for low-income homes, to name but a few. A work team can also be organized to help winterize homes for older or infirm members of the community. Naturally, not every autumn climate is conducive to planning outdoor activities in the *sukkah*. Even though living in the *sukkah* is supposed to remind us of the fragility of our material possessions, the rabbinic sources are practical. If it is raining enough to "ruin the soup," we are permitted to go inside. Even in bad weather we are encouraged to say *Kiddush* in the *sukkah*, but after that, personal comfort should dictate how long we stay exposed to the elements.

Getting the Most from Your Etrog

Acquiring an elegant *etrog* can involve much care and effort. In order to enhance *hidur mitzvah*—increasing the beauty of the mitzvah—special methods have been created to protect and preserve this special fruit. During Sukkot, your *etrog* can be stored in a special holder. Many available for purchase at Judaica stores are made of wood or silver and beautifully decorated. To make your own, simply take the box the *etrog* came in and cover it with decorative paper, rhinestones, shells, beads or whatever strikes your fancy. Be sure to save the packing materials in which the *etrog* is nesting, as they will provide protection for the fruit throughout the holiday.

Another use for your *etrog* after the holiday has ended is to stud it with whole cloves and use it to keep your closet or room smelling sweet or as part of your *Havdala b'samim* (spices). It can also be chopped up and made into a jelly or part of a chutney relish, and it can even be fermented into a beer or liqueur.

Making the Old New Again

Because Sukkot falls just before the rainy season in Israel, it is a natural time of heightened awareness about water resources and the impact of drought. The precious balance of the environment and the human impact on it were

Given the crisis surrounding global warming, Sukkot's focus on rain could be an appropriate moment to awaken our consciousness around the interconnection of people, land (and our overuse use of carbon resources) and rain. —N.C.M.

Throughout the history of Reconstructionist liturgy, there has been a consistent effort to sever the connection of morality to meteorology, dismissing or diminishing the biblical idea that rain falls in its season in proportion to the moral comportment of the Jewish people. Given this concern, we ought to be cautious about embracing the prayer for rain without appropriate caveats about the difference between petition and poetry. —R.H.

recognized long before industrialization and the modern concerns of global warming. *Midrash Raba* quotes Rabbi Shimon bar Yochai: "'Three things are of equal weight with one another: the earth (*eretz*), humanity (*adam*) and rain (*geshem*).' Said Rabbi Levi bar Hiyata, 'And each of the three is written [in Hebrew] with three consonants, to teach you that if there is no earth, there can be no rain, and if there is no rain, there can be no earth, and if the two of them are not, then there can be no man.'" (13:3–4)

The Talmud records a ceremony performed during Sukkot in the Temple era called *simḥat bet hasho'eva*, the Rejoicing at the Place of Water-Drawing. It is described as a carnival-like event that included acrobatics, juggling of torches, flute-playing, blowing the shofar and pouring libations of water in the Court of Women in the Temple. (B. Talmud *Sukkah* 53a) Though this ritual is no longer performed, it provides an evocative model for incorporating an awareness of water resources into our contemporary Sukkot celebrations.

The environmental organization Canfei Nesharim has put together a number of resources for awareness, study and celebration of water to be used in Jewish communities, including *sukkah* decorations, family programs and adult text study. One program includes a water-tasting event (with chocolate savored in between glasses of water

The Sukkot ritual described in the Talmud likely has roots in prebiblical pagan fertility rituals meant to draw down the blessing of rains and fertility for the land.
—N.C.M.

to "cleanse the palate") along with a study session about the value of water and the need for it to be protected. Other water-themed events might include setting up a rain barrel at your synagogue or organizing a river clean-up project or a day of water awareness.

Conclusion

As a biblically prescribed festival, Sukkot has long been a significant observance in Jewish tradition. It invokes historical events, underscores the importance of the harvest to us and to our ancestors, and provides an opportunity for physical interaction with our environment. In celebrating Sukkot, we are able to affirm the values of humility and justice that were brought to the fore of our consciousness during Rosh Hashana and Yom Kippur and to connect our life experiences to those of Jews throughout history. As early as the first century, Philo of Alexandria taught the social and moral importance of this holiday:

> The last of the annual feasts, called the Feast of Tabernacles, recurs at the autumn equinox. From this we may draw two morals. The first is that we should honor equality and hate inequality, for the former is the source and fountain of justice, the latter of injustice. . . . The second moral is that after all the fruits are made perfect, it is our duty to thank God who brought them to perfection and is the source of all good things. (Special Laws 2.204)

Shemini Atzeret/Simchat Torah

BARBARA PENZNER

At the center of the circle of Jewish community stands Torah. We lovingly grasp the Torah scroll, each of us seeking a personal relationship with its teachings. Centuries before the beginning of the custom of circling the synagogue while carrying Torah scrolls, the rabbi known as Yohanan ben Bag-Bag was quoted in *Pirkey Avot*

When I grasp the Torah scroll, my love is often not for its literal words and their plain meaning, but rather for the living Torah whose meanings have evolved so magnificently over the centuries. The actual text of the Torah often does not speak to me and is frequently offensive. I dance on Simchat Torah in the faith that the texts of the Jewish people will continue to be reinterpreted to express the most sublime values of every generation. —J.J.S.

(5.26) as saying, "*Hafokh ba vehafokh ba dikhula ba*"—"Turn it over and over again, for everything is in it." He intended to encourage Torah study as a lifelong pursuit, but the image of turning also conjures up the eternal cycle of Torah reading from year to year and the celebration of Simchat Torah as an annual culmination of that cycle.

A central element of Sukkot and Simchat Torah, the circle brings people together in processions, touching hands as they dance and creating sacred space. Circles represent wholeness and completion—in Hebrew, *shlemut*, from the same root as *shalom*, peace. Processing in circles evokes the ancient notion of the "sacred circle" that forms a protective space for everyone inside. As the multiple circles of Simchat Torah form around each other, intertwine, break up and recreate themselves, they remind us of our interdependence and of the potential for peace that we create together. As we dance together in times of joy, so we embrace one another in times of sorrow.

The Torah scroll is the tangible symbol both of the ancient words inscribed in it and the generations of commentary, midrash and discussion that comprise "Torah"

"Turn it and turn it," says Pirkey Avot, "for everything is in it." Many of us struggle to maintain the faith that if we keep looking in the Torah, we will find truths that speak to us in spite of the pain the text may sometimes cause us. Simchat Torah is a time to strengthen ourselves in that endeavor and to remind ourselves of our continuing commitment. In my own understanding, Simchat Torah is a time when God makes the Torah new for all the old and new souls who will meet Torah that year. —J.H.

more broadly as "Jewish teaching." We raise the Torah to remind us of its guidance to us as a community. We read the final verses of the Torah, with their description of the Israelites preparing to enter the Promised Land, and then we move back to *B'reyshit* (Genesis) and the story of Creation. We start over again each year, understanding that the circles of our lives always give us the promise of beginning anew.

The Celebration of Simchat Torah

Shemini Atzeret and Simchat Torah mark the end of Sukkot, even though technically they are not part of the Sukkot festival; they are a separate holiday unto

The end of the Torah narrative (Deuteronomy 34:6–12) leaves us with the image of Moses' 120-year-old body buried in a dry and dusty wilderness of browns, reds and yellows; the beginning of the Torah (Genesis 1:7–31) sets us down in the blues and greens of a lush, wet world. The desiccated wilderness of Moses teems with spiritual insight, ripe for the mind's picking. The newly created world of the first chapter of Genesis teems with wild promise, its freshness tickling our noses and beckoning to our hearts. —D.K.

Professor Ari Elon taught me to notice the monumental significance of the fact that we never enter the Promised Land in the cycle of Torah readings. Just as we are about to cross the Jordan into the land, we return to Creation. The experience of Torah-reading Jews through the ages has been the perpetual reenactment of wandering, of yearning for the ideal, of waiting for the Messiah. —J.J.S.

themselves. On Shemini Atzeret, we observe the beginning of the rainy season in the Land of Israel with prayers for rain. Reflecting a somber mood, sometimes with melodies reminiscent of the High Holy Days, Shemini Atzeret is a time for lighting Yahrzeit candles for those who have died and commemorating our lost loved ones with a *Yizkor* service.

Simchat Torah departs from the solemnity of Shemini Atzeret and exceeds the measured joyfulness of Sukkot.

Does Shemini Atzeret have a place in the Hebrew school curriculum? Absolutely! Not only can we teach the children about our tradition's long-standing prayer for rain in the right season, but we can also encourage the idea of school-wide *tzedaḳa* at this season going to organizations that work to provide clean drinking water, reforestation, wetland protection, flood/drought/storm relief and other rain-dependent initiatives. —D.K.

North Americans may have difficulty imagining what it is like to live in a climate where it does not rain for six months. It's reliably sunny for tourists in Israel on summer vacation, but by October, the wadis have dried up, the cisterns are empty, and the society is completely dependent for its food supply on rain over the next six months. No matter how joyously you have just celebrated the harvest on Sukkot, the feeling looking forward is one of profound vulnerability, not unlike the feeling on Yom Kippur. —J.J.S.

What "measured joyfulness?" Isn't Sukkot also *z'man simḥatenu*? For me, Simchat Torah, at the end of the entire Tishri cycle, is the culmination of the joy of Sukkot, moving to greater and greater joy out of the solemnity of the High Holy Days of Rosh Hashana and Yom Kippur. After all, in metaphorical terms, if we have done the work of Yom Kippur, if we have done *t'shuva*, reset our intentions and corrected our failings, if we have made up to those we have hurt and apologized for what we did not change and we are still here, we must have been successful. We are new, clean, forgiven. We are basking in God's renewed love for us and our renewed commitment to God. We have lots to celebrate! —E.W.

On Simchat Torah, the community reads together the ending and beginning passages of the Torah in the annual cycle, and celebrates by singing and dancing with the Torah scroll(s). Although ecstatic dancing on Simchat Torah is most often associated with Hasidic influence, such celebratory disorder has been associated with the festival in other times and places as well. The joy is not inebriated chaos, as on Purim, but rather a structured opportunity for embracing our most basic values and rejoicing in community.

Coming at the end of the many holidays in the month of Tishri, a month devoted to reflection and contemplation, Simchat Torah brings Jews together in large numbers one more time during the month with a kind of ritual of release. Energy may have faded since the crowds of Rosh Hashana and Yom Kippur have dispersed, but Simchat Torah brings Jews back together. As we prepare to return

I've thought a bit about "mandatory joy" over the years. In my experience, people often find it natural and unremarkable to enter a state of ritual sorrow when called on to do so, whether at a shiva minyan or on *Tisha B'Av*. But ritualized joy is harder to accomplish. On Simchat Torah, I find that ambivalence about Torah, feelings of inauthenticity (for example, we are not those Hasidim for whom ecstatic dancing comes so naturally), and shyness all bubble up. At least mine do. —M.H.

to the weekday routine and the simple regularity of Shabbat observance, we sense that our repentance and recommitment to Jewish life have been effective, and we acknowledge the power of Torah as our guide in everyday life.

Origins of the Holiday

Unlike the major holidays of Pesach, Sukkot, Shavuot, Rosh Hashana and Yom Kippur, Simchat Torah is not a biblically mandated festival. After the seven-day observance of Sukkot, the Torah mandates a final day of celebration called "Shemini Atzeret," meaning "the Eighth Day of Gathering." The holiday may appear to be the last

I never really "got" starting the Torah-reading cycle here, instead of, say, at Rosh Hashana or Shavuot, until I understood that with all of the preparatory spiritual work for entering a new year finally accomplished comes the opportunity to start anew. —M.H.

Those who observe all of the Jewish holidays often experience fatigue by the end of Sukkot. The difficulty of keeping up with one's work responsibilities is formidable, given all the days of holiday preparation and observance. Hosting meals in the *sukkah*, and even being hosted by others in their *sukkot*, is wonderful but potentially exhausting. The Simchat Torah celebrations can thus sometimes also be about the anticipated relief of the upcoming month of Heshvan, in which there are no holidays! —J.J.S.

day of the Sukkot holiday, but Shemini Atzeret has its own rituals that are distinct from those of Sukkot. For example, one is no longer expected to eat in the *sukkah* on Shemini Atzeret. Centuries after the creation of the Torah, and after holidays began to be observed for an extra day outside of the Land of Israel, Simchat Torah became the Diaspora's additional day of Shemini Atzeret. The unique rituals of Simchat Torah arose in the Middle Ages because of the historical designation of Simchat Torah as the day that ends and begins the Torah reading. Unlike the additional days of Pesach and Shavuot, Simchat Torah is the one "second-day" festival in the annual cycle that has acquired a tone, liturgy and rituals considerably different from the prior day.

Yom tov literally means "good day" in Hebrew, but it is normally used to mean "holiday"; in Yiddish, the

The Hasidic teacher Rabbi Noach of Lechowitz notes the contrast between the seven days of Sukkot, filled with beautiful rituals and adornments such as the *sukkah*, *lulav* and *etrog*, and the festival of Shemini Atzeret. He compares this to the difference between a wedding ceremony and the first time the newlyweds are alone together. At the wedding, the participants are dressed in their finest clothing; there is ritual and excitement, music and dancing. When the newlyweds are finally alone, they need none of these accoutrements—in fact, they would just get in the way. All of these distractions are discarded, and the newly married couple is left in a pure state of connection and intimacy. So too with God. On Shemini Atzeret, we do not need the vast profusion of ritual objects, of the symbols that we employ on Sukkot; rather we quietly rejoice in the feeling of deep connectedness that comes from standing in God's presence. —J.W.

phrase is pronounced "*Yontef*." How did the observance of the second day of a *yom tov* (*yom tov sheni*—for a full explanation, see the appendix) lead to the expansion of Simchat Torah as a distinctive holiday? On Pesach, Shavuot and Sukkot, the liturgy and rituals for the first day (and on Pesach, the last day) are repeated on *yom tov sheni*, with some minor alterations, such as different Torah readings. The festival of Shemini Atzeret presumably once shared its central rituals with its own second day. The Talmud (B.Talmud *Megila* 31a) notes that on the second day of Shemini Atzeret, the designated Torah reading was to be Deuteronomy 33–34, the final chapters of the Torah. At that time, the reading of *B'reyshit*, Genesis, was scheduled only on the following Shabbat, rather than also on the festival, as is our current practice. Not until later, when there was agreement that the reading of the entire cycle of the Torah should end and begin on the same day, did Simchat Torah begin to develop its own identity.

Development of the Cycle of Torah Readings

Prior to the ninth century of the Common Era, *Eretz Yisrael* and Babylonia developed different divisions for the weekly reading of the Torah. In Babylonia, the Torah was read in 54 *parashiyot* (divisions) every year. In *Eretz Yisrael*, the Torah was divided into more than 150 *sidrot* (sections; the exact number is uncertain), read consecutively over three years in a triennial cycle. Based on a reference in *Seder Rav Amram Gaon*, the earliest known version of the Jewish prayer book, we know that by the ninth century most communities followed the same annual cycle of Torah readings, although some communities continued the triennial practice.

The 11th-century *Maḥzor Vitri*, one of the earliest Ashkenazic prayer books, includes a special liturgy for Simchat Torah. By the 14th century, Simchat Torah had been accepted as a festival celebrating the ending and beginning of the Torah-reading cycle, even as it continued to include some of the Shemini Atzeret liturgy. Today, the holiday is observed by Sephardic Jews as well. Along with the *hakafot* (the parading of Torah scrolls in circles around the synagogue), the custom of reading the Torah at night (which was not a tradition at any other time of year) was established, thereby creating the observance of Simchat Torah that we know today.

In Israel and some other communities, Shemini Atzeret and Simchat Torah are celebrated together following the

I live in a rural area in California, where rain is often scarce, and where, in years of drought, our wells literally run dry. So praying for rain is an important part of our communal life. Since we're not the type of community to have a minyan for three separate holidays in a row, we've conflated the holidays a bit: We gather at sundown at the end of Shemini Atzeret and the beginning of Simchat Torah. First we go outside and beat willow branches on the ground as on *Hoshana Raba* (also pouring a big bowl of water on the ground, remembering *simḥat bet hasho'eva*, when vast quantities of water were poured over the altar in the Temple.) And we recite *T'filat Geshem*, also outside under the night sky. Then we go inside for Simchat Torah. The juxtaposition at that moment of our community's vulnerability and our joy is lovely.

—M.H.

seventh day of Sukkot. Other communities maintain the two days separately. For most liberal Jewish communities, the main event of Simchat Torah takes place during the evening service. In some of the congregations where Shemini Atzeret and Simchat Torah are observed on the same day, the different moods and liturgies are separated out between the morning observance (Shemini Atzeret) and the evening celebration (Simchat Torah). In others, the first part of the morning has the mood of Shemini Atzeret, while the Torah service reflects a more joyous mood. See the section "Communal Observance" for a description of the customs specifically related to Simchat Torah.

Torah as Central to Jewish Life

What Makes Torah Holy?

In Reconstructionist and other liberal settings, our conception of Torah is often colored by the question of its origins. If we do not believe that the Torah scroll from which we read each week comes from God's mouth to Moses' hand, then what makes it so special? How can we call

Reconstructionists can affirm Torah as holy because we connect to it as a source of meaning and wisdom in our lives, just as all the previous generations of Jews have done before us. In inviting Torah into our lives and locating our own lives within Torah, we connect as well to these earlier generations of Jews and their desire to understand what God expected of them. This connection, too, joining past, present and future, is one of the circles of Simchat Torah. —J.W.

Torah "holy"? Rabbi Mordecai Kaplan once said we affirm "that the Torah reveals God, not that God revealed the Torah." (*Future of the American Jew*, page 382) This thinking opens up possibilities for wrestling with the text, for taking the text seriously but not literally, rather than accepting every word literally or uncritically. Even as some may find certain sections of the Torah difficult to reconcile with modern sensibilities, we seek out those aspects of Torah that lead us to the divine. In our ongoing conversation with Torah, through commentaries from the ancient to the contemporary, we may come to an appreciation of the gift of Torah as a whole while otherwise wrestling with its parts.

There is always the danger of crossing the line from celebrating Torah to idolizing it. The Torah scroll itself, while approached with dignity and reverence, is not divine. It is the vehicle for our engagement with divine revelation—that is, moral guidance, ancient insight and the sacred story that shapes the Jewish people. As Kaplan has said, "The Bible is

For many years, our community's only sefer Torah was a scroll from the Westminster Synagogue's Memorial Scrolls Trust in London—a Holocaust survivor. Even though relatively few people were present when it was opened and read every Shabbat, in our whole community there was a special tenderness for the scroll itself and for all it had experienced. This was not idolatry, but something a bit more embodied than simply a relationship with the moral guidance, ancient insight and sacred story rendered by its content. —M.H.

Torah has often been seen as feminine, thus adding an erotic dimension to male Jews' embrace of the scroll. —D.D.M.

the earliest diary of the Jewish people." When we rise for the Torah, turn to face it or even kiss it, we express the same reverence one might show to a sage. It is possible for people to relate to the Torah with love and with reverence for it as an important Jewish symbol, regardless of the reaction one may have to specific passages.

Kaplan also compared the Torah to the U.S. Constitution. While we may add amendments to the Constitution, we do not actually change the original document. Likewise with Torah: While generations of Jews have interpreted the text, sometimes in radically different ways, we still preserve the original as the basis for Jewish life and learning. In this way "the Torah" is only one aspect of "Torah," the collective wisdom of the Jewish people. It is Torah in both the narrow and the broad sense that we celebrate and appreciate on Simchat Torah.

The Value of Torah Study and the Joy of Torah

The tradition on Simchat Torah of encouraging every member of the community to carry a Torah scroll or to be honored with an aliyah reflects the Reconstructionist values of inclusion and egalitarianism. Simchat Torah reminds us that the Torah "is not in heaven," (Deuteron-

Our community permits non-Jews to both dance with the Torah and come up to the Torah as part of a group (which includes Jews) for an aliyah on this day alone. On Simchat Torah, we celebrate our continuing and evolving relationship to Torah. Of course that relationship deepens over time. A number of non-Jewish members of our community, having been committed bystanders up until this point, have decided to pursue conversion in earnest after experiencing the opportunity to dance with and offer a blessing for the Torah on this one day. —E.W.

omy 30:12) and that throughout the year, everyone can learn, everyone can find meaning in Torah in the broadest sense. For Jews, lifelong Torah study demonstrates the unique ability of human beings to learn and grow; it reminds us of the wisdom we can tap from the lives and lessons of our ancestors. Likewise, Torah study is an open-ended activity. The rabbinic tradition introduced this proto-democratic notion into a culture that had been based in the dynastic elitism of both kings and priests. Torah study based on questioning and arguing over the text is available to all.

Whatever one's beliefs about the divine origins of Torah or its historical provenance, the joy of Simchat Torah needs no reinterpretation. The celebration of Torah as the constitution of the Jewish people (as Kaplan described it), as the source of abiding values, as the communal narrative of the Jewish people, or even as the basis for our reverence for learning and reflection, allows us to participate fully with our hearts and minds.

If we are to maintain the tradition of questioning and arguing over the text, then we must teach our children how to do these things. As education director and rabbi to my congregation, I find it at least as important as teaching young students to decode and/or rote-learn basic prayers in Hebrew. I now show our third to sixth-graders the animated film "Rashi: A Light After the Dark Ages" at the beginning of every school year. In the curriculum that I designed for our elementary grades, I included a number of text-based arguments framed as a give-and-take between Rashi (voiced by Leonard Nimoy of "Star Trek" in the film!) and his little grandson Ya'akov, who later became the famous commentator known as Rabbenu Tam. Arguing *l'shem shamayim* (literally, "for the sake of heaven"—for the advancement of knowledge) can then be seen as useful, playful and respectful all at once. —D.K.

Simchat Torah as Distinct from Shavuot

The role of Torah during Simchat Torah differs dramatically from that during Shavuot, the other annual festival with Torah at its center. On Shavuot, the high point of the synagogue service is the reading from the scroll of the revelation at Sinai and the Decalogue. (Exodus 19:1–20:23) Lacking time-honored home rituals like those of the Pesach Seder or the *sukkah*, Shavuot is celebrated through study and learning. But on Simchat Torah, it is neither the essence of Torah nor its meanings that we seek. Simchat Torah is a thanksgiving parade, in gratitude for having completed the year that has passed, and in hope for the year to come; it shares the theme of thanksgiving with Sukkot. Shavuot celebrates a one-time revelation; Simchat Torah celebrates the weekly interchange with revelation as we move through the annual cycle of Torah readings. Shavuot lifts us to contemplate the mystical and philosophical; Simchat Torah lifts us physically and emotionally as we rejoice with the Torah.

Celebrating at Home

Although Simchat Torah is most closely associated with synagogue rituals, the holiday has home rituals as well: giving *tzedaka*, candle lighting, and reciting the *Kiddush* and the *motzi* over two hallahs. One might be tempted to celebrate in the *sukkah* one last time, but Shemini Atzeret and Simchat Torah are designated as festivals separate from Sukkot. To mark the distinction, it is customary to eat inside the home, although some may still make *Kiddush* in the *sukkah*. The *Sheheḥeyanu*, the blessing of thanksgiving for having reached this moment, is recited on the evening of the holiday as well. In home rituals, Shemini Atzeret and Simchat Torah, observed separately or together, share identical liturgy. When chanting both the *Kiddush* and the *Birkat Hamazon* (the Grace after Meals), we acknowledge the holiday explicitly as *yom hash'mini ḥag ha'atzeret hazeh* (the eighth day of festivity) and *z'man simḥatenu* (time of our happiness).

In the traditional Diaspora reckoning according to the Talmud, when Simchat Torah falls on the ninth day after the beginning of Sukkot, it never falls on Shabbat. It may frequently occur on a Saturday night, providing an opportunity to add *Havdala* to the home and synagogue rituals. (See *Kol Haneshamah: Shabbat Vehagim*, page 629.) However, in Israel and those Diaspora communities where Simchat Torah and Shemini Atzeret are observed on one day, the combined holiday often falls on Shabbat. When welcoming the Sabbath, we include the Shabbat

How can you have one more meal in your *sukkah*? You've just prayed for rain! Perhaps your *sukkah* is now drenched. I'll never forget a Simchat Torah in Jerusalem many years ago when we brought our seventh *hakafa* out of the *shul* doors into the courtyard, only to be greeted by a clap of thunder and the first raindrops of the new year. What could be better? —M.H.

additions to the festival candle lighting and the *Kiddush*. (See *Kol Haneshamah: Shabbat Vehagim*, pages 531, 627.)

Celebrations at home are an ideal time to reflect on the blessings of Torah and learning during the past year, and to share ideas for Torah study in the year to come. Families may bring the joy of the celebration into the home with holiday decorations or special foods. When Simchat Torah has concluded, the time comes to take the *sukkah* down. This marks the end of all the Tishri holidays, so it would also be appropriate to put away the holiday cards that may be on display. Some families save the cards to decorate the *sukkah* in the year to come, carrying forward the joy in a circle from one year to the next.

Communal Observance

The Evening Service and Hakafot

Throughout history, different Jewish communities have greeted Simchat Torah with a range of responses from reserved decorum to ebullient ecstasy. Some congregations are packed on Simchat Torah; many Torah scrolls are brought into the congregation, and the dancing spills out into the street. In others, one Torah scroll is lovingly shared in a quieter atmosphere. The key theme of the cel-

What are the narratives that are central to your family? What are the stories your family wishes to carry forward and retell year after year? —J.W.

ebration is found in circles: the cycle of the year, the cycle of Torah, the circle of community. The circles of Sukkot, with processions with *lulav* and *etrog* encircling the congregation, are transformed into processions with the Torah scroll. As we read from the Torah on that night, we close the cycle of Torah readings by completing the reading of Deuteronomy. Some congregations begin Genesis once again that evening; others wait until the morning. Communities often honor those who are recognized as representing the Torah values they hold dear: teachers and students, and those who honor Torah and the congregation. In some congregations, a specific category of "Torah people" may be invited to carry the Torah scroll(s). The circles of Sukkot culminate on Simchat Torah with circles of community around Torah and with continuing the cycle of reading and study.

Some congregations begin the evening service with flag-making, family programs or activities that sum up the 54 Torah portions of the year, to give participants a full sense of the meaning of "completing the Torah." Such activities may include finding a key verse for each Torah portion, acting out a portion, or making up a one-liner (like a headline) to sum a portion up. The room may be divided into five spaces, one for each book of the Torah, so that participants can stand in the place of one book that describes them or that represents a characteristic that they want to attain. Or participants may be given texts about Torah and encouraged to discuss their own personal relationship to Torah. At some point during the celebration, some congregations may challenge those present to make a commitment to Torah for the coming year. This may take the form of participating in a *parashat hashavua* weekly study group; or of committing to regular attendance at Shabbat services, or to increased study or teaching, or reading from the Torah, portion by portion, at the Friday night Shabbat table or on one's own; or to learning to chant Torah or haftarah.

In some congregations, a note of levity is introduced into the *ma'ariv* (evening) service. Some follow the custom of chanting distinctive melodies for the prayers, including melodies from other holidays or popular songs. Some congregations bring in bands or other instrumental accompaniment to enliven the celebration.

After the standard evening *Amida* prayer for festivals, the liturgy turns to the ritual for removing the Torah scroll(s) from the ark. Instead of the usual Torah service, a composition of biblical verses known as "*Ata Horeta*" ("You have proclaimed") sets the stage. (See *Kol Haneshamah: Shabbat Vehagim*, pages 655–657.) Congregations often invite members to read or chant these verses, which are customarily repeated, one at a time, by the congregation. Other congregations open this part of the service with traditional Jewish or Israeli songs. During the chanting or singing, the ark is opened, and the Torah scroll(s) are ceremoniously removed from the ark as the time comes for the *hakafot*.

Seven *hakafot* take place on Simchat Torah evening and in the morning service. Traditionally, each *hakafa* begins with a few lines of the alphabetical liturgical poem, *Ana Adonay Hoshi'a na* (We pray, God redeem us now!), with the leader chanting each verse and the congregation joining in with, "*Hoshia na*" (see *Kol Haneshamah: Shabbat Vehagim*, pages 659ff). Congregation members carry the Torah scroll(s) in procession, circling the congregation once, followed by singing and dancing by the whole congregation.

Many congregations announce themes for each of the *hakafot* and offer the honor of carrying a Torah to a specific group (such as educators, people who have completed degrees or educational programs, people who have converted to Judaism, board members, students of a particular class, new members and, always, people who have never before held a Torah) for each *hakafa*. Different *hakafot* can be used to direct attention to an agenda for the coming year: a *hakafa* dedicated to peace, or to increased learning, or to justice, or to Israel.

The Torah scroll may be carried by the same person throughout a *hakafa* or it may be shared with others, depending on how heavy it is, how long it has been carried, and how many opportunities to carry a scroll are being offered. Everyone who can is encouraged to carry a scroll at some point. It is a great honor and, for those who have never held a scroll, it can be an indescribably moving experience. Many women, in particular, were never given access to a Torah scroll when they were children. Passing the Torah to someone who yearns to embrace it can be as meaningful as carrying it.

During the *hakafot*, ask to dance with a Torah. Let your dance be a reflection of the new wisdom you want to receive in the coming year. —L.H.L.

Those who are not carrying a Torah scroll join in the procession and celebration. Children often carry Torah flags in the procession. In some congregations, children under bar/bat mitzvah age do not carry a full-size Torah, but they may be given Torah ornaments, or miniature or toy Torahs, or *tzedaka* boxes to carry in the procession.

The service leader should be aware of the time and responsive to the energy in the room. Different *hakafot* can last for different lengths of time. A series of fast songs and lively dances may be followed by a set of slower melodies. While some people will not be physically able to dance or even to stand for the entire time, they should be welcomed to hold a Torah and to participate joyfully in their own way. For individuals who cannot stand easily or remain standing, the leader may give permission for them to sit during a *hakafa*, even though tradition calls upon us to stand in the presence of a Torah scroll. The leader should be attentive to who is included and who is not, and respond when people tire or drift away.

In some congregations, the *hakafot* take place after the reading of the Torah or even after concluding prayers, such as the *Aleynu* and the Mourner's Kaddish. In this way, the *hakafot* may continue on into the evening, beyond the time when some congregants can keep up with the festivities.

It is helpful to have a prepared song sheet to hand out if the hope is to involve the whole congregation in singing. —N.H.M.

Recalling the massive celebrations of Soviet Jews on Simchat Torah in the 1970s, many congregations have adopted the custom of taking a *hakafa* out of the building and into the night. The sight of Soviet Jews—who were secretive about their heritage and both fearful and reluctant to practice Judaism in public—courageously dancing in throngs on Simchat Torah night in full view of the Communist authorities inspired many Jews in North America to proudly take their Judaism to the streets as well. Undoubtedly, many Jews dancing in the street on Simchat Torah today have never experienced anti-Jewish feeling and have no memories of the Soviet Jewry movement. Their unself-conscious joy and comfort in singing Hebrew songs publicly is itself momentous and worthy of celebration.

In every age, different customs for this holiday have brought good humor and fun to the observance. Some may recall the old custom (called "*shnoderen*" in Yiddish) of auctioning off the honors (aliyot) of being called to the Torah on Simchat Torah. While this may not appeal to many congregations, it can be very entertaining and add to the joyful mood of the night if presented in a spirit of fun. The proceeds can be dedicated to *tzedaka*. Those who "buy" an aliyah often give it away to someone whom they want to honor. The basic intent, as always, is to rejoice in the spirit of the community's embrace of Torah and its values.

A Simchat Torah highlight for many congregations is the recently adopted custom of unrolling an entire Torah scroll, which is then held in a large circle by the participants, often encompassing the entire synagogue space. This is an awesome sight for those who have never viewed a Torah scroll from end to end, and many people look forward to this event on Simchat Torah. This requires enough individuals to hold the scroll without letting it fall, droop or pull at the seams. Individuals can stand behind the scroll, holding the top and bottom of the parchment, avoiding touching the ink. People may be encouraged to stand near their bar/bat mitzvah portions (past or future).

While the Torah is open, the rabbi or another Torah reader might walk from *B'reyshit* (Genesis) to *D'varim* (Deuteronomy), pointing out key passages, telling people which section they are holding, or choosing a verse for each person as their own verse for the coming year. In some congregations, the final passages of *D'varim* and even the opening passages of *B'reyshit* are read while the

Be careful! Unrolling the whole Torah scroll is not as easy as it sounds. Enough people must be present to support the scroll in its entirety with only a foot or so between each person. In our community, we ask people to hold the scroll using a tallit, in order to protect the parchment from the oil on our skin. Our space is large enough for us to unroll the entire scroll in one large circle, with the adults on the outside holding it, and the children of the community and me on the inside. We walk around the circle, from the opening word *B'reyshit* to the concluding words of *D'varim* and end up exactly back at *B'reyshit* again. It is quite something to see the two *atzey ḥayim* (holders) next to each other, but at their respective ends. This is a powerful physical experience of the cycle of Torah readings we are celebrating at this time. —E.W.

Another open-scroll activity is to have a scavenger hunt: We have the adults holding the Torah with the children on the inside of the circle. They are then encouraged to find visual clues in the text, such as the break between books. —N.H.M.

scroll is open and held vertically. This event brings everyone in contact with Torah, not only physically, but through finding a personal connection to a teaching of Torah. The sight of the entire community holding the Torah in a continuous circle makes tangible the verse, "*Etz ḥayim hi lamaḥazikim ba*"—"It is a tree of life to those who hold onto it."

Some congregations follow a custom on Simchat Torah of honoring the youngest students who are beginning their Jewish education. There are several ceremonies, including consecration, an aliyah for *kol han'arim* ("all the children"—see below in the section describing the morning service), and giving the children miniature Torah scrolls of their own. Bringing children into the synagogue to witness the joy of the adults and the love for Torah in the community can send a powerful message that Jewish education is a lifelong pursuit that should be approached with enthusiasm and unrestricted happiness.

The evening service ends when the last Torah scroll is lifted and then returned to the ark and the *Aleynu* and the Mourner's Kaddish are recited. In some congregations,

All of our Hebrew school students receive their books for the year on the evening of Simchat Torah under a *ḥupa*, in this case a large tallit held aloft by a rotating group of four adults. I invite each family to join me one by one under the *ḥupa*; they're escorted there by a tune from our in-house klezmer band. After quietly sharing a blessing intended for each family alone, I hand that family's children their books wrapped like a gift in fancy, wire-enhanced ribbon, topped with an Israeli chocolate bar or other Israeli sweet. —D.K.

the celebration may then go on into the night, with klezmer music, dancing, food and refreshments. Ideally, people will leave the celebration with a feeling of joy, and also a sense of personal connection to Torah in its broadest sense, as our people's ancient wellspring of learning, insight and direction.

The Morning Service and Torah Reading

In both the Shemini Atzeret and Simchat Torah morning services, *Hallel*, the series of psalms of praise for all holidays, is included. For Shemini Atzeret, it is customary to recite *Yizkor*, the memorial service, as well as *geshem*, a prayer for rain (for the Land of Israel). When both days are observed together, these additions combine to create a varied emotional terrain.

The Ashkenazic version of *T'filat Geshem* is a poignant liturgical poem composed by the classical liturgist Eleazar Kallir that makes use of biblical verses to plead for God's mercy in an appeal for rain in the coming season. The Sephardic version appears in *Kol Haneshamah,* thereby avoiding a listing of biblical miracles. While Reconstructionists may feel uncomfortable with aspects of the prayer and its assumption that God will withhold or provide rain according to our merit, it also contains deep spiritual lessons on which we can still draw today. In praying for rain for their crops, the ancient Israelites articulated their lack of control over this precious resource on which they depended for their very sustenance and livelihood. In our time, we often feel in control of our own destinies, but we too are subject to vast, unknowable forces. An accident, an illness, a terrorist attack, a natural disaster—these can forever alter the course of our lives. *T'filat Geshem* is an invitation to reflect upon our own powerlessness and continued dependence on God. —J.W.

When the two holidays are observed separately, the Torah reading designated for Shemini Atzeret is Deuteronomy 14:22–16:17, and the haftarah is I Kings 8:54–66. The Torah service on Simchat Torah morning follows the same procedure as the night before, beginning with *Ata Horeta* and continuing with the seven *hakafot*. Often, the morning *hakafot* of Simchat Torah tend to be less boisterous and less prolonged than those in the evening service. The procedures described below for the Torah reading may also be used in the evening service.

Much of the service is customarily devoted to reading from the Torah. Simchat Torah is one of the few days of the year with three traditional Torah readings: the end of *D'varim* (Deuteronomy 33:1–34:12), the beginning of *B'reyshit* (Genesis 1:1–2:3), and the *maftir* reading (Numbers 29:35–30:1), which is an additional reading for festivals that recounts the sacrificial offerings and therefore is not generally read in Reconstructionist congregations. The first reading comes from the final portion of the Torah, *V'zot Hab'rakha*. This is the only portion of the

The other days with three traditional Torah readings occur when Shabbat Hanuka coincides with *Rosh Ḥodesh*, and when *Shabbat Sh'ḳalim* (one of the four special *Shabbatot* prior to Passover) coincides with *Rosh Ḥodesh*. The regular Shabbat reading, the one for *Rosh Ḥodesh*, and the special readings each come from a different part of the Torah. —B.P.

Torah that is not read on a Shabbat. It recounts Moses' blessing to the twelve tribes of Israel before he ascends Mount Nebo to die. The story of Moses' death and the mourning of the Children of Israel is very moving, and it connects fittingly to the *Yizkor* service. The rabbis undoubtedly considered this an appropriate close to the holiday season, sending people home with blessings in their ears.

Just as on Simchat Torah night everyone is encouraged to hold the Torah, one goal on Simchat Torah morning is for everyone to have an aliyah. The first aliyot are usually offered to everyone in the congregation, either as individuals or in groups. One practice in large congregations is to set up several stations for reading these portions of the Torah. The verses can be repeated again and again until everyone has had an opportunity to recite the blessings. Alternately, the leader can invite particular groups for each aliyah (from the most mundane to the most creative categories), urging everyone to find their way to the *bima* for an honor. This is often a prime opportunity for adults who have never had an aliyah and who may be anxious about saying the blessings on their own to join a group in a joyous and nonstressful first time.

By ending with the death of Moses rather than the entry into the Promised Land, the Torah also invites us to consider the work of redemption that remains unfinished in the world. The story intentionally concludes before God's promise is fulfilled because it is not yet fulfilled in our lives: So long as there is poverty, hatred and suffering, the world is not yet redeemed. The incomplete story propels us back to the beginning of the Torah and the ongoing work of creating the world as it should be.
—J.W.

"Everyone" includes those who have not yet reached the age of bar/bat mitzvah. The tradition of *kol han'arim*, (all the children) is to call up all the children for one of the aliyot. They stand together under one or more large tallitot held aloft by adults, as one adult leads them in the Torah blessings. In some congregations, this aliya is followed by a shower of candy on the children, encouraging an association of Torah with sweetness.

The honors of coming to the Torah for the readings of the very last verses of *D'varim* and very first verses of *B'reyshit* are traditionally offered to individuals who embody the values of Torah and a commitment to lifelong learning. These two aliyot are usually considered great honors. The one who is called for the final reading from *D'varim* is known as *ḥatan* Torah (groom of the Torah) or *kalat Torah* (bride of the Torah). The one honored with being called for the first reading of *B'reyshit* is called *ḥatan B'reyshit* (groom of Genesis) or *kalat B'reyshit* (bride of Genesis), and receives the same recognition as the one honored with the last aliyah of the Torah.

Each community makes choices about inviting non-Jews to participate. "Everyone" may include non-Jews in some congregations and not in others. —B.P.

I've always been uncomfortable with the atavistic tendency of this practice, which suggests that the Torah is a "spouse" that a particularly righteous person "marries" through a devotional ritual. Simulating the marriage canopy is also automatically privileging a specific type of relationship and can be off-putting to non-partnered or unmarried congregants who are often very aware of this as a Jewish-congregational-life bias. —N.H.M.

Throughout the year, a particular reverence is associated with certain Torah readings, such as the Decalogue (the Ten Commandments) or the Exodus poem "The Song at the Sea." The most prominent readings are the ending and beginning of the Torah, and those who stand up for these readings represent deep dedication to Torah study and living Torah. In this way, one may envision these individuals as metaphorically "married" to Torah.

In the times when women were not called up to the Torah and marriage was always understood to join a man and a woman, the one called up to the Torah was called a *ḥatan* (bridegroom) of the "female" Torah. In Reconstructionist settings, both men and women are called up, and the recognition of same-sex orientations opens our eyes to alternative interpretations of this "marriage." Some congregations create a mock wedding atmosphere for these aliyot, even holding a *ḥupa* (marriage canopy) over the honorees and singing for them.

Traditionally, those honored as *ḥatan* or *kalat Torah* are called up for the aliyah with a unique and lengthy introduction. It invokes divine blessing, that "through this honor, may you be considered worthy in the eyes of our exalted God to see the next generation, and the one that follows after it, being occupied with Torah." (See *Kol Haneshamah: Shabbat Vehagim*, page 669.) As we conclude the reading of the Torah with these final verses, we pray for the continuity of our people—that as we end one year and begin another, so the Jewish people will continue from one generation to the next and the next. When this last aliyah is completed, the congregation shouts,

"*Ḥazak ḥazak venit'ḥazek*" ("Be strong, be strong, and we shall strengthen one another"), the refrain recited upon the completion of each book of the Torah.

As the first scroll, rolled to the end of the Torah, is lifted, the second scroll, rolled to the beginning of the Torah, is placed on the table, ready for the next reading. If a congregation does not have two Torah scrolls and cannot arrange to borrow an extra scroll for the holiday, the single scroll must be rolled back to the beginning. Because this can be time-consuming, the leader should be prepared with songs and/or other activities to keep everyone focused. Another option might be to read from a *ḥumash* (book containing the Torah text) or *tikun* (Hebrew text of the Torah readings) for the final reading from *D'varim*, and to use the prepared Torah scroll just for the reading from *B'reyshit*.

One year at Simchat Torah, our community had a shocking experience. It was a year of great tension in Israel and Palestine, and also a year of interpersonal strife in our local Jewish community. As we were rolling our fragile, warped Holocaust-survivor Torah scroll back to the beginning, the people at the two ends of the table tugged a little too hard and, with a loud snap, the scroll tore in half at a seam. The tear occurred right in the middle of *Vayera*, in the exact place that recounts the split between Sarah and Hagar. Now, many years later, there has been a great deal of healing in our community. And this year's rolling of the *sefer Torah* was done joyously and gently, with children and adults arrayed along the table, watching the text roll by backward, many with *yadot* (Torah pointers) in their hands, excitedly calling out and pointing as they recognized portions, words and letters. It was as sweet and affirming a moment as life can offer. It had been an even more fractured year in and around Israel. May our small experience portend a bit of healing there as well. —M.H.

You can read the end of *D'varim* and then the start of *B'reyshit* from the same scroll if it is unrolled around the room. —E.W.

The liturgical introduction to the honor of the first aliyah offers praises, saying that this person has "a heart ready to give interpretation, a spirit of justice and loving kindness, one who follows in the path of honesty. Since you are chosen as the first in fulfillment of this commandment, how fortunate you are, how great is your reward!" (See *Kol Haneshamah: Shabbat Vehagim*, page 671.) The values that we bring to Torah shape our interpretations and our actions. By calling up an exemplary individual to receive this honor, we demonstrate our community's commitment to living and teaching these values.

The reading from *B'reyshit* in the second scroll follows the account of the six days of Creation and the first Shabbat. Although it is usually chanted in its entirety as one aliyah, the reader customarily stops at the end of each day of Creation. The congregation chants, "*Vay'hi erev vay'hi voker, yom* . . ." ("It was evening, it was morning, the. . . . Day"), and then the Torah reader repeats the verse. The congregation is also invited to chant the entire section describing Shabbat (Genesis 2:1–3), followed by the reader. In this way, every member of the community not only participates in reading Torah, but also symbolically takes a role in Creation itself.

Some practice a special custom for lifting the second scroll. The *magbia* (one called to lift the Torah) crosses his or her arms, grasping the right handle with the left hand, and the left handle with the right. As the Torah is lifted, the hands come uncrossed, and the text on the parchment faces outward for all to see. This is a dramatic way of inaugurating the new Torah cycle. It also helps right-handed lifters, since the entire scroll is rolled onto the left handle. —B.P.

In congregations that do not often include the haftarah on Shabbat or holidays, it would be worthwhile to include it on Simchat Torah, in Hebrew or English. As early as talmudic times, the first chapter of the book of Joshua (1:1–18) was designated as the reading for the second day of Shemini Atzeret. The Book of Joshua is the first biblical book in the second section of the Hebrew Bible known as *Nevi'im*, or Prophets. It follows directly after Deuteronomy and picks up the story as Joshua leads the people into the land following Moses' death. The tradition of finishing the Torah on Simchat Torah may have been adopted intentionally to connect the ending of the story of Moses and the Israelites with this next chapter in the history of the people of Israel in the Land of Israel. Although the cycle of Torah continues by going back to the beginning, this haftarah permits us to glimpse for a brief moment the Israelites reaching their long-sought-after destination.

Conclusion

The final service on Simchat Torah may generate a wave of last-minute exuberance, and it may also leave a tinge of sadness as the heightened emotions of the Tishri holidays come to a close. At the end of Sukkot and Shemini Atzeret in ancient times, visitors who had brought sacrifices to the Temple in Jerusalem returned to their homes as the rainy winter season began. Talmudic rabbis discussed the need to rush home before the roads became too muddy for travel. In our day, we need to consider what emotions and lessons we want to take back with us to our routine lives. Having spent many hours in the synagogue this one month of the year, what do we want to remember of our reflections and revelations? What commitments do we want to pursue? What is our obligation to our community and its individual members? What will be the place of Torah, of study and of living out its precepts, in the coming year? Simchat Torah leaves us with a belief in our ability to come full circle, to face our endings and begin again, and to turn to Torah and to our community circles as our guide and support.

Eliyahu Kitov relates the following story, which expresses the overwhelming nature of the Tishri holidays in a slightly humorous vein. Rabbi Levi said: During every one of the summer months, God desired to give Israel a festival. During Nisan, God gave them Pesach; during Iyar, God gave them Pesach *Katan* (whoever could not bring the paschal lamb in its proper time could bring it a month later); during Sivan, God gave them Shavuot; during Tammuz, God wanted to give them a major festival, but they made the golden calf, and as a result, God cancelled holidays in Tammuz, Av and Elul. When Tishri came, God repaid them with Rosh Hashana, Yom Kippur and Sukkot. God said: Tishri repays the other three, but should that month not have its own holiday? God gave Tishri its own day—"on the eighth day it shall be an *atzeret* to you." (*Pesikta D'Rav Kahana*) —B.P.

Hanuka

Jason Gary Klein

The Book of Genesis tells a Creation story in which God uses words to create light out of a world of chaos. In Jewish tradition, light came to symbolize knowledge, goodness, hope and life. Like the wintertime stories of light among other ancient peoples, the story of Hanuka, the Jewish festival of lights, emerges as an annual celebration of bringing light into the world.

There is an appealing shared human experience here: The ancient German festival of Yule, Christmas, and the Hindu and Jain festival of Diwali all likewise celebrate light in a dark and cold season. While today many Jews today find it difficult to be a Jew on Christmas, these universal, embodied themes are the only way I see my way through the commercialization and kitsch of the holiday season. —J.M.

Origin of the Holiday

Hanuka is a relatively new holiday. It developed after the biblical period was over. That means we have more information about the historical Hanuka than we do regarding more ancient Jewish holidays, however, the history of Hanuka must be distilled from a patchwork of texts beginning with the apocryphal books (pre-rabbinic books not included in the Hebrew Bible) of I and II Maccabees. Later Jews, such as the Jewish Roman historian Josephus and the rabbis of the Talmud, were aware of these extra-biblical sources.

During the period of the Second Temple, Alexander the Great conquered most of the Ancient Near East and brought Greek culture with him. The Torah was translated into Greek. Although the Jewish people in the Land of

Jews seem to be fascinated by the problem of how to spell "Hanuka." Use one "k" or two? Start with a "Ch?" End with an "h?" I always answer that the correct spelling is "*ḥet*, *nun*, *vav*, *k̲haf*, *hey*," although even in Hebrew there's a question of whether to leave out the helping *vav*. Maybe the question of how to spell the name in English is appropriately prominent for a holiday that raises questions of intercultural relations and translations. —J.A.S.

Though the eight candles of Hanuka lend themselves powerfully to themes of the winter solstice, the precise timing of Hanuka is mapped onto actual historical events rather than onto the natural calendar. This is in contrast to most holidays described in the Bible, which (other than Yom Kippur), have deep ties to agricultural cycles and usually begin on either the new moon or the full moon. —D.W.

The scholar Yosef Yerushalmi notes that until the modern period, Jewish intellectual leaders were less interested in preserving history—recording dates and details of events—than in retelling religious narratives affirming God's relationship with Israel. The recovery of the historical Hanuka is itself a modern undertaking. —D.W.

Israel lived with relative autonomy, Hellenization was at odds with major parts of Jewish culture. As Alexander's kingdom split apart, Jewish culture in the Land of Israel became more diverse. Some Jews abandoned Jewish tradition to such a degree that they attempted to restore their foreskins surgically, while other Jews resisted Hellenization as much as they could. After the Seleucid dynasty conquered Syria, King Antiochus III conquered the Land of Israel between 201 BCE and 198 BCE. He allowed the Jewish community to live in accordance with their own laws (He even forbade non-kosher meat from entering Jerusalem!), and residents of Jerusalem and leaders of the community were exempted from many taxes. Ironically, in this period of relative tolerance, the most religiously, socially and politically elite members of Jewish society may have had the most to gain through Hellenization;

Some scholars speculate that the Hellenistic period is the period in Jewish history that most resembles the current period, with similar challenges and opportunities facing Jews living in modern, open Western societies. —D.W.

The books of Maccabees portray the so-called Hellenizers as opportunistic people who are willing to give up key elements of Jewish culture for personal gain. If we consider what those gains were, though, we might become more sympathetic to their choices. For example, the reversal of circumcision would have allowed some young Jewish men to attend the gymnasium, the school where students were introduced to the richness of Greek education and knowledge. In our own day, we tend to think of education as a central Jewish value, worthy of many personal and financial sacrifices. Perhaps the Hellenizing parents who advocated for the reversal of circumcision and other forms of assimilation were making a similar choice. —E.R.S.

even Jewish priests serving in the Temple became immersed in Greek culture and custom.

A few dozen years later, King Antiochus IV Epiphanes tried to enlarge his kingdom by conquering Egypt. A few miles from Alexandria, he stopped when he realized that his military might paled in comparison to that of the Romans. Perhaps in his desire to fortify the edges of his empire, the new Antiochus returned to the Land of Israel, imposed Greek culture on it, and outlawed Jewish traditions such as Shabbat observance and circumcision. By 169 BCE, Antiochus IV had made the Temple in Jerusalem his own by destroying Jewish ritual items, establishing statues and altars of the Greek pantheon, and sacrificing pigs.

Antiochus's conquest of Jerusalem was both military and religious/cultural, and the Jewish community responded to it on both fronts. Maccabees I and II tell us about the family of Mattathias—from the priestly Has-

One wonders whether the fierce opposition between embracing Hellenization and remaining loyal to Jewish traditions actually predated the persecution imposed by Antiochus IV. Jews might have continued to integrate Hellenistic practices and make them our own. After the Maccabean revolt, the Maccabees' descendants, the Hasmoneans, continued the process of Hellenization. Jewish civilization has always evolved in this way. We adopt new beliefs and practices, and not long after we start to assume that our grandparents believed and practiced as we do. —J.J.S.

The decision of Antiochus to limit the religious freedom of the Jews was so atypical for a Hellenistic monarch that it calls his motives into question. Some scholars have posited that he understood the civil war that had broken out in Jerusalem as a rebellion against him and therefore punished the Judeans for this perceived revolt. Antiochus' action demonstrates how cycles of victimization perpetuate themselves. After being humiliated by the Romans, Antiochus re-established his authority and power by oppressing the Judeans. —E.R.S.

monean clan—who resisted Hellenization, amassed a guerilla army to fight against Antiochus's forces during the years 169 BCE to 166 BCE, and tried to convince the Jewish people to reject assimilation. In ancient Judea, social climbers eventually became intermediaries between pagan authorities and the Jewish community. With increased status and wealth came an increased expectation of "fitting in" with a Hellenized society. So the Hasmoneans' revolt can also be understood as that of a lower socio-economic class rising up against a higher one. The Hasmoneans won, driving out the Syrian army.

At last, the Temple was rededicated on the 25th day of the month of Kislev in 166 BCE. ("Hanuka" means "dedication.") The holiday of Sukkot, which celebrates the original dedication of the Temple and which was considered the holiday of all holidays during the biblical era, was then celebrated in the Temple, albeit about ten weeks late. The Hasmoneans instituted the Hanuka celebration to mark their military victory and the establishment of a free Jewish state.

The Hasmonean dynasty that ruled Judea following the

Alas, the Hasmoneans did not merely "try to convince the Jewish people to reject assimilation." Their legacy is a difficult one: religious zealotry, violence, and what today is called "*k'fiya datit*," or religious coercion. Perhaps it is fortunate that most Jews don't know the history recounted here, and see Hanuka merely as a celebration of religious freedom. —J.M.

Which side of this conflict has your sympathies—the forces that saw all Hellenization as sinful, or those who were attracted by the theater and gymnasium? No wonder Hanuka has been reinterpreted in North America as a celebration of freedom of religion—the freedom of the Maccabees to practice Judaism. In fact, Mattathias and his sons were also interested in *limiting* the freedom of Jews to experiment with a different culture. This is very complicated for contemporary liberal Jews to grasp. —J.J.S.

rededication of the Temple lasted about a century, until the Roman-appointed King Herod conquered it. Ironically, the dynasty that the Maccabees created also became Hellenized and corrupted by its own power, perhaps in part because both kingship and priesthood were occupied by one family.

The Rabbinic Understanding of Hanuka

The Babylonian Talmud, compiled several centuries later, has a sparse explanation for Hanuka within a discussion about lighting Shabbat lamps. After comparing the light-

By sitting with the complex history of Hanuka in which the anti-Hellenizing Maccabean rulers themselves later adopted Hellenic practices, I have come to appreciate the way in which all of our lives are shaped by larger cultural forces that we may not always recognize or acknowledge. —N.C.M.

The story of the miracle of the oil likely has its origin in II Maccabees 1:18–31, which describes the rededication of the newly rebuilt Temple in the late sixth century BCE under Nehemiah. It describes how priests hid the holy fire from the altar of the destroyed Temple in a cistern in 586 BCE. When their descendants returned 70 years later, they found an oily substance called naphtha, which was used to rekindle the flame of the altar in the rebuilt Temple. This story is explicitly recalled at the time of the rededication of the Temple in 166 BCE, 350 years later. The naphtha serves as a link between the dubious legitimacy of the new Temple and the universally acknowledged claim of the old. Similarly, the invocation of the narrative in II Maccabees serves to validate the priesthood and leadership of the Maccabees. Just as those who built the Second Temple re-established Temple worship "as it ever was," so, too, did the Maccabees. Seeing the Hanuka lights in this context transforms our homes into micro-temples, and gives testimony to Judaism's continuity through its civilizational evolution. —J.M.S.

Hundreds of years after Hanuka was already an annual institution, the rabbis of the Talmud were asking, "What is Hanuka?" and "Why do we celebrate it for eight nights?" That has always been fascinating to me. How could they be celebrating a

ing of the Hanuka lights to lighting those for Shabbat, the rabbis ask: "*Mai Hanuka?*"—"What is Hanuka?" The Talmud tells the story of the "Greeks" defiling the Temple and the Hasmoneans prevailing over them. According to the rabbis, when the Jews re-entered the

holiday without knowing why? It seems so unlikely that I believe the only reason they raised the issue in the Talmud was to provide an opportunity to dramatically alter the public rationale for Hanuka celebration to downplay the military theme and place the focus of the celebration on God and the miraculous. —S.C.R.

The Talmud is a complicated source for understanding history. In the rabbinic text, geopolitical complexities are collapsed—sometimes under the threatening eye of an external censor, sometimes to meet internal mandates—into a simpler narrative about a stylized oppressor who interferes with the full observance of Israelite or Jewish religious practice. The effect is powerful in literary and religious terms, but confusing in historical ones! —D.W.

Why did it take eight days for new oil to be prepared? The pure oil that was used to light the lamps in the Temple could not be prepared as quickly as other oil. Less pure oil, which could be used for offerings, could be made by crushing or grinding olives. For the purest oil, the flesh of the olives was bruised slightly and then the olives were placed in baskets, and the baskets placed on top of each other. Without added pressure, the oil would drip slowly down, without any additional impurities, making it exceptionally clear. This would take a full week. —B.P.

Another midrash describes how Adam became despondent as the days grew shorter and shorter, as he feared that the sun was going to disappear entirely. Believing that he was responsible for this misfortune, Adam fasted and prayed for eight days. When the light began to return, Adam established an eight-day holiday to celebrate this natural cycle of the seasons. The rabbis add that while Adam established this holiday "for the sake of heaven," his descendants made it a holiday for the idols. (Talmud, *Avoda Zara* 8a) Jews light lights not to banish the darkness, but to be reminded of the miracles of everyday life. Light at the time of the solstice reminds us that we will survive the winter darkness. —B.P.

Temple to dedicate it, they found a single cruse of pure oil, only enough to last for a day, but they lit it anyway, and the oil lasted eight days, long enough for new oil to be prepared. Thus, the rabbis transformed a national holiday marking a military victory into a Jewish holiday that celebrates the triumph of faith.

The Talmud describes the debate between Hillel and Shamai—great rabbis of the first century BCE who disagreed on hundreds of matters of Jewish observance and philosophy, including the way to light the Hanuka candles. Shamai lit all eight lamps on the first night and counted down the remaining days until just one candle was lit. That parallels the Sukkot sacrifices in which the

The rabbis made this change, of course, because of their own historical circumstances: Under Roman occupation, they were nervous about celebrating the overthrow of occupation. This is yet another example of Judaism adapting to the times. —J.M.

The Temple remained in service from the rededication until the Great Revolt against the Romans resulted in its destruction in 70 CE, but the aftermath of the Bar Kochba revolt in 132–135 CE was even more devastating for the Jews of Judea, leading to the ravaging of the land and exile for most residents. Both revolts were fueled by the goal of political and religious independence from foreign powers. The rabbis' shift toward the spirit then defused the dangers of political activism and pointed toward a path of political accommodation that would guide Diaspora Jewish leaders for nearly two millennia. When Zionism and other forms of Jewish political activism emerged in the modern period, so too did a new understanding of Hanuka. —D.W.

Hillel's custom models the fundamental rabbinic principle that our actions should always increase holiness and never decrease holiness. It is a philosophical attitude about ritual, customs, spiritual practice and even study that can be used as a fundamental rule for almost all of life's choices as well. —S.C.R.

sacrifices of 13 bulls on the first day tapered down to seven by the final day of the holiday. Hillel began by lighting one lamp on the first night of Hanuka and adding a lamp each night until eight were lit. Hillel's custom prevailed; perhaps increasing the light night by night was preferable for those living through the shortest days of the year in the Northern Hemisphere.

By the first century of the Common Era, Josephus was calling the holiday "*Phota*"—"Light"—in Greek. Archaeological evidence indicates that Hanuka lamps were lit from Hasmonean days forward. Generally these were single-bowled oil lamps. Long before the custom of lighting multiple lamps night by night took hold, a single lamp

Hanuka may be seen as Judaism's answer to seasonal affective disorder (SAD), or as its winter solstice practice. In the longest darkness of winter, we kindle a growing number of lights to remind ourselves that spring will come and life will emerge once more. In this context, placing the Hanuka lamp in the window serves a different purpose of *pirsum hanes*, publicizing the miracle and making it a more universal miracle of hope in the midst of despair and darkness. —J.M.S.

The importance of light in the Hanuka observance (we do, after all, call this "*Ḥag Urim*," "the Festival of Lights") offers a hint to its attraction to Jews throughout the generations. Living in the Northern Hemisphere, this time of year feels dark and even frightening. As the moon dims during the final days of Kislev, the night sky grows darker. It should come as no surprise that many cultures observe festivities at this time of year to bring in more light (including the Roman Saturnalia, Christmas and solstice celebrations). When the rabbis of the Talmud composed the tale of the cruse of oil, it was not only to dissociate the holiday from its military roots. They were also eager to envelop the otherwise pagan custom of lighting flames within a Jewish context. This is a beautiful illustration of Judaism as an evolving religious civilization. As with many other rituals whose roots lie in pagan observance, the rabbis embraced the practice and sanctified it, putting God (or godliness) at the center. —B.P.

was lit. Lighting one lamp is all that is required to fulfill the *halakha* to this day.

The specific legal requirements of the holiday are laid out in the Talmud and echoed by later codes such as the *Mishneh Torah* and the *Shulḥan Arukh*. The texts discuss several issues:

- The blessings said while lighting the Hanuka lamp,
- Whether the lighting of the lamp or its display for the public is the focus of the mitzvah, and
- The priority of purchasing the oil for the Hanuka lamp compared with obtaining *Kiddush* wine or Shabbat candles if one can only afford one.

Priority goes to the Hanuka lamp over *Kiddush* wine for the sake of remembering the miracle because reciting *Kiddush* in the absence of the Hanuka lamp could increase the risk that we will forget the Hanuka miracle. Shabbat candles, which the rabbis understood as utilitarian because they provided light by which to eat dinner, have the highest priority for the sake of peace in the family. In each case, light is seen as brightening our experience both literally and metaphorically.

The Significance of Hanuka

Hanuka and Purim are often paired as two minor Jewish holidays established after the redaction of the Torah and

We can approach a miracle as a suspension of the laws of nature or as the record of an encounter or event that our ancestors found awe-inspiring or redemptive. —D.W.

thematically linked through the Jewish people's miraculous triumph over a powerful leader who aimed for their destruction. Hanuka, unlike Purim, has no biblical origin at all. (The story of Purim is told in the biblical Book of Esther; the books of Maccabees are outside the Jewish biblical canon.) In order to explain the celebration of Hanuka, the rabbis of the Talmud wove together extra-biblical stories of which they were aware with evolving Jewish tradition around the miracle of the oil. Hanuka blessings and prayers invoke gratitude for *nisim*, miracles.

Rabbi Mordecai Kaplan used Hanuka as an example of the importance of religious ideals in a civilization's survival and success. Even though the Maccabees might have thought that God gave them the victory, Kaplan asserted that it was "their devotion to the service of their God that gave significance to their victory and made the memory of it worth preserving." Kaplan argued that the Jewish people's successes are marked by inspiring commitment not just to values that we call Jewish, but to values that are

Mordecai Kaplan tried to achieve many goals in this interpretation. He was keenly aware of the Zionist reclamation of Hanuka as a nationalist holiday, and as a committed cultural Zionist, he shared the aim of building up Jewish pride. However, he tried to infuse a progressive religious vision into the Zionist movement, which was heavily informed by secular, even anti-religious thinking. He also wanted to ensure that the reclamation of Hanuka and of positive Jewish identity was not directed solely toward Jews living in the Land of Israel, but rather toward a connection with Jews around the world and with non-Jews as well. —D.W.

ultimately universal. Thus, we should not fear influence and interaction with surrounding cultures, even when they are the majority. However, Kaplan differentiated between passive and active assimilation. Passive assimilation happens when the norms and values of the other culture are accepted uncritically. Active assimilation occurs when a minority group appropriates "elements of the culture of the majority and so relates them to its own sancta that they stimulate the creativity and will to live of the

Grace Paley's short story "The Loudest Voice" describes a common experience of second-generation American Jews, the precise audience for whom Kaplan initially formulated Reconstructionist Judaism. In the story, a Jewish student, the child of immigrants, is selected to narrate her New York City elementary school's Christmas pageant because she has the loudest speaking voice in the class. Her parents are torn between pride at her selection for such an important part by her non-Jewish teacher and chagrin at the content of what she is narrating. Paley's humorous, touching story illustrates the tensions about which Kaplan theorized. —D.W.

The process of active assimilation continues to take place every day in contemporary Jewish life. Every time we make a conscious choice to incorporate something spiritual or meaningful from our surrounding majority culture into Jewish life and create a new Jewish tradition, we are participating in the process of active assimilation, something that helps keep Judaism relevant, contemporary and evolving. Using the importance and ubiquitous nature of Christmas as a backdrop against which to elevate the importance of Hanuka is itself an act of assimilation. —S.C.R.

American Jews continue to wrestle with passive and active assimilation ranging from gift giving on Christmas to adapting Jewish mindfulness and meditation practice from American Buddhism. The thoughtful integration of new practices may ultimately be the best recipe for Jewish survival in the future—helping to keep Judaism fresh and current. —N.C.M.

minority." (*The Meaning of God in Modern Jewish Religion*, page 339)

The history of holidays is one lens through which we may describe the evolving religious civilization of the Jewish people. After the destruction of the Second Temple nearly 2,000 years ago, Yom Kippur surpassed Sukkot as the holiest festival day of the year. Hanuka, which had been considered a minor festival, took on new meaning after the establishment of the State of Israel. The rabbis of the Talmud emphasized the miracle of the oil in order to de-emphasize the military victory—perhaps as a self-conscious nod to the Roman occupation of the Land of Israel, or perhaps as a veiled criticism of the later corruption of the Hasmonean military victors. The founders of the modern State of Israel

To the early Zionists, Hanuka represented an instance of Jewish activism. Investing the holiday with importance helped them to build up positive Jewish identity and to promote political activism. It was a repudiation of the rabbis' political quietude and an effort to convince Jews to fight politically and later militarily for the restoration of the historic Jewish homeland. —D.W.

Hanuka has also evolved for North American Jews in response to our unprecedented integration into the larger culture and our close, friendly ties with Christmas observers. —J.A.S.

The scholar Daniel Boyarin argues convincingly in his book *Unheroic Conduct: The Rise of Heterosexuality and the Invention of the Jewish Man* that until the Zionist movement, Jewish manhood was proudly defined in terms of intelligence, gentleness, sensitivity and morality, as opposed to the manhood of brutish non-Jewish men, who relied on their cruel physical prowess. The Zionist transformation of Jewish masculinity has triumphed around the world in non-Orthodox settings, and while Jewish men are now athletically competitive and able to defend themselves, there are values that have been lost in the process. —J.J.S.

found inspiration in the military victory of the Hanuka story, the victory of the few over the many, no matter how unlikely the traditional story might be. The stereotypical Zionist image of European Jews as lambs going to the slaughter during the Holocaust was supplanted by the image of Jews with strong bodies working the land and serving in the Israeli Defense Forces. So Hanuka earned a new position of prominence in contemporary Israel as a reminder of previous military triumphs. The understanding of Hanuka will continue to evolve in light of shifting relationships between Israel and its neighbors, and of Israeli self-identification as a triumphant underdog.

Another connection between Hanuka and the State of Israel is the Maccabi World Union (MWU), which was founded as a union for Jewish sports associations around

How interesting that in Israel as in North America, Hanuka has taken on more prominence than its status as a minor holiday might suggest. In Israel, although one is permitted by *halakha* to work on Hanuka, schools close for a weeklong vacation. —B.P.

In the several years in which I have lived in Israel through the month of December, the utter absence of Christmas lights and decorations in Jewish areas has been shocking, even though it has not been unexpected. It made me realize how important the Christmas season is to my experience of the significance of Hanuka. In the United States, Hanukah is magnified by its place in the holiday season. I am also hyper-aware that in United States, Hanuka is an act of cultural resistance to the oppressiveness of Christmas. In Israel, by contrast, even though Hanuka is unrivaled, it feels less important—like simply a time of vacation with a little evening candle lighting. —J.J.S.

Tensions—between body and mind, body and spirit, activism and faith—permeate religious cultures. The Hellenistic fixation on the body was one reason the rabbis of the talmudic period emphasized study over physical prowess. The 19th-century Zionist embrace of physical labor, exemplified in the writings of A.D. Gordon, set aside rabbinic preoccupations, and thereby mirrored larger cultural trends such as "muscular Christianity" and the founding of the YMCA movement. —D.W.

the world. The MWU is "a Zionist organization that utilizes sports as a means to bring Jewish people of all ages closer to Judaism and Israel in addition to various informal educational activities in a manner that surpasses politics and sectarianism." (http://maccabi.org/about) Its name comes from the association of the Maccabees of Hanuka with physical prowess, but it is also ironic because Hellenism was more associated with a body-centered culture.

Home Observance

Since Hanuka lasts eight days and does not carry with it traditional restrictions on work, the ritual preparation needed before the holiday is limited to readying a *ḥanukiya*. When families use Hanuka as an occasion to exchange gifts, holiday preparations include making or purchasing gifts.

In my Orthodox family of origin in the 1950s, there were no Hanuka gifts. There was Hanuka *gelt*, a bill or two slipped into my hand by aunts and uncles. Presents were regarded as *goyish*. My father did have a custom of taking me to the toy department at Macy's in Midtown Manhattan on the day after Christmas, when everything went on sale, and allowing me to choose one item. We never called it a Hanuka present. It was just a bargain. Jews were lucky because we could wait for the sales. —J.J.S.

In some households, *tzedaḳa* is given in honor of individuals instead of giving them gifts. —D.W.

Hanuka is largely a home-centered holiday focused around the lighting of the Hanuka lamp. The central symbol of Hanuka is the *ḥanukiya*, the nine-branched menorah (candelabrum) that includes one light for each day of the holiday plus a *shamash*, a "helper" light. The traditional form is a modified version of the menorah from Temple times that included seven branches, one for each day of the week.

Hanuka begins the evening of the 25th day of the month of Kislev, which can range anywhere from November 26 to December 25 on the Gregorian (standard Western) calendar. The holiday begins at nightfall, which is when the *ḥanukiya* is traditionally kindled (after three stars are visible in the sky), though it may be lit anytime throughout the night. The first candle to be lit is on the far right side of the *ḥanukiya*, and—night by night—candles are added from right to left, following the direction of the Hebrew alphabet, perhaps harking back to the God of Genesis creating light with words. When the lamps are lit, the newest one is always lit first, so they are lit from left to right using the *shamash*, which is lit first.

On each night of the holiday, the lighting is preceded by reciting blessings. On every night of the holiday, the

The practice of lighting candles teaches us something about respect for seniority as well as welcoming newcomers. The candle representing the first night is always the first to be inserted into the *ḥanukiya*. But the newest candle is always the first to be lit every night. —B.P.

With an eye toward creating a more egalitarian Hanuka blessing, I recite the words, "*she'asa nisim lahoreynu*" ("who did wonders for our parents"), rather than "*avoteynu*" ("our fathers"). —N.C.M.

blessing ending, "*asher kid'shanu b'mitzvotav v'tzivanu l'hadlik ner shel Hanuka*"—"who has sanctified us with mitzvot and commanded us to kindle the Hanuka light"—is said followed by a blessing ending, "*she'asa nisim la'avoteynu bayamim hahem baz'man hazeh*"—"who did wonders for our ancestors in those days at this season." The first time one lights Hanuka candles each year, a third blessing, the *Sheheḥeyanu*, is added in appreciation for reaching the holiday season.

As the candles are lit, traditional Jews recite a paragraph known by its opening words, "*Hanerot halalu.*" The passage teaches us that the candles are lit as a reminder of the miracles and wonders done for our ancestors in those days and at this time. The candles,

It is so evocative that we are not to use the light of the Hanuka candles for any utilitarian purposes. Against the darkness of the window, we are just to look at them. *Sefer K'dushat Levi*, written by Rabbi Levi Yitzhak of Berditchev in the 18th century, comments that while we are marking an event that entailed great human initiative and effort by the Maccabees, our present-day observance entails doing almost nothing, only looking at the light in the darkness and standing in the presence of the miraculous. This, he teaches, is the exact inverse of Passover, when the story of the miraculous liberation from slavery in Egypt took place entirely by the strong and outstretched arm of God. Our present-day observance of Passover requires a great deal of human effort. In both cases, we experience the importance of pairing human effort and action with divine assistance, support, inspiration and connection to the mysterious power that enables the miraculous to surface. —M.M.

The candles should not be used for any *practical* purpose, but for frivolous ones … such as a competitive game of dreidel. … Game on! —D.W.

according to the passage, are holy, and are not to be used for any purpose (such as reading by them) besides looking at them and remembering the story of Hanuka. By contrast, lighting Shabbat candles had a practical origin—

In the decade following World War II, my family worried about publicly proclaiming our Jewishness by placing the *ḥanukiya* on the window sill even though we lived in New York City, where 25 percent of the population was Jewish. Most of my grandparents' families were slaughtered in the Holocaust, and we also collectively harbored their oft-repeated stories of the pogroms they witnessed before they left Eastern Europe for America. We also worried about the fate of the State of Israel, recently established and surrounded by hostile neighbors. The story of the triumph of the weak over the mighty indeed felt like a miraculous fable. —J.J.S.

December can be a charged and often invisible time to be a Jew in North America, in a Christmas drenched-culture in which most storekeepers, bank tellers and people on the street wish everyone "Merry Christmas," regardless of religion or culture. Hanuka extends the challenge to be "out" as Jews during this time. The Talmud states that in order to publicize the miracle of Hanuka, one should light the Hanuka candles so that they can be seen from the street, and if they wouldn't be seen from the street at one's window, then one lights them at the outer limits of one's property. We are offered the challenge of taking our identities as Jews, along with the lessons and themes that Hanuka offers, out into the streets, not in defensive or aggressive ways, but with all the clarity and radiance of flames in the darkness. —M.M.

Just a word of caution: I have a friend who lit his *ḥanukiya*, placed it in his window and then went out to the theater with his wife, only to return to discover that his curtains had caught on fire from the candles. They had to call the fire department to extinguish the flames in their burning house. —S.C.R.

In 1993, in Billings, Montana, someone threw a rock through the living room window of the home of a Jewish family displaying their menorah on Hanuka. The communal response was extraordinary: The newspaper printed an image of a menorah and urged residents to display it as an act of solidarity, and non-Jewish religious leaders urged their followers to do the same. The photographer Frederic Brenner later captured the unified repudiation of intolerance in a panoramic image of

extending the light of the day into the night, having something to see by and enjoying a candlelit dinner.

Once the lights are kindled, it is customary to display them in a publicly visible place, such as in a window. This is called *pirsum hanes*, publicizing the miracle. In that location, the Hanuka menorah stands at the threshold of private and public. It is to be lit in the home, but its light overflows into the public domain.

Billings residents from all walks of life—Native Americans in traditional headdress; Catholic priests in robes; firefighters and police officers in uniforms; and citizens of all ages, races and ethnicities—holding up menorahs. —D.W.

In certain Jerusalem neighborhoods, the custom of placing lights in a prominent and visible location is built into the very walls of the courtyard. Along the sidewalk you will find niches in the stone walls that are meant for the placement of special Jerusalem *ḥanukiyot*. The *ḥanukiyot* are actually simple glass boxes soldered with tin. They are made by craftspeople who learned the art from Christians, who fashioned similar lanterns for carrying the "Holy Fire" during the Orthodox Christian observance of Easter. The practice of displaying Hanuka candles was not always possible in countries where Jews were at risk. In Jerusalem, Jews proudly publicize the miracle openly, even outside the house. Walking the streets of Jerusalem just after sunset, when candle lighting is to take place, I have watched the lights appear in home after home. —B.P.

Since according to tradition the Hanuka candles are kindled before sunset on Friday, and thus almost a full hour before dusk, some have the tradition of creating a disposable aluminum foil *ḥanukiya* that uses Shabbat candles, so that they burn at least half an hour into the night. —J.M.S.

On Friday it is customary to kindle the Hanuka lights before the Shabbat candles since lighting a fire is traditionally forbidden on Shabbat, and lighting Shabbat candles is associated with the start of Shabbat. At the end of Shabbat, it is traditional to wait until dusk (the time when we can see three stars) to light the *ḥanukiya* and then to say *Havdala*.

With the popularity of boxes of 44 Hanuka candles—exactly enough for the whole holiday—and the invention of the electric candelabrum, some of the wonder of what it meant for a small amount of oil to burn for days on end may be lost to us. Households that are willing to invest a little more preparation time before lighting Hanuka candles can use a *ḥanukiya* made for oil or prepare glasses (empty jelly jars or wine glasses look particularly nice) with oil (olive oil is most authentic, but other oils work as well) and wicks (those not inclined to make their own cotton wicks can usually find easy-to-use floating wicks at a Judaica store). Two or three ounces of oil go a long way, and instead of candles burning for 20 to 40 minutes, you might find yourself with a *ḥanukiya* that burns into the middle of the night, if not longer. We have the opportunity to embrace *hidur mitzvah,* beautifying the *ḥanukiya* even further by using a mixture of water and food coloring under the oil in each glass or using specially decorated glasses—such as shot glasses bearing a school's logo for those on a university campus.

Some families light one *ḥanukiya* as a household, while others allow each member of the household to light his or her own *ḥanukiya*. The latter custom may create great enthusiasm in young children as they prepare to light their own *ḥanukiyot*. Either way, the *ḥanukiya* provides an appropriate backdrop for the singing of Hanuka songs, eating together, playing dreidel and exchanging gifts.

Maoz Tzur, a medieval liturgical poem, is the most classic Hanuka song. When sung in their entirety, its verses celebrate deliverance not only from Antiochus, but from other enemies of the Jewish people as well. *Kol Haneshamah* is a good starting point for the variety of Hanuka songs in Hebrew, English, Yiddish and Ladino, but Hanuka has also inspired contemporary singers, including Adam Sandler and Peter, Paul and Mary, to write new music suggesting how some of the values of the

In my childhood, the centerpiece of our home Hanuka observance was gathering around the piano and singing every Hanuka song in the collection of Jewish music by composer Harry Coopersmith. We always ended by singing *Maoz Tzur* in four-part harmony. We always opened with "In the Window," written by Judith Kaplan Eisenstein: "In the window, where you can send your glow / from my menorah on newly fallen snow / I will set you (one, two, three ...) little candle(s) / on this the (first, second, third ...) night of Hanuka." —B.P.

The last of the six verses of *Maoz Tzur* can be challenging for Reconstructionists, as it asks for God to wreak vengeance on our foes and bring about the messianic age, denigrating our current situation as unending evil. Accordingly, only two verses of "*Maoz Tzur*" appear in *Kol Haneshamah*. This change offers us an opportunity to offer our hopes for how the world may change for the better as we bask in the glow of the Hanuka candles. —J.M.S.

story connect with contemporary life. Any of these songs can be fun to sing, but the lyrics are also teaching tools about the lessons of the holiday.

While there is no requirement to eat a specific food such as matza on Passover, today it is customary to remember the story of the oil by eating foods that have been fried in oil. Ashkenazic Jews typically eat potato pancakes (*l'vivot* in Hebrew, latkes in Yiddish) with any number of ingredients and any number of toppings; applesauce and sour cream are generally the most popular. Sephardic Jews typically eat donuts (*sufganiyot* in Hebrew) filled with jelly or with *dulce de leche*. The custom of eating dairy foods has its origin in the story of Judith, which is associated with Hanuka. Judith triumphed over the Babylonian general Holofernes by giving him curds to eat, after which he drank a great deal of wine

Cooking and serving creative latkes (my current favorite is sweet potato/ginger latkes) have become important to me as a way to connect with the holiday. Doing so brings out my culinary creativity and serves as an excuse to bring family and friends around a table. —N.C.M.

Filled donuts have taken over as a signature Hanuka food for all the Jewish communities of Israel, a tradition that may have originated in Europe or the Middle East. I have made it my annual custom to try a new, olive-oil-heavy recipe in honor of Hanuka. Some of the memorable dishes: pasta with garlic and olive oil, slow-cooked green beans with tomato and olive oil, even a surprisingly good olive oil cake! —J.A.S.

Like the first two books of Maccabees, the book of Judith is another apocryphal book not included in the Hebrew Bible. —D.W.

Not all versions of the story of Judith mention curds. This may be a later interpolation, influenced by the story of Yael killing Sisera after serving him milk. Judith's courage and fortitude offer a female counterpart to the bravery of Judah Maccabee. —B.P.

and fell into a deep sleep during which she decapitated him. The story, which echoes the biblical story of Yael killing Sisera in the Book of Judges, is set in the Babylonian period. As in I and II Maccabees, the book of Judith appears in the Apocrypha, and these books were written at about the same time. Potatoes arrived in Europe in the 16th century, so prior to that, Hanuka customs probably involved eating cheese or other dairy products. Because of the story of Judith, there are Sephardic communities in which the opening and closing days of Hanuka are considered special holidays for women.

Playing with a top ("dreidel" in Yiddish; "*sevivon*" in Hebrew) has probably been associated with Hanuka for about 200 years. It originated when Jews transformed a European children's top game by imagining it as a game that students learning Torah played to fool Antiochus' guards when Torah study was forbidden. Today's dreidel is a four-sided top with one Hebrew letter on each side. In the Diaspora, the letters are *nun, gimmel, hey* and *shin*, standing for, "*Nes gadol haya sham*"—"A great miracle happened there." In Israel the *shin* is replaced by a *peh*,

Playing with the dreidel is also an activity that does not violate the prohibition of not deriving any benefit from the lights of the *ḥanukiya*. Traditionally speaking, gambling for coins by spinning the dreidel is child's play and hence not useful. —J.J.S.

The dreidel is a reminder that much of life is shaped by chance. We simply cannot control everything, and we may be better served by not worrying about what we can't control and enjoying the happenstance of our lives instead. —J.M.S.

and the acronym stands for, "*Nes gadol haya po*"—"A great miracle happened here." The dreidel game can be played with small pieces of candy, nuts, chocolate *gelt* or small change. During each round, the players ante up a piece of the currency, and one player spins the dreidel; the outcome determines what he or she must do. "*Nun*" (which is said to stand for "*nisht*"—"nothing" in Yiddish) means that he or she neither gives nor receives anything. "*Gimmel*" (which is said to stand for "*ganz*"—"everything" in Yiddish) means that he or she receives the whole pot. "*Hey*" (which is said to stand for "*halb*"—"half" in

Our family has a traditional Hanuka game, but we have lost the reason for its association with the holiday. We call it "nut bowling," though it's closer to "nut marbles." A nut such as an acorn or hazelnut is placed toward the end of a long hall or foyer. This is the "target nut." Each player gets a bunch of nuts and takes a turn rolling the nuts from the other end of the hall, trying to hit the target nut. Whoever hits it gathers all the nuts that have been rolled, and a new target is placed. My family once celebrated Hanuka evening with my teacher Ari Elon in Modi'in, the home of the Maccabees, and we introduced him to this game. I learned that not only is Ari an amazing teacher of midrash, he's an incredible nut bowler! —J.A.S.

In Eastern Europe, other games were also associated with Hanuka, especially card games. One rabbi gave these games an ethical meaning: Once, Rabbi Yisroel of Rozhin entered his *bet midrash* on one of the nights of Hanuka and found his students playing cards. The students were embarrassed, but the rabbi told them, "Keep playing. It's Hanuka today. ... But you should know that one can gain intelligent ethical instruction from card games: If you have a terrible card in your hand, you try to get rid of it. Just so, a person with a terrible ethical trait should likewise try to get rid of it. Whoever has a good card hides it. Just so, one who has a talent or good qualities should, heaven forbid, not have pride about them, but should hide those advantages with the trait of humility." —J.A.S.

Yiddish) means that he or she takes half of the pot. "*Shin*" (which is said to stand for "*shtel*"—"put" in Yiddish), means that he or she must add to the pot. Older children and adults playing the game may allow the winner to designate the winnings to a favorite *tzedaka* fund at the end.

In the 21st century, it is hard to imagine American celebrations of Hanuka without exchanges of presents. Historian Jenna Weissman Joselit points out that early in the 20th century, at a time when Hanuka was not widely

Historian Jenna Weissman Joselit notes also that there is always some tension between elite prescriptions—what "authoritative" leaders say should be done—and lay practice—that is, what Jews do. The participation rates regarding Hanuka, including the giving of gifts, suggest that the holiday has become very important to laypeople for their own reasons, distinct from what leaders—religious, Zionist or other—say. —D.W.

Several phenomena—families comprised only of Jews having Christmas trees, the market for greeting cards celebrating both holidays, the myriad December customs with which bicultural families negotiate the holiday dilemma—can be seen as highly ironic. Hanuka, after all, is the holiday that celebrates Jewish resistance to assimilation. However, if we take a closer look at the Hanuka story, we see that the books of Maccabees describe a range of choices that different leaders of the Judean community made regarding the challenge of living in two civilizations. In the 21st century, Jewish communities are becoming increasingly multicultural, and Jews increasingly embrace multicultural identities. Perhaps we should consider reconstructing Hanuka not as a festival of resistance, but rather as a holiday that celebrates the fact that Jews have always negotiated the different appeals of separatism on the one hand and participation in the cultures in which they live on the other. It is only by trial and error and a willingness to experiment that we, as individuals and communities, can find the balance that is right for us. —E.R.S.

observed in the American Jewish community, fitting into American society meant that Jews exchanged Christmas gifts. After World War I, Jewish newspapers encouraged gift giving on Hanuka and eventually revived contemporary Hanuka observance. As the years have gone by, the proximity of Hanuka to the highly commercialized Christmas season has helped to cement this association. Of course Hanuka is a minor holiday compared to Rosh Hashana, Yom Kippur, Pesach, Shavuot and Sukkot. Only its proximity on the calendar to Christmas, one of the two major Christian holidays, has resulted in comparisons between Hanuka and Christmas, which will inevitably be unbalanced.

The message of Hanuka creates an opportunity for particularly thoughtful gift giving. Instead of creating the expectation that one present will be given to each child on

When I was growing up, my synagogue had a Hanuka home decoration contest every year and encouraged every family to create its own personalized decorations. The synagogue gave prizes and ribbons to the families with the best or most creative decorations, and the process helped make the celebration of Hanuka that much more special and significant for everyone. —S.C.R.

Other ways to give gifts without buying them for family members are many: Siblings can offer a service (such as babysitting or cutting the grass) to other family members in place of a gift. Children can decide individually or together on a *tzedaka* donation in celebration of the holiday. Children can select a gift to be donated for children in need. —D.W.

Larry Bush, the editor of *Jewish Currents* articulated a Hanuka practice that I admire. He and his family focus on a different *tzedaka* (gift to a particular charity) each night, thereby creating an opportunity to learn together as a family and to clarify important values to each other. —N.C.M.

every night of the holiday, families may consider exchanging gifts, or honoring their families or friends by making gifts (for example, arts and crafts projects, latkes or *sufganiyot*), or making donations to organizations that support Hanuka's themes, such as civil rights and renewable energy. Given the preeminence of chocolate "*gelt*," Hanuka provides an appropriate platform for considering issues of labor and global poverty as more people recognize the importance of fairly traded or directly traded chocolate. In addition, Hanuka's emphasis on the triumph of the little guy can serve as a reminder to patronize local businesses. Sometimes, but rarely, Hanuka coincides with the American holiday of Thanksgiving. The years 1899, 1918, 2013 and 2070 are such years, assuming that Thanksgiving continues to be celebrated on the fourth Thursday in November. Such intersections may be particularly apt times to reclaim some of the ancient messages of the psalms of thanksgiving that we chant in *Hallel.*

International Human Rights Day, December 10, often falls during Hanuka. This can be a special opportunity to tie the theme of Hanuka to contemporary struggles for human rights. In our congregation we substitute a reading of the Universal Declaration of Human Rights for the haftarah on our Human Rights Shabbat. —B.P.

Synagogue Observance

The structure of synagogue services on each day of Hanuka is based around the regular weekday or Shabbat liturgy with appropriate additions for the holiday. These include the paragraph *Al Hanisim* (for the miracles) in the *Amida* (the same paragraph is added in *Birkat Hamazon*), the full reading of the *Hallel* psalms, and special Torah readings each day of the holiday from *Parashat Naso* that recall the dedication of the *Mishkan*, the portable tabernacle in the wilderness. The liturgy thus links the celebration of the rededication of the Temple to the original dedication of the *Mishkan*. On Shabbat Hanuka, the regular weekly Torah reading is traditionally read, followed by the special portion for Hanuka, which is read from a second scroll. The haftarah is the same haftarah as for *Parashat Beha'a'lot'ḥa* (Zechariah 2:14–4:7). It includes the prophet's vision of the menorah and the line, "*Lo b'ḥayil v'lo b'kho'aḥ ki im b'ruḥi. . . .*"—"Not by might and not by power, but by my spirit"—framed as a biblical foreshadowing of the talmudic emphasis on Hanuka as a holiday that primarily celebrates not military power, but

Another custom is to place the *ḥanuḳiya* in the prayer space, adding a new candle each evening as at home. When davening on a weekday evening, Hanuka candles are lit just prior to the *ma'ariv* (evening) service so that they can burn the minimum of a half hour. On Shabbat morning, the unlit candles in the *ḥanuḳiya* add to the festive atmosphere. —B.P.

The historical narration of *Al Hanisim* is quite unlike the evocative liturgical poetry found in much of the rest of the siddur. —D.W.

faith and hope. When the first and last days of Hanuka coincide with Shabbat, the haftarah for the second Shabbat of Hanuka is I Kings 7:40–50, which describes King Solomon adorning the Temple lamps. Because Hanuka always spans the end of the month of Kislev and the beginning of the month of Tevet, one or two days (depending on whether Kislev has 29 or 30 days that year) will be *Rosh Ḥodesh*, the beginning of the new month, with an additional Torah reading and additions to the liturgy. When this coincides with Shabbat, communities that have multiple Torah scrolls traditionally read from three of them—one for Shabbat, one for *Rosh Ḥodesh*, and one for Hanuka. Some Sephardic traditions repeat Psalm 30 at the end of the morning liturgy each day throughout Hanuka.

Beyond synagogue services, the Jewish community has many opportunities for communal o bservance of Hanuka. Religious schools often use the theme of the physical might

Hanuka, or dedication, is a perfect time to gather for *ḥanukat habayit* (dedication of a new home). Such a gathering may include hanging mezuzot and telling stories of the home's transition and its former life, along with enjoying the normal Hanuka foods and festivities. One may even choose to hold a *ḥanukat habayit* years after moving in, as long as dedicating the home to Jewish practice is a goal of the ceremony. —J.M.S.

Communal candle lighting, for which guests bring their own *ḥanukiyot*, can be quite awe-inspiring. Of course proper precautions must be taken to prevent a fire. —B.P.

For several years my synagogue has held a "Celebrity-Judged Latke Baking Contest," where people compete by sharing their unique latke baking recipes (with samples, of course) and celebrities (from the congregation and local community) are judges. —S.C.R.

of the Maccabees to host a "Maccabiah," a color war of relay races and other athletic contests that may also be interlaced with game-show-style questions about the holiday itself or about a broader scope of Judaica. Friends may gather to share recipes for latkes or *sufganiyot* or to have a community contest to determine who makes the best Hanuka fried treats. The *oneg* after Friday night services during Hanuka may not be limited to the usual pastries, but might also include an olive oil "taste test" staffed by the community's teenagers, complete with baguettes for dipping and two or three kinds of gourmet olive oil to sample. Some college campuses have hosted latke-hamantashen debates that have become beloved annual events around the times of Hanuka and Purim. While precise customs vary, two people—often academics—are chosen for these debates, and each must advocate for the merits of one of the foods, which becomes the basis of an often laugh-out-loud funny debate between them. Whether on the college campus or in a synagogue community of learners, such a spectacle can connect teenagers and adults to a holiday whose observance—through family gift exchanges—often centers solely on children.

The Latke-Hamantash Debate originated at the University of Chicago in 1946. For some interesting academic takes on this annual event, see *The Great Latke-Hamantash Debate,* edited by Ruth Fredman Cernea (2006). —B.P.

A synagogue games night also fits in with the traditional practices of the holiday. —J.A.S.

Themes for Adults

The story of Hanuka we may have learned as children was likely an "us vs. them" story in which the Greek-Syrians were the bad guys and the Maccabees were the good guys and the leaders of the Jews. The reality of the history is much more complex. While the Greek-Syrians may have been proponents of Hellenization, the Jewish community did not homogeneously fight against their influence. Like Jewish communities throughout the ages, the Jewish community in the Land of Israel in the second century BCE was highly influenced by its surroundings. For some Jews, this meant adopting Greek practices, such as attending the gymnasium, eating non-kosher food or even attempting to reverse their circumcision. For some Jews—epitomized by the Hasmoneans—anything associated with the Greek-Syrians was utterly offensive to their tradition and to their

Hanuka is a history-based holiday. History writing ordinarily places humans (often, at least in the past, great men) at the center of the story, while religious narratives tend to place God at the center. Though history is assembled out of a set of facts, the narrative often turns on unexpected developments, both positive and negative, that can defy expectation. History can still inspire awe. —D.W.

The books of Maccabees indicate that even the first generation of Maccabees did not fully reject Hellenistic culture. In order to negotiate with the Seleucids and the Romans, these rebels needed to speak Greek and be well-versed in the diplomatic and political rules of the Hellenistic empires. This pattern is familiar from radically traditionalist movements today. Fundamentalists of all traditions use technology and cutting-edge political strategies to spread their messages and gain political power, even while decrying the corrupting forces of modernity in all its aspects. —E.R.S.

God. Most Jews, we might imagine, fell somewhere in the middle between these two extremes. In fact, history bears this out, since Jewish tradition permitted writing Torah scrolls in Greek and naming Jewish children after Alexander the Great in spite of his being Greek because the Jewish community prospered so much under his leadership. The military battles that took place were likely just as much civil wars within the Jewish community as battles between the Jewish rebels and the Greek army.

American culture has forged an association between Hanuka and Christmas. While the scheduling of each of these holidays around the winter solstice in the Northern Hemisphere inevitably links them through themes of light in the midst of darkness, Hanuka has not until recent times occupied a central role as a Jewish holiday. The relative importance of Jewish festivals has evolved over the millennia, so it is fair that the relative centrality of Hanuka for one generation may not be appropriate several gen-

Many Jews find themselves isolated or singled out at this time of year. It can be an uncomfortable time to be a Jew. Often this is a time of a year when co-workers might ask probing questions about Jewish beliefs and practices. The "December Dilemma" can also create tension for interfaith families seeking to honor parents, maintain their own cultural practices and discern how and what to teach children. As individuals and families experience these challenges, synagogue communities may be helpful in reaching out and creating supportive educational programming in order to share dilemmas and open dialogues to help resolve them. —B.P.

Our American Hanuka traditions teach us that being Jewish is fun. Decorating the house, hosting parties, cooking and serving special foods, playing dreidel and other games, and giving presents can be a joyful way for families to share a Jewish moment. —B.P.

erations later. Jewish authenticity need not be the same to every Jew or the same to every generation; the words "ancient" and "authentic" are not necessarily synonyms, and the Judaism of each generation must serve the Jewish people of that generation. Nonetheless, when the symbols of Jewish tradition are reduced to *ḥanukiyot* and dreidels, something may be lacking. We may be considering whether to give our children elaborate gifts or to lobby for the inclusion of Hanuka songs in a public school's holiday performance, but more important are some of the age-old themes of Hanuka that remain relevant today: To what degree are we as Jews special, and to what degree are we normal? To what degree do we want to be accepted just like everyone else, and to what degree do we want to be accepted on our own terms? What kinds of roles and

One of the gifts of sexual and gender diversity is the enrichment of religious language for everyone. In this light, I see Hanuka as the quintessential "coming out" holiday—not just for LGBT people, but also for anyone who has felt pressured to hide, to conceal or to conform. So, rather than viewing this holiday as being about Jewish specialness in particular, I like to see it as celebrating specialness, difference and pluralism in general. The Maccabees were not the heroes I learned about in day school, but they were standing up for difference and distinctiveness—and that is a message that still resonates today. —J.M.

One of the most memorable conversations I have had as a teacher was with a class of ninth-graders in preparation for Hanuka. We arrived at exactly this question of evolution from the outside in or inside out. As the students talked through their reactions to so-called "Hanuka bushes" (not okay, from the perspective of many of them) and to decorating the house with blue winter lights (okay), we sidled up to the notion that, given millennia of cultural mixing, our lines between "authentic" and "inauthentic" Jewish practice are necessarily idiosyncratic and arbitrary. This does not mean that we should refrain from drawing these lines for ourselves, but that we should be extremely cautious about extending them to others. —H.S.V.

responsibilities come with being "just like everyone else?" With being "special?" How do we find a place on the spectrum between isolation and assimilation that feels right for us and establishes the values we want to transmit to our children? To what degree should Jewish tradition evolve from the outside in, and to what degree from the inside out?

Some of the lessons of Hanuka can apply to all of us. The value of faith is central to the Hanuka story. Faith comes in many forms in the story: the faith that Hellenizing the entire Jewish people would not be good for the Jews, the faith that there is something worth fighting for, the faith that the few can find success over the many, the faith to light the menorah in spite of the small quantity of pure oil that remained.

Another theme is the triumph of the spirit. In spite of their faith, their hope and their optimism, there was little evidence to suggest that the Maccabees would be victorious in war or that the oil would last beyond one day. Yet these things may not be the be-all and end-all of the story. As the prophet says, "Not by might and not by power, but by spirit alone. . . ." The physical victory was not as important as the spiritual victory: remaining committed to their people

In reflecting on the miraculous nature of the Hanuka lights, Rabbi Yehuda Aryeh Leib Alter, the Gerer Rebbe and late-19th-century author of the *S'fat Emet*, described the Hanuka candles as embodying the divine light that illuminated the Temple. He said that with the right intention, lighting the Hanuka candles could be a path to recovering the hidden light and purity within our own souls. —N.C.M.

and to a tradition they could not fail, regardless of the outcome of the war. Maimonides taught that even if one does not light Hanuka candles oneself, when one sees someone else's candles, one should still say the blessing, "*she'asa nisim*" ("who did wonders") over the light itself. The spiritual message is alive in that blessing.

There is also the Hanuka theme of miracles. Reconstructionists and other liberal Jews are usually not associated with a theology in which God literally suspends the forces of nature to act in the universe. Yet we should not let our rationalism obscure our appreciation for the everyday miracles in our lives. From the structure of our bodies that allows us to breathe without conscious effort to the power of the connection between two people to the wonders of nature, we are surrounded by miracles. At the coldest and darkest time of year in the Northern Hemisphere,

A rejection of supernaturalism does not require a repudiation of feeling a sense of holiness, humility, mystery or gratitude at the interconnectedness of all things. —D.W.

How would you live if you really believed you were created in the image of God (*b'tzelem Elohim*)? Hanuka is an invitation to find the divinity inherent in our physical existence, and to let that awareness shine through each moment of embodied life. We are wrong if we think that we are not this body, and we are wrong if we think that we are only this body. We are both spirit and matter. Our courageous choices can help us to illuminate this paradoxical awareness, and Hanuka can be a time for increasing that light of awareness in our lives. —M.K.

While the timing of Hanuka is determined by history, its placement near the winter solstice and the practices associated with it are nonetheless connected to nature. Lighting candles at a dark season, cultivating faith and renewal during a period of darkness, and connecting to the earth's turn toward the sun are all deeply powerful. I am grateful there is a Jewish holiday for this season. —D.W.

Hanuka calls us to be thankful "*al hanisim, v'al ha'purkan, v'al hag'vurot, v'al hat'shu'ot, v'al ha'neḥamot sh'asita lavoteynu v'imoteynu bayamim hahem bazman hazeh*"—"for the miracles, the redemption, the salvation, the might and the comfort you provided for our ancestors in those days and at this time." These blessings were provided not just for our ancestors, but for us as well.

Since the primary symbols of Hanuka are those of light illuminating the darkness and hope illuminating despair, acts of *tzedek* (righteousness) and of social justice are particularly appropriate around the holiday.

The small amount of oil in the Hanuka story lasted well beyond any reasonable expectation for such fuel, but we are not so lucky today. Our current rates of fossil fuel consumption and of global warming raise serious issues about how we expect to sustain our planet. Community

One campaign, started by the Philadelphia-based Shalom Center, was the "Green Menorah Covenant," which focused on seven actions a household can commit to doing and promoting to heal the planet. Jewish ritual during Hanuka and other holidays can push us to make more progress in the critical area of sustainability. —N.C.M.

What if each night of Hanuka, each of us took a different step to reduce our carbon footprint and stretch our limited resources a bit further? For example, on the first night, change a regular bulb to a fluorescent one (150 pounds of CO_2/year); on the second, use mass transit or your feet instead of driving (one pound of CO_2 for each mile not driven); on the third, commit to recycling (2,400 pounds of CO_2/year by recycling half of household waste); on the fourth, check your tires to improve gas mileage (20 pounds of CO_2 for each gallon of gas saved); on the fifth, install a low-flow showerhead (350 pounds of CO_2/year); on the sixth, move the thermostat down two degrees (1,000 pounds of CO_2 per winter); on the seventh, wash clothes in warm water instead of hot (500 pounds of CO_2/year); and on the eighth, email your elected representatives to fight the lies and obstructions about climate change. Not only would such steps have a meaningful impact on our own carbon footprints, they would enrich the meaning of Hanuka as well. —J.M.

campaigns challenging us to reduce our carbon footprint can be especially meaningful against the backdrop of Hanuka, particularly because they may challenge us to aspire to voluntarily simplifying our lives, even in the face of December shopping and sales.

Many Jews of that time resisted the Hellenistic worship of the body. A friend once suggested why eating oil on Hanuka flies in the face of the Hellenistic value of body worship: Fried foods make us gain weight. So what? However, the more we learn today about proper diet and exercise, the more we understand that the way we treat our bodies is linked to Judaism's highest value of preserving life. Inspiring Jewish pride on college campuses by deep-frying battered sandwich cookies and candy bars may not be appropriate every day of the year, but making it an annual tradition may be a contemporary version of *pirsum hanes,* publicizing the miracle. That said, Hanuka, with its association with olive oil (a "good fat"), could provide a safe context in which communities could have important conversations about self-image, body consciousness, healthy eating and exercise.

Hanuka today reminds us to consider the issues of acculturation vs. assimilation (The struggle within the Hanuka story was a civil war as well.) and challenges us to search for light—knowledge, goodness, hope and life. Even as Hanuka serves as a reminder of a story nearly 2,200 years old, celebrating it reminds us to bring more light into a world that is often shadowed by darkness. Sometimes we can create that light with oil and wicks; sometimes we can create it through our deeds. And sometimes, all it takes, as it did for God at the moment of Creation, is the right words.

Purim

Barbara Penzner

Purim is a holiday that embraces opposites. It is filled with satire in dress, behavior, skits, music and stories. Purim is a holiday of masks, not the least of which is the façade of a carnival that conceals serious messages; Purim is an adult holiday masquerading as a children's party. The story itself is a farce pretending to be one of the more serious and historical books of the Bible. Even the name of the holiday, "Purim," which means "lots," as in "lot-

Purim for Children: Care should be taken when teaching the holiday of Purim to young children. While adults can understand the complexities of a farce, young children cannot, and they are frightened when they hear of a villain who wants to murder Jews. We try to avoid exposing pre-school children to the Holocaust, yet inquisitive young children may want to understand why Haman wanted to kill all the Jews. Purim is in many ways an adult holiday. —L.P.

tery," identifies this holiday with the arbitrary wins and losses of our lives, with risks, gambling and chance.

The festivities surrounding Purim are the most outlandish and whimsical of the Jewish calendar. Most Jews associate Purim with costumes and carnivals, *graggers* (noisemakers) and hamantashen (three-cornered, filled cookies that evoke the three-cornered hat of Haman) that appeal to children. But it would be wrong to dismiss Purim as a holiday only for children. Whether considering the deeper messages of the Megillah, the scroll containing the Book of Esther, or joining in the self-mocking atmosphere of a Purim *shpiel*, a satirical skit or short play, adults deserve to celebrate and enjoy Purim. Perhaps by putting on a mask for one day, we can learn something

Across cultures and over time, carnival traditions—especially the aspects of masquerade and reversal—have fulfilled both subversive and conservative social functions. When nobility masquerade as peasants and peasants pretend to be kings, when men play women and women dress up as men, the hierarchies of ordinary social organization are actually reinforced because when the carnival is over and things return to "normal," the categories of social organization have been reified and are stronger than ever. The experience of upside-down does, however, leave a trace effect, and girls may smile to remember how it felt to wear pants, as the peasants may remain inspired by the feeling of seeing one of their own as king. See *Rabelais and His World: Carnival and Grotesque* by Mikhail Bakhtin and *The Politics and Poetics of Transgression* by Peter Stallybrass and Allon White. —L.H.L.

Purim is a story about passing—the pretense of being a different sort of person for protection, advantage, and even adventure. —D.D.M.

The Talmud taught: "Wherever you find God's majesty, there do you find God's humility." (B. Talmud. Megillah 31a) That is, all of our descriptions of God are partial, inadequate glimpses. God is greater than we can conceive, so we only see God masked, robed in one quality or another. When we mask ourselves on Purim, we, too, imitating God, reveal aspects of ourselves that may otherwise be invisible. —J.S.S.

about the masks we wear every day and in the process discover some of the contradictions in our own lives.

The Story of Purim

Megilat Esther, the Scroll (or Book) of Esther, can be found in the third section of the Hebrew Bible, *Ketuvim* (Writings). The story it tells takes place in Shushan, the capital of ancient Persia. While elements of the tale reflect Persian culture, most scholars have determined that this book is more fiction than history. As the story of a foiled antisemitic plot, the Book of Esther has become an archetype for retelling later incidents when plots against the Jews were "miraculously" prevented from coming to fruition. In fact, the story's ending, with thousands of Persians being slaughtered by a small Jewish minority and hundreds of others Judaizing (either becoming or pretending to be Jews), turns the tale on its head. Like the holiday of Purim, the Book of Esther contains everything—and its opposite.

The tale opens with an extended banquet hosted by the Persian King Ahasuerus. After months (!) of feasting and

The story contains concentric circles of excess. It describes luxurious and over-long royal parties, mirrored by the lesser parties of the lesser people. Ironically, the sense of universal drinking creates a democratizing effect, as if everyone were equal in revelry. —L.H.L.

drinking, the king commands his queen, Vashti, to appear before his guests "wearing the royal crown" and presumably nothing else. When Vashti refuses, the king's advisers urge him to banish his wife in order to prevent other women in the empire from disobeying their husbands. Once Vashti has been removed, King Ahasuerus must fill the vacancy. He mandates an elaborate audition system and orders that "all the beautiful young virgins" (Esther 2:3) be brought to the king's harem.

At this point, our heroine, Esther, is introduced as a beautiful young virgin with Jewish ancestry who joins the harem. Her foster-father, Mordecai, keeps watch over his

The biblical text states that the king orders Vashti to appear "wearing her crown." The rabbis interpret this order to mean: wearing *only* her crown. —L.H.L.

Vashti has been partying with the women, and we thereby understand that the parties are sex-segregated. —E.R.S.

The king is advised to banish his queen lest the women of the realm follow her example of disobedience and threaten the power dynamic between the sexes everywhere in the kingdom. This anxiety indicates awareness that the sexual power structure is fragile; if not well policed, the balance could be upset. Vashti's refusal establishes the rule: "appear when you are called, and only when you are called." Vashti and Esther are, therefore, not opposites but rather synonyms or literary doubles. They break the same rule. Vashti does not appear when she is called, and Esther appears (with a vengeance!) when she is not called. Esther vindicates Vashti. Also made clear is that for the author of Esther, men control the infiltration of one sex into the space of the other. —L.H.L.

There is something subtly disturbing about the language describing the relationship between Mordecai and Esther. In 2:7 he is described as her *omen*, a peculiar male form of a word for a wet nurse. Back in Numbers 11:12, Moses has an outburst in which he complains, "Am I supposed to carry [the Israelites] in my bosom like an *omen* carries a suckling baby?" But Esther is no suckling baby. Later in the same verse we learn that she is "shapely and nice to look at," and that when her parents died, Mordecai "took her to be his daughter." If I were observing a bond like this forming in my congregation, I might have some worries. —M.H.

young ward, inquiring daily about her welfare. Esther, whose given name is the Hebrew Hadassah but who goes by a more Persian name, does not reveal to anyone in the palace that she is a Jew. When her turn to "meet" the king arrives, Esther wins Ahasuerus over and is named queen. A subplot is inserted at this point, in which Mordecai saves the king's life by informing Esther that he has overheard a plot to assassinate the king.

The arch-villain Haman is then introduced as the king's highest official. Just as Mordecai's pedigree connects him to King Saul, Haman's ancestry goes back to the Jewish archenemy King Agag, the Amalekite whom Saul was commanded to kill (I Samuel 15), thereby setting up a

Esther's name has been linked to Ishtar, the Sumerian/Babylonian goddess of love and fertility. But her Persian-sounding name also maps nicely onto the Hebrew root *s-t-r*, to hide or conceal. —D.K.

Mordecai is strategic. Only after he locates his niece close to power and reports the plot on the king's life is he represented as taking the risk of asserting his Jewish identity by refusing to bow down. He prepares well for the confrontation with power. —L.H.L.

On *Shabbat Zakhor* (right before Purim) 2002, I served as a scholar-in-residence at Congregation Bet Am Shalom. It is the day on which traditionally we are commanded not to forget that Amalek ambushed us when we wandered in the wilderness, because Haman was an Amalekite. Teaching a text by Rebbe Nahman of Bratslav on forgiving evil, I was challenged energetically about how foolish this was with regard to the evils of terrorists. Harry Waizer, who was in the World Trade Center five months before on September 11 and who was making his first appearance in synagogue after countless surgeries, stood up and said: "Perhaps the problem stems from King Saul—not that he *didn't* kill King Agag, but that he *did* massacre the Amalekites. What if Saul had broken the cycle of violence and had disobeyed God's command to wipe out Amalek? How might the subsequent history of Israel and the descendants of Agag have been altered?" —J.J.S.

classic battle between the forces of good (Mordecai) and the forces of evil (Haman). Irked by Mordecai's refusal to bow down before him, Haman determines to obliterate the entire Jewish nation in Persia. He easily convinces Ahasuerus to proceed with the plan, and the news is sent throughout the empire. When Mordecai hears of the plan, he enjoins the Jews of Persia to enter a period of mourning. In a comic scene, Esther sends clothes out to Mordecai so that he shouldn't embarrass her, while he replies with news of the impending destruction that has apparently not been mentioned to the queen. Finally, Esther dramatically agrees to take up the Jewish people's case with the king, despite potential danger to herself.

Esther succeeds in passing the first trial by charming the king in a scene filled with sexual innuendo, and she invites him and Haman to a feast. Haman is delighted by

Esther changes from mourning attire into finery to seduce her husband into "touching the royal scepter," the signal that he forgives her transgression into his space. On the model of other biblical heroines, Esther uses her sexuality to acquire political power. Her own desire is pretense, and her fancy clothes belie her true feelings. She is sad on the inside but removes her mourning attire to be seductive. Esther's dolling herself up is therefore an emotional masquerade. This detail in the story supports the early psychoanalytic insight that femininity itself is masquerade (first theorized by Joan Riviere in "Womanliness as a Masquerade," *International Journal of Psychoanalysis,* 1929). —L.H.L.

Mordecai warns Esther that if she does not do what she can to save her people, she will not escape their fate, a warning that has an uncanny resonance in our own post-Holocaust time. Power and influence were not enough to protect many German Jews from the decree against them. Esther poignantly agrees to intervene, with the statement of resignation, "If I perish, I perish." Until this point, Mordecai has been orchestrating events. Now Esther takes over. She orders the Jews to fast; she devises the plan; and she gives the marching orders. She becomes a stateswoman. —L.H.L.

the invitation, but his good mood is eradicated when he sees his nemesis Mordecai. Haman's wife Zeresh suggests that he build an immense gallows upon which to hang Mordecai.

Meanwhile, during a sleepless night, the king is reminded of Mordecai's success in foiling the assassination plot, and the king chooses to honor him. In another comic scene, Ahasuerus consults Haman on the proper way to honor a loyal subject. Thinking that he is the intended honoree, Haman describes an elaborate ceremony that he is then forced to bestow on Mordecai.

From that point on, Haman's fortunes are reversed. At a feast that Esther hosts, the queen identifies Haman as the villain of the story and simultaneously reveals her Jewish identity. Haman is hanged on the gallows intended for Mordecai, and Mordecai is elevated to Haman's previous office. But annulling the decree to kill off the Jews is not so easy. To counter the edict, Ahasuerus must send out a counter-decree permitting the Jews to defend themselves. All plans have been turned on their heads.

To celebrate the day that "had been transformed from one of grief and mourning to one of festive joy," (Esther 9:22) Mordecai institutes an annual holiday with specific ritual practices, and Esther records them in a scroll.

The Megillah calls the gallows an *etz gavoha*—literally, a big tree. (5:14) Whose is bigger is a central Purim question. —M.H.

Origins of the Holiday

Megilat Esther is one of the five books/scrolls in the *Ketuvim* (Writings) section of the Bible designated to be read on Jewish holidays. (The others are *Shir Hashirim*/Song of Songs on Passover, Ruth on Shavuot, *Eykha*/Lamentations on *Tisha B'Av*, and *Kohelet*/Ecclesiastes on Sukkot.) Yet Purim bears little resemblance to these other holy days. More analogous to Purim in some basic and surprising ways is the holiday of Hanuka. Both stories originate after the editing and closing of the Torah, the source of the major holidays of the Jewish calendar. Purim is the only biblically ordained holiday outside of the Torah. Hanuka is not biblical. It is recorded in the book of Maccabees, which is preserved in the Apocrypha—biblical-era books that did not become part of the Hebrew Bible (but are included in the Roman Catholic Scriptures). Therefore, the rabbis permitted everyday activities, including work, to proceed on these two holidays, giving them a different status than the biblical pilgrimage festivals and Shabbat. Without the usual restrictions on work, a variety of playful customs developed for both Purim and Hanuka.

Some scholars contend that both festivals arose during the period of Greek rule over the land of Judea (332–63 BCE), when Jews were subject to great empires that alternately tolerated and outlawed Jewish religious practices. The events of Hanuka took place in the Land of Israel, while the story of Purim is set in the Diaspora. In fact, the book of Maccabees refers to the holiday of Purim as "the day of Mordecai." Both holidays deal with overcoming an enemy ruler, and both commemorate the victory and its triumphant celebration. They are the two ancient holidays for which one recites the paragraph "*Al Hanisim*" ("for the miracles") in the *Amida* prayer during the holiday, though the specifics of the prayer differ for each. Thus, despite their lack of origins in the Torah, both festivals survived, acquired new meanings and grew in popularity after the destruction of the Temple.

Both Purim and Hanuka bear similarities to non-Jewish festivals, ancient and modern. Hanuka features lights at a time of darkness, typical of winter-solstice celebrations and the Roman Saturnalia. While Purim may look to us like Mardi Gras, it is reminiscent of the carnival holidays of many other cultures as well, and its origins may be traceable to a Persian or Babylonian carnival festival that

There are important differences in the vision of empire in the Megillah and Maccabees as well. In 1–2 Maccabees, the Seleucid emperor is portrayed as anti-Jewish. In Esther, Ahasuerus is not anti-Jewish. When he approves Haman's idea, he is not purposefully authorizing an anti-Jewish plot since Haman never names the people he proposes to kill. At the end of the book, Ahasuerus remains contentedly married to a Jew and appoints another Jew as his second-in-command. Rather, the arch-villain in Esther, Haman, is a member of another ethnic minority within the Persian empire, not a "natural" member of the ruling imperial elite. These differences articulate different ideals of Jewish political life. Hanuka celebrates and argues for Jewish sovereignty and autonomy, while Esther argues for Jewish success and safety within a larger empire. —E.R.S.

Mardi Gras, like other celebrations of carnival (a word that means "refraining from meat"—*carne*), is linked to Lent, formally balancing religious excess and restraint. The Scroll of Esther similarly represents both feasting and fasting, and the holiday's mandate to feast (the Purim *se'uda*) is balanced by the injunction to fast on the preceding day (*Ta'anit Esther,* The Fast of Esther). —L.H.L.

took place around the vernal equinox. It is likely that Jews adapted carnival customs of Christian Europe during the 15th and 16th centuries for their Purim celebrations, including appointing a Purim king (later, a Purim rabbi), similar to the jester pope. This custom survives today in the form of Purim Torah, a parody of traditional texts, and the Purim *shpiel,* a satirical play or series of skits.

Although a serious reading of the story might lead one to see Purim as a holiday of revenge, reading the story of Esther as a comedy provides a more joyous, self-mocking message. Historically, Jews have enjoyed the day as an escape from their usual worries. Unlike other dates in the calendar that recall past persecutions (such as *Tisha B'Av* or *Yom Hashoah*), Purim has a happy ending. The story itself provides a fantasy view of a topsy-turvy world, where the Jews not only escape from their would-be destroyers, but also turn the tables on them. At one point in the tale, many Persians "profess to be Jews" in order to save themselves—in marked contrast to historical reality, when conversion to Judaism was banned and "passing as a Jew" would have been unheard of. With its unusually

The happy ending of the Purim story is another reason to link Purim to Hanuka. —D.D.M.

In another interesting reversal, Esther "passes" as a non-Jew. —L.H.L.

raucous celebration, Purim permits us to laugh at ourselves and at our history and to behave in ways that would be discouraged the rest of the year.

Preparation for the Holiday

Purim falls on the 14th day of the Hebrew month of Adar. The Jewish calendar provides for an additional month, Adar II, seven times in every 19-year cycle in order to keep the Jewish holidays in their proper seasons. In a leap year, Purim is observed in the second Adar rather than in the first, so that it always falls one month prior to Pesach.

Playing with the topsy-turvy theme of Purim (whose name itself means "lots,") some years ago my congregation created a Purim Monopoly game. The board is drawn on a bedsheet and spread across the shul floor every year, with big fuzzy dice and cards that say things like, "King A. really gets off on your perfume. Move ahead two squares ..." or, "Impaled—you're out." —M.H.

My friend and academic mentor, a Catholic nun who had received permission from her Mother Superior to move out of the campus convent, decided to rent an apartment in a tranquil, mostly Jewish, neighborhood recommended by her *frum* (ritually observant) dentist. On the afternoon of moving day she called me, obviously upset. Unknown to her when reserving the moving van, she had inadvertently chosen Purim as the day to move into her satellite convent. "Did I make a terrible mistake?" she asked me with alarm in her voice. Her new street, she explained, was anything but quiet and her Jewish neighbors anything but modest in their behavior and dress. "Give it a day," I advised. "It'll pass." —D.K.

Purim never falls on Shabbat and, unlike major festivals, does not end with a *Havdala* service, so it is a holiday that often is enjoyed over several days' time. Shushan Purim, observed on the 15th day of Adar, refers to the date when Purim is celebrated in Jerusalem and other ancient walled cities. The Megillah itself names both—Adar 14 and Adar 15—for the celebration, leading some scholars to believe that there were originally two traditions for the actual observance of Purim. In the Megillah, the Jews of Shushan, a walled city, were forced to postpone their own celebration because of extended fighting there. Today, Shushan Purim applies only to those cities that were encircled by a wall in the time of Joshua (Megillah 1:1), limiting it to a few contemporary cities, most notably Jerusalem.

Spiritual preparation for the holiday begins on the Shabbat preceding Purim, known as *Shabbat Zakhor*, when a second Torah reading is added to the regular

I like to think of the month that separates Purim and Pesach as a period of women's folk *omer*. Just as Jews formally count the days from the end of Pesach, marking the Exodus, to Shavuot, marking the receiving of Torah, so, too, many women over the generations have begun their Passover preparations when Purim is over, counting the days until Seder. (I remember my grandmother saying every year, as Purim came to a close, "Oy. It's Pesach.") The days between Purim and Pesach are anticipatory time, women's time, leading up to the liberations of the Exodus. The story of Esther's heroism prepares us for Shifra and Puah, who defy orders and save babies; Yocheved makes a basket; Miriam watches in the reeds; Pharaoh's daughter takes a slave-baby home. The grand acts of liberation of the Exodus are preceded by quiet preparatory acts of women's heroism. Purim and Pesach are a balanced set—the former about human heroes and the latter about God—linked by attention to the details of cleaning, historically often supervised by women. —L.H.L.

Shabbat portion. The reading, Deuteronomy 25:17–19, recalls the deeds of Amalek, the archetypal enemy of the Israelites and, by extension, of the Jewish people. In this Torah portion, we hear the perplexing commandment to "blot out the memory of Amalek," and "not to forget."

The haftarah of *Shabbat Zakhor* recounts the story of King Saul's defeat of the Amalekite King Agag (I Samuel 15). This haftarah connects Haman the Agagite with his ancestor, King Agag of Amalek.

The day before Purim (or on Thursday, if Purim begins on Saturday night), is *Ta'anit Esther*, the Fast of Esther. The origins of this fast are unclear. Although the story indicates that Esther proclaimed a three-day fast (Esther 4:16), her own fast took place in the month of Nisan, at the time when Haman's plot was announced, nearly a full year before the month of Adar. Some suggest that *Ta'anit Esther* recalls the fast of Jews in Shushan as they prepared to defend themselves. Just as Jews fast on *Tisha B'Av* to mourn the Destruction of the Temple in Jerusalem, so the Fast of Esther brings up images of the fate of the Jews if Haman had not been defeated.

Like many minor fasts sprinkled throughout the Jewish year, this fast is not well known or practiced in the liberal Jewish community. Unlike the major fasts of Yom

Kippur and *Tisha B'Av*, it is customary to refrain from food and drink only from sunrise to sundown on a minor fast day. On Purim the fast ends when the festivities begin. Some liberal Jews include the Fast of Esther in their Purim preparations as a way of neutralizing often exaggerated behaviors on Purim. Again, the theme of opposites contrasts a sober fast with the raucous party. The solemnity of a fast can give us an opportunity to consider how to prevent our rejoicing on Purim from leading to extreme behavior.

Home Preparation and Rituals

In the Book of Esther itself, we find the basis for the essential elements of the Purim celebration:

Liberal Judaism does well to restore the significance of *Ta'anit Esther*, the Fast of Esther. Kolot: Center for Jewish Women's and Gender Studies at the Reconstructionist Rabbinical College, has promoted the observance of *Ta'anit Esther* as a Day of Social Justice that each year honors a modern Esther, a Jewish woman who advocates for justice. JOFA (The Jewish Orthodox Feminist Alliance) has encouraged us to use the Fast of Esther to attend to the problem of the *aguna* (abandoned wife) in the Orthodox community, and the Mistabra Institute has urged the Jewish community to address specifically the global problem of trafficking in women, especially appropriate since Esther is effectively "trafficked" when virgins are gathered for the king's harem. —L.H.L.

Ta'anit Esther is being reconstructed in some communities as a day to focus on preventing domestic violence and abuse, and to honor women who, like Esther and her predecessor Vashti, have been able to prevail in ways large and small over men who have chosen to use their physical strength, status, and/or financial power to intimidate or restrain them. This fast day also presents us with an opportunity to contribute money, perhaps equal to the cost of the food we're not eating, toward domestic violence prevention. —D.K.

> . . . to observe the 14th and 15th days of Adar, every year—the same days on which the Jews enjoyed relief from their foes and the same month which had been transformed for them from one of grief and mourning to one of festive joy. They were to observe them as days of feasting and merrymaking, and as an occasion for sending gifts to one another and presents to the poor. (Esther 9:21–22)

Rabbinic Judaism identified four mitzvot of Purim: hearing the reading of the Megillah, feasting and making merry, sending *mishloaḥ manot* (gifts of food) to friends and neighbors, and giving *tzedaka* to the poor. While the Megillah reading takes place in the synagogue, many of Purim's observances apply to the home.

The custom of *mishloaḥ manot* (also known as *sh'laḥ manot* or *sholaḥ monos*), while known today as a Purim custom, was likely also an aspect of other holiday celebrations. The biblical Book of Nehemiah speaks of sending *manot* on Rosh Hashana (Nehemiah 8:10–12). Even the Book of Esther prefigures this custom, when it refers to the *manot* (here, food rations) that Esther received in the palace (Esther 2:9). Over time, this custom became associated solely with Purim. In this way, Purim uniquely reminds us to cultivate our relationships with friends and acquaintances as well as to reach out to strangers.

Jewish custom gives the minimum requirement for *mishloaḥ manot* as two cooked dishes. Many families provide baked goods, nuts, candy and dried fruit on a decorated plate or basket. In some communities, making hamantashen is an annual congregational or school event. Some congregations encourage the sharing of plates of goodies among congregants, or delivering baskets to senior members, nursing home residents or others. All of these practices serve to bring members of a community closer and encourage people to show appreciation to friends.

In addition to sharing with friends, we give to strangers on Purim. Giving *tzedaka* is embedded in Jewish practice before every Shabbat or festival occasion. The mitzvah of

Some congregations have developed a fundraising mechanism for the benefit of the congregation or other beneficiaries that prevents anyone from receiving an overwhelming number of gifts, by providing a *mishloaḥ manot* service. Anyone can create a list of those within the community to whom they would like to send and contribute a given amount for each name. The recipient gets one plate, listing all the people who contributed in their honor. —B.P.

Another congregational practice is to create *mishloaḥ manot* communally through Hebrew school classes and by voluntary donations of baked goods and other items. A delivery service can bring a basket to every single member of the congregation during the days leading up to Purim. It takes some work to make this happen, but there is something special about getting a small package delivered to your door from a fellow congregant to tell you how important you are to the community. —E.W.

A friend of mine saves cartoons and jokes all year long to include with her *mishloaḥ manot*, making her gift the most fun package of the year. —M.H.

matanot l'evyonim (gifts to the poor) is a particular Purim form of *tzedaka*. On Purim, we give not only out of righteous obligation, but also in order to share our joy. The traditional custom is to give to at least two poor people. Prior to the Megillah reading would be an opportune time for individuals and families to consider recipients for the funds already in the family or community *tzedaka* box. Jewish organizations such as MAZON: A Jewish Response to Hunger, Bend the Arc, American Jewish World Service or a local Jewish relief fund are among those to which one might choose to send donations. One might also bring non-perishable food items to the local food pantry in honor of Purim.

The fourth mitzvah of Purim is *matanot l'evyonim* (giving gifts to the poor), not the more general obligation of *tzedaḳa*. This provides an opportunity to think creatively and substantially about what the poor and less fortunate in your community may need. Some congregations have the tradition of asking for food donations as an "entrance fee" to the Megillah reading. For others, this is the one time where passing the hat takes place in the context of communal Jewish worship. One year in my congregation, the B'nai Mitzvah class held the Megillah "hostage" and collected "ransom" before the reading could begin in order to engage the community in fulfilling this mitzvah. One of my favorite things to do each year is to hand-deliver the monetary and food collections from the Megillah reading to our local food pantry/soup kitchen on Purim. Even though this is just one of many ways that we interact with this organization over the course of the year, this transaction, a mitzvah mentioned in the Megillah, is profoundly concrete. —E.W.

The food customs of Purim—including *mishloaḥ manot*, *matanot l'evyonim* and a *se'udat mitzvah*—maintain a balance, unique to Purim, between giving to friends and giving to the poor. The usual Jewish consciousness of addressing want and creating justice is, on Purim, matched by our attention to protecting our intimate circles of gift exchange on which people routinely depend for support, regardless of financial circumstance. —L.H.L.

Collecting *tzedaka* at Purim may also be related to *maḥatzit hashekel*, the gift of a half-shekel as described in the Torah. (Exodus 30:13) The Torah describes two kinds of donations toward building the *Mishkan* (Tabernacle) in the wilderness: free-will offerings and half-shekel offerings. While the former allowed people to give as much or as little as they desired, the latter was defined as a token offering of a half-shekel given by every person. The deadline for giving the half-shekel was the first day of the Hebrew month of Nisan, making Purim an ideal time to fulfill this mitzvah. Having no traditional restrictions against handling money as there are on Shabbat and holidays, Purim is one of the rare times in the year when large groups of Jews who are gathered in the synagogue may collect money. Some communities follow the custom of passing a *tzedaka* plate or box around before or even during the service. The funds are then donated to the needy. Collections for the local food pantry serve a similar purpose. In this way, *tzedaka* is practiced publicly, yet without great fanfare. The idea of the *maḥatzit hashekel* is intended to minimize class and economic distinctions, and to model philanthropy on a grand scale, and it transforms many small contributions into a few large gifts, thereby

I understand the tenor of Purim giving to be reckless, without one's usual prudence about giving *tzedaḳa*. There is a story about someone who, on Purim, would leave money sticking out of his pockets and walk the street, encouraging poor people to, as it were, pick his pockets. In that spirit sometimes on Purim I walk around town and hand around $20 bills to homeless people I bump into, or I impulsively send off a somewhat-larger-than-I can-afford gift to a project that isn't usually on my radar.
—M.H.

modeling how collective responsibility is supported by individual responsibility.

Another traditional Purim event is the *se'uda*, a holiday feast. This is an occasion not only for gathering and eating, but also for extending the party atmosphere to Purim afternoon. While this is often a family or home event, communities also host Purim celebrations, including food, Purim *shpiels* (plays) and carnivals. An entire genre of Purim Torah has emerged over the centuries, lampooning and parodying traditional Jewish ritual and liturgy. There is no Kiddush for Purim, except for the hearty Purim Kiddush that uses Hebrew plays on words to encourage drinking more wine. In Reconstructionist communities the celebration usually includes plenty of contemporary humor in English, games and Purim *shpiels*.

The most prevalent food on Purim is hamantashen (Hebrew: *ozney haman*), sweet triangular pastries, recalling either Haman's hat or ears or pockets (*tashen*), depending on the language. Hamantashen often have fillings of prune, poppy seed or fruit preserves, prompting debates about which fillings are best. In addition to hamantashen, different Jewish communities over time assigned other foods to the Purim feast, including chickpeas and kreplach. Vegetarian fare is meant to replicate Esther's menus while she was in Ahasuerus' palace.

My beloved friend and teacher, Ella Russell, made the most beautiful and delicious hamantashen in our community. All of her friends and neighbors, Jewish and not, looked forward to her Purim gifts. When she became ill with a brain tumor, she invited specific people over during the year and laboriously taught them her recipe and her particular touches, so that her gift would be carried on. —M.H.

Although the Megillah makes no mention of what she ate or even that she observed Jewish dietary laws, traditional interpreters assumed that she avoided non-kosher foods by eating beans and lentils.

Communal Observance

When you are looking for a congregation or community, its celebration of Purim will often tell you more about a group than its observance of Yom Kippur. Each commu-

Purim seems to be the exact opposite of Yom Kippur, the holiest and most solemn of holidays. Or is it? For centuries, commentators have relished an outsized pun that binds these two special days in the Jewish calendar. Yom Kippur, also known as *Yom HaKippurim*, thus becomes via wordplay *Yom k̦'Purim*—a day like Purim. How so? One possibility is that on Yom Kippur we face the uncertainty that hovers over our individual lives—uncertainty about our own life's duration, trajectory and purpose. On Purim, we confront the uncertainty that hovers over the life of the Jewish people. When we make room, as adults, for Purim, we confront some of the same questions we face on Yom Kippur but on a different scale: How long will the Jewish people survive? By what means? Who or what will rescue us in troubled times? What is the trajectory and purpose of Jewish life? —D.K.

Purim, the holiday of frivolity, and Yom Kippur, the holiday of solemnity, have traditionally been linked by their nomenclature, in that the rabbis noticed that *Yom Kippurim* can be parsed as *Yom K'Purim* ("a day like Purim"), a day when we masquerade as fully repentant. One rabbinic tradition teaches that Purim is the only holiday that will continue to be observed in the messianic era, making the point that while a time may come when we no longer need to repent, we will always welcome opportunities to express joy and gratitude. —L.H.L.

The connection between Purim and Yom Kippur may hint at a deeper meaning in the Purim story: that of the hidden face of God. God's name is not mentioned anywhere in the Megillah, and Esther's name is a play on the word "hidden." The Babylonian Talmud (*Ḥulin* 139B) suggests that Esther's name is a reference to a verse in Deuteronomy: "But I [God] will surely conceal my face (*haster astir panay*) on that day

nity spices up the Purim service with its own form of folly. Carnivals, costume parades and Purim *shpiels* can all contribute to a fun evening for children and adults. Purim songs in English and Hebrew add to the joyous and silly atmosphere. How does a holiday that is so similar to Mardi Gras and Halloween maintain its distinctively Jewish character?

The heart of the Purim service is the reading of *Megilat Esther*, the Scroll of Esther. The Talmud records that the Megillah (literally, "scroll") was initially read only during the day, and the custom of the evening reading was added later. While some would argue that the daytime reading is the more important one, most liberal Jews are accustomed to attending the evening reading and celebration. Leading up to the reading from the Book of Esther, the weekday evening service is often peppered with silly melodies to the

for all of the ill that they have done—for they turned to other gods." (Deuteronomy 31:18) Is God's hidden face in the Purim story the result of something the Jewish people have done for which repentance is required? Or is it due to the fact that this is the first story we have of the Jewish people outside the land of Israel? They are not in a position to worship God according to tradition; do they require extra vigilance and care in maintaining their traditions and avoiding outright assimilation? —E.W.

The observance of Purim has classically been among the most egalitarian in that women share an obligation equal to men to listen to the Megillah reading with the rationale that "women were implicated in the miracle." The rabbis debate whether women's "inclusion" is due to Esther's heroism or simply that women, like men, were spared the genocide. The rabbis established early on that women should drink four cups of wine because they "were implicated in the miracle." Women are similarly obligated to light Hanuka candles because "women are implicated in the miracle." Perhaps because of this similarity, the apocryphal Book of Judith becomes associated with Hanuka, attaching a sexually powerful heroine, by analogy to Esther, to the Hanuka story. —L.H.L.

usual prayers. These tunes set the topsy-turvy mood for the evening.

For congregations with a service on the morning of Purim, the weekday service proceeds as usual. Unlike other holidays, the *Hallel* prayer is not recited on Purim. Some traditional interpreters argue that this reflects the fact that the events of the story took place outside of the Land of Israel, or that the redemption of Purim was not complete. Others, arguing from a more practical standpoint, claim that the reading of the Megillah takes the place of *Hallel*. More appropriate additions would be parodies of *Hallel* and other Jewish songs.

The Book of Esther is made up of ten chapters, traditionally chanted in Hebrew but often read in English as well so people can hear the trope but follow the story. But the way we read the Megillah is unlike any other reading of sacred text during the year. It is noisy and rowdy and highly dramatic. When the name of the arch-villain Haman is mentioned, everyone is encouraged to make

The combination of the halakhic mandate to hear the Megillah and the practices that have evolved to make it difficult if not impossible to understand what is being read have led to a paradoxical, Purim-like situation in which we are mandated to listen but prevented from hearing. As a result of this paradox, the versions of the Purim story that most Jews know are paraphrases that magnify the opposites in the story and either downplay or amend its theological oddities. —E.R.S.

Ma'yan, the Jewish Women's Project of the JCC in Manhattan, has designed "Purim Flags" with bells and encourages us to shake our flags and thus ring the bells when the names of Vashti and Esther are read, balancing the nasty noise of the groggers for the villains with congratulatory bells for the heroines. —L.H.L.

noise to "blot out" his name. This practice builds on the previously mentioned biblical injunction (*D'varim* 25:19) to "blot out" the name of Amalek. In medieval times, before *graggers* or noisemakers entered the scene, people wrote "Haman" on the soles of their shoes and "stamped out" the name every time it was mentioned. Individuals can make or bring their own noisemakers, or the synagogue can provide them. This custom should create an atmosphere of fun, as everyone behaves in a way not normally permitted.

There is more to the reading of the Megillah than making noise. When a congregation is fortunate enough to own an actual parchment scroll of the story, written without vowels like a Torah scroll, the reading becomes more of a reenactment than a repetition. The reader folds the scroll, rather than rolling it, and holds it like a proclama-

How strange that we drown out the name of Haman every time it is mentioned! If we truly wished to follow the injunction to blot out the memory of Amalek (Deuteronomy 25:19), wouldn't it be more fitting never to mention Haman's name again, and so let his name be lost to history? In recalling the Purim story year after year, aren't we instead keeping his memory alive? To truly wipe out Haman's name, we must blot out his legacy of hate. We cannot do this simply by forgetting him, for that approach can lead to complacency in the face of evil and allow cruel leaders to stand unopposed in our own times. Instead we must actively recall and disparage his memory, so we may fulfill the mitzvah of blotting out Haman, and all those who seek to harm and oppress the innocent. Perhaps this is why the same verse that commands wiping out the memory of Amalek concludes, "You must never forget." —J.W.

A noisy *gragger* can easily be made from a plastic 2-liter soda bottle by putting a handful of dried chickpeas inside. Substituting grains of rice makes a much quieter but still effective one. —D.K.

tion. While there is a special *trop*, or cantillation melody, for chanting Esther, at certain key verses a different melody is used to dramatize the meaning. When Haman's ten sons are listed, the reader draws attention to the event (as well as to the reader's own skill) by chanting the entire passage in one breath. In some congregations, players may act out the story during the telling, and other characters' names may be highlighted with specific noises or actions (such as applause for Mordecai and catcalls for Esther). All of these customs make fun of the usually serious demeanor of synagogue services and add to the atmosphere of farce.

Whether the story is told in Hebrew or English, it is worthwhile to maintain enough decorum to pay attention to the story. Recognizing the tendency for the reading to get out of hand, some communities may engage in a decision-making process about holding separate Megillah

At the Reconstructionist Rabbinical College, there is a well-established tradition that the reader of chapter nine not only chants the passage in one breath, but also while she or he stands on her or his head! —J.J.S.

Our congregation has an entire repertoire of shared Megillah sound effects:

For Vashti: Oo la la! For Ahashveros: Hiccup! Hiccup!
For Mordecai: Our Hero! For Esther: Hurray!
For Haman's wife: Hold one's nose and say: eeew! —E.W.

While communities define "enough decorum" in widely different ways, I argue that there is a limit. There are synagogues where the noise is expected to stop in precisely five seconds, when the rabbi or other designated person lowers the flag, so that there is absolutely no spontaneity. Whatever one's interpretation of *ad d'lo yada*, it has to involve *some* loosening of limits. —J.J.S.

readings for adults and for children. This practice could also permit use of some of the adult themes (mentioned below in "Purim for Adults").

The best expression of farce on Purim can be found in the creation and performance of a Purim *shpiel*. Often a highlight of a congregation's celebration, the *shpiel* usually pokes fun at political events or cultural heroes. While we refrain from "demonizing" our enemies the rest of the year, on Purim the use of comedy allows us to turn politicians, celebrities and other cultural icons into "Haman" for a night. At the very least, the *shpiel* can be a cathartic response to the major evils and minor struggles of our lives. One version of the *shpiel* is a "scholarly" debate over which are better, hamantashen or latkes.

A central aspect of the Purim *shpiel* is the opportunity to dress up and play different roles. Observing the theme that "things are not what they seem," adults and children alike often masquerade for Purim. The usual Esther, Mordecai and Haman garb has given way to all kinds of costumes that are not specific to the Purim story. Congregational leaders often prepare elaborate surprise costumes for the annual Purim celebration, and some synagogues

Costumes purport to conceal, but they often reveal a lot. We are always "dressing up" to create or enhance one persona or another, but we usually are constrained by our social roles and boundaries. When we overtly don a costume, we have greater freedom to transgress boundaries, and our choice of costumes can be revealing, intentionally or inadvertently. Significantly, on Purim we are not held responsible for our choices; we are allowed, even encouraged, to be transgressive and outrageous.

—J.J.S.

announce themes for the congregation to follow. Purim offers us a rare chance to put on masks, or even to try out an alter ego. Congregations sometimes have contests for the best costume. In the story of Esther, Mordecai himself puts on different costumes, including sackcloth and ashes when he learns of Haman's plot and royal robes when Haman is defeated. These two examples represent starkly divergent images of the Jew as victim and victor. The story itself gives us permission to try on different roles, and to have fun doing it. The festival of Purim underscores the idea of a synagogue as an organic community, a place where people can be themselves on a variety of levels. Having fun and laughing at ourselves has a place in Jewish life at least as much as being reflective or serious.

Drinking Alcohol

In the Talmud one finds the classic reference to alcohol on Purim, quoting Rava, who said that one should drink enough on Purim so that "Blessed is Mordecai" (*Barukh*

Costumes and dressing up on Purim also provide a Jewish counterpoint to the secular observance of Halloween, for which costumes seem to get bloodier, more grotesque and more horrific each year. Purim costumes in our community run the gamut from characters from the Megillah to comic book characters, embracing all sorts of silliness. But Jasons in hockey masks, Grim Reapers and headless vampires dripping blood don't bother coming. —E.W.

Mordeḥai) and "Cursed is Haman" (*Arur Haman*) are indistinguishable (*ad d'lo yada*—until one doesn't know [the difference]). (*Megila* 7b) This statement has engendered a variety of interpretations that either encourage or discourage excessive drinking. While some would argue that one would have to be very drunk to mix up the good guy with the bad guy, others might say that even light drinking could lead to this confusion. The true meaning of this statement is obscured even more by the fact that in *gematria* (the practice of assessing a numerical value to letters), "*Barukh Mordeḥai*" and "*Arur Haman*" have exactly the same value. Rava's statement also reminds us of the nature of Purim as a holiday of opposites.

In the biblical text, Mordecai and Haman are as much alter-egos as arch-enemies. They are both members of ethnic minorities who rise to positions of power and influence in the royal court. They are both the sources of violent decrees and the declarers of holidays or special occasions. In the end of the story, the facility with which Persians become Jews testifies to the story's contention that in Shushan, the two are not so far apart, and the bridge between them is not impassable. —E.R.S.

Jewish teachers of *musar* have long stressed the discernment required to avoid unintended consequences—intending to do good but causing evil, or intended evil with positive consequences. (See Moses Luzzatto (an 18th century ethicist), *Mesilat Yesharim*, chapter 20.) On all other days we tremble about our inability to control outcomes, but on Purim, we let go and laugh about blessings that end up as curses, and vice versa. —J.J.S.

The connection between Purim and intoxication undoubtedly has early origins. One needs to look no further than the Esther story itself for the source of drunken carousing on this holiday. Feasting and drinking provide a steady motif for the story, and they are mentioned in nearly every chapter. (Esther 1:3, 2:18, 3:15, 5:6, 6:14, 7:1, 8:17, 9:17,22) Of course, nowhere in the Megillah or Jewish law is getting drunk considered a mitzvah. Drinking alcohol is only one part of the general party atmosphere.

However, some have taken this custom of drunkenness to dangerous extremes, almost elevating drinking to a commandment in itself. In approaching our observance of

Alcohol abuse is a serious, often deadly problem, and I in no way want to minimize it, but ... there are still some Jews, like me, who are still learning how to have *fun.* Over thirty years ago, my therapist told me that I knew how to work well and love well, but that I needed to work on learning how to play. For me, it's easy to blame this on a certain kind of Orthodox upbringing in which *bittul Torah* (wasting time that could be spend on something worthwhile like Torah study) was a serious sin. While others have different personal histories, many of us are a little too serious. As we address concerns about uncontrolled revelry in the synagogue, let's not ignore the serious and significant problem of the playfully-challenged! —J.J.S.

The *Orḥot Tzadiḳim*, a five-hundred-year-old *mussar* (a Jewish movement aiming at moral instruction and invigoration) text, offers a positive teaching on the spiritual efficacy of wine: "This is how wine should be used: one should use it as a cure for sorrow, in order to strengthen oneself in Torah by learning it with joy, for when one is steeped in sorrow, one cannot learn. And even a *bet din* (court of law) which is in sorrow cannot adjudicate correctly. Sorrow also impairs one's concentration in prayer. Also, when one is steeped in sorrow, if someone asks for a favor, one is unable to fulfill that request. And it is written (Isaiah 49:8) 'In time of [favor] I will answer you.' It is to these ends, then, that a wise man should drink wine ..." [*Sefer Orḥot Tzadiḳim*, "The Gate of Joy," p. 175, translated by Rabbi Shraga Silverstein, Feldheim Publishers 1995] —M.H.

Purim, we need to consider the fact that drinking to excess can lead to risk-taking and self-destructive behavior. After all, Rava and his colleagues did not have to worry about drinking and driving. In addition, the practice of binge drinking among teenagers and college students is a real concern. The existence of JACS (Jewish Alcoholics, Chemically Dependent Persons, and Significant Others) has disabused us of the tired notion that Jews are not alcoholics. Out of sensitivity to Jews in recovery, communities may want to consider asking whether alcohol has a place in the community's celebration. At the very least, we need to consider whether public drunkenness is a behavior that we desire to promote among our children.

This topic can be an important focus for community decision making around Purim. In considering a communal event or even one's own private observance, here are some questions to ask. Will children or teens be present? Will alcohol enhance or endanger the celebration? Will it be a major or a minor part of the event? Will the presence of alcoholic beverages make it uncomfortable or impossible for any individuals to participate? Would anyone miss alcohol if it were left out of the celebration? If including

The rabbis were aware of the dangers that could arise from the excesses of Purim celebration. A story in the Talmud (B. *Megila* 7b) tells of two rabbis who become so drunk on Purim that one slit the other's throat. When he woke up to find his friend dead, he prayed, and the friend was restored to life. The next year, when he invited his friend to celebrate Purim together once again, the friend declined, saying, "A miracle does not take place on every occasion!" While we should certainly enjoy our Purim celebrations, we are warned of the risks of indulging in excess and are cautioned not to count on being spared the consequences of our actions. —J.W.

alcoholic drinks, is it possible to create a safe atmosphere for everyone? Can the community arrange for designated drivers? Will there be non-alcoholic alternatives?

Ad d'lo yada is a statement about confusing what is good and bad, right and wrong. But it does not need to lead to dangerous behavior. There are certainly ways of celebrating Purim that take this to heart, aside from drinking to excess.

Purim for Adults

While some people have experienced Purim only as a holiday for children, this is an unfortunate development. Many themes of the holiday can be understood better by adults than by children. Not only that, but who says that only children are allowed to play in shul? Purim is a holiday that invites us all to put on masks and to laugh at ourselves.

George Bernard Shaw reputedly said, "We don't stop playing because we grow old. We grow old because we stop playing." —L.H.L.

When we want to say in Yiddish that someone told every detail of the story or made a big deal of an event, we refer to the *ganze* megillah— "the whole story." When we read the whole story of Esther, we find it is an odd book to be included in the Holy Scriptures. Most glaringly, the name of God is not mentioned anywhere in the text. In fact, while most biblical texts would attribute the reversals of the story, including Haman's plot being foiled and Haman himself being hanged, to a divine miracle, *Megilat Esther* makes no such claim. Some hand-written Megillah scrolls begin each column with the Hebrew word "*Hamelekh*" (the king), trying to insert God back into the story. Some would argue that this is a case of God working behind the scenes. Reconstructionists are comfortable with the divine working through human beings. But when one reads the story carefully, one may also conclude that God really doesn't belong here in the same way as in other books of the Bible.

The lack of any mention of God in the Book of Esther may reflect the Jews' entrance into history: God no longer explicitly appears or intervenes in the world as God did for earlier generations of Israelites in the stories that form the mythic backdrop for Jewish history. At the same time, the rabbis discern a number of oblique references to God in the Megillah—most notably Mordecai's assertion that if Esther fails to act for the Jews, help may yet come from another place (Esther 4:14)—but they are all implicit. Just as God is hidden within the Book of Esther, perhaps the story of Purim suggests that God is hidden within the world, contained in the actions of individual people. Perhaps human beings serve as masks behind which God's presence in the world is concealed. —J.W.

The Greek versions of Esther as well as the Aramaic Targum do not share these anomalies. In the Greek and Aramaic versions of the story, God is quite present, and Esther and Mordecai pray and observe distinctive Jewish practices. —E.R.S.

Outside of the Torah, traditional Jews do not claim that the other books of the Bible were given by God. Many of the events in the Bible, including those in Joshua, the Books of Samuel and Kings, can be corroborated as historical. But the Book of Esther, while located in a historical setting in the capital of Persia, does not attempt to tell us history. Most biblical scholars deny that it has any historical truth, or even a basis in particular people or events. Like some other biblical books, particularly books of the Writings (*Ketuvim*), it plays a completely different literary role. Just as the Song of Songs brings love poetry into the Bible and the Book of Proverbs provides moral teachings, Esther highlights the art of comedy as holy literature.

When reading the Book of Esther, one of the main themes to remember is that things are not always as they seem. This book mocks us in our piety and runs roughshod over our exalted values. Even in their distress, neither Mordecai nor Esther pray! King Ahasuerus, often described as a fool, is in actuality a hedonist. He is either feasting or drinking in nearly every chapter of the story (see Esther 1:3, 2:18, 3:15, 5:6, 6:14, 7:1). The book opens with a feast that takes place over 180 days (1:4) and is followed by seven more days of feasting. Esther appears to be a model of piety by contrast.

Rebecca Kohn's novel *The Gilded Chamber* is a fully elaborated fictional account of the Book of Esther. This extended contemporary "midrash" does for Esther what Anita Diamant's *The Red Tent* does for Genesis. —L.H.L.

But Esther's presumed piety begs the clichéd question: What's a nice Jewish girl doing in a palace like this? The "beauty pageant" that we usually describe to our children is actually a harem, in which the king "tries out" a new concubine every night, in a sort of Scheherazade motif. The book never describes Queen Esther's ritual observances, except for her fasting when her life is in danger. No one in the story seems concerned that Esther's husband was not a Jew! Yet the author of Esther feels no need to justify Esther's behavior, any more than he or she condemns King Ahasuerus' drunkenness.

In a literary analysis, the Book of Esther is best understood as a farce. This can make the violent aspects of the story easier to bear. The story is a kind of Jewish communal fantasy blown out of proportion. For Jews who lived under oppression and fear, or who experienced brutality

Communal fasting and wearing mourning attire signify a collective appeal to God.
—L.H.L.

A close study of Jewish history reveals that our ancestors were not as pious as our teachers of piety may have taught. If one were motivated, one could even make a strong case that impiety is a traditional Jewish value. We shouldn't believe those who try to whip us into behavioral shape by invoking our pious ancestors. The Book of Esther may serve us well by reminding us that we are not the first Jews to dress immodestly and seductively, not the first to marry non-Jews, not the first to drink alcohol in some quantity, *and* that, somehow, Jewish civilization has survived until now . . . without making any predictions about the future! —J.J.S.

Rather than read Esther's story as a "farce," we can read it as a Jewish reconstruction of a Persian folktale, featuring Esther and Mordecai (Jewish variations on either Ishtar or Astarte and Marduk), heroes who strategically challenge "might" with "right." —L.H.L.

and exile, the Book of Esther and the Purim holiday provided comic relief. The tables are turned on our enemies several times during the story, with some reversals more humorous than others. In fact, the book acknowledges this theme of reversals explicitly:

> And so, on the 13th day of the twelfth month—that is, the month of Adar—when the king's command and decree were to be executed, the very day on which the enemies of the Jews had expected to get them in their power, the opposite happened (*v'nahafokh hu*), and the Jews got their enemies in their power. (9:1)

The reversals are taken to extremes when Haman is impaled on the stake that he had erected for Mordecai. This comeuppance reinforces the comic scene earlier in the tale, when Haman leads Mordecai on a horse in the manner in which Haman expected to be honored himself. (6:7–10) When Haman is gone, Mordecai wears his adversary's robes (1:6 and 8:15) and puts on the king's ring, taking Haman's place as chief adviser.

Violence in the Purim Story

Those who accept these particular examples as humorous may find the details of chapter nine of the Book of Esther more difficult. Chapter nine describes the killing of thousands of Persians in Shushan and the provinces. But if we think of this story as a farce, then the notion of 75,000 Persians being killed is absurd, and the additional description of people "professing to be Jews" (8:17) even more of a historical impossibility. If the Book of Esther is not history but rather fantasy, then chapter nine is only a cartoon. Of course, some may oppose cartoon violence as well. Rather than excising or repressing these troubling texts, it would be worthwhile to address them in a forum outside of the Purim celebration.

It is important to face squarely the violence in *Megillat Esther*. Yes, it is a fantasy. Yes, it reflects the justifiable anger of our oppressed and disempowered ancestors. But it reflects and transmits a sense of victimization that can lead to actual violence when Jews have power, as in the State of Israel. —J.J.S.

One way to raise our consciousness about the potential dangers of violent fantasies is for the reader of chapter eight to chant the passages in a whisper, which is a traditional custom when reading the curses in the Book of Deuteronomy. It is possible to create a culture that is aversive to vengeful violence without making explicit, overt political statements. —J.J.S.

I have damaged Purim joy in our community several times over the years by highlighting my discomfort with this part of the story during the Megillah reading. My worst judgment call was making people stand up, opening our ark and reading an *al ḥet* (penitential prayer similar to those read on Yom Kippur) that I had composed for hating enemies, for rejoicing in mass slaughter and so on, beating my chest as I did so. Another year I poured fake blood all over myself as these words were being read. Having made my point—a little too sharply—I now refrain. But in truth I find this problem of celebrating violence, even in a mocking spirit, hard to overcome or transform. —M.H.

During the congregational Megillah reading, I ask everyone to put down the *graggers* during the death-filled ninth chapter. It provides enough of a shift for children and adults alike to recognize that there is a serious message that should not be celebrated, yet it doesn't interrupt the flow of the reading too much. —N.H.M.

Some use the observance of *Ta'anit Esther* as a way of acknowledging the dark side of the Purim story. As noted earlier, a literal reading of the massacre in chapter nine undoubtedly shocks the modern Jewish reader. As Elliott Horowitz has discussed in *Reckless Rites: Purim and the Legacy of Jewish Violence,* the propagandistic use of the Book of Esther has had powerful consequences throughout history because of its image of Jews as violent. Just as many of us remove drops of wine from our cups when we recite the ten plagues at the Pesach Seder and remember the suffering of the Egyptians, we ask: How can the Jews be blind to such bloodshed? Only when we recognize our own dark desires for revenge, and feel compassion even for our enemies, can we turn to rejoicing. Therefore, by fasting we acknowledge the tragic and violent acts by our own people that echo the violence of the Purim story. Only after we have purged ourselves of these disturbing aspects of the story can we enter into the holiday and take pleasure in its satirical atmosphere.

Jewish tradition forbids us from taking any pleasure in our enemies' affliction, warning "*binfol oyvekha al tismah*"—"Do not rejoice in the downfall of your enemies." (Proverbs 24:17). For much of history, the Jews have been powerless victims of a series of oppressors. It is against this backdrop that the closing chapters of the Book of Esther can be understood. Without other means of defending themselves, the Jews repeatedly turned to the one recourse they had at their disposal: story. Through reframing their suffering and asserting their ultimate triumph over their oppressors, the Jews found a way to overcome their circumstances. In giving unrestrained voice to the impulse for revenge, the Megillah violates the precept not to rejoice in the downfall of our enemies, embodying the Purim spirit of '*v'nahafokh hu*'—of temporarily turning Jewish norms on their head. —J.W.

Another troubling aspect of the story is the inescapable connection between Haman and Amalek (Esther 3:1), and the practice by many Jews of identifying contemporary "enemies of the Jews" with the biblical archenemy Amalek. Although many sages and scholars have declared that Amalek is a historical, or even a metaphorical figure, some continue to see Amalek behind every action against Jews. Some make a similar problematical link between the Egyptians of old and current Arabs.

The Torah and haftarah readings prior to Purim compound these difficulties. One might consider the paradox of the Torah's command: "Blot out the memory" and, "Do not forget." This choice of Torah readings echoes the theme of "everything and its opposite." However, while the Torah instructs us to "blot out the *memory*" of Amalek (Deuteronomy 25:19), rather than destroying

In 1994 the dark side of the Book of Esther led to an actual, notorious deed, when extremist Baruch Goldstein murdered 29 Muslims as they prayed in the mosque at Machpelah, a site in the city of Hebron that is holy to Jews and Muslims alike. By performing this act on Purim, Goldstein sent a message that he was heeding the call of the Purim story and fulfilling the command to destroy Amalek. Liberal Jews are not alone in condemning this horrific act. Rabbis of all backgrounds consider this interpretation of both the Purim story and the role of Amalek deeply misguided. After all, we are told to "blot out the memory" of our archrival, not literally to destroy him or those we identify with him. In addition, many modern sources contend that we cannot identify any living person as Amalek, with some specifically arguing that the Arabs are not the embodiment of our archrivals. Muslims consider Goldstein's act an offense against Ramadan, since it occurred during that holiday. It was roundly condemned by most Jews in Israel and elsewhere. —B.P.

him and his descendants, the message found in the haftarah is more extreme. In the Book of Samuel, the prophet Samuel instructs Saul to destroy all of the Amalekite people. Reconstructionists utterly condemn such a brutal and uncompromising demonization of human beings. At the very least, such texts require discussion and reinterpretation.

In other times, Jews made effigies of Haman that were to be hanged or burned. For Jews who lived with a fear of oppression in a way that we in North America do not experience, Purim provided a cathartic release. But vilifying the fictitious Haman is still a step removed from perpetrating violence against any human being. On Purim, noisemakers are our weapons. Rather than delete these passages, we can use them to impart to our children the idea that they are indeed troubling, and not to be taken literally.

By acting out all this unsavory energy in such a contained setting, maybe it helps to keep us from acting more of it out in real life. But I don't think that Purim does much to encourage compassion for our enemies. To the contrary, if anything. Probably the most salutary aspect of the celebration is the hangover the next day, and perhaps the vague transgressive sense left over from all that carrying-on in front of the ark. Maybe some people can make the leap from being sick to their stomachs to being queasy about dancing in enemy blood. Or maybe that's just "spin" I tell myself since I am responsible for making Purim happen in our *shul* year after year. —M.H.

Purim as a Celebration of Diaspora Life

One distinctive aspect of the Purim story to which contemporary Jews who live outside of the Land of Israel can relate is the experience of being a Jewish minority. Purim is, in fact, the only holiday tradition that celebrates an event that took place in the Diaspora once the Israelites had established a kingdom in the Land of Israel. It is surprising that neither the Land of Israel nor the Temple is referenced in the story. In a way, the happy ending of the story affirms that, all in all, life in the Diaspora is not so terrible. At Mordecai's instruction, Esther hides her identity. Yet later he calls upon her to identify herself courageously, saying, "Perhaps you have attained to royal position for just such a crisis." (Esther 4:14) The story of Esther invites discussion of the role of influential Jews throughout history and the compromises they may have made, both as Jews and as notables in the majority culture. It also provides fertile ground for considering Rabbi Mordecai Kaplan's idea of "living in two civilizations."

While Purim has become the Diaspora festival par excellence, the Hebrew version in the Bible was probably written in Judea. It probably represents a Judean fantasy of life in the Diaspora. If we consider this possibility, then Jewish residents of the Diaspora like Mordecai, who are hardly distinguishable from their gentile peers, might be targets of the satire as well as its heroes. —E.R.S.

The importance of Purim was elevated among Jews living in times and places in which they had to conceal their identity. Among Conversos (the hidden Jews of Spain), Esther was venerated as an intercessor; in some places, the holiday was known among crypto-Jews as "The Festival of Saint Esther." —L.H.L.

In *The Meaning of God in Modern Jewish Religion*, Kaplan grouped Purim and Hanuka together in the chapter titled, "Jewish Religion as a Means to Jewish National Survival." Kaplan wanted to overcome what he considered an anachronistic interpretation of these holidays. Too often, Jewish knowledge and observance of Purim and Hanuka are limited to commemorating the victories over our physical enemies in what Kaplan considered a narrow focus on Jewish national survival. Kaplan envisioned both Purim and Hanuka more broadly as opportunities to summon us to appreciate and reinvigorate the spiritual values of Judaism.

Among the themes of Purim, Kaplan saw in the story of Esther a Diaspora tale about the oppression by a majority group (Persians led by Haman) of a minority (Jews), and the Jewish battle for equal rights for minorities. Kaplan saw Jewish spiritual values as the key to the resistance to oppression and the capacity to flourish as a minority peo-

In the early years of Hadassah, the women's Zionist organization, Purim and Hanuka were the only two holidays the organization observed since they were considered national and not religious, and hence also not divisive. —D.D.M.

For Jews seeking to respond to the suffering they experienced in the Diaspora and make sense of it, the story of Purim represented a direct line of connection between the Bible and their own experience of exile. In the Middle Ages, many Jewish communities created their own local Purim observances (such as Purim of Shiraz or Purim of Castile) to mark episodes where those communities narrowly escaped calamity. These local Purims were celebrated annually in addition to the Purim of Esther and Mordecai. —J.W.

Imagine Purim as a holiday that focuses us on how to address the oppression of minorities around the world, including minorities in the State of Israel. Thank you, Dr. Kaplan! —J.J.S.

ple. He saw Purim as a time to emphasize those values and to inspire creativity and compassion in Jewish life. Kaplan proposed that the outcome of the Purim story should be to look beyond a mere concern for survival and to imagine and create a Judaism that reflects the best that we as a people can be.

Mordecai and Esther, whose names echo the Babylonian gods Marduk and Ishtar, represent two heroic individuals who were immersed in a foreign society while affirming their Jewish identity and pride. Did the Jews narrowly escape, or did Esther's position in the government make the happy ending possible? And even after she reveals herself as a Jew, does Esther change her habits? Does Ahasuerus build a synagogue in the palace? What does it mean that Esther identified as a Jew, beyond her kinship with Mordecai and her courage in saving her people?

Purim Through a Feminist Lens

The story of Esther cannot be told without acknowledging Vashti, the king's defiant wife in chapter one of *Megilat Esther*. When Vashti stood up to the drunken king, refus-

In hiding her identity at court, Esther is like Joseph and Moses, who are other biblical hidden Jews whose access to power proves helpful to their people. The ethics of minimizing signs of one's Jewish identity to be more comfortable in secular governments has been a concern even in the history of the United States. Secretary of State Madeline Albright's reputed lack of knowledge of her own Jewish origins disturbed many journalists, and Monica Lewinsky—because of her access to the royal scepter—was referred to as "Queen Esther" in parodies on the Internet and in the Israeli press. —L.H.L.

ing to appear before him (presumably in scanty garb at best), Ahasuerus' courtiers claimed that she had threatened the stability of married life throughout Persia. (1:17–18) In the context of the farce, this absurd idea adds to the comic tone of the story. However, in today's context, Vashti's refusal strikes a blow for women's equality and respect. One might add that Vashti and Esther each resisted the king in her own way and asserted her own identity. With so few Jewish women as protagonists of biblical tales, we might find important lessons from both of these role models. A substantial literature explores the Book of Esther from a feminist perspective, dwelling on the relations between men and women, on the roles of women in the Diaspora and on the stereotypes reflected in the Esther story.

Conclusion

In some ways, Purim is one of the most complicated Jewish holidays. Because *v'nahafokh hu*, the reversal of fortune, is a central theme, Purim offers everything and its

Esther is a heroine who seduces a powerful man to achieve political goals. In this way, she resembles Tamar, Yael, and Ruth (as well as the villain Delilah). Among the messages that these stories send is that female sexuality is powerful and potentially dangerous. Over the generations, little Jewish girls, dressed up as Esther for Purim, have been encouraged to emulate the beautiful queen. We would do well, as a community, to discuss the implications of the story with our children, and clarify that 1) beautiful women are not necessarily threatening and 2) there are other ways for girls and women to achieve their goals without appealing to their sexuality. These messages still run deep in our culture. —L.H.L.

opposite: fast and feast, joy and sorrow, giving and receiving, hiding and revealing. It would be a mistake to take any aspect of this holiday at its face value. Yet the story invites us to peel away the mask and all the layers underneath it, to arrive at those principles and values that we truly cherish—and then to laugh at them.

The celebration of Purim provides a rich variety of Jewish practices that encourage giving and sharing, dressing up and playing roles and, above all, approaching this one day with a sense of humor and self-awareness, so that we do not fall into the trap of taking ourselves too seriously. It is for this reason, perhaps, that we find in the midrash the idea that in a future messianic time, when all the other festivals are abolished, Purim will remain. (Midrash Proverbs 9:2) Even in a perfect world, we will need to laugh, especially at ourselves.

Perhaps the writer of this midrash imagined that a truly messianic time will be a time when every human being has internalized the idea of God, just as the Purim narrative does. At that future time, talk about God will be unnecessary. At such a time, your conception of God will no longer compete with my conception of God, just as today we understand that your internalizing of the oxygen supply doesn't compete with mine; your breathing doesn't compete with my breathing. —D.K.

Pesach Theology

Spiritual Dimensions of Pesach

Richard Hirsh

Pesach is one of three festivals (along with Sukkot and Shavuot) that comprise the *r'galim*, festivals of the biblical calendar when Israelites were expected to make a pilgrimage on foot (*regel*) to Jerusalem.

Pesach, Sukkot and Shavuot orbit around the Jewish master story of the Exodus as told in the Hebrew Bible and expanded upon by later rabbinic tradition in lore, law and liturgy. Pesach is the core narrative, inaugurating the larger Israelite (later, "Jewish") story of the liberation of the Israelites from Egyptian servitude. Shavuot emerges in the later Jewish tradition as the festival commemorating the revelation of the Torah at Sinai although the Hebrew Bible does not make this association, seeing Shavuot solely as an agricultural festival of first fruits (See Seth Goldstein's chapter on "Shavuot" in this *Guide*). The Hebrew Bible links Sukkot to the story of the Exodus, since the booths (*sukkot*) were interpreted as symbols of the 40 years of desert wandering between the Exodus and the arrival in the Promised Land. The sukkot are then said to represent the transient shelters one might imagine being used during such a trek. (See Nina Mandel's chapter on "Sukkot" in this *Guide*.)

Of these three *ḥagim* (holidays), Pesach is the core holiday, in terms of historical, spiritual and theological significance, as well as in terms of narrative, liturgy and frame of reference for much of Jewish tradition. Pesach is the most widely observed of these three, primarily through the ritual meal of the Seder. The Haggadah (Seder manual) is among the most widely interpreted of Jewish liturgical works, with multiple medieval and modern versions in circulation.

Each of the *r'galim* also has a place in the agricultural cycle. Sukkot is linked to the fall harvest, Shavuot to the summer grain harvest, and Pesach to the coming of spring—to planting and beginning anew. One of the names for Pesach is *Ḥag Ha'aviv*, the holiday of spring, which ties annual agricultural renewal to the rebirth of the Jewish people through their escape from Egyptian slavery.

The centrality and ubiquity of Pesach make it an exceptionally rich resource for contemporary spiritual exploration.

History and Myth

For generations, the story of Pesach has been passed down as history: Moses, the ten plagues, the parting of the Red Sea, the miraculous deliverance. Our ancestors recited the story of the Exodus to affirm their belief that it was a true historical event, and to sustain faith in the God who, according to the Torah narrative, made it all happen. This tracing of the events back to the will and actions of God accounts in part for the curious absence of Moses in the texts of many traditional Haggadot.

In our time, the Seder tale is more often seen as a sacred story or a holy myth, rather than as a historical record. Moderns are skeptical of miracles. We are troubled by the moral implications of plagues and punishments. We resonate to imagery of God that is associated with freedom and liberation, but we pursue an enlarged vision that seeks and supports the liberation of all peoples who suffer under oppression.

"Myth" is a rich but sometimes uneasy term for us, since a common association of "myth" is with "false." But in spiritual discussion, myth is not an issue of true or false; it refers to sacred narratives that help to bind a community and define its identity.

Is the Pesach story true? No, not if by "true" we mean an accurate account of events that happened more or less the way they are described in the Torah. But our ancestors, those who wrote the Bible and those who crafted the various Haggadah texts, did not write history. They wrote of their experience or understanding of, and even a belief in, a power greater than themselves that stood for freedom and against oppression.

But that power is garbed in imagery that is both elevating and disturbing. We resonate with the God who is imagined as demanding, "Let My people go!" but we draw back from the imagery of the God who is imagined as calling down a series of plagues culminating in a plague of death. When we remember, however, that the imagery of God is as mythic as the narrative in which it is embedded, we can reframe the ways that we respond to that imagery. These stories tell us less about God than about what some of our ancestors thought about God. They do not necessarily tell us anything about God, or what we, in our time, may choose to think about God. Put differently, our ancestors have conveyed various conceptions of God; it is up to us to sift and sort through them as we search for what can be sustaining beliefs about God.

Those ancient writers used mythic and poetic language couched in the context of their experience. We do not live in the worlds in which they lived, but we are descendants of the family that the Exodus story created: the Jewish people. We do not narrate the Exodus story because it is historically accurate. We tell the story (the mitzvah of Pesach *is* to tell the story) because it is our story, and in the telling, the discussion and the questioning, we discover eternal ideas, issues and insights that can inform our own understanding of oppression and liberation.

Three Dimensions of Pesach

Pesach is widely understood to be a celebration of the "going out from Egypt" of the ancient Israelites. Extending out from this is the broader theme of "liberation," which then often becomes the even more general idea of "freedom." Both of these nuances have an individual as well as a collective meaning. We are given the opportunity to consider their meanings in terms of our personal experience as well as in terms of the past, present and future experience of the Jewish people.

In Jewish tradition, Pesach has three phases. The first and last serve as spiritual bookends, singular experiences meant to be experienced once only. Bracketed in the middle are observances meant to be reenacted annually—revisited, with the perspectives and experiences of the prior year lending them new meaning, insight and interpretation.

In rabbinic tradition, these three observances are known as *Pesach Mitzrayim* (the Pesach of/in Egypt), *Pesach Dorot* (the Pesachs observed since the Exodus from Egypt up until our own day and beyond) and *Pesach L'atid*, the Pesach to be observed when the Messiah comes.

Finding Spirituality in the Singular Moment

One of the questions raised by the three phases of Pesach is how we weigh the meaning of transcendent and transformative events in our lives. These events may be from the past, moments whose significance emerges in retrospect, even if at the moment we experienced them they seemed routine. These events may be from the future, where their significance is anticipatory, and yet they shape our present experience. The classical Jewish expectation of the coming of the Messiah is an example of this. And these events may be of the present moment, when right in the midst of a profound experience we know that something transformative is happening and that we will not be the same person we were.

Some of the most intense and meaningful turning points in life result from a singular experience that, however meaningful, cannot be repeated. Such experiences may be anticipated, even planned for, but just as often and perhaps more so, they catch us by surprise. It may be a chance meeting with someone, a conversation through which we gain a new insight or have an assumption challenged, an encounter with a poem or a piece of music or a work of art, a confrontation with the miraculous (perhaps the birth of a child) or an overture to mortality (perhaps a threatening medical diagnosis).

We know from the Torah story as well as from later rabbinic tradition that not all Israelites chose to leave when the opportunity of the Exodus presented itself. *Pesach Mitzrayim* suggests that we cultivate an awareness or anticipation of the possibility of surprise, and that we be prepared amid our daily routines for singular opportunities that might be missed. In a similar way, the idea of *Pesach L'atid,* the Pesach waiting to be celebrated "when the Messiah arrives," can function to support the importance of hope and of remaining open to the transformative potential of the future. Many progressive Jews view the traditional idea of "the Messiah" as an outdated supernatural myth, and thus, they often dismiss it. Rabbi Mordecai Kaplan, however, taught that the underlying idea in the imagery of the Messiah is dissatisfaction with the world as it is and a belief in the potential for the world to be better. From this perspective, the idea of a Messiah may be seen as a metaphor or a poetic myth that affirms our belief in the possibility of improvement in the world.

Finding Spirituality in Serial, Sequential and Steady Moments

If *Pesach Mitzrayim* and *Pesach L'atid* are singular events, the Pesachs that we observe annually (*Pesach Dorot*) are a series of familiar rites and rituals. Evoked through a script, the story gains power through repetition, familiarity, anticipation and reenactment. *Pesach Dorot* is the Pesach some of us grew up with, others came to later in life, and some have only recently encountered. This Pesach symbolizes the daily, weekly, monthly and annual routines whose familiarity often provides the comfort and security of the familiar, and a sense of stability amid the inevitable changes of life. *Pesach Dorot* challenges us to cultivate an appreciation for those things that are reliable in our lives, things whose very taken-for-granted nature often makes us forget to appreciate and celebrate them.

Because Pesach is so often connected to family gatherings, over the course of a lifetime we become aware of how familiar seats at the table can one year become vacant, and how new seats (or sometimes highchairs) have to be found for those who may not have been there the previous year. *Pesach Dorot* helps us to be mindful of the subtlety of change and the nuances of difference that reside within the framework of the familiar—or, put differently, of the subtle and often imperceptible shifts that take place even in moments that we define as "static." As an example: How do we become different people between the time we sit down at the Seder and, hours later, when we rise up at its completion? The Seder took place; what changed in us while that was happening?

Sacred Time

Defining the boundaries of time and establishing the rhythm of the calendar are prerogatives of power. Enslaved people have their time determined by those who rule over them; liberated people define time on their own terms.

The overture to *Pesach Mitzrayim* speaks to this issue: "The Lord spoke to Moses and Aaron in the land of Egypt: This month shall mark for you the beginning of months; it shall be the first of the months of the year for you." (Exodus 12:1–2)

Among the remarkable occurrences associated with the Exodus, this simple yet powerful gesture of redefining time as a consequence of liberation is one of the most significant. It is notable that this declaration regarding time comes from God to Moses and Aaron *in* the land of Egypt, rather than after the Exodus. The end of Israelite enslavement begins not with the redefinition of space—leaving Egypt—but with the redefinition of time. Even before they departed, the Israelites ceased to have their identity defined by an alien calendar. Their liberation begins not in space but in time.

The biblical view of time as linear, purposeful and redemptive is established with the Exodus. With the beginning of the redemption of the Israelites comes a new meaning of time. No longer is time to be viewed solely as a repetitive, predictable cycle (as in the annual flooding of the Nile). Time itself now becomes the dimension through which God enters the world to make possible new things. Pesach challenges us to break loose from the rhythm of the routine and the ennui of the expected and to embrace the opportunities of the unimagined.

Jewish tradition celebrates time as a gift, as an opportunity to sanctify minutes, days, weeks, months and years by filling them with acts that advance God's hope for the world and those of us within it. In marking Jewish time as beginning with liberation, the Torah seeks to awaken within us an awareness to use our time wisely, both individually and collectively.

Pesach is a particularly powerful moment in which to consider the ways in which time is determined for us and the ways in which we determine time. It is also a chance to consider the ways in which we choose to live within the boundaries of our calendars. Can we find moments of liberation or freedom even within the busiest of days or weeks?

Perhaps more significantly, what, for each of us, is "the first of the months of the year?" How do we determine the day or date or season when our life began? Does that moment reside in the past, the present or the future?

What Are We Waiting For?

Myth shapes our understanding of our lives. We are rooted in our self-understanding as a people that emerged from slavery (*Pesach Mitzrayim*) and that strives to bring full redemption (*Pesach L'atid*). We live amid the generations (*dorot*) that are in the in-between, generations that derive meaning from the journey from Egypt to complete redemption. This not only provides a meaningful narrative for our lives as Jews. It also imparts a sacred vocation. We can live our lives with a commitment to furthering the cause of redemption.

Anger, Aggression and Ambivalence

A primary dynamic of Pesach can be found in the ambivalence the tradition embodies around the feelings of anger and aggression that the story of the Exodus calls forth. As we read in Exodus 15 of the salvation of Israel and the simultaneous destruction of the Egyptians, these contrasts become vivid.

In what the Torah records as the Song of/at the Sea, we note that there is no ambivalence on the part of the poet: "Horse and driver God has hurled into the sea . . . they went down to the depths like stone . . . they sank like lead in the majestic waters . . . who is like You among the celestials, Adonay?" We sense no moral ambiguity, no emotional self-consciousness and no measure of regret at the utter destruction of the enemy.

Later rabbinic tradition could not rest content with this text as it stands. The rabbis who created the Haggadah and defined the ritual requirements of the Seder also crafted midrash to explore and expand the Exodus narrative in ways that domesticate this unrestrained celebration of the destruction of the enemy.

For example, when we recite the ten plagues at the Seder, it is customary to remove one drop of wine or juice from our cup for each plague. Insofar as innocents suffered as the price of our going free, our celebration is diminished, and we cannot consume a full cup—or so go most explanations in modern Haggadot.

The tradition of removing drops of wine as a nod in the direction of innocent Egyptians is ratcheted up a notch in the midrash that is also often cited in those same modern Haggadot: The very moment the Israelites passed through the sea and the Egyptian troops pursued them happened to be when, in the rabbinic imagination, the angelic choir began to sing praises to God. In the midrash, God silenced them, saying, "My creatures (the Egyptians) are drowning, and you would sing?"

But there is a different version of this midrash, one not often quoted in modern Haggadot, in which the angels commence their song of praise at the moment when the Israelites are up to their necks in the Red Sea. It is at *that* moment that God calls out: "My creatures (the Israelites, not the Egyptians) are drowning, and you would sing?"

These competing midrashim neatly encapsulate one of the key questions with which contemporary religions continue to wrestle: To what degree should religious tradition accept and then strive to restrain the very real and universal human tendencies toward aggression, defensiveness and the marginalizing of others with whom we disagree, even those who would wish us harm or actually strive to harm us? Conversely, to what degree should religious traditions encourage us to transcend and transform our negative feelings and related expressions of hatred and violence toward others? Put differently, should religion "accept us as we are," with our very human capacity toward the negative, and thus seek to constrain us, or should religion "accept us as we ought to be," strive to shape and strengthen our capacity toward the positive, and thus seek to expand us?

There is ambivalence in Pesach as to how to address the conflicts among anger, aggression and ambition. Pesach is thus one way in which Jewish tradition expresses and recognizes the paradoxes, dilemmas and conflicts of human nature and of our communal and historical existence. Pesach challenges us to examine the degree to which we want and even need to celebrate survival even when, and perhaps especially when, survival comes at the price of the destruction of an enemy who can only be defeated, not debated. (If we replace "Egyptians" with "Nazis" in the above-cited midrashim, we may come closer to the experience of our ancestors in Egypt who sang at the sea.) And Pesach simultaneously reminds us that notwithstanding our own experience, we are to "know the heart of the stranger because we were strangers in the land of Egypt."

Pesach was not intended to be an exercise in easy assurances. Instead, each year as we encounter the story, we are left to struggle with often troubling implications of the imaginations of the biblical writers, and of the associations and connections they left for us to discover amid the grand narrative we know as the Torah.

Vulnerability and Protection

The first Pesach recounted in the Torah (Exodus, chapter 12) describes the rituals observed by the Israelites on the night before their departure from Egypt, the night of the tenth plague, the death of the Egyptian firstborn. Since the people have not yet left, the meaning of this Pesach cannot be liberation or freedom, nor can it recall "the going out from Egypt" since the Israelite people are still in Egypt at that point.

More accurately, then, the theme of *Pesach Mitzrayim* is "protection" (which is likely the underlying ancient meaning of the word "*pesach*"). The various rituals of *Pesach Mitzrayim* suggest the warding off of demonic forces. These rituals include the shared sacrificial animal, the requirement that those clustered in homes stay within until daybreak, the expectation that all Israelite males in those homes be circumcised, and the placing of blood on the lintels of the doorway. As later rabbinic tradition suggests, once the *mashkhit* ("destroyer") is let loose by God, it cannot differentiate between the intended targets (the Egyptian firstborn) and the innocent bystanders (the Israelite firstborn). The only recourse is to take steps to deflect the destructive force through a series of quasi-magical rituals of protection.

In this ancient myth, which is replete with moral and theological complexities, Pesach anticipates one of the most common human experiences: the awareness of the fragility and vulnerability of life. We commonly become aware of the inevitable transience of life and of the ubiquity of mortality during the journey from childhood to adolescence to adulthood. But even at our most rational and reasonable, the right set of circumstances can easily evoke a primal sense of fear that causes us to invoke ritual, prayer and other practices that are as much a plea for intervention as they are strategies for coping.

Protection comes in a variety of ways, and can be imagined under a series of images, including "refuge," "shelter" and "shield." Just as on the night of the tenth plague the threat was tangible and not imaginary, so, too, we are aware of moments when we truly are exposed to danger, when we are actually at risk. While we have generally distanced ourselves from rituals whose efficacy relies on the magical or the supernatural, we are no less in need of the stability and security that being within the circle of a community can confer. While a community of people cannot guarantee us protection, it can perhaps provide a way for us to endure a period of vulnerability until the danger has passed, or lessen the impact on us of some form of harm, or provide a context in which we can extract meaning even at moments when we are aware of a loss of control.

Dual Dimensions of Divinity

The larger story of Pesach begins in the early chapters of Exodus. The rapid narration begins with the birth of the infant Moses, the story of his deliverance in a rescue from the Nile, and his move into the royal palace of Pharaoh after he is adopted by Pharaoh's own daughter. Before we are even out of the first three chapters of Exodus, Moses has become an adult, killed an Egyptian overseer, and fled to the wilderness in search of refuge.

It is several years later, when Moses seems settled and sedentary as a shepherd, that he has the encounter that changes his life. During his rounds of pasturing the flocks of his father-in-law, he comes upon the bush that burns but is not consumed. This is the moment when Moses first learns the true name of God, and is called upon to return to Egypt. There, he is to announce the message of deliverance to the enslaved Israelites, and to demand of Pharaoh that he let God's people go.

In the encounter at the bush (Exodus 3:14), when Moses asks God for the divine name as a sign of authorization that he can present to the Israelites, the Torah depicts God's reply as "*Ehyeh Asher Ehyeh*," usually translated as "I am that I am," but more precisely rendered as "I will be (present) as I will be (present)." Curiously, this name is rarely used again in the Bible, displaced by the more familiar divine names "YHVH" (usually rendered as "Lord" or "LORD" in English Bibles) and "*Elohim*" (usually rendered as "God"). The open-ended possibilities of "*Ehyeh Asher Ehyeh*" may have been too challenging for a tradition to control, and perhaps the default to "YHVH" or "*Elohim*" is a concession to the need for some degree of stability and certainty in thinking about divinity.

That noted, it remains the case that both "*Ehyeh Asher Ehyeh*" and "YHVH" seem to be related to a Hebrew root word that means "to be, to exist," but in neither case is the derivation totally clear. We remain uncertain as to what these names for the divine actually mean, even as we are pointed in a direction that suggests what they may mean.

This imprecision in names is an appropriate as well as accurate reflection of a generally consistent Jewish teaching that while we can hover around some general sense of what the nature of God is, and can even perhaps identify moments in which God seems to be evident, we can never fully know the essence of God or be assured of accuracy in assuming the presence of God.

We might imagine that the two names for God imply two essential ideas: The name "YHVH" may be experienced as something like "Being" (existence itself, all that is) and "*Ehyeh Asher Ehyeh*" as "Becoming" (fluid, future-focused, changing). So for example, the medieval Jewish theologian Maimonides, influenced by Greek philosophy, could reference God as "the unmoved mover," the Deity whose very essence is stability, and who remains constant and unchanging. Conversely, the modern Jewish theologian Abraham Joshua Heschel, influenced by Hasidic tradition, could imagine God as "the most-moved mover," the One who is, in Heschel's terms, "in search of man," the One who reacts and responds and changes in relationship to human behavior.

Monotheism suggests that it is a misunderstanding to think that one needs to choose between a God who is "Being" and a God who is "Becoming," or between a God who manifests compassion and a God who demands justice. But sometimes this presents significant spiritual difficulty. The God who liberates the Israelites appears to be the same God who decrees and carries out the death of the Egyptian firstborn. "I am the God who creates light *and* darkness, good *and* evil," says Isaiah (45:7). Monotheism forces us again and again, when asked to choose between one dimension of God and another, to say, as Rabbi Lawrence Kushner teaches, "God is both."

Texts and Contexts

Familiar biblical stories often reach us through secondary sources, such as the siddur (prayer book) or the Pesach Haggadah, where biblical texts are lifted out of context, sometimes amended, and at other times edited, with the meaning shaped by where a quotation begins and ends.

The Haggadah distills the Torah narrative of the ten

plagues down to eleven words (the tenth plague is described in two words: *makat b'khorot*/killing of the firstborn) and omits the narrative in which the plagues are embedded. Recounting the plagues from the Haggadah rather than from the Torah yields an impoverished reading.

When read in the context of the Torah and the Hebrew Bible, the narratives of the plagues take on a more complex meaning. While we focus on the story as told in Exodus, both Psalm 78 and Psalm 105 narrate the plagues as well—with the notable difference that each psalm mentions only seven plagues. The dissonance in detail is significant, pointing to an underlying shared tradition among the ancient Israelites of a mythic narrative of the plagues but an absence of agreement as to the number and sequence.

In contrast, the narrative in Exodus is a carefully edited literary construction whose deliberateness points us again to the mythic and poetic rather than historical nature of the story. There are several ways in which to interpret the editorial architecture of the "signs, wonders and plagues." One is to see in the constructed nature of the narrative an implicit message that whatever affliction challenges human dignity, decency and life itself results from a series of interconnected factors rather than from a single root cause. Rather than grouping all social ills under one heading, it may be more helpful to define which are "signs" of warning, which are "wonders" that make us pause and take notice, and which are "plagues" that immediately threaten life itself. Some will come with warning and some will appear unannounced. One thing we do know: We do not have the luxury of using the many challenges to freedom still facing us to allow our "hearts to become hardened." Liberation is an ever-current challenge of the present in anticipation of the future.

Pesach

Celebrating Pesach

David A. Teutsch

Pesach is the most observed of all Jewish holidays in North America. The power of the Seder has multiple sources. It is at once a family event at home, an opportunity to absorb a central Jewish narrative, a link across generations, and a celebration of Jewish life and commitment.

The power of Seder may stem from the role of the Passover story in our self-definition as Jews. The theme of remembering that we were slaves or strangers in Egypt is among the most repeated in the Torah. Who are the Jews? We are the people who "understand the heart of the stranger," who have the experience of otherness. We believe to our core in the possibility of liberation. —J.A.S.

History

The biblical story of the Israelites' first Pesach is a familiar one. According to the Book of Exodus, after the Egyptians enslaved the Israelites, God visited nine plagues upon Egypt, but Pharaoh refused to let the Israelites go free. On the eve of the Tenth Plague, the Israelites smeared lamb's blood on the doorposts of their homes to protect themselves from the coming plague. They ate of the lamb they had roasted and huddled in their hovels while the tenth plague, the death of the firstborn, swept across Egypt. Then Pharaoh ordered their quick departure, and they took valuables of the Egyptians with them, fleeing so

The exodus narrative itself—an enslaved people achieving liberation so that they may serve the God of freedom and justice—is deeply powerful. So too is the ethical mandate arising from the story: to remember that we were once strangers who were oppressed and so, to treat all strangers justly. This ethical theme is the most often repeated verse in the Bible, mentioned no fewer than 36 times. —D.W.

On the 14th day of Nisan, the Israelites slaughtered the paschal lamb and then placed its blood on the doorposts of their homes. Was it the blood itself that protected the Israelites, or were they protected by the act of faith itself that God would "pass over" their houses? —J.G.K.

Before the Children of Israel could set forth from Egypt, they needed to become a people. The Pesach rituals as described in the Book of Exodus (see chapter 12) provided all the elements necessary to help the slaves form a covenantal community: sharing what they had with those who had less; eating a sacred meal together with their neighbors; marking their homes in solidarity with one another and in defiance of their oppressor; and uniting, not only to fight a common enemy, but in pursuit of a common purpose. —B.P.

quickly that they did not have time to allow their bread to rise. We cannot establish the historicity of the first Pesach, but its power as a formative myth remains at the center of Jewish self-understanding.

When the Israelites settled in the Land of Israel and built the Jerusalem Temple, Pesach became one of the *sh'losh r'galim*, the three pilgrimage festivals. On these holidays, Israelites went up to the Temple from all over the country to offer sacrifices in rites carried out by the *kohanim*, the priests in the Temple. On Pesach the rites of sacrifice included that of a lamb brought by the head of the clan.

Whether or not the events of the exodus story actually occurred is secondary to the importance of how deeply the story has entered into the practical lives of Jews and, more broadly, Western civilizations. It has become the archetypal story of hope and salvation for generations of oppressed peoples, and the lack of archaeological or historical documentation has not changed that fact. —N.H.M.

How important is historicity? For some, the statement, "We cannot establish the historicity of the first Pesach" may come as a shock. This begs the question: Can we find meaning in the exodus if it didn't "really happen?" Our traditions are based on truth, which is eternal, rather than on history, which is always interpreted subjectively. The inner truth of the exodus story relates to the human condition and to our ability to rise up against oppression, confront injustice and become liberated from the chains of tyrants. That truth continues to unfold throughout history, no matter the circumstances. —B.P.

Many biblical scholars posit that originally there were two separate springtime holidays that merged into what we know as Pesach. One holiday, Pesach, was intended to keep away evil spirits by smearing blood on tents or shelters. The Festival of Matza marked the early spring harvest. While the Festival of Matza was rooted in agriculture, the early Pesach ritual may have had its origins in seminomadic life. —T.K.

Once it had been slaughtered on the altar, the family head would return to the clan gathered on the edge of Jerusalem, and they would roast the lamb, which was a long, slow undertaking. Gathered around campfires, the elders would tell the story of the exodus from Egypt, and the younger generations would listen. Eventually evening would fall, the meat would be done, and the roast lamb would be eaten with unleavened bread and *maror*, a bitter herb. While that combination of foods was probably a common meal in that time, those foods came to signify the key events of the first Pesach—the bitterness of slavery, the Israelites' protection from the tenth plague and their flight from Egypt. The Mishnah (*Pesaḥim* 10.5) records these three foods as the essential ones for the Pesach Seder.

Exodus states that an animal from the flock must be slaughtered, while Deuteronomy says that an animal from the flock or cattle may be used. Exodus says that the meat of the animal must be roasted, while Deuteronomy tells us that the meat must be boiled. Second Chronicles 35:13, anticipating rabbinic talmudic methodology, tells us that the animal must be boiled in fire! —T.K.

It is easy to understand how, as the Jews began urbanizing, such Seders shifted from being typical meals to becoming exceptional ones.

When the Second Temple in Jerusalem was destroyed in 70 CE, the Pesach pilgrimage ended. So did the ritual sacrifice of a lamb and the clan meal near Jerusalem. A new ritual was needed to replace them. Some clans returned to the practice of sacrificing and roasting a lamb for themselves in the areas where they lived. The rabbis, who gradually emerged as the dominant Jewish leaders after the destruction of the Second Temple, opposed this practice because they believed that sacrifices could be properly offered only in the Temple. Eventually the rabbis were successful in eliminating the practice.

Annually offering the paschal sacrifice ended within Jewish tradition, but it continues in outlying traditions descended from Judaism. Once, I was privileged to witness the Samaritan Pesach that took place in the mountain region north of Jerusalem that was their ancestral home. We observed the modern Samaritan men of the clan drawing knives from beneath their cloaks and slitting the lambs' throats, almost in unison, in a split second. Later, they roasted the meat over very large pits and shared it with their community. It was an experience that allowed me to reimagine our own ancient tradition. —B.P.

The early rabbis were faced with a dilemma. They needed to observe the Seder, but the inherited rituals no longer worked as they had. How were they to structure the storytelling that is the key observance of the first night of Pesach? They borrowed the structure of the Greek symposium meal, a leisurely and ceremonial feast eaten while reclining. During the symposium meal, much of the conversation was connected to the foods served at the meal.

Sephardic Jews (descendants of the Jews of Spain) traditionally eat roast lamb at the Seder in commemoration of the first Pesach and the ancient Israelite custom, but because of concern about the appearance of engaging in the controversial sacrifice of a lamb after the destruction of the Temple, Ashkenazim (descendants of Jews from middle Europe) traditionally avoid eating roast lamb at the Seder. —D.A.T.

The interpretation of Pesach in the Mishnah, offered by the early rabbis following the destruction of the Temple, was not only an effort to establish a practice of Judaism that was not based on animal sacrifice at a centralized shrine. It was at the same time an effort to assert a Jewish interpretation of the Pesach symbols in the face of emerging Christianity, which had its own understandings of the holiday, its symbols, and, indeed, the significance of the destruction of the Jerusalem Temple. The Haggadah asserts a new, limited and polemical meaning for the paschal lamb. —D.W.

A major shift was the de-emphasis of the role of Moses in the narrative of liberation: Moses is not mentioned in the rabbinic version of events laid out in the Haggadah. This shift suited the political context in which the rabbis lived. Political revolts against oppressive empires in both the 60s of the Common Era and then again in the 130s not only led to the destruction of the Second Temple, but also forced the deportation of most Judean residents and the despoliation of Judean land. The rabbis deemed the prudent path forward to be a focus on study and religious observance, rather than on radical challenges to established authorities. —D.W.

Frequently apple dishes and greens were elements of the symposium meal, and this was reflected in the apple-based *ḥaroset* (the variety served at most Ashkenazic Seders) and the *karpas*, a green. The rabbis restructured the telling of the exodus story so that it no longer centered on the paschal lamb. Additional foods, such as greens and *ḥaroset*, became mandatory parts of the Seder, and the Temple sacrifices were commemorated by a roasted lamb bone (paschal sacrifice) and roasted egg (festival sacrifice), which were not eaten. All these elements were added to the Seder plate, which retained the *maror* (bitter herb) from the Israelite Seder. Why was the matza not on the Seder plate? It had its own plate because of its large size.

Before the advent of printing, few people owned Haggadot, the scrolls—and later, booklets—explaining the

I am fascinated by the multifaceted issues raised by the phenomenon of Jews, an oppressed and occupied people, borrowing the cultural forms of the Roman/Greek oppressors in order to tell the story of Israelite liberation from oppression. —J.A.S.

It has seemed strange to me throughout my entire life that even though the Haggadah says that eating the "paschal lamb" is one of the three essential elements of Pesach, I have never seen lamb served at a Pesach meal. Every year, I feel as though something is missing and that I am somehow not fulfilling one of the essential mitzvot of the festival. Perhaps if we talked about why we Ashkenazic Jews don't eat lamb at the Seder, it would make more sense that we still read about the importance of the mitzvah itself. —S.C.R.

In 1974 I was living in French Hill in Jerusalem, and our Moroccan immigrant neighbor had a lamb tied up outside our front door in the month before Pesach. I was in pretty deep shock when I realized what that lamb's destiny was to be. —S.P.W.

elements of the Seder ritual, because handwritten ones were too expensive. Families told the exodus story without the benefit of a written text—a practice that made for local differences and led to the evolution of an oral tradition unconstrained by a canonized text. This created another challenge for the rabbis: How could they ensure that the key elements were included in the Seder in the absence of a standardized text? Perhaps that is the origin of the ancient chant now often found near the beginning of Haggadot that consists of the elements of the Seder in

While most families would not have had access to printed Haggadot, we must also keep in mind that before the advent of printing, and even after it, memorization was a prevalent mode of engaging with Jewish text. Educated Jewish males often knew key passages of the Mishna by heart. The tenth chapter of Mishna *Pesaḥim* clearly outlines all the components of the Seder, including, verbatim, the Four Questions and the explanation of the Pesach, matza and *maror*. One remaining vestige of the oral preservation of the Haggadah is the memorization by the youngest child of the *Ma Nishtana*, the Four Questions. Children learned to recite the Four Questions at age 3, and they might well have learned new passages each year and recited them at the table until they memorized the entire *magid*. I see the Seder as a communal, liturgical, formal recitation, punctuated and accompanied by discussion, to be sure, but wedded to a script. I believe that since the advent of printing (and the diversification of Jewish practice through the different movements), the Seder has actually become *more* varied as different print editions have been created. For more than 1,000 years, the oral tradition actually preserved the Seder and its components in a remarkable degree of sameness. This may be evidenced by comparing the text of the Mishna to the texts of traditional Haggadot across Ashkenazic and *Mizraḥi* communities and across time. —V.M.

The chant that lists the order of the Seder (referred to as "*Simaney Haseder*" ("Signs of the Seder/Order") first appears in the 12th-century *Maḥzor Vitri*. It is attributed in that work to Rabbeynu Shlomo ben Yitzhak, better known by the acronym Rashi, who lived in the 11th century. —V.M.

order. Memorizing the chant provided a way to preserve the sequence of the major Seder elements. Since "Seder" means "order," preserving the structure is important. Over time, the story recounted at the Seder centered less on the biblical account of the exodus and more on the rabbinic midrash that interpreted it, eventually leading to the Haggadot that were produced in the early days of Hebrew printing.

The Mishna and Talmud also preserve early Seder liturgies that have become the core of the standard Haggadah. Beginning with the Four Questions and including Rabban Gamaliel's explication of the three main Seder foods (*pesaḥ*, or paschal lamb; matza, or unleavened bread; and *maror*, bitter herb), these passages were enshrined in Jewish text study. However, the rest of the Haggadah continued to evolve, not only through rabbinic influence but also by absorbing the practices of everyday Jews throughout history. Today's contemporary Haggadot reflect a 2,000-year-old tradition of reinterpretation and renewal. —B.P.

Telling the Pesach story through the recitation of rabbinic midrash is an integral component of the *magid* as it is described in the Mishna. Mishna *Pesaḥim* 10.4 says, "Explain '*Arami Oved Avi*'—'My father was a wandering Aramean.'" This passage (Deuteronomy 26:5–9) was originally a formulaic narration of our history offered in thanksgiving as part of bringing the first fruits to the Holy Temple in Jerusalem. Once the Temple was destroyed, the sacrificial rites of blood, grain, wine and oil became nonoperational, but the liturgical rites, being purely words, were still somehow salvageable. It was an act of conscious reconstruction to lift the text of "*Arami Oved Avi*" from its place in the defunct ceremony and reassign it to a prominent place at the Seder table. Reciting and learning these particular verses is as much about redeeming their ritual context as it is about learning their narrative content. —V.M.

In the Orthodox world in which I was raised, every word of the inherited text of the Haggadah is meticulously read as if it is as immutable as the Torah or the traditional liturgy. It is always startling for me to be reminded that the Haggadah text has evolved fluidly like all other aspects of Jewish civilization. —J.J.S.

Passover Preparation

One of the mitzvot that is undertaken well in advance of Pesach is giving *tzedaka* to enable those who might not otherwise be able to do so to make sufficient provision for the holiday for themselves and their families. This mitzvah is known as *ma'ot ḥitin*, money for wheat (i.e., matza). Many cities have *ma'ot ḥitin* funds that collect money to help the poor in their vicinity. Rabbis often collect money for this purpose and disburse it through their discretionary funds. Pesach is a holiday marked by many special food and holiday celebrations. Providing *ma'ot ḥitin* money helps to provide the means for joyous celebration to those who might not otherwise be able to fully enjoy the holiday.

Ma'ot ḥitin can be a powerful teaching tool for families by connecting familial celebration to shared communal responsibility. —N.C.M.

Preparation for Pesach and the month of Nisan, which is considered the New Year, takes place throughout the month of Adar. Just as the month of Elul at the end of summer prepares us for the Days of Awe (that other Jewish New Year) through self-reflection and repentance, the month of Adar prepares us for the season of love and spring through practices of generosity. These include the gifts of food to friends during Purim, gifts for the poor on Purim, the collection of food for the needy for Pesach (*ma'ot ḥitin*), and the invitations to the Seder—"Let all who are hungry come and make Pesach with us." While the month of Elul asks us to examine how much we have to grow, the month of Adar reminds us how much we have to give. Thus, the Jewish year is balanced between awe, *yir'a,* and love, *ahava,* at these temporal poles that are six months apart. —V.M.

More observant Jews begin their preparations far in advance of Pesach because they want to rid their households of all *ḥametz*, leavened foods. The first step in this process is consuming such foods that are already in the pantry or freezer, a process that can take a month or more. Closer to the start of Pesach, a process of meticulous spring cleaning is undertaken to get rid of crumbs wherever they might have ended up. For a full description

I like to think of hamantashan baking as the first step in getting ready for Pesach. It is the perfect opportunity to use up any flour and other baking ingredients on my shelves. —N.H.M.

The period of time when we use up the food in our homes can be one of spiritual reflection on scarcity and abundance. How long could we eat comfortably just from the groceries in our homes at this moment? What would it be like not to have the luxury of a choice of foods? An "empty cupboard" challenge—to buy nothing or only essentials in the lead-up to Pesach could put us in touch with those still oppressed by global food insecurity. How much sweeter would our own liberation be if we forced ourselves to experience some degree of scarcity? —N.H.M.

The first day of Nisan is mentioned in the Mishna as one of four new years—the New Year for Kings. A new year of a king's reign in ancient Israel would begin on the first day of Nisan, regardless of when he ascended to the throne. We can thus see the cleaning in honor of Pesach as being similar to preparing for the arrival of a king. Over the cold winter, we tend to stay in the house, to sleep more, to eat more, and to accumulate more unnecessary stuff. Clearing away physical clutter also allows us to be spiritually present and light for the beginning of our spiritual journey from winter and narrowness (Mitzrayim, Egypt, has the same root as *tzar*, narrow) to the wide-open space of the wilderness and the Land of Israel, represented by the spring and summer. Again in late summer, many people clean before Pesach's calendric opposite, Rosh Hashana, readying themselves for the next seasonal shift to fall. —J.M.S.

of Pesach kashrut, see the separate section that follows "Celebrating Pesach." Some Jews do modified versions of these two processes. Some give their sealed containers of *ḥametz* to food banks, soup kitchens or other organizations serving the needy. Some Jews remove any *ḥametz* that they consider edible without becoming concerned about inedible crumbs. Others just remove bread, crackers, cake and the like. Those who take the more arduous approach sometimes find it a helpful way to focus on the upcoming holiday, while others see it as a huge task from which they feel liberated only once the house is clean and the food prepared.

Regardless of the form of this observance, on the night before the first Seder, it is customary to do a symbolic search for *ḥametz* while carrying a candle for light and a feather and wooden spoon for sweeping up the *ḥametz*. This search, called *b'dikat ḥametz*, is a wonderful experience for children regardless of the degree to which *ḥametz*

Men have long been involved in Pesach cleaning, since the commandment around eliminating *ḥametz* is binding on both men and women. However, in both Jewish and majority societies, housekeeping and cooking traditionally have been within the province of women, and Pesach has been famously taxing on them. At least until recent times, much of the chore of cooking has fallen on women, and both published literature and family stories illustrate how exhausting those last 24 hours leading up to the holiday can be. —D.W.

Some follow the custom of using the dried-up *lulav* branches (palm fronds) from Sukkot instead of a feather for *b'diḳat ḥametz*. This is, perhaps, an early form of reuse and recycle! —B.P.

One can't overstate the cathartic nature of deep cleaning! Jewish legal tradition places such an importance on *b'diḳat ḥametz* that it says that one should interrupt one's meal and even Torah study to do this process. (*Shulḥan Aruḳh* 431) —N.C.M.

is removed from the house. When children are going to take part in the search, family members place a few pieces of *ḥametz* (such as hard crackers) somewhere that the children can find them and sweep them up. Of course, the adults will want to keep careful track of where they have placed the *ḥametz* so that they can make sure it is all collected. The ritual begins with a blessing that ends, "*v'tzivanu al bi'ur ḥametz*"—"commands us to remove *ḥametz.*" After the *ḥametz* has been gathered, the ceremony ends with a pronouncement that any leaven that has been missed is to be considered "null and ownerless, like the dust of the earth." The complete text of this formula can be found in *A Night of Questions: A Passover Haggadah*, page 7, as well as in most other Haggadot.

When we swept up the last piece of bread in the candlelit darkness, my father recited the Aramaic formula as if it were a magical incantation. He was declaring all remaining *ḥametz* null and void, and it felt as if his voice were disintegrating any remaining crumbs. —J.J.S.

The following morning, the remaining *ḥametz* is burned in an open fire, usually outdoors, and another nullification formula is recited. If children are present, using the fire to roast marshmallows after the *ḥametz* has been burned will make this an unforgettable experience for them. When the

I have developed the practice of buying a new wooden kitchen spoon at Pesach, using it throughout the year and then burning it when I do *bi'ur ḥametz* (burning the *ḥametz*) as a way of making a fresh start. —N.H.M.

After days and weeks of cleaning out all of the *ḥametz*, the nullification of any remaining, overlooked crumbs affirms that we have done the best we can, and that it is good enough. We work hard, but we need not achieve perfection. —J.J.S.

I experience a definite psychological benefit from the rituals of *bitul ḥametz* and *bi'ur ḥametz* (nullification and burning of the *ḥametz*). I see the ritual as a psychological throwing up of one's hands. Each year, I reach the point where the Pesach preparation I've done will just have to be good enough because I've reached my limit. And each year, *bitul ḥametz* is there to affirm that it really is enough. —M.F.

My father and I would place the bundle of bread pieces into my mother's metal wash pail and take it down to the Bronx sidewalk to burn it. We lived in a Jewish neighborhood, but few of our neighbors were ritually observant, and this annual practice felt like a rite of passage in which I joined my father in a public act of Jewish pride. Afterward, we would walk around the corner to the grocery store to buy a kosher-for-Pesach bar of Israeli Elite bittersweet chocolate. Might that be why I have a strong preference for semisweet chocolate to this day? —J.J.S.

B'diḳat ḥametz also provides a great opportunity for children to learn about fire safety. Some synagogues have firemen available to teach basic fire safety skills while the *ḥametz* burns. —J.M.S.

Seder takes place on a Saturday night, *b'dikat ḥametz* is traditionally carried out on the preceding Thursday night, and the burning takes place on Friday morning, with Shabbat meals consisting of foods that are kosher for Passover so that Seder food can be prepared on Friday. In this way, the restful atmosphere of Shabbat is not disturbed by Pesach preparations. Why the search and burning rituals?

Some Jews may not do the regular burning at all when Pesach begins on a Saturday night. They choose to eat year-round food Friday night and early Saturday morning, particularly so that they can eat regular bread as a centerpiece for their Shabbat meals and eat their first matza at the Seder. —J.G.K.

My mother would set up a bridge table in the hallway outside the kitchen on which I could eat Rice Krispies and milk if I could finish by 8:45 a.m., after which we carried out any leftover *ḥametz* to be burned. If I overslept, I could eat neither *ḥametz* nor matza until the Seder in the evening. Fruit, cheese and gefilte fish were the stuff of lunch. —J.J.S.

When I was growing up, my parents created a symbolic hunt for *ḥametz* on the morning before the Pesach Seder using a feather and a spoon and finding crumbs that they had placed conspicuously around the house. We then took the *ḥametz* to our back yard and burned it in the family barbecue grill. To this day, this ritual is a highlight of Pesach for every young child in our extended family. —S.C.R.

The plain matza that is used at the Pesach Seder is not eaten on a Shabbat that immediately precedes Pesach in order to keep the experience of its taste fresh for the Seder. —J.A.S.

Common traditional practice is to eat hallah on a Shabbat immediately preceding Pesach, but to do so over a towel or in the bathroom so that the crumbs can easily be cleaned up. In order to avoid this uncomfortable situation, communities may choose to host a kosher Shabbat meal at an offsite location. —J.M.S.

When I was a child, we did *b'diḳat ḥametz* in the religious school wing of the synagogue building, and it was a memorable annual ritual. —J.G.K.

There are several possible reasons. These rituals have great pedagogical value. They create a ritualized end to the process of ridding the house of *ḥametz*. And, since it is possible to become obsessive about the process of house-cleaning, the ritualized pronouncement that nullifies any remaining *ḥametz* can be comforting, as even careful people are bound to miss something somewhere.

Traditional Jews "sell" their *ḥametz* through a contracted installment sale that is canceled immediately after the end of Pesach. They designate their rabbi or someone else skilled in this transaction who then sells their *ḥametz* to a non-Jew in a sale that is effective hours before the start of the Seder.

Selling *ḥametz* is a great model for those with perfectionist tendencies because it limits our compulsiveness. I wonder why such measures are reserved only for Pesach. —S.P.W.

We have found it more meaningful to draw up our own contract and sell it to a non-Jewish friend or neighbor than to ask our congregational rabbi to do it for us. This provides an opportunity to share a bit of Jewish life that is usually hidden from view. It also provides a counterbalance to the heavy Pesach emphasis on Jewish insularity. Kashering your house for Pesach can be an exercise in expunging all non-kosher-for-Passover "contaminants," a category into which non-Jews tend to fall if we are not careful. —J.J.S.

The disposal of *ḥametz* poses a three-way conflict: I don't want to own *ḥametz* on Pesach; I'm unable to donate opened or perishable items to my local food bank; and throwing away food is costly, and it violates *bal tash'ḥit*, the prohibition against waste. One recent Pesach, I arranged to "sell" our community's *ḥametz* to a local pastor in exchange for a donation to the local kosher food bank. When the holiday ended, I "bought back" the community's *ḥametz* with a donation to her church's food pantry. —M.F.

Those whose lives are connected to the larger Jewish world may also be aware that there is a separate prohibition against eating *ḥametz* after Pesach if it was owned by a Jew during the holiday, so the fact that the sale of *ḥametz* took place may remain relevant for weeks after the holiday concludes. —J.G.K.

Since traditional Jews are not supposed to own *ḥametz* on Pesach, the selling allows them to avoid giving up valuable possessions (anything from a fine collection of scotch to a large cookie factory) and to have another guarantee that they do not possess *ḥametz*. Some argue that this is a halakhic (Jewish legal) nicety and that those not committed to *halakha* need not bother with it. But liberal Jews who take the "do not possess *ḥametz*" rule seriously may find this a meaningful way of fulfilling that commitment. The contract of sale does legally change who possesses the *ḥametz*, so it is not simply a legal fiction.

Another custom is to stop eating matza a month before the Seder so that eating matza at the Seder is a fresh and meaningful experience. People who *kasher* their homes for Pesach do not eat bread after the burning of the *ḥametz*, making it less likely that *ḥametz* will get near the food being prepared for Pesach.

Those who do not *kasher* their homes for Pesach can start cooking and freezing food far in advance of the holiday. Some observant people who have two kitchens available to them *kasher* one of them for Pesach a few weeks in

Hasidic interpretations around the removal of *ḥametz* focus on removing the behaviors, thoughts and practices in our lives that inflate us (and our egos) with an expanded sense of self-importance. —N.C.M.

The selling of *ḥametz* is undertaken by people who have not physically emptied their houses or apartments of *ḥametz*. —J.A.S.

It is customary to stop eating *ḥametz* and not to possess it a few hours after sunrise on *erev* Pesach. —J.G.K.

advance of the holiday so that they can start cooking for the Seder there. But most people who *kasher* their homes for Pesach cannot begin cooking until their kitchens are kosher for Pesach and their Pesach dishes are unpacked. That typically happens the evening before the Seder, making the last 24 hours before the holiday an intense period of preparation and cooking in homes that host Seders.

Some firstborn adults observe the Fast of the Firstborn on the day leading up to the Seder. It commemorates the Torah's account of the Egyptians' loss of life due to the tenth plague, the plague of death of the firstborn, and the sparing of the Israelites' firstborn. If someone who would observe this fast attends a *siyum*, a celebration marking the end of study of a book when the eating of a celebratory meal is expected, this takes precedence over the obligation to fast, which is why many congregations arrange a *siyum* on that occasion.

A *siyum* is usually conducted after morning services, before the latest time for *bi'ur ḥametz*, usually around 10 a.m., so that one last taste of *ḥametz* can be eaten before we enter into full Pesach mode. —J.M.S.

My older brother is the firstborn male in our household and the first male grandchild on both sides of our family. Though not particularly observant, he takes the responsibilities of being the eldest male very seriously, including attending the *siyum* for firstborns most years. For him, it is the rare occasion that acknowledges and crystallizes his status in the family. —D.W.

Preparing for the Seder

The Seder ritual has several elements that must be prepared for in advance. Perhaps the most basic is ensuring that enough copies of the Haggadah are available for everyone to use. The choice of Haggadot is amazingly large. Traditional Haggadot come with different kinds of commentary, illustrations and translations. And the variety of contemporary Haggadot is almost endless—including feminist, family and abbreviated Haggadot, Haggadot emphasizing social justice, and Haggadot with commentary. Visiting a good Jewish bookstore should provide more than a dozen choices, and new ones come out every year. When selecting a Haggadah, it helps to think about the people who will be present at one's Seder. How traditional are they? How knowledgeable? Are their concerns

It is ironic that there might be a Haggadah specifically focused on social justice when this holiday, beyond any other, is about speaking truth to power and about liberation from oppression. I hope that every Haggadah is inherently a social justice text. —J.G.K.

Though contemporary Jews take the great range of available Haggadot for granted, the diverse reinterpretations of content—as opposed to illustrations and creative translations—is a relatively new phenomenon. —D.W.

primarily spiritual? Or are they focused on social justice or on Jewish learning? Will they care about illustrations or the quality of the translation? What about egalitarianism or theology? It is very helpful to find a good match between the Haggadah and the group.

Once the choice of a Haggadah is made, it can be useful to think about what is missing. Additional readings are available online and through many Jewish organizations; some publish a new Haggadah supplement every year. Some additions deal with issues in current events. Others

The purchase of Haggadot, especially if one is inclined to take the mandate of hospitality seriously and to invite a lot of people to one's Seder, can be a significant and sometimes burdensome investment. It is a relief to find a Haggadah that feels like a good fit. —D.W.

When I was in college, we used to create a Seder for our friends in which every person had a different Haggadah so that each part of the Seder could be shared with a different emphasis. It helped keep everyone's interest and made for very lively discussions throughout the evening. Some families with young children like to use the Haggadah that their children use in their religious school or early childhood center to make sure that the Haggadah is age-appropriate. —S.C.R.

With so many choices of Haggadot, the leader may decide to incorporate selections from a variety of publications. Some families give everyone different books, while others select a very basic text for everyone to use and then share different Haggadot around the table. Many families have a tradition of creating their own photocopied version of the Haggadah, collecting favorite readings and songs over the years. If we are to take seriously the notion that we should feel as if we ourselves were taken out of Egypt, then the version we choose ought to be renewed in some way to make the experience unique each year. —B.P.

deal with perennial challenges. Some, such as ones that include a fifth cup of wine, interpret particular aspects of Jewish tradition. Others connect loosely to one of the themes of the Seder. It is also possible to add poetry not originally designed for a Seder, to write new material, or to read selected sections aloud from Haggadot other than the one that has been distributed at the table. *A Night of Questions* and some other Haggadot offer many ways to use the same Haggadah.

Creating your own Haggadah (perhaps by excerpting from various ones) can be an empowering process. It can result in a Haggadah that matches your taste and approach. —N.C.M.

Another way to engage all the participants is to invite different individuals or families to prepare a section of the Haggadah in advance. Like a potluck meal, this kind of Seder builds on the special talents and interests of everyone involved. It can also lead to surprises for everyone. Be sure to state expectations and limits clearly, indicating how much time the section should take, and the ages and backgrounds of other participants. —B.P.

Some people choose to make their own family Haggadot year after year. Such Haggadot can include traditional Seder texts, pictures, poetry, essays and personal writings. Sometimes participants are allowed to take these creations with them as yearbooks of sorts. —J.G.K.

When Seder leaders prepare, they should think through how the evening should go, what questions should be asked, and what themes highlighted. What objects on the table need to be explained? If children will be present, how will they be involved in the Seder? How long should the Seder last? Where should discussions take place? A

A hearty yes to truly planning the Seder! Inclusivity does take more thought than domination. —S.P.W.

As a child growing up in Argentina, I hated the Pesach Seder. My uncle would read the Haggadah in Hebrew, which we did not understand, and he never paused to give an explanation. As the evening went by, we became tired and fidgety, which made my uncle angry with us, and the evening unfolded as a very unhappy event for all the cousins present. That might be why I carefully prepare to lead the Seder in my home every year. I plan for weeks, carefully choosing readings, explanations, and a major theme for discussion, doing my best to have not only a meaningful evening but a joyous one as well. —L.K.

Since the goal of the Seder is to experience the redemption of the Exodus, it is a great idea to utilize some experiential education tactics to enhance the Seder. A few of my favorites are: giving everyone a question to ask related to a step of the Seder, to be revealed and discussed when the Seder arrives at that step, and asking a few people to pick a character in the Exodus story, and then having them retell the story in that character's voice. Another approach is to assign roles that accord with "the four children" for people to take on during the telling of the story: 1. Critical Thinker (*Ḥakham*)—What are the assumptions built into this text? How does each of these connect to the experience of redemption? 2. Agitator (*Rasha*)—Why bother? What is in these texts for me? What assumptions underlie these texts that I question? 3. Simplifier/Reductionist (*Tam*)—Summarize this in a one-page report. What does it all boil down to? 4. Non-Questioner (*She'eyno Yode'a Lish'ol*)—one who attempts to formulate answers to others' questions rather than adding a personal voice to the questioning. —J.M.S.

One of the smartest suggestions anyone ever gave me is to feed young children who are present at a Seder before the Seder starts. That way, they will be able to sit through the Seder itself without the constant nudging that comes from hunger. —S.C.R.

well-planned Seder will encourage everyone's participation; the Seder leader will guide the group rather than dominate it.

Over time, the number of ceremonial objects at the Seder has expanded. Many Seder plates have places for five objects:

- *beytza*, the roasted egg, signifying the festival offering in the ancient Jerusalem Temple;
- *z'ro'a*, the roasted lamb bone (or a roasted chicken bone if a lamb bone is unavailable, or, for vegetarians, a roasted beet or roasted sweet potato), signifying the protection of the Israelites during the Tenth Plague in Egypt and the paschal sacrifice in the Temple;

Sometimes no amount of planning can guarantee a participatory ritual. My late uncle reveled in asking: "When do we get to eat the festive meal?" right up until the chopped liver was brought out from the kitchen. For him, the point of the Seder was family and food; he could not tolerate a discussion of the themes of slavery, redemption, activism or springtime renewal. —D.W.

"*Z'ro'a*" literally means "arm" and so is associated with the biblical metaphor of God saving the Israelites with the outstretched arm of redemption. —J.A.S./J.G.K.

The sweet potato is better known as the "Paschal Yam," of course! —M.F.

There is another story regarding the use of the beet. In Buchenwald concentration camp in 1945, a woman recorded: "It hit me suddenly that the Haggadah could have been written for us. If I only changed the tense from past to present, it was written about us … At this time, the scene in the barracks was bad, there was fighting, cursing and yelling … so when I asked the women to be quiet, it was like a miracle, this absolute silence in the barracks. I started the Seder by asking why is this night different. And I said that every night we quarrel and we fight and tonight we remember. There were close to a thousand women there. I picked up the slice of sugar beet, and I said, 'This is the bread of our suffering …' And then we made a vow that if we survived, a beet was going to be on our Seder table." So some homes add a roasted beet to the Seder plate each year. —T.K./L.K.

- *maror*, bitter herb, which is most commonly horseradish, signifying the bitterness of slavery; horseradish continues to spread in the garden under adverse conditions, as the Israelites did in Egypt;
- *ḥaroset*, a mixture of fruit, which might include apples, dates, nuts, figs, wine, sugar and cinnamon, depending upon which tradition Jews follow, that signifies the mortar used by Israelite slaves in Egypt; and
- *karpas*, greens—usually parsley, but whatever is available can be used—signifying the beginning of spring and the rebirth of the Israelite people after their crushing experience of being enslaved in Egypt.

The Lurianic kabbalists of Tzfat considered the five-ingredient Seder plate to be incomplete. They added *ḥazeret*, an additional kind of bitter herb (sometimes sliced horseradish, sometimes romaine lettuce or another bitter

Jewish cookbooks have many wonderful *ḥaroset* recipes. I make a *ḥaroset* that includes all the foods mentioned in the Song of Songs, the biblical book of love songs traditionally recited on the Shabbat that falls during Pesach. —J.A.S.

When my family makes *ḥaroset* from figs or dates or other sticky fruits, we serve it shaped into pyramids, drawing the connection between *ḥaroset* and mortar in a very concrete way. —B.P.

My family—on both the Hungarian and Russian sides—used boiled potatoes for *ḳarpas*. Potatoes aren't green, but they were available locally in early April, when green vegetables were hard to come by. —J.J.S.

One kind of bitter herb—like romaine lettuce or endive—can be dipped into *ḥaroset* for the *maror*, while a second kind—like grated horseradish—can easily make up the filling of Hillel's sandwich for *ḳoreḳh*. —J.G.K.

vegetable). The six ingredients can be laid out as the points of a six-pointed star composed of two triangles, with one representing creation, revelation and redemption, and the other representing God, Torah and Israel. Both five-ingredient and six-ingredient Seder plates are available. Many are beautifully designed, aiding in *hidur mitzvah*, making more attractive the mitzvah of the Seder as we re-experience the going forth from Egypt.

The text's interpretation of the six points corresponds to the points of the "Star of Redemption" expounded by the 20th-century philosopher Franz Rosenzweig. My understanding is that the Seder plate of Isaac Luria (who lived in 16th-century Tzfat) associated the six points with six of the lower *s'firot* (aspects of divinity): *Z'ro'a* for *ḥesed*/caring, egg for *g'vura* /fortitude, *maror* for *raḥamim*/compassion, *ḥaroset* for *netzaḥ*/endurance, *ḳarpas* for *hod*/majesty, and *ḥazeret* for *brit*/covenant (more often called *y'sod*/foundation). The seventh lower *s'fira, Malḳhut/Sheḳhina*, is symbolized by the plate itself. *Sheḳhina* is God's presence that dwells with us, even in exile. We ask for the presence of the *Sheḳhina* in our daily prayers. The three matzot represent the upper three *s'firot—Eyn Sof*/infinity, *ḥoḳhma*/wisdom, and *bina*/understanding. I like to imagine that ten items on the table can also be related to the journey from ten plagues in Egypt to ten utterances at Sinai. —J.G.K./J.A.S.

Other kabbalistic representations have the *z'ro'a, beytza,* and *maror* representing the *s'firot* (kabbalistic emanations) of *ḥesed* (loving kindness), *g'vura* (strict judgment) and *tiferet* (the balance point between them), respectively. The *ḥaroset, ḳarpas,* and *ḥazeret* represent the *s'firot* of *netzaḥ (eternity), hod* (wonder) and *y'sod* (foundation) respectively. The three matzot represent the three upper *s'firot* of *ḥoḳhma* (wisdom), *bina* (discernment) and *da'at* (knowledge). Thus the orange, in the center of the Seder plate, could represent *malḳhut,* God's immanent and feminine presence in the world. —J.M.S.

I have found that the three most common Jewish ritual objects people collect are Hanukah menorahs, mezuzot and Seder plates. Some people put out several different kinds of Seder plates on their tables both to serve as ritual objects and to add ritual beauty to the festival table. —S.C.R.

Starting in the 1980s, the custom arose of placing an orange on the Seder plate as a gesture of solidarity with Jewish gay men and lesbians. The orange is on some level about overcoming alienation. Whether this is about the need to include women fully in Jewish life, about the importance of equality for gay men and lesbians or about the fruitfulness of women is a matter about which people who observe this custom differ. Whatever the original reason, the meaning of the orange on the Seder plate is likely

Rabbi Rebecca Alpert's book, *Like Bread on the Seder Plate*, points out that the custom of putting an orange on the Seder plate originated when someone observed that being lesbian and Jewish was as incongruous as placing bread on a Seder plate. In one response to this outrageous comment, lesbians and their allies began putting bread on their Seder plates. In time, the custom shifted to putting an orange on the Seder plate instead, since oranges are neither traditional nor forbidden. —J.G.K.

An orange is a symbol without meaning in traditional Pesach liturgy, whether it is the original biblical or the renegotiated rabbinic holiday. As a new symbol, the orange can signify ideas about inclusion that are easily incorporated into the Seder. Rebecca Alpert suggests that the origins of this practice are far more transgressive, and that the original phrase was directed at lesbians, who were judged as belonging to the Jewish community as much as bread belongs on a Seder plate. Enacting that challenge radically alters boundaries rather than gently expanding them. The many symbols of Pesach provide an excellent opportunity to discuss who and what make up the Jewish community, and how commitments are translated into action. —D.W.

Susannah Heschel says that she was the first to put an orange on the Seder plate after seeing a crust of bread on a Seder plate at Oberlin College. The story that developed later is that the original incident took place in response to someone who said, "They belong on the *bima* as much as bread belongs on a Seder plate." She used an orange because using bread during Pesach is transgressive. Of course, other contemporary midrashim carry different versions of the tale. —D.A.T.

to evolve. The origin of any innovation is less important than how it comes to be understood over time. When a new issue regarding freedom or justice arises, the symbols and rituals of the Seder can be expanded to make room for it.

Also on the Seder table are three matzot, sometimes under a special, three-layered matza cover that is often graced by beautiful embroidery. A midrash suggests that the three matzot represent *kohen*, *levi*, and *Yisrael*—priests, levites and Israelites—brought together to show the unity of the Jewish people. A more technical explanation is that two complete pieces of matza (the equivalent of the two loaves of bread on the Shabbat table during the rest of the year) are needed for the recitation of the *motzi*, the blessing beginning the Seder meal, when the Seder falls on Shabbat. Since the third matza is broken early in the Seder to be set aside for the *afikoman*, three matzot are needed in order for there to be two whole matzot at the beginning of the meal. With three matzot needed when the Seder occurs on Shabbat, the rabbis made three matzot the standard for every Seder night so that people would not have to remember to prepare the matzot differently on Shabbat.

Adding components to the Seder plate can be a way of both personalizing and contextualizing Pesach in the spirit of identifying with the struggles of the ancients. Another recent addition to the Seder plate is a dish of olives to symbolize a hope for peace between the people of Israel and Palestine. —N.H.M.

The Seder table also holds a container of salt water, signifying tears and historically evoking the dipping of food into salt water at the symposium meal. We dip the *karpas* into the salt water before eating it, reminding us that new life can follow a period of tears and loss.

The cup of Elijah is the fifth cup, the cup of redemption and a reminder of messianic hope. It is filled with wine at the beginning of the Seder. In recent years, many Jews have begun including on the table a water-filled cup of

The saltwater and the water for Miriam's cup signify the waters that burst forth as new life emerges. Just as women figure prominently in the birth story described in the first few chapters of the Book of Exodus, so at the Seder, women are heroes of resistance as well as midwives, nurturers and witnesses to the birth of this people. —S.P.W.

The Pesach drama both begins and ends with saltwater. We start with saltwater tears and end as the Israelites pass through the split sea and the Egyptian army is drowned in saltwater. —J.A.S.

The tradition at our Seder is to start with the cup of Elijah empty and then to pass it around the table so that each of the participants can add a little of their own wine until the cup is full. This reminds us that for redemption to come, all of us must do our part. All of us have a role—men and women, young and old. Similarly, an empty Miriam's cup can be passed and filled while recalling the names of those for whom we pray for healing. —N.H.M./S.C.R.

A medieval custom of having fish on the Seder table was associated with Miriam. Just as the Seder plate's egg is associated with Aaron (the priest making the holiday sacrifice) and the bone with Moses (who affirmed that God would reach out to redeem the people), a third kind of cooked food is associated with Miriam. In just one verse of the Hebrew Bible, the three siblings are named one after the other: "And I will set before you Moses, Aaron and Miriam." (Micah 6:4) The word "*eshlaḥ*," translated as "set" here, has the same root as "*shulḥan*," which means "table." The three siblings, co-equal in this verse alone, can be set before us at the Seder table. —J.G.K.

Miriam as a reminder of the aspect of redemption present in everyday life, for water sustains our lives daily. Each of these cups is available in artistic designs. Family heirlooms can also be used for the cups.

Each person at the Seder traditionally drinks four cups of wine or grape juice. The wine or juice may be sweet or dry, red or rosé or white, but many insist that it be certi-

Bringing Miriam into the Seder is, on the one hand, natural. Miriam played a role in the exodus narrative, nurturing her younger brother Moses in his early years and partnering with him in leading the Israelites in the years of desert wanderings, including drawing forth a wellspring out of which this ritual arises. On the other hand, what makes it slightly odd is the notable absence of Moses and their elder brother Aaron from the traditional Haggadah. The rabbis omitted their roles in order to shape the postbiblical ritual in the wake of the Bar Kochba revolt in a way that plays down political activism. For the rabbis, the individual to make more visible was Elijah, harbinger of the ultimate redemption. If Miriam is to be introduced into the Seder, Moses and Aaron should be acknowledged as well, as they are in *A Night of Questions.* —D.W.

I was 11 years old when I was actually permitted to drink wine, and I became intoxicated. With all that wine available, someone should be the designated driver, even if it is a religious ritual. —J.J.S.

fied as kosher for Passover, an issue dealt with in the section on Pesach kashrut that follows. Some say the four cups represent the four freedoms. The first cup is drunk after reciting the holiday Kiddush near the beginning of the Seder, so it sanctifies the day. The second cup is drunk at the end of the telling of the story of redemption from Egypt, so it is linked to past redemption. The third cup is drunk at the end of the *Birkat Hamazon*, the Grace after Meals; it marks the redemption of the present that is embodied in the food we eat. The fourth cup is drunk near the end of the Seder, which focuses on future redemption.

The four cups can also signify the four worlds in the mystical tradition. The structure of the Seder then moves through the worlds of body, heart, mind and spirit. This reminds us of the mystical notion that the deepest level of exile was the exile of awareness. As we bring attention and awareness to the various levels of human experience, we are also liberating awareness itself. —S.P.W.

I have structured the four cups so that the first represents sacred time; the second, personal liberation from bad habits or desires; the third, communal freedoms and obligations to tackle challenging issues where we live; and the fourth, planetary liberation—what we need to do locally and globally to create a more healthy, sustainable, and just world. —N.C.M.

The drinking of the four cups can model responsible alcohol consumption. Drinking wine recalls the template of the Greek symposium upon which the Seder is based. The four cups put us at ease with those around us, creating a social and convivial atmosphere. But with two of the cups to be consumed toward the end of the gathering when people are getting ready to leave, there is a danger of traveling while intoxicated. It may be advisable to use dessert wine of a low alcohol content or grape juice for the last two cups to avoid this problem. It is also helpful to include plenty of singing after the fourth cup. —J.M.S.

The wine and grape juice we consume during the meal are not counted toward the four ritual cups. A considerable amount of wine and grape juice is needed for the Seder.

The Seder is designed to stimulate curiosity, invite inquiry and encourage participation. When children are to be present at the Seder, collecting objects related to the Seder that they can play with at the table will help to keep them engaged. Children's songs for the Seder can be rehearsed in advance. Somewhat older children can learn to recite the Four Questions. The exodus story should be told in a way that children will understand. A Sephardic

In fourth grade at yeshiva, I was required to memorize the Four Questions in Yiddish, to the delight of my Yiddish-speaking *bubby*, with whom I could not otherwise communicate. Alas, to this day, the *Fir Kashes* (Four Questions) and the Yiddish lullaby "*Rojinkes mit Mandeln*" ("Roses and Almonds") constitute the entirety of my Yiddish repertoire. —J.J.S.

I do a yoga-based *magid* for children that grownups can also enjoy. It can be a real energy boost during all that sitting time. It is not hard to find poses that link to the story, and it is great fun. —S.P.W.

When our children were young, we held the first part of the Seder on couches in the basement or living room, allowing them to move around freely. This custom also echoes the ancient origins of the Greek symposium. After the storytelling of the *magid*, we would come to the formal table for the meal and conclude the Seder there. —B.P.

custom is to keep nuts and raisins handy so that they can periodically be thrown to the children. An adult can be asked in advance to work on a skit with the children in another room and then bring them back so that they can present the skit.

For young people, one of the Seder's most engaging elements is the hiding of the *afikoman*. The Mishnah states, "*Eyn maftirin aḥarey hapesaḥ afikoman*," which was taken by later rabbis to mean, "Don't eat anything after eating the Pesach Seder's *afikoman* matza." We now know that "*afikoman*" is a word borrowed from Greek that means "late-night parties," so a better translation would be, "After eating the paschal sacrifice, don't go out partying." But the custom of eating the *afikoman* is a long-standing one. Traditionally the person who "stole"

In our family, we send the children off to prepare a skit in order to give them time to move around and play, and also to provide an opportunity for adult conversation regarding some of the darker sides of the Pesach story. —T.K.

the *afikoman* could bargain for a prize for its return because the *afikoman* is the final food eaten at the Seder. Sometimes the Seder leader turns the *afikoman* over to someone else to safeguard. If the *afikoman* is captured, the person in charge of the *afikoman* must redeem it. Many families have an agreement that the ransom will take the form of giving *tzedaka*, with the amount and the beneficiary to be negotiated. Some Seder leaders hide the *afikoman* and then give a prize to the person who finds it. Some families hide one "*afikoman*" matza piece for each child present at the Seder, preparing one prize or gift for each child in advance.

I remember going to my grandfather's house for Seder every year as a child and the excitement of knowing that regardless of who found the *afikoman*, each child would receive a shiny silver dollar as a prize (with a double portion for the one who actually found it). Over the years, inflation has caused the amount of the prize to go up in our family, but the excitement remains the same for every child who hunts for the prized matza. —S.C.R.

While the text of the traditional Haggadah emphasizes divine rather than human agency in liberation, real liberations usually come about through organized human effort. In that spirit, in my family the children form a "union" and bargain collectively for a generous *afikoman* ransom. —J.A.S.

Like the ancient disagreement between the House of Hillel and the House of Shammai, in our day we have the disagreement between the *afikoman* stealers and the *afikoman* finders. —J.A.S.

Before the Seder, we prepare an envelope for each child who will be present with a piece of matza inside, and we hide most of the envelopes at age-appropriate levels before the Seder. When it is time to find the *afikoman*, older children who have already located their envelopes are drafted to help the younger children find theirs. —D.W.

Conducting the Seder

Every Seder leader has his or her own way of leading the Seder. The key mitzvah of the Seder is to feel that you have gone forth from Egypt. An effective leader will keep that in mind while balancing the intellectual, affective, spiritual and activist elements of the Seder. If the guests do not all know each other, introductions should be made before the Seder begins. Some Seder leaders review the items on

There is a tradition for the Seder leader to wear a *kittel* to designate the purity and seriousness that the leader brings to that role. In a situation where leadership is shared, it may be helpful to have a tallit or another ritual item that is passed around to whoever is leading that part of the Seder. —J.M.S.

The primary role of the convener of the Pesach meal is actually threefold: to ensure that conversation flows around the topics of Pesach (convener of the symposium), to lead the rituals (supplanting the priestly role), and to organize teaching and text study (a rabbinic role). —N.C.M.

Too many Seder leaders feel that they have to read the Haggadah out loud, verbatim. Noam Zion teaches that much of the Haggadah is akin to a teacher's preparatory notes for a class. Reading those notes aloud is neither required nor advisable. —M.F.

One family we know has everyone write his or her name inside the cover of the Haggadah each is using. Each year, the accumulation of names not only reminds the family of Seders past, but also attests to the notion of *l'dor vador*, continuity from one generation to the next. —B.P.

The Seder officially opens with the declaration, "Let all who are hungry come and eat." Likewise, the Torah instructs families to share their lambs with their neighbors who have none. Therefore, many families make a point of inviting people who have no other Seder to attend. This might include complete strangers, such as students or those in the military who are far from home. —B.P.

the table to ensure that the participants understand their significance. Other Seder leaders start almost immediately with the holiday Kiddush (*kadesh*), which includes a version of *Havdala* when the Seder falls on Saturday night. The Seder continues with hand washing (*urḥatz*) and then with dipping the green in salt water (*karpas*). It is the custom in some families to pause at *karpas* to eat not only the green, but also an expanded course of vegetables and dips, and, in some families, gefilte fish as well. This allows the main part of the Seder to last longer because people are not hungrily awaiting the meal. Many people like to eat matza with their fish, but matza should not be eaten until the meal, when *motzi* is said. Some people serve egg matza instead; others eat without it.

Virtually all Haggadot then proceed with the Seder ritual in the same order. The middle matza is broken for the afikoman. Then the heart of the Seder, the *magid* (telling; at the Seder, telling about the going forth from Egypt), begins with the tale of the Four Children, which illustrates the need to tailor the story to the people who are listening

It is practical to make *karpas* a real appetizer course. I like to follow dipping parsley in saltwater with dipping artichokes in olive oil and strawberries in whipped cream.
—J.G.K.

to it. Much of the Seder ritual is designed to stimulate questions and conversation. The Four Questions, which have changed over time, were originally backup questions to be asked if none of the people at the Seder asked any questions of their own. In our time, singing the Four Questions has become so popular that they are included no matter what questions are asked otherwise. While traditionally the youngest person capable of it at the Seder asks the Four Questions, this task can be assigned to anyone, or the group can sing them together. Some leaders answer the questions before moving on to the rest of the *magid*. The Seder narrative may draw heavily on the midrash; it may stay closer to the biblical account; it may

The Talmud insists that someone be stimulated to ask a question at the Seder, thereby inviting the leader to begin telling the tale of the exodus. Throughout Jewish history, various customs have been introduced to provoke questions, especially from children. The Four Questions were originally provided as a kind of script in case no one had a question. We once attended a Seder where the leader hung matza from the ceiling with crepe paper, which succeeded in getting people to ask questions. —B.P.

My wife, Merle Potchinsky, developed a playful style of *magid* that has become popular at our Seders. Before Pesach, we write random phrases from popular culture, children's songs and poetry on strips of paper. At the Seder, the group is divided into teams, with each assigned a section of the Pesach story. Each team pulls some of the strips from a hat. The teams have a few minutes to prepare a skit telling their part of the story in a way that incorporates the random phrases. —J.A.S.

Singing *Dayenu* is perhaps the least negotiable part of my family's Seder, and is absolutely the high point. This expression of gratitude, sung with a catchy melody, is understood by all to be the main point of our gathering. —D.W.

consist of telling the story without relying on the Haggadah; or it may focus on ties to current issues of social justice. The *magid* concludes with the singing of "*Dayenu*" and the first part of "*Hallel*," and drinking the second cup of wine.

The meal begins with ritual hand washing, the *motzi* made over the two whole matzot, the eating the *maror* (bitter herb) dipped in *ḥaroset*, and the Hillel sandwich (*korekh*). Originally the Hillel sandwich contained the

In my family the eating of the *maror* is an opportunity each year to talk about the ongoing enslavements that still exist in our world. Human trafficking is more prevalent than ever; economic enslavement is rampant; and more men, women and children are enslaved in one form or another today than at any time in human history. —S.C.R.

I can't think about *ḥreyn* (Yiddish for a horseradish condiment, usually chopped and blended with beets), which my family uses for *maror*, without considering the *ḥaroset*, which my *bubby* made extra sweet with wine and cinnamon. My uncle loved the horseradish to be as hot as possible. He would pile the horseradish high on a piece of matza, pop the whole thing into his mouth in one bite, and then grin broadly while the rest of the family shrieked in pain as we imagined the fire coursing through his sinuses. He shunned the moderating sweetness of the *ḥaroset*, preferring the heat of remembered bitterness to any temperance. I, on the other hand, would build a veritable tower of *ḥaroset*, crowning it with the smallest possible dot of red horseradish, as we said the blessing over bitter herbs. As a child, I wanted only sweetness, no matter the intended symbolism. I now strive for a middle path. My spoonful of horseradish is equally balanced by a modest dollop of *ḥaroset*. Chewing, swallowing, wincing only a little, I take into myself an essential teaching of Judaism—that the bitterness and the sweetness are intertwined, that our *simḥas* are balanced by our sorrows, and that our freedom is brought home to us most powerfully by the recollection of our bitter enslavement. —D.W.

For more than 60 years, Avi Morrow, a Montrealer, has been making and distributing his own horseradish every spring, to an ever-growing list of friends and acquaintances. It is a powerful—and pungent!—way to establish and maintain connections. —D.W.

three elements of the Seder meal required in biblical times—matza, *pesaḥ* (roasted lamb from the paschal sacrifice) and *maror*. Since there is no longer a *pesaḥ*, a second piece of matza is substituted. Some people add *ḥaroset*. How can matza substitute for the *pesaḥ?* Both are symbols that signify the redemption from Egypt.

Then comes the meal itself (*shulḥan orekh*). Customs regarding foods to be included in the meal vary widely. Many include soup with matza balls. Some eat a separate fish course. The entrée is usually meat or fowl. Salad and a variety of vegetables are often present. Dessert follows.

Nearly every one of the ritual symbols of Pesach serve as symbols of both slavery and liberation. For example, matza is both the "bread of affliction" and the symbol of our haste in pursuing freedom. *Maror* can represent both the tears of our enslavement and the tears of joy at liberation, as well as the tears we still shed for the millions who remain captive and enslaved today. —S.C.R.

Entire commentaries can be written on the topic of matza balls alone. Which is better, heavy or light, big or small, *Bubby's* or Grandma's? My father always insisted that the best matza balls are heavy, like the ones my mother made, but with a dollop of schmaltz in the middle, like the ones his mother used to make when he was little, so that the hot, flavorful fat would burst into the soup and into his mouth at the first bite. —D.W.

Before serving the matza ball soup and the fish, my mother's custom was to serve cold egg soup. The egg on the Seder plate has no corresponding ritual in the Seder itself, so this first course provided a means to incorporate it into the meal. —B.P.

I think the secret of the best Pesach cakes is not to try to replace flour with starch or matza meal and instead to focus on flourless cake recipes. —J.G.K.

Because most Jews do not serve leavened products at the Seder, chocolate mousse, fruit salad, or kosher-for-Passover cakes can be used. (For more information on Pesach food, see the Pesach kashrut section that follows.) The meal is concluded with eating the ransomed *afikoman* (*tzafun*, hidden).

The Seder ritual then proceeds with the *Birkat Hamazon* (Grace after Meals) and the third cup of wine. The

Pesach hot beverages are associated with some great Jewish history. For a long time, Moroccan Jews did not eat white sugar on Pesach for reasons similar to why Ashkenazic Jews restrict their eating of *kitniyot*, and some Moroccans still drink tea with dates on Pesach. In North America, the Maxwell House Coffee Co. published a Haggadah in the 1930s largely to broaden its reach into the Jewish community and to affirm that its coffee is kosher for Passover. The Maxwell House Haggadah, which was free at some supermarkets, remains the classic Haggadah for many American Jews. —J.G.K.

With younger children, it can be fun to have the adults quickly drink down the wine from Elijah's cup while the children are searching for the *afikoman*. When the children see the wine cup empty, it adds to the drama of Elijah's visit. —T.K.

Preparing, serving and cleaning up after the Seder meal are major undertakings, even when the gathering is small. This would be a good time for all to demonstrate appreciation for the work that has gone into the Seder and to offer to help out in the kitchen! —B.P.

future redemption section includes the opening of the door for Elijah. Elijah, who, according to the biblical account, ascended to heaven in a chariot, is traditionally understood to be a harbinger of the Messiah. According to some strands of Jewish tradition, it is on the Seder night that the Messiah will arrive, so that is one reason to open the door. An infamous libel held that Jews used the blood of Christian children to make matza, so Jews opened their doors to demonstrate that nothing untoward was happening at their Seders. The ritual remains today in part because it engages young people. The Seder proceeds with the second part of *Hallel* and drinking the fourth cup of wine or juice. The Seder concludes with singing of songs that are connected to the holiday such as "*Ḥad Gadya*," "*Adir Hu*" and "*Eḥad Mi Yode'a*."

Traditional Diaspora Jews conduct two Seders, as they observe two full holiday days at the beginning of the holi-

A powerful contemporary teaching on this passage is included in "The Body in Question," an episode of the 1990s television show "Northern Exposure." In it, Fleischman, the Jewish doctor exiled to rural Alaska, has a dream about an Old World Pesach Seder in which he gets up to open the door to find a man in a modern-day suit standing there and claiming to be Elijah. In the dream, Elijah challenges Fleischman: "What would you do if Elijah were really here? Would you open the door wide to him or slam it in his face?" Fleischman, grappling with the question of faith versus science, wakes up and ponders the question quite seriously.
—D.W.

Elijah's cup was the most exciting part of the Seder for me as a child. He was the closest thing to a Jewish ghost or Santa Claus. It was years before I had enough courage to open the front door for Elijah unaccompanied. And then the adults would try to convince me that he had taken a sip from his cup when it appeared to be as full as ever. Elijah represented sacred mystery for me long before he ever came to stand for hope. —J.J.S.

day and two full holiday days on the seventh and eighth day of the holiday. Jews who follow Israeli practice, including many Reconstructionist and Reform Jews and some Conservative Jews in the Diaspora, conduct only one Seder. They observe only the first and seventh days as full holiday days, and they observe seven days of Pesach rather than eight. For an explanation of the rationales for these choices, see Appendix I. Some liberal Jews conduct two Seders not because they consider themselves obligated, but because it gives them a chance to share the Seder with different groups of family members and friends. Sometimes they make the second Seder more freeform and thematic, and they keep the first Seder more traditional. Some also go to themed Seders—Seders focused on feminism, interfaith affairs, justice and so on—on other nights of Pesach or at another time in the weeks before or after Pesach.

On the second night of Pesach, *s'firat ha'omer*, the counting of the *omer*, begins. If a second Seder is conducted, *s'firat ha'omer* takes place during the Seder. If a second-night Seder is not conducted, the counting of the *omer* is said as part of *ma'ariv*, the evening service, or on its own; the *omer* is then counted each evening. The *omer*

A creative second Seder might be built around favorite memories and experiences of Pesachs past, or children could write a play of the exodus narrative in the afternoon and act it out for *magid*. —D.W.

counts the days for seven full weeks from the second night of Pesach until Shavuot, which is the 50th day. Keeping track of the count is made easier if you use an *omer* counter; some set an alarm to remind them to do the counting. The blessing that precedes the counting ends, "*vetzivanu al s'firat ha'omer*"—"commands us to count the *omer*." The announcement of the number of the day in the count follows. In ancient times, these seven weeks marked the time from the planting to harvesting the first grain, a time of considerable anxiety, since the right amount of rain and sun was necessary to create a bounteous harvest. Later the seven weeks came to be understood as the time from the liberation from Egyptian slavery to the mythic receiving of the Ten Commandments at Mount Sinai. The process begun in Egypt culminates at Sinai, where the covenant is affirmed. Jews repeat this process through celebrating Pesach, counting the *omer*

The weeks between Pesach and Shavuot are still associated in traditional circles with various catastrophes in Jewish history, including the suffering of Rabbi Akiba's students during the Bar Kochba revolt in the second century and the massacre of the Jews in the Rhineland during the First Crusade in the eleventh century. It is customary not to celebrate at parties or get haircuts during this period—except on the 33rd day, *Lag B'Omer*. —J.J.S.

and observing Shavuot. The counting of the *omer* in the Northern Hemisphere spans most of spring. Kabbala, the Jewish mystical tradition, attributes meanings to the weeks and the days of the week, providing another way to add meaning to the counting.

What is the connection between liberation and Torah? Genuine liberation enables us to accomplish things in the world without being enslaved to outside forces, to the past, or to inner forces of trauma, habit or ignorance. The work of such liberation is sometimes called "praxis," which the Brazilian educator Paolo Freire defined as "reflection and action upon the world in order to transform it." Torah is praxis; it is a dialogical process of releasing ourselves from assumptions and limited perspectives in order to reveal a more divine truth and act for *tikun olam*. Thus, *Pirkey Avot* 6.2 teaches: "Only those who engage in *talmud Torah* are free." —J.A.S.

The mystical tradition of *omer* counting creates an opportunity to spiritually prepare ourselves for Shavuot by reflecting on how we are living out 49 different qualities in our lives. Several contemporary *omer* calendars have been created, such as Rabbi Yael Levy's "Journey through the Wilderness" and Simon Jacobson's "Counting the Omer." —N.C.M.

Our family always looks forward to counting the *omer*. In the midst of our other Pesach preparations, we plan a customized *omer* counter each year that allows us to mark the 49 days until Shavuot. The counter changes from year to year, depending on what is happening in the world and in our family's life. For example, when we were spending a year living in Israel, we cut out 49 domes, arches and other architectural elements that our children could assemble night by night into a Jerusalem cityscape. Another year, we created an abstract picture showing the Israelites—represented by small squares of colored paper—crossing through the Sea of Reeds and heading toward Mount Sinai. And another time we cut out seven colorful Jewish stars, each comprised of a central hexagon that would start the week, and six small triangles that would form the star as they counted off the days of that week of the *omer*. Now that our children are older, they are excited to have an active hand in creating the *omer* counter. Every evening, we gather to say the blessing, and then one of the children tapes the newest piece to the kitchen wall, adding to the design. The best designs are freeform giving the children freedom about choosing and placing that evening's piece, rather than putting a particular piece in a specific spot. Each year our children—and we!—are excited to count our way through the *omer* and to watch the image take form on our wall night by night as we count our way to Sinai. —J.W.

Observing a full holiday (in Hebrew, "*yom tov*"; in Yiddish, "*yontef*") is similar to observing Shabbat in terms of creating a joyous, restful atmosphere and in terms of many of the patterns of observance. However, traditionally observant people recognize a few distinctions. While the traditionally observant would neither start nor regulate a fire nor cook on Shabbat, those activities are recognized as permitted on holidays (unless they coincide with Shabbat) even by the most stringently observant. Jews who would not carry objects outdoors on Shabbat will carry them on *yom tov*.

Pesach Worship

The evening service on the first day of Pesach is relatively brief. Structured like the weekday service, it uses a different *nusaḥ* (musical structure) and contains the *Amida* used on the *sh'losh r'galim*, the three pilgrimage festivals. Some congregations do not have an evening service on Seder night because the focus of the evening is on the Seder, whether it takes place in a community setting like a congregation or in a home.

Traditionally on *yom tov*, observant people will transfer fire from an existing flame to a new fuel source/wick, but they will not light a new flame with matches or a lighter. Different people apply this principle in different ways to electric stoves and ovens, depending on their approach to electricity as "fire." —M.F.

The first parts of the morning service on the first day of Pesach—*Birkhot Hashaḥar*, *P'sukey D'zimra*, and the Shema and its blessings—are the same as for Shabbat. The *Amida* is the one for the *sh'losh r'galim*. The *Amida* is followed by the singing of the full form of *Hallel*, consisting of Psalms 113–118 and a brief introduction and conclusion. *T'filat Tal*, the prayer for dew, is inserted in the *Amida* during *shaḥarit* in liberal congregations; Conservative and Orthodox congregations add *T'filat Tal* in *Musaf*. *Hallel* marks the divine presence associated with the *sh'losh r'galim* and, to a lesser extent, with holidays that developed later in Jewish history.

The main Torah reading on the first day of Pesach is from Exodus (12:21–51), which recounts the first Seder in Egypt and the liberation of the Israelites. Many congregations observe the custom of reading the *maftir* portion from a second Torah scroll. That reading (Numbers 28:16–25) describes the basic rules for observing Pesach—not eating leavened bread, observing the first and last days of Pesach as full holidays on which no work is done, and

I always look forward to the prayer for dew; it reminds me of how much our sustenance and ability to live are dependent on natural cycles. Precipitation and its lack, especially in a time of planetary warming, cannot be taken for granted. —N.C.M.

making special sacrifices in the ancient Jerusalem Temple. The haftarah for the first day is from Joshua. The traditional reading is 5:2–6:1 and 27; some Reconstructionists read 5:2–15. This haftarah recounts the circumcision of the Israelites in the wilderness and the observance of Pesach there. There are five aliyot from the first Torah and one from the second Torah.

Those who begin Pesach by observing two days of full *yom tov* have a morning service on the second day like that of the first day. The main Torah reading then is Leviticus 22:26–23:44, which puts Pesach in the context of the five annual holidays specified in the Torah—Pesach, Shavuot, Rosh Hashana, Yom Kippur and Sukkot. The *maftir* reading from the second scroll is the same as the one on the first day. The haftarah (II Kings 23:1–9, 21–25) concerns King Josiah's efforts to remove idolatrous worship from the Temple and his reinstitution of Pesach observance after his predecessor had undermined it.

The afternoon service is similar to that on weekdays, though the festival *Amida* replaces the weekday *Amida*. The Torah is read during *minḥa* only on Shabbat.

The Reform *Ḥumash*, *The Torah: A Modern Commentary* edited by Rabbi Gunther Plaut, gives Isaiah 43:1-15 as the haftarah for the first day. —J.A.S.

In my minyan, it is customary on the first day of Pesach to replace a formal *d'var Torah* with a discussion in which people are invited to share a highlight from their Seder the night before. —D.A.T.

The Torah is read from two scrolls during *shaḥarit* on every day of *ḥol hamo'ed* (the intermediary days). There are four aliyot from the first Torah and one from the second. On the first day, the reading from the first scroll is Exodus 12:21–51; on the second day, Exodus 13:1–16; on the third, Exodus 22:24–23:19; on the fourth, Exodus 34:1–26; and on the fifth (for those who observe a seven-day holiday), Numbers 9:1–14. On *Shabbat ḥol hamo'ed,* the reading is Exodus 33:12–34:26. All of these readings are from different places in the Torah that address the observance of Pesach. The reading from the second Torah, Numbers 28:19–25, remains the same for all of *ḥol hamo'ed.* It summarizes the Pesach offerings in the ancient Temple. There is no haftarah on *ḥol hamo'ed* except on Shabbat.

It frequently happens that Shabbat falls on one of the days of *ḥol hamo'ed* Pesach. When this occurs, the service uses the *Shabbat Amida* with Pesach insertions and includes the short form of *Hallel.* The Torah reading is Exodus 33:12–34:26. This passage describes Moses' plea to God that he see God's glory, which God permits; God then renews the covenant. Pesach is mentioned as the seven-day holiday of matzot. The *maftir* reading from the second scroll is again Numbers 28:19–25. There are seven aliyot during the first Torah reading as there always are on Shabbat, and there is one aliya from the second scroll, elevating the importance of this Shabbat over non-holiday Shabbatot. The haftarah is Ezekiel 37:1–14, which contains the vivid image of dry bones that God brings back to life—Ezekiel's way of saying that God will redeem Israel no matter how hopeless its situation might appear. *Shir Hashirim*, the biblical book Song of Songs, is customarily read on the Shabbat of Pesach.

The seventh day of Pesach is a full *yom tov*, so the service is similar to that of the first day. However, only a half *Hallel* is said. If the seventh day of Pesach falls on Shabbat, *Shir Hashirim* is read. Some congregations include some or all of *Shir Hashirim* after the haftarah; others read it later in the day. *Shir Hashirim* is associated with spring and romantic love. While the rabbis suggested it was about the love between God and the Jewish people, the plain meaning of the text is graphic enough to make one doubt that explanation for the book's inclusion in the *Tanakh* (Hebrew Bible); one influence on the choice of inclusion may have been the book's popularity. Those who observe seven days of Pesach also include *Yizkor* (a memorial service) in the morning service, usually before the Torah is placed back in the ark, but it can be moved to

Shir Hashirim contains some of the *Tanakh*'s most beautiful and evocative love poetry. Its reading—particularly if done in a thoughtful and/or creative way—can be an opportunity to celebrate love, sensuality and the desire for human connection.
—N.C.M.

As on any *yom tov,* it is traditional to begin the day (on the previous evening) with candles, festival Kiddush, and a festive meal. There is a Hasidic tradition of a special Seder for the seventh night focused on the crossing of the sea, which is understood to have happened on the seventh day of the original Pesach. Some even pour water on the floor and carefully dance through it. Our congregational seventh-night Seder includes the dance "*Yesh Lanu Tayish*" in which the two lines of dancers represent the walls of the split sea.
—J.A.S.

other places in the service as well; some congregations that do not do a separate *musaf Amida* often place *Yizkor* after the returning of the Torah to the ark and before *Aleynu*. Those who observe Pesach for eight days include *Yizkor* in the eighth day's service rather than on the seventh day. The seventh day's haftarah is II Samuel 22:1–20.

The Torah reading for the seventh day of Pesach is Exodus 13:1–15:26; many liberal congregations begin the reading at 13:17. The Torah portion traces the exodus from Egypt to the Red Sea and includes *Shirat Hayam*, the Song of the Sea, a victory poem that is one of the oldest compositions in the Torah. *Shirat Hayam* is chanted in a special *trop* reserved exclusively for this section of Torah, and it is customary to stand while it is read. By tradition, the crossing of the sea occurred on the seventh day of Pesach. The reading from the second scroll is Numbers 28:19–25, which enumerates the Pesach Temple sacrifices. There are five aliyot from the first Torah and one from the second scroll. The traditional haftarah is II Samuel 22:1–51; liberal congregations usually read II Samuel 22:1–20. This is a celebratory poem attributed to David that is a clear parallel to *Shirat Hayam*.

According to midrashic tradition, the moment of the crossing is a revelatory moment, when *all* Israelites, and not just their prophetic leader, came into direct contact with the divine. This narrative gives me hope and reinforcement for my own personal spiritual growth. —N.C.M.

Those who observe eight days of Pesach treat the eighth day as a full *yom tov*. The service is very similar to that of the seventh day, but it includes *Yizkor*. The Torah reading from the first scroll is Deuteronomy 15:19–16:7. It has a particularly extended section on how Pesach is to be observed, and continues with the description of the other *r'galim* (pilgrimage festivals), Shavuot and Sukkot. The *maftir* from the second scroll is again Numbers 28:19–25.

Ḥol Hamo'ed

Ḥol hamo'ed consists of the middle days of the festival. In the Israeli pattern of observance, Pesach lasts for seven days, and the first and last days are full *yom tov* days; the middle five days are *ḥol hamo'ed*. In the traditional Diaspora observance, Pesach lasts for eight days, and the first two and last two are full *yom tov* days; the middle four are *ḥol hamo'ed*. On *ḥol hamo'ed*, all kinds of work are done. The festive mood of the holiday continues, however, and there are more social events and shared meals than on non-holiday weekdays. The weekday service includes an addition to the weekday *Amida*, a Torah reading and in those congregations that include it, *Musaf*. *Kol Haneshamah* (the Reconstructionist prayer book series) and Reform prayer books do not include *Musaf*.

Just as Shabbat is a weekly opportunity to turn inward toward our communities, our families and ourselves for one day, Pesach is an annual opportunity to do this for an entire week as we are guided by dietary restrictions and social opportunities. —J.G.K.

The shortened form of *Hallel* is used on *ḥol hamo'ed* as well as the concluding *yom tov* of Pesach. This reflects the traditional understanding that the Egyptians drowned when the Red Sea closed upon them. Rather than rejoice at the victory, some midrashim say, God demanded that the angels not celebrate the death of these beings created in the image of God. The shortened *Hallel* reminds us to feel compassion and regret when anyone—even an enemy—is hurt or dies.

The Pesach dietary restrictions are observed in the same way on all the days of Pesach.

Food During Pesach

Because Pesach observance restricts some foods that are usually eaten, a variety of Pesach foods have been developed to take their place. Pesach rolls, matza balls and *matza brei* are a few examples. Different specialties come from different parts of the world. The only time that matza must be eaten is at the Seder itself. Not everyone likes matza, and there is no obligation to eat matza on the other days of Pesach. Fish, eggs, nuts, fruit, salad, potatoes, meat, dairy products and many kinds of vegetables

There is no obligation to eat matza after the Seder, but those who wish to make "bread" the cornerstone of their holiday meals—particularly on Shabbat Pesach and the final day(s)—may find themselves eating additional matza. —J.G.K.

can make a satisfying diet for the week. It is easy to find recipes in cookbooks, on the Web and in other media. While some people enjoy making Pesach desserts that are quite elaborate, some of the best desserts for Pesach are ones that can also be eaten the rest of the year. Some supermarkets carry a large selection of foods that are certified kosher for Passover. A trip to such a supermarket will demonstrate how many different kinds of prepared foods are available for those who wish to observe Pesach in a more traditional way.

The unfortunate result of the kosher-for-Passover binge is that supermarkets often sell these items at a tremendous markup. One may want to limit the amount of specialty kosher-for-Passover items purchased and concentrate on year-round kosher staples, such as fruits, vegetables, dairy and meat. Some of the kosher-for-Passover adaptations are not very tasty, anyway. —J.M.S.

While many American Jews conclude Pesach with a trip to the pizza parlor or bagel shop, a custom called "*Maimouna*" that originated among North African Jews has become quite popular in Israel. Various traditional foods are associated with *Maimouna*, but the most characteristic aspect of the holiday is a tradition of visiting with neighbors. Doors are left open, and anyone in the neighborhood may come in to socialize. Some see *Maimouna* as an especially appropriate time for interfaith socializing, recalling that in some North African communities, the Jews' Muslim neighbors would bring them gifts of bread at the end of the festival. —J.A.S.

Pesach Kashrut

Robert Tabak
and David A. Teutsch

Pesach is in many ways a food-centered holiday. Many Seder rituals involve special foods, and the laws for kashrut on Pesach add restrictions that do not exist during the rest of the year. The practice of Pesach kashrut varies widely, depending on the traditions of families and communities. Of course, people make all sorts of personal choices regarding how and when to observe different aspects of the traditions about Pesach food.

Please don't skip the section on Pesach kashrut because you don't keep kosher on Pesach. The various spiritual and psychological meanings of *ḥametz* are worth exploring no matter your current practice. —J.A.S.

The kashrut for Pesach maintains all the procedures for kashrut in general (covered in *A Guide to Jewish Practice*, Volume I, pages 519–548, and not repeated here). The additional rules for Pesach stem from the Torah. According to that narrative, on the first Pesach, the Israelites ate roast lamb, bitter herbs and matza. (Exodus 12:8) One of the biblical names for Pesach is *Ḥag Hamatzot*—the Holiday of Matza. The Torah instructs us to eat matza during Pesach and to avoid *ḥametz* (leaven) on all the days of Pesach. (Exodus 12:15) The rabbis interpreted this to mean that we must eat matza at the Seder, but that but we are not obligated to eat it at other times during Pesach if we would prefer not to. The other obligation, according to the rabbis, is to absolutely avoid all leavened products throughout Pesach. The rabbis extended the category of leavened goods far beyond baked goods, and much of Pesach kashrut has to do with that extension, which includes not eating, owning or benefitting from *ḥametz*.

Unlike the rest of kashrut, laws surrounding *ḥametz* govern not only what we may eat, but what we may own as well. —J.G.K.

As explained below, the original prohibition involved exclusively leavened grain products. —J.A.S.

Jews who observe Pesach kashrut follow a broad variety of practices regarding what they will eat during the holiday. Mordecai Kaplan suggested that following the positive commandments is more important in creating a Jewish life and Jewish identity than following the negative ones. Several ways to observe Pesach kashrut are described below, along with suggestions for selecting a personal approach that responds to individual situations and values. Many choices and decisions—sometimes confusing, sometimes complex—are part of the process of developing this personal practice, so, after studying this guide, it will probably be helpful to talk through your choices with your rabbi.

Mordecai Kaplan was writing for first- or second-generation Americans, for whom liberating themselves from unproductive traditional strictures and integrating into American society were important projects. Thus, he de-emphasized the "negative commandments" (thou-shalt-nots) and advocated avoiding practices that separated Jews from non-Jews. Our generation is largely unburdened by Old World strictures and is fully integrated in the larger society. We have different needs and concerns. We should seek practices, either "thou-shalts" or "thou-shalt-nots," that have ethical or spiritual resonance and/or strengthen the bonds of Jewish community. —J.A.S.

While consulting with a rabbi can always be an opportunity for learning and growth, I don't believe that Pesach kashrut is beyond the abilities of laypeople to figure out, nor do I think that it is a category of practice uniquely requiring rabbinic guidance. —J.A.S.

Understanding Ḥametz

Ḥametz involves the leavening or souring of any of the five species of grain—wheat, oats, barley, spelt and rye. Leavening involves either the fermentation or the softening of dough to allow it to rise. In their unleavened form, any of the five species of grain or any combination of them can be used to make matza. Flour made from a ground grain and water can become *ḥametz* by rising from contact with yeast in the air or through the addition of a leavening agent (*se'or*). The fermentation process is essential for making bread, crackers, cereals, cake and muffins. It is also necessary for making beer (including ale and stout), grain-based whiskey (such as scotch, bourbon and rye) and a variety of other foods. None of these foods or beverages is ever kosher for Pesach. Wheat germ, couscous and tamari made from wheat are also never kosher for

The Talmud (*Pesaḥim* 35a) says that flours made from the five grains will leaven (create a sourdough) when wet, while others will spoil. —J.A.S.

It's not just that the five grain species can be used to bake matza; one of them *must* be used in order for the matza to be kosher (fit) for fulfilling the mitzvah of eating matza on the night of the Seder. The content of *ḥametz* is the very stuff of matza. The only difference between *ḥametz* and matza is the time involved in the making of them. —V.M.

Most vodkas (and thus gins), made from grain alcohol, are not kosher for Passover. Potato vodkas may be certified for Pesach use. —J.G.K.

Tamari and soy sauce usually contain fermented wheat, which would make them not kosher for Pesach by the traditional rules. However, there are wheat-free tamaris, and these could be kosher for Pesach for those who eat soybeans, which are *ḳitniyot* (explained later in this section). —J.A.S.

Pesach. Because of the pervasiveness of leavened ingredients in manufactured foods, one cannot assume that they are leaven-free without investigation.

Even the most miniscule quantity of *ḥametz* renders an entire container of food unusable on Pesach. The year-round observance of kashrut has a provision that if a bit of milk or cheese accidentally gets into a meat dish or vice versa, and the bit is less than one part in 60, then it is not considered to affect the kashrut of the food or its vessel. No such rule pertains to *ḥametz* on Pesach unless it was in your possession before the holiday and nullified by the declaration made when *ḥametz* was hunted for and burned on the eve of the holiday. And it is also forbidden to own or benefit from *ḥametz* during Pesach. This is why cleaning before Pesach traditionally is meticulous, and why year-round dishware must be set aside unless it can be totally purged of even a trace of *ḥametz*.

Since Jews should not own *ḥametz* during Pesach, all matza must be made before the holiday. Making kosher-for-Passover matza necessarily produces *ḥametz* from bits of the dough that do not make it into the oven. —J.G.K.

Meticulous preparations and adherence to Pesach kashrut standards have provoked more than one person into commenting that if Pesach is about going from slavery to freedom, the preparations are about going from freedom to slavery! —N.H.M.

Ḥametz is often identified with the *yetzer hara,* the evil inclination. The attempt to completely rid ourselves of *ḥametz* has significance from that perspective. —D.A.T.

Many symbolic meanings have been attached to *ḥametz* to deepen the meaning of the practice of avoiding it during Passover. It may be associated with a puffed-up ego or the *yetzer hara*. It may be symbolic of living off the stores of past wealth or the complacency of a settled life. It might symbolize all sorts of psychological and spiritual accretions that grow around our pure soul-essence. We keep *ḥametz* present all year. All the things it may symbolize have legitimate uses in our life. But we can take the days of Pesach to practice being their master, not their slave. —J.A.S.

Fermented foods that do not contain grain are not *ḥametz*. That is why wine can be kosher for Pesach. It is also possible to find kosher-for-Pesach cider vinegar and similar foods.

One of the consequences of the *ḥametz* regulations is that people who might be willing to eat some foods in restaurants or non-kosher homes during the rest of the year will often avoid doing so during Pesach. People who usually eat lunch out might bring their lunches from home during Pesach.

One is not supposed to benefit from *ḥametz* during Pesach. Some strict observers insist upon kosher-for-Passover milk to ensure that they are not benefitting from *ḥametz* used after the start of the holiday. Alternatively, they can buy milk before the holiday begins and freeze it, or they can use powdered milk.

Why Are We Allowed to Eat Matza?

While the two ingredients of matza are flour and water, matza is baked quickly so that it does not have a chance to

Since cows eat *ḥametz*, their owners, if strictly observant, will not drink milk the cows produce after the start of the holiday since the owner would be benefitting from the cow's eating *ḥametz* on Pesach. To avoid this, the owner would set aside milk before the start of the holiday and use it until the holiday is over, selling the milk produced during the holiday to non-Jews. Most Jews are not concerned about this form of benefit from *ḥametz,* perhaps because most of us are so removed from the realities of farm life. —D.A.T.

rise. Most matza is made from wheat, but other varieties of matza are made for those who cannot eat wheat for health reasons. The matza used for the Seder must have only flour and water for ingredients. There is an Ashkenazic (descended from German and East European Jews) custom of not eating *matza ashira*—matza enriched with other ingredients, such as fruit juice, eggs or honey—unless one is infirm, ill or pregnant. Sephardim (whose ancestors came from Spain and Portugal), *Mizraḥim* (Jews from Eastern lands) and many Ashkenazim will eat *matza ashira* any time except after saying *motzi* at the Seder. A small number of Jews eat only *sh'mura matza*, which is guarded from the moment of harvest to ensure that it was never exposed to moisture and which is then often handmade. Some people use *sh'mura matza* only at the Seder. Handmade matza harks back to premodern times.

Once flour has been baked into matza, it is no longer a candidate for becoming *ḥametz*. That is why we can use matza meal (ground matza) to make matza balls, *matza brei* (fried matza) and other foods that are cooked in liquid. Some Hasidic Jews avoid these foods because they

We don't eat enriched matza at the Seder because the Torah calls the matza to be eaten with the Pesach sacrifice "the bread of poverty/affliction." —J.A.S.

When people refer to *sh'mura matza* today, they are usually referring to the large, circular, hand-baked matza. All matza marked "kosher-for-Passover" is guarded. —J.G.K.

follow a stricture called "*gebrochts*" (Yiddish) or *matza sh'ruya* (Hebrew) prohibiting the consumption of foods that include any form of moistened matza. Many kosher-for-Pesach baked goods use matza meal, often along with baking powder, eggs, potato starch and other ingredients. Many of the foods that evoke the strongest Pesach memories are in this category.

The Kitniyot *Question*

There is a category of foods called *kitniyot* that everyone agrees are not *ḥametz* but that most Ashkenazim, as a

Those who do not eat *gebrochts* generally make an exception on the eighth day of Pesach in the Diaspora, a curious manifestation of coinciding gray areas of observance (the rabbinic institution of an extra day of the holiday and the custom of not eating moistened matza against the background of a biblical commandment forbidding *ḥametz* for one week), even for Jews who may self-identify as ultra-Orthodox. —J.G.K.

The word *gebrocht* (also *gebrokt*) literally means "broken." Those who refrain from breaking matza into their soup refer to this restriction as "not eating *gebrocht*." My Hasidic grandfather would spread a napkin beside his plate and eat his matza over the napkin so that no crumbs would fall into his food and run the risk of getting wet and possibly generating *ḥametz*, on the off chance that there was a pocket of unbaked flour in the matza. On the eighth day of Pesach, however, when the prohibition against eating *ḥametz* is no longer of the stringent category of Torah law, my grandfather would sit back, break his matza into his soup with great ceremony and enjoy! But, because the *gebrochts* on his plate might render the plate *ḥametz*, he would only enjoy this daring combination on a Pesach that preceded a Jewish leap year, so that the following Pesach would be 13, not twelve, months following. This was because the dishes in which he would enjoy this *gebrochte* matza with soup would have to sit for more than one year (twelve months) in order to be absolutely and indubitably kosher for Pesach for the next Seder. —V.M.

matter of custom, do not eat. These foods include rice, millet, beans, peas, soybeans and corn, as well as products made from them, such as tofu, soymilk, rice milk, hummus and tehina. Sephardic Jews eat rice and beans on Pesach. The proof that *kitniyot* are not *ḥametz* is that observant Ashkenazim will eat in the homes of Sephardim and simply avoid those particular foods. If *kitniyot* were *ḥametz*, observant Ashkenazim would not eat from the Pesach dishes of Sephardim. At least one Conservative ruling in Israel holds that Sephardim and Jews from Eastern lands (*Mizraḥi*) constitute a majority of Jews there, and that, as a result, Israeli Ashkenazim are permitted to eat *kitniyot* there, but most Israeli Ashkenazim do not eat *kitniyot*.

It is not clear why Ashkenazim do not usually eat *kitniyot*. Perhaps it is because when ground, such foods can resemble flour, which is subject to the restrictions regarding *ḥametz*. Perhaps it is from fear that grains may have contaminated these foods during harvest or storage.

When Distillery No. 209 in San Francisco created a kosher-for-Passover gin in 2010, the company created it based on a sugar cane alcohol (rum) and carefully adjusted the aromatic ingredients so that they did not include *ḳitniyot*. It was easy to make the factory kosher-for-Passover because their year-round product contains *ḳitniyot*, not one of the five forbidden grains. —J.G.K.

I wish that it were true across the board that Ashkenazim would eat in the homes of Sephardim. Unfortunately, it is not the case all of the time. —J.G.K.

Another Conservative responsum in Israel suggests that we do away altogether with the *minhag* of not eating *ḳitniyot* on Pesach. —J.G.K.

Whatever the original reason, the vast majority of Ashkenazim who observe Pesach kashrut do not eat *kitniyot*, with vegans being the largest exception for reasons of health. *Minhag* (custom) sometimes has more power than law.

Where there is a sufficiently large Sephardic population, as in Israel, products containing *kitniyot* that are certified kosher for Pesach can be found. In the United States,

In halakhic Judaism, a *minhag* (custom) must be maintained unless rabbinic authorities declare it a *minhag shtut* (a foolish or mistaken custom). Precisely because the Talmud explicitly says that one may eat *ḳitniyot* on Pesach, the rabbinic authorities assumed that the Ashkenazic custom wasn't just a mistaken ignorance of *halaḳha*, but an ancient custom with some acceptable basis. For Jews who don't follow *halaḳha*, the role of *minhag* is more complicated. —J.A.S.

The idea that a *minhag* can have more power than law seems especially relevant to Pesach. Some Jews who do not observe any form of kashrut the rest of the year feel strongly about observing the Pesach customs of their youth. The holiday and its rituals seem to speak to a level of Jewish identity unlike any others. —N.H.M.

Although my ancestry is Eastern European, I eat *ḳitniyot* on Pesach because the benefit of connecting myself with my Ashkenazic ancestors through the prohibition seems significantly smaller than the cost incurred in reducing the culinary joy of the festival. In fact, I think Jews should generally adopt practices of various historical Jewish communities based on the civilizational usefulness of those practices, not on where their ancestors came from. —J.A.S.

where the Jewish community is overwhelmingly made up of Ashkenazim, such products are uncommon.

The *kitniyot* issue is important for vegans. While vegetarians who eat eggs and dairy products can easily eat a balanced diet during Pesach, this is much more difficult for vegans. When vegans eat *kitniyot*, the beans, rice and nuts can help to ensure that they have a healthy diet during Pesach.

Contemporary Approaches to Pesach Kashrut

Among American Jews, a wide range of Pesach kashrut observance exists. Some Jews only refrain from eating bread during the Pesach Seder. Others forgo bread when

Benjamin Ben Baruch, a Reconstructionist activist in Detroit, suggests that Ashkenazim add a bowl of rice to the Seder plate as a reminder of the diverse customs of the Jewish people. —R.T.

Concerns about health also come up around *kitniyot* because of the high fructose corn syrup (HFCS) industry and its detractors in the United States. Although opinions vary as to whether HFCS should be permitted on Pesach or not, kosher-for-Passover Coca-Cola has prompted an often non-Jewish cult following. People stock up on cane-sugar-sweetened soda each spring. Doing taste tests between year-round and kosher-for-Passover sodas can allow us to ask, "Why is this sugar different from all other sugars?" and teach us about different customs regarding how we eat on Pesach. My students love this—the opportunity to see if they can taste the difference and which soda they prefer, as well the conversations about processed sugars, biochemistry and health. —J.G.K.

they are at home throughout Pesach, but eat it when they are out. Still others do not eat bread anywhere for the entirety of Pesach. Many Jews avoid eating all forms of food they recognize as *ḥametz*. Many check ingredients to avoid eating significant amounts of *ḥametz* that are sometimes invisibly mixed into packaged foods. Others eat only foods that are certain to be kosher for Pesach, and they eat only from dishes and utensils that are also kosher for Pesach. This is the only way to completely avoid *ḥametz*. This *Guide* lays out approaches that are as simple and inexpensive as possible, but individuals must decide what works for them.

Those observing more of the holiday food restrictions may find that it helps to make them more conscious of Pesach even on workdays. That in turn can encourage further thinking, conversation and action on the major themes of Pesach. This kind of observance can also be understood as a spiritual discipline. For some people, connection to the Jewish people (*klal Yisrael*) is a motive for greater observance. Of course, it is much easier to observe Pesach kashrut more fully when others in one's family and community observe similarly. Shared meals are an important part of Pesach celebration, and they are possible only when there are comfortable ways to bridge differences in observance.

Although we observe Pesach kashrut in our home pretty meticulously—changing all our dishes and pots and eating kosher-for-Passover food—we welcome food into our home prepared by people whose kitchens have not been kashered for Pesach. We do not want our ritual observance to exclude others. —J.J.S.

On the other hand, some Jews experience Pesach observance as a problematic barrier between themselves and others; this is particularly the case when they live and work in relatively nonobservant environments. They may find some aspects of Pesach observance burdensome and fruitless. Some factors that affect observance include the history of Pesach observance in the person's family and the memories associated with that observance; the role of Pesach as a counterbalance to Easter celebrations; the part Pesach can play in acculturating children or grandchildren to Judaism; and the desire to observe in a way that allows parents, children and other relatives to eat comfortably in each other's homes during the holiday. Individuals' patterns of observance change over time. A change in family situation, geographic location, spiritual life, and a host of other factors can result in shifts in observance.

People living in dormitories, assisted living situations or other situations where food is provided for them may be unable to organize or pay for separate meals. When that is the case, they may try to avoid drinking beer and whiskey and eating bread, cake, cereal and other foods that are clearly *ḥametz*—leavened goods made from the five grains. They may bring their own matza to the dining room to supplement the meal if matza is not made available by the institution. Often, a request to an institution

In my rural Jewish community, the schoolchildren often complain about the burden of having to explain to their peers why they are bringing matza and other kosher-for-Passover products for their school lunches. —N.H.M.

well in advance of the holiday will result in the kitchen making some degree of accommodation for Pesach observers.

Deciding how much to do requires seeking a balance, given the time and expense involved in maximal Pesach observance. We should not be impoverished as a result of our Jewish observance. As one source puts it, *Torah ḥasa al mamon Yisrael.* (The Torah takes pity on the finances of Israel.)

When food is served in communal settings, it is important to use a kashrut standard that will allow everyone present to partake of the meal. It is permissible to use packaged, kosher-certified foods even for a community Seder.

Foods Kosher Without Certification

Many foods require no separate kosher-for-Passover certification. These include fresh and frozen meat; fresh fish; baking soda; pure, caffeinated tea without flavorings; whole nuts; pure, fresh and frozen fruit juices; fresh fruits

The book learning one does to become a rabbi is quite different from the practical learning one does in order to live as a Jew. I traveled home to my parents' house for every Seder until I was in my mid-40s. When I would return to my own home in the middle of *ḥol hamo'ed*, I was nearly fully provisioned for the rest of the holiday, as long as I augmented my mother's brisket and kugels with some salads and vegetables. I didn't host my own Pesach Seder until a few years ago. As I shopped and planned the menu, I was stunned to discover that baking soda, that key leavening ingredient, was kosher for Passover. I had to "hit the books" again to make sense of that. —D.W.

and vegetables; and potatoes and other edible roots. By contrast, dried fruit, because it is often treated with chemicals and sometimes left outside to dry (where it can be exposed to *ḥametz*), usually needs a *heksher*, certification by a recognized authority that the fruit is kosher for Pesach.

Many foods and kitchen products are kosher for Pesach if bought before the holiday (see the section on *ḥametz* above). These include cocoa powder, detergents, some brands of coffee and tea, milk, sugar, butter, cottage cheese, cream cheese, unflavored yogurt, quinoa, peanut butter with no ingredients except peanuts and salt, and canned tuna and salmon with no ingredients added except water and salt, extra virgin olive oil, safflower oil and canola oil. Cheeses with no added foods or flavorings are also kosher for Pesach, but mozzarella and ricotta, which contain vinegar, require a *heksher*. Some observant Jews accept frozen vegetables with no additives of any kind as kosher for Pesach, but the contents of the package should be inspected to ensure that they contain nothing but the vegetables.

Since peanuts are usually classified as *ḳitniyot,* why can peanut butter and peanut oil be eaten on Pesach? The form they are in when they are consumed is so altered from the raw state of peanuts that they will not be confused with forbidden products, and the process of their preparation ensures that there is not a meaningful admixture with grain products. —D.A.T.

Many Ashkenazim avoid eating peanut butter and peanut oil on Pesach. Customs among Ashkenazic Jews vary with regard to oils and butters made from *ḳitniyot.*

Pure salt, baking soda and unground spices need no *hekshe*r, but powdered garlic and garlic salt do need a *hekshe*r. Other food may not require a *hekshe*r, but this can change from year to year, depending on manufacturing and handling processes. Several of the kosher certifiers and a number of rabbinical organizations put out new guides annually to provide up-to-date information.

Prescription medicines as well as nonprescription pills and capsules are kosher without a *hekshe*r.

Nonfood products that need no *hekshe*r include paper plates, plastic ware, new tablecloths and any other item you are sure contains no *ḥametz* among the ingredients.

This section is based on information accurate for the United States at the time it was written. Conditions may change. Foods produced and sold in other countries, including Canada, may be processed differently. Annual bulletins from several reputable sources are available to keep the Jewish community up to date. A rabbi can provide guidance in locating current information.

While I own beautiful Seder plates bought both here and in Israel, my favorites are the ones made by my children more than 40 years ago. —L.K.

How amazing that we in the United States live in a nation where we trust the ingredient labels of prepared foods because the Food and Drug Administration regulates labeling. We tend to take this for granted. It is a significant indication of the relationship that Jews have with our government. This has not always been the case. —J.J.S.

Foods Requiring Certification

Many manufacturers make matza throughout the year marked with a regular *heksher*. Such matza is not kosher for Pesach, so a careful look at the *heksher* is needed to ensure that it refers to Pesach. Many manufacturers produce a variety of products associated with Pesach. If a consumer wishes to avoid *ḥametz*, all such foods require a Pesach *heksher*. These include cakes, cookies, cereals, cake mixes, candy, most canned goods, gefilte fish, most dried fruit, ice cream and other frozen desserts, gelatin, hot dogs, salami and other processed meats, ketchup,

The advent of commercially produced kosher-for-Passover packaged foods has considerably lightened the burden of Pesach preparation, but it has brought new complexity to our choices. I avoid kosher-for-Passover cereal and cake that look too much like what I eat the rest of the year because even though they are certified as kosher, they do not provide the psychological distance from such foods that I seek on Pesach. Some Jews are participating in a trend that avoids many prepackaged foods in favor of cooking food for Pesach from scratch. —D.A.T.

Sometimes stick-on "kosher-for-Passover" *hekshers* are applied to convey the information that the products were owned by Jews who recited the formula for the nullification of unseen *ḥametz* before Passover began, so that any minuscule amount of *ḥametz* the products may have contained was nullified before the holiday began. —J.G.K.

The English terms "kosher for Passover" or "may be used for Passover" are synonymous with a Pesach *heksher* in Hebrew. —R.T.

While strictly kosher, these commercially made kosher-for-Passover products tend to be expensive, marginally healthy or even overtly unhealthy, and not so enjoyable. Every time I stand in the "kosher for Passover" aisle, I am struck by how marketers seem to rely on and even to promote a sense of deprivation that results from avoiding leavened goods during Pesach. —D.W.

alcoholic beverages (including wine), margarine, mayonnaise, pickles, prepared horseradish, seasoned salt, soft drinks, soup, vanilla extract, vinegar and flavored yogurt.

New products emerge and manufacturing procedures change, so these lists are indicative but not exhaustive. A general rule of thumb is that products that have multiple ingredients and/or are processed in some way will need a *hekhsher*. Unless you know that something does not require a *hekhsher*, you should assume that it does.

Why Are Some People More Careful About Kosher Certification During Pesach?

One of the characteristics of Pesach observance is that traditionally no amount of *ḥametz* is acceptable during Pesach. Trace amounts of *ḥametz* can remain on cooking utensils, in pots and on manufacturing equipment. Minute quantities can also get mixed in with otherwise kosher foods during harvesting or transport. As a result, many

Stores often place stick-on "kosher-for-Passover" labels on packages. These labels can be misleading because the people placing them on the packages often do not have the knowledge to do it properly, so stick-on *hekhshers* should not be trusted. —D.A.T.

people—even those who pay little attention to kosher certification during the rest of the year—buy only products with a *hekhsher* for Pesach during the holiday.

One example of this issue is kosher wine. Many Jews who as a matter of principle drink *stam yayin* (noncertified wine) the rest of the year are aware that the *ḥametz* issue requires them to buy kosher-for-Passover wine for Pesach. (For an explanation of the kashrut of wine during the rest of the year, see *A Guide to Jewish Practice, Volume 1, Everyday Living*, pages 546–547.) The large number of Jews who do so is evidenced by the wide array of kosher-for-Passover wines now available.

Kosher certification—a *hekhsher*—for Pesach is complex. It involves the meticulous checking of all ingredients as well as supervision of the process by which all equipment and utensils have been kashered (made kosher) for Pesach. This requires considerable knowledge of both kashrut issues and all the scientific questions raised by food preparation techniques. Issues about vinegar, flavorings, preservatives and other additives, for example, affect a host of food products. A brand that was kosher for Pesach one year will not necessarily be kosher for Pesach the next due to changes in ingredients, processing methods

Some people are more careful about what they eat on Pesach because the messages of the Passover holiday and its traditional observance speak to them in ways that ordinary kashrut may not. —J.G.K.

or the manufacturing facility used, so it may be important to look for the *heksher* each year.

A *heksher* for Pesach generally involves the trademark of the supervising organization plus a "P" to indicate that the certification is for Pesach use. (See *A Guide to Jewish Practice Volume 1, Everyday Living*, page 546 for examples of kosher symbols.) But care is needed here, since "P" is sometimes used to mark a food as pareve—as neither milk nor meat—and thus may not indicate that the product is kosher for Pesach.

Preparation for Pesach Kashrut

The process of using up food and cleaning the home can begin well before Pesach. That reduces the work on the eve of the holiday. Some people who host large Seders complete the process of kashering two or three days in

Food in fully sealed containers can be kept for a year or more, but matza, for example, is not generally sold in a hermetically sealed container. —D.A.T.

Orthodox authorities granting a *hekhsher* sometimes use the resulting income to pursue a conservative political agenda that conflicts with progressive religious values. In determining my own food practices at Pesach and at other times, this reality weighs heavily on me. As much as possible, my shopping list and diet during Pesach are comprised of all natural ingredients and foods I prepare myself. —D.W.

In my experience, "P" has a standard meaning of "kosher for Passover." "Pareve" is almost always spelled out. —J.G.K.

Many people start preparing for Pesach right after Purim. —D.D.M.

advance so that they can start preparing kosher-for-Pesach foods. Key to decreasing the stress of preparing for Pesach is having a plan and a schedule for the days leading up to the holiday.

In cleaning the house, particular attention should go to the rooms where food is consumed. One should make sure to vacuum under furniture; fastidious Jews vacuum behind cushions and dust inside surfaces. Backpacks, briefcases, purses, lockers, drawers and pockets that might contain food or wrappers need to be emptied.

An important step in preparing the home is using up and/or giving away all of one's products that contain *ḥametz* and putting aside any products about which there could be doubt. Some people "sell" (usually undertaken through a contract arranged by a rabbi on your behalf

I approach the daunting task of Pesach cleaning with a spring cleaning sensibility and with a deeply spiritual understanding of *ḥametz*, which in my life is too frequently clutter. I think about areas of the house where things are piled up or otherwise out of order. I think though what needs to be cleared away and what needs to be transformed or reordered so that I can feel more liberated from the things that are weighing me down or holding me back. In this way, Pesach cleaning has great personal meaning, and I feel much less resentment about the enormity of the task or panic about how quickly the holiday is approaching. If I invite anyone to our home to eat, I explain my practices around cleaning and kashrut so that they can decide whether they want to eat in our home. —D.W.

Many Jewish communities conduct food drives for non-Jewish food pantries in the days before Pesach. —R.T.

If the day after Pesach falls on Shabbat, then the time at which sold *ḥametz* becomes permitted is also extended by a day to Saturday evening. —J.G.K.

If you observe Pesach for only seven days and the rabbi who arranges the sale of *ḥametz* observes the holiday for eight days, you cannot use the *ḥametz* you sold on the eighth day because it does not become yours again until the beginning of the ninth. —R.T.

with a non-Jew) their remaining *ḥametz* after carefully putting it aside; this is a sensible approach for someone with a well-stocked bar or food pantry filled with items that cannot be discarded without violating the value of *bal tash'ḥit* (avoiding waste).

The kitchen is invariably the room that needs the most attention. Shelves, counters, tables and drawers need a careful cleaning. Counters and sinks can then be kashered by pouring boiling water over them. If there is worry that this might damage a counter or if a section of the counter is made of a particularly porous material such as wood, the counter should be covered with paper, plastic or a tablecloth.

Any dish, pot, utensil or surface that could have absorbed *ḥametz* during the year must be purified before it can be used for food on Pesach. Since the process of purifying is difficult and time-consuming, most people who make their homes kosher for Pesach simply keep a separate set of kosher dishes, utensils, pots and pans that they use only on Pesach; if they keep kosher during the year and eat meat, they usually have two sets of Pesach dishes—one for dairy and one for meat. Once the kitchen is clean, it is then a matter of putting away the year-round dishes and bringing out the Pesach dishes.

There may be reasons, such as limited storage space or tight finances, why it would be advantageous to *kasher* items used throughout the year for use during Pesach. Such kashering must remove any remnant of *ḥametz* and any lingering smell, taste or appearance of any food previously in contact with the item to be kashered. Any such item must be thoroughly cleaned and then not used for 24 hours before kashering. After that, it is possible to kasher glass items such as pitchers, drinking glasses and dishes by rinsing them.

Metal items that are one solid piece and made of only one material can be kashered after cleaning by heating them to a point hotter than they were at any time while they were being used. With pots used for boiling liquids, one can achieve this by filling them with water and boiling the water until it spills over the edges of the pot, but utensils used with oil or for broiling need to be blow-torched, a process that is not worth the bother and the danger. For that reason, baking pans cannot be kashered in any practical way.

Porous materials like china and pottery cannot be kashered by boiling. Dishes made of Pyrex and Corelle can be kashered by immersing them in boiling water. If plastic can take the heat, it can be kashered by a brief immersion in boiling water. Cutlery can be kashered by immersion in boiling water, but this should be done cautiously since the process can permanently discolor the cutlery. Any item made of more than one material cannot be kashered unless the two pieces can be separated for clean-

The prevalent Sephardic custom is to kasher glass by using boiling water. The prevalent Orthodox Ashkenazic custom is to soak the glass in cold water for three days, changing the water every 24 hours. —J.G.K.

My grandfather would kasher his teeth for Pesach by removing them and boiling them in a pot on the stove. False teeth, of course! —V.M.

ing because otherwise there is no way to fully clean the parts where the two materials meet. Expensive dishes and silverware that have been put aside and not used for one full year are considered kosher, so this is a simple way to prepare for Pesach use a set of dishes inherited from a relative or friend.

Preparing appliances for Pesach use begins with a thorough cleaning. The refrigerator should be defrosted, emptied and thoroughly wiped down with a detergent solution. Dishwashers should not be used for 24 hours and then they should be run through their hottest cycle—empty except for detergent. Ovens should be thoroughly cleaned. Where available, this should be followed by running the self-cleaning cycle of the oven; if the oven does not have a self-cleaning cycle, it should be cleaned with oven cleaner and then left on at its highest temperature for one hour. Convection ovens can be kashered in the same way as other ovens. Toaster ovens cannot be kashered for Pesach.

Stovetops should be thoroughly cleaned. Electric burners, once thoroughly cleaned, should be left on long enough to carbonize anything left on them. (Keeping them red hot for five minutes will accomplish that.) Gas burn-

Why leave an appliance idle for 24 hours before kashering it? Nothing changes chemically during that period. The primary reason is to provide a psychological break, distancing those who use the kitchen from its year-round use. —D.A.T.

The process of kashering stoves and ovens can generate a great deal of heat. It is advisable not to do all the heating at the same time because it may overheat or melt something adjacent, and electric burners may overload their electric circuit. In any case, it is advisable to stay in the kitchen and monitor the process. —R.T.

ers, after cleaning, should burn for 15 minutes at their highest setting.

Microwave ovens should be cleaned and left idle for 24 hours. Then a bowl or cup of water should be placed inside and heated to boiling. Once the water starts to steam, the microwave should be run for five more minutes.

Conclusion

This guide cannot cover every detail, and circumstances change. While the basic principles will remain constant, it is important for those intending to maintain Pesach kashrut to research changes in food production and technology that may affect specific details of the process. A local rabbi can provide up-to-date information and help sort out any areas of doubt or confusion that one might have.

No two households maintain exactly the same standard of Pesach kashrut. To what extent you will observe the holiday and in what ways are personal decisions that you will need to make for yourself, but it is important to consider the impact of your decisions on loved ones and members of your community. If the choices you make one year seem to be not quite right, you can make adjustments the following year. A standard Pesach greeting is: "*Ḥag kasher v'sameaḥ*"—"A kosher and happy holiday." It is important to find ways of dealing with Pesach kashrut that will add to the holiday's spiritual meaning without significantly reducing the joy of the celebration.

There is also the Yiddish greeting, "*A ziessen Pesach*," "May you have a sweet Pesach." Given the central role that food plays in this holiday, this locution seems very apt.
—D.W.

Rabbi Alan Yuter likes to wish people a Purim *kasher* and a Pesach *sameaḥ*. On Purim people often overuse alcohol and attempt to justify it with Jewish law. On Pesach, people often overdo kashrut in a way that hurts others and attempt to justify it with Jewish law. We should emphasize keeping Purim kosher and Pesach happy.
—J.G.K.

Shavuot Theology

Jacob J. Staub

The festival of Shavuot ("Weeks" or "Pentecost") is also known in our tradition as *z'man matan toratenu*—"The Time of the Giving of Our Torah." While the holiday's origins lie in an agricultural harvest celebration, in our time it has become primarily a commemoration and reenactment of the revelation of the Torah at Mount Sinai to Moses and the Israelites.

How are we to understand the traditional claim that the Torah is divinely revealed? And what exactly is the Torah that was revealed? A literal reading of the Book of Exodus, chapters 19 and 20, suggests that it was the Ten Commandments that Moses received on two tablets. For the last 2,000 years, however, the rabbis have claimed that the entirety of the Pentateuch was dictated by God to

Moses, so that every word, every letter, every repetition and contradiction in the Five Books of Moses (the written Torah) has meaning and significance. In the rabbis' view, when the Five Books of Moses are correctly interpreted, they yield the oral Torah and the massive expansion of *halakha* (Jewish law) and *aggada* (non-legal teaching) that is compiled in the Talmud and the books of midrash. The rabbis were so bold as to claim that God revealed the oral Torah as well as the written Torah to Moses at Sinai, so that all post-Sinai interpretations through the ages rediscover what was already revealed at Sinai.

The belief that every letter of the Pentateuch was divinely revealed remained standard Jewish belief up until modernity. Instead of stifling innovation, however, this belief has served as the foundational premise that supported and authenticated all innovation. If the Torah is divinely revealed, prior generations believed, then it must be true. Thus, whatever one knows to be true must be contained in the Torah, which must be reread to find hidden meanings. Rabbis read apparently unsubstantiated laws and customs out of—or back into—the Torah text on the basis of intertextual syllogisms and other principles of interpretation that they established. Since Jewish philosophers assumed that Moses had access to perfect philosophic and scientific truth, they sought and often found answers to perennial questions hidden in the Torah. Kabbalists mined the divine footprints in the Torah for esoteric clues to inexpressible insights about the nature of reality.

To us it may appear as if premodern Jews were disingenuous when they claimed that their innovations were actually embedded in the text given at Sinai and for all we know, some of them may indeed have been merely abiding by cultural norms when they claimed ancient validation for their own beliefs. In most cases, however, we should trust their sincerity. If you believe that a text is divinely authored, then it is reasonable to infer that the depth of its wisdom is timeless and all encompassing. This was a non-negotiable belief; when Spinoza questioned it in the 16th century, he was excommunicated.

In the 19th century, the academic field of biblical criticism began to flourish, originally among Protestants. Not only did Bible-critical scholars not assume that the Bible is divinely authored; they also questioned the claim that the Five Books of Moses were written by Moses, and that they were a single text at all. They studied the language, syntax and outlook of the Pentateuch and concluded that it is actually a set of documents that were once independent and that were subsequently woven together into a fairly seamless whole. Instead of assuming that contradictions were portals to divine wisdom, they seized upon them as clues to the identification of different authors. Each document they identified and isolated has its own distinctive linguistic identifiers and a coherent view of God and the meaning of life.

Jewish scholars entered the field of biblical criticism in the middle of the 20th century. While they noted and revised many Christian biases in the field, they mostly accepted the basic assumption that different sections of the Bible were written and edited by different groups of people with differing outlooks, and that the five books we now call the Torah were edited into their current form no earlier than the Babylonian exile following the destruction of the First Temple (586 BCE), and perhaps later.

The enterprise of liberal Judaism assumes that the Torah was not literally revealed in the sense that every letter and word was dictated by God and thus is binding upon us for all time. But if the Bible is just a book written by human beings, why do we continue to treasure it, and why do we choose to live according to its teachings?

Most of us highly doubt that a tape recorder at Mount Sinai would have recorded the voice of God, or that 2 million Israelites (assuming small families for the 600,000 adult men referred to in the Torah) stood at the foot of the mountain in a dramatic thunderstorm. How can those of us who are skeptical about those things reenact the mythic revelation at Sinai on Shavuot? First, we can acknowledge that some of our myths retain more power than others. This is not because we believe that the events occurred as they are described, but rather because our values and self-understanding are easily embedded in them. Mythic power derives from intuitive, experiential truth, not from historical accuracy.

The story of the Exodus from Egyptian slavery resonates deeply with our commitment to working against injustice and with the value we place on our own internal liberation. Biblical and rabbinic sources would not have approved of our association of Pesach with democracy, religious pluralism, feminism, or any of the other meanings of freedom we bring to the Passover Seder. Like prior generations, we ascribe our values and insights to the story. Sometimes we are aware that we are innovating; sometimes, not.

Shavuot is not as easy to reinterpret. It celebrates the revelation of the Torah, which, according to rabbinic traditions, contains the *halakha* by which we are supposed to live. First, we may not have had revelatory encounters with the divine, or we may not believe in their possibility. Second, if we do not regard *halakha* as authoritative, we may resist celebrating a narrative that affirms that God gave us the commandments at Mount Sinai.

Non-Supernaturalistic Understandings of Divine Revelation

There are strands of rabbinic teaching that may be helpful here. One of them asserts that there is a *bat kol* (a divine voice) that perpetually "sounds" at Mount Horeb (Sinai), saying: "Return, you wayward children." It is the cause of our yearning for the Infinite: However stuck we are in our wayward ways, there is a whisper, a subliminal vibration that stirs within us and moves us to yearn to get closer to God. That is, revelation was not a one-time occurrence. The call continues to "sound" today, at every moment. The variable is whether we are open to hearing it.

This is an approach to divine revelation that does not require that we believe in a God who reveals the Torah with specific content at a specific moment in history. Rather, we might understand the revelation at Sinai—whatever its content—as the response of Moses and the Israelites when they discerned the divine presence there.

Another rabbinic teaching states that what was revealed at Sinai was the *aleph* of "*Anokhi*"—that is, the first letter, silent in Hebrew, of the first word of the first commandment—the "I" in "I am the Lord, your God." The German Jewish philosopher Martin Buber understood this to mean that what transpired—and transpires—at Sinai is an I-Thou encounter between humans and God, in which we are completely open and receptive to a powerful and indefinable divine presence that we sense intuitively. Such experiences of the holy dimension can be transformational. People have new insights and feel changed; they understand the meaning of their lives differently, with new imperatives. Buber posited that the Sinai experience involved a community that had (and has) such an encounter together, the results of which are a *brit* (covenant), and a set of ritual and ethical norms and sacred narratives that constitute the Torah. God doesn't speak; rather, we hear.

This connects to yet another rabbinic teaching: "The Torah speaks in human [not divine] language." At Sinai, each individual heard according to his or her capacities. Thus, the content of revelation is filtered through the human vessel. We verbalize and conceptualize intuitions and encounters for which we have no words or concepts, interpreting them according to who we are, what we know and the beliefs of our culture. Two different people, standing side by side, received two different revelations.

None of these interpretations preclude a belief in the reality of God or divine revelation. They suggest, however, that by definition, the divine is beyond human ability to express in words, since language is a human convention that refers to things that are not God. All accounts of encounters with God must be understood as reflections of particular people who hear in a particular socio-historical context. They reveal more about those who receive the revelation than about the revealer.

How, then, can we know whether or not God exists? We cannot. That is why it is called faith. Scientifically, you can neither prove nor disprove the existence of God. The evidence we have consists of our own experiences and the accounts of others who describe their encounters with God, including the Israelites in the biblical period.

Rabbi Mordecai Kaplan understood the Torah and the mitzvot as the expressions of the highest ideals and most sublime values of the Jewish people. If you believe with a perfect faith that you should love your neighbor as yourself, or that you should not work on the seventh day, then it is what you will hear God commanding. As Jewish civilization evolved through the centuries, adapting to changing cultural and socio-historical circumstances, values changed and so did the content of what people heard God saying. From this viewpoint, the content of revelation and the interpretation of Torah will never cease to evolve because we limited humans will never achieve the kingdom of heaven on earth. Fortunately, revelation and inspiration are ongoing.

The Authority of Torah for Liberal Jews

If you don't believe that the text of the Torah was literally written by God, and if you don't believe that the oral Torah and the 613 mitzvot are literally divine commandments, then why would you continue to read and interpret the Torah and observe some if not all of the mitzvot?

1. Tradition. Reconstructionists believe that belonging to the Jewish people is the basis for all other aspects of Jewish civilization. Belonging precedes behavior and belief—not only for Jews, but also for all communities and nations. What you share with all other members is citizenship or membership. In our community and our family, we become acculturated. We learn the language that shapes the contours of reality. We acquire beliefs and values. We are rendered culturally specific. The Jewish people's narratives, rituals and practices shape us and become our spiritual home. When I fast on Yom Kippur, I'm doing what my parents and grandparents did, even if I interpret the practices differently from them, and even if I modify them or change the words. That's okay—they were interpreting the same practices differently from their grandparents. Traditions are the constants that allow for continuity, even as they change over time. Even when we don't want to live as our parents did, we still want to acknowledge our connection to our origins.
2. Accrued sanctity. Using my mother's Shabbat candlesticks and my grandfather's tallit (prayer shawl) is not only meaningful and emotionally

powerful. These material objects convey an accrued holiness because of the prayers and aspirations they have expressed over the decades. This is also true of a newly purchased tallit or pair of candlesticks because they are ritual objects that have been used to express the yearnings of countless millions over the centuries. The same can also be said of the rhythms of the Jewish calendar, liturgical blessings, colloquial expressions, melodies, recipes and texts. The Torah, however we define it, is a sacred heritage. This is the case not because it is God-given, but because it was and is produced by people who have sought to experience the deepest and richest levels of reality.

3. Limiting autonomy. It is good to belong to a community that expects its members to show up sometimes on Shabbat mornings. I am not compelled by that expectation to show up every week, but I am somehow rendered accountable; I need to think about what I'm doing (or not doing) to celebrate Shabbat this morning. I am grateful to belong to a community that adopts Jewish texts, values and practices as a starting point, rather than to a group of individuals who are starting from scratch. In short, nonhalakhic Jews can enrich their lives by regarding the Torah as a sacred inheritance worth celebrating.
4. Practice as an instrument of revelation. Studying sacred texts, practicing rituals, and working to effect prophetic values may be activities in which we

engage because we believe them to be divinely revealed—*or* they may be the instruments by means of which we are able to experience what we might call revelatory moments, moments in which we are transported beyond ourselves and connected to a presence that is divine.

Ongoing Revelation

When we celebrate Shavuot, then, we need not limit the celebration to an event that occurred (or did not occur) in the 13th century BCE. If the giving of the Torah is ongoing, then new interpretations we discover at a *tikun leyl Shavuot* are part of the oral Torah. According to one interpretation, they, too, were actually revealed by God to Moses at Sinai. If in our study we feel transformed by an experience of the sacred, then we ourselves are standing at Sinai. Reconstructing our understandings of divine revelation and the authority of Torah enables us to see ourselves as links in the chain of tradition even though inherited understandings of those beliefs no longer make sense to us.

Shavuot

SETH GOLDSTEIN

Background

The festival of Shavuot is a celebration of Torah, the foundational text of the Jewish people. It is from this text that

At its beginning, the holiday of Shavuot was not about Torah at all. It was the quintessential agricultural festival, when every Israelite in Temple times would bring first fruits to the Temple as a tribute. When the Temple was destroyed, the rabbis went to great lengths to transform the holiday of Shavuot into a day that commemorates the giving of the Torah on Mount Sinai. Separation from the Land of Israel necessitated making the focus on something we carried with us into exile—namely, the Torah. The Torah itself makes no explicit connection between the date of Shavuot and the giving of the Torah, nor does the Torah say to commemorate the giving of the Torah, as we are commanded to do regarding the moment of the Exodus. Torah is meant to be with us always, and we reenact our receiving of the Torah at least weekly with its reading. —J.M.S.

Shavuot should also be about celebrating nature and seeing God in the unfolding of spring and summer and in the promise of a renewal of life. When we focus exclusively on Torah on Shavuot, we rob the holiday of its depth and beauty. In biblical times, the holiday instilled in people a sense of wonder and gratitude at nature's rebirth and, even more, at the fact that humanity can sustain itself upon nature's bounty. A number of Jewish farms and educational centers have sprung up that have revived the Jewish connection to the land, even outside of the Land of Israel. We would greatly enhance the community's knowledge of Shavuot by following their lead and making it the pre-eminent nature holiday. —J.M.S.

the tree of Jewish knowledge, life and lore has sprung. "Torah" has multiple meanings within Jewish tradition. It refers to the content of the first five books of the Bible (*Ḥumash*). It refers to the scroll upon which the five books are written and used in Jewish liturgy and ritual. But Torah is also an expansive term, referring to the chain of interpretation of Jewish texts, to the entire unfolding body of Jewish tradition, and to the commitment to Torah as a basis of living one's life in a way that manifests holiness. To accept the Torah today means associating with the Jewish people, agreeing to engage seriously with Jewish tradition, and working toward reinvigorating Jewish life and practice. Accepting Torah means that we bind our-

Torah is called *etz ḥayim*, "a tree of life." —J.A.S.

Many of us use the term "Torah" to refer also to texts written by non-Jews when they are helpful to us in our ethical and spiritual journeys. —J.J.S.

In 1942, Judith Kaplan Eisenstein and Ira Eisenstein collaborated on a cantata—a combination of the spoken word and singing—that was performed by confirmation students at Shavuot services at the Society for the Advancement of Judaism. It was titled, "What is Torah?" The cantata answered its own question with these explanations:

> Torah is the creation of the world. …
> Torah is the Sabbath. …
> Torah is the pastoral life. …
> Torah is the epic of Egyptian slavery and emancipation. …
> Torah is ethical idealism. …
> Torah is a parchment scroll. …
> Torah is a study room, a lullaby, a prayer. …
> Torah is a land. …
> Torah is a light unto the nations. …

—D.W.

selves to living in consonance with Jewish principles and values.

The Jewish calendar has two holidays primarily dedicated to celebrating Torah: Simchat Torah and Shavuot. While Simchat Torah focuses on the Torah scroll and the liturgical reading of Scripture, Shavuot is dedicated to the *idea* of Torah and to the importance Torah plays in Jewish life.

Shavuot (literally, "Weeks") is, with Pesach and Sukkot, one of the three pilgrimage festivals of ancient Israel. It falls in late spring on the sixth day of Sivan and celebrates the story of the revelation at Sinai and the giving of the Torah as told in the Book of Exodus. The story of Sinai tells the traditional story of the origin of the Torah. After the Exodus from Egypt and the liberation from slavery, God gave the Torah to Moses on Mount Sinai, and he then brought it to the people. Jewish tradition's mythic understanding of history holds that each generation of Jews was at Sinai, not only those who are

Jewish principles and values have evolved over the millennia and continue to change. Therefore, which principles and values we ought to live in consonance with is not always clear. That is a good thing. The influence of Jewish traditions upon us is dynamic, and it requires that we query the teachings of our heritage. —J.J.S.

spoken of in the Torah. When we mark Shavuot, we symbolically take our place at the foot of the mountain, ready to accept Torah, to receive revelation.

In a contemporary understanding, what does it mean to accept Torah, to receive revelation? The story of Sinai is a narrative fundamental to Jewish self-understanding; it is a story of monumental truth. As surprising as it might sound from a traditional perspective, whether or not the events at Sinai happened in the way the Torah describes them is not important; we do not read the Torah as a history book. What is relevant is the truth contained within the story of Sinai: that Judaism rests on a *brit* (covenant), a sacred relationship that binds us to each other and to the divine. Torah is central to these relationships.

Reconstructionism views the Torah as a humanly created document. Developed over generations, the Torah

Some midrashim portray the *Bat Kol*, the divine voice, as communicating not only at the time of Moses, but also at every moment, so that revelation is contingent on our ability in every generation to receive and interpret the message. —J.J.S.

I love the Midrash that says all Jewish souls once stood together at the foot of Mount Sinai. Therefore when we meet another Jew for what appears to be the first time, it is appropriate to say, "Nice to meet you again!" —S.C.R.

Every time we hear the Torah read in synagogue, we may also have a moment at the foot of the mountain. —J.G.K.

Some of us would say that the Torah was written by humans as a result of our encounter with the divine. It is a record of what we see and hear and understand in those encounters. Seen in this way, the human discovery of the transcendent includes the transcendent. —J.J.S.

contains the collective wisdom and truth of a people. Originally created as oral histories, stories and laws, the works that became the Torah were eventually written down in several different documents that were then later redacted into one whole. This was probably done after the destruction of the First Temple in Jerusalem in 586 BCE, when the conquering Babylonians sent the Jewish community into exile. When the Persians restored the Jews to their homeland in 538 BCE, the Jews brought with them a text that, as recounted in the books of Ezra and Nehemiah, was placed at the center of the community.

Though ascribing human authorship to the text, many Reconstructionists and other liberal Jews do not see the text as any less sacred than do those who hold the traditional understanding that the whole Torah was given at Sinai. The authors of the Torah use the language of divine

Many scholars place the final redaction of the Torah well into the Second Temple period, following the Jews' return from Babylonia in 538 CE. —J.A.S.

The ancient Israelites who composed the Torah encountered the divine and recorded that experience through their own cultural lenses. We honor their sacred encounters, even as we honor our own experiences—experiences that look and feel different, that use different imagery to capture them, and that are similarly subject to our own cultural limitations. A contemporary rejection of supernatural revelation doesn't end the Jewish people's relationship with God or Torah; rather, it creates opportunities for new images and practices. —D.W.

origin and agency to describe their experiences and their values. These same stories become our stories, and we share many of the same values. Much in the same way that Americans find transcendent values in the Declaration of Independence and the U.S. Constitution—texts created by humans that nevertheless ascribe a divine origin to the rights contained within them—Jews find transcendent values in the Torah authored by humans. Also like the Constitution, the Torah serves as the basis for an ongoing chain of interpretation as each successive generation roots itself in the teachings of the Torah and tries to discern meaning and relevance for its day. Through this act each generation commits itself to the *brit* of Sinai.

A *brit* is a relationship—God and the Jewish people are inextricably linked, and each has rights and responsibilities. The covenant is a web of relationships based on trust and compromise, love and commitment. The *brit* of Sinai is unique in that it is both "vertical" and "horizontal."

The Torah contains our ancestors' account of their personal and collective experience of the divine. Such an experience can hardly be captured in words. It requires imaginative and attentive reading, as opposed to a literal understanding. When we read from the Torah, we catch a glimpse of our forebears' experience. When we discuss, interpret, create and imagine Torah for ourselves, we enter into our own experience of the divine. —B.P.

Even when we find the values of the Torah's authors distasteful, we don't just walk away. We wrestle with their values and transform them. This is not unlike the way we acknowledge that we are the children of our parents, in both the ways in which we are similar to them and the ways in which we have reacted to them and distanced ourselves from some of their beliefs, values and practices. —J.J.S.

The story of Sinai speaks of Israel as a collective that is making a covenant with God, a divine power. Thus, a vertical agreement was made, symbolically represented by the fact that the revelation took place on a mountain, with Moses ascending to God and then descending to the people. Yet at the same time, the covenant is horizontal. In making the vertical pact with God, each individual within that collective made the same pact. When individuals make the same *brit*, they make a *brit* with each other at the same time. The covenant creates Jews individually and the Jewish people collectively. In the language of Leviticus 19:18, the covenant creates the neighbors whom people must love as they love themselves: The covenant creates a sacred community.

As with any relationship, a *brit* involves a limitation of power. In a traditional understanding, the covenant binds

There are those who understand the term "neighbor" in Leviticus 19:18 to refer only to other Jews (as the main text suggests), and those of us who consciously interpret "neighbor" to refer to all people with whom we live in shared communities. The importance of loving our non-Jewish neighbors as we do our Jewish neighbors may be all the more crucial today as our world seems to become increasingly less tolerant of differences—especially religious differences. —S.C.R.

The feminist theologian Judith Plaskow adopted the limitations that come from covenant as the central argument of her groundbreaking book, *Standing Again at Sinai: Judaism from a Feminist Perspective*. She urges us to reimagine this central moment in the Jewish people's narrative. She insists that how we understand God shapes how we treat each other and how we build our communities. Plaskow pushes us to work through all the connections between the immanent and the transcendent so that we move closer to fully egalitarian, fully inclusive communities. —D.W.

One basis for a Jewish politics may be the notion that covenantal relations provide an opposing and preferred social paradigm to power relations. —J.A.S.

both the Jewish people and God. The Jewish people agree to live by a set of rules and obligations, and God agrees to cast the divine lot with this people and to protect and provide for them. God and Israel are each limited in the actions that they may take in relation to each other. In a contemporary framework, when we apply ourselves to the *brit*, we agree to be mindful of Jewish tradition and to weigh its importance and teachings. Jewish tradition is changed by the determination of contemporary Jews as to the direction in which it should go. In the Reconstructionist formulation, the past has a vote, but not a veto. Traditions make Jews, and Jews make (and remake) Jewish traditions.

The same is true of the horizontal nature of the covenant among the Jewish people. We are regulated regarding our relationships with others. We must act with *tzedek*/justice and *ḥesed*/loving kindness, caring for those

Contemporary thinkers often struggle with the ongoing state of the covenant, since it is clear that God does not seem to protect and provide for us as the Torah promises. The Holocaust has brought this question to the fore. Do we want to assume, with some traditional teachings, that Jewish suffering results from the misbehavior of Jews? Or do we acknowledge that whatever God does, God does not intervene supernaturally in human history to protect us? It is often puzzling to find meaning in the term "*brit*" when we don't know the terms of the mutual agreement. —J.J.S.

in need. We must not act solely out of self-interest, and therefore, we must balance self-interest with the needs of others. These obligations, rooted in Jewish tradition, are binding upon us today. The concept of *tikun olam* (repair of the world), extends these obligations to include our relationship with all of humanity. The celebration of Shavuot marks the affirmation of our commitment to both the vertical and horizontal aspects of the covenant.

We live out these two aspects of the covenant through the mitzvot. "Mitzvot" literally means "commandments," but the term can also be understood to mean "sacred acts and obligations." These are the ritual and ethical practices that define our relationships with each other and with God. The covenant contains within it mitzvot that are

The nature of religious authority continually vexes liberal religious thinkers. The premodern Jewish understanding that the Torah was revealed at Sinai enabled centuries of rabbis to assert that Jewish law, interpreted through them, was binding because of its divine origin. The three Abrahamic traditions historically debated which revelation—the Torah at Sinai, Jesus' revelation as recorded in the Christian Gospels or Mohammed's revelation recorded in the Koran—was true and would afford its followers eternal salvation. When we set aside supernatural revelation, we also set aside any claim on behavior "because God said so." Mordecai Kaplan and other early Reconstructionist thinkers urged the reinterpretation offered here to avoid getting caught up in distracting discussion of origins. They focused instead on the nature of obligations that individuals voluntarily choose to take on within their communities. They argued that religious leaders and doctrine should be persuasive, not coercive. In our contemporary environment, with its commitment to radical individualism, such voluntary divestment of autonomy is countercultural. Our environment makes the discussion of commitment centrally important. —D.W.

both *beyn adam lamakom* (between a person and God) and *beyn adam laḥavero* (between people). Through the mitzvot, which are rooted in Torah and derived through interpretation, we are able to bring holiness into the world.

Biblical Origins

While the specific observances of Shavuot are few, the themes of the holiday are deep. As with the other festivals, Shavuot has both an agricultural and a historical basis. As an agriculture festival, Shavuot marks the end of the spring grain harvest in the Land of Israel. The historical association is more ambiguous because no link exists between the Torah's story of the revelation of Sinai in the Exodus story or in other references to the holiday. (Exodus 34:22, 23:16, Deuteronomy 16:10, Numbers 28:26) The association of Shavuot with the giving of the Torah has developed with the unfolding of Jewish civilization.

In the Torah, Shavuot is known by several names, highlighting its agricultural roots as a springtime harvest festi-

Mitzvot are practices that we engage in for the sake of experiencing a connection to something greater than ourselves—community, tradition and the divine. Mitzvot are also a means to cultivate our human capacity to embody the sacred qualities of heart and mind—wisdom, love and kindness. —S.P.W.

val. In references to the pilgrimage festivals, the holiday is called "*Ḥag Hakatzir*," "Harvest Festival" (Exodus 23:16) and "*Ḥag Habikurim*," "Festival of First Fruits" (Exodus 34:22)—both relating to the holiday as the time of the first fruits of the grain harvest. This is reiterated in the Book of Numbers, when the holiday is called "*Ḥag Hashavuot*," "Festival of Weeks": "On the day of the first fruits, your Festival of Weeks, when you bring an offering of new grain to God, you shall observe a sacred occasion; you shall not work at your occupations." (Numbers 28:26)

Shavuot is intimately connected with the agricultural dimension of the holiday of Pesach. The name "Shavuot" (from the Hebrew root "*sheva*," meaning "seven") does not refer to any intrinsic theme of the holiday, but rather to the holiday's timing as falling seven weeks after Pesach. As recounted in Leviticus (23:9ff) and Deuteronomy (16:9ff), from an agricultural perspective, Pesach marks the beginning of the Israelite grain harvest. At a time when the spiritual life of the community centered on the ancient Temple overseen by a class of priests, on Pesach one would bring the first sheaf of barley—the first grain to ripen and be harvested—to the Temple as an offering. One would then count seven weeks—the counting of the

Shavuot provides an opportunity for contemporary Jews to reconnect with the holiday's agricultural roots. One approach is to create a communal meal from the harvest of people's gardens (or a synagogue community garden). Another is to integrate themes of *bikurim* (first fruits) into the liturgy. —N.C.M.

omer (see below). On the day after the seven weeks, one would bring an offering of two loaves of bread, the "first fruits" of the wheat harvest, along with other sacrifices. Shavuot thus marked the end of the spring harvest.

According to the Torah, originally there was no fixed date for Shavuot; it was counted from the beginning of the grain harvest. Later, the date of its occurrence was fixed by counting from the second day of Pesach. The dates of the festivals eventually came to depend on when the Sanhedrin, the ancient rabbinic court, would establish the new month based on testimony from witnesses who observed the cycles of the moon. Thus, an exact date was not set. Over time, as the rabbis instituted mathematical models for determining moon phases and thus the calendar, the dates of the festivals became fixed. Since Pesach is fixed to begin on the 15th day of the month of Nisan, Shavuot begins on the sixth day of the month of Sivan.

The purpose of the spring harvest was to ensure a new lease on life for the coming season. Not only were the Israelites able to harvest essentials of barley and wheat, they were also able to begin the sacrificial bread offerings anew—an important symbol of spiritual stability and relationship. —N.C.M.

Before worship was centralized in Jerusalem, one would offer the first sheaf of barley to God at the local altar site and would then return home to collect the harvest. When worship was forbidden outside of Jerusalem, *Ḥag Hakatzir*, the Harvest Festival, became Shavuot, (literally, "Weeks"). If a farmer took the first sheaf to Jerusalem and then traveled back to the farm, the harvest would be lost. So the offering for this spring festival was deferred by seven weeks, allowing farmers to reap the harvest and then to travel to Jerusalem to make an offering. —T.K.

While not as explicit as that of Pesach (the Exodus) and Sukkot (the wanderings), a historical basis for Shavuot exists in the Torah, centered on the ancient ritual of first fruits (Deuteronomy 26), which is to take place after the Israelites have settled in the land. Israelites were to bring their harvest, make an offering, and recite:

> My father was a fugitive Aramean. He went down to Egypt with meager numbers and sojourned there; but there he became a great and very populous nation. The Egyptians dealt harshly with us and oppressed us; they imposed heavy labor upon us. We cried to God, the God of our ancestors, and God heard our plea and saw our plight, our misery and our oppression. God freed us from Egypt by a mighty hand, with an outstretched arm and awesome power, and by signs and portents. God brought us to this place and gave us this land, a land flowing with milk and honey. Wherefore I now

German Biblicist Gerhard von Rad believed that the first-fruits declaration in Deuteronomy 26 is the oldest ritual creed in the Bible. It tells us how our ancestors viewed their own history. Notice that the recitation stresses God's saving acts and does not mention Sinai or Torah. —T.K.

bring the first fruits of the soil that You, O God, have given me. (Deuteronomy 26:5–10)

The speech is a condensed religious narrative of identity that ends by expressing gratitude for having reached and settled the land, and, thus, for having received the privilege of growing fruit in its soil from which the offering can be made. While the Torah does not explicitly tie this to Shavuot, the Mishnah (in *Bikurim*) directly applies this to the yearly Shavuot offering. In the Deuteronomy passage itself, the allusion to "first fruits" reminds us of Shavuot. Thus, in this ritual, a connection is made

The passage from Deuteronomy 26 is the essential biblical assertion that God is a promise keeper. From the moment when God promises to give the Land of Israel to Abraham and his descendants until this moment in the Torah after the 40 years of wandering in the wilderness following the Exodus, all of biblical history led to this moment of acknowledging that God has fulfilled God's promise to the Jewish people. This is at the same time an assertion of faith that God's promises of future redemption will be kept, as well. —S.C.R.

The traditional Haggadah text includes most of the text from Deuteronomy 26 as one framework of the story of enslavement and Exodus. It is the base text upon which the midrash in the *magid* (telling) section of the Haggadah is based. This is a none-too-subtle hint that Passover and Shavuot were meant to be inextricably linked to one another, and to the Temple worship. —J.G.K./J.M.S.

between first fruits and the acquisition and settlement of the land.

Biblically, therefore, the three pilgrimage festivals can be seen as completing a cycle in which Pesach marks the Exodus from Egypt and the ending of slavery, Sukkot marks the wanderings in the desert, and Shavuot marks the settlement in the Promised Land and a new life for the Israelites.

Rabbinic Development

After the destruction of the Second Temple in Jerusalem and the exile of the Jewish people in 70 CE, this practice became obsolete. The biblical association of Shavuot is with harvest, first fruits and becoming landed. In a situa-

There can be a tension between the centrality of the Land of Israel in the biblical view and the association that many of us make between Jewish values and landlessness, cultivated over the millennia by Jews in the Diaspora. Are we grateful for the gift of the land? For those who recite the traditional *Birkat Hamazon* (the prayer after eating a meal), this is a daily issue. "You should eat and be satisfied and bless your God for the good land that God has given you." Perhaps the land need not be the Land of Israel; perhaps we are thankful for the fruit of the earth wherever that may be. —J.J.S.

tion of exile, separated from the land, the holiday required a new meaning. The substitute for land became Torah. Shavuot became associated in the midrash and Talmud with the revelation at Sinai, the giving of the Torah and the covenant between God and Israel. Sacred text became a "portable homeland" in contrast to the actual settlement of the land. (And, as mentioned above, the Torah itself was developed during a period of exile.)

The story of the revelation in Exodus (Exodus 19–20) does not give an exact date for the events of Sinai, save for a reference to the "third month," which is Sivan, since the Torah calls Nisan the first month. Based on calendric calculations, the rabbis in the Babylonian Talmud determined the date of the revelation to be the sixth day of Sivan. (Babylonian Talmud *Shabbat* 86a–88b) The actual date of the biblical Shavuot is still unclear, since the biblical text refers to the counting of the seven weeks as beginning "the day after the Sabbath." (Leviticus 23:15) The talmudic text records a dispute on whether this means the Shabbat that falls during Pesach (the date of which can change from year to year) or the day of the festival itself. (Babylonian Talmud, *Menaḥot* 65a–b) The latter is the determinative position, thus fixing the date of Shavuot as

The association of land and Torah is found in rabbinic liturgy: The second *b'rakha* of *Birkat Hamazon* (Grace after Meals) speaks of Torah in the context of thanking God for the land, while the *b'rakha* that precedes the morning Shema speaks of the land in the context of thanking God for Torah. —J.A.S.

the sixth day of Sivan—seven weeks after the 15th day of Nisan (Pesach).

The association between Shavuot and the idea of covenant has its textual precedent in early rabbinic post-biblical works, especially the book of Jubilees. Jubilees is one of several works that are considered extracanonical—books that are biblical in theme, content, style and historical context, but that were not included when the *Tanakh* was given its final form. While not part of the biblical canon, they still hold relevance as a source for insight and guidance, and they are evidence of the rich Jewish thought of that period. The book of Jubilees is a work from the first century CE that retells the early narratives of the Bible. It makes a connection between the festival of first fruits and the covenant of Noah:

> And God gave to Noah and his sons a sign that there should not again be a flood on the earth. God set a bow in the cloud for a sign of the eternal covenant that there should not again be a flood on the earth to destroy it all the days of the earth. For this reason it is ordained and written on the heavenly tablets that they should celebrate the Feast of Weeks in this month once a year, to renew the covenant every year. (Jubilees 6:15–17)

Additionally, the covenant with Abraham in Genesis 17, in which Abraham's name is changed from Abram and the rite of circumcision is instituted, is said to have occurred during the Feast of First Fruits. (Jubilees, chapter 15)

Other references in rabbinic literature affirm the association of Shavuot with the giving of the Torah. For example, "Mar son of Rabina would fast . . . except on Shavuot, Purim and the eve of Yom Kippur—Shavuot because it is the day on which the Torah was given." (Babylonian Talmud, *Pesaḥim* 68b) Early liturgy referred to Shavuot as "*z'man matan torateynu*," "the time of the giving of our Torah," just as Pesach was referred to as "*z'man ḥerutenu*," "the time of our freedom" and Sukkot was referred to as "*z'man simḥatenu*," "the time of our joy." (See the minor talmudic tractate *Sofrim* 19:4.)

This association was important for the development of Jewish civilization. It ensured that Shavuot would continue to be observed in the absence of the Temple and its sacrifices. But by moving emphasis away from the first fruits of the harvest to the fruit of Torah, the rabbis enacted a larger shift from Canaan to Sinai, from land to text.

To the rabbinic community living after the destruction of the Temple in 70 CE, in exile and not in control of the Land of Israel, the central institution of the Jewish people became sacred text. Holiness became democratized—the Jewish community could no longer depend upon a central location and a central institution to connect with the divine. The basis for communal leadership shifted from genealogy (priests) to knowledge (rabbis). Aspects of holiness were made accessible to all in their own homes and daily lives. The home became a *mikdash m'at*, a little sanctuary. And text, unlike land, is portable. The emphasis on text over land made a Diaspora Judaism possible.

I like to imagine that when the home came to be understood as a *miḳdash m'at,* the role of high priest was inherited by the woman of the house, who traditionally orchestrated kashrut and food service. —J.G.K.

For the rabbis, the cycle of the holidays was thus slightly altered—Pesach would mark the Exodus from Egypt and the ending of slavery; Sukkot would mark the wanderings in the desert; and Shavuot would mark the cycle's completion not through land, but through Torah. Torah becomes the prime mediator of the covenant between Israel and God.

Themes and Concepts

The idea of revelation is central to the celebration of Shavuot. Among the many midrashim that deal with the nature of revelation, several emphasize the fact that revelation occurred in the desert, and not in Canaan. It is this factor that makes the Torah potentially accessible to all. "The Torah was given publicly and openly, in a place to which no one had any claim. Everyone who desires to accept it, let him or her come to accept it." (*Mekhilta De'rabi Ishmael, Baḥodesh, Yitro,* 1) A Torah given in the wilderness is not confined to a place or even a specific group of people. It is accessible to all who wish to attach

The rabbis' reinterpretation of the meaning of Shavuot highlights how the evolution of Jewish civilization has enabled its ongoing existence and relevance. —D.W.

The giving of the Torah in the desert also symbolizes the great potential that can come from a seeming barrenness. Places and people are more than meets the eye. —J.G.K.

As Hasidic sources teach, the expansive and stripped down wilderness (*midbar*) is also the state of mind in which one can be metaphorically removed from distraction to hear the ongoing words (*dabar*) of divine revelation. —N.C.M.

themselves to it. So while it is given to a specific group, this does not mean that it is inherently exclusive.

The precise nature of the revelatory experience has been a question for Jewish theologians throughout time. What they often see as most important is that revelation as an act of speech (as described in Exodus), is meaningless without an act of listening. The onus is on the listener, then, to interpret and apply what is heard. Yet, as humans we are flawed, and we may differ in how we make sense of things, both among ourselves and across history. Tradition teaches that there are "70 faces" of Torah, and what was a valid interpretation at one time may be modified in the future. The idea of interpretation is embedded in our understanding of Torah, even from the early talmudic rabbis, who deemed that the act of revelation resulted in the giving to Moses of both the *Torah shebikhtav*, the written Torah (the text) and *Torah sheb'al peh*, the oral Torah (its interpretation).

In keeping with the Reconstructionist movement's rejection of the idea of the exclusive chosenness of the Jewish people, I understand the Torah as given to all. It is the revelation that introduced the notion of right and wrong into the world through the mitzvot and ethical commandments that challenge all human beings to live their lives in accordance with ethical ideals. —S.C.R.

A rabbinic midrash suggests that there are 70 names for God. It interprets the Hebrew word "*shema*"—"listen"—by breaking it down into "*shem*," meaning, "name," plus the letter "*ayin*," which has the numerical equivalence of 70 in Hebrew *gematria*. —S.C.R.

Rabbi Abraham Joshua Heschel talks of revelation as a timeless mystical moment. From that perspective, "as a report about revelation, the Bible itself is a *midrash*." (*God in Search of Man*) —N.C.M.

Our task regarding revelation is to engage in a continuous quest of interpretation, looking at the world not as it is, but as it should be. The Hasidic Rebbe Menachem Mendel of Kotsk noted that Shavuot is called the time of the giving of the Torah rather than the time of Jews receiving the Torah. He noted that while the Torah was "given" once, it is constantly being received anew in every generation. More important than the actual nature of revelation is the outcome of the revelatory experience. It is a commitment to listening, to seeking, to moving forward, to the creation of meaning. This is what defines the revelatory experience and gives continuity to the covenant.

Shavuot focuses on text and not on land because arrival in the land implies a final resolution—an end to listening, an end to the wilderness. The Torah itself ends before the Israelites arrive in the Promised Land: At the end of Deuteronomy, the Israelites are still in the wilder-

Revelation is all about relationship. All relationships evolve and change. Think of the evolution between parent and child or between partners. For the change to be wholesome, we need to cultivate a deep appreciation for ourselves as well as for the other. —S.P.W.

We are taught that the Torah is being given over and over again, forever. In the blessings that we recite before reading from the Torah in synagogue, we bless God for "giving" the Torah, not for "having given" the Torah ("*noten Hatorah*," not "*natan Hatorah*")—as a reminder that the revelation is constantly being renewed. —S.C.R.

Rabbi Toba Spitzer teaches, "The God of the Torah and the God of our daily experience of the world is not an abstract, unchanging, and immutable Unmoved Mover, but That which allows the universe to unfold in all of its dazzling complexity." This understanding of God presumes that change is holy—for God, for the universe, and for us humans acting within it. —D.W.

ness. The story of the transition into the land is reserved for the Book of Joshua, but the Book of Joshua is not in the Torah. In our yearly liturgical reading of the Torah, the Israelites never make it into the land. As they stand poised on the west bank of the Jordan River, we turn back once more to the beginning of the Torah and its story of Creation.

Rather than being a location of incompleteness, this place is one of limitless potential. And the power that drives us forward toward fulfilling that potential is God. Mordecai Kaplan, the great American 20th-century philosopher, connects this with the ancient belief in *olam haba*, the world to come. *Olam haba* is the ancient rabbis' language for the world as it ought to be. God is "what the world means to the man (sic) who believes in the possibility of maximum life and strives for it." (*The Meaning of God in Modern Jewish Religion*, page 328)

In each generation, we are all individual receivers of Torah. The midrashic text *Pesikta D'Rav Kahana* (12:25) notes that each individual at Sinai heard revelation according to his or her capacity. Thus, each person heard the same words, but in a way that made sense to each. The obligation is on each of us to listen for Torah in our own day, and to hear it according to our capacity, in a way that is meaningful for us.

Olam haba is also the world that is coming—the *now*. Everything is already present in this very moment. —S.P.W.

Yet we do not go it alone. As we listen, we balance our desire for individual choice with our communal obligation, and we balance our inherited traditions with our contemporary mores and values. While Reconstructionism affirms this idea of ongoing revelation, this does not mean that we are free to do whatever we desire. We are free to make choices, but we are always working within certain boundaries and limitations. We are bound to each other in the work of world building. We are bound to tradition, to history, to text. We are bound by the momentum to move forward in our construction of a better world. We are bound by covenant.

On Shavuot we celebrate Torah, and we celebrate covenant. Shavuot is a time in which we turn our attention to the covenants that bind us: our covenant with the Jewish people, our covenant with our local Jewish communities, our covenant with the Jewish past, and our covenant with the Jewish future. To celebrate Shavuot is to celebrate the fact that we are all part of something greater than our individual selves.

We are bound to keep our obligations, but I prefer the notion that we are connected to them. "Bound" can be an oppressive term, but connection is simply a statement of the truth of how things are. —S.P.W.

The Counting of the Omer

The observance of Shavuot is preceded by the observance of *s'firat ha'omer*. The *omer* (literally, "sheaf") is the seven-week period between the second day of Pesach and Shavuot, and it refers to the biblical barley offering (see above). This was a time of trepidation about the possibility that the weather would disrupt the growth of the grain, so the days from planting to harvest were counted with care.

In rabbinic literature, Shavuot is given another name, *Atzeret*, which means "assembly," but which comes from a root meaning "stop." By using this name, the rabbis emphasize the link between Pesach and Shavuot. *Atzeret* implies a concluding festival, just as the festival at the end of Sukkot is called Shemini Atzeret. Shavuot thus stands on its own, yet it is linked to the themes of Pesach. This is clear in the Torah, where Shavuot marked the end of the grain harvest of the crop planted at Pesach—a harvest that was set by literally counting the days between the two holidays. Despite the de-emphasis of the agricultural basis in favor of the historical understandings, the link between the Pesach and Shavuot is maintained.

Shavuot is also a festival of liberation. The liberation from slavery marked at Pesach is linked to the giving of the Torah at Shavuot. Just as with the harvest, Pesach begins a process of liberation that culminates at Shavuot. The physical movement out of Egyptian slavery is therefore only the first step in liberation; the giving of the Torah is the final step in liberation. Freedom does not simply mean the absence of oppression. In order to be truly free, a society must have a system of norms and regulations that can guarantee those freedoms and protect the individuals who make up that society.

The Israelites who left Egypt could not truly be free until they accepted the Torah. Communities need norms and guidelines to inform the lives of their members. In this way, people create a community rather than remaining a group of individuals. The ancients spoke of this acceptance of Torah through the story of the revelation at Sinai as recounted in the Book of Exodus. It was in this story that the authors of the Bible imagined that God spoke to

In the Torah we learn that Israelites were liberated from bondage in Egypt not simply to be free, but to enter into service with their true God, *Adonay*. The political philosopher Isaiah Berlin teaches that there are different types of freedom: freedom *from* oppression (such as hunger and persecution) and freedom *to* act. At Shavuot, I think about what I am free to do, and what obligations I choose to take on in order to protect myself and others from various oppressions. —D.W.

In order to be truly free, we need to be able to hear voices other than our own. We need to think and argue, as we do when we study Torah. In order to be truly free, we need to be able to act for the repair of the world (*tikun olam)* as we do when we perform the mitzvot of Torah study. —J.A.S.

On Shavuot we rise to a level of consciousness (spiritual liberation) that enables us to take on the obligation to serve others in community more fully. —N.C.M.

We could not be free without Torah because Torah is the acknowledgment of our interconnection with all life and with each other. To imagine we are separate is a delusion; it cannot be the basis for freedom. —S.P.W.

the Israelites from Mount Sinai—"revealing" the Torah—and the Israelites accepted the yoke of its obligations with the words, "*Na'aseh v'nishma*"—"We will do and we will hear." (Exodus 24:7) The *omer* thus links the first stage of the journey to freedom at Pesach to the second stage at Shavuot.

The contemporary practice of *s'firat ha'omer* involves literally counting each day after sundown, after reciting the appropriate *b'rakha*. With the influence of Jewish mysti-

Our ancestors said they would do before they would hear, before they necessarily understood what their commitment would entail. Perhaps to this day, following communal customs and norms happens the same way; when we belong, we may behave a certain way even if we do not yet fully grasp the significance of our actions. —J.G.K.

Na'aseh v'nishma, "We will do, and *then* we will understand." We can dive in head first, entering into an experience in order to understand it. While being prepared intellectually is useful for many pursuits, the spiritual life often requires taking an intellectual risk. Our rational minds may limit our choices to what "makes sense" while preventing us from embracing those experiences that touch our hearts. —B.P.

The practice of counting the *omer* appears to be a simple and mathematical ritual. However, the practice requires attention and intention. Before counting, we need to know what day it is. If we announce the day before reciting the blessing, we have actually fulfilled the mitzvah already! To preserve this ritual accounting as a holy act, the solution is for the leader (or anyone else) to announce what day was counted *the day before*. Then, after the blessing is pronounced, the actually counting becomes a new experience. All this attention just to say a number! —B.P.

It is striking that we count up, not down, to Shavuot. When we count down, we risk losing sight of the current moment: When will school end? How long until the kids leave for camp? Perhaps counting up allows us, in the words of Psalm 90, to treasure each day in order to bring our hearts wisdom. This reminds me of Hanuka, when we add a candle each day as suggested by the school of Hillel, in keeping with the dictum *ma'alin bakodesh*, we should always increase the amount of holiness. —J.G.K./L.B.

The counting of the *omer* can be an opportunity for *hidur mitzvah*—beautifying the mitzvah through an *omer* calendar, either purchased or crafted on one's own. —J.A.S.

cism, this period has become a time for self-reflection and inquiry as we make our own personal journeys from Pesach to Shavuot, from liberation to revelation. In Kabbala, Jewish mystical thought, God, as the *Eyn Sof* or Infinite One, passes through ten *s'firot* (emanations or essences) to sustain the spiritual and physical world. A diagram of these is known as the Tree of Life. The *omer* is seven weeks long, and each week is assigned one of the seven lower *s'firot* from the kabbalistic Tree of Life. Each day of the week during the *omer* is also assigned one of these *s'firot*. Thus, each day becomes an opportunity to engage with the intersection of two of the *s'firot* and to ponder how our lives reflect them.

Tradition also associates this period with a plague that struck the disciples of Rabbi Akiba, and so the *omer* period is also associated with some mourning practices. It is the custom of some to refrain from shaving or cutting

Some contemporary Jews utilize a practice known as "*tikun midot,*" the "fixing" or refinement of character traits or divine qualities based on the *s'firot*, during the seven weeks. Each week, a character trait is focused on for contemplation and action. For example, during the first week of the *omer* period the primary *s'fira* is *ḥesed,* loving-kindness. One might then focus on the quality of generosity and adopt practices that embody generosity throughout the week. —M.K.

One Jewish tradition ascribes the plague that struck Rabbi Akiba's students to their unkindness to one another. As we make our way from liberation to revelation, we are reminded that Torah learning that does not lead to loving practice is empty and even dangerous. —J.A.S.

their hair during this period, as well as from engaging in celebrations such as weddings. As tradition teaches, the plague lifted on the 33rd day of the *omer* ("*Lag B'Omer*"). Some maintain these mourning practices only for the first 33 days of the *omer*, while some maintain them throughout the entire seven weeks. It is traditional to suspend many of these restrictions on *Rosh Ḥodesh* and, more recently, it has become the custom to suspend them on *Yom Ha'atzma'ut*. Some of these restrictions are not widely observed among liberal Jews, but many more traditional Jews do observe them, and this has an impact on planning celebrations and major events throughout the Jewish community.

Lag B'Omer itself is a minor festival, and is generally observed through outdoor activities, picnics, bonfires, and so on. Many Israelis follow the custom of visiting the grave of talmudic sage and mystic Rabbi Shimon bar Yochai, whose Yahrzeit is observed on that day. (For more on *Lag B'Omer*, see the section on *Lag B'Omer* in the Minor Holidays section of this book).

Tikun Leyl Shavuot

Unlike the Seder of Pesach or the sukkah activities of Sukkot, no major ritual is associated with Shavuot. Rather, the focus is on study and text.

A unique observance of Shavuot is the *tikun leyl Shavuot*, an evening or all-night study session on the evening of Shavuot. The practice has been traced to the kabbalists, the medieval Jewish mystics, and it is referred to in the Zohar, the major medieval work of Jewish mysticism. The traditional custom is to stay up all night in study, though some contemporary communities may wish to observe the practice for only part of the evening. Some communities hold a separate *tikun* for teens or other affinity groups.

Various reasons are given for the practice of the *tikun*. One legend holds that the Israelites overslept on the morning when they were to receive the Torah and that they had to be awakened by Moses. We stay up all night to make up for the Israelites' error and to demonstrate our willingness to accept the Torah today. Another tradition speaks

My favorite moment of the *tikun* is always the early morning prayers that follow a night of study. There is something powerful about experiencing a full night of darkness and then reciting the morning prayers just as the sun begins to rise. The combination of the early prayer hour and the exhaustion of a full night's study creates a unique spiritual experience that I find unparalleled in the cycle of the Jewish year. —T.K.

Some say that studying at night, not all night, is enough for a *tikun leyl Shavuot*—and that praying in the morning when we have not rested sufficiently is not appropriate. One risk of an all-night *tikun* is that it can become an endurance contest that divides a community based on age and health needs. Communities might want to experiment with a *tikun yom Shavuot*, in which the time from noon—after morning services—until night is filled with Torah study. —J.G.K.

of midnight as a time in which the heavens open, ready to receive prayer. One can also imagine that as the kabbalists sought mystical experiences of the divine, the feeling of slight disorientation that overtook them from the lack of sleep set the day apart in a physical sense, as well. How-

The practice of *tikun leyl Shavuot* as a ritualized practice outside of the Zohar dates to the early 16th century. A vivid description of the first known *tikun leyl Shavuot* appears in a published letter by Rabbi Shlomo Halevi Alkabetz, author of *L'kha Dodi*. He described the *tikun leyl Shavuot* led by Rabbi Joseph Caro in Salonika in 1530 or 1534. Caro studied a series of texts (including sections from the *Tanakh* and Kabbala), mainly reading through them, and was transported to mystical realms. He repeated the experience with a larger audience on the following night. The *tikun leyl Shavuot* was originally intended as a spiritual experience, not primarily an intellectual one. The *tikun* was part of a larger cycle of midnight observances that became popular among the circle of Tzfat kabbalists that included Alkabetz and Caro in their number. Scholars have suggested that the availability and popularity of coffee in the mid-16th century fueled the ability and interest to have these late-night spiritual experiences. —J.M.S.

I have fond memories of staying up all night at a *tikun leyl Shavuot* in Jerusalem and walking to the Temple Mount at the break of dawn along with thousands of others. As we streamed into the Old City, we watched the early light of the sun turn the Jerusalem stone to gold. It was the closest experience I can imagine to arriving in Jerusalem among the pilgrims in Temple times. —B.P.

The kabbalistic practice of learning as a path to communing with the divine can also take place on a weekly basis at midnight, which is seen as a moment of opening to the higher realms of the divine presence. —N.C.M.

ever, the main idea of the *tikun* is that on a day dedicated to remembering and renewing the covenant, which is mediated by the Torah and text, we should deepen our relationship to the words of the Torah. Jewish practice puts a great emphasis on Torah study—as is written in Mishnah *Peah* 1:1, "*Talmud Torah k'neged kulam*"—"The study of Torah is equal to all"—because through the study of Torah we are moved to engage in our world in a positive way.

Historically, "*Tikun*" was the name of a book studied on Shavuot. It contained excerpts from the corpus of classical Jewish literature—the first and last verses of each Torah portion, the opening and closing of each Mishna tractate, and selections from the Zohar. In contemporary practice, "*tikun*" refers to the event, and the content and structure of the *tikun* are much more expansive.

If we are to keep Torah as the focus of the holiday, the experience of *tikun leyl Shavuot* should be the primary religious experience of the holiday. The act of engaging in Torah study while forgoing sleep is so strange and wonderful that it imbues the receiving of Torah with wonder and delight. While this is difficult with children, one may allow them to stay up until 10 P.M. or midnight to participate in the magic of the *tikun*. The level of honesty, openness and questioning in communal study that takes place during a good *tikun leyl Shavuot* is unparalleled in the Jewish year. It is especially good when the gathering can be hosted at a home rather than a synagogue. Different people can be asked to lead different hour-long sessions, perhaps broken up by a game of Torah-based trivia. Thus, *tikun leyl Shavuot* can become the home-based experience for Shavuot that the Seder is for Pesach. —J.M.S.

"*Tikun*" also refers to the idea of repair—the notion that our actions here on earth have a real effect on a cosmos that contains so much brokenness. —J.G.K.

The nature of the *tikun* can vary from community to community, and it is subject to creative interpretation. A community may wish to dedicate the evening to one topic of interest or importance to that community. Communities may divide the night into time periods, with each period dedicated to a different topic. Different members of the community may serve as teachers, sharing with others an interest that is important to them. Some communities may offer an "open house" in which members of the community can come and study any topic of their choosing. A broad selection of texts can be studied, and they can be drawn from a wide variety of sources. Participants may delve deep into traditional Jewish texts or focus on the work of a single philosopher. Communities may study music or learn songs, or they may draw on other aspects of the Jewish arts, such as theater, dance or film. The evening can be a mix of individual and group activities. Discussion groups, panel presentations or guest speakers can all be added to the mix. The *tikun* is designed for communal rather than individual study, and the structure and content of the *tikun* are limited only by the community's interest and imagination. Snacks are usually available during the *tikun*.

Why stop at snacks when *Pirkey Avot* teaches us that Torah and physical nourishment go hand-in-hand? Even for communities that do not cook on Shabbat, Shavuot provides an opportunity to share freshly made food communally at the synagogue. It doesn't have to be complicated; pizza bagels and chocolate chip cookies are among my personal favorites. —J.G.K.

Tradition and Rituals

Communal observances and restrictions on work are the same for Shavuot as they are for the other pilgrimage festivals, which, while sharing a general prohibition against work as on Shabbat, are not as restrictive; cooking is permitted on the pilgrimage festivals. Two other general customs related to Shavuot are decorating the home and synagogue with greenery and eating dairy foods.

Numerous reasons exist for the custom of decorating with greenery. This custom harks back to the holiday's agricultural roots, and we remind ourselves of the harvest and offerings associated with Shavuot. Also, the Mishna (*Rosh Hashana* 1.2) states, "At four seasons of the year, the world is judged . . . at Shavuot, for fruit of the tree." In connection to the Sinai story, the greenery reminds us of the green pastures around the mountain, implied by the verse "neither let the flocks and herds graze." (Exodus 34:3) And Torah is metaphorically known as the "tree of life." Just as trees provide raw materials to sustain life, so, too, does Torah provide sustenance.

This custom is an opportunity to add an environmental consciousness to Shavuot. We are reminded of the "physical surroundings" of the story of revelation—mountain, wilderness and pasture—and of our connections to our own natural surroundings. Communities may wish to observe this practice and embellish it by using locally grown and harvested plants and fruits, or by creating more elaborate decorations (as in the sukkah).

Eating dairy foods on Shavuot is also linked to various sources. A verse from the Song of Songs, "Honey and milk shall be under your tongue" (4:11) is understood to refer to Torah. Another mythic reason from *agada* (rabbinic legend) is that immediately after the Israelites received the

In modern Israel, the customs of Shavuot reverted to agricultural themes, emphasizing both greenery and first fruits. Processions of farm animals, decked out in flowers and led by the children who care for the animals, are still popular festive events on some kibbutzim. —B.P.

My firstborn child arrived just before Shavuot. While holding and nursing her during the holiday, I realized that the Israelites were spiritual infants when they left Egypt. Former slaves, they had not yet developed a sense of their own power, and they were dependent on God for food, water and protection, just as newborns are dependent on their parents for the basic necessities of life. Because our ancestors were mere infants, their main source of sustenance was milk! Thus, we recall the infancy of our people by eating dairy foods. —B.P.

Another explanation for eating dairy products on Shavuot is the association with the calving season. —J.J.S.

The rabbis made further comparisons between milk and Torah: Both are pure; both are nourishing. Just as milk stays good only in plain containers, not in gold or silver, so Torah stays good only in those who are humble. Baruch Sienna, with whom I once worked and studied, liked to offer a Shavuot challenge: What other foods are similar to Torah and why? Artichoke? Chocolate? —J.A.S.

Torah and the dietary laws contained within, they did not have any meat that was properly prepared. They therefore ate dairy foods. This practice can be observed individually through personal food choices throughout the day and communally through a common meal with dairy entrees and dairy desserts. Blintzes and cheesecakes were East European Jewish favorites.

Erev *Shavuot*

Shavuot is welcomed with candle lighting and evening services. The *erev* Shavuot service is a standard Shabbat/festival *ma'ariv* service, with appropriate insertions for Shavuot. There are a variety of ways to make the service more meaningful and appropriate for the themes of the holiday:

- *Kol Haneshamah: Shabbat Veḥagim* includes a unique service, *Kabbalat Ḥag*. *Kabbalat Ḥag* for Shavuot includes psalms and songs both appropriate for all festivals and relevant to the themes of Shavuot.

Other reasons for eating dairy include the connection between Sinai and Zion—a land of milk and honey—or the idea that the Israelites, newly out of Egypt, are like a baby being nourished by its mother for the first time. God nourishes us from her breast, the mountain, with words of Torah, symbolized by milk. —J.G.K.

One Jewish cookbook on my kitchen bookshelf offers a recipe for a Mount Sinai cheese ball, with a pecan half on top, representing the two tablets. —B.P.

- Selections from the Book of Ruth (see below) can be incorporated into the service.
- Since the timing of Shavuot often coincides with graduation dates for high school and college, the Shavuot service could be a time to honor those celebrating such a milestone. The service could also be a time to honor those who have completed a significant course of study, or converted to Judaism in the past year, or completed the requirements for confirmation. (See below.)
- The decorating of the sanctuary in greenery can be a part of the service itself, with those in attendance helping to decorate. Along with this, environmental themes and reflections of the holiday's biblical agricultural origins can be highlighted.
- The service could serve as the introduction to the *tikun*, thus ending with the *b'rakha* for Torah study or another appropriate reading.

Shavuot Day

Shavuot morning services are often held at sunrise just before the *tikun* concludes. Some communities begin the services later, and some offer both options.

The morning service is a standard Shabbat/ festival *shaḥarit* service. The festival *Amida* is recited, including the insertions for Shavuot. After the *Amida* and before the Torah reading, Hallel, the series of celebratory psalms, is recited.

The primary Torah reading for Shavuot is Exodus 19–20, which recounts the revelation at Sinai and includes the Ten Commandments. Various traditions exist for the reading of the Ten Commandments, including using a special *trop* (melody) and having the entire congregation stand while the Ten Commandments are read. The haftarah for Shavuot is Ezekiel 1:1–28, 3:12, which recounts the prophet's ecstatic vision of the heavenly hosts and chariot. The haftarah parallels the Torah reading in that they both describe direct mystical experiences of the divine—the Israelites at Sinai and Ezekiel along the Chebar River in Babylonia in the sixth century BCE. The effort to re-experience revelation on Shavuot is reflected in those texts. Shavuot is one of four times during the year when we recite the Yizkor memorial service.

Shavuot is one of the biblical festivals that, while biblically ordained for one day, became a two-day *ḥag* in the Diaspora due to the difficulty of disseminating the news of the holiday's date according to an ancient calendar based on the cycle of the moon. For those communities that observe two days of Shavuot, the *erev* Shavuot and Shavuot day services are the same on both days, but a *tikun* is not held on the second night, and different Torah and haftarah readings are selected for the second day. See the Appendix to this volume of the *Guide* for a complete discussion of the issue of one-day versus two-day *ḥag* observances.

Piyyutim

It is the custom of some to include special *piyyutim* (liturgical poems) in the Shavuot service, usually as an introduction to the reading of the Torah on Shavuot Day. The most popular from the Ashkenazic liturgy is *Akdamut*, an Aramaic alphabetical acrostic *piyyut* composed by Meir ben Isaac Nehorai in Worms during the eleventh century. *Akdamut*—from the words "*akdamut milin*," "before the words"—is a song of praise to God's greatness, and it can be chanted or read responsively when it is included.

The Book of Ruth

The Book of Ruth is read on the second day of Shavuot during morning services. For those observing a single day of Shavuot, Ruth may be read during morning services or studied at any time during the holiday. One possibility is to use the Book of Ruth as a subject for the *tikun*. Some read Ruth on Shavuot afternoon. Selections from Ruth can also be an alternative *musaf* on the first day.

Various explanations are given regarding why Ruth is associated with Shavuot. A clear thematic connection is that of covenant and acceptance, for Ruth is the mythic antecedent to what will later be called conversion—refer-

In many communities Shavuot is a time when individuals who have converted to Judaism as adults share with the community their own personal spiritual journeys and what inspired them to choose Judaism as their spiritual civilization. In keeping with the tradition of reading the Book of Ruth, this contemporary sharing of a Jew by Choice is often the most moving experience of the festival itself. —S.C.R.

ring to one who chooses Torah, covenant and peoplehood by her own free will. This is symbolic of both the Torah and midrashic stories of revelation, in which the Israelites accepted the Torah from God of their own free will. It also applies to the ability of those who are not born into the Jewish people to choose freely to accept the covenant. The story of Ruth also reminds us that as contemporary Jews, we are continually making an active choice to associate with the Jewish people, and it is only through our active and voluntary commitment to uphold the covenant of the past and to pass it to the next generation that the Torah continues to be a living and relevant document.

According to the end of the Book of Ruth, Ruth is an ancestor of King David. The midrash states that David died on Shavuot (*Rut Raba* 3:2). Since the traditional belief is that the Messiah will be a descendant of David, celebrating the giving of the Torah can remind us of our messianic hopes and our obligation to work toward the messianic age so that one day we will live in a world in which the Torah's vision of peace (*shalom*), justice (*tzedek*) and loving kindness (*ḥesed*) will be fulfilled.

Another theme of the Ruth story is the harvest. Key scenes in the story of Ruth take place during the harvest season, and Shavuot marks the end of the spring wheat harvest. In the story, Boaz generously allows Ruth to glean what she needs from his fields. This reminds us of our obligations to help those in need—obligations that are specifically outlined in the Torah as agricultural obligations. After the description of Shavuot in Leviticus 23, we are enjoined:

> When you reap the harvest of your land, you shall not reap all the way to the edges of your field, or gather the gleanings of your harvest; you shall leave them for the poor and the stranger. I am Adonay your God. (Leviticus 23:22)

While most urban and suburban Jews may not have fields, the obligation to help those in need is clear. Reading Ruth at the time in which we mark the giving of the Torah reminds us that these obligations are at the center of living a life dedicated to Torah.

Other Contemporary Observances

Confirmation

Originating in the Reform movement in the late 19th century, confirmation is a ritual affirmation of Jewish identity for high-school age Jewish youth. It is commonly celebrated when a student is 16 or 17. Originally intended to replace the bar/bat mitzvah ceremony, since it was felt by the leaders of Reform Judaism that a child of 13 was not mature enough to be considered a "Jewish adult," confirmation has been maintained in many communities to "book-end" a Jewish youth's teenage Jewish experience.

From the earliest practice of Jewish confirmation ceremonies, both girls and boys were confirmed. Early Reform leaders preferred confirmation in part because it redressed the exclusion of girls from the bar mitzvah ritual. —D.W.

Confirmation provides an opportunity for students to confirm their Jewish identity as they prepare to leave their community of origin for study or other pursuits. The ceremony usually follows a period of Jewish study and engagement (Hebrew High School program, youth group, etc.), and it is celebrated on Shavuot to fit with the theme of affirmation and acceptance of the covenant. It is fitting, too, since Shavuot falls at the end of the school year, much as Simchat Torah falls at the beginning of the school year and is thus commonly marked as a time of celebration of the consecration of new students. Reconstructionist congregations may want to observe confirmation, and the manner of celebration is open and up to communal interpretation and standard setting. Confirmation often includes song and dance. Elements may include students leading the service, delivering a *d'var Torah*, or making a public statement about their Jewish identity and an affirmation of the covenant. Indeed, the content of the confirmation service is often developed by the students themselves. Sometimes confirmation is held on the Shabbat closest to Shavuot.

Kabbalat Gerim *(Welcoming the Convert)*

The process of conversion is an individual pursuit in which a person undergoes a period of study and personal ritual to mark the joining of the Jewish people. A person's conversion to Judaism should be a communal celebration as well, as the community welcomes its newest member. Congregations may wish to institute a ceremony of *kab-*

balat gerim, welcoming the convert, to publicly welcome those who have chosen to join the Jewish people. Because of its themes of the Book of Ruth and the acceptance of Torah, Shavuot is a fitting time. Congregations may wish to invite the newly converted to lead the service, share some words of Torah or speak about their personal journeys to Judaism.

Ketuba

Since Shavuot is about covenant, it evokes the imagery related to another covenant in Judaism—the covenant of marriage. Indeed, kabbalistic imagery is explicit in this regard. Shavuot then becomes a celebration of the sacred partnership between God and the Jewish people. This is evoked in the Sephardic tradition of writing a *ketuba*, a marriage contract, between God and Israel that is read during the Torah service of Shavuot, after the ark is opened and before the Torah is removed. The language is drawn from the traditional *ketuba* text, and it speaks of the ways God and Israel are bound and obligated to each other, and of the responsibilities each has toward the other. Communities can adopt this exercise and adapt it to focus on individual community covenants. Communities may wish to write a communal *ketuba* that spells out the obligations the members of that community have to one another and what the community will provide. These may change every year as communities change every year. Rather than write a new document, communities may wish to use the time on Shavuot to examine their own sacred texts—their mission statements and other foundational texts—as a means of reaffirming the congregational covenant as well.

Conclusion

While the ritual and sancta of Shavuot are not as elaborate as those of some other holidays, Shavuot embodies some of the deepest parts of what it means to be Jewish. To celebrate Shavuot is to celebrate our connection to our past, to our tradition and to our ever-unfolding relationship with God and Torah.

In the Book of Ruth, which is read on this holiday, Ruth the Moabite turns to her mother-in-law, Naomi, as she is about to return to Judah after dwelling in Moab for some time. Naomi's husband and two sons—including Ruth's husband—have all died, and although Naomi tells her daughters-in-law Ruth and Orpa to remain in Moab, only Orpa complies. Ruth, on the other hand, declares to her, "Wherever you go, I will go; wherever you lodge, I will lodge. Your people shall be my people, and your God shall be my God." On Shavuot, when we read these words, we, too, are affirming Ruth's commitment: that the Jewish people shall be our people, the God of the covenant, our God. We commit ourselves once again to stand at Sinai as part of the Jewish people.

Minor Holidays, Days of Mourning and Fast Days

DAVID A. TEUTSCH

Many special days on the Jewish calendar commemorate historical events. Some of these are days of joyous celebration, and others mark destruction, loss and deep sadness. The pages that follow describe some days that recall painful chapters in Jewish history, some that mark triumphs, and one, *Tu Bishvat*, that stands outside the historical cycle altogether. Many of these days have significant observances outside the synagogue, and they bring together men and women, adults and children. We begin by turning our attention to our most somber day of mourning.

The History of Tisha B'Av

The end of self-rule and the destruction of the sacrificial system centered in the Second Temple in Jerusalem came when a Roman army invaded Judea and destroyed the Temple in the second half of the first century (customarily dated to 70 CE—the 70th year of the Common Era, which Christians call *anno Domini*, "the year of our Lord"). As long as the Temple had stood, the *kohanim* (priests) had played the primary role of religious leadership. With the Temple gone and the Temple sacrifices eliminated, a period of chaos ensued. The rabbis then gradually emerged as the dominant Jewish leaders. It was they who established *Tisha B'Av*, the ninth day of the month of Av, as an annual day of mourning marking the destruction of the Second Temple. Because Av comes in midsummer, many Jews overlook this observance. *Tisha B'Av* is widely observed in Jewish summer camps because it is the only holy day besides Shabbat that falls during the North American camp season.

The commemoration of *Tisha B'Av* at Orthodox summer camps in the early 1960s left a lasting impression on me. I mourned deeply the destruction of the Temples and was acculturated to associate all Jewish historical misfortunes, including the Holocaust, with the chant of *Eykha* (Book of Lamentations). Prior to 1967, viewing Jewish history as a vale of tears felt satisfying and identity forming to me. —J.J.S.

To understand *Tisha B'Av*, it is important to keep in mind the centrality of the Temple during the First and Second Temple periods. From the perspective of the people at that time, sacrifices and rituals in the Temple could achieve atonement, bring ritual purity and help secure God's blessing for a good harvest. The Temple was the locus for the key observance of such holidays as Pesach—the sacrifice of the paschal lamb that was a precursor to the Pesach meal. Shavuot meant the offering of the first fruits of the farming season, and Sukkot, celebrating the fall bounty. Yom Kippur without the scapegoat and the high priest entering the inner sanctum of the Temple was unimaginable at the time of the Temple's destruction.

The ultimate purpose of sacrifices in Temple times is reflected in the root of the Hebrew word for sacrifice, *korban*, which means "to bring close." The role of the priests in the Temple was to facilitate the process of bringing the people close to God through the rituals of the sacrifices and offerings. The great trauma of the destruction of the Temple was due in part to the sudden and profound sense of loss and desperation that the people must have felt at having their mechanism for drawing close to God suddenly torn away and destroyed. —S.C.R.

Writing in the twelfth century, Maimonides understood the loss of sacrificial worship through the destruction of the Temple as having led to spiritual progress. Moses understood that the Israelites would not have followed him if he had asked them to give up animal sacrifice. Instead, he instructed them to devote their offerings to God instead of to idols. Without the Temple, the rabbis replaced sacrifice with prayer, a purer form of worship. —J.J.S.

Are there institutions in contemporary Jewish life today whose loss is unimaginable? The rabbinate? Synagogues? The State of Israel? If Judaism survived the loss of the Temple in Jerusalem, perhaps no one thing is indispensable. —J.J.S.

The sense of loss when each Temple was destroyed must have been nearly unbearable. The sacrificial system at the core of biblical religious observance was never restored thereafter, despite a careful recording of all the Temple procedures by the rabbis of the Talmud in the hope that the Temple would be rebuilt in messianic days. Prayers for rebuilding the Temple and restoring its rituals have been part of traditional rabbinic prayer from that day to this. However, Reform, Reconstructionist and some Conservative prayer books omit these prayers because the possible reinstitution of sacrifices is seen as a past stage in the evolution of Jewish worship.

The loss marked on *Tisha B'Av* involved more than ritual. Many people lost their lives in the conflict with the Romans, which lasted several years and ended in 73 CE with the mass suicide at Masada, the last fortress to fall. Jewish self-government was destroyed, only partially and

Historians tell us that the Temple was destroyed by the Romans because of relentless provocations by Jewish zealots who refused to settle for anything less than independence from Rome and full Jewish control of the Land of Israel. An unwillingness to compromise and accept less than our ideal can lead to undesired and even catastrophic consequences. —J.J.S.

Mourning the death of a loved one can feel like an earthquake in the soul. It takes time for healing and settling to take place. The destruction of the Temple was an earthquake in the soul of the Jewish people. Delving into the ways in which the rabbis made meaning following this tragedy is uplifting, even as we mourn. *Tisha B'Av* offers healing and demonstrates the resiliency and creativity of the soul of the Jewish people. —L.T.P.

Even for those who would willingly re-establish the sacrificial system, rebuilding the Temple would have catastrophic political implications because it would require the destruction of the Dome of the Rock, an important Muslim shrine built on that site. —J.J.S.

gradually to be reorganized through the rabbis, who established an academy and court system at Yavneh with the consent of the Roman rulers. Indeed, the term "rabbi" (in Hebrew, *rav* or *rabi*) came into regular use only after the Temple's destruction because it marked the emergence of the rabbis as sages, teachers and judges who became the key Jewish leaders of that period. Eventually the Romans

The Jewish general Josephus, writing for his Roman masters, included the dramatic narrative of the death of 960 Zealots at Masada, but that narrative has no parallels in Jewish texts. Archaeological evidence confirms the presence of the Zealots on Masada and of the Roman besiegers at the mountain's base, but not the dramatic ending described by Josephus. The ancient rabbis, who included many stories in what became the Talmud, either did not know of the mass suicide or suppressed stories about it because they did not want to encourage political resistance. They shifted focus from political to spiritual redemption, deferring it to a vaguely defined *olam haba*, the world to come. The high cost of political rebellion was a lesson the rabbis learned all too well through the failure not only of the Great Revolt, but also of the Bar Kochba revolt (132–135 CE), which ultimately proved even more devastating for Jewish fortunes in Judea than the destruction of the Second Temple. In the early 20th century, Josephus's tale became a powerful shaping narrative within Zionist and Israeli circles. —D.W.

The rabbinic reconstruction of communal religious practice following the destruction of the Temple is an extraordinary example of the vitality and evolution of Jewish civilization. The rabbis understood themselves to be acting in continuity with Jewish tradition. They were conscious of the calamity that had befallen the Jews and the need to recreate a world of meaning that would sustain the Jewish people, but they did not share our modern sensibility that humans are empowered agents who can act in history and alter structures by means of our own rationales and reasoning. In our day, making major structural changes honestly requires us to acknowledge what we are doing and why. Our time calls for bold and self-aware action in the face of radically changing circumstances—action that acknowledges both continuities and breaks with the past. —D.W.

Recent scholarship increasingly questions the historicity of the Yavneh story, understanding it as a myth of origin for the later rabbinic movement. —E.R.S.

The rabbis at Yavneh are often portrayed as the sole survivors of the Roman onslaught—survivors who reconstructed Judaism from memory as Jerusalem burned. While their importance cannot be underestimated, the reality was likely more complex. Diaspora communities in Egypt and Babylonia were already in existence from the time of the first exile in the sixth century BCE, and Jews remained in the Jerusalem area even after the destruction in the first century. —N.H.M.

recognized rabbinic authority, allowing a degree of self-rule and thereby easing conflict and aiding tax collection. This kind of accommodation between the Jewish people and ruling authorities gave rise to the rabbinic dictum, "*Dina d'malkhuta dina*," "The law of the kingdom must be obeyed." This rabbinic concession paved the way for Jewish self-rule within Diaspora kingdoms throughout the rabbinic and medieval periods. Without the principle of *dina d'malkhuta dina*, Judaism as we know it could not have emerged. The ability of the Jewish people to adapt and sometimes to thrive under foreign rule has been a key to Jewish survival.

Over time, *Tisha B'Av* became the central day of mourning on the Jewish calendar. Later generations layered their tragedies onto it. Associations grew to include not only the destruction of the Second Temple in 70 CE, but also the destruction of the First Temple in 586 BCE, the

The dictate *dina d'malkhuta dina* emerged following the failure of the Bar Kochba revolt and a rabbinic orientation away from political activism. Such political quietism persisted until the modern era, when Jews created the Zionist movement and also became active in such universally oriented social movements as socialism and Communism. —D.W.

Allowing Jewish law to be subservient to the secular law of the land in which Jews found themselves was key to the flourishing of Jewish creativity. —S.C.R.

The ninth day of Av has become a holy vessel strong enough to contain the sorrows of many of the tragedies that have befallen our people throughout our history. Just as the time frames placed on mourning practices such as shiva and *sh'loshim* help us to mourn and move on, this annual container invites us to remember and grow from these historical tragedies without becoming stuck in ongoing grief or mourning. A vessel for grief becomes a vessel for healing and for transformation. —L.T.P.

final crushing of the Bar Kochba rebellion against Roman rule in the Land of Israel in 135 CE, the expulsion of the Jews from Spain in 1492 and the Chmielnicki pogroms of 1648 in the Ukraine. Each of these events was of historical importance, and each involved enormous suffering and death for Jews. The Mishna, seemingly without any historical basis, associates the ninth day of Av with a tragic event described in the Torah—the day when Moses declared that the people would not enter the Land of Israel for 40 years. (*Ta'anit* 4.6) When *Yom Hashoah V'hag'vura*, a day to remember the Holocaust, was instituted, the Knesset (Israeli parliament) debated whether to mark this tragedy, too, on *Tisha B'Av*, but ultimately decided to select a date in spring prior to *Yom Ha'atzma'ut* (Israeli Independence Day) instead. (See below.)

Tisha B'Av takes place 40 days before Yom Kippur, an auspicious number in Jewish tradition. The Children of Israel spent 40 years traversing the wilderness after the scouts persuaded them not to enter the land right away. Moses spent 40 days on Mount Sinai in communion with the divine presence. In these 40 days, we reflect on the journey of our lives, so we can prepare ourselves for the spiritual peak of Yom Kippur. —B.P.

Some individuals suggested that, should a new memorial day be created, it should not be layered onto *Tisha B'Av*, but rather commemorated on Kristallnacht, the Night of Broken Glass that in November 1938 signaled the intensification of the Nazi program against the Jews. —D.W.

It is certain that fasting took place on *Tisha B'Av* after the destruction of the Second Temple, and there is some evidence that *Tisha B'Av* became a fast day after the destruction of the First Temple. *Tisha B'Av* has been the main day of mourning on the Jewish calendar since that time.

Pondering the Meaning of Tisha B'Av

Traditionally *Eykha*, the Book of Lamentations found in the Bible, is chanted on *Tisha B'Av*. It records the horrors inflicted on the Israelites in 586 BCE, when the Babylonians conquered the land and destroyed the First Temple. Its theology is straightforward: God inflicted this terrible punishment because Israel was sinful. Many rabbis of the

The Talmud identifies the midsummer weeks surrounding *Tisha B'Av* as a time of cosmic danger, when evil spirits roam and demonic forces incite people to violence and hostility. It is possible that the rabbinic understanding of the ninth day of Av as the date of tragedy after tragedy was layered onto earlier beliefs regarding the dangerous nature of midsummer. The penitential rituals of *Tisha B'Av* would have been understood as effective means for expressing contrition and regaining divine favor and for staving off supernatural and cosmic dangers. —E.R.S.

Collective mourning for the Jewish past, especially for the Temple, with its animal sacrifices and priestly class, runs counter to our modern sensibilities. It is a constant challenge for progressive Jews to find meaningful ways of commemorating *Tisha B'Av* while at the same time remaining true to our core beliefs and values. —S.C.R.

Many of the biblical prophets believed that God could control the actions of the ancient nations and empires. They prophesied about the ways in which God would maneuver the enemies of Judea to attack Jerusalem as a punishment for the sins of Jerusalem. —T.K.

talmudic period described the destruction as a result of *hastarat panim*, the hiding of God's face, in response to Israel's sinfulness. Traditional Jewish theology holds that if Israel faces its wrongdoing and repents, God will restore at least a remnant to Israel's rightful place. Many contemporary Jews do not experience the world as reflecting a direct causal effect between human wrongdoing and cosmic punishment. Our theological differences should not interfere with our confronting the reality of the collective losses of the Jewish people and mourning them. Remembering our history, mourning our losses and resolving to fight the forces of evil in the world make the observance of *Tisha B'Av* a powerful annual event.

The prophet Ezekiel (11:22–23) described a vision in which he saw the presence of God, the *kavod*, lifting itself up and out of the Holy of Holies of the Temple. The presence, appearing as a cloud, floated over to the Mount of Olives. As soon as God departed from the Temple, the structure became vulnerable to enemy attacks. —T.K.

A balanced view of history indicates that, contrary to popular belief, Jews have not always been victims. Nevertheless, the tragic occasions of Jewish history are deserving of recollection. Though *Tisha B'Av* is a minor holiday, not only in traditional terms but also in its rare observance in the liberal Jewish community, it provides one day a year to remember the saddest events of our past. Whether these events actually took place on this calendar date is irrelevant. For those whose experience of Judaism is overwhelmingly joyful and fun, *Tisha B'Av* is an essential corrective. —B.P.

Acknowledging our own suffering helps us to empathize with the suffering of others—to experience news of war, oppression and genocide as if they were happening to us. —J.J.S.

While some passages in *Eykha* invoke covenantal transgression as the cause of Israel's suffering, the majority of the book does not. Rather, most of *Eykha* sympathizes with Israel and protests the extremity of her suffering while portraying God as a brutal, enraged and destructive force. The haftarah read on the Sabbath following *Tisha B'Av* reiterates the excessive nature of Israel's suffering, declaring that Israel has "received at the hand of God double for all her sins." (Isaiah 40:2) —E.R.S.

The 19th- and early-20th-century Reform movement did not observe *Tisha B'Av* because early Reform thinkers understood the destruction and exile as necessary to fulfill the destiny of the Jewish people—to disperse across the world and bring the Jewish vision of ethical monotheism to all humanity. After the founding of the State of Israel, the Reform commitment to Zionism grew, and today the observance of *Tisha B'Av* exists in some form in many Reform congregations.

Some have suggested that with the advent of the State of Israel, *Tisha B'Av* should no longer be observed, that we should put mourning for the loss of Jewish sovereignty behind us. But many reasons to observe *Tisha B'Av* remain. *Tisha B'Av* marks the pain that flows from avoidable cruelty among people and among nations, as well as from war and from the flaws in social systems that prevent many people from experiencing personal liberty and social justice and from having their basic needs met. The advent of the State of Israel has not ushered in messianic

A close reading of the Bible makes it clear that under the rule of the Israelite kings, including David and Solomon, things were not ideal. The hope that the establishment of the State of Israel is a step on the way to messianic restoration is unrealistic and misguided. We work to right wrongs and injustice because by definition we do not live in a perfect world. —J.J.S.

At the Conservative movement summer camp where I grew up, some promoted a tradition of breaking their fast after *minḥa* (the afternoon service) in an effort to resolve the cognitive dissonance between historic destruction and the establishment of the contemporary State of Israel. —J.G.K.

days; Israel is still far from achieving its messianic vision of justice, plenty and peace. We still have much to mourn on *Tisha B'Av*, and the resolve to make things better is no less important.

According to the Babylonian Talmud (*Yoma* 9b), the sin that caused the destruction of the Second Temple was *sinat ḥinam*, baseless hatred among Jews; the rabbis viewed *sinat ḥinam* as an egregious offense. One dimension of *Tisha B'Av* is concern with the way we treat those around us in both speech and deed. In connecting *Tisha B'Av* with *sinat ḥinam*, the rabbis made this an occasion to contemplate the mitzvot *beyn adam laḥavero*, between

From its earliest days, the Zionist movement drew upon and modernized the ancient Jewish belief in messianic redemption. This impulse continues to infuse elements of contemporary Israeli policy and politics, even as it blends uneasily with the realities of a modern nation-state in a highly politicized region of the world. —D.W.

What about outrage that *has* a basis? The rabbinic teaching that we should avoid *sinat ḥinam* is often misused to silence real, heartfelt disputes among Jews with regard to what is right, just and sacred. We should not shrink from criticizing other people, including Jews, but we should be attentive to our tone and motivation. We may be angry, but we should seek change, not gratuitous hurt. —J.J.S.

Rabbi Abraham Isaac Kook inspired contemporary Israeli bumper stickers that read "*b'ahavat ḥinam yibaneh*," "with generous, unwarranted love it will be built." The metaphor of building the messianic age through love remains even for Jews who do not believe in a literal rebuilding of a third Temple. —J.G.K.

individuals and those around them. We have almost endless ways in which we can treat each other well and harm each other. However, the rabbis were teaching that transgression is not only a question of action. It is also about the destructive ill feelings toward others that we carry around in our hearts. These feelings are corrosive to the person who has them, and they leak out, damaging others in unintended ways.

The Israelite corruption described by the prophets in the Bible was not only personal; it was national. So are many of the problems the world currently faces—hunger caused by war and environmental abuse, homelessness resulting from the shredding of governmental safety nets, a lack of minimally adequate healthcare because of the unfair distribution of resources, business and government corruption driven by greed and lust for power. We may not fear divine retribution, but we have reason to fear the actions of governments, nations, corporations and groups. *Tisha B'Av* provides an opportunity to confront such issues and to resolve to take action on a regular basis

For centuries, some Jews have practiced *ḥesed* (loving kindness) meditation, sending blessings to all of Creation, orienting their hearts to kindness and good will. Many find that the practice makes them better able to regard and treat others more benevolently.

—J.J.S.

to try to make things better. Those designing the observance of *Tisha B'Av* today face the challenge of moving beyond ritual for its own sake in order to motivate participants to change their personal lives and to act for the good of broader society, particularly around the issue of *sinat ḥinam* (baseless hatred).

When the Temple stood, Yom Kippur was an opportunity for purification on three levels: of the Temple itself, of the nation Israel and of each individual. With the destruction of the Temple, the first two purifications lost their mechanism and their meaning, and Yom Kippur has become exclusively focused on personal atonement. *Tisha B'Av* now serves as a framework for collective reflection and repentance. —D.W.

The rabbis' emphasis on the role of *sinat ḥinam* in the destruction of the Temple is a challenging legacy. While many liberal Jews reject the literal truth of this assertion, it can be embraced as an invitation to do the work of *musar*—of examining our own hearts, attributes and inclinations as we interact with others from day to day. Meaningful observances for *Tisha B'Av* or for the nine days or three weeks leading up to that date might involve personal *musar* work as well as communal *tikun olam* efforts. —L.T.P.

The Jewish community today is seemingly in constant upset over discussions about Israel and its search for peace with its Palestinian neighbors. The relentless external threats to Israel's survival raise such powerful emotional issues for many Jews that they have generated a modern equivalent of *sinat ḥinam*—expressions of hatred by one Jew against another simply because of differing political positions on Israel and its domestic and foreign policies. —S.C.R.

The Observance of Tisha B'Av

A period known as The Three Weeks stretches from the minor fast of the 17th day of Tammuz until Tisha B'Av. Some Jews avoid celebrations (including weddings) and stop shaving, cutting their hair and listening to music during The Three Weeks.

In Hebrew, the period of The Three Weeks is called "*beyn hametzarim*," "between the narrow places." —J.G.K.

Entering a season that begins with *Tisha B'Av* (or the three weeks leading up to *Tisha B'Av*), extends through the *Yamim Nora'im,* and concludes with Simchat Torah is a yearly invitation to literally live out the message of Psalm 30—to turn our weeping and mourning into dancing. Our tradition teaches us that there is a time for each of these purposes. These days and practices, meaningful in and of themselves, also coach us on how to embrace times to mourn and times to dance—how to deeply experience the range of human emotions and to confront head on the blessings and the misery of the human condition. Mourning together on *Tisha B'Av* strengthens us for the other times when we need to mourn as individuals and as a community. *Tisha B'Av* can serve as a paradigm for how to employ the gifts of ritual and community when calamity befalls us and when life is particularly chaotic. —L.T.P.

Rabbi Joseph Soloveitchik taught that when we approach *Tisha B'Av*, we go through the same phases of mourning as we do when we have lost a close relative, only in reverse order, with mourning gradually increasing until it peaks at *Tisha B'Av*. —J.G.K.

From the beginning of the month of Av, the period of The Nine Days begins; *Tisha B'Av* is the ninth day. The Nine Days are the last part of The Three Weeks. Some Jews who do not observe the prohibitions for The Three Weeks (not shaving or cutting their hair, not scheduling weddings or listening to music, and avoiding large parties) observe some or all of those prohibitions during The Nine Days; some Jews also refrain from eating meat and drinking alcoholic beverages (except for Kiddush) during The Nine Days. The Three Weeks mark the period of siege before Jerusalem fell and the Second Temple was destroyed. The Nine Days mark the period from the breaching of Jerusalem's walls until the destruction of the Temple.

Just as the Talmud teaches that from the beginning of the month of Adar (when we celebrate Purim) joy increases, it also teaches that from the beginning of the month of Av, joy decreases. Our sages could have taught, "From the beginning of the month of Av, sorrow increases," but they did not. The standard by which we measure ourselves is joy. —J.G.K.

Sephardic Jews heighten their observance of prohibitions during the week of *Tisha B'Av* itself rather than from the very beginning of the month of Av. —J.G.K.

Exceptions to the restrictions on eating meat and drinking alcoholic beverages include Shabbat and *seudot mitzvah* (festive meals celebrating a mitzvah, such as a *brit* ceremony) or when celebrating a *siyum* (completing the study of a tractate of Talmud). —J.G.K.

The Shabbat before *Tisha B'Av* is called Shabbat *Ḥazon* after the opening words of the haftarah from the Book of Isaiah. The *parasha*, the section of Torah read that day, is the opening section of Deuteronomy. The haftarah and Torah portion reflect basically the same theology of divine punishment for sin as that of *Eykha* described above, and Isaiah warns of physical destruction and human humiliation and decimation. This intensifies the mood as *Tisha B'Av* approaches.

Tisha B'Av is a 24-hour fast day that begins at sundown. Many of its observances are the same as those of Yom Kippur, which is *d'orayta* (required by the Torah). *Tisha B'Av*'s observance is *d'rabanan* (ordained by the rabbis rather than biblical in origin). While Yom Kippur (known as *Shabbat Shabbaton*, the Sabbath of Sabbaths) is traditionally observed for 25 hours, as is Shabbat, *Tisha B'Av*, which is never observed on Shabbat, lasts only 24 hours. Work is prohibited on Yom Kippur, but *Tisha B'Av* always falls on a weekday, and work is permitted.

Adults traditionally observe the fast on *Tisha B'Av*; minors, those who are ill and women who are pregnant or nursing are exempt. If the ninth day of Av falls on Shabbat, *Tisha B'Av* is observed immediately after Shabbat.

"*Ḥazon*" means "vision." Here it refers to the prophet's vision of impending destruction. During The Nine Days or on *Shabbat Ḥazon,* some congregations foreshadow *Tisha B'Av* musically by singing *Adon Olam* or *L'kha Dodi* to the tune of *Eli Tziyon*, a common *Tisha B'Av kina*. —J.G.K.

Even though *Tisha B'Av* is observed for one hour less than Yom Kippur, it often feels longer because sunset falls later in the day than on Yom Kippur. —J.J.S.

The fast is postponed until then because fasting and mourning are contrary to the spirit of Shabbat, which takes precedence over other observances. When *Tisha B'Av* is observed on a Sunday, *Havdala* is not recited at the end of Shabbat; instead, it is recited at the conclusion of *Tisha B'Av*, since it would be inappropriate for the sweet smell and joyous tone of *Havdala* to launch *Tisha B'Av*. The fast is preceded by a substantial meal, *se'uda mafseket* (literally, "meal of pausing," the last meal before a fast). At the meal before *Tisha B'Av*, it is customary not to serve alcoholic beverages or elaborate foods, so that the meal has some of the somber tone of *Tisha B'Av*.

Once *Tisha B'Av* begins, some Jews avoid wearing leather, jewelry, belt buckles and other metal objects, which were considered ostentatious and in earlier times were reminiscent of war. An effort is made to wear simple, plain clothes. Many Jews also refrain from bathing and showering, wearing perfume and makeup, and having

On ordinary Saturday evenings, many Jews delay *Havdala* in order to prolong the joy of Shabbat. In the frequent years when the ninth or tenth day of Av begins on a Saturday evening, the striking transition from the joy of Shabbat to the gloom of *Tisha B'Av* leaves no room for prolonging the spirit of Shabbat into the work week. On those evenings *Havdala* consists of acknowledging separation in the silent Saturday evening *Amida* and reciting the blessing over a flame or lamp. The spices are omitted entirely, and the blessings over wine and separation are postponed until Sunday night. —J.G.K.

On weekdays, some people include hard-boiled eggs and ashes in the pre-fast meal. —J.G.K.

Leather shoes in particular are traditionally not worn on *Tisha B'Av*. —J.G.K.

sexual relations. Even though work is permitted on *Tisha B'Av*, some Jews avoid signing contracts and negotiating agreements because *Tisha B'Av* is not a day associated with good outcomes. Traditional Jews limit Torah study, a pleasurable activity, to themes of the day, and they avoid sports, movies and other forms of entertainment altogether in order to preserve the day's somber mood. Some communities strategically place black cloth or ribbon on the *bima* or pews in the sanctuary to remind their members that this is a day of mourning. Some Sephardic (descendents of Spain and Portugal) congregations put black mantles on their Torah scrolls; some congregations put a black curtain on the front of the ark.

As on Yom Kippur, the evening service usually begins at sundown or soon thereafter. It is chanted plaintively with a melodic line different from that of any other *ma'ariv* (evening) service. Sometimes special *kinot* (dirges; mournful liturgical poems) are read, or songs on the theme of the day are sung. *Eykha* is always chanted in a special *trop* (melody). Sometimes five different people each chant one of the five chapters of *Eykha*; some con-

The two major fast days on our calendar are radically different. Some consider Yom Kippur a joyous fast when we are undistracted by food. On *Tisha B'Av* we fast because of events so terrible that eating is not possible. —J.G.K.

I grew up reciting *Tisha B'Av* prayers with no melody at all, just reading the words aloud one by one, which I have found to be strikingly different from the chanting on autopilot to which we may be accustomed. —J.G.K.

gregations read all or part of it in English translation. In keeping with the spirit of mourning, many people listen to *Eykha* while sitting on low stools or on the floor with the lights dimmed, sometimes reading the text by candlelight. This somber atmosphere creates a suitable opportunity for reflecting on the themes of the day. In some communities, a *d'var tzedek*—a talk focused on justice or righteousness—is given on a contemporary issue demanding action. In other communities the service is preceded by a lecture, film or discussion related to the themes of the day. Some communities have the custom of maintaining silence after the service until people are some distance from the building in order to better preserve the mood invoked by the service.

On *Tisha B'Av* we remember a time when Israel's prayer utterly failed, and we remember the resulting pain. That is why in both the morning and evening service it is

Communities might use The Three Weeks to explore and make a commitment to new areas of *tikun olam* for the coming year. *Tisha B'Av* can be a day when people share these discoveries and prioritize their work in the realm of world repair, as well as create a space for service projects. —L.T.P.

Tisha B'Av can also be a time to engage questions of theology. If traditional teachings bring up questions of God's hidden face or of prayer failing our people, we might engage in exploring and writing on where we find God's face in suffering or on how we bring godliness into tragedy. We might also acknowledge the prayers that are omitted on this day and create new ones that encourage us to bring godliness to each situation and build a world where we all are able to seek and experience God's presence. —L.T.P.

customary to omit the *titkabal* line from the Kaddish. It asks, "May the prayer and supplication of the whole house of Israel be acceptable to their creator in heaven." It is not a day to ask that our prayers be accepted.

Traditional communities schedule extra time for their early morning service on *Tisha B'Av* to allow time for reading *Eykha* once again. Some include *kinot* as well. Reconstructionists insert a fast-day version of *Avinu Malkeynu* after the *Amida*. (See pages 139–143 in *Kol Haneshamah: Limot Ḥol.*) Both the Torah portion (Deuteronomy 4:25–40) and haftarah (Jeremiah 8:13–9:23) speak of the destruction. Additional readings are often added to the service. (See pages 473–477 in *Kol Haneshamah: Limot Ḥol.*) While most adults wear a tallit for *shaḥarit,* donning tefillin, normally a morning activity, is usually postponed till *minḥa* in the afternoon. This dis-

What does it mean to have a prayer "accepted"? Even in the most adverse circumstances, the Slonimer Rebbe teaches, when we pray for comfort with an open heart, or for strength or faith or endurance, our prayers are always accepted. When you open your heart, things shift substantially, even when the external outcome does not go your way. —J.J.S.

Unlike on the minor fast days, traditional communities do not recite *Avinu Malkeynu* on *Tisha B'Av*. Also omitted are the *Taḥanunim*, supplications after the *Amida*, perhaps because the mourning humbles us enough or because the word "*moed*," "festive season," is used to describe the day in Lamentations 1:15. There is also a legend that the Messiah will be born on *Tisha B'Av*, and that *Tisha B'Av* will become a holiday in messianic times. —J.G.K.

The *Minḥa Amida* on *Tisha B'Av* contains a special fast-day paragraph and an elaborate version of its 14th blessing expressing the hope for the rebuilding of Jerusalem and comfort for its mourners. The idea of imagining and working toward a real city of peace echoes the social justice themes we see throughout the holiday. —J.G.K.

ruption is partly because the wearing of tefillin is a source of pleasure that some consider an adornment, and partly because according to the Targum (an Aramaic translation/interpretation of the Bible), tefillin are symbols of God's glory, and according to the midrash, God's glory is obscured on *Tisha B'Av*.

The Contemporary Significance of Tisha B'Av

A key prophetic idea is that religious practice ought to lead to ethical living. The religious failure involved in observing ritual while shirking moral responsibility is a central concern of *Tisha B'Av*. When the observance of *Tisha B'Av* consists only of fasting and prayer, it fails to

The tone of *Tisha B'Av* shifts in the afternoon, allowing for the mourning to begin abating. The afternoon service includes words of consolation. Rabbinic tradition teaches that the Messiah will be born on this saddest of days, a message that we can interpret as a vision of hope and peace arising from the ashes. The survival of the Jewish people despite these tragedies permits us to end our fast and return to everyday life. When the personal or communal observance of *Tisha B'Av* is compressed into a shorter period than a full day, it is worthwhile to consider how to bring this hopeful vision into that observance. —B.P.

Some hold that until noontime on *Tisha B'Av*, you should act as one who has lost a close relative before the funeral—one who is in the state of *aninut,* in which one is exempt from regular work and from putting on *tzitzit* and tefillin. From midday onward, we transition to *avelut*, the type of mourning associated with shiva, when we don *tzitzit* and tefillin. —J.G.K.

satisfy this core concern. What might ethical actions look like? A congregation could organize volunteer projects aimed at feeding the hungry and housing the homeless or at supporting civil rights. It could hold a teach-in on social issues, such as sex trafficking or the repression of certain ethnic groups. If individuals cannot bring their congregations to undertake such ethical actions, those individuals can act on their own. Observances similar to those of Martin Luther King Jr. Day, a day of service, are appropriate to *Tisha B'Av*.

One of the questions that arise is whether the beneficiaries of our *tzedaka* and social action should be limited to Jews or to one's country of residence. While the tragedies marked by *Tisha B'Av* are all focused on Jews, the message of *Tisha B'Av* is far broader than this might lead one to believe. (For a more extensive discussion of *tzedaka* priorities, see *A Guide to Jewish Practice: Volume I—Everyday Living*, pages 424–449.) Mourning our losses should inspire us to become co-creators of a world

The appropriate focus of social justice work and ameliorative activities—whether directed toward an individual, a community or issues on a broader level—is an ongoing debate among liberal Jews. In premodern times, our ancestors lived in segregated communities, so their *g'milut ḥesed* activities were almost always directed at fellow Jews. We liberal Jews live in integrated communities and share concerns and commitments with non-Jewish friends and neighbors. When the prophets railed that we should feed the hungry, were they talking about the Israelite hungry or anyone who is hungry? Where should Jewish time and money be directed? For a discussion of these issues, see *A Guide to Jewish Practice: Volume I—Everyday Living,* pages 442–449. —D.W.

where no one experiences such losses. Construing the response more narrowly may well involve the sin of *sinat ḥinam,* of furthering baseless hatred. The rabbis sometimes expressed the hope that the end of *Tisha B'Av* would someday mark the beginning of messianic days; it is up to us to bring them. The fast we are asked to keep is one that protects widows and orphans, feeds the hungry and frees those who have not yet attained their freedom. Mourning what is lost should inspire us to build a better future for our world.

From Tisha B'Av *to Rosh Hashana*

On each of the Shabbatot from *Tisha B'Av* to Rosh Hashana, special haftarot are recited. These are known as

One way to commemorate the destructive power of *sinat ḥinam*, "baseless hatred of Jew against Jew" is to use *Tisha B'Av* as an annual Day of Reconciliation, bringing together Jews of different political opinions (especially related to Israel) to demonstrate civility and the real meaning of being part of a caring community. —S.C.R.

Another possible approach to the issue of *sinat ḥinam* is to create an opportunity for interfaith dialogue between clergy and lay members of all faiths. Such experiences lay the groundwork for a truly modern vision of the messianic age, when all people recognize the godliness in the other. —S.C.R.

Tisha B'Av precedes the month of Elul, when we begin the personal process of *t'shuva* in preparation for Yom Kippur, but *Tisha B'Av* is a time to talk about communal *t'shuva*. We can mourn for communal loss and examine our communal role in neglecting precepts of godliness, as well as our role in the contemporary acts of *sinat ḥinam* in which we participate knowingly or unknowingly. —N.H.M.

Shiva D'neḥemta, the seven haftarot of consolation. The first of these special Shabbatot is called Shabbat *Naḥamu* (Sabbath of consolation) because its haftarah opens with the word "*naḥamu*" and continues, "Be comforted, be comforted, my people." (Isaiah 40:1) The haftarot of consolation bring us gradually from the pain of the losses marked on *Tisha B'Av* to recognition that we can lead lives of spiritual seriousness, integrity and caring, and that such conduct can help us reconnect to the divine.

Faculty members at Camp JRF in the Pocono Mountains had a custom for *Shabbat Naḥamu* of preparing an *oneg Shabbat* for the camp counselors of "comfort foods," from macaroni and cheese and guacamole to chocolate chip cookies and ice cream. It is customary to refer to the month of Av as *Menaḥem* Av, comforting Av, from the very beginning of the month. We anticipate rebuilding even as we approach the destruction of *Tisha B'Av*, and the particular gastronomic delights on *Shabbat Naḥamu* provide some balance to our bodies and our spirits after our week of Jewish national mourning. —J.G.K.

The haftarot of consolation can also be read as God's repeated attempts to console Israel in the aftermath of the rupture and alienation of *Tisha B'Av*. Throughout the seven weeks, God encourages us to be consoled, but it is only on the seventh week that Israel finally accepts God's attempts at consolation, saying, "I greatly rejoice in God; my whole being exults in God." (Isaiah 61:10) Whereas God is portrayed on Rosh Hashana as a mighty sovereign and Israel is portrayed as God's subject people, in the weeks leading up to the holiday, it is God who is the supplicant, inviting Israel back into relationship with God. —E.R.S.

This season is an excellent time to mine Jewish tradition and other sources on the question of what brings comfort in the face of loss and tragedy. The recitations of these haftarot might be accompanied or replaced by other texts that bring healing, comfort and expansiveness into our narrow places of grief, pain and hopelessness.
—L.T.P.

The last month of the year is called Elul; on all its Shabbatot, haftarot of consolation are recited. For all of Elul, it is customary to sound the shofar at the end of *shaḥarit;* the shofar sound reminds us of the spiritual tasks to be undertaken in preparation for the Days of Awe. Some begin reciting special prayers called *s'liḥot* from the beginning of Elul. Others wait until the Saturday night a few days before Rosh Hashana to begin reciting *s'liḥot.* Thus the period from *Tisha B'Av* until Rosh Hashana prepares us for the High Holy Days that follow. (For more details, see the section of this volume on the *Yamim Nora'im.*)

Yom Hashoah V'hag'vura

The Holocaust is by any reckoning one of the darkest times in Jewish history. The murder of 6 million Jews is the most traumatic event in recent Jewish history. While

Taking a few minutes each day during Elul for reflection will enrich the experience of the High Holy Days. The task of *t'shuva*, return/repentance, that is central to Rosh Hashana and Yom Kippur is monumental and can be life-changing. However, lives are not changed in one service, one day or even Ten Days of Repentance. The month of Elul can begin a process of self-assessment, mindfulness practice and moral scrutiny that will form the foundation for the drama of the *Yamim Nora'im*. In addition to hearing the shofar and reading the *S'liḥot* prayers, many contemporary books, recordings and tools are available to focus our attention during Elul. —B.P.

The English word "Holocaust" comes from a Greek word meaning "sacrifice by fire"; the Hebrew word "*shoah*" means "whirlwind." —J.G.K.

we should never forget that Jews were not the only targets of Nazi genocide—the Roma people, homosexuals and the Nazi's political enemies were also singled out—the annihilation suffered by the Jewish people was on an unprecedented scale. The highly developed culture of European Jewry, at that time at the center of Jewish life, was irrevocably destroyed, and the United States and Israel emerged as Europe's successors as centers of Jewish life and culture. *Yom Hashoah* (Holocaust Remembrance Day) is the solemn commemoration day that recalls the horrific losses during the Holocaust.

Israel's Knesset established *Yom Hashoah* in 1951 and fixed its observance on the 27th day of Nisan (which occurs in April or May) or, if that day falls adjacent to Shabbat, on a nearby day. Prior to the Knesset's decision, several other dates were considered. One was the 14th day of Nisan, the anniversary of the Warsaw Ghetto uprising, which had the advantage of commemorating one form of Jewish resistance, but that day is the day before Pesach, a principal reason it was not selected. As mentioned above, *Tisha B'Av*, another possibility, was rejected because so many people wanted the Holocaust memorial to be on a day of its own, when that one enormous loss could be contemplated. A third possibility was the tenth day of Tevet, a pre-existing minor fast day that was selected for this observance by Israel's Chief Rabbinate in 1949. Most Jews have followed the Israeli Knesset's lead; some Hasidim and ultra-Orthodox groups do not, and they include remembrance of the Holocaust either on *Tisha*

B'Av or on the tenth day of Tevet. It is striking that it was the Knesset, rather than a religious group, that made these calendar decisions. This is a sign of Jewish sovereignty re-established after almost 2,000 years.

Yom Hashoah is normally commemorated around the world by solemn gatherings either on the day itself or a nearby day when it is easier for people to gather. While there is no established format for these gatherings, several common acts are usually part of the observance. Usually six memorial candles are lit, representing the 6 million Jewish lives that were destroyed. The Mourner's Kaddish and *El Maley Raḥamim* ("God full of mercy," a prayer for the deceased) are recited. The special *El Maley* includes the phrase "*neshamot shenehergu bashoa*," "lives destroyed in the *Shoah*." (See *Kol Haneshamah*: *Shabbat Veḥagim*, page 640.) For more than 50 years, these rituals

Situating the commemoration of the *Shoah* as part of the narrative of the rise of Israel was consistent with other actions by the government of Israel's first prime minister, David Ben-Gurion, who saw Israel as the culmination of Jewish history.
—D.W.

Some communities light eleven candles to commemorate the estimated 11 million victims—across religions, ethnicities, and beliefs—of Nazi persecution. (Total deaths in World War II, including civilian and military casualties, exceeded a staggering 55 million.)
—D.W.

were usually accompanied by testimony by Holocaust survivors, but the rapidly dwindling number of survivors has resulted in remarks often being offered by children and grandchildren of survivors as well as by historians, rabbis and community dignitaries.

Although some rabbis have suggested that *Yom Hashoah* should become a fast day, that has not generally occurred, and other suggestions about a selecting a haftarah or Torah reading for the day have not been widely adopted. Jewish religious schools, day schools and youth groups often study the Holocaust in the week prior to *Yom Hashoah* and conduct a memorial service on that day. Many observances take place in the synagogue on *Yom Hashoah*. Readings can be found in most modern weekday siddurim. (See *Kol Haneshamah: Limot Ḥol*, pages 449–457.) These commemorations can include

In some ways, remembering the destruction of the Holocaust is a modern version of remembering that we were slaves in Egypt. Just as the Torah is constantly reminding us to remember slavery so that we stand up for those who are enslaved, remembering the Holocaust must challenge us to stand up for all who continue to be murdered in the genocides of Darfur, Rwanda, the Congo and throughout the world. —S.C.R.

As a child in the 1980s, I was anxious about going to religious school on the day we commemorated *Yom Hashoah* because I anticipated that we would be bombarded by terrifying stories and images that in retrospect were probably not age-appropriate. As a teacher, I witnessed a religious school principal telling 150 elementary school students on the first day of school that they were here because "Hitler killed 1.5 million children." We should be careful to talk about the *Shoah* in age-appropriate ways and to teach its history in developmental stages, taking care not to impose our own anxiety or guilt on our children. —J.G.K.

films, lectures, discussions and solemn rites. Some North American congregations plan suitable programs or remarks for the Shabbat preceding *Yom Hashoah*. In some localities, local or state governments sponsor public observances.

In Israel, a national memorial takes place in front of Yad Vashem—Israel's Holocaust museum, archive, and education and research center—after sundown when the day officially begins. Other memorial observances take place throughout Israel. During the morning, sirens sound throughout the country. People come to a stop where they are, even on the highway, and stand at attention for two minutes of silence. On that day, flags are flown at half-mast, public entertainments are closed, television stations carry Holocaust documentaries and related material, and radio stations' music selections are attuned to the day.

Regardless of the specific programs that individual synagogues create in commemoration of *Yom Hashoah*, the essence is always the mitzvah of memory, the obligation to remember the destruction of European Jewry and the inhumanity of which human beings are capable. Facing that inhumanity and standing up for our ancestors and family who were murdered should bring us to action. —S.C.R.

When *Yom Hashoah* begins, public entertainment venues in Israel close. —J.G.K.

I have a vivid memory of being in Israel in the late 1970s on a summer youth trip and hearing the sirens for *Yom Hashoah*. Our bus pulled over by a gas station on a minor highway, and we all got out. In just a moment, we shifted our energy from adolescent gossip to absolute, solemn silence. I noticed a group of Christians coming out of their tour bus and the Arab gas station attendants stepping back from their work. In that moment, we were all unified in our respect for the value of human life. On that day, I did not just experience a nation coming to a halt to commemorate a tragedy. I looked into the eyes of sisters and brothers for the first time and appreciated the interconnectedness of us all. —T.K.

The 27th day of Nisan falls six days before *Yom Hazikaron*, Israeli Memorial Day for those who have fallen in the defense of the nation, and it falls seven days before *Yom Ha'atzma'ut*, Israeli Independence Day, celebrated on the fifth day of Iyar. In establishing this order, the Knesset gave these three days an implicit relationship to each other. It is common to hear speakers declare that the State of Israel rose out of the ashes of the Holocaust. In some ways the institution of these three days in close conjunction with each other is reminiscent of a cycle of special days marking historical events of national importance that was created during the last period of Jewish sovereignty that occurred while the Second Temple existed (530 BCE to 70 CE).

Yom Hashoah, Yom Hazikaron and *Yom Ha'atzma'ut* are similarly important to the contemporary State of Israel. The March of the Living, sponsored in part by the

While no one would argue that *Yom Hashoah* is unimportant to and within Israel, the destruction of the European Jewish community also has significance independent from the establishment of the State of Israel. The timing of *Yom Hashoah* does not easily allow for that independent commemoration to emerge. —D.W.

The location of Yad Vashem on Mount Herzl, the same mountain where government leaders and soldiers are buried, also physically reinforces this relationship. —J.G.K.

In the early days of the State of Israel, many were opposed to highlighting a connection between the Shoah and the establishment of the state. Some leaders wanted to focus on the heroism and strength of those who fought to establish Israel and were uncomfortable with the image of the brokenness represented by traumatized Holocaust survivors. In later decades, a new public appreciation for the role of the survivors emerged in the Israeli consciousness. —N.H.M.

Israeli government, brings Jewish teens from around the world to Eastern Europe to march from the infamous death camp Auschwitz to Birkenau. The experience includes a large commemoration on *Yom Hashoah* inside Auschwitz, after which the teens are flown to Israel for an intensive program. Some regard the implied relationship between *Yom Hashoah* and *Yom Ha'atzma'ut* as theologically and historically problematic, though each observance taken separately is highly important.

"Never Again!" is a frequently heard refrain on *Yom Hashoah*. Some people take it to mean solely that Jews should do everything in their power to prevent others from destroying us, but many others see that understanding as too narrow in a time of relative Jewish safety and prosperity. An expanded understanding of the phrase includes the commitment not to sit by while others are dying as a result of persecution, war, disease or famine.

Many Jews still live consciously or unconsciously in the shadow of the Holocaust. Some interpret contemporary events through the lens of that horror. Others recoil from focusing on it at all. As with *Tisha B'Av*, the focus of a day of remembrance offers us a vessel through which we can purge our horror and sadness. It is a container. *Yom Hashoah* can be the day when we read Holocaust history, literature or theology. It might be a day to celebrate particular lives that were lost or the culture that was lost, just as a Yahrzeit is a time to remember as well as a time to mourn. It may be a day when we proudly and productively assert our Jewish identity. It may be a day when our *tikun olam* efforts focus on the plight of Jews around the globe. It may be a day when we stand up as a religious practice against genocide, torture and cruelty, even if it feels as if we are too small to make a significant difference. It is another opportunity to counter the misery and cruelty of the world with gestures and deeds of love, justice and redemption. —L.T.P.

Yom Hashoah is a day for rededication to those efforts, and many *Yom Hashoah* observances, particularly in liberal congregations, are accompanied by social justice activities that translate the commemoration of the Holocaust into concrete actions, such as collecting food for a local food bank, furthering campaigns to bring attention to egregious human rights violations, and collecting money to combat disease in a developing country. Of course, these actions should be undertaken in addition to any necessary efforts to combat antisemitism.

Yom Hazikaron

Yom Hazikaron, Israeli Memorial Day, for those who have fallen in the defense of the nation, was originally observed only in the State of Israel, but the day has come

North American Jews may not be aware of the importance of *Yom Hazikaron* to Jewish Israelis. Unlike Memorial Day in the United States, *Yom Hazikaron* is probably the most heartfelt and personal observance on the calendar for the majority of Israelis. For nearly every Jewish family, this day is a solemn reminder of the loss of a family member or close friends in the service of their country. Parents of soldiers worry daily about their sons and daughters who are fulfilling their military duty at age 18. When Israelis visit the United States, they are often shocked that Jews do not mark *Yom Hazikaron*. Recognizing the significance of this cultural landmark in Israeli life is a key to understanding the everyday experience of our people in Israel.
—B.P.

to be marked in other places as well. In Israel, where there is near-universal military service, the day evokes particularly powerful emotions because almost everyone has had a relative or friend who has died in service to the country. The observance begins in Israel with a one-minute siren in the evening and a second siren sounding in the morning, during which people stand at silent attention. National services mark the day, and the Israeli flag is flown at half-mast. In great numbers, families and individuals visit the graves of family members and friends who died during military service.

Yom Hazikaron was for two years observed on the same day as *Yom Ha'atzma'ut*, Israeli Independence Day, but this proved difficult and, since 1951, *Yom Hazikaron* has been observed on the fourth day of Iyar, the day before *Yom Ha'atzma'ut*, except when one of the observances would fall on a Friday, Saturday or Sunday, in which case both are moved to the nearest other days.

For very different reasons, neither ultra-Orthodox Jews nor the Palestinian citizens of Israel—two significant populations with increasing numbers—usually serve in the Israeli army. —J.G.K.

In our time it seems particularly important for Diaspora Jews, particularly for those of us living in relative comfort and safety, to mark *Yom Hazikaron*. In so doing, we acknowledge the sacrifices made by countless men and women for the sake of the modern State of Israel. This may also be the time to focus on the highest ideals of the IDF and to pray for the safety of those who serve in the IDF and for their ability to live out their highest ideals in the face of so many challenges. —L.T.P.

Yom Ha'atzma'ut

Israeli Independence Day is celebrated on the fifth day of Iyar, the day that Israel's Declaration of Independence was signed in 1948. The day represents the restoration of Jewish sovereignty in the Jewish homeland after a gap of nearly two millennia. A national ceremony launching the day in Israel takes place on Mount Herzl. The ceremony is broadcast on Israeli television. Local celebrations take place, often including fireworks, in almost every city square. For most Jewish Israelis, *Yom Ha'atzma'ut* is a day of celebration, picnics, barbecues and frivolity. Men, women and children all participate in the many joyous events of the day. Israeli flags hang from balconies across the country, and *Hatikva*, the national anthem, is sung to mark the emergence of Israel as a democratic country. In the Diaspora, *Yom Ha'atzma'ut* is often celebrated in the evening or on a nearby Sunday.

Some Arab Israelis and most Palestinians refer to the day as *Yam an-Nakba*, Arabic for "Day of the Catastrophe," and mark the day as one of mourning, though many Palestinians observe *Yam an-Nakba* on May 15, the secu-

Jewish sovereignty is deeply important—a fact that is powerfully illustrated by the events leading up to and comprising the Holocaust. But sovereignty that means autonomy for Jews also means power over non-Jews. Jewish aspirations for autonomy, long-standing and legitimate, have come to fruition in the form of a modern nation-state in a particularly contested territory. This makes for many complications. No simplistic approach to this situation will ever be sufficient. —D.W.

The Passover Seder ritual of spilling wine from the second cup to temper our joy when reciting the ten plagues because of the loss of Egyptian life is a lesson to take

lar date of the signing of the Declaration of Independence. What for Jews is a day of celebrating the return of Jewish sovereignty in the Jewish homeland is for them a day of mourning their losses.

The Israeli Chief Rabbinate has stated that *Hallel* ought to be recited on this day, so it is added to *shaḥarit* (the morning service) across Israel and in some places elsewhere, though some recite *Hallel* without its introductory blessing. Reciting *Hallel* on *Yom Ha'atzma'ut* is controversial in some quarters because, according to the early rabbis, *Hallel* is recited to mark divine intervention, such as on Pesach, Shavuot, Sukkot and Hanuka. Not everyone agrees that *Yom Ha'atzma'ut* should qualify. This is particularly so for some Hasidim and the ultra-Orthodox Neturei Karta, who hold that the state should not have been created before the coming of the Messiah. Some reli-

with us into the contemporary period as well: The creation of Israel came with a real cost of hundreds of thousands of Palestinians being displaced from their homes. *Yom Ha'atzma'ut* may be a joyous day for us, but the *Naḳba* reminds us that this joy, as on Passover, has its limits. We appreciate the State of Israel, yet we seek an Israel that upholds our highest values as Jews. It is not enough to celebrate Jewish sovereignty without working for peace and justice; otherwise, we risk losing the values we hold most dear. —J.G.K.

I love Israel, and I want Israel and its friends to use their power as effectively as possible to help bring about a two-state solution. My personal *Yom Ha'atzma'ut* observance includes omitting one of the eight sections of *Hallel* with the hope of restoring it one day when there is a permanent resolution to the conflict. May that day come soon! —J.G.K.

gious Zionists recite a special *Al Hanisim*, a prayer inserted in the weekday *Amida* on Hanuka and Purim. Some add a haftarah, and many congregations include extra psalms, songs and readings. (See *Kol Haneshamah: Limot Ḥol*, pages 456–471.) Some also sound the shofar. The liturgy for *Yom Ha'atzma'ut* has not been standardized, and Israeli prayer books demonstrate a variety of approaches to the prayers and poems for the day. Some include a *Kiddush* written specifically for *Yom Ha'atzma'ut.*

In addition to liturgical changes, Jews outside Israel often observe *Yom Ha'atzma'ut* by eating Israeli foods, including humus, pita, olives and falafel. Israeli films,

At Kehillat Mevakshei Derech, a liberal Jerusalem synagogue founded by Rabbi Jack Cohen and his colleagues in 1962, I remember attending *Yom Ha'atzma'ut* dinners that included lighting holiday candles with a blessing, prayers, songs and celebration. The evening's highlight was a panel of speakers who represented the different *edot* (ethnic communities) and aliyot (group arrivals to Israel since the late 1800s) of Israel's history. It was a stirring reminder of the diverse culture of the Jewish state and the many challenges that each group faced in leaving their homes and arriving in their homeland. —B.P.

Given the lack of standardized liturgy for *Yom Ha'atzma'ut*, this is an opportunity for each community to explore its members' relationships to this day and to Israel and to take the time to create new liturgy for the occasion. It is an ideal time to have a teach-in about Israel. —L.T.P.

dancing and music are featured, as well as lectures and discussions about Israel. Such discussions tend not to focus on controversies regarding war and peace, the treatment of Arabs and other minorities, the social welfare system or other difficult topics, but it remains important to explore such issues at other times of the year.

Minor Fast Days

Examples of fasting (*tzom*) are found throughout the Bible. Sometimes they are accompanied by *ina nefesh,* afflicting the body, usually by abstaining from washing, bathing, sexual intercourse and anointing, and by wearing sackcloth and ashes. According to the Torah, Moses fasted as a purification rite on Mount Sinai. (Exodus 34:28)

Israel Independence Day provides an occasion each year not only to celebrate the miracle of Jewish rebirth and renewal after 2,000 years of expulsion, but also to create interfaith dialogues on Israel and the pursuit of peace with its Palestinian neighbors. —S.C.R.

It may be valuable on *Yom Ha'atzma'ut* to explore the difficult issues that Israel faces. Whether it is wise to do that depends on the community and what makes sense for it, but intellectual honesty demands that we not shy away from hard conversations. We rejoice that Israel was created, but it came with a cost. —J.G.K.

Another national holiday observed in Israel and sometimes in Diaspora Jewish communities is *Yom Yerushalayim,* which marks the unification of Jerusalem during the June 1967 war. Observed on the 28th day of Iyar, just over three weeks after *Yom Ha'atzma'ut,* the holiday is celebrated in Israel with parades, school assemblies and special public programs. —D.A.T.

Frequently people fasted to avert a calamity, which may be why they fasted when a king died. (See I Samuel 31:13 and II Samuel 1:12.) Fasting is usually an act of penance and supplication. King David fasted to seek God's mercy when his son was ill, but stopped fasting after his son died. (II Samuel 12:21–23) In the Book of Joel, people fasted to end an attack by locusts, and in the Book of Jonah, the Ninevites fasted as a form of repentance to ward off destruction by God.

Adults observe the minor fast days on the Jewish calendar by fasting from dawn until nightfall, but ill people and pregnant or nursing women are generally exempt from these fasts. If a minor fast day falls on Shabbat, the fast is observed the next day.

One cycle of fasts is said to commemorate the destruction of the First Temple and Jerusalem. There is no historical record indicating that these observances fall on the days of the actual events, but the Book of Zechariah attests to these fasts. (See, for example, Zechariah 8:19 and 7:3–5.) The fast days include the tenth day of Tevet (the beginning of the siege of Jerusalem in 586 BCE), the 17th day of Tammuz (the breaching of the walls), *Tisha*

The exception to fasts being shifted to Sunday if they would fall on Shabbat is the Fast of Esther, which moves back to Thursday instead of forward to Sunday, because when the Fast of Esther would fall on Shabbat, Sunday is Purim. —J.G.K.

B'Av (discussed above; the actual destruction of the Temple) and the third day of Tishri (*Tzom Gedalya*, a fast marking the assassination of Gedalia, the governor of Judah appointed by the Babylonians). The three minor fast days (tenth day of Tevet, 17th day of Tammuz and third day of Tishri) were never observed in Reform congregations and are largely ignored outside the Orthodox community. Since the establishment of the State of Israel and particularly after 1967, when the Temple Mount in Jerusalem became accessible to Israelis, these fast days have been increasingly ignored since they commemorate a destruction that the existence of the State of Israel has remediated. Only a small number of non-Orthodox Jews observe these fasts in our time.

Jewish tradition associates other events with these minor fast days, such as Moses' breaking of the first set of the tablets on the 17th day of Tammuz. The creating of the Septuagint—the Greek translation of the Hebrew Bible, considered by those who thought the Hebrew Bible should never be translated to be an evil that befell the Jewish people—is linked to the 10th day of Tevet. —J.G.K.

In an attempt to connect contemporary Jews to historic events, some have advocated observing *Tzom Gedalya* in memory of the late Israeli Prime Minister Yitzhak Rabin. In 586 BCE, an Israelite assassinated Gedaliah ben Achikam, who had been appointed governor of Israel following the destruction of Jerusalem. In 1995, a Jewish religious extremist assassinated Rabin because of his efforts to make peace with the Palestinians. —B.P.

Ta'anit Ester (the Fast of Esther) immediately precedes Purim and commemorates events described in the Book of Esther (also known as the Megillah). These include Esther's fasting in advance of appearing before King Ahasueras and the general fasting in response to the king's decree that the Jews of Persia were to be killed. (See Esther 4.) The annual commemorative fast is decreed in Esther 10:31. Given the legendary nature of the Book of Esther, relatively few non-Orthodox Jews observe this minor fast day.

The Fast of the Firstborn is observed on the day before Pesach by firstborn adult children in commemoration of

I observe *Ta'anit Esther* as a reminder of Baruch Goldstein's terrible misuse of the Purim festival as an excuse to murder Muslim worshippers in Hebron in 1994. (See the section of this *Guide* on Purim.) The fast is designed to atone for the violence underlying the holiday and for Goldstein's crime. The fast also serves as a balance to the potential for wanton behavior that Purim celebrations may engender, bringing a spiritual foundation to an otherwise raucous party. —B.P.

Ta'anit Esther is commemorated in some circles today as a time to take action on areas of ongoing oppression of women, such as human trafficking and domestic violence. Jewish feminist organizations have encouraged linking the Fast of Esther to raising awareness of the contemporary sex slavery industry that is in full force worldwide, and notably in Tel Aviv. —N.H.M./J.J.S.

The Fast of the Firstborn can be suspended by engaging in the study of a concluding passage of Jewish text. Such an occasion is marked by a *siyum*, a feast celebrating completion of a book. Because eating at a *siyum* is a mitzvah, the fast may be broken. When this occasion falls on the morning of the Seder, providing a *siyum* for firstborns or others can heighten the anticipation of the holiday. (When the Seder falls on or after Shabbat, the Fast of the Firstborn usually takes place on Thursday.) I generally choose a selection of text that speaks to the themes of Pesach, rather than adhering to the requirement of actually finishing a book. When we eat the pastry after our study, we are mindful that this is the last taste of *ḥametz* before the holiday. —B.P.

the Israelites having been protected from the tenth plague, which according to the Torah killed all the Egyptian firstborn except Pharaoh. (See Exodus 13:1.) Originally only firstborn males observed the fast; a commitment to egalitarian principles suggests that firstborn females should observe the fast as well. Those obligated to observe this fast are exempt if they eat a festive meal marking a *siyum*, completion of a book of study, so these ceremonies take place in many more traditional congregations following *shaḥarit*.

Small groups of Jews observe other minor fasts. These include the seventh day of Adar, traditionally given as the date of the death of Moses, which is observed by some *ḥevrot kadisha* (groups that prepare bodies for burial; singular: *ḥevra kadisha*), and *Yom Kippur Katan*, (little Yom Kippur) the last day of each Hebrew month. Some Jews fast every Monday and Thursday, a custom found among those observing *musar* traditions. (For more on *musar*, see *A Guide to Jewish Practice: Volume 1—Everyday Living*, pages 78–79.)

In some traditional Sephardic communities, firstborn daughters observe the Fast of the Firstborn as well. —J.G.K.

Two cycles annually of daylight fasts, each on three days (Monday-Thursday-Monday) are particularly associated with the weeks following Passover and Sukkot as if to add balance to the intensity of weeklong celebrations. —J.G.K.

In addition to the annual fasts described above, one-time fasts are observed on several other occasions. It is traditional for a couple to fast on their wedding day as an act of purification to prepare them for their marriage. Those who witness a Torah scroll being dropped customarily fast for a period as penance. One-time fasts have occasionally been declared in response to drought and other natural phenomena that cause problems for the people who live through them.

Most minor fast days are not commonly observed in our time. However, seeking to remember, to do penance and to become pure is even more important in times of affluence and self-satisfaction. That challenge remains with us. We now turn to two independent minor holidays.

There are many variations on the custom kept by some observant people of fasting in response to local events, such as dropping tefillin. Such fasting is often linked to giving *tzedaka* equivalent to the value of the meal(s) missed; some people give *tzedaka* in place of fasting. —J.G.K.

Jewish tradition is not alone in using fasting as a spiritual practice. In fact, many people choose to fast or to engage in a cleansing for medical and spiritual healing. For those who find this practice meaningful, it is helpful to understand the Jewish roots of fasting beyond the observance of holy days. —B.P.

While most modern Jews ignore the minor fast days and do not experience fasting as a natural aspect of their religious lives, increasing numbers turn to the mikvah—the use of ritual immersion—as a symbol of physical, spiritual and communal transformation and as a response to personal challenges of trauma in their lives. —S.C.R.

The supplicatory prayer *Avinu Malkeynu,* which is associated with the High Holy Day season, is also associated with the liturgy of minor fast days because it echoes the penitential theme of fast days. —J.G.K.

Tu Bishvat

Tu Bishvat takes its name from the date of its observance on the Hebrew calendar—the 15th day of the month of Shevat, which falls in January or February. *Tu Bishvat* is also known as the New Year for Trees, which is how it is described in the Mishna (*Rosh Hashana* 1.1) because it is the date from which the age of trees was counted, determining when fruit tithes were owed in the days of the Temple. This date was selected because trees flowered after it. In Israel, where the winters are relatively mild, the date also marks the beginning of the tree-planting season. *Tu Bishvat* has no holiday restrictions; even the most observant do work and conduct business transactions as usual.

Because *Tu Bishvat* is connected to the agricultural cycle of the Land of Israel, it is customary to eat fruit grown in Israel on that day. This can include dates, figs, grapes, almonds, pomegranates, carob and oranges. Some people also make a point of eating olives or honey, since these are also typical products of Israel.

In some parts of Europe, it was the custom to eat 15 different kinds of fruit on *Tu Bishvat*, perhaps because the "*Tu*" of *Tu Bishvat* means "15." It is customary to eat a fruit one has not eaten during the previous year so that the *Sheheḥeyanu* blessing can be recited. In some places, Psalm 104 and 15 additional psalms (Psalms 120 to 134) were recited; these include the "psalms of ascending" (*shirey hama'alot*) associated with walking up to Jerusalem to offer sacrifices.

Sephardic Jews (descendants of the Jews of Spain and Portugal) often held a *Tu Bishvat* seder, a custom that originally came from kabbalists (Jewish mystics), most likely those of 16th century Tzfat, a town in northern Israel. Influenced by the much older Pesach Seder, this seder, too, incorporates four cups of wine or grape juice. The four cups progress from white to pink to darker pink and finally to red. Traditional forms of the *Tu Bishvat* seder are based on the four worlds described in kabbala: *atzilut* (spirit), *b'ria* (intellect), *yetzira* (emotion) and *assiya* (physical action). They are understood as part of the primordial structure of the world embedded in the *s'firot*, the ten emanations connecting God (*Eyn Sof*) to our world. The traditional form of this seder can be an opportunity to introduce kabbalistic thinking, but this difficult material is often daunting. This may account for the emergence of alternative seders.

Different forms of fruits are associated with each of the four cups of the *Tu Bishvat* seder. Some begin with a fruit with a hard outer shell (such as almonds or oranges), continue to a fruit with an edible outside but an inedible pit (such as dates or olives), and then continue to fruits that are edible through and through (such as grapes). The forms of the fruits are metaphors for our own boundaries and vulnerabilities. The fourth cup may be associated with an *etrog* or no material fruit at all. —J.G.K.

The order of the cups and of the associated mystical worlds varies among *Tu Bishvat* seder traditions. The tradition I follow reverses the order, so we end with the world of *atzilut*, spirit. —J.G.K.

The seder liturgy and rituals of *Tu Bishvat* are recorded in the book *P'ri Etz Hadar* (literally tree of beautiful fruit or citron [*etrog*] tree), published in 1753. —D.A.T.

In recent years *Tu Bishvat* seders have become more common, perhaps because of environmental concerns, a desire for deeper spirituality and the flexible and open-ended nature of the holiday's observance. A *Tu Bishvat* seder can be built on many different themes, and many contemporary versions of the *Tu Bishvat* haggadah are available; a large number can be found on the Web. They differ considerably in ritual, target audience and style, but many of them have environmental themes that are universalistic in nature. Some congregations and *havurot* hold seders; some Jews conduct seders in private homes.

Tu Bishvat teaches us that we can create and refine communal rituals of meaning that draw from religious sources but address other interests and needs. What other cultural creations might we want to create? —D.W.

During the first decades of the State of Israel's existence, *Tu Bishvat* was celebrated in the Diaspora by eating fruit from Israel and donating to the Jewish National Fund to plant trees in Israel. Israeli Jews planted trees with their own hands and sang songs to celebrate the first budding of the almond trees. Jews in Israel and the Diaspora were united by this joint commitment to greening the state. In the late 20th century, North American approaches to *Tu Bishvat* influenced Israelis to introduce the *Tu Bishvat* seder and to include a more general environmental focus for the holiday. This shift demonstrated the growing mutuality between Diaspora and Israeli communities as we share common concerns and contribute to each other's cultural growth. —B.P.

Many contemporary synagogues use the celebration of *Tu Bishvat* as an opportunity to have discussions and public forums on issues affecting the environment. Our synagogue announced its "Greening Initiative" on *Tu Bishvat*, as well as our policy urging members to eliminate plastic bottles from their lives. —S.C.R.

In contemporary Israel, the festival has its own songs, and it is customary to plant trees. For some Jews outside of Israel in recent times, *Tu Bishvat* has come to be a day with activities designed to connect Jews to the agricultural cycle of the Land of Israel. *Tu Bishvat* is a cultural Zionist celebration rather than a political one.

Rosh Ḥodesh—*Celebrating the New Month*

The Hebrew months correspond to lunar cycles. The beginning of the new moon is called *Rosh Ḥodesh,* literally, "head of the month." The Hebrew word for month, *ḥodesh*, is from the same root as that of *ḥadash*, "new." The exact date of *Rosh Ḥodesh* is announced on the preceding Shabbat during a prayer called *Birkat Haḥodesh,* blessing the month, which is part of the Torah service. Because a lunar cycle is 29½ days, some months are one

In Israel today, *Tu Bishvat* has become a time in which young people build bonfires and party late into the night. —T.K.

The celebration of *Tu Bishvat* in North America invites us to pay attention to the gifts of nature in the dead of winter and to appreciate the understanding of Judaism as "the evolving religious civilization of the Jewish people." As we move from the taxes/tithing teachings of the Mishna, to the mystical layer courtesy of the kabbalists, to the cultural Zionism of modern Israel, to the universal imperative to take care of our fragile earth, we witness the richness of a tradition that evolves with respect to both meaning and practice. With *Tu Bishvat*, we can embrace the layers from each civilization, enriching our practice of this minor festival and our understanding of our rich and evolving traditions. —L.T.P.

day longer than others, and some have two days of *Rosh Ḥodesh*, while others have only one. In biblical times, *Rosh Ḥodesh* was determined by observing when the first sliver of the new moon appeared. The rabbis declared the new month after interviewing witnesses who had observed the appearance of the moon. Signal fires then passed this information across ancient Israel. This signal system eventually proved unreliable in Israel, and it was completely unworkable in the Diaspora, where the method was replaced by astronomical calculation during talmudic times. Jewish calendars now indicate when *Rosh Ḥodesh* starts, and whether it is observed for one day or two.

Work is permitted on *Rosh Ḥodesh*, but there are liturgical changes. They include the recitation of the shorter form of *Hallel*, a Torah reading with four aliyot (Numbers 28:1–15, except when *Rosh Ḥodesh* falls on Shabbat, in which case the weekly Torah reading is followed by reading Numbers 28:9–15 from a second Torah scroll), the recitation of *musaf* in some congregations, and additions within the *Amida*. Some of these changes reflect biblical commandments; for example, the *musaf Amida* replaced the *Rosh Ḥodesh musaf* sacrifice (Numbers 28:15).

Those who engage in agriculture are fully aware of the lunar cycle. Most Jews live in cities and live lives that substantially reduce contact with nature's rhythms. *Rosh Ḥodesh* provides an opportunity to reconnect to those rhythms. It is a good time to take a walk, to observe the night sky and to observe the change in seasons.

In recent years, women's groups have formed to celebrate *Rosh Ḥodesh*. Such groups gather on *Rosh Ḥodesh* or in close proximity to it. These groups also provide opportunities for mutual support, for study and discussion, and for any other activities each group can agree upon.

The day before *Rosh Ḥodesh* is known as *Yom Kippur Katan*, the "Small Day of Atonement." Some Jews (in our

I note *Rosh Ḥodesh* as a time for renewal and gratitude. In our household, we have three *Rosh Ḥodesh* greetings: *Ḥodesh tov* (A good month), *Yare'aḥ same'aḥ* (Happy moon) and *Levana s'meḥa"* (Happy moon, using the rabbinic term). —B.P.

While Jews intercalate the calendar, adding an extra month of Adar in seven out of 19 years to keep the holidays in their seasons, Muslims follow the lunar calendar but do not intercalate, so the Islamic calendar loses roughly eleven days per year compared to the solar calendar. Nevertheless, the awareness that our neighbors' months begin on the same days as ours makes *Rosh Ḥodesh* an opportunity for Jewish-Muslim dialogue. —J.G.K.Many reasons are offered for why *Rosh Ḥodesh* has become a women's holiday. One thread focuses on the powerful connection between the moon's cycles and women's menstrual cycles. —D.W.

Rosh Ḥodesh has become an opportunity to engage Jewish girls in serious conversations about their bodies and about how to live responsible adult Jewish lives through the vehicle of *Rosh Ḥodesh ḥavurot* for girls, support groups that help girls to navigate the challenges of their emerging teen years. —S.C.R.

Rosh Ḥodesh groups were one of the keys to my full embrace of Judaism as an adult. The opportunity to study together, to tell stories about our mothers and grandmothers, and to be there for one another in times of joy and sorrow enabled me to integrate the wisdom of Jewish traditions with my own journey as a Jewish woman. —T.K.

time, mostly Hasidim) observe this as a fast day in order to reflect on bad deeds and achieve contrition. It began among the kabbalists of Tzfat during the late 16th century, and later developed its own liturgy.

Kiddush Levana or *Birkat Levana* ("Sanctification of the Moon" or "Blessing of the Moon") is another monthly ritual. It is performed outdoors at night no earlier than the third day of the Hebrew month and not later than the appearance of the full moon. It must occur on a night that is clear enough for the moon to be plainly seen, and it is customary for the ritual to take place on Saturday evening. The central blessing of *Kiddush Levana* can be found in the Talmud (*Sanhedrin* 42a), and the rest of the liturgy developed around it. The increasing size of the moon is associated with a growing presence of the *Shekhina*, the immanent, feminine aspect of God, and with the

Rosh Ḥodesh groups have offered inspiration and support to many women. It is a further blessing that adolescent girls have been introduced to the concept of the women's *Rosh Ḥodesh* group, where learning, nurturing and identity building can be found within the Jewish community at a time of life when it is most needed. – L.T.P.

Liberal Jews might want to experiment with various practices for this Yom Kippur *Katan*. It might be a time for journaling or for other methods of self-reflection with respect to *musar* practice or more general reflection as we bid goodbye to one month and prepare to welcome another. The contrast of this day of intense introspection with the celebration of *Rosh Ḥodesh* may add meaning and depth to both days and support individuals or groups in a monthly process of spiritual renewal. —L.T.P.

The returning of the waxing moon each month is also associated with the restoration of the Jewish people after times of trouble or persecution. Since the blessing of *Kiddush Levana* is framed with verses of protection, some LGBT people associate the ritual with coming out, since the moon can come out each month, over and over again, and still remain protected and whole. —J.G.K.

renewal of nature. One version of the liturgy can be found in *Kol Haneshamah: Shirim Uvrakhot*, pages 122–129. The ritual can bring people together to appreciate the natural world, and it can conclude with song and dance. In some places, men's groups have formed around the observance of *Kiddush Levana.*

For Further Reading

David A. Teutsch

Books about the Jewish holidays abound. Michael Strassfeld's *The Jewish Holidays: A Guide and Commentary* is clear, thorough and modern; it describes traditional practice, suggesting contemporary observances and attending to spiritual meaning. *The Jewish Way: Living the Holidays* by Irving Greenberg recounts the narrative of the holidays in a way that reflects his contemporary theology. Hayyim Schauss wrote a classic, *The Jewish Festivals: A Guide to Their History and Observance*, the first widely used book to take a more historical view of the holidays. A three-volume work by Eliyahu Kitov, *The Book of our Heritage*, is written from a very traditional perspective, but it is full of midrashim and traditional Jewish interpretations that often bring fresh insights. Arthur Waskow's *Seasons of Our Joy: A Modern Guide to the Jewish Holi-*

days is a highly creative work that emphasizes contemporary interpretation and the importance of *tikun olam.* Mordecai M. Kaplan considers and interprets the significance of every holiday in his book *The Meaning of God in Modern Jewish Religion.*

The Jewish Publication Society has produced a series of anthologies, many of them edited by Philip Goodman. They contain holiday stories, poetry, activities and music, as well as the primary texts out of which each holiday developed. For parents and teachers, these remain a useful tool.

For those interested in traditional observance, a Conservative approach can be found in *A Guide to Jewish Religious Practice* by Isaac Klein and also in a more recent volume, *The Observant Life: The Wisdom of Conservative Judaism for Contemporary Jews*, edited by Martin S. Cohen and Michael Katz. Orthodox practice is described in the *Mishnah Berurah*, which is available in a Hebrew-English edition; the *Mishnah Berurah* is based on the earlier *Shulḥan Arukh*. For a more liberal perspective than the one described here, the most up-to-date book is Mark Washofsky's *Jewish Living: A Guide to Contemporary Reform Practice*. For those seeking contemporary rituals, prayers and poetry, the website at www.ritualwell.org is a helpful resource.

Since most holidays have roots in biblical or apocryphal texts, it is helpful to read the accounts in those texts and the commentaries on them. Examples of these include Nahum M. Sarna's *The JPS Torah Commentary: Exodus* and Adele Berlin's *The JPS Bible Commentary: Esther*. *The Apocrypha*, translated by Edgar J. Goodspeed with an introduction by Moses Hadas, is also an excellent resource.

For background on particular objects, practices, people and texts, *The Encyclopedia Judaica* and the much older but still useful *Jewish Encyclopedia* are invaluable.

Further information on the liturgy of the holidays may also prove useful. Some prayer books, such as the multi-volume *Kol Haneshamah*, for which I served as editor-in-chief, and *A Night of Questions: A Passover Haggadah*, edited by Joy Levitt and Michael Strassfeld, contain extensive commentary and explanations. Books about the liturgy include *Justice and Mercy: Commentary on the Liturgy of the New Year and the Day of Atonement* by Max Arzt and *My People's Prayer Book* and *Prayers of Awe*, two series edited by Lawrence A. Hoffman. The number of siddurim and Haggadot available is so large that the excellent ones cannot all be listed here; a trip to a good Jewish bookstore to survey them is recommended.

—D.A.T.

Appendix: Explanation of Observance of 'Yom Tov Sheni,' *The Second Day of Major Holidays*

The Babylonian Talmud describes the necessity of two days for every holiday (except Yom Kippur) when it is observed outside the Land of Israel. In talmudic times, the annual calendar depended on the monthly sighting of the new moon in Jerusalem, and holidays could not be fixed until the Sanhedrin (the Jewish high court) had determined that the new Hebrew month had begun. This method sufficed when the announcement of the New Moon could be transmitted short distances. Even using bonfires from mountaintop to mountaintop, the word could reach the large Jewish communities in Babylonia and Egypt within the same day.

However, soon the rabbis were forced to use messengers on foot rather than bonfires, and outside the Land of Israel one could not be assured of receiving the notification from the Sanhedrin in time to celebrate a festival on the proper day. Therefore, the rabbis instituted the practice of *yom tov sheni shel galuyot*, adding a second full day to the first day of the festival for Jews outside the Land of Israel. Since the general timing of holidays could be anticipated to fall on one of two days, a community that celebrated two days would be assured of giving the correct day due sanctity, whichever one was the "true" holiday.

By the middle of the fourth century, when the Byzantine Christian rulers forbade the proclamation of a calendar, the great sage Hillel the Younger published the Sanhedrin's mathematical formula for calculating the months. A fixed calendar provided stability for Jewish communities no matter where they lived. Nevertheless, by then the practice of *yom tov sheni* had become standard, and its practice, part of *halakha* (Jewish law).

In the modern period, beginning with early Reform Judaism in the 19th century, the second day of festivals began to be dropped in liberal Diaspora Jewish communities. Today, all Orthodox and most Conservative synagogues retain the additional day, while almost all Reform and Reconstructionist communities have dropped it. The only exceptions usually found in Reform and Reconstructionist practice are the two days of Rosh Hashana (because it is a two-day holiday in Israel, as well) and the second Seder of Pesach. For those who keep the second day, it marks an important distinction between those who live in the Land of Israel and those living in the Diaspora, since the holidays celebrated in the Land of Israel do not require the extra day. For much of Jewish history, living outside the Land of Israel was considered "divine punishment" for alleged transgressions of the Jews. After the establishment of the State of Israel, such theological interpretations of history are superfluous, if not offensive, to Jews, and the centrality of Israel suggests that all Jews ought to share the same calendar.

The chart below shows the pattern of celebrating eight or nine days of Sukkot and Shemini Atzeret in different times and places.

Observance of Sukkot, Shemini Atzeret and Simchat Torah in Different Times and Places

Biblical	Sukkot Full Holiday 1	Sukkot *Ḥol Hamo'ed* 2	Sukkot *Ḥol Hamo'ed* 3	Sukkot *Ḥol Hamo'ed* 4	Sukkot *Ḥol Hamo'ed* 5	Sukkot *Ḥol Hamo'ed* 6	Sukkot *Ḥol Hamo'ed* 7	Shemini Atzeret 1	
Talmudic Period Diaspora	Sukkot Full Holiday 1	Sukkot Full Holiday 2	Sukkot *Ḥol Hamo'ed* 3	Sukkot *Ḥol Hamo'ed* 4	Sukkot *Ḥol Hamo'ed* 5	Sukkot *Ḥol Hamo'ed* 6	Sukkot *Ḥol Hamo'ed* 7	Shemini Atzeret 1	Shemini Atzeret 2
Medieval Diaspora & Contemporary Orthodox Diaspora	Sukkot Full Holiday 1	Sukkot Full Holiday 2	Sukkot *Ḥol Hamo'ed* 3	Sukkot Ḥol *Hamo'ed* 4	Sukkot *Ḥol Hamo'ed* 5	Sukkot *Ḥol Hamo'ed* 6	Sukkot *Ḥol Hamo'ed* 7	Shemini Atzeret 1	Simchat Torah
Contemporary Israel, Diaspora Reconstructionist & Reform	Sukkot Full Holiday 1	Sukkot *Ḥol Hamo'ed* 2	Sukkot *Ḥol Hamo'ed* 3	Sukkot *Ḥol Hamo'ed* 4	Sukkot *Ḥol Hamo'ed* 5	Sukkot *Ḥol Hamo'ed* 6	Sukkot *Ḥol Hamo'ed* 7	Shemini Atzeret Simchat Torah 1	

Biographies of Contributors

SYLVIA BOORSTEIN, PH.D., is a co-founder and faculty member of the Spirit Rock Meditation Center in Woodacre, Calif. She has been teaching meditation since 1985. Her books include *That's Funny, You Don't Look Buddhist: On Being a Faithful Jew and a Passionate Buddhist; Pay Attention, for Goodness Sake: The Buddhist Path of Kindness;* and *Happiness Is an Inside Job: Practicing for a Joyful Life.*

RABBI LESTER B. BRONSTEIN has served as rabbi of Bet Am Shalom Synagogue in White Plains, N.Y., since 1989. He has been a member of the Reconstructionist Rabbinical Association board and the Reconstructionist Commission on the Role of the Rabbi.

RABBI MICHAEL FESSLER (RRC '01) is co-rabbi of Congregation B'nai Tikvah-Beth Israel in Sewell, N.J. He moderates the listserv of the Reconstructionist Rabbinical Association.

RABBI RICHARD HIRSH (RRC '81) is executive director of the Reconstructionist Rabbinical Association, a former editor of *The Reconstructionist*, and a former congregational rabbi. He teaches at the Reconstructionist Rabbinical College.

RABBI MARGARET HOLUB is rabbi of the Mendocino Coast Jewish Community in Northern California. She was founding chair of "Honor the Image of God: Stop Torture Now," a campaign for Rabbis for Human Rights-North America. She spent her sabbatical at the Desmond Tutu Peace Centre in Cape Town, South Africa.

LEAH KAMIONKOWSKI is a certified public accountant. A former vice president of the Jewish Reconstructionist Federation, she is a member of Kol HaLev in Cleveland.

TAMAR KAMIONKOWSKI, PH.D., is the vice president for academic affairs and associate professor of biblical civilization at the Reconstructionist Rabbinical College.

RABBI DONNA KIRSHBAUM (RRC '08) served as rabbi of the String of Pearls Jewish Reconstructionist Congregation in Princeton, N.J., for five years. She now resides in Omer, near Beersheva, in Israel. Kirshbaum is the lead author of four holiday guides published by Jewish Women International—*Rethinking Purim/Shavuot/Sukkot/Shabbat*: *Women, Relationships & Jewish Texts.*

RABBI JASON GARY KLEIN (RRC '02) has served on the board of the Reconstructionist Rabbinical College, as president of the Reconstructionist Rabbinical Association and as a faculty member at Camp JRF. He serves as director of Hillel at UMBC (University of Maryland, Baltimore County).

RABBI MYRIAM KLOTZ is director of yoga and lay

programs at the Institute for Jewish Spirituality in New York and co-director of Yoga and Jewish Spirituality Teacher Training at the Isabella Freedman Jewish Retreat Center's Elat Chayyim Center for Jewish Spirituality in Falls Village, Conn.

LORI HOPE LEFKOVITZ, PH.D., is the Ruderman Professor and Director of Jewish Studies at Northeastern University in Boston. She previously served as director of Kolot: The Center for Jewish Women's and Gender Studies at the Reconstructionist Rabbinical College. Her most recent book is *In Scripture: The First Stories of Jewish Sexual Identities*.

RABBI NINA H. MANDEL (RRC '03) serves Congregation Beth El in Sunbury, Pa. She is also a lecturer in the Department of Philosophy and Religion at Susquehanna University in Selinsgrove, Pa.

RABBI MIRIAM MARGLES (RRC '06) is an artist, composer, educator and activist. She serves as the rabbi of the Danforth Jewish Circle in Toronto and leads workshops in the United States and Canada. She is co-founder of Encounter, which is dedicated to strengthening the capacity of the Jewish people to be constructive agents of change in transforming the Israeli-Palestinian conflict.

RABBI NATHAN C. MARTIN (RRC '06) currently serves as director of student life at the Reconstructionist Rabbinical College. Martin has long had an interest in understanding how Jewish tradition can inform our work to create a more sustainable planet for future generations, and he is active in the Jewish environmental movement.

He also has a strong interest in Jewish mysticism and in the cultivation of a healthy and balanced inner life.

RABBI VIVIAN MAYER (RRC '96) is director of the Mekhinah-Year Program and Bet Midrash at the Reconstructionist Rabbinical College. She formerly served as rabbi of Congregation B'nai Israel in Danbury, Conn.

RABBI ELA MEROM (RRC '10) lives in Israel, where she founded Eden MiKedem, a progressive, spiritual and highly musical congregation in Tel Aviv.

JAY MICHAELSON, PH.D., is a well-known author, a contributing editor at *The Forward*, and a founder of Nehirim, a national community for lesbian, gay, bisexual and transgender Jews and their families and friends. His most recent book is *God vs. Gay? The Religious Case for Equality*. A graduate of Yale Law School, he received a doctorate in Jewish thought from the Hebrew University in Jerusalem.

DEBORAH DASH MOORE, PH.D., is the Frederick G.L. Huetwell Professor of History at the University of Michigan in Ann Arbor, and director of the Jewish studies program there. She previous taught at Vassar College. She served as general editor of *City of Promises: A History of the Jews of New York, which* won a 2012 National Jewish Book Award.

RABBI BARBARA PENZNER (RRC '87) serves Temple Hillel B'nai Torah in West Roxbury, Mass. A past president of the Reconstructionist Rabbinical Association, she lived in Israel for two years as a Jerusalem Fellow and worked as a consultant to the Combined Jewish Philanthropies of Boston.

RABBI LINDA T. POTEMKEN (RRC '97) is the rabbi of Congregation Beth Israel in Media, Pa.

RABBI STEVEN CARR REUBEN is senior rabbi of Kehillat Israel Reconstructionist Synagogue in Pacific Palisades, Calif. He is the author of five books on aspects of intermarriage and on raising ethical children, and he has published many articles.

RABBI YAEL RIDBERG (RRC '97) is the rabbi of Congregation Dor Hadash in San Diego, and a past president of the Reconstructionist Rabbinical Association.

RABBI JEREMY SCHWARTZ (RRC '97) has been spiritual leader of Temple Bnai Israel in Willimantic, Conn., since 2000. He previously served as the assistant director of Kolel: The Adult Centre for Liberal Jewish Learning in Toronto. His teaching interests include prayer, the siddur, modern Hebrew poetry and the theology of *tikun olam*. He has published translations of the writings of Zionist A.D. Gordon and Israeli writer Ari Elon.

RABBI HUGH SEID-VALENCIA (RRC '04) is director of the Israel and Jewish studies curriculum at the Kehillah Jewish High School in Palo Alto, Calif., where he has served since 2003.

RABBI JONATHAN P. SLATER is co-director of programs for New York's Institute for Jewish Spirituality. He has served congregations in New York and California, and he received a doctorate in ministry from the Pacific School of Religion in Berkeley, Calif., where he studied the nature of rabbinic authority among Conservative rabbis.

RABBI JOSHUA M. SNYDER (RRC '08) is executive director of the Goucher College Hillel in Baltimore. A former veterinary student, Snyder has written on Jewish connections to animals.

RABBI TOBA SPITZER (RRC '97) serves Reconstructionist Congregation Dorshei Tzedek in Newton, Mass. A past president of the Reconstructionist Rabbinical Association, she has done a variety of rabbinic and educational work on Jewish approaches to issues of economic justice and the role of money in our everyday lives.

RABBI JACOB J. STAUB, PH.D., (RRC '77) is professor of Jewish philosophy and spirituality at the Reconstructionist Rabbinical College, where he oversees the program in Jewish Spiritual Direction. He previously served as vice president for academic affairs there.

ELSIE R.STERN, PH.D., is associate professor of Bible at the Reconstructionist Rabbinical College. She is the author of *From Rebuke to Consolation: Exegesis and Theology in the Liturgical Anthology of the Ninth of Av Season,* and a contributor to the *Jewish Study Bible* and *The Torah: A Women's Commentary.*

RABBI ROBERT J. TABAK, PH.D. (RRC '97) is a chaplain at the Hospital of the University of Pennsylvania and editor of the Reconstructionist Rabbinical Association's newsletter.

RABBI ELLIOTT M. TEPPERMAN has been rabbi of Bnai Keshet Reconstructionist Synagogue in Montclair, N.J. since 2002, when he graduated from the Reconstructionist Rabbinical College. Dedicated to social justice, he has been an activist in congregation-based community organizing.

RABBI DAVID A. TEUTSCH, PH.D., is the Wiener Professor of Contemporary Jewish Civilization and director of the Levin-Lieber Program in Jewish Ethics at the Reconstructionist Rabbinical College. A past president of the College, he was editor-in-chief of the *Kol Haneshamah* prayer book series.

RABBI DEBORAH WAXMAN (RRC '99) is the vice president for governance of the Reconstructionist Rabbinical College, where she is also a faculty member. A Columbia University graduate, she received her doctorate in American Jewish history from Temple University. Her dissertation was titled, "Faith and Ethnicity in American Judaism: Reconstructionism as Ideology and Institution, 1935–1959."

RABBI JOSHUA WAXMAN (RRC '03) is the spiritual leader of Or Hadash: A Reconstructionist Synagogue in Fort Washington, Pa., and he serves as a spiritual director at the Reconstructionist Rabbinical College.

RABBI ELYSE WECHTERMAN (RRC '00) has served as spiritual leader at Congregation Agudas Achim, a Reconstructionist community in Attleboro, Mass., since 2001. Prior to that, she served as a congregational consultant at the Jewish Reconstructionist Federation in Philadelphia. She has authored numerous articles and stories.

RABBI SHEILA PELTZ WEINBERG (RRC '86) is outreach director and a staff member teaching meditation at the Institute for Jewish Spirituality in New York. She has previously served as a congregational rabbi, a Hillel director and a community-relations professional.

Index